Grave concerns: death and burial in England 1700 to 1850

Grave concerns: death and burial in England 1700 to 1850

Edited by
Margaret Cox

CBA Research Report 113
Council for British Archaeology
1998

Published 1998 by the Council for British Archaeology
Bowes Morrell House, 111 Walmgate, York YO1 2UA

British Library Cataloguing in Publication Data
A catalogue for this book is available from the British Library

ISBN 1 872414 85 0

Typeset by AMA Graphics Limited, Preston

Printed by Pennine Printing Services Limited, Ripponden, West Yorkshire

Front cover The Doubt 'Can These Dry Bones Live?' by Henry Bowler (reproduced with permission of the Tate Gallery)

Back cover An archaeologist evaluating the archaeology within the crypt of St Pancras Church, Euston Road, London. (Photo: The St Pancras Project, Bournemouth University)

Contents

List of illustrations

List of tables

Acknowledgements

Cover illustration: *The Doubt: 'Can these dry bones live?'*, by Henry Alexander Bowler (1854), reproduced by permission of the Tate Gallery. Bowler's quotation is from Ezekiel 37, in which God shows the prophet the valley of dry bones and asks: 'Son of man, can these bones live?'. In this painting the question is posed by a young woman who leans on a tombstone inscribed: Sacred/to the/MEMORY/ of/John Faithful/Born 1711 died 1791/'I am the Resurrection and the Life'. Faithful's bones lie exposed to her gaze. At the foot of the chestnut tree another stone is inscribed 'RESURGAM' (I will rise again). A butterfly, traditional symbol of resurrection, perches on Faithful's skull. On the stone at the foot of the tree Bowler depicts a germinating chestnut, a symbol of natural regeneration and an alternative to the supernatural or religious resurrection proclaimed on the standing stone (Tate Gallery 1984, 130). Whether the woman's doubts are answered is not clear.

Dedication

This volume is dedicated to the many scholars who have given of themselves to advance this subject area, in particular to two whose contributions have been more significant than most: Jez Reeve and Julian Litten.

Acknowledgements

This volume owes much to many different people and organisations. Firstly, the *Grave Concerns* Conference (April 1997) would not have taken place without the sponsorship and efficient organisation of the Continuing Education Department, School of Conservation Sciences, Bournemouth University. Particular thanks are due to Katherine Barker, Anne Gifford and Jackie Collishaw. No conference can be a success without a cohort of enthusiastic and knowledgeable speakers and these include those who have not contributed to this volume: Dr Sue Black, Dr Robert Dunning, Dr Harold Mytum, and Dr Ruth Richardson. The conference attracted many delegates including archaeologists, histori-ans, social scientists, students, the general public, and members of the undertaking profession. They too played a part in contributing to some stimulating, contentious, and lively discussion.

Speakers who have contributed to this volume include Louise Bashford, Dr Lynne Bell, Eric Boore, Dr Vanessa Harding, Lucy Kirk, Paul Kneller, Robert Janaway, Dr Julia Lee-Thorp, Julian Litten FSA, Dr Tony Pollard, Jez Reeve, Dr Louise Scheuer, Helen Start, Gwynne Stock, Dr Sarah Tarlow, and Dr Susan Young. They are all thanked for producing papers within a very short deadline and facilitating the publication of the conference proceedings within a year of the conference: an almost unheard-of achievement. Additional contributions to the volume were sought in order to cover relevant areas not addressed during the conference. Authors of these include Angela Boyle, Graham Keevill, Dr Julie Rugg, Dr James Thompson, and Bill White. These heroic contributors produced papers within even tighter deadlines than those mentioned above. Numerous people have assisted by refereeing papers and they too are sincerely thanked for such quick, considered, and invaluable responses to the editor's requests.

Editing a volume can be a thankless and exasperating task but this would have been unthinkably awful without the invaluable contribution and expertise of Dr Kate Macdonald, who gallantly undertook the sub-editing role. She is particularly thanked for her patience, diligence, and tenacity even when confronted with that most elusive of academics, the overdue and guilt-ridden contributor! I am also indebted to the publications team at the CBA, in particular Christine Pietrowski for her seemingly endless enthusiasm for subjects that less enlightened publishers might shy away from. Ruth Richardson is thanked for many hours of interesting discussion and debate and for drawing Bowler's *The Doubt* to my attention as a contender for the frontispiece, an inspired suggestion when tackling a subject area that engenders both 'doubt' and 'Grave Concerns'.

Margaret Cox
Bournemouth University
September 1997

Biographical notes

Louise Bashford

Louise Bashford currently works as an Assistant Field Officer with Archaeology South-East, a division of the Field Archaeology Unit, University College London. She took her degree in Ancient History and Archaeology in 1994 at Birmingham University, and her research concerned the funerary beliefs displayed in the burial practices of Mycenaean Greece.

Lynne S Bell

Lynne Bell is an FRD Prestigious Post-Doctoral Fellow at the Archaeometry Research Unit, Department of Archaeology, University of Cape Town, and begins as a Wellcome Post-Doctoral Fellow at the Department of Palaeontology, Natural History Museum, London, in March 1998. Her background is in archaeology, forensic osteology, and mineralized tissue biology. Her principal research interests include diagenetic microtaphonomy, stable light isotope dietary tracking, and DNA survival.

Eric Boore

Eric Boore is an independent research archaeologist who was formerly employed in the Field Archaeology Department at Bristol City Museum and Art Gallery. He has worked throughout Britain on rural and urban sites of the Romano-British and medieval periods and on prehistoric sites in Holland. He has also been involved in several projects at Bristol Cathedral. His main interests are in church archaeology, particularly post-medieval burial vaults and their occupants. He is a member of the Bristol and Gloucestershire Archaeological Society.

Angela Boyle

Angela Boyle has degrees in archaeology and osteology. She has worked for the Oxford Archaeological Unit since 1990 as Unit Osteologist, also undertaking stratigraphic analysis and the identification and analysis of artefacts. She lectures on aspects of osteology and archaeology at the Department of Continuing Education, Oxford University, and has published a series of bone reports on material ranging in date from the Neolithic to the 19th century. Her current research interests include Neolithic and Bronze Age burial in the Upper Thames Valley. She is a member of the Osteoarchaeological

Research Group, the Association for Environmental Archaeology, and the Palaeopathology Association.

Margaret Cox

Margaret Cox is presently Senior Lecturer in Archaeology at Bournemouth University and Course Leader for MSc Forensic Archaeology. During the 1980s she was an historian and osteoarchaeologist on the Christ Church, Spitalfields Project. Her experience and specialism in the field of funerary archaeology was enhanced and enriched by working in a complex conservation and environmental background in the early 1990s. She has published extensively and is currently preparing a book on health and disease in England, prehistory to the present, with Charlotte Roberts, and another on women's health and maternity from the Roman period to the 1930s. She is a Member of the Institute of Field Archaeologists, Forensic Sciences Society, American Association of Physical Anthropologists, Association of Environmental Archaeologists and the Forensic Advisory Search Group.

Vanessa Harding

Vanessa Harding is Senior Lecturer in London History at Birkbeck College, University of London. Her research and publications have focused on medieval and early modern London, especially on the development of the built environment and uses of urban space. She has published on London's demography and on burial choice and location. She is currently completing a book on death and burial in 16th and 17th century London and Paris, as part of a wider investigation into the nature of metropolitan society and social structure.

Robert Janaway

Robert Janaway is currently a lecturer in achaeological sciences at the University of Bradford. Originaly trained as an Archaeological Conservator at University of Wales, Cardiff he has pursued a research interest in the taphonomy of inhumation burials and associated textile finds. He was the principal organizer of the joint professional colloquium on archaeology and forensic science held in Leeds in 1987, the basis for *Death, decay and reconstruction* (edited by Boddington, Garland, and Janaway). He became involved with the Christ Church Spitalfields project, taking part in the last few weeks of excavation and preparing a report of the extensive textile finds which were published in 1993. While maintaining an interest in textiles from post-medieval burials, his recent research has included applications of this work to criminal investigations and purely archaeological topics such as archaeological textile evidence from South Asia.

Graham Keevill

Graham Keevill has been project manager at the Oxford Archaeological Unit since 1990, and has wide experience on survey and excavation sites throughout England. He was the Dean and Chapter's Archaeologist at Carlisle Cathedral (1988–90) and was appointed Project Co-ordinator for the Historic Royal Palaces and OAU in 1993, leading recording and excavation work on the Tower of London, Hampton Court Palace, Kew and Kensington Palaces. He has published extensively, and was a member of the Council of the Institute of Field Archaeologists (1990-93) and has been Honorary Treasurer of the Society for Church Archaeology since 1995.

Lucy Kirk

Lucy Kirk, a graduate of the Institute of Archaeology, University College London, is a field archaeologist with main research interests in the study of human remains and the archaeology of the Americas. She is currently working on the London Road, Kingston-upon-Thames skeletons as well as analysing material from an Anglo-Saxon cemetery and a medieval leper hospital cemetery. She is also working part-time for an MSc in Forensic Archaeology at Bournemouth University.

Paul Kneller

Paul Kneller is a lecturer in Laboratory Sciences at Bournemouth University and trained as an analytical chemist. Research interests include new designs of equipment for flow injection analysis. He is part of the university safety team as the COSHH coordinator, researching health and safety at archaeological sites and scenes of crime.

Julia A Lee-Thorpe

Julia Lee-Thorp is a Senior Research Fellow in the Archaeometry Research Unit, Department of Archaeology, University of Cape Town. She has undergraduate and postgraduate training in both chemistry and archaeology, and opened up the field of stable isotopes in the mineral phase of bones and teeth, the subject of a PhD thesis in 1989. Currently she specializes in applications of stable light isotope tools to questions about diet and past environments of relevance to palaeoanthropology, archaeology, and quaternary environments. These interests have also lead her to do research into the mineralogical chemistry of ancient bones and teeth. She has published extensively in these areas.

Julian Litten

Julian Litten is a leading authority on ecclesiastical antiquarianism and has published widely on funerary archaeology and antiquities. His 1991 publication, *The English Way of Death: The Common Funeral since 1450*, is the standard work of reference on the subject. In 1984 he was commissioned by Portsmouth Cathedral to design the coffin for the Unknown Mariner from the *Mary Rose*, and in 1987 was consultant to Westminster Abbey for its reorganization of the Undercroft Museum with its unique collection of royal funeral effigies. He is a member of the Cathedrals Fabric Commission for England, a Fellow of the Society of Antiquaries of London and of the Society of Antiquaries of Scotland.

Tony Pollard

Tony Pollard was formerly a Project Manager with Glasgow University Archaeological Research Division (GUARD). He received his doctorate from Glasgow University in 1995 with a thesis on marine exploitation in prehistoric Scotland. He is currently Projects Manager with Archaeology South-East, a division of the Field Archaeology Unit, University College London. He is general editor of *The Scottish Archaeological Review* and joint editor, with Jane Downes, of *The loved body's corruption: archaeological contributions to the study of human mortality* (in press).

Jez Reeve

Jez Reeve directed the archaeological excavation of the crypt of Christ Church, Spitalfields, London 1984–6 and has acted as an archaeological consultant on a number of development proposals affecting crypts and burial grounds. She is currently Head of the Greater London Archaeology Advisory Service, English Heritage, Chair of the Institute of Field Archaeologists, and Secretary to the Society of Church Archaeology.

Julie Rugg

Julie Rugg manages the Cemetery Research Group at the University of York. Her principal research interests include the early history of cemetery development, and more current social policy issues with respect to cemetery and crematorium development. Publications include *The Management of Old Cemetery Land* (with Julie Dunk), *Burial Space Needs in London* (with Halcrow Fox and the Landscape Partnership), and 'The origin and progress of cemetery establishment in Britain', in *The Changing Face of Death* (eds P Jupp and G Howarth). She is currently writing for the forthcoming *An Illustrated History of Death*.

Louise Scheuer

Louise Scheuer is an Honorary Senior Lecturer in Anatomy at the Royal Free Hospital School of Medicine, University of London. Her main interests are in the juvenile skeleton, the skeletal biology of historical populations, and forensic osteology. She has taught anatomy to medical students and archaeological and forensic osteology to post-graduate groups. She also acts as a consultant osteologist to the police. With Sue Black (MacLaughlin) she was awarded a Leverhulme research grant for the conservation and re-evaluation of the St Bride's crypt skeletal collection, and they are currently working on a book on the anatomy and development of the juvenile skeleton.

Helen Start

Following an archaeological degree at the University of Birmingham and an MSc in osteology at the University of Sheffield, Helen Start has undertaken several archaeological and osteological projects including the Quaker Burial Ground at 84 London Road. She is now an osteo-archaeological research assistant for ARCUS at the University of Sheffield. Her current research areas include analysis of skeletal material from the burial ground at Newcastle Infirmary (1753–1845) and ethics in burial archaeology.

Gwynne Stock

Following (very) early retirement from television broadcast studio engineering Gwynne Stock has developed a long-standing interest in landscape archaeology into a special interest in post medieval burial grounds. He advises South Gloucestershire Council with their Churchyard Conservation Project, is a member of the Association of Burial Authorities' Steering Group, and is an Attender of the Religious Society of Friends. He has recently been awarded a post-graduate research diploma by Bournemouth University for his work on Quaker burial practice.

Sarah Tarlow

Sarah Tarlow is a Lecturer in Archaeology at the University of Wales, Lampeter. She is the author of a forthcoming book on the changing understanding of death from the Reformation to the 20th century in Britain. Other publications include responses to the First World War and work on the archaeology of death. A co-edited volume (with Susie West of the University of East Anglia) on social approaches to early modern and modern archaeology in Britain is also nearing completion. Currently she is working on responses to the Reformation in England and Scotland, on 19th century cemetery landscapes, and is beginning to explore the archaeology of Utopias.

James Thompson

James Thompson is Senior Lecturer in Psychology at University College London Medical School, University of London. He is a Chartered Clinical Psychologist, and is Director of the Traumatic Stress Clinic at the Middlesex Hospital, which specializes in the treatment of survivors of disaster and major traumas. His research interests are in the treatment of trauma and perceptions of threat and risk. He has published *The Experience of Illness, Psychological aspects of nuclear war*, and over 80 scientific papers.

Bill White

Bill White trained as a chemist and worked for many years in the pharmaceutical industry. Concurrently he obtained a diploma in archaeology and went on to specialize in work on human skeletal remains. Following the publication of *The cemetery of St Nicholas Shambles* in 1988 he has studied 1,500 skeletons from archaeological sites of all periods from London, and is currently working on a further 500 skeletons from the 1994 excavation of Stratford Langthorne Abbey.

Susan Young

Susan Young is a retired consultant epidemiologist, and previously worked in clinical infectious diseases and microbiology, latterly for the Public Health Laboratory Service. Her main interests are in the management of infectious diseases and their role in public health. Since her involvement at Christ Church, Spitalfields she has been instrumental in mass exhumation of burials, and in health and safety at work for funerary archaeologists and undertakers. She is a fellow of the Royal College of Physicians, London, and a Fellow of the Faculty of Public Health Medicine, Ireland.

Introduction

The choice of the period 1700–1850, for a review of death and burial, reflects both the existence of a significant corpus of relevant data and material and the importance of the period from an epidemiological, demographic, socio-economic, and religious perspective. If one were writing a book on the subject of death and burial during the 'long 18th century', there would be every opportunity to develop a framework and structure the research and results logically around this. The framework could be thematic, geographical, chronological, denominational, or some other relevant criteria. However, when organizing a conference, such as that held by the School of Conservation Sciences, Bournemouth University from the 19 to 20 April 1997, both life and scholarship prove far less straightforward. Despite assigning different sessions to different themes, and requesting that authors address particular subject areas, the interests and coverage of different contributors inevitably overlap. This is hardly surprising as they come from wide-ranging backgrounds including history, archaeology, clinical medicine and psychology, and the social sciences. Some cross numerous conceptual and thematic boundaries, some begin their research in eras, even centuries, before 1700 and others end theirs after 1850. Furthermore, some stray far from England's shores.

As a consequence of the vagaries of human nature, the dynamic nature of research, and all that makes any kind of academic research both worthwhile and unpredictable, the contributions to these proceedings, as of any conference, cross-reference, cross-fertilise, and overlap. Also, as would be expected in such an embryonic and wide-ranging subject area, they occasionally take issue with aspects of other contributions.

What is presented here is by no means a definitive statement of where we are in understanding death and burial in 18th and early 19th century England; a two-day conference could not achieve such an aim. Indeed it is worth drawing the reader's attention to the fact that the conference was initially planned as a one-day meeting. However, so great was the interest shown by both potential contributors and delegates that it was decided to extend the conference to two days. This is a reflection of not only the burgeoning interest in death and disposal but also in post-medieval archaeology in general. Further, the value of post-medieval archaeology as a provider of archaeological analogues, and as a means of examining and developing both archaeological and other scientific theories and methodologies is now fully appreciated.

Lacking the academic freedom of the sole author about to assemble her structural framework, what follows is organized to optimize the significance and relevance of individual contributions to the overall conference theme, with additional contributions included to elaborate on topics without which the editor felt the volume would be seriously disadvantaged. Perhaps the major deficiency in the volume, and bias reflected in the contributions, is an emphasis towards the intramural burial context to the disadvantage of the extra-mural. This reflects the limited research and contributions to this area rather than any editorial bias.

This volume is divided into four sections. Firstly, an introduction to funerary practice in post-medieval England using both historical and archaeological evidence. Secondly, a more archaeologically-orientated section looking at case-studies which are sub-divided into (i) the Anglican tradition and (ii) a nonconformist view: that of the Quakers. This is followed by a consideration of health and safety issues facing archaeologists excavating post-medieval mortuary contexts, and the volume concludes with a section on concerns, research priorities, and the way forward. None of these sections are definitive or mutually exclusive and some papers would fit equally well into more than one section.

Zusammenfassung

Über die Bedeutung der Gräber im nach-mitteralterlichem England von 1700–1850

Tod und Beerdigung:

Im April 1997 versammelte sich eine Gruppe von Archäologen, Historiker, Anthropologen und Sozialwissenschaftler bei einer Konferenz an der Universität in Bournemouth, um die Todesursachen und die Beerdigungen in England zwischen 1700 und 1850 zu besprechen. Dieser Bericht bezieht sich auf die Konferenz und ist die erste Publikation, die sich mit diesem Thema befaßt und dabei eine Palette von Quellen und Forschungsmethoden benutzt.

Die Mitbeteiligten, darunter die bekannten Experten Julian Litten, Jez Reeve und Louise Scheuer befassen sich mit der damaligen Begräbniskultur und -textilien, dem Todesalter, der Entwicklung der Friedhöfe und der zwichenmauerlichen Beerdigung. In dieser Publikation gibt es Berichte über die jüngsten Arbeitsvorgänge in St Nicholas, Sevenoaks, den Quäker-Friedhof in Kingston-upon-Thames und Bathford, Christ Church Spitalfields und St Augustine-the-Less, Bristol. In Betracht genommen werden Gesundheits – und Sicherheitsprobleme für Archäologen, die im Bereich der Beerdigungen tätig sind, wobei man sich auf Pocken und traumatischen Nachstreßeffekt konzentriert. Der letzte Abschnitt befaßt sich mit der Untersuchung des gegenwärtigen Wissens und mit dem Fortschritt der Dinge, wobei man im besonderen die Einstellung des Historikers auf den Tod mit dem Stand der wissenschaftlichen Analyse des Archäologen über die Überreste des Skeletts, ergänzt.

Die Publikation Über die Bedeutung der Gräber, im nach-mittelalterlichen England 1700–1850 ist ein erster, wichtiger Schritt in der Zusammenkunft der Vielfalt des Fach – und Spezialwissens, das dazu notwendig ist, um die Komplexität des Themas 'Tod und Beerdigung' im 'langen 18 Jahrhundert' vollständig zu verstehen.

Sommaire

'Grave Concerns' [A propos de sépultures]: mort et enterrements en Angleterre post-médiévale, 1700–1850

En avril 1997, un groupe d'archéologues, d'historiens, d'anthropologues et de spécialistes des sciences humaines se réunirent pour une conférence à l'université de Bournemouth afin de parler de la mort et des enterrements en Angleterre, de 1700 à 1850. Le présent rapport, basé sur la conférence, est la première publication traitant de ce sujet à l'aide d'une grande variété de sources et de méthodes d'enquête.

Les collaborateurs, y compris les experts reconnus, Julian Litten, Jez Reeve et Louise Scheuer, se penchent sur l'industrie funéraire, les textiles utilisés pour les enterrements, l'age à la mort, le développement des cimetières et les inhumations à l'intérieur des églises. On trouvera des rapports sur les récents travaux à St Nicholas, Sevenoaks, les cimetières Quaker de Kingston-upon-Thames et de Bathford, Christ Church, Spitalfields et St Augustine-the-Less, Bristol. La santé et la sécurité des archéologues funéraires est prise en considération, en mettant l'accent sur la petite vérole et la névrose traumatique. Une dernière section examine l'état actuel des connaissances et les développements futurs et se penche en particulier sur la manière dont l'analyse scientifique des ossements humains par les archéologues complète l'étude de la mort et des enterrements par les historiens.

'Grave Concerns' marque un important premier pas, celui qui réunit les nombreux domaines d'expertise et de spécialisations requis pour une bonne compréhension des complexités de la mort et des enterrements pendant le 'long 18ème siècle'.

Part I   Funerary practice in post-medieval England

Funerary practice

Funerary practice in post-medieval England provides a flavour of the enormously complex area of
relationships between the living and the dead,
social behaviour, and private practice. Aspects discussed include the funeral itself, the textiles
involved in burial, the monuments that were
erected to mark the grave, changes to the organiza-
tion and structure of the places where the majority
were interred, and the last resting place of the more
marginal members of society.

We begin with an overview of the English funeral,
contributed by the doyen of this complex and final
rite of passage, Julian Litten. This chapter deals
with the more public and commercial aspects of this
complex, evolving, and dynamic social ritual, which
appears to become increasingly commercialized and
secular through our period. Julian's picture of 'the
most lucrative trade ever invented', an industry
denying its clients freedom of choice, is not quite so
apparent in Rob Janaway's overview of funerary
textiles. Archaeological evidence, despite problems
of differential survival, suggests a greater degree of
individual expression in death than that suggested
by historical documents.

Individual expression, in this case of emotions,
personal loss, and of relationships, is a theme also
apparent in Sarah Tarlow's appraisal of the use of
gravestones in Orkney. The benefit to scholarship of
work on such remote geographical areas is that,
unlike in most areas of the British mainland, many
18th century Orcadian burial grounds and monuments survive, largely unaffected by later interments. Sarah's work also considers some of the
problems involved in addressing socially constructed emotions through material culture.

The 19th century saw a dramatic shift away from
burial grounds sited around city churches to cemeteries specifically laid out to cater for the burgeoning population of urban dead. Julie Rugg argues
that this represents a response to health problems
and the indignities imposed upon the dead, subsequent distress to the bereaved and bystanders, and
economic and financial opportunism. This shift is
complex in origin and expression and is largely
responsible for the present urban landscape encom-
passing the dead among the outer limits of town-
scapes in a relatively marginalized situation from
the one that it replaced. What is clear from Vanessa
Harding's contribution is that the disposal of the
mortal remains of marginal members of society has
always merited particular attention by those
responsible for managing places of interment. Traditional notions of status and entitlement could,
and frequently did, lead to the marginalization of
certain categories of people, both in death as in life,
within the construct of the Parish. By the 18th century these boundaries were being undermined by
wealth and transience. Archaeologists could usefully note the effect of such change on burial practice as previous certainties become far less secure.

1 The English funeral 1700–1850 *Julian Litten*

A Swiss observer, N Misson, provides significant evidence for the early development of the undertaking industry in London. Writing in 1719 he described the registration of deaths, the dressing of the corpse, the etiquette of 'viewing', the street procession, and the church service. His minute detail suggests that he had probably himself attended the funeral of a 'person of quality', that is, of middle or upper middle-class status (Misson 1719, 88–93).

First, Misson tells us, the death was notified to the parish minister who was responsible for ascertaining the cause of death from those who laid out the body. Ministers filed a 'certificate' with the parish clerk whose duty it was to publish a record of deaths and their estimated cause. In the City of London such returns were made to the Company of Parish Clerks who produced monthly Bills of Mortality, covering all the city churches. As the majority of the certificates were completed by 'good women' with no medical experience whatsoever, the reliability as to the cause of death is highly questionable. It was shortly after the registration of the death that the undertaker was called in.

Undertakers seem never to have enjoyed a popular press. In 1631 the antiquary John Weever lamented over the vain pomp provided by the trade:

> But funerals in any expensive way here with us, are now accounted but as a fruitless vanitie, insomuch that almost all the ceremoniall rites of obsequies heretofore used, are altogether laid aside: for we see daily that Noblemen, and Gentlemen of eminent rank, office, and qualitie are either silently buried in the night time, with a Torch, a two-penie Linke, and a Lanterne; or parsimoniously interred without the attendance of any one of the Officers of Armes, whose chiefest support, and maintenance, hath ever depended upon the performance of such funerall rites, and all exequies (Weever 1631, 17).

The first recorded operative trading as an undertaker per se covered by the time span of this paper, and, indeed, the earliest of a number of late 17th century trade cards in the British Library, was William Boyce, 'in ye Grate Ould Bayley Near Newgeat, London'. His trade card of *c* 1675–80 (Fig 1.1) is headed by a reproduction of his shop board: to the left, and hanging from a hook, an upholstered coffin, with the initials B I A, an hourglass and skull and crossbones on the lid, the whole above another skull and crossbones, while to the right is the badge of Richard II, a white hart couchant sporting a crowned collar with attached

chain. The accompanying legend reads: 'By William BOYCE / Coffinsmaker at ye Whight / Hart & Coffin in ye Grate Ould / Bayley Near Newgeat / London You May Be Furnished / With all sorts & sizes of / Coffins & Shrouds Ready Made / And all other Conveniences / Belonging to Funerals' (British Museum: Boyce).

Contemporary to William Boyce was William Russell, an heraldic painter and coffin-maker, also trading in London. Far more ingenious and innovative than Boyce, Russell entered into an agreement with the College of Arms in 1689 whereby, for an arranged fee, its members would attend certain funerals of persons of rank furnished by Russell. This was a shrewd move on his part for it meant that not only did he secure the blessing, and guidance, of the College, but also avoided their

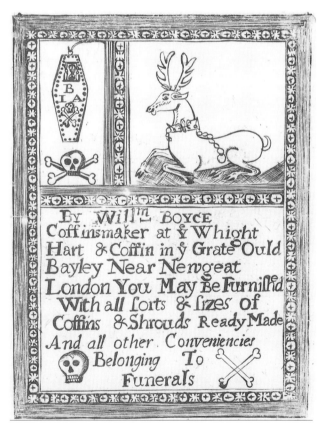

Figure 1.1 Trade card of William Boyce, coffin-maker (c 1680). This is presumed to be the earliest extant trade card of a coffin-maker. Boyce was based under the sign of the White Hart & Coffin in the Great Old Bailey, Newgate, and limited his venture to the supply of coffins to the undertaking trade (copyright: The British Museum)

censure. However, as an heraldic painter, Russell was probably already known to the College and may well have once worked for them directly or received work on contract. Whatever the association, Russell's agreement with the College was an astute political ploy and must have been seen by him as an exceptional opening into the mysteries of the College's funeral practices. However, the College of Arms did not privatize all of their dealings, as they remained the funeral furnishing establishment for the royal funerals until 1751 when a private undertaker, a Mr Harcourt, was requested by the Lord Chamberlain to furnish the funeral of Frederick, Prince of Wales, though it is possible that private companies had been previously involved in some small way in royal funerals. It is doubtful that the College of Arms provided, for example, coffins, and it would seem probable that they contracted this out to the trade, to people such as William Russell.

Yet neither Boyce nor Russell enjoyed an absolute monopoly, for there were others in business at that time, such as William Grinly of Fleet Street whose trade card of *c* 1700 was advertising 'At ye lower corner of Fleet lane at ye Signe of ye Naked Boy / & Coffin you may be Accommodated wth. all things for a / Funeral as well as ye meanest as those of greater Ability / upon Reasonable Terms more particularly Coffins Shrouds / Palls Cloaks Sconces Stans Hangings for Rooms / Heraldry Hearse & Coaches Gloves wth. all other things / not here mentioned' (V&A 1700). The trade card of Eleazar Malory, *c* 1720 (Fig 1.2), shows a selection of funeral accoutrements, with the legend 'Joiner at the / Coffin in WhiteChapel, near Red / Lion Street end, maketh Coffins, / Shrouds, letteth Palls, Cloaks and / Furnisheth with all other things / necessary for funerals, at Reaso / nable Rates, Also Appraiseth and / Buyeth all sorts of Household Goods' (British Museum: Malory). Also practising at this time were Arthur Granger, also *c* 1720, at the Crown & Coffin, Whitechapel, and John Clarke, at the Four Coffins, Jermyn Street, St James's in *c* 1725.

In the early years of the trade there were no written rules or codes of practice; practically anyone could set themselves up as a coffin-maker or undertaker, and many did. The extant trade cards reveal that the furnishing of funerals in the early 18th century was, in the main, restricted to those already involved in carpentry, joinery, cabinet-making, and the upholstery trades. Territorial boundaries seem to have been honoured, especially in London and the larger conurbations, for funeral furnishers appear to have limited their operations to those parishes in which they were situated, and while most of the later 18th century trade cards advertised 'Funerals performed in all parts of Great Britain', it is doubtful that this offer was ever taken up. Fourteen trade cards issued by London undertakers during *c* 1670–*c* 1760 are recorded by Ambrose Heal (Heal 1925), and as none indicate any other craft affiliation it could be assumed that

they were able to make a living and furnish from stock all that went to provide for a funeral.

When the College of Arms hindered the grant of a new Charter to the Upholders Company in 1722, a group of enterprising London undertakers made an attempt to form their own livery company. A contemporary trade card, designed by George Bickham, for the United Company of Undertakers was produced in anticipation. It was an elaborate coxcombery (Fig 1.3): Youth and Age, represented as Bacchus and Clotho, sit on an oval cartouche in front of a display of banners, bannerols, and pennants, flanked by Time and Eternity, while below is a pair of weeping cherubs, each resting on an upholstered child's coffin. The inscription reads: 'Funerals Performed / To & from all parts of Great Britain; in ye/ Best, and most Reasonable Manner;/ By ye United Company of UNDERTAKERS;/ At their House, the Corner of Southampton Street / Bloomsbury, in Holborn / LONDON'. But was this no more than a co-operative of local Bloomsbury

Figure 1.2   Trade card of Eleazer Malory, joiner and coffin-maker (c 1720). Malory was more widely involved in the business of furnishing funerals than his description of 'joiner and coffin-maker' suggests. His trade card indicates that his coffins were provided lined and with grave clothes, and that he also hired out palls and cloaks to the trade (copyright: The British Museum)

Figure 1.3   Trade card of the United Company of Undertakers, c 1725 (copyright: Hon Christopher Lennox Boyd)

undertakers? Probably, for the United Company of Undertakers was never admitted at Guildhall, and the 'house' was none other than the business premises of Robert Legg Snr, upholder, appraiser, and undertaker. Whatever ensued between the Worshipful Company of Upholders and Legg, the United Company of Undertakers did not receive livery status, though the idea did excite sufficient interest to merit a caricature from William Hogarth entitled 'The Company of Undertakers' with the motto *Et Plurima Mortis Imago* – The Very Image of Death.

The Hogarth engraving was erroneously published by Bertram Puckle in 1926 as the 'Sign of the now extinct Company of Undertakers' (Puckle 1926, facing 128). Had he but read the caption he would have quickly understood the lampoon:

Beareth Sable, an Urinal proper, between 12 Quack-Heads of the Second and 12 Cane Heads Or, Consultant. On a Chief Nebulae, Ermine, One Compleat Doctor isuant, checki sustaining in his Right Hand a Baton of the second. On his Dexter and Sinister sides two Demi-Doctors, isuant of the second, and two Cane Heads isuant of the third; The first having One Eye conchant, towards the Dexter Side of the Escocheon; the second Faced per pale proper & Gules, Guardant. With this motto Et Plurima Mortis Imago.

While Legg and his compatriots were enjoying a short-lived grandeur within the spurious and ill-fated United Company of Undertakers, the Upholders' Company continued to support those of their members who furnished funerals as part of their everyday trade. By the mid 1730s the Upholders saw fit to make available to their members blank funeral invitation tickets for overprinting, designed by A N Coypel and engraved by Ja. Chereau, being a deliberately up-market plagiarism of that previously issued by the United Company of Undertakers.

Not all London funeral furnishers were anxious to become affiliated to either the Upholders' Company or the United Company of Undertakers. Robert Green, of St Margaret's Hill, Southwark was obviously content as a single operative furnishing undertaker. Green, who issued one of the most elaborate rococo trade cards of the time (Fig 1.4), offered a comprehensive service:

1752. Robert Green / Coffin Maker & Undertaker / at the four Coffins St. Margaret's Hill, / Southwark, / Sells and Lets all Manner of Furniture for

Figure 1.4   Trade card of Robert Green, coffin dealer and undertaker (1752). A number of trade cards were based on designs for engraved ornament, and this is one such example. Green was a funeral furnisher and warehouseman, his many and diverse wares being advertised in full on his trade card, and his premises identified in St Margaret's Hill, Southwark under the sign of the Four Coffins (copyright: The British Museum)

/ Funerals, on Reasonable Terms, / VIZ. / Velvet Palls, Hangings for Rooms, large Silver'd / Candlesticks & Sconces, Tapers & Wax Lights, Heraldry, / Feathers and Velvets, fine Cloth Cloaks and middling Do. Rich / Silk Scarves, Allamode & Sarsnett Hatbands, Italian Crape / by the Piece or Hatband, black and white Favours, Cloth Black, / or Grey; Baize and Flannel Do. Burying Crapes of all Sorts, / fine Quilting & Quilted Mattrices the best Lac'd, Plain & Shammy Gloves, Kidd & Lamb Do. &c. NB All Sorts of Plates & / Handles for Coffins in Brass, Lead or Tin, likewise Nails of all Sorts / Coffins & Shrouds of all Sizes ready made. Where Country Chapman / and others may be furnished in the most Expeditious/ Manner on the least Notice (British Museum: Green).

The majority of undertakers' trade cards concerned themselves with advertising their seemingly limitless wares; as a result, few contemporary illustrations survive depicting the interiors of funeral furnishing establishments of the 18th century. Trade cards tend to depict stylized street processions (of an elaboration which they were probably hardly ever asked to furnish) with occasional spurious hatchments, targes, and other heraldic devices. A proof engraving of a trade card of *c* 1730 exists of the St Paul's Churchyard upholsterer and cabinet-maker, Christopher Gibson, who held a royal warrant as court supplier (V&A 1710). A well-dressed gentleman in the centre of the group, presumably Gibson himself, is shown attending two clients. To the left of the shop, a gilder prepares an armchair, beneath a pair of pall escutcheons and two hatchments. In the back room, beyond the baulks of cloth and the cutting bench, are five more pall escutcheons. Judging from this display of post mortem heraldry, the furnishing of funerals appears to have played an important part in Gibson's day-to-day business.

Less rare are views of the exteriors of undertakers and funeral furnishing premises. Probably the best-known image of a coffin-maker's shop sign appears in Hogarth's engraving *Gin Lane*, of a suspended coffin and figure of Father Time. An engraving from 1737 by John Kip of St Clement Danes, Strand shows a shop-front of a furnishing undertaker not dissimilar to that of Messrs Barnard's premises in an anonymous watercolour of *c* 1840 in Brighton Museum. The addresses on the extant trade cards, invitations, memorial cards, and contemporary trade indexes for London undertakers of the period *c* 1700–1850 indicate that the majority of coffin-makers and funeral furnishers were situated off the high street, thereby maintaining a discreet but not inaccessible presence. However, this is not particularly important as house visits from the undertaker to the client was the standard means of conducting business. In this way the undertaker/funeral furnisher gauged at first hand the social status and standing of his client and thus estimated the quality of the funeral to be supplied.

The funeral trade had three distinct branches: coffin-making, undertaking, and funeral furnishing. The coffin-maker did that which his name suggests: he made coffins. He might also have performed funerals, but not necessarily so. In the main he sold his coffins on, mainly to those who advertised the performance of funerals as a sideline, but also to undertakers and, occasionally, to funeral furnishers. The undertaker, who might also be his own coffin-maker, provided for funerals at the lower end of the social scale, much like Charles Dickens's Mr Sowerberry in *Oliver Twist,* or Mr Mold in *Martin Chuzzlewit.* The funeral furnisher both bought in and/or made his own coffins, dressed and upholstered them, and performed the funeral. A coffin-maker, therefore, looked up to the funeral furnisher while respecting the undertaker, the undertaker respected both the coffin-maker and the funeral furnisher, but might have looked down on a coffin-maker who performed funerals; the funeral furnisher needed the coffin-maker, and probably ignored the existence of the undertaker.

From surviving trade cards, pattern books, bill headings, trade directories, and livery company admissions lists it is apparent that Southwark, Whitechapel, Limehouse, and Spitalfields appear as the four main centres in London accommodating the funeral furnishing trading houses and manufactories during the 18th and early 19th centuries. Southwark specialized in the production of coffin furniture, that is the metal fittings for coffins, such as depositum plates, handles, and lid motifs. Whitechapel and Limehouse developed an expertise in the production and wholesale manufacture of coffins and fabric-covered outer cases. Factories were close to the docks, the majority of iron foundries, brass founders, and tin-platers being sited in Southwark and the timber yards at Limehouse and Whitechapel. Moreover, Whitechapel bordered onto Spitalfields, the Huguenot centre for linen, velvet, and silk weaving, particularly those items known as 'black stuff', the crepe, Utrecht, and Genoese velvets closely associated with the funeral furnishing trade. Yet while certain coffin-makers and upholders occasionally furnished funerals, there is no evidence to show that the same can be said for iron founders and tin-plate manufacturers. To keep transport costs down, a number of funeral furnishing warehouses were situated close to the manufacturers; it has already been noted that Robert Green had his premises in St Margaret's Hill, Southwark, and so did Tuesby & Cooper of Borough High Street.

In the main, the average undertaker was little more than a speculative carpenter or joiner who, by direct contact with the metalworking and soft furnishing trades, or via such houses as Robert Green's and Tuesby & Cooper's, was able to buy in all that was required to furnish a funeral. However, those upholsterers and drapers who ran a funeral furnishing branch to their main business, while able to provide the soft furnishings such as coffin linings and coverings, shrouds, palls, gloves, cloaks, and mourning hatbands from their own stock in trade, would have contracted out to the coffin-maker the provision of the coffin, to a funeral furnisher or funeral furnishing featherman for the plumes, and to the 'black' jobmaster for the hire of the hearse, carriages, and horses.

The undertaker and the funeral furnisher's relationship with the client involved elements of hire and outright purchase. Obviously the coffin, with its linings, grave clothes, and metal furnishings was purchased outright, as were the mourners' gloves. The mourning hatbands and scarves were generally hired for funerals below the rank of tradesman, and purchased by those higher up the social scale. The pall, cloaks, feathers, and house/church drapery were hired as they would be of no use to the client once the funeral had been performed. None of Robert Green's clients, for example, would have needed to retain the large silvered candlesticks and sconces. Conversely, in heraldic funerals, the armorials would have been of no use to the funeral furnisher: these would be treated as an outright purchase on the part of the client, and those displayed by Christopher Gibson in his St Paul's Churchyard premises were there as advertisements rather than returned hired goods. Green's hire service enabled the less wealthy town undertaker to furnish a funeral in the London fashion if required to do so, and Richard Chandles of Shrewsbury, trading in c 1750, was able to offer to the country undertaker items from his warehouse to enable them to perform funerals 'after ye same manner / as by ye Undertakers at London, at Reasonable Rate' (Christopher Lennox-Boyd Collection), with the country undertaker transferring the hire cost, plus a small handling charge for his own services, to the client.

While the possibility of hiring was a boon to the small town and country undertaker, it would not have been cheap to set up in business as a funeral warehouseman, as he would have needed at least four complete sets of funeral accoutrements to make a reasonable living. This stock would have included eight velvet palls (four adult size, four children's), four hundred yards of black baize for room hangings, twenty-four silvered candlesticks, forty-eight plumes of black ostrich feathers, one gross scarves, forty-eight cloaks, one gross gloves of various quality and sizes, canvas and paints for heraldic achievements, two gross of assorted candles, one hundred yards of crepe, one gross black and white rosettes, shrouds and miscellaneous grave clothes of varying sizes, coffin mattresses, about one hundred and sixty-eight coffins, sheet lead for coffin shells, one gross yards of velvet for coffin case covering, and a multitude of copper, brass, lead and tin-dipped stamped iron coffin furniture; all with, perhaps, a small stock of

repousséd painted copper coronets and three-dimensional coronets of all degrees for the funerals of the nobility. He may also have had four funeral carriages. Assuming items to the value of £500 would need to be hired by an undertaker at, say, £50 to furnish the funeral of a member of the middle class, he would recoup this outlay by charging his client £100, with the funeral warehouse receiving the £50 hire charge and the undertaker making £50. From this £50 he would be required to pay for the hire of the horses, mutes, and the coffin bearers, perhaps ending up with a profit of, say, £25. Suitably maintained, it would have been possible for a complete set of funeral accoutrements as outlined by Robert Green to have serviced 50 funerals before requiring replacement, earning for the warehouseman during their 'lifetime' a total of £2,500.00. If it cost £500 to buy a set of accoutrements, and £600 to replace them, the warehouseman was making £1,900 profit, a c 300% mark-up against expenditure. Items replaced were more often than not disposed of within the trade, being acquired by the lesser undertakers, such as Dickens's Mr Sowerberry, who carried out funerals for the lower end of society.

The investment made by such funeral warehousemen to provide such feigned pomp and parade must have been substantial. Unfortunately, the profit to be made induced those on the fringes of the trade to exploit the system. In 1843 Edwin Chadwick asked Mr Dix, a successful London undertaker performing upwards of eight hundred funerals a year, to explain how such anomalies came about and how the hiring system worked in practice:

Dix	'. . . frequently perform funerals three deep, that is, I do it for one person, who does for another, who does it for the relatives of the deceased, he being the first person applied to.'
Chadwick	'The people, then, generally apply to the nearest person?'
Dix	'Yes, they do. Everybody calls himself an undertaker. The numerous men employed as bearers become undertakers, although they have never done anything until they have got the job. I have known one of these men get a new suit of clothes out of a funeral of one decent mechanic' (Chadwick 1843, 51).

Daniel Defoe informs us that 'Generally speaking, most tradesmen have some peculiar ways to themselves which they either derived from masters who taught them, or from experience of things, or from something in the course of business' (Defoe 1645), but we learn from R Campbell in his *London Tradesman* of 1747 that this did not strictly apply to undertakers:

a set of men who live by death and never care to appear but at the End of Man's Life ... their Business is to watch Death, and to furnish out the Funeral Solemnity, with as much pomp and feigned sorrow as the Heirs or Successors of the deceased chose to purchase: They are a hard-hearted Generation, and require more money than Brains to conduct their Business; I know no one Qualification peculiarly necessary to them except, that is, a steady, demure and melancholy Countenance at Command: I do not know that they take Apprentices in their Capacity as Undertakers, for they are generally Carpenters, or Herald Painters besides; and they only employ, as Journeymen, a set of Men whom they have picked up, possessed of a sober countenance, and a solemn Melancholy Face, whome they pay at so much a Jobb' (Campbell 1747, 329–40).

Again, the commentator Thomas Lamb had a poor opinion of the trade; in his two-volume work of 1811, *On Burial Societies, & the Character of an Undertaker,* he furnishes the reader with a dismal description of the trade:

He is master of ceremonies at burials and mourning assemblies, grand marshal at funeral processions, the only true yeoman of the body, over which he exercises dictatorial authority from the moment that breath has taken leave to that of its final commitment to the earth. His ministry begins where the physician's, lawyer's and divine's end ... He is bed-maker to the dead. The pillows which he lays never rumple. The day of interment is the theatre in which he displays the mysteries of his art (Lamb 1811).

These comments were later ratified by Charles Dickens and, in 1840, by Douglas Jerrold:

Happy is the Undertaker above all the race of trading men – his commodities, as provided and supplied, defy the voice of cavil. His articles, six, eight, ten feet below the earth, are not to be questioned. He boldly charges for the 'best mattress and pillow'; for the grass has begun to grow above them, or the masons has built them over, and who should doubt their quality? No man (that is, no tradesman) has a more exquisite notion of the outward proprieties of life – of all its external decencies, luxuries, and holiday show-making, than your Undertaker. With him, death is not death, but, on the contrary, a something to be handsomely appointed and provided for; to be approached ... with an attention, a courtesy, commensurate with the probability of profit' (May 1996, 4).

When Edwin Chadwick's comments on the trade are examined it becomes abundantly clear why funeral warehouses were needed. The number of persons whose sole business was that of undertaker whose names appeared in the Post Office Directory for the year 1843 for the metropolis was 275. However, a much larger number than were named in the Directory retained the insignia of undertakers in their shop windows, for the sake of the profits of one or two funerals a year, bringing the total to 730. They merely transmitted orders to the furnishing undertakers and took their percentage. One early 19th century funeral warehouseman was J Turner of Farringdon Street, a 'Coffin Maker, Plate Chaser, Furnishing Undertaker and funeral Featherman'. His nine-page catalogue of 1838 contains a wealth of information for the funeral historian, listing 111 coffins of thirty differing types, twenty sizes of off-the-peg shroud (each available in four qualities of material), fifteen styles of ruffling, winding-sheets, mattresses, coffin furniture, and palls (Turner catalogue, Guildhall Library). Turner was also able to provide bearers and attendants' fittings, together with hearses, coaches and horses if required, and to any part of the country.

Taking items at random, for 17 shillings one got a 'good inch elm Coffin, smoothed, oiled, and finished one row round of black or white nails, a plate of inscription, four handles, lined and pillow', whilst £9 could secure Turner's *pièce de resistance,* a '1½ inch Oak case, covered with superfine cloth, finished three rows all round, and six ornamental diamonds, with best nails, lead or brass plate, glory and urn, four pairs of cherub handles, and four dozen rays and stars'. This, together with an 'Elm Shell, covered with 4lb lead, lined, ruffled, and pillow', would provide a item fit for the grandest vault, and would have been sold to the client for about £25. Added to this would be a further £25 for two mutes with gowns, staves, hatbands, and gloves, six pages with hatbands, gloves, truncheons, and wands, six mourners' cloaks, hatbands, and gloves, six coffin bearers with hatbands and gloves, and the hire of a hearse and three mourning coaches, each pulled by four horses with palls. In this way the £9 coffin would end up as part of a £50 funeral, with the undertaker probably clearing ten guineas for his trouble. There was little interference from those ordering the funeral regarding the manner of its execution for it was the undertaker/funeral furnisher who decided on what was considered customary and fashionable in any given situation. He alone selected the wood for the coffin, the lining, the shroud, the coffin furniture, the quality of the pall, the number of attendant mutes/bearers/pages, and the grandeur of the street procession (Fig 1.5). The standard instruction from the client was to 'provide that which is customary'; a pathetic comment, in which the trade's development of funeral etiquette for each rank in society was recognized and the client's control over the funeral cost surrendered to the trade. Occasionally the trade overstepped the mark and offered the bereaved a funeral of the type that was above their station. While this was accepted by the pretentious, it usually put at risk the possibility of the undertaker receiving future

Wm Hogarth del.t   *J. Ireland sc*

You are desired to Accompany ɣ Corps of   *from*
h late Dwelling in   *to*
on   next at   *of the Clock in the Evening.*

Perform'd by Humphrey Drew Undertaker, in King-street Westminster.

Figure 1.5   Trade card of Humphrey Drew, undertaker, by William Hogarth (c 1720). It was not infrequent for funeral furnishers to solicit designs for their trade cards from well-known artists. Here Hogarth shows an idealized interpretation of a funeral entering St Paul's Church, Covent Garden. The funeral depicted is that of a person of quality, as indicated by the escutcheons on the pall. The coffin is raised on the shoulders of bearers, the ensemble enveloped by a huge pall whose hem is supported by pall-bearers (copyright: Litten Collection)

patronage from the family. In short, undertaking had become a necessary, rather than a popular, trade. It provided a public service and was, therefore, tolerated. The undertaker of the late Georgian period does not stand up to close examination. In the main they were greedy, with a greed so rapacious that they were not averse to reducing some of their clients to penury by charging for an inflated spectacle which few could understand at prices that few could afford. This was especially heinous, since many items charged for were, in essence, only hired, to be put back into stock to be 're-sold' time and again. Conversely, the funeral furnishing trade, that is to say the 'quality undertaker', rarely overstepped the mark.

The funerals performed by the trade in the second quarter of the 19th century were anything but simple. However, the question arises whether the undertaker was aware of the significance of the many trappings he insisted on providing. The following conversation is recorded between Edwin Chadwick and a London tradesman:

Chadwick   'Are you aware that the array of funerals, commonly made by undertakers, is strictly the heraldic array of a baronial funeral, the two men who stand at the doors being supposed to be the two porters of the castle, with their staves, in black; the man who heads the procession, wearing a scarf, being a representative of a herald-at-arms; the man who carries a plume of feathers on his head being an esquire, who bears the shield and casque, with its plume of feathers; the knights-companions-at-arms; the men walking with their wands being supposed to represent gentleman-ushers, with their wands; are you aware that this is said to be the origin and type of the common array usually provided by those who undertake to perform funerals?'

Undertaker 'No, I am not aware of it.'

Chadwick 'It may be presumed that those who order funerals are equally unaware of the incongruity for which such expense is incurred?'

Undertaker 'Undoubtedly they are' (Chadwick 1843, 267).

Regarding the corpse, it received no hygienic treatment during the 18th and early 19th centuries, as 'embalming' was reserved for members of the royal family and the aristocracy. Bodies were merely washed, dressed, and cased, being buried within seven to twelve days of death, the encoffined remains being kept in the main reception room of the house until the day of the funeral; 'chapels of rest' in funeral parlours attached to undertakers' workshops were not introduced until c 1875. The inner joints of the coffin were caulked with Swedish pitch, to prevent leakage of obnoxious gasses and liquid emissions associated with death, and the base was covered either with a mattress or a thin layer of bran beneath the fabric lining to absorb the discharged fluids associated with primary decomposition. Once cased, the space between the shrouded body and the lid of the coffin was filled with aromatic bran spiked with Oil of Rosemary and balsam, to mask the odour of death. In the matter of triple-shell coffins, it was not unusual for a layer of powdered charcoal or plaster of Paris to be applied to the lid of the inner coffin prior to the fashioning and soldering-up of the lead shell. From the ledgers of Messrs Banting, the royal undertakers between c 1775–1935, it is apparent that the inner coffin was covered with cambric before being soldered down and that the outer case was lined with cambric before the lead shell was deposited in it (Litten Collection: Banting).

Nothing was published on the undertaking trade and coffin-making before the beginning of this century, the first book appearing in 1905 by Paul Hasluck under the title of *Coffin-Making and Undertaking* and has one of the shortest overviews on the subject yet published: 'Undertaking is a business which, especially in country districts, may with advantage be allied to that of the builder, wheelwright, or cabinet-maker, the necessary experience, except in a few extra details, being very similar to that requisite in all branches of woodworking. Undertaking may be interpreted not only as coffin-making, but as including the management of funerals throughout' (Hasluck 1905, 9). However, it is to the dynastic and parochial burial vaults one needs to descend if one wishes to trace the development of the coffin from c 1700–1850. A detailed study in the early 1980s of nearly one thousand coffins of the period 1728–1852 in the vaults beneath Christ Church, Spitalfields revealed a wealth of information on coffin-making, as well as on shrouds, coffin linings, and coffin furniture (see Reeve & Adams 1993; Molleson & Cox 1993).

The inner coffin was usually of elm, 1 or 1½ inches thick, planed, smoothed, and oiled, butt-jointed with recessed lid, and covered in cambric. These sections were both glued and screwed together, the base within the side planks, the screw holes countersunk, and infilled with putty. To support the recessed lid, a length of beading was affixed with glue and tacks around the upper inner side, 1 or 1½ inches from the top, depending on the thickness of the lid. This lid was anchored to the sides by screws through the sides. Prior to fixing this lid the inner joints, base, and sides were caulked with Swedish pitch, the base covered with a shallow layer of wood shavings, sawdust, and bran over which the bottom sheet was tacked if a mattress was not being used, the side lining was affixed, then a ruched or broderie anglaise frill; finally, the pillow and the shrouded body. If there was to be no viewing of the remains, the coffin was at once covered with plain or waxed cambric, glued, and gimped into place.

The lead shell had to be bespoke. Few coffin-makers had the talent to fashion such an item, so an order would have gone out to a local plumber. Eleven ways of cutting and fitting the lead have been recorded, but the two most commonly used were the 'shoe box' and the 'smooth wrap'. To produce the latter, the inner coffin was placed on to a sheet of milled lead which was then cut so as to be three inches large all round the coffin itself; this was then turned up and tacked to the wood. A shaped length was placed on the lid and likewise folded over the edge and tacked into place. All joints were then soldered and smoothed, the tack-heads soldered so as to maintain the water-resistance and airtight qualities required of the coffin. A diaper design was then card-wired on the shell using a template and a straight-edge. Finally, the lead depositum plate was soldered into place. The 'shoe box' type was similarly fashioned, though the sides were affixed before the lid.

Whether the undertaker or funeral furnisher produced a bespoke outer case or took one from stock is not known, though logic argues in favour of the latter. Outer cases of the period c 1725–75 and later were sumptuously upholstered and provided with elaborate cast brass coffin furniture. Veneers were used only to mask carpentry mistakes. One such instance was discovered during the 1983–4 excavations at St Augustine the Less, Bristol masking a split at the shoulder caused by overzealous saw-cuts when kerfing. Cases made and upholstered by cabinet-makers, as distinct from coffin-makers, have had greater attention paid to the affixation of the velvet, those in the Poulett vault at Hinton St George, Somerset and the De La Warr vault at Withyham, Sussex housing examples of this type. The coffin of the Fourth Earl De La Warr (d 1795) was padded with shoddy (woollen cloth) prior to the fitting of the velvet, shoddy and velvet being gimped to the chamfered edge of the base of the case. The velvet, or baize for lesser mortals, was used sparingly, tucked in upon itself at the angles of the coffin and the width of the side planks at the top. The lid was similarly upholstered though sometimes the velvet did intrude on the underside surface. Great care had to be taken in fitting the cotter-pins securing the grip and grooves were cut on the inside of the case into which the cotter-pins were bent, so as not to come into contact with the lead shell. The upholstery pins, escutcheons, lid motifs, and depositum plates were affixed to the case prior to the insertion of the lead shell, their appearance being enhanced if applied to a fully-upholstered case.

The positioning of the lead shell was a delicate operation, care being needed to avoid piercing or damaging the lead in any way. Having been placed on three lengths of webbing, six men would be required to lift the shell and put it into the case; the webs were then cut, as it would have not been possible to withdraw them owing to the weight of the shell. Finally, the lid was put into position and screwed or bolted down. The trade never solved the issue of the aesthetic positioning of the lid screws/bolts: too often they either interrupt or abut the upholstery pins around the edge of the lid, lending credence to the opinion that the majority of such outer cases were upholstered by coffin-makers and delivered finished to the funeral furnisher. Some tradesmen endeavoured to mask the countersunk screw-heads with small discs of velvet.

Not all coffin-makers went to the expense of buying two-foot widths of wood; some made up their cases from twelve-inch or six-inch planks, relying on the velvet upholstery to mask their techniques. A number of such cases of this type were seen in the vaults at Christ Church, Spitalfields and St Marylebone Parish Church as well as in the vaults beneath St Paul's, Shadwell and St John's, Wapping. A classic example survives at Hinton St George, Somerset with the coffin of Colonel William Poulett (d 1805). The black velvet has perished, exposing the sides of the case which, on examination, proves not to be a single plank but four six-inch boards, butted and held into place with thin iron straps (Fig 1.6).

Figure 1.6   Coffin of Colonel William Poulett, d 1805. Poulett vault, Hinton St George, Somerset. Copyright: Rector and Churchwardens of Hinton St George and with acknowledgement to the Countess Poulett (photo: Eric Boore)

While the coffin enjoyed a number of variants, the differential in styles of grave clothes is even more marked. Some undertakers dispensed with the full-length shroud, preferring to adapt the coffin lining to serve this purpose. Once the coffin had received its primary lining and edging frill, two rectangular sheets, the length and width of the coffin, were tacked to the base at its sides. With the body safely ensconced, and the fitted pillow beneath the head, these 'side sheets' were folded over the remains and either pinned or roughly sewn into place. The upper section of the sheet was left parted, exposing the features to view, and remained so until the time came to secure the lid. In this way was the body was placed in the coffin dressed in a shift and bonnet. It was not only a neat way to 'finish' the interior but also gave to the corpse the appearance of being asleep, if not bedded down for the night. The confusion caused by the nomenclature in some late 18th and early 19th century trade catalogues regarding 'winding sheets' was ironed out at Spitalfields when it was realised that this meant 'side sheets'. Turner of Farringdon Street stocked twenty lengths of shroud, from infants through to adults. A six foot shroud of 'common quality' cost 2s 8d, of 'middle quality' 3s 8d, of 'fine rose' 4s 9d, and 'superior rose fully trimmed' at 6s 3d. The 'fine rose' would have been on linen with buttoned rosettes, similar to one of c 1850 in the Castle Museum, York.

There were two categories of soft furnishings at Spitalfields: the dressing of the coffin and the grave clothes. The coffin dressings were of plain cloth, devoid of decoration. Side linings, however, were either plain, or with punched or pinked edges. The majority of the linings and mattress covers were either bleached woven cotton or wool, as were the grave clothes and frills, though there were three instances where there were silk fittings in satin weave. The mattresses and pillows contained a variety of stuffing material: wool, feathers, and hay, and only two out of the one thousand coffins examined had both pillow and mattress surviving. Further, there was only one recorded surviving example where a pad had been bound to the loins to absorb body fluid emissions, a type of post mortem Peaudouce, and few surviving instances where modesty drawers had been used. The limbs of a number of the remains had been tied, probably for ease of transfer from death-bed to coffin, in particular legs were bound either at the ankle or the big toe, and/or the arms secured to the side of the body. These ties were sometimes torn strips of material or, more commonly, commercially produced ribbon. It is clear, then, that the 18th century undertaker had ribbon available in the same way that the modern funeral director has bandage. The embarrassment of jaw relaxation was most frequently addressed by reliance on the draw-strings of the bonnets and caps. Some bodies had been placed into their coffins in their day clothes; this is an unusual occurrence in English undertaking and may have been the result of death through infectious disease and the reluctance of those dealing with the corpse to wash and dress it in the usual way. Surprisingly, quite a number were laid out with their dentures *in situ*.

At the very top end of the funeral furnishing scale the richly-upholstered outer case was of 1½ inch Spanish mahogany, the interior lined with cambric, the exterior padded with shoddy and covered with rich scarlet Genoese or black Utrecht velvet, four pairs of gilt grip-plates and grips, panelled two rows all round of gilt-headed upholstery pins, seven dozen gilt escutcheon drops, a gilt metal Urn and Glory, and a burnished brass plate of inscription. Indeed, this style of coffin remained popular well into the first quarter of the 19th century, and one was provided for Sir Francis Bourgeois for deposit in his Dulwich mausoleum within a few days of his death on 7 January 1811. Most funeral furnishers have their idiosyncrasies, and it is possible in some dynastic vaults to recognise coffins produced in the same workshop. So it is with the Bourgeois coffin, where the urn was placed just below the plate of inscription, whereas the majority of funeral furnishers fixed it lower down, almost above the occupant's knees. The Bourgeois coffin represents the highest quality of undertaking available at the time and could well have been provided by the society funeral furnishers, Messrs Jarvis & Sons of Great Marylebone Street, just two roads away from the house where Bourgeois died. Their trade card of c 1810 depicts a similar coffin (V&A 1810).

The bought ledger for 1746–7 of Richard Carpenter, an undertaker located in Fleet Street, London, shows how a business was carried out in the middle of the 18th century (Guildhall Library: Carpenter). Carpenter dealt with one coffin-maker, and all thirty-nine coffins ordered between July and September 1747 were standard stock sizes held by his supplier. They were bought plain, so that he could provide the finish. A second expensive item was the burnished brass inscription plates, whose cost equalled that of the coffin. He rented items from other suppliers, the largest outlay to those who hired out the black ostrich feathers. In addition, glovers, linen drapers, and wax chandlers provided him with other goods. Carpenter had a local plumber on call to provide lead shells, and, for those higher up the social scale, he engaged the services of an heraldic painter. Overall, his ledger reveals that those engaged in the undertaking trade, as opposed to the funeral furnishing trade, in the mid 18th century did not have the capital to equip their own establishments with items required for furnishing funerals. Most were middlemen, who 'undertook' to organize and arrange funerals of quality only when called upon to do so; it was not their standard stock in trade.

By the last quarter of the 18th century London practices were being emulated outside the capital. John Miller of Ipswich branched out in the 1790s and annexed a funeral furnishing department to his drapery business. The most elaborate funeral he staged was that of Captain Kennedy on 28 May 1810, 'a military style funeral' at a cost of £289 0s 9d. It was not until 15 May 1815 that he mounted his first 'heraldic style funeral' when he was asked to 'provide that which is customary' for the late Charles Berners, and here he had to rely on the funeral warehouses of Messrs Mott & Witt and Messrs Cresall. Miller's relations with London funeral warehouses were seldom pleasant; in the case of the Berners funeral he challenged Moss & Witt's bill of £582 11s 1d, saying that the invoice indicated a great deal of 'padding' and that the arrangements could have been provided for £200 less. Moss & Witt refused to lower their charges, and Miller placed the matter into the hands of his solicitors who negotiated a settlement of £400, a saving to Miller of £182 11s 1d. From then on he only uses Messrs Cresall as his supplier.

Not all coffins, however, were put to funerary use. When the medieval roof of St Botolph, Hadstock, Essex was being recorded in 1974 it was discovered that a number of coffin boards had been used for running repairs during the 18th century. Mrs Delany, in her *Autobiography*, records that, in *c* 1720:

> Sir William Pendarvis's house was the rendezvous of a very immoral set of men. One of his strange exploits among other frolics, was having a coffin made of copper (which one of his mines had that year produced), and placed in the midst of his great hall, and instead of his making use of it as a monitor that might have made him ashamed and terrified at his past life, and induce him to make amends in future, it was filled with punch, and he and his comrades soon made themselves incapable of any sort of reflection; this was often repeated, and hurried him to that awful moment he had so much reason to dread (quoted in Girouard 1987, 181).

On 6 February 1771, Colonel Luttrell arrived at Mrs Cornely's Masquerade at the Pantheon, London dressed as a coffin. R S Kirby, who was present at the event, recorded that Luttrell cast such a 'pall of gloom' over the proceedings that he was obliged to leave shortly after his arrival (French 1985, 116).

In 1769 Thomas Pickering, a tin-plate manufacturer based in Southwark, patented a method of raising patterns in sheet iron which was forever to affect the production of coffin furniture. His hand-operated presses were able to raise highly detained patterns on particularly thin sheet iron which, when tin-dipped and burnished, resembled repoussé silver. However, Pickering was not the first manufacturer to be producing coffin furniture from tin-dipped sheet iron, as examples on coffins of *c* 1720–30 prove. Many other tin-platers emulated Pickering's process; most were inferior, but some were far superior, and it is regrettable that we do not know the name of the manufacturer of a truly

splendid set of stamped gilt copper grip-plates with integral coronets and chinoiserie bells on the 1777 coffin of the 2nd Earl De La Warr at Withyham, Sussex. A similar set was discovered in February 1997 in a private vault of the 1780s at the west end of St Mary's Church in Walthamstow, Essex. Three coffin furniture pattern books of the period 1783 to 1826 survive in the Victoria & Albert Museum, with that of 1783 containing designs by 'JB' (possibly the ironmonger, John Butts, at the Gridiron, near Hungerford Market, in the Strand?) issued through Tuesby & Cooper, Coffin Furniture Ironmongers of 221 Borough High Street, Southwark, by far the finest (V&A 1783). That of 'AT' of *c* 1821–4 is almost as fine, though the plates are not so highly finished, with 'EL' of 1826 coming in at a deserved third in the field. Be that as it may, far more items matching designs in 'EL' have been discovered on coffins of the period; either their prices were keener or their distribution and service to the trade better.

From these catalogues we learn that coffin furniture has its own terminology. Coffin plates are described as 'breast plates', or 'depositum plates', handle back-plates as 'grip plates', handles as 'grips', lid decorations as 'motifs', upholstery pins as 'nails', and panel decorations as 'escutcheons' or 'drops' (V&A 1783, 1821, and 1826). Stamped iron depositum plates, tin-dipped and designed in the form of a concave oval cartouche encircled by a garland of flowers, first appeared at the end of the 17th century; so did grip-plates, which were similarly oval with a repoussé design of winged cherubs' heads, When Tuesby & Cooper published their catalogue in 1783 there was already a considerable variety of 'finishes' available for coffin furniture: bronze, gilt copper, copper, brass, silvered (tin-dipped stamped iron, though silver leaf was sometimes applied on top of the tin), Black (more expensive than 'silvered', being tin-dipped stamped iron with two or more coats of matt black paint), and 'coloured' for childrens' coffins (tin-dipped stamped iron, painted with two or more coats of matt off-white with certain details highlighted with water-gilding or matt mauve). Opposite the title page comes some very useful information:

> N.B. A Sett of Coffin Furniture contains a Breast Plate, Flower Pot and Angel, 3 Pr. of Handles & Pins to fix them. If order'd with 4 Pr. of Handles & 20 Yds of Lace &c the Price is advanced in Proportion. Large Wrt. Cast Gripes to any of the Setts will be 1/-pr. Sett advance (V&A 1763)

A 'Flower Pot and Angel' was the trade's nickname for certain lid motifs of a vase of flowers (foot end of lid) and a winged angel with trumpet (head end of lid).

The tin-dipped stamped iron coffin furniture had one drawback: it was not suitable for cut lettering. This would not have served for vaults, and so the stamped and scribed lead depositum plate remained the more usual item in such instances.

Towards the end of the 18th century both pewter and pure tin, natural or silvered, were also being used, though the nobility appear to have remained loyal to brass, it being more convenient for the engraver to work, especially if one's coat-of-arms was to appear on it.

Although the majority of depositum plates were rectangular, a few followed the dictates of heraldry. Thus the plate for a young girl or spinster was lozenge-shaped, shield-shaped for a boy or young man, rectangular with central cartouche for a married woman or widow, and rectangular with central rectangular panel for an adult male, married man, or widower. However, not every coffin-maker, undertaker, or funeral furnisher knew this and one could end up with the embarrassment of an elderly widower being given the plate of a type used for a young maiden, and vice versa.

While the transportation of the dead was the responsibility of the trade, few could afford the outlay required to purchase hearses and carriages, and maintain stables; consequently there grew up in most towns a branch of the carriage hire trade know as 'black' jobmen. It was they who developed vehicles especially for the purpose, whereby the encoffined corpse could be borne to the grave with more solemnity, pomp, and ceremony than the deceased could have expected when alive, and hired out their vehicles to the funeral trade. To some extent the timing of the funeral depended not only on the minister and the sexton, but also on the availability of hired transport. Most of the vehicles were utilitarian, but some were magnificent. The following description appeared in the *Quarterly Review* of 1844 in a short story entitled 'Inheritance':

> Suddenly, a huge black object was dimly discernable entering the avenue and dragging its ponderous length towards the castle . . . the snow ceased, the clouds rolled away, and the red brassy glare of the setting sun failed abruptly on the moving phenomenon, and disclosed to view a stately full-plumed hearse. There was something so terrific, yet so picturesque in its appearance, as it ploughed its way through waves of snow – its sable plumes nodding and gilded skulls grinning in the now lurid light of the fast-sinking sun – that all stood transfixed with alarm and amazement (*Quarterly Review*, **146**, 1844)

During the 1780s and 1790s the foot procession in London was beginning to wane for, as they wound their way along the busy thoroughfares of the city (more, it has to be said, as an advertisement to the onlooker of the panoply available from Mr So-and-So's undertaking establishment, than a continuance of a medieval tradition), no one could have ignored the increase in commercial traffic and the concomitant bustle of a town pursuing its daily occupation. Even the meanest undertaker succumbed to the hire of an enclosed vehicle, in an attempt to retain some dignity; but as this involved an extra cost to the mourners, a number of lower-class funerals continued to be shouldered through the streets well into the 1840s. In general, enclosed horse-drawn hearses, close-upholstered in velvet and with tiered ostrich plumes on the roof, were in widespread use by the 1820s; to complete the cortege, mourners' coaches could also be provided, though it was acceptable for one's own coach to be used, provided it was in a dark livery. But while a quiet conquest had achieved in the space of four decades the abolition of a two thousand year old tradition, few could have afforded to match such a grand funeral car as that provided by the royal undertakers, France & Banting, in January 1806 for the obsequies of Viscount Nelson.

The Nelson funeral was atypical of its time, it being the fourth state funeral allowed for a commoner since the Reformation, the other three having been for Sir Philip Sidney, General Monck, and John Churchill, Viscount Marlborough. The entire arrangements were left to France & Banting, being given carte-blanche – or, rather, carte-noire – to provide far more than that which was customary. No expense was spared in draping the Painted Hall at Greenwich for the lying-in-state, the canopy above the encoffined remains supporting twelve fantastic plumes of dyed ostrich feathers. The outer case of the composite coffin was fashioned from Spanish mahogany by France & Banting's chief cabinet maker, Mr Chittenden, with water-gilded coffin furniture provided by the Piccadilly silversmith, Mr Holmes, under the supervision of Mr Bidwell. However, Nelson's remains do not float in rum; on repatriation, the body was laid out, dried, embalmed, dressed in standard grave-clothes, and placed into a silk-lined elm coffin, around which was soldered a lead shell, then a second inner coffin and a second lead shell, and, finally, the velvet-covered outer mahogany case. While Nelson stood 5' 1" in his stockinged feet, the finished coffin measured 6' 8" in length, 26" across the shoulders, and took twelve men to carry.

The burial of the poor was of increasing anxiety to the socially conscious during the latter part of the 18th century. Burial clubs and societies, such as the Society for Burials based at Whitechapel, had been in existence since the time of Queen Anne. Some funeral furnishers also ran their own clubs: Edward Evans, at the Four Coffins in the Strand, promised to 'perform 2s in the pound chaper than any of the Undertakers in Town or elsewhere' (*sic*), while John Middleton, also based in London, promised for twopence a week subscription, 'a strong Elm Coffin, covered with fine Black, and finished with Two Rows all round close drove with Black Japanned Nails, adorned with rich ornamental Drops, a handsone Plate of Inscription, Angel above the Plate and Flower beneath, and pair of handsome handles with wrought Grips . . . For use, as handsome Velvet Pall, Three Gentleman's Cloaks, Three Crepe Hat bands, Three Hoods and

Scarves, and Six Pairs of Gloves. Two Porters equipped to attend the Funeral, a man to attend the same with band and Gloves.' (cited in Laqueuer 1983, 109–31). All 'very handsome', no doubt. However, while a few burial clubs were corrupt, more so those associated with public houses in the inner-city slum areas, the majority assiduously executed their duties, occasionally branching out into other areas of personal finance, such as money-lending and insurance.

In an age when success was measured by material possessions and monetary wealth, the late 18th and early 19th century funeral was regarded as a public manifestation of one's acumen. The trade was acutely aware of this and devised a 'sliding scale' system of charges, itemizing the differential in class of funeral. This seeped down through all levels of society, but stopped short of the pauper class. A pauper funeral was, therefore, something to be avoided, not only because of its profound simplicity, but also for its significance in exhibiting one's failure to maintain a position, however lowly, in contemporary society.

As the 19th century approached, the number of grand in-house lyings-in-state among the landed gentry began to wane as funeral parlours were becoming established. That of Matthew Russell of Brancepeth, Co Durham, arranged by the London funeral furnishers, Dowbiggen & Holland in 1822, must have been one of the last of its kind. However, the nobility maintained the tradition well into the 19th century, probably because it was expected of them by the trade, and one of the last known such events, again, furnished by Dowbiggen & Holland, was in 1853 at Belton House, Lincolnshire for John, 1st Earl Brownlow.

By the 1850s the grand funeral, with its seemingly endless procession of black carriages, was no longer popular among the upper classes. They looked for a simpler, but no less dignified, approach and the trade knew that it had to acquiesce or lose custom. First, the number of mutes and attendants were reduced, then the number of funeral carriages, and then the number of horses employed to pull the hearse; only in the poorer parts of the larger cities did the old-fashioned panoply survive, buying-in a spectacle which the relatives erroneously believed emulated the obsequies of their betters.

Public acceptance of funereal simplicity came with the death of W E Gladstone in 1898. Gone were the black shoulder-scarves, mutes, feather-men, and prancing horses; instead, Messrs Banting's men wore simple frock coats and top hats for the burial at Westminster Abbey. William Wickham, Gladstone's grandson, was deeply impressed and in a congratulatory letter to his uncle, Herbert Gladstone, was able to say: 'I felt that everything was perfect and quite ideal. Not only was it grand, solemn and impressive but it was also simple. It made one feel that though many were there to mourn, no one was there to gaze as at a show. It was too simple to be tawdry and too grand to be unworthy' (quoted in Jalland 1996, 203).

The funeral furnishing trade of the period 1700–1850 has little to be proud of. It was led neither by entrepreneurs nor by high fashion, rather it entrenched itself in the middle ground of steadfast conservatism and quasi-respectability; it provided a sham, and sustained such, being a trade born out of necessity rather than vocation. Since the establishment of the first undertaking shop in the third quarter of the 16th century, the seeds were planted for what was to become the most lucrative trade ever invented – the trade in death. And, in the main, it has remained so ever since.

2 An introductory guide to textiles from 18th and 19th century burials *Robert Janaway*

Introduction

Textiles had an important role in furnishing 18th and 19th century funerals. In addition to the textiles that were used to dress the body and to cover the exterior and interior wooden surfaces of the coffin, textiles were needed for aspects of the funeral such as palls, mourning dress, silks for mutes, and gloves. During this period there was considerable development of businesses furnishing the funeral trade, with integration of wares including coffin and coffin fittings manufacture and associated textiles.

The extent of the industry by the end of our period is seen in *The Ecclesiastical Art Review* of 1878 which describes the firm of Messrs Dottridge Brothers. Their main establishment was at the junction of East Road and City Road, London EC1, with branch establishments in West Ham Lane, London Bridge, King's Cross, Victoria Park, and Birmingham. At the principal branch there were a number of departments, including the Funeral Department, which dealt with palls. The most fancy of these were made of 'rich purple velvet, bordered with gold fringe, inset with texts of Scripture, and having the sacred monogram I H S worked in gold thread in the centre' (*The Ecclesiastical Art Review* 1878, 42). The Chief Wareroom contained mural ornaments including breastplates, handles, lid ornaments, crosses, clips, side-bands, etc, while the Drapery Department 'stored various assortments of cloths, silks, cambrics, flannels, gloves &c. so as to suit the purses and tastes of mourners' (*ibid*). The firm was directly involved in the production as well as retail of these goods with a Stamping Room with presses for embossing tin (plate?) and other metals. Metal finishing included 'acid pickling, burnishing, electo-painting [*sic*], coppering, bronzing, lacquering and Japanning' (*ibid*). The Coventry Room contained 'a number of sewing machines &c. worked by fair fingers; while other tidy and lively young damsels are actively engaged in pinking, goffering and embroidering' (*ibid*).

The archaeological evidence

In the last fifteen years a number of excavations and clearances of vaults, and, to a lesser extent earthen burials, have produced archaeological evidence of a range of textiles used to furnish 18th and 19th century burials. From the excavations at Christ Church, Spitalfields (Reeve & Adams 1993; Molleson & Cox 1993; Cox 1996a) and St Nicholas's, Sevenoaks (Boyle & Keevill, this volume) it is clear that there was a well developed industry providing textiles to the funeral trades.[1]

Ethical considerations

There are a number of problems associated with the excavation and study of textiles from graves of this period. In addition to the purely practical problems resulting from health and safety issues, the cost of excavation, conservation, and storage of the archives, important moral questions need to be considered. The study of clothing on the dead, whether it be in an archaeological or forensic context is by its very nature intimate and intrusive. There are dilemmas which are fundamental both in terms of preparing a body for burial and for scientific study after exhumation, namely that the body needs to be handled, manipulated, and undressed. This issue has recently been addressed by a television documentary on approaches to funerals (*Modern Times*, BBC2, broadcast April 1997).[2] If those who are intimate with the deceased in life dress them for death it can be a positive part of mourning, as shown on the *Modern Times* programme. However many surviving relatives are not willing, capable, or given the option of performing this task. There is a long tradition of washing, laying out, and dressing being performed by a non-related party, with professional undertakers retaining the services of women for this purpose (see Richardson 1988; Litten 1991). This arrangement, which began before the 18th century, gradually gained acceptance until it is almost universal in current undertaking practice provided it is done in a dignified and respectful manner. With archaeological exhumation it is not possible to ascertain the precise wishes of the deceased or their immediate family, however the balance of probability is that most corpses of the 18th and 19th centuries had already been in the hands of a respectful stranger. Thus, while there are still important issues relating to whether/ and in what circumstances bodies should be exhumed from their final resting place, the study of the funerary textiles should not raise any additional moral issues if conducted in a suitably respectful manner.

No crypt and churchyard clearance within the UK has been conducted as a pure research project;

the dead are either exhumed by archaeologists or specialist contractors prior to development or reuse of the site. In this respect the issues are very different from those raised by Clyde Snow's attempted exhumation of Butch Cassidy and the Sun Dance Kid in Bolivia.[3] Against this background it is important to consider the academic justifications of studying this type of textile material.

It is not possible to study archaeologically the whole range of textiles that were used in the funeral, just those that were interred with the body and which survive in an identifiable form for analysis after one hundred to three hundred years. This in itself biases the sample towards burials in lead coffins that are often, but not exclusively, deposited in intramural vaults. There are exceptions and well-preserved textiles have been observed from single-shell wooden coffins and earth burials. (Issues of preservation and taphonomic processes are discussed further below.) However, the nature of the majority of these caskets and the location of their burial represent the more expensive funerals that were available during this period.

Individuality or conformity?

An important issue that can be studied by the examination of these textiles is variability in furnishing the burial, which may represent choice, an individual and personal expression against the promotion of conformity driven by commercial interests of the undertakers and other funeral professionals. The view of Litten (1991, 26) is that there was little individual choice of coffin, linings, or handles. This is certainly borne out by the archaeological and documentary evidence (eg Spitalfields and the trade catalogues, where there is choice but within prescribed limits). However, earlier assertions (Janaway 1993, 94) that the body was usually dressed solely in textiles provided by the undertaker needs to be questioned in the light of current evidence.

Clothing, in addition to being among a person's most intimate and personal possessions, is one of the principal mechanisms of stating individuality, group membership, or rejection of group stereotype in post-medieval Europe. How the deceased is dressed and whether there is a conflict between individual expression and social and commercial pressure towards conformity is at the heart of a power balance between the individual/consumer and the undertaker/provider. In the UK during the late 20th century the traditional funeral, largely led and directed by the funeral industry, is being rigorously questioned in terms of contemporary beliefs, morality, economics, and environmental impact. In this context it is important to document the origin, nature, and development of the diverse aspects of the professionally-run funeral for non-aristocratic members of the population.

The bulk of documentary evidence for the 18th, 19th, and early 20th centuries comes from trade catalogues and directories. In order to examine the hypothesis that commercial interests led to a reduction of individual expression, by providing a universal funeral uniform of shroud/cap etc and that individual family members had less and less active participation in preparing the body for burial, then the documentary evidence will need to be augmented by archaeological data.

In addition to the textiles from Christ Church, Spitalfields and St Nicholas's, Sevenoaks textiles have also been recorded from St Marylebone Parish Church, London, St Barnabas, West Kensington (Black & Scheuer unpublished), and St Nicholas's, Bathampton, Bath & North East Somerset (Cox & Stock 1995). The current archaeological data has a strong London/south-east bias and generally dates from the first half of the 18th century until just into the second half of the 19th century. Little material has been recorded and published from after 1860 in the UK, which reflects the cessation of intramural burial in the 1850s.

Within these limitations it is possible to recognise certain characteristic textile types that were provided as sets for dressing both the body and coffin. These include shrouds, caps, winding sheets, pillows and mattresses, and coffin linings, frills, and coverings (Fig 2.1). According to Litten (1991) the body of the deceased was washed and usually dressed in textiles provided by the undertaker, and it was unusual for the deceased to be buried in their own clothes. However, a number of British archaeological sites provide good evidence not only of textiles provided as part of the funeral furnishings but also items of personal clothing. At Spitalfields sixteen burials were recorded with the body dressed in their own garments, sometimes under a shroud, while only twelve bodies with only shrouds were recovered. Items of clothing ranged from an 18th century silk-faced man's waistcoat to an early 19th century lace-trimmed dress. From St Nicholas, Sevenoaks the body of a 19th century silk weaver was recovered. He was wearing a hooded cotton nightshirt with evidence of darning. From St Marylebone Parish Church there were two instances of burials with specific personal clothing: one man was dressed in military uniform, while another, an octogenarian, was laid out in a *macaroni* outfit 'more suited to a man sixty years his junior' (Litten 1991, 73). From St Barnabas a woman was buried with her husband's military uniform (Black & Scheuer unpublished) (Figs 2.2 and 2.3).[4] The body of David Dallas, who died in 1829 aged 28 years, was interred at St Nicholas, Bathampton in a heavily fulled woollen suit. The jacket had shoulder pads and the trousers had plain metal buttons down the outside seams (Cox & Stock 1995, 40).

During the 18th and 19th century it was normal practice for the coffin to be kept open at home for two or three days allowing friends and relatives to view the body (Dezallier-D'Argenville 1731, quoted

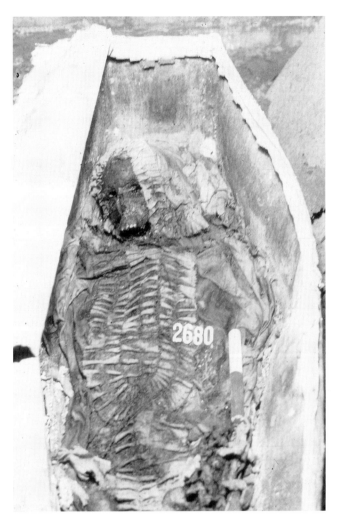

Figure 2.1 Body as excavated (skeletonized despite lead coffin) showing cap and shroud in wool, furnished for the funeral (photo: Christ Church Spitalfields Archaeological Project)

by Litten 1991, 80). This clearly necessitated careful presentation of both the body and the coffin interior. Any clothing worn by the corpse that was not covered by a shroud (see below) would have been in clear view.

While the personal clothing associated with the burials from these sites may not comprise the overall bulk of textiles, they do represent a significant group of material. The importance of this clothing is that it does demonstrate that the funeral trade did not force every corpse to be attired for the afterlife in a uniform set of grave clothes, lacking in individuality. For the more determined client, there was free choice and expression, perhaps despite the market forces and a drive for conformity promoted by the undertakers.

Act for Burial in Wool

During the 17th century the choice of material used for shrouds acted as an indicator of status, with different linen cloths being favoured (Litten 1991, 72). In 1666 an Act of Parliament was passed in order to promote the domestic woollen industry (18 & 19 Car II c4); this decreed that all persons had to be buried in shifts, shrouds, and winding sheets made of woollen material rather than linen and free from 'Flax, Hemp, Silk, Hair, Gold or Silver or other than what is made of Sheep's Wool' (Litten 1991, 74). This Act, strengthened in 1680 (32 Car II c1), remained on the statute books until 1814 (54 Geo III c78). The very wealthy could, if they wished, pay the £5 for default, and there is some evidence that this practice did occur (Cressy 1997). One effect of the Act was to encourage the practice of grave clothes and coffin linings being supplied as sets by specialist workshops (Litten 1991, 74). This trend is most noticeable with the surviving Spitalfields material, where the norm was for shrouds, caps, and other grave clothes to be made of the same fabric, with the same punched decoration as the textiles furnishing the coffin interior in any one burial. Other aspects of these Acts are discussed by Cox (this volume).

Preservation of textiles and sample bias

Textile materials decay differentially according to burial environment, and there are always sample biases due to differential preservation among archaeological textiles (Janaway 1996a). The excavation of non-earthen post-medieval burials can yield large quantities of material. This is largely as a result of the relatively short time between deposition and excavation but also because of the specific environmental conditions associated with coffins from within vaults (Janaway 1993). At Spitalfields the majority of material recovered was wool, cotton, and silk, with linen as a minor fabric. This partly reflects differential survival, as the proteinic fibres in wool, hair, and silk are usually the most robust in archaeological environments, although they will decay in aerated deposits, or alkaline burial conditions (Janaway 1996a; Janaway *et al* forthcoming). The cellulose-based fibres, linen and cotton, are easily degraded in the presence of moisture and air over a relatively short timescale (Janaway 1996a). Cellulose is most susceptible to acids, while wool degradation is promoted by alkalis (*ibid*).

Inside the coffin, textile decay is unavoidably linked to the biochemical breakdown of the cadaver (Janaway 1989), as demonstrated by the relatively poorer condition of the woollen textiles from inside compared with those of the outer coffin coverings. The rate and nature of cadaveric breakdown is governed by a large number of factors (Janaway 1996a). Important among these are the interval between death and the coffin being sealed, whether the seal was originally gas-tight, and the speed and scale of coffin breakdown in relation to the time of excavation. It is self-evident that coffin construction will play an important part in this (Mant 1989). In

Figure 2.2 Lt Colonel Francis Chesney's Royal Artillery coatee which was draped over the body of his wife, Everilda, who died aged 48 in 1840 and was interred beneath St Barnabas' Church, West Kensington (photo: S Black and L Scheuer)

Figure 2.3 Gold epaulettes from Lt Colonel Chesney's coatee, St Barnabas, West Kensington (photo: S Black and L Scheuer)

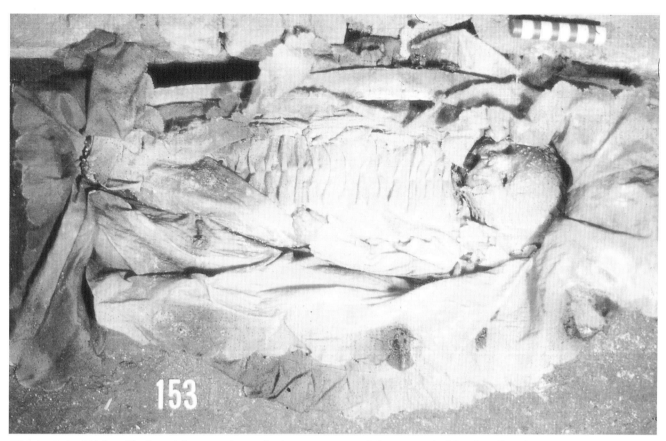

Figure 2.4   Body of baby with extensive soft tissue preserved due to sealed lead coffin, from Christ Church, Spitalfields. The textiles included woollen cap, shroud, and winding sheet, all furnished as part of the funeral (photo: Christ Church Spitalfields Archaeological Project)

most cases lead coffins probably had good gas-tight seals when first interred. However, the lead will break down in time for two principal reasons: downward pressure due to the practice of stacking a large number of coffins on top of one another, and corrosion of the lead. At Spitalfields many lead coffins were no longer gas-tight when excavated, although the contents sometimes had a greater moisture content than adjacent all-wooden coffins. Some coffins retained a great deal of liquid, and had sufficiently low rates of gas exchange with the outside to retain anaerobic conditions until their opening by the excavators; in extreme cases anaerobic conditions can lead to a very high degree of soft tissue preservation (Fig 2.4).

With vault-buried wooden coffins, whether single or double-shelled, the degree of sealing would depend on the quality of the timber, how quickly the boards warped, the degree of insect attack, and the quality of the joints (Mant 1989, 67). The use of pitch on coffin interiors would have the advantage of providing an elastic sealing medium.

The Spitalfields excavation has produced a relatively large number of burials with poor or no textile preservation (Fig 2.5), while a small number of either anaerobic lead coffins or very desiccated burials provided the most complete 'sets' of textiles. The airflow in the north parochial vault led to desiccation and natural mummification of the bodies in

wooden coffins, which were associated with textiles preserved in good condition (Fig 2.6). Overall, the bulk of identified textile samples from inside coffins came from 72 lead and 30 wooden coffins. Of the latter, nine contained mummified bodies (Fig 2.7) (Janaway 1993). In general, it should be anticipated that future excavations of non-earthen 18th and 19th century burials will yield significant textile remains.

The nature of burial textiles: review

The textiles that were deposited in a vault in association with the body and coffin had three basic practical functions: to finish the exterior of the coffin, to finish the interior of the coffin (which would have been open for viewing the body), and to clothe/cover the body.

The coffin

Coffin construction and outer cloth covering

During the 18th and early 19th century outer coffins were usually of elm and covered with wool baize or silk velvet (Litten 1991, 90). The use of cloth covering for coffins started to decline with the

Figure 2.5   Skeletalized body with no soft tissue or textile survival (photo: Christ Church Spitalfields Archaeological Project)

introduction of French polishing in the second quarter of the 19th century (*ibid*). Cloth-covered coffins survived into the 20th century in more conservative areas. The cloth-covered coffin was finished with decorative metalwork and round-headed tacks.

Silk velvets were high status coverings and were usually associated with aristocratic burials, either black or scarlet in colour during the 18th century with midnight blue, holly green, and turquoise being added in the early 19th century. Woollen baize was of lower status and appears to have been either black or scarlet (op cit, 112). At Spitalfields the majority of outer coffin covers were of wool baize dyed dark green or black. It is difficult to distinguish between these shades after excavation as the outer covers were normally very heavily soiled and black dye will bleed as dark green.

Coffin linings and other textiles used in furnishing coffin interiors

These textiles formed the finish for the interior of the coffin, or the interior of the innermost shell of double and triple-shell interments. The primary linings were on view to the mourners when the coffin was open. The wood on the inner coffin was caulked on the base and sides with Swedish pitch and an

undersheet tacked in place before fixing the side lining, the side sheets, and ruched frill (op cit, 92). The lining was glued to the sides and sometimes the base with an adhesive while the side sheets were fixed at the top, hanging loose and curtain-like at the sides. The ruched frill, ruffling, was used to conceal decoratively the top of the lining and/or the wooden bead around the top of the coffin (see Fig 2.7). They usually had pinked/scalloped edges with punched decoration. The tucks were usually held with tacking stitches and secured by iron tacks. The fabrics were plain woven, either wool or cotton. The function of the top bead was to support the inner lid.

Mattresses and pillows were placed at the base of a coffin underneath the body. At Spitalfields there were fewer pillows than mattresses recovered (although when in a very decayed state discrimination between them could be difficult). Where both mattress and pillow were placed in the coffin they were part of a set of textiles, with the same covering and stuffing.

Mattresses were usually shaped to cover the whole of the coffin base (Fig 2.8). The primary function of the mattresses is to soak up body decomposition products. They consist of plain woven cloth covers, often decorated with frills or rosettes, which were then stuffed with a number of materials

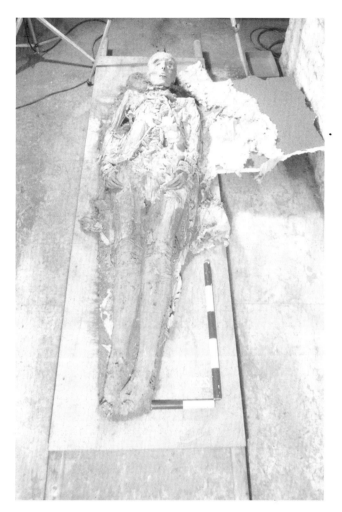

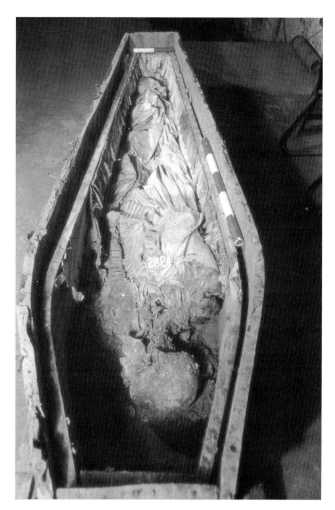

Figure 2.6 Natural mummification from the north parochial vault, Christ Church, Spitalfields. This woman was interred wearing an elaborate linen dress with lace trim and ribbons, silk stockings, cotton cap, and wrapped in a winding sheet (photo: Christ Church Spitalfields Archaeological Project)

Figure 2.7 Naturally mummified body from the north parochial vault, Christ Church, Spitalfields, interred in a double wooden coffin. Ruffling can be observed from around the top of the inner coffin, linings, and shroud (photo: Christ Church Spitalfields Archaeological Project)

including wool, hair, and straw. It is interesting that this decoration would only be visible when the coffin was empty, but, with the body inside, especially if a winding sheet or shroud was used, the mattress would be hidden. It is significant that this is an example of elaboration and expense which would not aid the presentation of the body to the mourners. A layer of sawdust or bran in the base of the coffin would serve the same function.

The pillow was used to support the head (Fig 2.9). It was cloth covered, with various stuffing materials of either wool, feathers, or hay. The covers were usually plain woven of either wool or cotton and matched the other coffin lining fabrics. Most burials with pillows did not have mattresses, with the exception of two at Spitalfields.

Coffin bases were filled with sawdust or wood shavings. In some instances, after viewing and prior to the lid being 'closed down', the remaining space in the coffin was filled with sawdust and/or bran to absorb liquid and odour from the body's

decomposition. It might be assumed that sawdust or bran coffin packing was not necessary where a mattress was used, however, from Spitalfields there were six examples where both a mattress and sawdust were recorded as being present.

The body

Textiles associated with laying out the body

There is only evidence for broad trends regarding the laying-out of the body. Variations which have been recorded appear to be related more to differences of individual practice, just as today, than to any general differences between treatment according to age at death, sex, or changes through time. There is only one recorded example of a pad being bound to the loins at Spitalfields. The rest of the loin coverings are 'modesty clothes' used to cover the body's sexual organs, recorded at

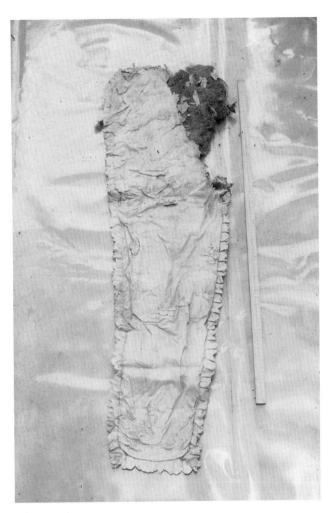

*Figure 2.8   Mattress from Christ Church,
Spitalfields (photo: Christ Church Spitalfields
Archaeological Project)*

both Spitalfields and Sevenoaks. In modern practice a pad is used to absorb the decomposition fluids
that are evacuated from the anus soon after death.
The body is stripped and washed and lower
garments and sheets in contact with the body at
death are often soiled and are discarded. It is then
necessary to cover the body, normally by clean
underclothes, to cover nakedness. There was no
general evidence of underclothes at either Spitalfields or Sevenoaks.

A number of ties were used to stop the body from
moving out of position in the coffin. In particular
the legs were tied together, either at the ankles or
by tying the big toes together, and the arms were
sometimes tied to the sides of the body. In modern
practice medical bandages are used; at Christ
Church, Spitalfields the ties were sometimes torn-
up strips of other materials or, more commonly,
they were plain commercially-produced silk ribbons. It is clear that the 18th and 19th century
undertaker had plain silk ribbons to hand in the
same way as a modern undertaker has bandages.
The exceptional use of fancy ribbons or strips of
cloth would seem to represent the use of things to
hand.

The function of trussing a body in this manner
was to keep it in a neat, seemly position while being
viewed, and to prevent the limbs banging against
the coffin sides while the coffin was being moved,
which would be distressing during a funeral procession. The problem of the jaw dropping open was
addressed in a number of ways. It could be tied up
by silk ribbons, or a special cloth could be pinned to
the cap, called a 'jaw cloth'. One example shown in
an excavator's notes from Spitalfields had a piece of
cloth, like a triangular bandage, wrapped twice
around the jaw and head and tied under the chin. A
cap was then placed on top of this, not shown in the
drawing. In some instances the under-chin ties of
caps were probably sufficient. An identical example
is recorded from Sevenoaks.

Clothing the body

In an account of 1731:

> We went to see a dead man laid out, and it would
> be a pity not to give you an account of his state.
> He was dressed in a long flannel shirt edged with
> lace, with flounces all down the middle, and five
> or six more on either side of the chest, all sewn
> with wool, in accordance with an Act of Parlia-
> ment which forbids the use of linen or cotton for
> this purpose. The sleeves end in cuffs. This shirt
> is put over the head and does not surround the
> body in one piece but is fastened at the back. The
> body is laid out in a coffin resting on a bed of bran
> or sawdust. The face is shaved, the head dressed
> in a bonnet, fastened at the top, and a cravat and
> gloves of flannel are worn. When the lady is laid
> out, it is in a mob-cap and an embroidered head-
> band, and neatly pressed flounces. The shirt
> comes right down over the feet, and threaded
> through with woollen thread at the ankles, with
> tassels at the end. (Dezallier-D'Argenville 1731,
> quoted by Litten 1991, 57)

According to Litten (op cit, 81) in the 18th and early
19th centuries the majority of commercially-produced grave clothes were manufactured in London
but by the 1830s, with the increase in the use of
cotton, Lancashire became increasingly important
as a production centre. Not all grave clothes were
bought ready-made but were often made by women
of the household, as is attested by *The Workwomans
Guide* of 1832, which gives instructions for making
caps and shrouds (op cit, 82).

With the repeal of the Act for Burial in Wool
in 1814 (54 Geo III c78) a variety of textiles
became available for shrouds and winding sheets,
including alpaca, calico, cambric, cashmere, eta-
mine, flannel, holland, linen, muslin, poplin, satin,
serge, silk. Calico, cambric, flannel, linen, silk,
and swansdown were used for linings (Litten 1991,
81). However, the bulk of the excavated sets of
textiles used in furnishing burials that have

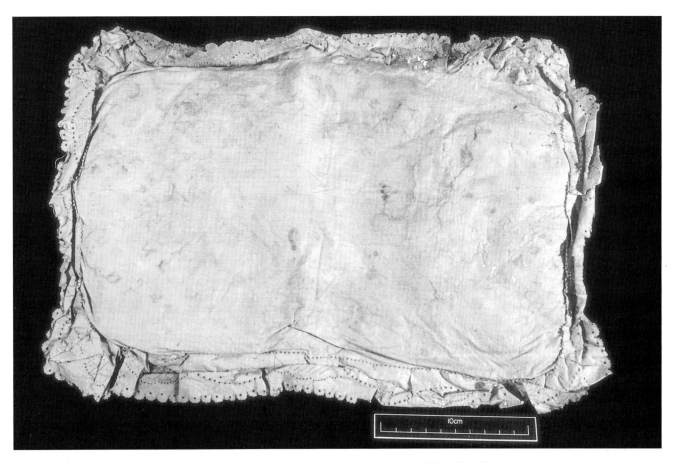

Figure 2.9   Pillow from St Nicholas, Sevenoaks (photo: University of Bradford)

been examined by the author, dating from the mid 18th to mid 19th century, are either plain woven wool or plain woven cotton. At Spitalfields the use of cotton for shrouds, coffin linings, ruffling etc did not make its appearance until after 1815. Where an individual was buried in items of clothing this often reflected a wider range of fabrics, for instance silk (satin) ribbons, silk facings to jackets or waistcoats, and linen (as well as cotton) for shirts and shifts.

The body which was clothed in either garments, a shroud, or both, was placed in the coffin, and the winding sheet was folded over to cover the body. Winding sheets of the 18th and 19th centuries consisted of large flat sheets, often with decorative borders in punched work, laid in the base of the coffin with the sheets extending over the sides. Before the coffin was closed they were folded inside the coffin to cover the body. The material could be either wool or cotton, and was usually the same fabric as the lining, and shroud (if present). These large sheets, big enough to wrap the body in, often consisted of two loom widths of material stitched together at the selvedge in order to give the necessary size. The punched designs ranged from simple to complex (Fig 2.10). Litten (op cit, 79) uses the term 'coffin sheet' for these items, however some confusion is caused by trade directories of the 19th century still referring to 'winding sheets'. For example, the trade catalogue of J Turner, Funeral Furnisher of

Farringdon Street, London (1838) quotes for the following textile items: 'Shrouds, Ruffling, Winding Sheets and Tacked Mattresses' (*sic*; see Litten, this volume). Other textile materials from his catalogue include palls, scarf and hood, cloak and band, silk band, gloves, velvets for hearse, horse velvets, and hammercloth.

Winding sheets differed from side sheets in that the former was a larger piece of cloth which extended under the body and was held in position by the weight of the corpse, rather than being nailed in place along the lower edge. Side sheets allowed undertakers to dispense with the full-length winding sheet. Once the coffin had received its primary lining and edged frill, two rectangular sheets, both the length and width of the coffin, were tacked to the base at its sides. Once the body had been placed in the coffin and the fitted pillow positioned under the head, these sheets were folded over the remains and either pinned down, or roughly sewn in place. The upper section of the sheet was left parted to expose the features to view and remained so until the time came to secure the lid. In this way the body was put into the coffin wearing just a shift and bonnet. It was not only a neat way to 'finish' the interior but also gave the dressed corpse 'the appearance of being in bed' (Litten 1991, 79).

The face cloth was a rectangular piece of cloth used to cover the face, often with punched decora-

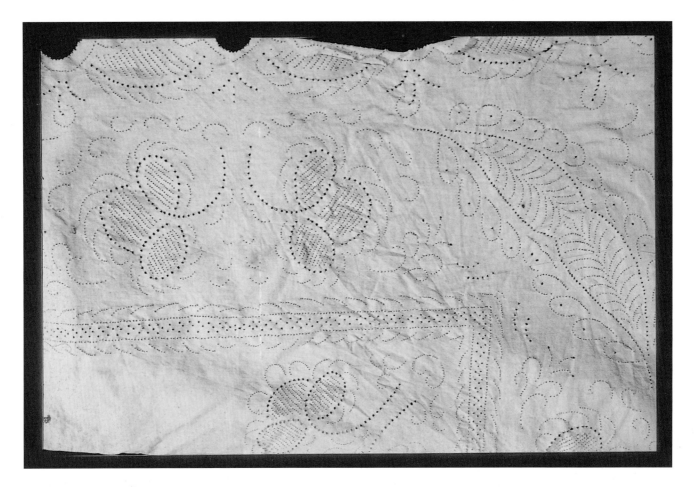

Figure 2.10   Detail of punched decoration on cotton winding sheet (photo: The Natural History Museum, London)

tion and pinked/scalloped edges, usually made of the same material as the shroud, lining, and frill. Five face cloths were recorded from Spitalfields, there was at least one example from Sevenoaks (Fig 2.11), and this practice was also evident at Bathampton (Cox & Stock 1995, 140).

There is little evidence for coins being used to close eyes. Certainly the bodies were not generally buried with coins on the eyes, although there was one example from Spitalfields. However it should be noted that not all burials had face cloths while many could have been buried with them, so no conclusions should be drawn from the limited evidence for this practice.

The preparation of the body, use of jaw cloths, face cloths, and general presentation of the body, supports the view that during the 18th and 19th century it was normal for the coffin to be open prior to the funeral.

Dressing the body

The body coverings can be divided into two groups:

1   Material which comes as part of a set of burial fabrics: frills, linings, winding sheets, shrouds, etc. Shrouds are backless but with sleeves, and cover the body from the neck to the feet. They are decorated with gathered frills on the region of the chest, and often with punched decoration.

2   The deceased's own clothes, wigs, stockings, etc. The garments that have been recorded include shifts, shirts, chemises, civilian jackets, trousers, and waistcoats. Military uniforms have also been recorded.

In practice, provided the remains are not too fragmentary, it is usually possible to distinguish between the two categories, eg a cap made for the funeral and provided as part of a set of fabrics can be quite distinct from one made for everyday wear (Figs 2.12 and 2.13); in some cases we cannot identify items which were bought especially for burial, eg stockings. It is worth noting that some garments had monograms or evidence of repair. The main criteria used to make this distinction were based on the range of cloth types in any one burial, the presence/absence of punched decoration, and the degree of finish (hems, stitch types, etc).

'Burial clothes', made of similar cloth to the linings and frills etc, often had pinked, scalloped edges with punched decoration. They lacked hems and very coarse tacking stitches were used in a generally crude construction. They often had decorative strips of gathered material attached to the front

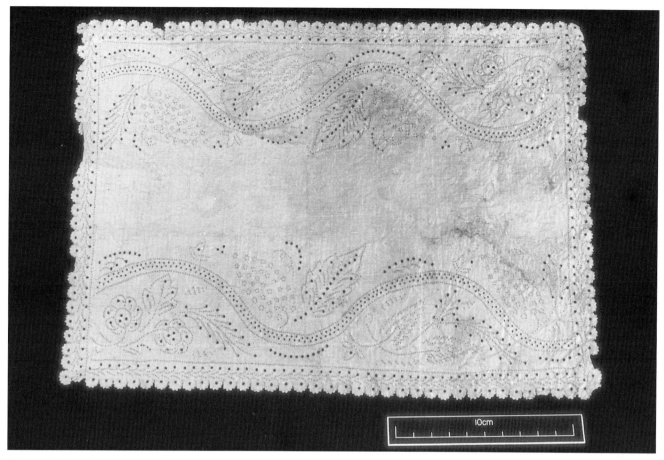

Figure 2.11   Cotton face cloth with punched decoration from St Nicholas, Sevenoaks (photo: University of Bradford)

faces. Of course, with some items, such as the back-less shrouds, their funerary nature was self-evident. Where items of normal clothing were included, the quality of construction and needle-work, even of the poorest quality, is infinitely better than that of the funerary textiles (Fig 2.14). The latter do not have buttons or buttonholes, being fastened when necessary with either ties or copper alloy pins, and lack linings, facings, pockets, or lace. In general the decoration on normal garments was not plain-punched, as this would not stand up to wear without having the edges over-sewn, as in *broderie anglaise*.

Head coverings

Textiles associated with the head consisted of caps and wigs, as well as face cloths and cloths associated with support of the jaw. According to Litten (1991, 76) the cap or bonnet had been a feature of grave clothes since the 1630s. *The Workwomans Guide* of 1838 gives details of how to make head gear for the grave. Cap: 'If the usual cap is not put on, the following is made for a man: it is of flannel, cut exactly like an infant's foundling cap. a quilling of punched flannel is put round the face, and a band of it is laid on behind, and across the top of the

head, strings of the same, are also sewed in'. Cap for a woman: 'This is of flannel: the round part is plat-ted up to the front, and a quilling of the bordering put on, a band of the same laid on at the back, and strings' (quoted in Litten 1991, 82).

Caps could be either made of the same material and decoration as the shroud, winding sheet, lin-ings etc, or manufactured separately, either espe-cially for the funeral or as items of normal dress. From Spitalfields there were ten caps from the 18th and 19th centuries that were part of sets of funeral textiles, while there were at least five caps which were not part of a set. Of these one was a knitted night cap (not recovered) which is similar to one recovered from Sevenoaks (Fig 2.15).

Shrouds and clothing for the body

At Spitalfields it was impossible to make generali-zations about how the body was covered because of the combination of differential preservation of tex-tile materials and differential recovery and record-ing by the excavators. For instance there are two burials in the archive which had only gloves or stockings recovered! Only sixteen bodies were dressed in one or more garments while eleven were covered by only a shroud. Two had both garments

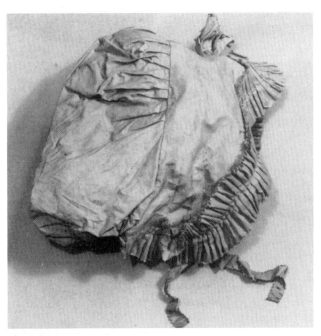

Figure 2.12   Cap made for the funeral at Christ Church, Spitalfields (photo: The Natural History Museum, London)

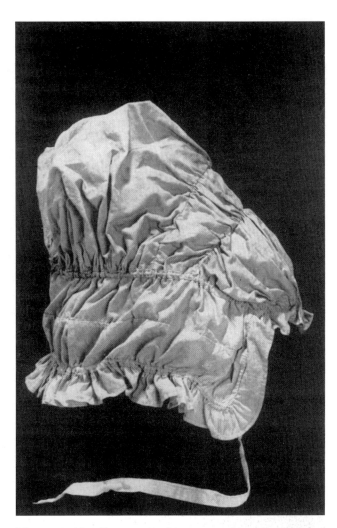

Figure 2.13   Cap, part of a personal wardrobe, Christ Church, Spitalfields (photo: The Natural History Museum, London)

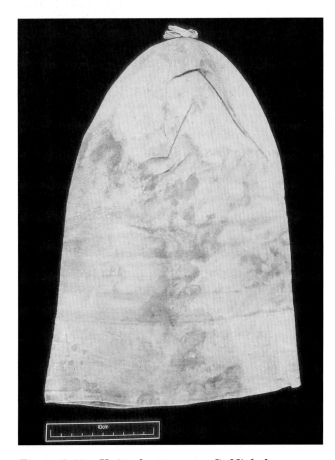

Figure 2.15   Knitted cotton cap, St Nicholas, Sevenoaks (photo: University of Bradford)

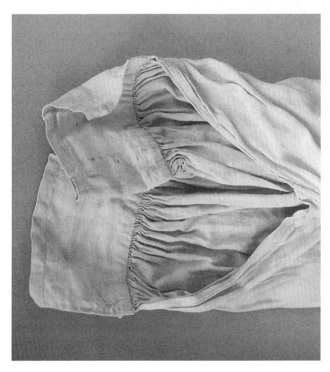

Figure 2.14   Detail of shirt cuff from Christ Church, Spitalfields (photo: University of Bradford)

Figure 2.16   Shroud from Christ Church, Spitalfields (photo: The Natural History Museum, London)

and a shroud. Six burials with shrouds had caps while six burials in garments also wore caps.

Shrouds are backless garments with sleeves, usually with ruffling to decorate the front (Figs 2.16 and 2.17). They are crudely sewn with long tacking stitches and a number of the edges are often cut with pinking shears. At Spitalfields when the body was dressed with a shroud and cap they were made of the same material, and were of similar construction and quality. There were two instances where a body was dressed in personal clothing (excluding gloves, stockings etc) with a shroud on top:

The burial of an 82 year old woman buried in 1843; she was wearing a fragmentary cotton garment with a frill at cuff and neck opening, fastened with cartwheel buttons. It was not possible to ascertain whether this was part of a night gown or some other garment. On top of this was a cotton shroud (Janaway 1993, 111).

A burial of unknown identity and date of death was interred with a cotton shroud covering, cotton stockings, a cotton, long-sleeved, open-fronted jacket, fastened with a tie at the neck, all worn over a shift (op cit, 114).

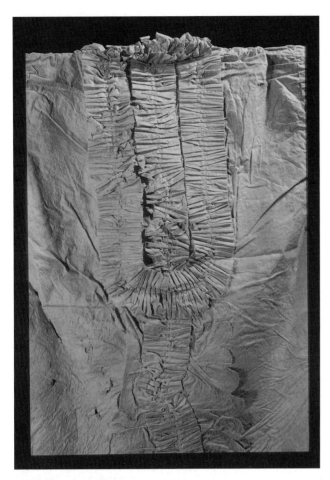

Figure 2.17   Detail of a shroud front from Christ Church, Spitalfields (photo: The Natural History Museum, London)

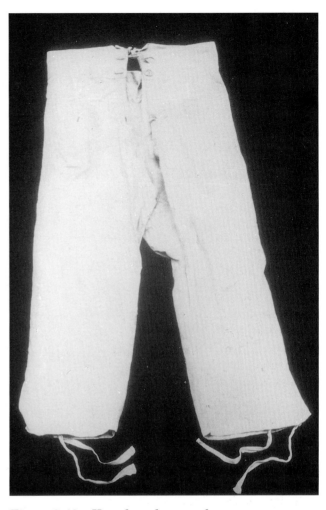

Figure 2.18   Knee-length pants from a young man, George Robert Davis, died 1836 aged 18, from St Barnabas, West Kensington (photo: S Black and L Scheuer)

There are many more examples of burials with personal garments but no shroud. Fifteen were recorded from Spitalfields, and some of these are described below:

Silk satin and twill facing and pocket flap and lining from a man's coat or waistcoat, with button holes.

Silk facing of collar edge or coat tail and three buttonholes from a man's coat from the burial of a 58 year old man buried in 1795.

Small fragments of a linen garment, with fragment of cuff with cartwheel button, recovered by excavator but with insufficient detail for further reconstruction. There was evidence of a very degraded cotton stocking on legs.

Linen shirt fastened at the front with alternating cartwheel and mother-of-pearl buttons, with a cotton cap and cotton stocking.

Fragments of a cotton shirt cuff band and three cartwheel buttons.

A complex, high quality women's garment; made of linen, with lace trim to cuffs and neck. Tied with ribbon, terminating in lace-trimmed lappets under the bust. Cuffs drawn with silk satin ribbons. Worn with silk stockings and a cotton/silk cap.

Long-sleeved, cotton, open-fronted jacket, fastened with cartwheel buttons at cuffs and neck and worn with a cotton cap.

Cotton gown from a baby boy buried in 1825, open-fronted, fastened with tie at neck, long sleeves with triangular gusset under arms; worn with cap of linen and silk.

Open-fronted wool jacket with long sleeves, fastened with four buttons, worn with wool garments on lower body described by the excavator as 'leggings', but not recovered, from a 52 year old buried in 1837.

Cotton open-fronted shirt, button on collar only, cuffs drawn with cotton ribbon, triangular gusset under sleeve worn with cotton cap and cotton stocking, from a 68 year old female buried in 1823.

64 year old male, buried in 1847, wearing a linen shirt with long sleeves worn under an open fronted cotton jacket worn with cotton cap and cotton stockings (op cit, 117).

This evidence, taken alongside the data from other site such as Sevenoaks and St Barnabas, West Kensington (Fig 2.18), indicates that the use of shrouds may not have had the dominance that might be inferred from trade catalogues of the period.

Gloves and mittens

At Spitalfields three burials were excavated where the body was wearing gloves. There were two males buried wearing knitted silk gloves with a short cuff. One burial had a pair of mittens made from woollen cloth, part of a set of funeral textiles to accompany a cap, shroud etc, with scalloped edges and punched decoration.

Stockings

Seven pairs of stockings were recovered from Spitalfields, and in all cases they reached to above the knee. They were generally knitted, with a seam up the back of the leg. Four pairs were of undyed cotton, with a characteristic double narrow red stripe around the top. Similar pairs are recorded from Sevenoaks and St Barnabas (Fig 2.19). One Spitalfields burial with an elaborate lace trimmed dress, dating to the early 19th century, had a pair of quality knitted silk stockings with a decorative clock. Two pairs of knitted woollen stockings were also recovered.

In addition to the stockings worn by the corpses, one burial at Spitalfields had a single, knitted, woollen, footless sock which had been rolled up so as to provide an extra support for one side of the head. This had possibly been removed from the body during laying-out, and was simply to hand. This is an example of a purely fortuitous inclusion of the deceased's clothing in the coffin.

Children

In general children are under-represented in the site groups of intramural burials which provide much of the textile data (see Cox 1996a). At Spitalfields there were only two child burials with good textile preservation. Both were from well sealed lead coffins. One was buried in a woollen cap, shroud, and winding sheet, made especially for the funeral and similar to adult burials (see Fig 2.4). The second had a pillow, cap, and gown that had not

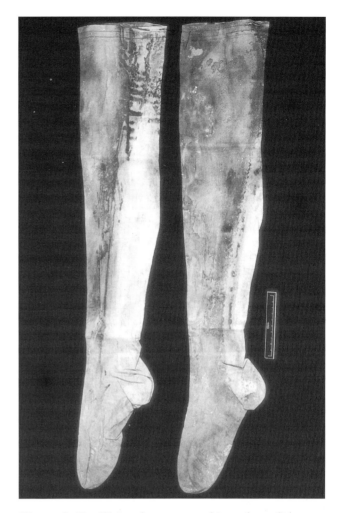

Figure 2.19   Knitted cotton stockings from St Nicholas, Sevenoaks (photo: University of Bradford)

been made for the funeral and which resembled a christening gown and cap.

Discussion

With the data available to date it is not possible to make definitive statements concerning textiles used in burials of this period, but some trends are emerging. There are no indications as to the direct relationship between the use of shrouds etc as opposed to personal clothing. The body could simply have clothes with a winding sheet, or a winding sheet and shroud, or winding sheet and shroud with clothes underneath. The nature of the shroud was such that it covered the whole body from neck to feet, thus no clothing underneath would be visible.

It has been stated (Janaway 1993, 108) that in the event of an individual dying from what was thought to be an infectious disease there may have been was reluctance on the part of the person laying out the body to disturb the clothing. However, the bulk of the evidence that has accrued to date indicates that personal items of clothing included in the burials are day wear rather than the sort of garments that might have been worn in the sick bed. It appears that the personal wishes of the deceased or their surviving relatives were probably a more significant factor; for instance a favourite garment, wedding dress, ball-gown, or uniform might be used. A good example from Spitalfields was a female who unfortunately lacked surviving biographical details from the coffin plate. This woman was clothed in an elaborate linen long-sleeved dress, trimmed with satin ribbons and lace (see Fig 2.6). Additional clothing included a pair of knitted silk stockings and a lace-trimmed cotton cap. The body was also wrapped in a winding sheet. The use of a winding sheet, rather than a shroud, would allow the dress to be seen when it was turned back while the body was being viewed. Not all burials where the bodies were dressed in their own clothes were of such quality. Another burial from Spitalfields was elaborately furnished with a double shell wooden coffin, decorated mattress, winding sheet, and shroud. However, under the shroud (and not visible to the mourners) was a repaired cotton shift, a short-bodied, long-sleeved jacket, and knitted cotton stockings. An unusual case from St Barnabas, West Kensington revealed a military uniform buried with the officer's wife (see Figs 2.2 and 2.3).

What is clear from the data is that there was considerable variation in the way in which the body was dressed and presented in the coffin. There is danger in over-extrapolation from a limited number of sites. How the dead were prepared for burial and how surviving relatives wished their last image of the deceased to appear in the open coffin gives a valuable insight into contemporary attitudes to death. While the funeral industry has grown to have very coercive powers in the 20th century, it is clear that not all burials of the 18th and early 19th centuries were dressed in uniform shrouds and caps, showing as much individuality as the blue suits of Maoist China. While there is good evidence for the growing power of the funeral professionals it is important that it is not overstated for this period.

Quote from death notice

3rd October 1850; Died lately at Kewstoke near Weston-super-Mare, aged 84, Mr Hugh Haimains. By his own desire he was buried in his first wife's wedding gown, which was an old fashioned light chintz printed cotton; and, by his own request, also,

his wife's linsey apron was put in the coffin with him (Brown & Jones 1997, 27).

Acknowledgements

There are a number of statements in this paper which question some of the views put forward by Julian Litten. This is not to underestimate the considerable debt that the discipline and the author owe to him for his knowledge and enthusiasm. Thanks are due to Louise Scheuer and Sue Black for permission to use some of their unpublished data and photographs from St Barnabas, West Kensington. A debt is also owed to the excavators of post-medieval burial sites: without their efforts and commitment, in often difficult circumstances, no archaeological data would be available.

Notes

1. The excavations at Christ Church, Spitalfields recorded 1,000 intramural burials dating from 1729 to 1852. Over 500 textile finds were recovered ranging from complete garments to small scraps. These are published in Janaway 1993, but see also Molleson & Cox 1993, 198–203. About 500 burials dating from 11th to mid 19th centuries were excavated from under the church floor in St Nicholas, Sevenoaks (Boyle & Keevill, this volume). Initial observations indicate that much of the textile material dating to the 18th and 19th centuries is similar to that from Christ Church, Spitalfields. Both sites are referred to extensively throughout this paper. It is anticipated that a full catalogue of the Sevenoaks material will be produced in the next twelve months.

2. This television programme broke new ground in terms of aspects of preparation of the dead for burial or cremation being shown to the general public. This included both embalming by a professional undertaker, collection of a relative from a hospital morgue, and two sisters dressing their dead father for burial.

3. This was filmed for a television programme in 1992 which has been broadcast on a number of networks in the USA and UK, eg Nova, Wanted: Butch and Sundance. Forensic anthropologist Clyde Snow journeys to Bolivia to dig up bones that may reveal the fate of Butch Cassidy and the Sundance Kid (Science Broadcast Programme Schedule, North Carolina 14 May 1997).

4. The woman, who died aged 48, was buried with the uniform of her husband Francis, R Chesney (Royal Artillery). It consisted of cap, coatee with gold epaulettes, two pairs of trousers, shoes, and lace gloves (see Figs 2.2 and 2.3; Black & Scheuer unpublished).

3   Romancing the stones: the graveyard boom of the later 18th century *Sarah Tarlow*

Orkney gravestones

This paper addresses a particular problem which confronted me in my research into commemorative monuments in Orkney. For archaeologists Orcadian monuments usually mean the islands' spectacular prehistoric tombs and standing stones, but the focus of this research is on the monuments of more recent periods: memorials of the last 450 years.

In the summer of 1992 a number of graveyards around Orkney were recorded, with the help of students and local people (Fig 3.1). I wanted to look at changes through time and space in the terms by which people understood death. In all, five graveyards were recorded and over three thousand stones. Four graveyards were in rural areas and one was attached to St Magnus Cathedral in Kirkwall (Figs 3.2, 3.3, and 3.4). The following winter I

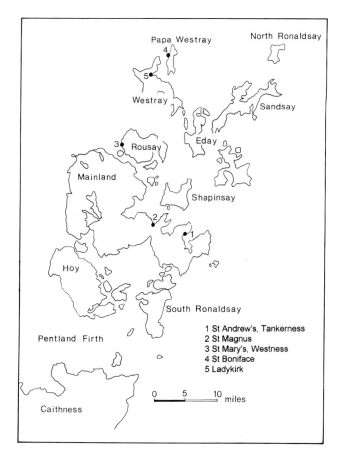

Figure 3.1   The Orkney Islands, showing the location of the graveyards included in this study

spent a few long and dreary months making several kilos of paper into a database, and then finally in the spring I sat down with considerable anticipation intending to press a couple of buttons and see the emergence of neat trends covering, in attractive battleship curves, the period from the 16th century through to the 20th. Naively, I envisioned being able to document changing monument styles and inscriptions and correlate them with age and gender through time. But things didn't work out like that. The problem was that the number of stones from each decade not only varied, but differed drastically. For example, while it is possible to make an assessment of which gravestone motifs or shapes were most popular for, say, women in the 1880s when you have a set of a hundred or more stones, if you have a set of one, as was the case for some of the decades of the 18th century, the pie charts are certainly more dramatic, but utterly meaningless. I found little difficulty in detecting statistically valid trends over the last two centuries. The problems came when trying to extend any of these trends back into the 18th century or earlier. There simply weren't enough stones to do the kind of statistical analysis that had been planned.

While it was apparent that the graveyards contained more 19th than 18th century stones, I didn't truly realise until all the records were assembled just how few pre-19th century stones there were. For each decade of the 19th century, there was an average of 189 stones. For each decade of the 18th, there was an average of six. The number of stones continued to increase from the last two decades of the 18th century up to a peak in the 1890s, from which time there was a steady decrease, which accords with the decreasing population of Orkney through the first two thirds of the 20th century. The dramatic rise in numbers began around the turn of the 19th century. The number of stones belonging to each decade increased fivefold between the 1780s and the 1820s (Fig 3.5).

My first thought was that I was dealing with the results of poor preservation. At least three of the five graveyards recorded had suffered some 'tidying' this century, and older, unstable stones dating from before 1800 might well have been cleared out. I saw one 18th century stone forming part of the churchyard steps at one graveyard. The most unstable of all could be lying flat under several inches of soil. No excavation was undertaken in the graveyards, since they were all still in use. But differences in the sample, or in the preservation of the early

In the map (Figure 3.1):

1 St Andrew's, Tankerness
2 St Magnus
3 St Mary's, Westness
4 St Boniface
5 Ladykirk

Figure 3.2   St Boniface, Papa Westray (photo: Sarah Tarlow)

Figure 3.3   St Mary's, Westness, Rousay (photo: Sarah Tarlow)

Figure 3.4   St Magnus, Kirkwall (photo: Sarah Tarlow)

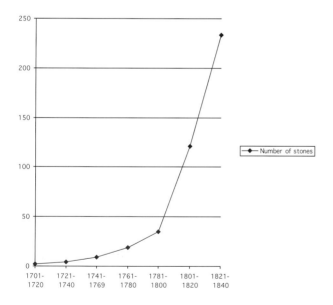

Figure 3.5   Number of monuments recorded at all five churches and graveyards dating to the 18th and first half of the 19th century, arranged by decade

stones, could not account for the scale of the change in absolute numbers. It seems that at the turn of the 18th century there really was a gravestone boom.

The nature of the boom

In the 17th and early 18th century, nearly all memorials to the Orkney dead took the form of large slabs or mural monuments which were put up inside church and cathedral buildings (Fig 3.6). Church of Scotland rules did not allow intra-mural monuments, and on the Scottish mainland these rules were generally obeyed: memorials were put up around the enclosing wall of the graveyard or free-standing in the graveyard itself. Where this happened the use of memorials in churchyards was attributed to a development from forms previously found inside the church. Thus, 'the slab in the floor became the flat stone in the graveyard; the monument set against the church wall became the headstone; the large tombs which often carried an effigy on top became in the churchyard the box tomb, altar stone or table stone' (Gordon 1984, 101; following Ariès, 1981). In Orkney the development of graveyard memorials did not follow this pattern. Tracing the development of a single tradition of commemorative monuments from the ostentatious intramural memorials of the 17th century to the early graveyard stones of the late 18th century is not possible. Very few prestigious memorials exist outside the church building. Only in a couple of parishes where family mausoleums were built in the graveyard was there any change from the burial and commemoration of the dead inside the church,

Figure 3.6   Late 17th century memorial slab from inside St Magnus Cathedral (photo: Sarah Tarlow)

that the earliest of the 'boom' stones bear little information about who erected them – often not even a name – attributing class identities to individual erectors is not straightforward. Even later on, attribution of class is fraught with ambiguity. Historians recognise the difficulty of finding criteria which enable individuals, families, or groups to be assigned to a class group. Mostly it is easier to say who the erectors of gravestones were not, rather than who they were. The gravestones of the boom are not erected by the upper class and upper middle classes, nor are they fashioned in the style favoured by the families of those classes who are responsible for most of the early modern commemorative monuments. Nor, for the most part, do they seem to have been erected by the very poorest people, although it may be that some of the unworked, uninscribed stones were put up by the very poor, who might have been illiterate.

The finish and the inscriptions on some of the early stones suggest that they are home-made. The stones from the 1780s, which marked the beginning of the boom, often have rather crudely cut letters in inconsistent cases and approximate spelling (Figs 3.7 and 3.8). This suggests that the carvers, while not being illiterate, were unpractised, probably the products of local parish schools, who had had little cause to use their skill in writing. This points to the lower middle classes; smallholders, better-off tenant farmers, and traders. Some of the other inscriptions, however, seem to be professionally cut, suggesting greater affluence, and where the stones bear more detailed inscriptions, the professions which appear on them; schoolteachers, merchants, low-ranking clergy, legal, and administrative officers, indicate the middle classes.

Such findings are not unique to Orkney. In many places around Britain and throughout much of Europe there was a similarly rapid increase in the number of commemorative monuments. In Orkney this explosion is particularly noticeable because nearly all stones from before this period were erected inside the church or cathedral building, so most outdoor Orkney graveyards have a negligible number of gravestones dating to the period before the end of the 18th century. Elsewhere in Scotland, the Church's repeated proscriptions of the practice of intra-mural burial appears to have been better respected, resulting in a significant tradition of memorials in graveyards dating from the early 17th century, most noticeably in regions like East Lothian (Gordon 1984; Willsher 1992). However, even in these areas the numbers of these memorials were not very great in comparison to the gravestones of the 19th century (Mytum 1990). The boom was obviously part of a large and widespread phenomenon, and demands some kind of explanation.

One of the problems in trying to approach this question is that the nature of the literature on later historical graveyards in Britain is frustratingly incompatible with the kind of question being asked. The study of gravestones has largely been art

in the pre-Reformation Catholic pattern. Until the early 19th century the churchyard was empty enough of memorials to allow grazing of animals, and for entertainers and hawkers to set themselves up there. The records of the Kirk Session reveal that guards who policed the town fairs built bonfires in Kirkwall Cathedral graveyard, and the ministers tethered their horses there. Even inside the church or cathedral, the overall numbers of memorials were small. In Kirkwall only a few families habitually put them up – and those families were the county gentry – lairds, the large landowners, and wealthier burgesses. The boom consists not only of a growth in the overall numbers of gravestones which exist, but in a change from gravestones being predominantly inside the church building to being almost exclusively outside in the churchyard. The attitude to the graveyard as sacred space changed in the early 19th century, and in Orkney ordinances were passed forbidding the grazing of animals, singing of songs, and making of fires in the kirkyard.

The questions this paper addresses are who erected the 'boom' gravestones and why. Both of these questions are complex and problematic. Given

Figure 3.7 Late 18th century graveyard stone (photo: Sarah Tarlow)

Figure 3.8 Late 18th century graveyard stone (photo: Sarah Tarlow)

historical in nature. It is dominated by studies which focus especially on the graves of the famous or the rich; the remarkable at the expense of the unremarkable. The literature on the history of graveyards tends towards the anecdotal, only rarely conveying any sense of how widespread or how typical particular expressions or modes of expression actually are. The most famous social history of death, for example, Phillippe Ariès's *The Hour of Our Death* (1981), covers the history of death in Europe from classical antiquity to the present day. However, because most of its evidence is drawn from fine arts and literature, it necessarily focuses on the history of elite groups. There is no discontinuity or radical change in tradition for Ariès because the subjects of his study are memorial monuments to kings and bishops, made by famous sculptors; large-scale popular movements which do not produce unique works of art are not his concern.

One line which might be taken is to explain the rising number of gravestones as a product of a general rise in population. Does an increase in the number of memorials coincide with an increase in the number of people dying? To some extent, yes. The population of the entire county of Orkney in 1755 was about 23,000. In 1851 it was closer to 31,000 (Barclay 1965). However, most of that increase took place in the period 1820 to 1860, about 40 years after the increase in the number of gravestones began around the end of the 18th century. Although in most areas there was a slight increase in population over this period, even in those rural parishes which had a stable or even declining population in the second half of the 18th century, there was an increasing number of stones from the turn of the century. This is also in spite of the fact that many Orcadian men in the late 18th century were dying abroad or at sea, as employees of the Hudson Bay Company or as fishermen, and being buried away from the parish church.[1] The rise in population over the period 1820–60 would predict a rise in the number of stones in the period 1860–1900, given an average life span of around 40 years: this is, in fact, what happened. So while the population increase might help to explain the rising number of memorials in the second half of the 19th century, it does not work for the first. Nor can an increase in population by itself explain why people chose to put up gravestones. Since the rise in numbers of stones is out of all proportion to any imaginable rise in numbers of deaths, the boom must be explained in terms of motivated human practice.

Getting and spending

For economic historians, one of the popular lines of approach to the revolution in the consumption of material culture at the time of the Industrial Revolution is to explain the consumer boom in terms of greater spending power, and more easily accessible consumer goods. This argument suggests that more efficient means of mass production makes consumer goods more financially and logistically accessible to more people. Graveyard historians such as Willsher (1985) have attributed the 19th century pattern of commemoration to technological developments, enabling the production of cheap, mass-produced stones, at the same time as developments in transport made national and international distribution an economically viable prospect. The concurrent development of a cash economy provides people with a disposable income enabling them to purchase the gravestones they had, we assume, always wanted. Such technologically-driven approaches have been criticized by historians, economists, sociologists, and even archaeologists for several reasons. In particular, the focus on production and supply rather than demand leaves unanswered the fundamental question of why people want things. The mere availability of a product does not mean that people would necessarily want to buy it. Such explanations presuppose that the desire for consumer durables is a fundamental human attribute, and only when prices were low and the money economy operative could it be indulged. However, the increase in spending power does not, by itself, explain why in the late 18th century people chose to buy gravestones, or indeed any other consumer goods.

Nor does the getting and spending idea fit with the evidence. In Orkney, at least, mass-produced gravestones of a standard manufactured design did not become available until the 1810s, some twenty years after the upturn in numbers of stones began. The new gravestones at the beginning of the boom were home-made, and the stones used were local: no place in Orkney is far from the shore or some other ready source of inscribable flagstones. Due to the lack of trees in Orkney, flagstones are also the commonest building and roofing material, and would be easily obtainable from a quarry or an old building. Thus the materials to construct a memorial had always been available at little expense. Unshaped and unprofessionally inscribed gravestones had existed in Orkney churchyards in very small numbers since the 17th century and these home-made stones constituted most of the late 18th century boom stones. The distribution of commercially produced stones was subsequent to the increase in demand: availability did not occasion demand, nor did it actually facilitate the acquisition of a gravestone. Moreover, the commercially manufactured gravestones were not cheap. During the 19th century the expense of putting a body in the ground and marking the spot reached bankrupting levels. A death could financially ruin a family, hence the foundation of and subscription to special savings plans and funeral societies to provide for these huge expenses (Litten 1991). The memorial stones were a significant part of the financial responsibility of the family. The acquisition of a commercially produced gravestone should not be compared with the acquisition of one commissioned from a mason, but with a non-professionally inscribed undressed flagstone from a local source. The gravestones of the 18th century graveyard are not derived from the intramural memorials of the gentry, but from the poor graveyard stones of the preceding century. It cannot be argued therefore that new commercial technology, new traders, or new materials made it easier to obtain a gravestone. The financial outlay as a proportion of income was greater, not less than before. We are forced to conclude that the gravestone boom came about because of a change in people's desires, which was later harnessed by the producers and marketers of the industrial revolution. Only now, in the late 18th century, did significant numbers of people want to put up memorials to their dead. There was a major change in attitude to the dead, and it is this change in attitude, commemorated by the prodigious boom in gravestones, that needs to be explained.

Emulation and status

The discussion of consumer demand has been essentially what Colin Campbell (1987) calls 'other-directed.' That is to say, people's motivation for acquiring things; clothes, houses, cars, imported food, and so forth, is to do with their social position. The justification for these kinds of approaches is that the goods concerned are ostentatious: they are to be seen and noticed by other people. These theories maintain that the display of material wealth was a means of raising one's social status, or maintaining a high position in society. This is a compelling argument as far as the aristocratic gravestones of the first half of the 18th century and earlier are concerned. These earlier memorials were two metres or more in height, elaborately carved with scenes, motifs, heraldic, and other designs. They were beautifully inscribed with epitaphs in Latin or Greek immortalizing the memory of individuals, whose family connections, profession, and personal characteristics were meticulously set forth. Monuments were positioned along the interior walls of the choir of the church or cathedral building, where every living soul in the parish would see them at least once a week. It certainly seems likely that such monuments were involved in the negotiation of status relationships. Although the use of heraldic rules and devices, and classical languages gave full access to the meaning of the stones only to the select few who knew Latin and could interpret the codes of heraldry, other people would have recognised at least their partial exclusion and, in a general way, the elite status of such monuments. (This is not the theme of this paper, so will not be developed further here. The ways in which ostentatious memorials functioned in the reproduction of status relationships have been examined and developed by Finch, 1991.)

But approaches which centralize the negotiation of status relationships work less well for the gravestones of the late 18th century. The gravestone boom coincided with many social and material changes, and to look at the boom contextually it is necessary to see it as associated with the social and economic changes which took place then. In recent years many scholars of the Industrial Revolution have argued that the change in consumer attitude is of more crucial importance than simple questions of demography or spending power (eg Braudel 1967; McKendrick, Brewer, and Plumb 1982; Weatherill 1988). Within these terms, the acquisition of 'nonessential' material culture items by the middle classes has been interpreted as an attempt at status enhancement by means of emulating their social betters. Is it appropriate to interpret the middle class demand for gravestones as a desire to enhance their social status by means of emulation? The model of the spread of ideas by emulation or imitation is very widespread in archaeology (eg Miller 1985; and see Fig 3.9), and comes into numerous archaeological interpretations of material culture, including grave monuments, both historically and prehistorically (eg Curl 1972, 8; Rowell 1970, 49).

I do not believe that this model of self-aggrandizing emulation of one's social superiors is an appropriate way to understand the gravestone boom of the late 18th century, or, for that matter, a sufficient explanation of the consumer revolution and I will try to explain why not. This discussion draws heavily upon Colin Campbell's book *The Romantic Ethic and the Spirit of Modern Consumerism* (1987).

Models of social emulation are based upon certain assumptions:

1 (After Thorstein Veblen) That commodities have social and symbolic meanings beyond the satisfaction of economic needs (Veblen 1957; Diggins 1978).
2 That the material goods signify personal wealth, which is in turn an index of social status (Veblen 1957).
3 That each person aspires to the social class above that which they presently occupy.
4 Middle ranks of society will imitate (emulate) higher ranks and be imitated by those lower than them (implicit in this is that a person's motivation for such emulation is the power of a universal and pre-existing envy or ambition (McKendrick *et al* 1982: 14–16; Leibenstein 1982, cited by Campbell 1987).
5 Those in the highest social ranks are thus those whose tastes and values will eventually spread

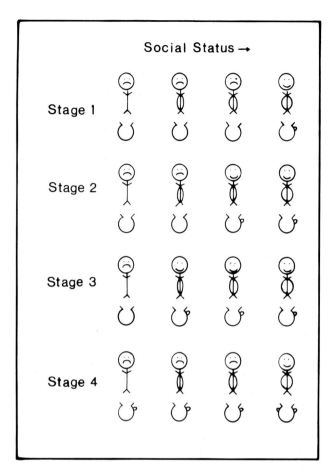

Figure 3.9   The spread of ideas by emulation (from Miller 1985, 186, courtesy of Cambridge University Press)

throughout society. They are also the locus of innovation.
6 The consumption of material culture is significant in the articulation of social emulation.

Veblen's recognition of the social significance of material goods enriched economics, and is fundamental to modern archaeology (eg Frankenstein and Rowlands' 1978 model of the 'Prestige Goods Economy'). However, his suggestion that this significance has solely to do with the communication of a message of status, unproblematically construed as a correlate of wealth, is unnecessarily restrictive.

This analysis suggests (points 3 and 5) that the tastes, values, and attitudes of the elite of society represent the ultimate pinnacle towards which everyone is striving. Morley follows this construction when he claims that it was during the 19th century that the middle classes adopted aristocratic values, somewhat coloured by a 'definite middle class tinge' (Morley 1971, 11). However, in this historical context, it seems unlikely that the middle classes were emulating the aristocratic classes. Is it probable that the same class within which developed socially and religiously puritan, anti-aristocratic movements including the 'Protestant ethic' (Weber 1930), should also aspire to associate themselves with those very symbols of degenerate luxury? In popular religion and literature, the 'social betters' whom, Morley's model suggests, the lower middle classes were supposed to have wished to emulate were held up as examples of dissolution because of their idleness and immorality. The middle classes had a deep antipathy towards what was perceived to be the aristocratic ethos of luxury (Campbell 1987, 31–5). There is also much to suggest that many of the changed tastes which characterized the consumer revolution were middle class in origin. Novel-reading, for example, was a middle class, rather than an aristocratic taste (Watt 1957).

It is a strange snobbery that while developments among the aristocracy are interpreted as innovative and intellectually-based responses to social or philosophical problems, commentators are unwilling to attribute to the middle classes anything but a desire to keep up with shallow fashion. Social history and archaeology are bound to be more involved with the upper classes than the middle and lower ones, simply because they leave more, and more durable, traces. But assuming that the history of the middle classes is merely the shadow of the history of aristocracy is a distortion against which we should guard.

In the case of gravestones, it is worth noting that the stones which the Orkney middle classes erected at the time of the gravestone boom were quite unlike the stones which the upper classes had been putting up during the preceding two centuries. The 'middle class' stones are small, free-standing headstones, or flat slabs. They do not carry much biographical information, perhaps not even a full name. They are in the churchyard rather than in the choir of the church. They bear little or no decoration. Crucially, they differ from the earlier stones by being less ostentatious, less elaborate. Is it really credible that this is because the middle classes are trying to emulate the gentry but, through lack of money or taste, are unable to 'get it right'? I think not. It makes no sense that the growing numbers of memorial stones for the middle class dead should emulate a class to which the middle classes were antagonistic, at a time when the values of the middle class are supposed to be triumphing over the aristocratic ethic. It is at odds with the prevalent view of the late 18th and early 19th century, as Marx, Weber, and others have characterized it: that modern capitalism arose with the emergence of the middle class ethic at the time of the Industrial Revolution.

One strand of thought about graveyard commemoration in the 19th century is that 'part of the new wealth of society was expended on the funerals and on monuments necessary to establish respectability' (Curl 1972, 20). The maintenance of social respectability was clearly important to middle class Victorians. Such an argument has the virtue of attributing aspirations to the particular material culture of death to 'fitting into' rather than clawing up the social order, and it permits the interpretation that respect or love for the deceased might have a role to play. However, these accounts do not go further than the equation of expenditure with respectability, which fails to address the particular pattern of expenditure which characterized 19th century practice. Why was the domain of funerary culture given such particular emphasis in the 19th century? Concentrating financial investment in one area of material expression should make us question why death should be such a powerful context that 'respectability' in other areas might be compromised. Being publicly perceived to be bankrupted by the expense of a funeral did not strengthen one's social status, where such status is gained through the display of wealth. In fact, to throw oneself and one's children into poverty through expenditure on funerary and mourning accoutrements was to invite social censure in the Victorian Age (Richardson 1994). Why should families who could otherwise be identified as 'working class' (presumably through other aspects of their lives), choose to put resources particularly in this one area of expression? Curl's implicit assumption that expenditure in funerary practice is motivated by social position does not account for its particular context. He touches on a more contextually specific explanation when he comments that funerary practice also functioned to impress on others the love, esteem, and honour in which the deceased was held by the bereaved (Curl 1972, 20). It is not a general 'middle class status' which is being sought, or consolidated, but a particular attitude towards death and bereavement, and the relationship between the dead and the bereaved which is being elaborated.

Social communication and private pleasures

Social communication is not enough to explain why a person makes or acquires material culture. Things have meanings for the individual, maybe meanings created and enhanced through advertising, daydreams, or aspirations for the future. If I buy a car, my motivation is more complex than a simple desire to elevate or enhance my status in society. I'm buying dreams. If I were able to buy this car it would be fulfilling a desire, not to impress the neighbours, but to buy a dream. My point is that the acquisition of material goods has a highly personal, internal, as well as an 'other-directed' dimension, at least in the context of modern British history. This argument associates consumer behaviour with broadly 'Romantic', rather than Rationalist, frames of reference: imagination, emotion, self-expression, and self-consciousness. Insofar as the erection of a monument is a visible action and a communication, there is clearly an 'other-directed' element in the acquisition and erection of grave monuments. However, people's motivation for this behaviour in the specific context of the funeral is rarely advanced beyond the implication that it indulges a latent and universal desire for social climbing (eg Mytum 1989). In this chapter it is suggested that the erection of a gravestone has a more self-conscious and emotional side than is generally suggested in the literature. Campbell (1987) argues that the opposition of Romantic and Rationalist trends in modern British history is a red herring and in fact the two strains actually share many concerns. However, the assumption that the two are opposed has, until recently, prevented the recognition of romanticism in consumer behaviour. This romanticism involves the self-conscious creation of illusion in the form of day-dreaming or fantasising. Novel material items are consumed for the potential they offer the consumer to experience in reality what has been pleasurably experienced in the creative imagination.

The development of the concept of and attention to 'self' has been exhaustingly examined in the literature of social history, most notably by Michel Foucault (eg Foucault 1979; 1981; 1985; 1986). In economic history, the Industrial and consumer revolutions are fundamentally involved with the developing awareness of self. In intellectual and social history, the cults of sensibility and romanticism are based in the internal, dreaming, feeling self. The link between romanticism and consumerism has been elaborately discussed by Campbell (1987): here I consider what the popularity of sensibility and romanticism had to do with putting up stones in a graveyard.

Before the boom, most burials which took place in the Orkney kirkyard were marked only with a small mound of earth, which flattened as the coffin and its contents decayed beneath it. In fact before the late 18th century the bones of the dead might well be moved elsewhere in the graveyard in order to make space for fresh interments. The absence of a memorial implies that knowing the location of the actual physical remains was not of primary importance. Even the memorials to those buried inside the cathedral are not necessarily positioned immediately above the remains of those whom they commemorate. The gravestone immortalized the memory of the worthy dead. It did not mark their bodies or facilitate visiting their remains. Although in general, philosophical terms the 'skull beneath the skin' exercised a fascination and figured a moral and religious lesson for the people of the 17th century, the body of the dead individual held a greater interest for the Romantics than for the sons and daughters of the Baroque (Tarlow, forthcoming).

The late 18th century monuments did not necessarily bear any inscription at all. Where there was an inscription, it frequently only took the form of initials and possibly a date. The stone did not immortalize the memory of the deceased. It would mean little to a future observer without access to additional information, no date, no name. But what it did do was mark the position of the physical remains. The monuments of this period are frequently flat slabs, which not only mark the space of the corpse, but also effectively 'seal' the plot (or 'lair', as it is known in Scotland) making it difficult to use the plot for burying anyone else, or to move the remains (Fig 3.10). Before the 19th century, the use of a small piece of land to bury all the dead of the parish was facilitated by the removal of old bones. But from this period on, the lair was being seen more and more as belonging to the deceased and their family in perpetuity. So one of the purposes of marking the grave was to secure the ground from further intervention. Putting up a gravestone is also a way of marking family property, staking a claim to land which belongs to you and your heirs. The possession of a grave plot was surely important to families that they should want to mark out their claim in this way.

One other, and, for the purposes of this paper, central corollary of the marking of the lair was that it became possible to visit the actual remains of the dead. This had not generally been possible before. Even the aristocratic monuments inside the church were not usually positioned immediately above the burial. In the graveyard the frequently temporary resting places of the dead went unmarked and, although the graveyard as a whole was made sacred by the presence of the (collective) dead, the body of

Figure 3.10 Late 18th century flat slab, St Boniface (photo: Sarah Tarlow)

the dead individual was not commemorated. Before the late 18th century there is little evidence in Orkney that the graves of the dead were habitually visited by their survivors. The churchyard was put to a variety of civil and religious uses, including giving respect to the dead at their interments, but there is little indication that one would expect the specific grave to be attended again. Now the existence of headstones enabled the graves of individuals to be visited. In 1758, the Kirk Session decided that the gates to the St Magnus Cathedral graveyard should not be locked by a key, but left on 'snecks' [latches], so that people could freely enter into the Kirkyard and walk in it.[2] There is a concern here that the actual physical remains of the dead should be accessible to their survivors. Lawrence Stone notes such a concern with the physical remains of the dead as illustrated in the response of the diarist Arthur Young to the death of his fourteen year old daughter, 'Bobbin', in 1797. Stone recounts Young's expression of terrible grief, and his formulation of a plan to bury her under the family pew in church 'fixing the coffin so that when I kneel, it will be between her head and her dear heart' (Bentham-Edwards 1898, 277–82, quoted in Stone 1977, 248). 'There is an obsession here' writes Stone 'with the physical remains . . . which occurs again and again in the eighteenth century' (Stone 1977, 248–9).

Love and marriage

To recap: the gravestone boom is involved with the development of a desire to visit the grave, with a growing feeling that the remains of the dead should not be disturbed, and that the space of the grave should belong to its purchaser in perpetuity. All of these represent a change in the relationship between the living and the dead, as individuals. The post-Reformation understanding of the relationship between the living and the dead centred on the preparation of the living to follow the dead to judgement and then to glory, or to everlasting damnation. In either case, the relationship between life and death was largely the relationship between present (earthly) state and future (Heavenly or otherwise) state, and between the living as a class and the dead as a class. Communication between the two states was in the form of a journey undertaken at death. The changes which occurred in the late 18th century related to changes in attitudes towards that relationship. The living bereaved related to their dead as individuals, and the relationship after death corresponded to the kind of relationship in life. Essentially, the association was individual and emotional, and the relationship was not between past and future states, but a synchronic relationship between a living and a dead person.

The 18th century was a time of major change in personal and family relationships. The changes in commemorative practices are associated with the rise in the 18th century of an affective individualism, involving changes in the individual's perception of him/herself in relation to others, and changes in his/her behaviour towards them. Lawrence Stone (1977) characterizes 'affective individualism' by a high degree of self-awareness, sentimentality and feeling, increasing desire for autonomy in social, religious, and political life and humanitarian reform. Affective individualism also resulted in fewer, but more intense social and familial relationships. In the family, the development of an affective individualist ethic began to undermine traditional patriarchal and hierarchical relationships, promoting free choice of marriage partner and kinder treatment of women and children.

The causes of the growth of affective individualism are, as Stone says, 'not . . . a mere intersection of curving lines, but the shift of a whole system of values' (Stone 1977, 258). It won't be possible to pick out any single 'prime mover', partly because the economic, social, and ideological changes of the 18th/19th century are enabled and reinforced by each other, but also because to give primacy to economic or political changes would risk attributing to ideological and emotional history a purely legitimatory role. However, I do believe that the economic changes of the 18th century, resulting in greater individual autonomy, articulated with popular philosophical and ethical developments to promote the spread of affective individualism throughout society. The development of capitalist relations of wage labour enabled individuals to become more autonomous, and at an earlier age, than in the early modern period. This in turn facilitated a greater degree of personal choice in regard to, for example, marriage partner. So middle class adults who died around the turn of the 19th century were linked by strong emotional ties to their spouses, generally chosen for primarily sentimental reasons, and children.

Given this emotional context, at the death of a family member the feelings of the bereaved individuals were often very profound. 'Emotional' situations such as death are organised in society in ways which stress certain 'appropriate' responses and ties. However, it is important not to see these emotions as somehow false because we can point to how they were constructed, and what contradictions they served to mask ideologically. Grief at the death of a beloved husband or wife is no less deeply and painfully felt for being socially constructed.

Conclusions

So why, at the end of the 18th century, did the practice of putting up stone memorials to the dead became so popular and so widespread? The gravestone boom was a real phenomenon, too exaggerated to be the product of differential survival, nor is there any evidence that a rise in population was a significant factor. Supply-led economic arguments offer no explanation of why people were motivated to erect monuments to their dead, nor would such arguments fit with the Orkney gravestone boom, which began before commercially produced gravestones were readily available in the islands, so any explanation must take into account the motivation of the people, broadly middle class people, who wanted gravestones.

The traditional explanation of the middle class consumer boom which characterized the Industrial Revolution attributes a general acquisitiveness to the desire to emulate or imitate one's social superiors. The motivation for emulating the upper classes at the time of the triumph of the middle class ideal is doubtful, and, in the case of Orkney gravestones at least, the gravestones of the boom differ in several important respects from the upper class memorials of the preceding two hundred years. The gravestones of the late 18th century do not seem to have anything to do with making claims about status, if status is considered in terms of material wealth. The earliest stones of the boom were not expensive, they are poor in comparison to the aristocratic memorials which preceded them. And yet their public position and the occasional inscription, written in accessible English, make us realise that, although we should look at people's attitudes towards death and bereavement, there is a desire that the monument will mediate relationships between living people, as well as between the dead and the bereaved. Although material culture, in this case, could be considered as an expression of class identity, it is not an ideology imposed from the outside, but a personal, internalized one, created and recreated by predominantly middle class activities such as novel-reading.

The way to understand these monuments must be as a public expression of deep, personal feelings. To erect a monument is a way of showing how much an individual has meant to you, and showing that to the rest of the community. It enables you, by marking the grave, to go on making gestures of grief such as visiting the beloved remains, laying flowers, and being able to indulge in meditation and prayer, essential activities of the man or woman of feeling. The stone is also about the relationship between a living and a dead individual. From the late 18th century, family and matrimonial relationships were characterized by bonds of affection. Commemoration of a dead person is a way of demonstrating feelings of bereavement, melancholy, and the strength of familial or romantic love felt by the bereaved. The stone is a memorial to the deceased, but also, crucially, a memorial to a relationship. The significance of the stone was personal and emotional, and the fact that it was publicly visible should not make us cynical about the feelings of bereavement experienced by those who erected them. The stone was a way of making a statement about the strength of feeling of the bereaved individual. It was also in its own right an indulgence of such feelings, and permitted grief and melancholy to be further indulged.

The public nature of the stone ensured that those who knew of the bereavement would continually be made aware of your suffering, and permitted them the sentimental pleasure of empathising with your bereavement, or meditation on the life and death of the deceased. What the 18th century stones did not necessarily do was to commemorate the deceased for future generations. I cannot now know who 'AS 1795', for example, might be. The stones would only have been fully meaningful within a small community for at most a couple of generations. This is a significant change from earlier periods where the information on the stone gave full names and often long lines of aristocratic descent, incorporating family coats of arms. In those cases it was by association with dead aristocratic forebears that the status of the living family was enhanced. In the late 18th century there was a change to a situation where less emphasis was placed on the links with aristocratic ancestors and more on personal links with individuals in life. The gravestones are monuments to those personal links. Considering the minimal amount of information on most of them, it is significant that the most common piece of additional information is the initials of a spouse, and a heart. The move from inside to outside the church might also be associated with the greater stress on personal links with living individuals. The graveyard is just as public as the internal space, but the association with the impersonal, institutional aspect of the church is perhaps weaker.

I have tried to show in one, historic, example how complex the human response to death is, and some of the problems and deficiencies in considering the material culture of death only in economic or broadly Marxian terms. I am not trying to say that economics is unimportant, nor that human emotions are somehow universal. On the contrary, because emotions are socially constructed, and constructed through, among other things, material culture, archaeologists can address some of the social aspects of the creation and reproduction of a society's emotional life. Death is an emotional experience – both bereavement and the anticipation of our own inevitable mortality – and archaeological approaches to this area are problematic. Nevertheless, an attempt to meet the challenge presented by these more emotional aspects of human experience will lead to richer, deeper archaeologies.

Notes

1   The Hudson Bay company employed almost exclusively Orcadian men in the years between 1745 and 1820, taking about 10% of the adult male population of the islands.
2   Petition of Thomas Loutit to the Kirk Session, 1758.

4 A new burial form and its meanings: cemetery establishment in the first half of the 19th century

Julie Rugg

Introduction

In the first half of the 19th century, a significant change took place to an aspect of funerary practice that had remained virtually unchanged since the 8th century AD. The establishment of cemeteries introduced the possibility of large-scale burial outwith the control of the Church of England. By 1820, urban churchyards and burial grounds had come to be characterized by sordid huddles of rank overgrowth and stone. Cemeteries, by contrast, were often attractively landscaped and offered strictly regulated interment along pathways where promenading was encouraged as a genteel recreation. The introduction of cemeteries was not an inevitable development. There can be no doubt that from the end of the 18th century the churchyard was seen increasingly as an unsatisfactory place of burial, but it took a particularly unusual combination of circumstances to provoke widespread cemetery foundation and to ensure the continuation of that trend. This chapter, by looking at towns and cities across Britain, will demonstrate that the early history of cemeteries was by no means a simplistic affair, and that the cemetery then, as now, held a number of meanings. This place of burial could, among other things, be an expression of religious independence, a place of security, and an indicator of taste and civilisation. These meanings in themselves did not remain static, even over the three decades preceding 1850.

Cemeteries: an inevitable development?

The establishment of new and different burial grounds, increasingly referred to as cemeteries, occurred in the context of rapid population growth and urbanization. Examples of increases could be startling. For example, Sheffield's population increased from 46,000 in 1801 to 92,000 in 1831. This doubling in size was by no means exceptional: Birmingham, Leeds, and Leicester had a similar rate of growth, and Manchester increased by as much as 150 % (Cook & Stevenson 1980, 181). This expanded population was for the most part inadequately housed, crushed into insanitary courts and cellars. As a consequence, the national death rate that had shown consistent decline from 1780 began, from 1810, to increase (Flynn 1965). The statistician William Farr noted in 1840 that life expectan-cies were up to 20 years higher in rural districts compared with the worst urban areas (Woods & Woodward 1984). Urbanization was increasing the death rate, creating greater numbers of dead to be interred.

Existing burial provision, in private grounds, parish churchyards and vaults, and nonconformist burial grounds, was entirely insufficient to accommodate the newly massing dead. The level of burial provision in Hull was fairly typical. For much of the first half of the 19th century, the town had been reliant on the Holy Trinity churchyard at Dock Green, situated in the heart of the town. The three-acre ground had been opened in 1783 and still had space for further burials although there were fears about its continued use since it had taken most of the cholera victims of the early 1830s. Alternatives were limited. The Holy Trinity Church at the Market Place had a 1.5 acre burial ground attached, but this had been in use since 1300 and was so full that its surface was well above the level of the street. The half-acre St Mary's Churchyard was in a similar condition. The St James's Church on Mytongate had only a small churchyard, but it contained vaults with room to accommodate 5000 coffins. Vaults were also available at the Wesleyan Chapel on Humber Street, and the Independent Chapel on Fish Street. All these sites were at the centre of the town, and between them took the majority of interments. Between 1838 and 1845, these numbered just over 9000 (Smith, 1850; Milner, 1846).

Similar levels of provision can be described for many towns and cities in Britain at the time. It is no surprise that in these circumstances, burial was not satisfactorily undertaken. Overcrowding was chronic. The 1851 report on burial conditions in country towns concluded that there was a heavy reliance on burial grounds that had already been in use for centuries (*Report on a General Scheme . . . 1851*, xxiii). For example, in York the burial grounds 'have been places of sepulture for ages past, and the soil almost humanised with interment' (*York Herald*, 28 August 1836). The situation was exacerbated by the limited space afforded to burial in most towns. In Bristol, an average of 2,400 bodies a year were buried in only ten acres (*Matthew's Annual Bristol Directory and Almanack* 1843), and in Birmingham 3,500 interments were taking place annually in twelve acres of land (*Report on a General Scheme . . . 1851*). As a consequence, burial tended to be partial. In some grounds the coffins were by necessity stacked rather than interred, since there was no longer sufficient fresh earth for burial. This meant that corpses were frequently exposed to view, and passers-by were subject to 'the revolting sight of half-decayed human limbs and ghastly countenances that show the work of death but half complete' (*Falkirk Herald*, 8 November 1849). With churchyards frequently situated in the densest parts of town, the most casual passer-by could witness the desperate attempts of the gravedigger and sexton to bury where there was no room.

In these circumstances, it might be considered that burial reform was swiftly implemented. In many places where there is evidence of poor conditions, a new cemetery was indeed laid out before 1850, but the strength of the causal connection is open to question. Notwithstanding the appalling conditions in their churchyards, it was possible for communities to be apathetic about burials. For example in 1847 an editorial in the local newspaper in Rochdale pressed for the need for a new cemetery, describing local churchyards as 'either loathsome, as far as the nature of the soil is concerned, or nearly full with graves' (*Pilot and Rochdale Reporter*, 14 June 1847). Attempts to move on the issue met with an indifferent response, and it was another eight years before a new cemetery was laid out. Similar lack of activity was evident in other towns of heavy population growth, for example, Wigan, Bolton, and Stoke-on-Trent. Even in areas where conditions were bad, there was often a delay in action: in most places overcrowding must have been evident by 1820, but new cemeteries were not laid out until the 1840s. Toleration for appalling conditions could be very high, as a local doctor in Norwich commented: the 'regular and more fixed population' of the town was 'disregardful' of the 'obnoxious and deleterious sights daily presented to its view' (*Norwich Mercury*, 15 October 1845).

There was a second reason why there was not always a clear connection between poor burial conditions and cemetery establishment: in many cases there were more pressing reasons why a new cemetery was required. Much of the rest of the chapter will explore those reasons. Before doing so, however, sources and methods for cemetery research will be discussed.

Cemetery research: sources

Historians have generally drawn conclusions about the progress of burial reform by narrating attempts to pass national legislation that was intended to mitigate the evils of inner-city graveyard overcrowding. Much of this narrative concludes that burial reform was a difficult process, with cemetery establishment hampered by the operation of vested interest (Lewis 1852; Finer 1952; Wohl 1983). Pursuing the history of cemetery development through provincial sources, however, reveals a great deal of often unexplored material that points to a different conclusion: successful cemetery establishment appeared to be a common activity. Beyond question the most significant agency of new cemeteries were joint stock companies. These sold shares to finance the laying out of new ground and erection of the necessary chapel and office buildings. A typical example would be an enterprise established with a capital of £10,000, selling shares at £5, and opening a cemetery of around 10 acres on the outskirts of the town. Over 100 companies operated in towns and cities throughout England, Scotland, and Wales. It is clear that the institution was popular and widespread. Company formation was spread between a range of town and settlement types, including ports and dockyards (Bristol, Newcastle, and Hull), old market and manufacturing towns (Leeds, Halifax, and Sheffield), and spas and resorts (Brighton, Torquay, and Ilfracombe). Although cemetery company formation did tend to occur more frequently in the larger towns and cities, companies were also founded in smaller towns, including Bridgwater (Somerset), Hereford, Teignmouth, Wisbech, Chippenham, and Newport. These examples indicate the inadvisability of making an exclusive association between cemetery companies and urban sprawl.

Given the extensive nature of their foundation, study of the nature and chronology of the cemetery company is invaluable to an understanding of the progress of burial reform. In addition, analysis of company documentation provides a new range of material, including prospectuses, minute books, and annual reports, that offers a detailed view of the way in which communities viewed the issue of burial in their particular town. This material can often be supplemented by reports on the cemetery in local newspapers and town guides. Much of this chapter will demonstrate the information available from these sources, and the way in which they can be used to build up a rounded picture of cemetery development. In addition to these sources, the chapter has also relied on prosopographical material to understand the meanings of cemetery establishment: biographies of company directors have been researched, to enable conclusions to be drawn on the motivation of particular directorates. Using all these sources, it has been possible to classify each company as one of three types: nonconformist, profit-motivated, and public-health motivated. The chapter's conclusions rest on research into the chronology of each of these company types, and the associated mutability of meanings attached to cemetery development.

Early cemetery establishment – dissent and dissection

Modern cemetery development had its origins in two distinct and unconnected threads: the desire of nonconformist communities to have burial grounds independent of the Church of England, and fears concerning the security of the corpse at a time when body-snatching appeared to be increasing in intensity. Both trends pushed for the laying out of new burial grounds or cemeteries, and are reflected in the early history of the first dozen or so companies.

It is appropriate that the first cemetery company was founded in Manchester in 1820. Above all else, Manchester was a city of confidence and innovation, and its citizens were conscious of living in a town of world-wide importance. The Dissenting community in Manchester was particularly politicized in its awareness of the disadvantages they suffered compared with their Church of England neighbours. The grievance list was a long one: for example, Dissenters could not hold important local or national government offices, their marriages were not considered valid unless registered by the Church, their admission to university was restricted, burial in the churchyard could only take place according to Church of England rites, and they were compelled to pay the church rate (*Quarterly Review* 1835). Dissenters were increasingly militant in their call for religious equality, and early cemetery foundation was caught up in the passion of this movement.

The establishment of the Rusholme Road Proprietary Cemetery in Manchester was a direct response to burial grievance. Dissenting congregations in Manchester were expanding, and it was becoming evident that an independent cemetery was necessary. At the same time, nonconformist opinion on the issue of equality was being galvanized by local wrangles over the church rate. The rate was a tax levied in all parishioners, regardless of their denomination, to contribute to the upkeep of the parish church, its contents, and its churchyard. Nonconformists objected to paying the rate, and Manchester in 1820 saw one of the earliest moves against the levy. All parishioners, regardless of their religious affiliation, had the right to vote on the annual level of the rate, and in 1820 the nonconformists successfully packed the meeting to propose and support a vote against an increased rate to finance new church building in the city (Hadfield 1882). Thus the new cemetery 'for the use of all persons dissenting from the Established Church' (*Articles of Agreeement of the Rusholme Road Cemetery Company* 1820) was established in the direct context of a successful attack on the Church, and was no doubt an extension of the desire to break all Church monopolies.

The desire for independent burial ground was not wholly political. For the majority of Dissenters, the need for such a ground rested on three broad objections to current practice. Firstly, according to Church law ministers were obliged to refuse burial to the unbaptised, and this requirement placed many clergymen in a difficult position. It was certain that the children of Baptists, who were not yet baptised, and Unitarians who were not baptised according to the Trinity, could be refused burial. More scrupulous clergymen objected to burying any

Dissenters, since all had consciously rejected Church teaching. As a consequence there were a number of famous 'test' cases of clergymen refusing to bury Dissenters (Manning 1952). Although almost all were decided in favour of the bereaved, the situation remained that nonconformists could not be guaranteed burial in the local churchyard. Secondly, only Established Church ministers could preside over funerals in the churchyard. This meant that Dissenters being buried there would perforce be buried according to the rights of the Church of England. There was great strength of feeling on this matter. George Hadfield, leading Congregationalist and agitator for Dissenting rights, noted in his Memoirs that a cemetery was required for nonconformists, 'to get our own ministers enabled to provide at our funerals' (Hadfield 1882, 1). It had been known for some funerals to be presided over by a Dissenting minister standing outwith the boundaries of the churchyard (see *The Times*, 14 November 1834), but this was clearly an unsatisfactory compromise. Thirdly, Dissenters objected to burial in consecrated land. Wesley himself had declared against consecration, as being unauthorised by 'any law of God, or by any law of the land' (Collison 1840, 192).

The foundation of an entirely independent cemetery was evidently the best way to tackle these difficulties. Ten of the thirteen earliest successful cemetery companies were established by nonconformists, and this sort of company dominated the 1820–34 period. In all cases, the new cemetery was open to use by any denomination. Newcastle's Westgate Hill Cemetery Company declared itself on annual reports 'Open alike to the Whole Human Family without difference or distinction' (*Annual Reports of the Westgate Hill Cemetery Company*, dates various). Similarly, the Birmingham General Cemetery was open to 'all shades of religious opinion' (Manning 1905, 7). Openness was also promised on the issue of which minister should preside over the funeral. The Leeds General Cemetery company provided the services of a Christian minister, but permitted 'the substitution of one selected by the parties' (*First Annual Report of the Leeds General Cemetery Company* 1836). The Portsea Island Cemetery Company went further, and promised that anyone using their ground 'may inter their dead without any service whatever' (*Prospectus of the Portsea Island Cemetery Company* 1830, Fig 4.1). In none of these cases was the new cemetery consecrated. The directors of the Newcastle Westgate Hill Cemetery Company denied the need for such a ritual, declaring 'we want no mitred dignity and state, to declare our spot of ground to be hallowed for the dead' (Fenwick 1825).

Early cemeteries thus had a religious political significance. There is, however, another part of the root of early cemetery foundation that needs to be considered: the need for new cemeteries as a means of offering security from body-snatchers. Until the passage of Warburton's Anatomy Act in 1832, the

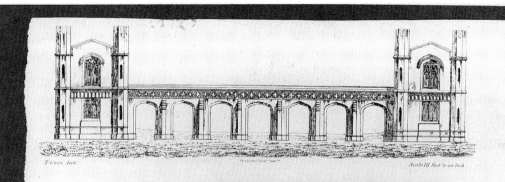

Prospectus of the Portsea Island General Cemetery,

WITH A VIEW OF ITS FRONT ELEVATION.

IT has for many years been a subject of regret, that in so large a population as these Towns contain, no suitable and convenient place of Sepulture, commensurate with the necessities of upwards of 50,000 persons, has been provided.

There is not to this day a place of interment sufficiently retired and secure, where the funeral obsequies may be performed without noise or intrusion; and where the remains of our departed friends may be deposited, without dread of being taken up again for anatomical purposes, or their graves trodden by the rude and hasty feet of an idle rabble.

It is however presumed, that the time is now arrived, when this accommodation may be secured; where our friends shall repose in perfect and uninterrupted security, until "the voice of the archangel and the trump of God" shall rouse from the long sleep of death, the myriads of the dead to a state of immortal vigour.

A suitable piece of ground having been offered for the purpose, a number of gentlemen met at the Society's Hall, November 24th, 1830, to consult on the subject; when it appeared to be the unanimous opinion, that the measure was not only desirable, but practicable.

They therefore appointed a provisional Committee,—to correspond with those Towns which had already established Cemeteries,—to examine the land proposed, and the probable expense of enclosing it,—and of erecting suitable buildings for the object. On the 8th of December another Meeting was held in the same place, and the Report of the Committee was presented; when it appeared, that the greatest success had attended such Institutions where they had been established. *

A sub-committee was appointed, to invite the attendance of other persons who may be friendly to the object,—to draw up a Prospectus,—to make further inquiries,—and to lay the result of their labours before a more general meeting, on the 16th inst.

A meeting was held accordingly, which was respectably attended; when it was resolved unanimously :—

That a General Cemetery or Public Burying Ground, for the accommodation of all parties in this extensive and populous neighbourhood, is highly desirable.

2. That the site of land consisting of nearly four acres, situated near the Nelson's Arms, on the London Road, being considered the most suitable for the purpose, be purchased accordingly.

3. That £3000 be raised by 600 shares of £5 each.

4. That the Committee be empowered to call a general Meeting of Shareholders.†

The plan now proposed to the public, is—to afford to all classes the privilege of committing their dead to the tomb according to their own views of the rites of Sepulture, in the most decent and becoming manner.

To secure this object, the above piece of land has been purchased; round which it is intended to erect walls, not less than thirteen feet high, to be surmounted by iron spiked rollers; to have a handsome entrance from the London Road; the whole front secured by an iron palisade with folding gates, conducting to the corridor or covered way; beneath which the mourners may leave the coaches and enter a commodious edifice, to be erected for the funeral service. This building to form one wing of the entrance, corresponding with a dwelling-house for the Chaplain on the other wing; the whole presenting a very interesting object.

The total estimated expense for land, walls, erections, gates, drains, planting, &c. is £5000; to be divided into 600 shares of £5 each, open to persons of all denominations; but no one individual to hold more than 20 shares in his own right.

The shares to be paid for by instalments in the following order, viz.—one pound on the purchase of each share, and one pound per share at the close of each quarter subsequently; till the whole be paid.

The property to be vested in Trustees, for the purpose of a general Cemetery or Burying-place, for ever.

A Minister is to be appointed, to officiate as Chaplain and Registrar, whose services will be at the command of such as wish to avail themselves of them, without charge or fee. On these occasions, it will be left with him to conduct the service as he shall think most for the edification of the parties present. Those who bring their own Minister with them, will be at liberty to use what form they please; while others, who prefer it, may inter their dead without any service whatever.

A correct register will be kept, containing every requisite particular for identifying each individual interred; while an index to the ground plan, will immediately direct to the spot where the remains are deposited. * Every precaution will be taken, by the residence of responsible and confidential persons on the spot; and by the method in which the vaults and graves will be secured, to preserve the sanctity of the tomb inviolate, and the ashes of the dead undisturbed.

The Cemetery will be neatly arranged, and planted with suitable shrubs, presenting an inviting retreat, which may be frequented with fond affection by the relatives and friends of those who slumber within its enclosure.

For the guidance of those disposed to become Shareholders, the Committee have made some general calculation of the probable income of the Cemetery; and they submit, that in a population of 50 or 60,000, about 1500 die annually; of these it may be fair to conclude, that, considering the superior advantages of this Cemetery, not less than 500 may be interred in it annually.

This, notwithstanding the moderate charges proposed, will produce
per annum, including vaults, brick-graves, &c. about £600
While the expenses will not exceed 150

Leaving a balance of £450
Which will pay on 600 shares of £5 each, 15 per cent. per annum.

ADVANTAGES OF THE INSTITUTION :—

1. The expense will be much less than in other burying grounds in the neighbourhood.

2. The privilege of adopting any form of service deemed most suitable at the interment of friends.

3. A correct register and index or ground plan for identifying the spot where the remains of any individual lie.

5. And above all, the superior security of those interred.

* At Liverpool a Cemetery was opened in February, 1825, at an expense of £7000; and though their charges for interments are low, they pay £10 per cent. interest on the shares; besides having paid off a debt of £3000 in 5 years. The following is a statement of their progressive prosperity, (including vaults and brick graves) :—

No. of Interments.		Annual Income.		
1825	204	£ 292	2	2
1826	424	1018	2	0
1827	561	1245	5	0
1828	706	1700	17	7
1829	743	1806	18	0
1830	probably 900			

† The Committee have to state, that, as they are only acting *pro tempore*, when a sufficient number of shares are taken, a General Meeting of Shareholders will be called, to appoint Trustees, managing Committee, Treasurer, and Secretary; and also to determine on the rules and regulations necessary for the proper management of the Cemetery.

☞ Shares may be obtained, on application to Messrs. Atkins and Son, Bankers, Portsmouth; Mr. T. Ellyett, Treasurer, and Mr. Garnett, Queen Street; Mr. Bilton, Union Road, Southport; or, to Mr. T. Owen, Architect, Southsea.

December 22nd, 1830.

Horsey, Printer, Queen Street, Portsea.

Figure 4.1   Prospectus of the Portsea Island Cemetery Company 1830 (the Sanderson Collection, Portsmouth Central Library) trade in cadavers was highly lucrative (discussed further by Cox in this volume and in detail in Richardson, 1987). A number of private anatomy schools had been established in London and elsewhere, and the demand for bodies for dissection was increasing (Lawrence 1988, 62). Although there are no statistics on the incidence of bodies stolen, there was clearly a public perception that body-snatching was a frequent occurrence. The insecurity felt by communities when faced with the threat of body-snatching or 'resurrectionist' activity was reflected in increased attention to the security of the corpse. Double and triple coffins were popular during this period, as were a range of gadgets designed to prevent the levering off of the coffin lid (Richardson 1987, 81).

It is important to understand the strength of feeling that was connected to the notion of a body being taken for dissection. Generally, anxiety was expressed on three counts. First, the dissection of the corpse was held to have serious consequences for the spiritual state of the dissected. Christian belief in the physical resurrection of the whole body after death was commonplace, and the dismemberment of the corpse was thought to be detrimental to this process. Such belief was supplemented by more indefinable solicitude for the corpse, deeply rooted in folklore. It was this feeling which, in part, motivated the crowds protecting the Tyburn corpses from the anatomists (Linebaugh 1977). The activities of resurrection men in dragging corpses out from their coffins by ropes around their neck was enough even in itself to violate this feeling, even without dissection taking place. Second, dissection was associated with the worst crimes. Without recourse to body-snatchers, anatomists could only make use of the corpses of executed felons, and dissection was often specified as part of the punishment. The final source of anxiety about disinterment and dissection was occasioned by its sexual connotations. The notion of the body of a mother, sister, or wife 'subjected to the gaze of lads learning to use the incision knife' was deeply harrowing, with dissection being thought akin to sexual assault (*The Times*, 9 December 1822).

As a consequence of the depth of revulsion felt against dissection, attention was from the early 19th century increasingly paid to the security of the place of burial. All the early company cemeteries were founded with an evident apprehension of the fear of resurrection men and showed some commitment to security. For example in Birmingham, the location of a medical school, the Birmingham General Cemetery Company directors expressed the intention to lay out a cemetery that would 'preserve and secure the repose of the dead', and be 'capable of being defended against violators' (Manning 1905, 8; Aris's *Birmingham Gazette*, 18 October 1832). The inhabitants of Liverpool, where two cemeteries were founded in the 1820s, were faced with a double risk from the resurrectionist. The city housed two medical schools, each teaching upwards of forty students. In one hugely notorious incident of 1826, barrels containing bodies were found on the dockside (*Gentleman's Magazine* 1826, 363). Liverpool had also become 'the centre of a most extensive traffic in subjects', supplying London, Dublin, and Scotland with cadavers (Cooper 1843, 396). Anxiety created by body-snatching activity formed the background to the establishment in 1825 of the Liverpool Necropolis, which promised 'entire security against trespassers of any kind' (*Liverpool Mercury*, 19 September 1823). The Liverpool St James Cemetery, opened four years later, also guaranteed 'perfect security' (*Minute Book of the Trustees of the St James Cemetery*, 10 August 1825).

Thus, two powerful but unconnected trends worked in concert to push for the establishment of new cemeteries. For the most part, the cemeteries were founded by nonconformist communities, but all the early sites constituted a response to common fears that the bodies of relatives would be stolen for dissection. From their origins, therefore, cemeteries could carry dual significance: a means of religious political expression, and a way in which to protect the corpse from violation. Neither meaning remained static. Anglican communities also adapted cemeteries to express their political allegiances, using their sites to promote connections with the Established Church and paying dividends directly to the clergy. After 1832, fears about the disturbance of the dead became attached to sextons and their boring rods, attempting to find fresh places for burial where there were none (Rugg 1992). After the mid 1830s, wider civic significances were attached to cemetery foundation.

Speculation in cemeteries

Many historians have defined the Victorian cemetery company as a somewhat tasteless adjunct of the heavily commercialized Victorian funeral, to be listed alongside ostrich feathers, mutes, jet jewellery, and Shillibeer's funeral omnibus as evidence of the 'Victorian celebration of death' (Morley 1972; Curl 1972). These historians are in agreement with the writer to the *Quarterly Review* that the joint stock cemetery was 'necessarily mercenary' (*Quarterly Review*, 1844, 449). It cannot be denied that some companies reflected a new cemetery image: burial as big business. The majority of these companies emerged during periods of extreme enthusiasm for joint stock finance, when any scheme that looked likely to make a profit was paraded for perusal by eager investors. This aspect of cemetery company development is perhaps more illustrative of Victorian finance than Victorian views on death and burial, but it is important to pursue this point for two reasons. First, detailed study of the setting up of the more speculative companies indicates the importance of ownership of the place of burial; and second it is this strand of pure profit motivation that led to the establishment of some of the more spectacular Victorian cemeteries, including perhaps the most famous of all: Highgate.

Speculative cemetery companies first emerged, and the majority flourished, during times of investment mania. There was no doubt that the companies were instituted to meet the soaring demand for investment opportunities which characterized the mid 1820s, mid 1830s, and mid 1840s. The mania of the mid 1830s was particularly important in widening out cemetery schemes from being purely nonconformist affairs. This mania saw a particular concentration on investment in domestic enterprises, including banking, life assurance, mining, steam navigation, and railway schemes, although all the manias were alike in their national absorption in investment opportunity (Hunt 1936). During these periods there was an almost hysterical search for new investment opportunities, and fraudulent exploitation of the sometimes unquestioning appetite for speculative ventures was inevitable. Charles Dickens parodied the boom in Nicholas Nickleby's 'United Metropolitan Improved Hot Muffin and Crumpet Baking and Punctual Delivery Company', 'the very name of which will get the shares up to a premium in ten days' (Dickens 1983, 69).

Financial success had followed the majority of the early Dissenting cemetery companies, and this made the format ripe for replication. The Liverpool Necropolis had been particularly successful, and it was circulated that the company had been able to pay off its £3000 loan, and still 'pay a £10 per cent [sic] interest on the shares'. Annual income had risen from £292 in 1825 to £1806 in 1829 (*Prospectus of the Portsea Island General Cemetery* 1830). As a consequence, sometimes outlandish scrip-sale schemes were set up to soak up interest in cemetery speculation. Almost all announced some hook or quirk to capture the imagination of the investor. For example, the Metropolitan and Suburban Cemetery Society proposed instituting in its ground a simplified burial fee by which 'at least 12 per cent per annum will be realised during 350 years' (*The Scotsman*, 28 January 1847). Both the Great Eastern and Western Cemetery Company and the Provincial and General Cemetery Company intended to set up 'chains' of cemeteries in all large towns and cities, although the Great Eastern planned to add to its attractions by making all the cemeteries accessible by river (newspaper clipping, undated, possibly 1845). None of these schemes came to fruition.

Perhaps more enduring were speculative schemes that were set up to tap into a particular locational market in large towns and cities. These types of schemes tended to be set up in places where there was an already well established cemetery in operation, and were restricted largely to Edinburgh, Glasgow, and Manchester. In Manchester, cemetery establishment on a frenzied scale erupted in April 1836, a key month for investment mania. During that month alone, the city saw the launching of many improbable schemes including a Zoo-

logical, Botanical and Public Gardens Company and a Joint Stock Exchange Buildings Company (*Manchester Guardian* 23 April 1836). On the last day of April, an amazed editor of the *Manchester Guardian* surveyed the number of cemetery companies that had been founded and asked 'Are we about to be visited by the plague?' (*Manchester Guardian*, 30 April 1836). But the interest subsided almost as quickly as it arose. Of the nine new cemetery companies floated, only two companies lasted more than a matter of weeks. Neither company was overtly profit-oriented, both had directorates composed of civic worthies, and both went on to establish cemeteries.

At one level, the speculative cemetery says little about attitudes towards death and the foundation of cemeteries. Approached from a different angle, however, a great deal can be implied. In particular, it should be stressed that the most companies of this type had a high failure rate. Certainly, some were only concerned with the sale of incompletely paid-up shares, or scrip, but there were some that appeared to offer a genuine long-term investment opportunity. It is clear that the public chose to withhold its support from this type of company, even when the need for cemetery land was acute. For example, during the mania of the mid 1840s, the *Renfrewshire Advertiser* carried a the prospectus of the Greenock Cemetery Company (*Renfrewshire Advertiser*, 15 February 1845). The directorate was evidently comprised of out-of-town speculators, and response to the company was heated. It was acknowledged that the town needed a new cemetery, but it was considered distasteful for speculators to exploit that need for the purposes of 'stock-jobbing and speculation' (*Glasgow Herald*, 17 February 1845). The company failed and in 1846 John Gray, a town councillor, successfully put forward plans for a cemetery that was backed by the town council. Certainly joint-stock investment in cemeteries was welcomed, but only if the scheme was proposed and owned locally.

Thus the majority of the speculative companies disappeared. But there was one type of speculative company that did make a long-term impact – companies that sold a luxury burial service. Included in this group were the London Cemetery Company, that opened both Highgate and Nunhead Cemeteries, the West London and Westminster Cemetery Company, that opened Brompton, and the South Metropolitan Cemetery Company, that laid out the Norwood Cemetery (Rugg 1992). There were only a small handful of companies of this type, but they have tended to receive most interest from historians. These companies were intentionally exceptional. For example, the London Cemetery Company was established with a capital of £80,000 at a time when most cemeteries were being laid out for £10–20,000. The company paid £3,500 for the seventeen-acre site at Highgate, situated on a hill and having fine views of the capital. The site had long been used as a promenading area, and after the cemetery was laid out, none of the 'pleasure garden' atmosphere was lost. Indeed, one commentator was shocked to note 'parties of pleasure' having picnics in the cemetery's consecrated area (Collison 1840, 170–1). The cemetery's main attractions in status terms were the vaults and catacombs built into a sunken Egyptian-design avenue at the highest point of the grounds. The success of Highgate led to imitators that also invested heavily in the landscape and encouraged the erection of suitably grandiose memorials. It is these sites that have tended to lead historians to conclude that new cemetery establishment was intended to cater solely for the middle-classes. Although this was not generally the case, the speculative 'luxury' cemeteries did probably encourage a particular status-conscious use of space in cemeteries once they were established, adding further meaning and significance to the site.

Cemeteries and the civic ethos

It may be argued that, if cemeteries were not a direct reflection of middle-class consciousness, then why were aesthetic considerations given such a high priority when company directorates looked to the layout of their sites? A report written by Thomas Grundy in 1846 indicates the depth of this concern. Grundy was one of the directors of the Northampton Cemetery Company, and the documents is a report of cemeteries he visited in an attempt to gain some ideas for the company's proposed cemetery. Grundy's tour was extensive, and included visits to Nottingham, Sheffield, Derby, London, and York. His comments were terse but telling. Taste figured quite strongly as an indicator of cemetery worth. Kensal Green Cemetery was 'not in the best taste', although Highgate had 'much taste'. Abney Park Cemetery was planted 'with great propriety'. Grundy concluded that the cemetery at Northampton should be laid out with attention to neatness and regularity, and that 'excessive ornament' should be avoided (Grundy 1846). Such a recommendation did not prevent a modest attempt to present the town with a suitably attractive cemetery, 'laid out with great taste from designs by Mr Marnock, of the Regent's Park Botanical Gardens'. The cemetery had a Norman chapel, and at the entrance of the grounds was 'a handsome lodge in the Elizabethan style' (Whellan 1849, 159).

This self-consciousness with respect to cemetery design had as its basis a general drive towards civic adornment. This enthusiasm was a marked feature of the 1800–50 period, and was manifest in the erection of municipal buildings, schools, churches, educational and cultural institutions, botanical gardens, hospitals and medical schools, and cemeteries. Indeed, the cemetery was very much part of this drive towards urban improvement since it fulfilled the key functions of all urban enhancement: laying out a new cemetery helped to reflect the success of the local economy, it constituted a vital element in the play of local rivalries with other towns, and it reflected philosophical ideas that saw cities as agents of civilisation.

The enthusiasm for civic expansion was based, in part, on economic expansion and industrial growth, and a conscious delight in the wealth produced. Britain was known as the richest country in the world, and every town and city considered itself to be an important contributor to that reputation. Furthermore, it was felt that the appearance of the town should reflect the wealth of its citizens. There was a marked increase in expenditure on urban improvement. In Leeds and the West Riding, for example, the period 1820–9 saw investment in public buildings reach £436,500, with at times between 30 and 40 building projects underway simultaneously (Grady 1987, 47 and 67). In addition to buildings adorning the centre of town, a well-laid out garden cemetery was also thought to be capable of conveying the importance and wealth of a city. For a town to lack such provision, or provision of adequate grandeur, was considered shameful. For example, at a meeting to discuss a new cemetery in Wolverhampton, it was commented that lack of action was not appropriate in a town 'noted throughout England for its commercial eminence' (Wolverhampton Chronicle, 12 September 1849). Similarly, a cemetery director in Hull expressed the hope 'to see the inhabitants of this wealthy port provided with a suitable cemetery' (Milner 1846, 48) (Fig 4.2). A peevish letter to the directors of the Leeds General Cemetery commented that the writer had visited the Portsea Island Cemetery, and felt aggrieved at its architectural superiority, which was a disgrace to Leeds considering its 'superior wealth' (Makins 1833).

Inter-town rivalry was a strong factor in inducing civic leaders to continue programmes of urban improvement. Often the proposal of a new building was accompanied by comments that improvements of a similar type had already been erected by a rival town. For example, the plan to open a new dispensary in Bradford was met with this comment in a local newspaper: 'Bradford is the only wealthy manufacturing town hereabouts in which such a one does not exist; and shall Wakefield, Huddersfield and Halifax excel us? Our pride says nay' (Leeds Intelligencer, 14 October 1824). Rivalries were also played out in cemetery establishment. For example in Doncaster, one attender at a public meeting on a proposed new cemetery commented 'other towns in the West Riding had cemeteries and he could not see why Doncaster should not have one' (Doncaster, Nottingham and Lincoln Gazette, 18 March 1842). Furthermore, it was not sufficient for the town simply to have a cemetery. The cemetery had to be of the finest design. All over Britain, local cemeteries were lauded as the most attractive, most dramatic, or most charming in the country. For example, A E Hargrove writing on burial in York declared 'no city in the kingdom possesses a more

TO THE CHAIRMAN & DIRECTORS OF THE HULL GENERAL CEMETERY COMPANY.

THIS PRINT OF THEIR BEAUTIFUL GROUNDS IS RESPECTFULLY DEDICATED

by their most obedient servant H Foster.

Figure 4.2   The Spring Bank Cemetery, opened in 1847 by the Hull General Cemetery Company. The cemetery was hoped 'to prove creditable to this large and influential borough' (Hull Advertiser, 4 June 1847) (author's collection) beautiful cemetery than ours' (Hargrove 1847, 11), a claim rivalling Brighton's Extra-Mural: 'no cemetery in England can boast of a more picturesque or pleasing appearance' (Bishop 1864, iv). Edwin Patchett, designer of the Church Cemetery in Nottingham, declared the intention to lay out a site 'equal to many and probably surpassed by few, Necropolitan places in the kingdom' (*Nottingham Church Cemetery: Report of Directors* 1855). Thus expenditure on cemeteries went far beyond basic utilitarian requirements.

The building of cemeteries also accorded with philosophical views in the civilizing nature of the urban landscape. The notion that the city constituted a means of education and refinement had its basis in the Victorian admiration of Greek culture. The increased wealth brought about by industrialization financed a pervasive expression of this passion. City dwellers were concerned to demonstrate that 'in the ardour of mercantile pursuits' they had not 'omitted to cultivate the perception of the beautiful and a taste for the fine arts' (Wemyss Reid 1883, 147). A garden cemetery was admirably able to reflect the 'urbanity' of its founders, in a way that was specific to cemetery foundation. Cemeteries were evidence that the 'barbarity' of old burial practices had been abandoned and that a new and sensitive sentimentality had been adopted:

> A beautiful spot, rich in the healing influences of picturesque nature, planted with congenial taste, kept with care, watched vigilantly, open as a quiet, not uncheerful, but not merely idle resort, enriched with well-designed memorials, and adorned with buildings fitted for their solemn purpose, appears to be the most rational choice possible as a resting place for the ashes of the dead. The living may there contemplate, remember, and mourn, but they will not shudder. (*Kentish Mercury*, 18 October 1845)

Cemeteries also, irresistibly to the Victorians, provided facilities for the pursuit of rational recreation. Indeed, the amenity value of a proposed new cemetery was frequently stressed. In Wisbech, for example, cemetery directors promised that the cemetery would be 'an almost public garden, where the beauties of vegetation, arranged and cultivated by art, might be enjoyed' (Walker & Craddock 1849). The ability of the cemetery to improve the mind was similarly highlighted. For example, Glasgow's Sighthill Cemetery directors intended that their site would be laid out so that the 'disposition of its walks and ornaments will form a scientific arrangement of all the forest trees and shrubs enduring our climate' (*Minute Book of the City Burial Grounds Institute and Père Lachaise of Sighthill*, 24 March 1840).

Thus, another layer of meaning can be added to the early 19th century cemetery. A garden cemetery was one of a list of amenities thought to be indispensable in a wealthy commercial or industrial town. Garden cemeteries were an invaluable asset in the forum of inter-town provincial rivalries, and constituted an essential portmanteau activity few towns could be seen to lack. The laying out of new grounds was replete with indicators of good taste, sentiment, and intelligence, appealing both to 'the man of feeling' and the person seeking rational recreation.

Cemeteries and public health

By the 1840s, a new meaning was becoming routinely attached to cemeteries: an essential public health measure. This decade saw a general agreement on the need to combat the supposed evils, both moral and medical, arising from chronic overcrowding in inner-city graveyards. Discussion of the burial debates of the 1840s is usually dominated by narration of the efforts of sanitary reformer, Edwin Chadwick, to introduce national legislation on the issue of intra-mural interments. These histories generally conclude that Chadwick was obstructed by the operation of a range of vested interests including the Church, the undertaking trade, and private cemeteries. Looking at more widespread material, however, reveals a national consensus on the importance of cemetery reform in the 1840s. As one commentator to *The Times* wrote:

> It is now time that every Englishman should see that the abolition of the Corn Law is not all that he requires; that free trade is not the only thing that will make him cheerful, and happy; that the Metropolitan Buildings Act is not all that can be enacted to supply him with purer air; that the erection of longer sewers will not take away all the unpleasant smells. It is true that they are all productive of some good, but are comparatively trifling compared with the subject of intramural interment. (*The Times*, 18 September 1846)

These feelings were being translated to new cemetery foundation around the country, with a general view on the importance of new cemeteries as a sanitary measure.

There was an awareness of the sanitary consequences of inner-city burials before the 1840s. It was clear, however, that by that decade a transformation had taken place in the way in which the whole issue of burials was discussed. The question acquired an unprecedented urgency. During the 1830s, cemetery company prospectuses often simply mentioned that there was only limited space in the existing sites, and that these sites were already overcrowded. Prospectuses in the 1840s, however, were much more likely to dwell on the sanitary and moral consequences of intramural interment, add some gory detail of the consequences of overcrowding, and give supporting scientific evidence. It is unlikely that conditions, chronically poor since the early 18th century, had seen significant deterioration. Rather, a radical occurrence broke the habit of finding this overcrowding acceptable. Credit for this change is due to the work of Dr George Alfred Walker. Walker's *Gatherings from Graveyards* was published in 1839, and treated its readership to an exposé of burial conditions of such force that it transformed the language then used to describe graveyards, and allowed an almost Gothic relish of the worst conditions which accelerated demand for change (Walker 1839). Indeed, by 1850 *The Times* could declare that the first legislation on burials was 'mostly owing to his exertions' (*The Times*, 23 August 1850).

Gatherings from Graveyards contained a history of burial, gave examples of the public health consequences of overcrowded graveyards, and offered descriptions of a selection of the burial grounds in London. What was radical about Walker's approach was the language used. All his medical case-studies were drawn out with sickening detail, and his descriptions of conditions in graveyards dwelt unremittingly on stench and gore. A single typical example gives a flavour of the work: in describing a graveyard in Southwark, Walker noted that:

A body partly decomposed was dug up and placed on the surface, at the side slightly covered with earth; a mourner stepped upon it, and the loosened skin peeled off, he slipped forward and had nearly fallen into the grave. (Walker 1839, 201–2)

Although his writing was at times melodramatic, Walker's conclusions were rarely questioned. Indeed, the doctor was called to give evidence on government public health committees. The *Lancet* accepted his assertions of the fatal consequences of breathing in graveyard emanations, and presented corroborating case studies. For example a Mr J C Atkinson, surgeon, wrote to the medical periodical praising the 'excellent and interesting *Gatherings from Graveyards*' and noting that in his area the recent death of a sick gravedigger, the attending doctor, and his servant were all due to 'miasm or effluvium from the grave' (*Lancet* 1840, 405). Provincial newspapers reproduced extracts from Walker's work, and he was referred to in cemetery company prospectuses. It was clear that by the beginning of the 1840s, Walker had 'succeeded in awakening an unusual degree of public attention to the subject of intramural interments' (*Lancet* 1839, 542).

It is no surprise, therefore, that the majority of cemetery companies established in the 1840s had public health concerns as their prime motivation. The directors of these companies were well informed on the issues surrounding intramural interments. For example in Paisley in 1845, the local newspaper had included extensive discussion of Walker's book and the subject of burials generally. The Paisley Cemetery Company prospectus referred to such debate and concluded that 'the social evils of interment, in the midst of towns are now universally acknowledged' (*Renfrewshire Advertiser*, 1 February 1845). Perhaps a more telling indicator of the cemetery company directors' understanding of the burial issue was the fact that in many of the new cemeteries, concern was expressed to make burial affordable. The sanitary reformer Edwin Chadwick had stressed that the key to the interment problem was the inability of the poorer classes to afford quick and sanitary interment, away from the heart of the city. Thus many of the public health cemetery companies offered to the poorer classes burial at cost. At Bradford, the cemetery's lowest burial fees were not to exceed the parish rate (*Bradford Observer*, 8 June 1854). The Sighthill Cemetery Company in Glasgow made a similar commitment: its fees were one twelfth of the price charged elsewhere in the city (*Minute Book of the City Burial Grounds Institute and Père Lachaise of Sighthill*, 25 February 1840). In addition, the companies promised that burial was to be of good quality. Despite being cheaper, interments would still be of 'equal security with the rich that their graves would not be disturbed' (*Norwich Church of England Burial Ground Company* 1845). Board of Health inspectors generally found that these companies were doing 'good service' in offering sanitary burial 'at moderate charges', successfully drawing burials away from the overcrowded urban burial grounds (eg Smith 1850, 71; Lee 1852, 10). Thus cemeteries established in the 1840s acquired, alongside other meanings, a utilitarian flavour in constituting a response to the need for new burial ground for sanitary reasons.

Conclusion

This chapter began by addressing the notion that the intolerable nature of interment in inner-city churchyards was a directly causal factor in the development of cemeteries. Certainly conditions were poor, but burial reform was by no means inevitable. Indeed, cemetery establishment as a public health measure was a relatively late development: it was twenty years after the first cemeteries were laid out that sanitary considerations became a dominant theme in company prospectuses. The weakness of a direct utilitarian link leads to the conclusion that burial reform is best explored in wider contexts, and this chapter demonstrates that cemetery development was richly significant in cultural terms, revealing much of the tenor of 19th century urban life.

Cemeteries became evidence of the desire for burial independent from the Established Church, and a means of affording protection to the dead. Cemeteries also connoted a degree of sophistication, and as such constituted a suitable vehicle for expressions of a town's wealth and sensitivity. Thus even in a short 30-year period, cemeteries could hold a number of interacting meanings for their promoters.

5   Burial on the margin: distance and discrimination in early modern London   *Vanessa Harding*

Introduction

This paper has two main themes. First, that in 16th and 17th century London there was a substantial consensus on the criteria for the location of burial, dominated by a metaphor of centrality and marginality. This can be illustrated by different treatments accorded in numerous city parishes to persons of greater and lesser importance within the parish community, and to those outside either the local or the moral community. Secondly, however, it argues that that consensus was being undermined by the fragmentation of urban society, as a result of increasing numbers, the mobility and transience of the population, and religious division. By the 18th century, a significant proportion of the population rejected or at least cared less about traditional burial locations and practices. In the broader frame, all aspects of burial, including that of spatial location, were increasingly commodified, as the criterion of wealth came to override more traditional notions of status and entitlement. It is important to understand both the consensus of the early modern period and the ways in which it was modified in the 17th and 18th centuries, in order to appreciate the motives and constraints underlying burial practice between 1700 and 1900. The romanticism of some 18th century treatments of death and the dead, and the utilitarian and hygienic perspectives of the 19th century, must be set in the context of much older and long-enduring beliefs about the importance of burial style and location.

The act of disposing of the dead is a key moment at which individuals and communities display their sense of personal and collective identity. In particular, by choosing where the dead may be buried they express both their sense of the relationship of the living and the dead, and their perception of the way in which the space they themselves inhabit can properly be used. These choices may also be constrained by the physical environment and a range of proprietorial and other interests, especially in an urban context. Burial of the dead in urban societies is likely to be a more contested issue, and hence perhaps may produce a more complex and nuanced expression of space and identity, than burial in rural communities.

Between the 17th and the 19th centuries, England changed from a largely rural society to one in which a high proportion of the population lived and died in towns and cities. London, on which the research for this paper has focused, contained less than 5% of the national population in 1550, but about 11% in 1700; by 1800 another 8% lived in substantial provincial towns and cities (Corfield 1982, 8–11; Houston 1992, 20). Nineteenth century urban growth was even more substantial. Large and rapidly-growing cities like London are subject to major spatial constraints, and also to significant social tensions. Urban societies of the past, perhaps especially in the early modern period, appear to have been particularly sensitive to space and the ways it can be used – public, private, sacred, secular; spatial arrangements, and the disposition of people in a formal context defined and declared social relationships. The disposal of the dead could epitomize social relations in a spatial dimension, and a simple metaphor of centrality and marginality, of inclusion and exclusion, could be applied to burial in the early modern city, which resulted in the reservation of favoured, centrally-located burial spaces for those seen as central to society, together with relegation of socially 'marginal' groups (including those who alienated themselves from the majority, such as religious dissenters) to extramural or distant burial grounds.

The period covered here, however, (c 1550–1800) was one of social, economic, and cultural change – transformation might not be too strong a word – on a large scale. 'Traditional' attitudes to the individual, the family, the structure of society, and the nature of authority were all challenged and revised. Religion, formerly a unifying force in social and cultural terms, had become a divisive one. Cities may well have been the most active locus for this process of transformation, and the complex metropolitan society of early modern London, the largest city in western Europe, was especially important (see Wrigley 1967). The flow of immigrants, the main motor behind the capital's growth, increased the diversity of metropolitan culture and society, but also placed great strains on that society's ability to assimilate the incomers. Perceptions of both space and social position were sharpened, while high mortality rates increased the frequency and urgency of disposal of the dead. Traditional burial practices had, to some extent, to give way to new expediencies, and one result was a greater discrimination between claims on the community's limited resources of desirable burial space. The continuing pressure of numbers in the long term, however, undermined traditional ideas of civic community, in relation both to the living and to the dead, and therefore the basis for discriminatory practices;

new kinds of social units, new kinds of relationships and hierarchies, had to evolve, and new values and criteria came to determine social distinctions.

Burial spaces and hierarchies of spatial preference

Early modern London accommodated a large and diverse population, reflecting the city's metropolitan role and the population's immigrant origins, but it can also be seen as a collection of small communities, wards, neighbourhoods, and especially parishes. For the purposes of burial and the disposal of the dead, at least up to the late 17th century, the parish was the primary community. Already a very ancient institution, the parish carried strong traditions of collectivity, including worship, shared responsibility for the income of a priest and the upkeep of the church, fundraising for communal purposes, and celebration. By this period parish congregations were organizing themselves to carry out numerous tasks, appointing churchwardens who held the funds and undertook day-to-day administration, and giving authority to a handful of local leaders who, acting collectively as the parish vestry, made policy decisions on behalf of the community. Each parish had its physical focus and embodiment in the parish church, an architectural palimpsest of the community's past, and a location invested with particular significance in public, private, and communal spheres. The burial, over many years, of the dead of the community in and near the church contributed to its special meaning and importance.

London had a multiplicity of local burial communities: even in the large metropolis, parishes could be quite small and intimate, with the possibility of a very strong identification between parishioners and a physical place. There were 97 parish churches within the city walls, another 16 in the immediate suburbs, north and south of the river, and a further 17 to 20 in the areas that became part of the metropolis in the 17th century (Lobel 1989; Harding 1990, 125). This does not add up to the exact total of parish churchyards, since some parishes had no burial ground and some had more than one. At least a dozen parish churches in the city of London were wholly surrounded by other buildings, and had no open-air burial space: they had to bury their dead inside the church and/or in one of the civic or other parochial churchyards (Harding 1989, 116). Some parishes had ancient burial grounds that were not immediately adjacent to the church, but only a few yards away, as at St Magnus in London. Few of these parochial churchyards were of any considerable size, and some can have been no more than a few square yards in extent. As the pressure on burial space increased with the expansion of population in the early modern period, several parishes (including St Botolph's Bishopsgate, St Bride's, Fleet Street, and Holy Trinity

Minories) acquired additional burial grounds, usually larger than the old and often some distance from the church. In the early years of use they might offer a less constrained environment for burial, but even so urban mortality rates caused them to fill rapidly (Harding 1989, 117–18).

In addition to the parish churchyards, London had an ancient burial ground near the city centre, at St Paul's Cathedral. This may at one time have been a shared burial resource for the whole of the civic community, but by the early modern period it was subject to constraints and competing claims and used for burial by only a part of the urban population. Several of the tiny parishes clustered round the cathedral buried their dead there; other individuals from further afield chose to be buried there, often to be close to ancestors or relatives. In addition, as the only large burial space in London before the 1560s, St Paul's had to accommodate overflow burials from other parishes in plague years. By the 1580s over-use of the churchyard was perceived as a serious problem (Harding 1989, 118–19; Harding 1992, 123). At the same time it retained a strong tradition of use by the community at large for purposes other than burial: assemblies and meetings, sermons and public addresses, private trysts and transactions.

The combination of parish, convent, and civic burial grounds had provided enough accommodation for burial up till the Reformation, apart from the exceptional mortality of the Black Death, but when new accommodation for the dead was required in the early modern period, tradition, sentiment, and vested interest all had a part to play in the process. With rapid demographic growth from the 1530s, and a series of severe epidemics in the 1540s, 1550s, and 1560s, the need for new burial space soon became pressing. It was relieved by a municipal initiative, the foundation of the so-called New Churchyard, on the northern fringe of the city, in 1569. This was intended to be truly a resource for the whole civic community, and it did receive bodies from all over the city, especially from city-centre parishes with space problems, and in plague years. It was relatively large (nearly one acre) and enclosed with walls and gates. For the next century it was the only such ground, but a number of parishes, particularly those in the rapidly-growing suburbs of London, acquired new burial grounds; these too were necessarily in locations peripheral both to the parish and to the city. A second, even larger, municipal burial ground, that of Bunhill Fields, was established in London during the plague of 1665, also in the northern suburbs of the city (see Harding 1993, 60–1).

With the opening of these and other new grounds in the later 17th century, and the large-scale revision of parishes and burial space within the city after the Fire of 1666, the special conditions of burial choice and location created by the network of parish churchyards began to change. The main part of this paper focuses on the practices and decisions about burial made up to around 1700, since this was clearly a crucial period within which enduring traditions were established, but will then return to the question of new factors and conditions influencing 18th-century burial practices.

Among the burial places belonging to a parish there was a hierarchy of desirability, created partly by distance but also by antiquity of use. All churches seem to have allowed burial within their walls (even where the church stood on vaults or cellars occupied by others), and the prices charged for different locations indicate that burial in the church was more desirable than burial in its churchyard; burial in a cloister or porch came between the two. Within the church, the chancel and chapels were normally the most highly favoured and priced; the nave, and then the aisles and less prominent parts of the church, came next. Where a parish had more than one churchyard, the older, which was usually also the nearer, was seen as the preferable location for burial; the prejudice against new grounds could be so strong that parishes had to try various ways of encouraging burial there (Harding 1989, 117–18). However, few urban churches had burial space all round them, so there is little evidence for a prejudice against north churchyards, attested elsewhere by the burial of children and suicides in such locations (MacDonald & Murphy 1990, 48–9).

St Paul's churchyard (which in fact lay to the north of the cathedral) remained the burial place of first resort for a number of parishes, and long traditions of use and association kept it in favour for others. But after the opening of the New Churchyard the Dean and Chapter attempted to restrict the burial of ordinary persons there, preferring (if they could) to keep the space for 'persons of worship and honour'. Burial in the New Churchyard in London was free, according to the original benefaction; this may in time have reduced the perceived status of burial there. It was also much used for burial in plague epidemics, and this, together with the social and environmental decline of the inner ring of suburbs may also have affected its desirability (Harding 1989, 118–19).

Centrality and marginality in early modern London

One theme of this paper is that social status and place of burial were intimately linked in the early modern city, and especially that metaphorical, social, marginality was expressed in the physical marginalization of the corpse. Given the places available for burial in early modern London, and the evidence for a hierarchy of desirability, how and by whom were they used in practice? How were the values of centrality and marginality articulated? Who belonged to which category?

Society does not have a single centre, and in the early modern city there were overlapping circles of belonging, to the household, to the family circle, the local community both small and large, and the moral community. Similarly, status is not a hierarchy determined by a single value; many factors contribute to it, including age, gender, public service, and long association, as well as wealth and rank. With so many burial locations, there was a range of responses to pressure. Within the parishes, some had more space and some very little, and there may have been different local traditions: a variety of practices can be observed. What matters is not so much the absolute numbers buried in one place or another, but the relative treatment of different categories of person within each burial community, so that general principles underlying local discriminatory practice can be perceived.

A considerable quantity of documentation survives for early modern London, including statements of policy or prescription about burial, but investigation of practice is dependent on zealous record-keeping. Parish clerks were obliged to register burials, but only a minority (possibly an officious minority) bothered to record further details such as the status, occupation, or parentage of the deceased and his or her place of burial, all of which is essential to this discussion.

Much of the writing so far on this topic has focused on the attitudes and choices of the autonomous individual, faced with his own death, which certainly contribute to our understanding of common attitudes towards death and the body, and help to establish for us the norms of contemporary behaviour. The desire that the physical integrity of the corpse be respected, and that it be interred in hallowed ground, in association with the bodies of deceased members of the family or community, and that it remain undisturbed, were assumed by contemporaries to be pretty well universally shared. This paper, however, necessarily considers the burial of individuals with little autonomy, objects rather than subjects in the discourse of death. Children, servants, the poor, criminals, and those defined as heretics usually had only limited control over their own bodies in life, and even less over what happened to them after death. Obviously, this was influenced by the norms for autonomous individuals, and it was those same individuals who as willmakers articulated their own desires, who as heads of households, churchwardens, vestrymen, and leaders of local society, had the power to determine the style and location of burial of most of the rest of society. But in making these decisions on behalf of others, these men were influenced not only by their sense of what was generally desired, but by their view of what was appropriate for individual cases.

Parishioners and strangers

The most obvious distinction, in the case of burial in the parish, is that between those who were parishioners and those who were not. Burial rights are fundamental to the idea of the parish: a parish priest has the right to bury his parishioners (and to receive their fees and offerings therefore); parishioners have the right to be buried in their parish by their priest. In the early modern period, by which time it was customary for fees to be paid to parish officials (churchwarden, clerk, and sexton) as well as to the priest, parish communities had begun to claim that even if members were buried somewhere else they still owed fees to the parish they belonged to, in lieu, as it were, of the parish's right to bury them.

In consequence, all parishes made a distinction between those who had parochial rights and those who did not; most commonly, this was to charge double the normal fee for burial. London had many temporary residents who lodged in inns and private houses, but whose means and status were equal to the leaders of the community. Although such persons were not entitled to burial in the parish, they could secure it on payment of the appropriate double duties (which might well be less than the cost of transport home). Similarly, Londoners who wished to be buried in a parish in which they were not resident, perhaps to be with family or friends, could do so, paying a fee in lieu of burial to the parish they died in and double duties to the parish of burial. Just as the presence of numerous transients, lodgers, and non-householders in the city was tending to undermine the traditional idea of the parish as a community of co-residents with mutual bonds and common obligations, so the ready acceptance of strangers for burial on payment of a fee in some sense undermined the idea of the parish as a burial community; burial location was no longer primarily an entitlement, a privilege earned by membership (see Harding 1989). Only in a few cases do we find parishes unwilling to accept the bodies of strangers at all. When the London parish of St Leonard Foster Lane obtained a new churchyard in 1579, they decided to limit burial there to parishioners; this must have meant that burials from outside would not be accepted, and possibly also that lodgers and inmates in the parish would have to be buried elsewhere (GL MS 9531/13, ff 90v–91). But in general, parishes were willing to accept strangers, provided they could pay.

If strangers had limited rights, not all parishioners were equal. The traditional view certainly gave credit for age and long residence: at Holy Trinity Minories a minute recording the decision in 1602 that in future all burials should be in the New Churchyard added 'always provided and excepted, that when ancient dwellers being head of a house either man or woman shall happen to die, that then it may be lawful for him or her to be buried either in the church or churchyard of the parish' (Lambeth Palace Library, MS 3390, f 101v). This was a parish that saw a huge rise in population in this period, with many incomers and probably a large 'floating' population. The distinction of 'ancient dwellers' made sense for them, as it might not have done in a parish with a more stable, and perhaps more affluent, population. At St Bride's, Fleet Street, another suburban parish, but one with a significant population of substantial citizens, gentry, and even nobility, burial places were priced on a sliding scale partly determined by public service: those who had served the office of churchwarden paid less for burial in the chancel and the body of the church than those who had not, and churchyard burial was priced inversely to contribution to the poor rate (Harding 1989, 122).

However, the main criterion for discrimination within the local community was that of wealth. This is implicit in the decision to charge different rates for different burial places, which made wealth the passport to favoured places, and ensured a certain exclusivity in death for the wealthier members of the community. Other factors also existed, as has been suggested, but wealth was increasingly taken as a proxy for all kinds of merit. Practical considerations – the length of time it took to disintegrate – made it reasonable to charge more for burial in coffins than in shrouds, but this also demonstrated that wealth could secure a better and longer defence of the integrity of the corpse.

Marginality within the household

If the archetype of the fully human social being in early modern urban society is the adult male householder, politically and economically enfranchised, and head of a family, were other members of his household regarded as more marginal, treated differently when it came to burial?

Gender, of itself, made no difference, despite the lesser social and political status which women were normally accorded, even though men and women sat separately in church and had opposite places in the funeral procession. The choice of burial 'near the pew where I used to sit', made by both men and women (eg GL MS 9171/15, f 237; PRO, PROB 11/62, f 364v), would have had some small effect of segregating their bodies, but the records of actual burials indicate that men were buried near the women's pews and vice versa, and that men and women were buried in the same graves. There is no suggestion that wives were treated differently from their husbands, and indeed those who could choose often asked to be buried together, though the serial monogamy common in London must sometimes have given the final survivor a difficult choice between deceased spouses. Only where gender is implicit in a particular status, as with widows (see below), is it closely linked with burial treatment.

Some studies of early modern societies have suggested that children, and perhaps especially infants, were not perceived as fully individual; with high child mortality (certainly borne out from burial records), adults simply could not afford to invest small children with individuality, and lavish on them the personal affection and interest that we do now (Stone 1979, 82–3). If this were really so (and considerable doubt has already been expressed about the thesis), we might expect to find it reflected in burial practices for children: modest ceremony, little commemoration, less attention to the niceties. However, the evidence tends to suggest otherwise. It is certainly true that children did not merit the most impressive treatment: St Bride's, again, said that its great bell was not to be pealed for children. Some parishes had special palls for children, but though they may have been cheaper to hire than palls for adults there is no suggestion that they were not of good quality. All parishes in fact charged less for child burial, primarily because of the smaller demand on space, but no parish excluded them from any part of the church. The key factor was the quality of the family from which the child came: children were buried in a manner appropriate to their family's status, and many wealthy householders could and did have their children buried together with adult members of the family (Walters 1939, 50, 291; Harding 1989, 121–3). Poorer families, including those dependent on parish charity, may not have been able to choose the burial place of their children, just as they could not for themselves. In these cases there may have been some further discrimination, that is poor children may have been even less favourably treated than their parents. At St Peter Cornhill in London there are one or two references to an 'infants' pit' in the east churchyard, and certainly a large number of children were buried in the east yard (Leveson Gower 1877, 145). Archaeological and historical evidence from Christ Church, Spitalfields exemplifies the continuing complexity of this issue in the 18th and 19th centuries. It seems that where a family vault had been purchased, infants and children were usually buried with their larger families (eg the Mesman vault), while if an individual or a couple were buried in a parochial vault, their deceased children could be buried elsewhere, as the Courtauld infants were (Molleson & Cox 1993, 209–10).

The observance of proper burial standards applied equally to abortives, stillborns, and chrisoms, children dying within a month or so of birth, some of whom might understandably have been regarded as not quite human, let alone not fully individual. Although there may be variations in the faithfulness with which they are recorded in burial registers from one parish to another, where they do appear they do not seem to have been subject to special discrimination. One child 'not baptissed at all' (sic), another 'not baptized but nammed Isacke' (sic), and a third born six weeks prematurely were all buried in the church of St Nicholas Acon in the 1650s and 1660s (Brigg 1890, 113, 117–18). In the parish of St Margaret Moses, the burials of 66 chrisoms and stillborn children were recorded between 1605 and 1666, a figure appropriate to the likely occurrence. The burial place of 18 is not given. Of the remainder, 29 were buried in the church, eight in St Paul's Churchyard, and eleven in the New Churchyard, that is, in similar proportions to the generality of burials. In several cases, where more detail is given, we can see that chrisoms and older children from the same family were buried close to one another (Bannerman 1912, 74–94). This subject is discussed further by Cox (this volume).

Another large group in early modern urban society was that of servants and apprentices. Sometimes in London the words are used interchangeably, and in both cases we are talking about young persons living in the household, under the authority of the household head, but apprentices were bound for a long term of years and came from families of similar or even higher status to the master's, while domestic servants, though they too might be indentured for a period, were of lower status and had lower expectations. Apprentices too were predominantly male, while domestic servants were mostly female. The proportion of domestic servants to apprentices in the population grew considerably over the 17th century. In both cases, however, they were concentrated in the wealthier areas of the city, where households were larger (Finlay 1981, 66–7; Earle 1994, 61, 124–5).

Although servants and apprentices were household members and shared the family's living quarters, they did not often share their burial accommodation. Heads of households paid burial fees and funeral charges for them, as for other dependants, and could therefore decide where they would be buried and with what degree of ceremony, and it seems that, in general, they saw them as different from the rest of the family, and not meriting equal treatment. Sometimes the choice was very obvious: in St Pancras parish in 1628, John Parker, merchant, buried his daughter Mary in the church, where two other of his children were already buried; his servant, also Mary, who died twelve days later, was buried in the churchyard (Bannerman 1914, 298). Colonel James Drax buried his son in a vault in the chancel of St John Zachary in 1654 and his maidservant in the farther churchyard two years later (McMurray 1925, 333). Analysis of the printed city parish registers for the 16th and 17th centuries indicates that somewhere between 70 and 85 per cent of servants (whose burial places are known) were buried somewhere other than in the parish church. This is a much higher proportion than the overall average in these parishes. In most of these cases servants were buried in the parish churchyard, but those parishes that, for reasons of space, had to bury some people outside the parish, buried a number of servants either at St Paul's (before around 1580) or in the New Churchyard. Twenty-two of the 38 servants dying in the parish of St Margaret Moses between 1636 and 1666 were buried in the New Churchyard (Bannerman 1912, 83–93). In the excavation of part of the New Churchyard in the late 1980s, the best preserved layers were the latest, dating from the mid 18th century, and included large numbers of young women, from whom the servant class was certainly drawn by that date, suggesting that it continued to be used for such persons.

Marginality within the local community

If servants were somewhat marginal members of the household, and were discriminated against when it came to burial, the same was true of marginal members of the local community: poor families and dependent individuals. These had a claim on the burial resources of the parish (if they were parishioners and not lodgers or vagrants) but with little money and influence they had to be content with what the authorities were prepared to allow them.

Widows may perhaps be located midway between 'marginal to the household' and 'marginal to the community'. The category 'widow' was often a status definition as well as one of gender; not all widows were poor, of course, but the poor widow was a prevalent stereotype. In the 16th and 17th centuries it became increasingly rare for the widows of poor men to remarry, and their economic position was likely to decline the longer they lived (Todd 1985), so that in early modern cities it can almost be taken for granted that a cluster of widows represents a concentration of poor households, and that a parish with a larger than average percentage of widows is a poor one. A distinction between widows by status is noticeable in the printed parish registers sampled: the widows referred to as Mistress or Dame, or as 'widow of' (and especially of a citizen or professional), were usually buried in different places from the women named as 'widow Brown' etc. In several parishes about half the widows were buried in the church, and about half elsewhere; the 'widow Browns', and widows described as pensioners of the parish, were in the latter group. In general, the larger the number of widows in a parish, the higher the proportion buried in the churchyard or out of the parish.

It is not easy to document the impact of moderate household poverty on burial location, though the prescriptions and prices certainly imply that those who paid for their own burial, but had little cash, were meant to choose less favoured locations. Few parishes, however, went as far as St Bride's, which set prohibitively high prices for favoured burial locations for those who had made little or no contribution to the poor rate, effectively confining such people to the more distant 'lower' churchyard (Harding 1989, 122). An attempt to correlate wealth, as measured by rental value of property in the tithe survey of 1638 (Dale 1938; see Jones 1980; Finlay 1981, 70–82), with the burial place of members of those households was only moderately successful: there are not really enough vital events within a short time to draw any clear conclusions, even in the parishes that have all the relevant information. In any case, it could be argued that any householder liable for tithe was modestly well off; it was those who lodged in rooms and shed dwellings whom we should be looking for. In one or two cases, pockets of poverty within parishes can be observed: in St Margaret Moses, for example, the former Castle Inn had been divided into tenements, known as Castle Yard, occupied by a number of unnamed lodgers and undertenants in 1638. Twenty-one of the 35 people who were buried from Castle Yard in the 17th century were buried in the New Churchyard (Dale 1938, 99; Bannerman 1912, 74–93).

In 17th century London parishes were both burial communities and also, as a result of the Elizabethan Poor Laws, major providers of relief and support for the poor. Poor rates brought in an annual sum, sometimes increased by rates-in-aid transferred from richer parishes, and by benefactions, which the elected overseers of the poor could use to provide various kinds of relief. Foundlings and pensioners on weekly doles were the most dependent, but many other families required assistance at some time; a large proportion of London's population lived at or below the poverty line (Archer 1991, 152–4). There must have been many for whom the cost of burial was beyond their means, and who therefore were dependent on the parish's goodwill and charity.

Several parishes were prepared to waive their burial fees for poor individuals, though they often used this concession to direct burials to less-favoured locations. In a number of them, the phrases 'no duties' or 'duties remitted' seem to occur mostly in relation to New Churchyard burials; that is, the normal duties payable to the churchwardens were remitted, but the individual obtained only a marginal location for burial (Bannerman 1913, 192; GL MS 4438, not foliated: entries for 2 & 9 September 1625, 7 November 1625). The parish of St Mary Colechurch waived the usual fee of 6s 8d charged to a sojourner (a temporary resident) who was buried outside the parish if he was poor, a significant encouragement to take that option (GL MS 66, f 13v).

Others were unable to afford even the payment to the gravedigger and the minister's fee for the burial service, which the parish therefore paid out on their behalf. The churchwardens of All Hallows the Great paid 3s 10d for the burial of widow Clarke 'that died poor' in 1622, a sum made up of the minister's fee of 1s 6d, the clerk's fee of 1s, 1s for a knell, and 4d for a grave in the churchyard; they waived the duty they themselves would normally have taken (GL MS 818/1, f 27v; GL MS 9531/13, pt 2, f. 378). In 1638–9 the parish of St Anne Aldersgate paid the parson's burial fees for 'old Smyth lying bedridd'/ (sic), and also bought him a winding-sheet for 2s

(McMurray 1925, 337, 348). Those who were buried at the parish's expense probably included all those who were dependent on parish pensions, and certainly all the foundlings taken into the parish's care. Like widow Clarke, they obtained only marginal locations by the standard of the parish concerned. At St Michael Cornhill, all six persons described as pensioners were buried in the churchyard, as were the five parish children (Chester 1878, 246–53). At St Margaret Moses, no pensioner was recorded as being buried in the church: all whose burial place is known were buried at St Paul's or the New Churchyard (Bannerman 1912, 74–84).

Plague was obviously a major cause of death in the early modern city, and an event that disrupted the normal workings of society and, it might be thought, normal burial practice. In fact, though mortality during the plague epidemics certainly placed severe pressure on the parishes, burial in plague years was for the most part fairly orderly, and followed traditional practice for as long as possible (Harding 1993). Nevertheless, it is clear that many parishes which did not normally bury there turned to the New Churchyard in epidemic years (Littledale 1912, 54–61; Bannerman 1916, 200–3; Hughes Clarke 1938, 104–5, McMurray 1925, 381–2; Brigg 1890, 119). In addition, several parishes used it for the occasional attributed plague deaths that cropped up throughout the century outside the main epidemics (Leveson Gower 1877, 166; Hughes Clarke 1943, 104). The pressure and panic of plague epidemics may well have sharpened the sense of who had local burial entitlement and who had not. In the plague of 1563, 24 people died in the parish of All Hallows Honey Lane. Twelve were the sons, daughters, and kin of householders, and all of these were buried in the parish; eleven were servants, and all were buried out of the parish, in St Paul's churchyard (Bannerman 1914, 259–60).

Outside the local community

Plague multiplied the number of deaths in the community, but it also increased the numbers of those whom the parish had to deal with, whether they had burial rights or not, because they happened to die in the street. Burial was one of the seven works of corporal mercy enjoined by the Catholic Church (Thomson 1993, 335), and long after the Reformation this charitable aspect seems to have tempered the harshness with which we might expect the bodies of such people to have been treated. We know that parishes tried to prevent pauper women from giving birth within their territorial bounds, so that they themselves would not be charged with the upkeep of the mother and child (eg McMurray 1925, 341–2, 346, 348), but they seem to have accepted the task of burying dead strangers less grudgingly.

Some of these were perfectly respectable but simply not parishioners, as 'Roger Powell, a journeyman-clothworker who fell down dead in our parish and was buried in new church yard' (Bannerman 1912, 84). Others, however, were vagrants and paupers. Early modern Londoners believed there was a severe vagrancy problem (Beier 1990, 122–7), and to some extent this is borne out by the references in burial registers to nameless persons who died in the street. They seem to have been buried cheaply, but not invariably in marginal locations. The register of All Hallows Bread Street records the burials at St Paul's and the New Churchyard of poor men and women who died in the street, but also the burial in the church of the twin children of 'a poor woman of Kent that fell in travell going through Watling Street' (Bannerman 1913, 167, 169, 171). Several other parishes also gave at least parochial churchyard burial to some poor strangers and foundlings, rather than automatically exiling them to the New Churchyard (Leveson Gower 1877, 190–1, 193, 197; Chester 1878, 250). We cannot tell what influenced such decisions – pity on the part of the parish officials, a contribution to the cost from some charitable parishioner, possibly just that these parishes found themselves less pressed for space at that moment.

Outside the moral community

The burial of poor strangers was a Christian duty, and whatever their personal circumstances they belonged to the moral community. Others, however, by their actions, separated themselves from that community, and could reasonably expect to be treated accordingly when it came to their burial. Suicides, traitors, and those deemed heretics were all penalised in some way for their transgression of the community's standards.

The exemplary vengeance wrought on the bodies of some suicides has often been commented on, and can be documented from a variety of sources. Bodies were physically abused, and in some cases explicitly condemned to be buried in the street or at a crossroads, with a stake through the heart (MacDonald & Murphy 1990, 18–20, 144–50). However, the full implementation of such sanctions was probably the exception rather than the general rule: London's parish registers suggest a varied response, perhaps according to circumstance. Of thirteen suicides noted from the burial registers and other sources examined for this study (up to c 1670), five were completely excluded from consecrated ground, three being buried in the street or highway, one 'in the field', and one at Mile End. Another five were buried in the New Churchyard, and one was buried in her parish churchyard without any service. The burial location of one is not given; the only one who apparently had a 'proper' burial in the normal place was a woman who stabbed herself but afterwards lived long enough to repent and receive the sacrament. Bishop's licences for Christian burial were obtained for several of these burials (Harding 1989,

120). The Bills of Mortality suggest that there were between ten and twenty suicides every year in later 17th century London, but the place or parish of burial cannot be traced from that source (Millar 1759). This issue is discussed by both Cox and Scheuer elsewhere in this volume.

Vengeance on the body was also part of the treatment of traitors, who were beheaded or hanged, dismembered, and their body parts, especially their heads, displayed in a public place – often, in London, on the bridge. The mid-16th century chronicler of London funerals, Henry Machyn, observed the vivid contrast between the funerals, on consecutive days, of a deceased Alderman and former mayor, and of a traitor. Sir Richard Dobbes's corpse was attended to the church by heralds, city officers, Aldermen, 60 mourners, and 30 poor men in russet gowns, and there honourably interred, while Captain William Stathum, condemned for treason, was drawn from the Tower to Tyburn before being hanged, quartered, and decapitated, his head being set on London Bridge the next day (Nichols 1848, 156). The bodies of lesser felons could however be recovered for decent burial, though unfortunately the parishes surveyed here have little data on this.

The corpse could also be the focus of confessional conflict: heresy and religious nonconformity could provoke extremes of hostility towards the body, of which the burning of heretics is the most obvious expression. In London, the period of severe persecution on explicitly religious grounds had ended by 1560, but in Paris the treatment of the dead remained a contentious issue throughout the early modern period. In isolated incidents in France in the 1560s, some bodies that had been buried according to reformed rites in Catholic churchyards were dug up and cast out; the bodies of victims of the massacre of St Bartholomew's Eve were thrown into the river. Even after official toleration they suffered all kinds of humiliations and penalties, and were largely confined to extramural burial gounds used also for the city's plague and pauper dead (Thibaut-Payen 1977, 157–85). Even before the revocation of the Edict of Nantes, the masters of Hôtel Dieu had stated as a principle that they only gave the bodies of heretics (Protestants) for anatomizing, though they did say that the flesh and bones must be returned for burial according to their religion (Brièle 1881, 218).

In London, the effective elimination of Catholicism at least reduced this area of conflict, and attention shifted to nonconformist and radical Protestants. The focus was different too. Whereas in Paris Huguenots had claimed burial rights along with Catholics in long-established sites in the city centre, in London Puritans and nonconformists voluntarily distanced themselves from traditional practices. There were two aspects to this: a generalized dislike of rituals and ceremonies, and the traditions that attributed significance to the place of burial; and a more radical challenge to the idea of the geographical parish as the basis for religious

congregation (see Stock, this volume). The first sentiment could be expressed by ministers as well as laypeople, and there are probably as many cases of congregations complaining that their ministers neglected the prayerbook services and rituals of burial as there are of laypeople resisting the performance of such ceremonies (Collinson 1967, 370–1; Maltby 1993, 265–7). The second view rejected compromise with the existing church and advocated the formation of separated or gathered church congregations, which explicitly distanced themselves from the inclusive parochial community (Tolmie 1977, 91). In both cases, however, attachment to the parish church was undermined, and geographically marginal location became a matter either of indifference or of positive choice.

Although, as has been shown above, the New Churchyard was often used for the burial of servants, strangers, and individuals of marginal status, it was also the place of choice for a few. It was consecrated, but was not owned by the established church, nor attached to any parish. From an early date, therefore, it was favoured by religious separatists. The Scottish minister James Lawson was buried there in 1584, and in 1590 the court of High Commission acted to curb its use by irregular or Dissenting congregations from across the city (Collinson 1967, 371). In the 17th century it appears to have been chosen by a small number of citizens of at least moderate standing, though their motives are not known (eg GL MS 9051/8, f 339; MS 9171/31, f 28). A few Dutch and Irish were buried there, perhaps for religious reasons, though others from the same parishes received local burial; so too were some Quakers (Bannerman 1912, 85; Littledale 1903, 141–2; McMurray 1925, 326; Hughes Clarke 1943, 115). A complex of religion, politics, and morality must have determined the burial in the New Churchyard of the executed Leveller Robert Lockyer, after an impressively well-attended funeral procession in 1649 (Gentles 1996, 219–20).

The nonconformist associations of the New Churchyard mitigated but did not entirely remove its identification as a burial place for the socially marginal. Perhaps more surprising was the rapid conversion, in practice, of the new plague ground of Bunhill Fields to a burial ground for Dissenters. There has been some debate over whether it was used for plague burial in 1665, but it was probably opened for use by October of that year at the latest, in the last months of the epidemic, when mortality in London was still running at 4,000 deaths a week (Harding 1993, 61). In the early 18th century John Strype noted that since the plague it had been 'chosen by dissenters from the Church of England, for interring their friends and relations, without having the office of burial applied by the book of Common Prayer said at their graves' (Strype 1720, book iv, 54). He lists a large number of tombs and monuments, the earliest dating from 1667, though there is nothing to say how many of these were

Dissenters. It is notable, however, that several ministers were buried there, and at least one inscription (from 1672) refers to prisoners and oppressors (op cit 55–9). Maitland (1756, 775) refers to 'one Tindal' taking a lease of the plague burial ground and converting it to a burial ground for the use of Dissenters, and there are references to it as 'Tindal's ground' before the end of the 17th century (eg Chester 1878, 259–60). It may be that in the 18th century the success of Bunhill Fields as a respectable place for Dissenters' burial saved it from being deemed a marginal and hence generally unattractive burial site, though it was actually more distant from the city centre than the New Churchyard.

Burial from the later 17th century

With the growth of a positive choice for the New Churchyard and other non-parochial locations in the 17th century we can see traditional criteria of desirability weakening. Several other factors contributed to this. The tendency to commodify burial has already been cited; the rise of the professional undertaker, to some extent replacing the role of neighbours and friends in organising the funeral, also dates from the later 17th century (Litten 1991, 17–19; Gittings 1984, 95). The growth of London helped to dissolve the parish community, as did the changes to the ecclesiastical map of the city after the Fire of 1666.

Between 1550 and 1700, the population of the metropolis grew from 60–75,000 to over half a million. The number of parishes increased, but in no way matched this demographic explosion. Only seven new parishes were created between 1550 and 1700, mostly by subdivision; sixteen 'outparishes', formerly almost wholly rural in character, were incorporated into contemporary representations of the metropolis by 1700. Whereas in 1500 more than half of the metropolitan population lived within the city walls, in parishes of less than 10 acres (4 ha), by 1700 less than a fifth did so (Harding 1990). Several of London's suburban parishes were each as large and populous as a significant provincial town. The ring of parishes around the city walls contained populations of 2,500 to well over 10,000; parishes such as St Martin in the Fields had populations in the tens of thousands; the huge parish of Stepney, which comprised most of east London, had had one smaller parish carved out of it before 1700 but still had over 40,000 inhabitants (based on extrapolation from annual burial totals in Millar 1759).

In these circumstances, the idea of an inclusive and comprehensive 'parish community' could hardly survive. In an earlier paper (Harding 1989, 113–15) the decline of explicit instructions about the place of burial in early to mid 17th century London wills was tentatively attributed to a change in will formulae, rather than a loss of interest in burial location. This argument remains valid, but the decline may also have been influenced by a weakening of attachment to the parish church and community for the reasons given above. It also appears that by the late 17th century more people were making wills prudentially, rather than close to the point of death, which could mean that burial was less of a concern at the moment the will was made. The decline in specific provision certainly continued to the end of the 17th century and beyond, though the great majority still made some reference to 'decent' or 'Christian' burial, at the discretion of their executors (see Table 5.1).

In the Great Fire of 1666, 86 parish churches in the city and western suburb were burnt. For up to ten years the populations of these parishes were temporarily dispersed; most parish registers record few if any burials between the summer of 1666 and the reopening of their church, and there was obviously a significant interruption to patterns of burial. A few burials in the ruined churches are recorded in the later 1660s and early 1670s, but most must have taken place in the extraparochial burial grounds. Thirty-five of the burnt churches were not rebuilt, and their parishes (often, but not always, among the smallest in area and population) were united with neighbouring parishes, and thereafter shared clergy, sacraments and services, and obligations. In some cases the sites of former churches and churchyards were built over, in others they became a burial ground for the united parish, but for all there was some break in the patterns of

Table 5.1: Burial choice in London, 1560–1700

	1560	1580	1600	1618	1640	1660	1680	1700
No reference to burial	2	3	3	3	3	5	11	3
Standard formula (no location)	19	16	29	32	31	34	32	42
Burial location specified	29	31	18	15	16	11	7	5
(with exact place)	(4)	(5)	(3)	(5)	(1)	(2)	(4)	(3)
Total	50	50	50	50	50	50	50	50

Source: 50 wills for each year, starting with the first registered that year, from the Archdeaconry and Commissary Courts of London: GL, MS 9051/2, f 282v ; MS 9050/4, f 185v; 9050/5, f 149; 9050/6, f 1; 9050/8 f 31; MS 9171/31, f 1; 9171/37, f 28v; 9171, f 1. For a fuller breakdown of the wills to 1660, see Harding 1989, 114.

use and association. By the end of the century the populations of the city's ecclesiastical parishes averaged over 1000, and were clearly getting too large for intimacy and the human scale.

The weakening of the parish's identity in the later 17th century was paralleled by an increasing diversity in the population of London and the religions they practised. It is clear that the nonconformist congregations of the Civil War and Commonwealth period were submerged, but not suppressed, by the Restoration. After 1689 they were free to establish churches openly, and by 1700 London supported a proliferation of independent churches. Tory anxiety about the strength of nonconformity in London estimated the number of Dissenters at 100,000 in the early 18th century; though this is clearly an exaggeration, the true number may have been over 40,000, with 74 Dissenting congregations noted in the capital (Port 1986, ix), though not all of these had individual burial grounds or rights. Of the early nonconformists, the Quakers were the most distinctive in their practices of worship and burial; the latter is discussed elsewhere in this volume (see Stock; Bashford & Pollard; Start & Kirk).

There had long been a significant alien community (mostly French- and Dutch-speaking Protestants) in London. They had had their own churches, but many worshipped in Anglican parishes and were buried there (eg Christ Church, Spitalfields), though a few chose, or were perhaps obliged, to accept burial in the New Churchyard (see above; Pettegree 1986). Immigration from France increased in the 1670s and 1680s, especially after the revocation of the Edict of Nantes in 1685. It is estimated that 40–50,000 French Huguenots came to Britain, and the majority of them settled in London, establishing churches and congregations in the northern and western suburbs, with a variety of confessions (Gwynn 1985, 35–8, 91– 109), though they could also assimilate with the Anglican community, as the case of Christ Church, Spitalfields indicates (Molleson & Cox 1993, 3–7). Another distinctive group were the Jews, who returned to England from the later 1650s, and who had established a sizeable community in the northwest of the city by 1695 (Diamond 1962, 71–3; Arnold 1962).

Together with the toleration of English Protestant dissent, these developments greatly increased the number of burial sites in London. By the 1680s and 1690s the city parish of St Dionis Backchurch was recording burials in its own church and yard and also at Bethlem (the New Churchyard), 'the Quakers' ground', 'the Swedes church', 'the Jewes burial place', and 'Tindells ground by Bunhill fields' (Chester 1878, 252–60). Maitland noted the inadequacy of the Bills of Mortality, based on the Anglican parishes, to capture the full number of annual burials in 18th-century London (Maitland 1756, 740; see George 1965, 35 and n 1). In the early 18th century, the Church of England made an effort to recover its control of Londoners' religious life with the Fifty New Churches Act, creating new parishes in the spreading suburbs of the metropolis. It was suggested that the number of annual burials should be a rough indicator of the need for subdivision and a new parish. Where the existing parish buried 350 or 400 a year, a new church was clearly needed; the largest parishes after the reorganization should only be burying 250 to 300 a year. All the new churches were to have churchyards, but intramural burial was not to be allowed (though this was changed as at Christ Church, Spitalfields; Cox 1996a). However, even the new grounds had a hierarchy of desirable locations, expressed in price, and the usual double charges for strangers (Port 1986, ix–x, xviii, nos 114, 415).

Conclusion

Social status and the location of burial were clearly intimately linked in early modern London: the grounds for discrimination might be complex, and varying local circumstances affected actual practices, but overall it is easy to see how perceptions of status helped to determine the place, as well as the style, of an individual's burial. Centrality was desirable, but access to it was limited; marginality was the fate of many. What is argued in addition, however, is that in determining status, monetary considerations were increasingly important; high mortality rates and frequent epidemics kept up pressure on burial accommodation, and ultimately, complex criteria based on traditional ideas of community membership and entitlement began to give way to pragmatic distinction by price. Although some important non-monetary distinctions remained, especially in regard to those outside the moral community, burial space, like so many other features of the early modern city, had in effect become a commodity that could be bought and sold. At the same time, ideas of community were themselves changing, and it appears that, for a range of practical and ideological reasons, Londoners no longer attached as much importance to place and parish that they had once done.

There are no absolutes in cultural practice, however, only shifts within a range of variation. The argument that burial practices were changing, and the monetary aspect was becoming more important, does not mean that by 1700 or even 1800 the site of burial or the treatment of the dead body had become matters of indifference. The popularity of family vaults, the increasing use of lead coffins, the prominent funerary sculpture of the 18th century, all indicate otherwise. The responses to the utilitarianism of the 1832 Anatomy Act and the 1852 Burial Act also show how strongly feelings could and can run on this subject (Richardson 1988). The Burial Act, closing almost all the parish vaults and churchyards in London, came about after long campaigning against 'the unwise and revolting custom of inhuming the dead in the midst of the living'

(Walker 1839, title page). Although there were said to be many who welcomed the measure (Holmes 1896, 206–25), there was also contrary feeling. Victorian Londoners could still feel the same strong attachment to places of worship and burial as their early modern predecessors, despite the decline in the residential population of the city, and the disappearance of parochial communities of the traditional kind. In 1841, when the closure of burial grounds and vaults was being discussed, an anonymous citizen of the parish of St Mary le Bow wrote to the parish clerk, thanking him for opposing the measure and appealing to those who favoured it to appreciate 'the anguish of mind of those when on a Death Bed to think that they will be prohibeted [sic] from being laid by the side of them who was there [sic] great Comfort in this life' (GL MS 7815).

Acknowledgements

This paper is based on one given at the 1995 conference on 'The social context of death, dying and disposal' at Sussex University, substantially revised for inclusion in this volume. It also includes some of my thoughts on the parish community in early modern London which I discussed in a paper at the conference of European Urban Historians in Budapest in 1996. I am grateful to Ralph Houlbrooke and Peter Jupp for comments on the original paper; to several colleagues including Penelope Corfield and Geoff Crossick for comments on the Budapest paper; to Steve Rappaport who subsequently read and commented on that paper; and to Margaret Cox for encouraging me to revise the material in this form.

Part II The archaeological contribution: case studies

i An Anglican perspective

The only major excavation of an Anglican post-medieval burial context published to date is Christ Church, Spitalfields. This site is not discussed in detail in this volume as it is adequately published elsewhere. Other sites are either presently unpublished, or have only been subject to limited archaeological examination and recording. Consequently, the interested reader has limited options when it comes to increasing their understanding of the archaeology of Anglican post-medieval funerary tradition, a situation which this volume ameliorates in a modest way.

Eric Boore introduces us to the Anglican tradition by way of his excavation of St Augustine the Less, an urban parish church in Bristol, and several family vaults from the West Country. Moving east Angela Boyle and Graham Keevill introduce us to the people buried within St Nicholas, Sevenoaks during the 18th and 19th centuries and consider the loss of information arising from a general curatorial bias towards the medieval at the expense of the post-medieval. A commonality between St Augustine and St Nicholas is that for different reasons both excavations were under-funded and full post-excavation analysis and reporting is yet to be undertaken. Continuing with scenarios that are (hopefully) unfamiliar to present-day archaeolo-

gists, the human remains recovered from beneath St Bride's, Fleet Street, London were made available by virtue of bombing during World War II. Louise Scheuer discusses the demography and cause of death of the people buried beneath St Bride's and her results reinforce many conceptual issues and methodological challenges first raised at Christ Church, Spitalfields.

Our understanding of the archaeology of post-medieval funerary tradition is biased by many factors. These include a tendency to allow the presumed doctrinal framework to shape our preconceptions of the background position, and neglect of both popular belief and practice. This issue is discussed in the final chapter in this section which also challenges archaeologists to increase their awareness of, and openness to, the wide range of contemporary funerary rites well represented in the sister literatures of history, the social sciences, ethnology, and anthropology. It suggests that the time honoured method of excavating funerary contexts and research strategies may well be inappropriate, and fail to realise the enormous potential of post-medieval funerary contexts. Awareness of advances in scientific methods, many from adjacent disciplines, such as forensic science, also have a contribution to make in this field and if we ignore them we do so to the detriment of the discipline we seek to advance.

6 Burial vaults and coffin furniture in the West Country *Eric Boore*

Be silent in that solitude,
Which is not loneliness – for then
The spirits of the dead who stood
In life before thee, are again
In death around thee – and their will
Shall overshadow thee: be still

(*Spirits of the Dead*, Edgar Allan Poe [1809–49])

Introduction

Research into life and death in post-medieval Britain has led to a greater awareness of the value and relevance of the study of burial vaults, their occupants, and associated sepulchral remains. Recent major studies have revealed the wealth of information available from a combined analysis by archaeological, anthropological, and historical approaches to the examination of funerary practice and funerary archaeology (Litten 1991; Reeve & Adams 1993; Molleson & Cox 1993). The appreciation of the importance of burial vaults, coffins and coffin furniture, and osteological analysis of human remains have confirmed the significance of post-medieval burial studies within the archaeological time-frame and banished the archaic attitude that had considered intramural vaults as 'nasty modern disturbances' (Litten 1985b, 9).

The excavation of the church of St Augustine the Less, Bristol provided the opportunity to record in detail the proliferation of intramural and extramural burial vaults and brick graves in an urban church in the post-medieval period. This phase of occupation was recorded within the context of the overall archaeological and historical development of the church and parish (Gilchrist & Morris 1996, 117). The associated coffin furniture and other sepulchral remains provided further evidence of funerary custom practiced during the late 17th to mid 19th centuries. The occurrence of vault burial has been recorded throughout the city in both churches and churchyards and reflects a level of prosperity prevalent in Bristol for the post-medieval period and the local popularity of this form of interment.

Faculty applications for internal alterations have enabled the examination and archaeological recording of larger family vaults in churches in the rural areas of south Gloucestershire and south Somerset. Extramural stone-walled graves have been recorded in a churchyard in north Somerset. The threat of redundancy, clearance of intramural vaults, and encroachments upon churchyards continue in both urban and rural areas. Further comparative work is necessary to establish local funerary customs, to provide information about the influences determining regional differences, and to preserve and protect where possible the remains of post-medieval burial vaults and their occupants.

St Augustine the Less, Bristol

In 1983 excavations on the site of the former church of St Augustine the Less, Bristol (ST 58497273) were undertaken in advance of redevelopment. The site is located in the western part of the city in the area formally known as Billeswick (Sabin 1956, XI). It was in Billeswick, to the west of the Norman walled town of Bricstow, that Robert Fitzharding, reeve, founded St Augustine's Abbey in *c* 1140 (Dickinson 1976, 122). The abbey became the Cathedral for the city in 1542. According to tradition the parish church of St Augustine the Less was founded by the abbots of St Augustine's Abbey in *c* 1240, and was required to meet the needs of the expanding local community. An increase in trade and population in Billeswick had developed around the new quays constructed along the improved waterfront to the east of the site. This occurred after the completion of a major engineering project described as the 'diversion of the river Frome' which took place between 1240–1247 (Lobel and Wilson 1975, 7). In 1480 the antiquarian William Worcestre described the church of St Augustine the Less as 'the ancient and original church of the said abbey which is now a newly-built church' (Dickinson 1976, 117). The arms of Abbot Newland (1481–1515) and Abbot Elyot (1515–26) were depicted on window glass within the church. At this time the church possessed north and south aisles and a west tower with an octagonal stair turret on its north-east corner. The main porch stood on the north side with a second doorway and rood stair on the south. The burial ground surrounded the church (Winstone 1962, 75).

In 1708 the chancel and aisles were extended and in the 19th century extensive internal alterations were undertaken. They included the introduction of underfloor heating in the chancel area and the building of a new vestry. To the west of the site the Royal Hotel partly replaced a Georgian terrace in 1868. In 1938 the parish of St Augustine the Less was united with St George on Brandon Hill. The building was damaged by fire during the air raids of 1940, which led to its closure in 1956 and demolition in 1962 without any record of the event. This may have been, in part, due to its alleged later rebuilding and prosaic comments by contemporary sources (Pevsner 1958, 388). However more recent commentators were more perceptive in regard to the potential of the site (Dickinson 1976, 126; Dawson 1981, 22). In 1971 the external churchyard was cleared commercially with some retrieval of coffin furniture. The churchyard had been considerably reduced at this time by various road encroachments.

The results of the archaeological survey and excavations carried out between June 1983 and July 1984 uncovered a complex archaeological sequence dating back to the Saxo-Norman period. The earliest occupation may be associated with the original foundation site of St Augustine's Abbey, if not within the area of a chapel dedicated to St Jordan, a contemporary of St Augustine (Bettey 1996, 2). The post-medieval period perhaps represents the church in its apotheosis with considerable redevelopment of the parish during the 18th century (Lobel & Wilson 1975, 23) and a proliferation of intramural burial vaults and brick graves (Fig 6.1). A list of parishioners described in the elections of 1714–15 suggests a prosperous parish including a shipwright, mariner, hooper, 'tyler', baker, pipemaker, merchants, and a surgeon (Sabin 1956, 256).

In the 19th century church Faculty petitions are mentioned in 1842, 1849, and 1876. They refer to such items as removal of monuments, rearranging of pews, and moving the organ and font. In 1849 the Faculty includes the concreting over of the aisle floors, rebuilding of the vestry, and removal of the north and south galleries. The insertion of a boiler-house below the south aisle of the chancel revealed the remains of the earlier 17th century vestry rooms. A schedule of memorials, wall tablets, and inscribed floor-slabs lists a total of 70 vaults with 126 names which include many family groups. The memorials range in date from the late 17th century to the early 19th century. Early ledger stones situated in the chancel floor are dedicated to Sarah Tie who died in 1689 and Sir Hugh Owen of Orielton, Pembroke, South Wales who died in 1698. The broken remains of his black marble ledger bearing his coat of arms were removed from the chancel area during the archaeological excavation. Other wall tablets of the 17th century were recorded in the south aisle (Boore 1985, 22).

The practice of vault burial was discontinued in part through considerations of health and hygiene. Many people in this period were victims of cholera and smallpox and earlier in the 17th century there had been 'the begininge of the pestilent plague in the parish of Little Sainte Augustine in bristoll' (Sabin 1956, 22). This may refer to an outbreak of bubonic plague. A reference to burial inside the church in 1881 states, 'In vaults beneath the floor of the church are about 800 leaden coffins, enclosing the remains of as many parishioners' (Nicholls & Taylor 1881, 238). This figure is not an unrealistic number and may even be an underestimation. However such a volume of interments inside the church would, with the passage of time, create particularly unpleasant conditions (Rodwell 1989, 160). The affluvia from coffin decay would have been intensified by the installation of under-floor heating systems in the 19th century (Mytum 1989, 288). These effects may have contributed to the need to concrete the aisle floors in 1849. Intramural burial declined in London after legislation was passed in the Metropolitan Interments Act of 1850, which was extended throughout England and Wales in 1853 which the creation of public cemeteries. However intramural burial could continue in burial vaults pre-dating the passing of these measures (Litten 1985b, 10). At this time there was virtually no available space left within the church of St Augustine the Less and the intensity of earlier vault construction may have not only undermined the aisle floors, but also necessitated remedial work on the main wall foundations and aisle pier bases (Boore 1985, 29).

Figure 6.1 Aerial view of St Augustine the Less, Bristol looking east showing the main church walls, intramural burial vaults, and brick grave burials c 17th–19th centuries (photo: Bournemouth University)

The problems of overcrowding were not confined to the interior of the church. The incumbent in 1819, Dr Luke Heslop, described the churchyard as being overcrowded which contributed to the founding on Brandon Hill of St George (ST 58137297) as a chapel of ease to St Augustine the Less. St George was consecrated in 1823. The high density of churchyard burial, particularly in the towns and cities, literally transformed the churchyard environment (Litten 1985b, 10 and Mytum 1989, 286). There was also a fear of graverobbers or Resurrectionists who sought specimens for the anatomical medical schools (Richardson 1988, 52). An incident of body-snatching was recorded in 1819 from the churchyard of St Augustine the Less. Fortunately the body was subsequently recovered though no arrests were ever recorded (Bailey 1991, 76). Intramural burial was also sought by the increasing professional, military, and mercantile classes of the 18th and 19th centuries (Rodwell 1989, 157 and Litten 1991, 221). The nearer the altar the greater the spiritual benefit and an increasing source of income for the incumbent and the parish (Litten 1991, 218 & 224). This is well illustrated by an epitaph at Kingsbridge, Devon from 1795:

Here lie I by the chancel door,
Here lie I because I'm poor.
The further in, the more you'll pay
Here lie I, as warm as they.
(Johnson 1984, 54).

Both vaults and brick graves also occurred in the churchyard, though whether this was dictated by financial considerations or lack of available space inside the church is open to question. Overcrowding in churches and churchyards and an increasing population in some cities led to the establishment of private cemeteries, such as the garden cemetery at Arnos Vale, south east of Bristol, which was opened in 1840, providing opportunities for grander graves than could be obtained at such churches as St Augustine the Less.

The documentary references to the many intramural burial vaults and sepulchral remains illustrate the increasing status of the parish and church of St Augustine the Less, particularly in the 18th century. In contrast by the late 19th century various encroachments had reduced the churchyard by nearly half. Over 2,500 burials were exhumed in 1892 and 1894 with many of the numbered graves dating to the 18th and early 19th century. The northern churchyard included burials of military and naval officers of the 19th century (BRO P/St Aug/R/6). In the early 20th century the church and parish went into decline as the inner city population decreased and the area became more industrialized with the construction of warehouses to the south and east of the churchyard. The church was, however, still able to raise its own choir in the early 1930s and a marriage was duly solemnized in the summer of 1939 (WH Phillips, pers comm). After the demolition of the church in 1962 and clearance of the churchyard in 1971 the site lay neglected and became covered with undergrowth and inhabited by urban foxes. Prior to demolition the internal burial vaults and brick graves had been cleared and some of the church furnishings, memorial tablets, and church bells were transferred to St George, Brandon Hill. In 1984 the church of St George was closed for regular worship and leased by St George's Music Trust. The church of St Michael the Archangel (ST 58517329) has now assumed the parochial responsibility for the combined parish of St Michael with St Augustine and St George.

The excavation of the site of the church of St Augustine the Less was undertaken by the former Archaeology and History Department of Bristol City Museum and Art Gallery with the aid of a Manpower Services Commission Community Programme sponsored by the City of Bristol. The excavations took place with the permission of the site owners, Beazer Property Developments Limited, previously M P Kent plc, who also made a generous donation towards post-excavation costs. A watching brief was carried out on site in 1988 with the permission of Sir Robert McAlpine Management Contractors Limited when the remaining foundations of the church were removed and the new extension to the Swallow Royal Hotel commenced (Boore 1988, 34). In 1991 the hotel extension was completed. All of the site records, finds, and archive belonging to the 1983–4 excavations and subsequent fieldwork were formally transferred from Bristol City Museum and Art Gallery to the School of Conservation Sciences, Bournemouth University in 1995. At the time of the excavation there was a limited interest in post-medieval burial and their contents, with some exceptions (Butler 1978, 185; Rodwell 1981, 154; Shoesmith 1981, 64). The intensity of the post-medieval burial features were initially viewed elsewhere, not in their own right but in their impact upon the survival of the earlier archaeological phases on the sites (Morris 1987, 181). Further research and field work has led to an increased appreciation of the importance and value of post-medieval burials and funerary archeology (Litten 1985a and 1985b; Roberts, Lee & Bintliff 1989; and Litten 1991). The unique excavation and publication of the large parochial and smaller family vaults at Christ Church, Spitalfields, London has revealed the potential of the vast fund of evidence, data, and information which can be obtained from post-medieval burial vaults (Reeve & Adams 1993; Molleson & Cox 1993). 'A landmark in church archaeology was created at Spitalfields' (Rodwell 1989, 160 and 1996, 201).

Total excavation of the internal area of the church of St Augustine the Less, Bristol revealed an intramural patchwork quilt of burial vaults and brick graves. The interior was a virtual honeycomb of vaults and brick graves dating from the late 17th to the early 19th century (see Fig 6.1). Interment in burial vaults was fashionable among local merchants, artisans, and the military throughout the 18th and early 19th century. There were 107 intramural burial vaults and brick graves. A further nine vaults and brick graves were recorded externally (Boore 1985, 29). The later watching brief recorded eight brick graves in the south west and north east corners of the churchyard along with other brick walls suggesting that more had lain on the north side (Boore 1988, 34). During the excavation all 116 burial vaults and brick graves were recorded individually using a standard feature context sheet adapted at the time to record dimensions, location, and relationships to other contexts. In spite of the general sealing layer of 1962 demolition material, individual contexts were given to the deposits within each vault and grave. This was important not only in the instances where coffins and inhumations survived *in situ* but also in relation to the distribution of coffin furniture and other sepulchral remains, particularly ledger stones and wall tablets. This method of recording, which was very time-consuming and probably not comprehensive, was also applied to the external trench excavated in the disturbed churchyard area. A proforma burial-vault context sheet would certainly facilitate recording in future excavations and surveys (Reeve & Adams 1993, 23). The 1962 demolition and clearance of the intramural burial features and the 1971 churchyard clearance had been carried out by commercial contractors. There are no surviving records of these activities although a small quantity of coffin furniture was rescued in 1971 (M W Ponsford, pers comm). The destruction of evidence at this time and the information lost is to be regretted, as is also the loss of the osteological and anthropological evidence and information relating to the parishioners of St Augustine the Less and the evolution of this part of medieval and post-medieval Bristol as a city. However, the large-scale disturbance and destruction of the site was not total. A succession of seven major phases of occupation were recorded on the site. This included a Saxo-Norman cemetery and a Norman stone church which was enlarged and rebuilt in the medieval and post-medieval periods through to the 19th century. The intensive sequence of burial vault construction during the 18th and 19th centuries did not completely destroy all evidence of earlier archaeological periods (Morris 1987, 181, fig 83).

In addition to the surviving foundations of the church and the post-medieval burial features numerous architectural fragments including voussoirs, decorative plaster, mouldings, window tracery, pulpit, and sepulchral remains were recorded. There were also 119 headstones, 34 wall tablets, 22 inscribed ledger stones, and a benefaction stone. Unfortunately much of this material could not be retrieved due to its sheer bulk and quantity. Pottery, coins, tokens, clay tobacco pipes, many decorated medieval floor tiles, and a considerable quantity of post-medieval decorated window glass were recovered. A large collection of coffin furniture

was retrieved and a selection of brick types of the 18th and 19th centuries were retained. Finally, a total of 137 stratified burials were found, dating from the late Saxon to the early 19th century. These included five lead shells which were subsequently reinterred at South Bristol Cemetery and a very large quantity of unstratified material including charnel deposits. The location and deposition of this material was recorded during excavation and included the remains of a skull which had undergone post-mortem examination. A fortunate survival and archaeological time capsule for the churchyard was found preserved beneath the later 19th century vestry built on to the south east corner of the church. This area, which measured $3.75 \times 3.25 \times 1.22$ m, contained an intense sequence of interments. In total 40 burials were recovered dating from the earliest inhumations to an intact *c* 18th century shouldered brick grave. The density of burial made it difficult to detect grave outlines, with one grave often cutting into another. Initial examination of a selection of the human skeletal remains has revealed evidence of osteomylitis, osteoarthritis, and possible leprosy (M Cox, pers comm). An interesting find amongst the disarticulated material, from a post-medieval context, was a bone-handled tooth-brush.

All of the 107 intramural burial features were individually recorded and planned. A more intensive recording system was adopted for a representative sample which included photographic recording and, where relevant, on unusual vaults elevation drawing was also undertaken. Initially the burial features were subdivided into three basic types (Boore 1985, 29) but they can now be assigned to two types following Litten's typology for intramural burial vaults of the period 1650–1850. Litten Type 2; 'the family vaults, often not much more than a double or triple-width brick-lined grave with its own barrelled roof, usually for the landed gentry', and Litten Type 3; 'the single-width brick-lined shaft, capped off by a ledger stone, a superior version of the family grave, patronised by the professional classes' (Litten 1991, 211). The Type 3 brick graves at St Augustine the Less were both rectangular and shouldered, that is coffin-shaped. The majority of the intramural vaults were brick graves which predominated in the body of the church although examples also occurred in the chancel area. The rectangular family vaults were mainly concentrated in or near the chancel though they also occurred in the nave and aisles. There were several variations including an oval shape with parallel ends, odd shapes produced when two vaults were knocked into one, and one example where the gap between existing vaults was joined up to create a new vault. The location and type of vault reflected the status and wealth of the deceased's family.

There were several examples of vaults cutting vaults and the subdivision and reuse of family rectangular vaults. The large vault below the 1708 chancel extension, complete with its own stepped entrance from the churchyard south, was sub-divided on two subsequent occasions. This vault was probably originally reserved for use by the incumbent (Litten 1991, 217). Space inside the church was at such a premium that at least two of the aisle pier bases were partly cut away by the insertion of vaults. The vaults were literally crammed in to meet the demand, emphasizing not only the desirability of intramural burial but also the wealth of the parishioners. The interpretation of the sequence of vault construction was complicated by their earlier clearance and disturbance in the 1962 demolition of the church. There does appear to be a pattern of vault construction in groups, particularly in pairs. This may have been caused by the time and expense incurred and the disturbance within the church during the excavation and construction of a vault or brick grave. Construction in pairs would help alleviate the problem of roofing and capping. There may also have been an element of speculation resulting from the combined interests of incumbent, brick-layer and undertaker.

The method and standards of construction varied from vault to vault, walls being of both single and double brick construction. Their bonding was mainly stretcher bond though English Cross, Flemish, and Monk bonds were all recorded. A unique vault contained one face with alternate niches giving a dovecote effect. This may have had some unknown personal significance to the deceased or, more prosaically, may have resulted from a shortage of bricks. A few family vaults contained brick floors which were bedded in sand, either in parallel rows or a herringbone pattern. Others may have originally possessed a thin skin of mortar while many, particularly the brick graves contained no trace of a floor other than the natural clay and sandstone. One vault possessed a floor of Pennant Sandstone flagstones. The floors of many of the shafts were covered with a granular deposit of decayed wooden shells, fabric covering, and loose coffin furniture. Later vaults were sometimes painted internally with a plain lime wash, which was also used to disguise pier base foundations when a vault was inserted below an arcade. The family rectangular vaults were often covered with barrel-vaulted brick roofs with the remains of the springing arches surviving in some examples. The brick graves were sealed with Pennant Sandstone flagstones or inscribed ledgers. The presence, location, or identity of a vault or grave was also indicated by the remains of white marble wall tablets. A unique discovery was an oval, white marble tablet which was set in a large rectangular slab of Pennant Sandstone, possibly a ledger or part of a monument. The preparatory layout for the epitaph had survived in charcoal on the tablet and is a rare example of the stone mason's art. This unfinished piece had been reused in the construction of the 19th century under-floor heating ducts.

The dimensions of the vaults varied considerably. One of the family rectangular vaults measured $2.6 \times 1.86 \times 1.59$m, a rectangular brick grave was $2.5 \times 1.14 \times 1.8$m, and a shouldered shaft $2.5 \times 1.04 \times 1.92$m (externally). These dimensions were taken from incomplete disturbed vaults. In some of the brick graves there were niches left in the internal wall faces to accommodate horizontal iron bars or timber bearers which would have supported coffins laid above the brick floor. In the large 'Vicar's' vault, below the 1708 chancel extension, were two lines of parallel single brick courses which presumably acted as runners and supports for the coffins. The most unusual and possibly the earliest family vault, occupying prime position in the centre of the early post-medieval chancel, was built against the chancel east wall. The walls were constructed of narrow red bricks which measured $0.25 \times 0.12 \times 0.05$m and were bonded in a white/pale grey mortar, painted with a red ochre wash. The vault measured $2.76 \times 1.90 \times 1.90$m and was probably sealed with a ledger stone. The broken remains of a black marble ledger to Sir Hugh Owen, who died in 1698, and Anne Lloyd, bearing his coat of arms, were discovered amongst the demolition material in the chancel area. His ledger and vault are referred to in later documentary sources.

In the floor of the vault, there were six rows of evenly spaced, upright, narrow slabs of Pennant Sandstone aligned north–south set immediately above a medieval stone coffin. Their purpose was not only to support the intended coffins in this vault but also to dissociate them from the stone coffin below. The stone coffin, complete with internal head-niche, contained the disarticulated remains of at least three individuals, and may have been discovered during excavation for the late 17th century burial vault along with other human remains. The importance of this high status medieval burial would seem to have been recognized. The disturbed medieval coffin was relocated at a greater depth beneath the 17th century vault with the addition of further human remains added to the stone coffin as a charnel deposit. This act may have been thought to add greater sanctity to the occupants of the 17th century vault immediately above and certainly influenced its construction. The vertical Pennant Sandstone slabs served to separate the important charnel deposit from the equally important occupants of this unusual vault while maintaining a certain spiritual relationship between the two groups of burials in death and beyond. Considering the location of the vault one could speculate as to whether it was Sir Hugh Owen who paid for or contributed towards the subsequent chancel extension of 1708. All of the post-medieval vaults were constructed of brick with one late medieval stone-bonded burial feature (Boore 1985, 31).

Many of the later vaults and brick graves cut through earlier inhumations and the disturbed remains were either ignored or collected together and redeposited elsewhere as a charnel group. This occurred at the west end of the nave. Between a contemporary group of 19th century brick graves and the west tower were crammed a large, mixed quantity of human remains in a form of charnel deposit. A similar practice may have been adopted in the chancel area when the central heating ducts were inserted in the 19th century. The remains of five triple shell coffins in varying degrees of preservation were found relatively undisturbed. Four were located beneath the central heating ducts in the chancel area and one in the chancel extension to the north of the Vicar's vault (Fig 6.2). These burials were extensively recorded *in situ* and subsequently reinterred at South Bristol Cemetery. A sixth lead shell was found in the eastern churchyard area during the 1988 watching brief (Boore 1989, 246). This ornate shell, decorated with panels on its sides and lid, bore an embossed lead shield depositum plate with the initials TT and the date 1818. It was similar to the lead shells found at the Barnardiston Vaults at Kedington church, Suffolk (WHB 1918, 44). A single surviving lozenge-shaped grip-plate and iron grip was attached directly to the lead coffin. The Burial Register for 1813–26 has an entry for a Thomas Thirkill from Bitton, South Gloucestershire who was buried in 1818 (BRO P/St Aug/R/2[c]). Thomas Thirkill is listed in the trade directories as 'Plumber and Water Closet Maker', at 26 College Street in St Augustine's parish (Matthew's Directory 1818, 145). The manufacture of lead shells would have provided a considerable income for plumbers during the 18th and early 19th centuries, and Thomas Thirkill may have supplied many lead coffins for interment in the church of St Augustine the Less, or in its churchyard. It was therefore appropriate that he himself should be so buried and having been a plumber would not have wished to enclose or hide the workmanship within an outer case. This lead shell was also reinterred at South Bristol Cemetery. Rectangular family vaults and brick graves were found in the churchyard, and there is documentary evidence to suggest that brick-built vaults were located throughout the burial ground. During the grave clearance of the northern churchyard in 1894 fourteen lead coffins were recorded suggesting the presence of vaults or brick graves although triple-shell interments have been found in earth-cut graves (Litten 1991, 103, fig 51). A shouldered brick grave capped with Pennant Sandstone, below the 19th century vestry, contained the remains of two adults who had been interred in single shell wood coffins. A similar interment was recorded in a brick grave in the north aisle. The surviving external brick vaults were constructed against the foundations of the church walls, with a rectangular family vault with a barrel-vaulted brick roof having been constructed beneath the north porch. There were no burial vaults or

Figure 6.2   Triple-shell coffins in vaults and brick graves in the chancel area at St Augustine the Less, Bristol (photo: Bournemouth University)

brick graves within the west tower space, south of the north porch, below the eastern arcade of the south aisle, in the north west chancel area occupied by the pulpit, or the south west chancel area north of an earlier doorway.

The burial vaults and brick graves at St Augustine the Less would have contained single-break coffins, with either single or double lids and triple-shell coffins, 'lead-lapped inner wooden shell with an outer wooden case' (Litten 1985b, 12). The lead shells were sometimes decorated with crosshatching. At St Augustine the Less, with the exception of the Thomas Thirkill coffin, the lead shells were of the triple shell type. The lead shell was placed within an outer case of oak or elm, often covered with fabric, either wool baize or velvet attached with circular headed copper-alloy upholstery pins (Litten 1985b, 12 and 1991, 100). The upholstery pins were often arranged in various patterns and may also have formed the initials of the deceased and date of death on the lid of the coffin (Shoesmith 1981, 91, fig 14; Barker 1986, fig 78; Mytum 1988, fig 1). Metal grips in iron, tin-dipped copper alloy, or brass were fixed at either end of the coffin and along the sides, usually eight in all, often attached to decorative grip-plates. The end grips were circular and the side grips rectangular, loop- or bow-shaped. On top of the coffin was the breast or depositum plate inscribed with the name and date of the deceased, and often accompanied with other lid motifs. Other metal fittings included false hinges or angle brackets, metal straps, and escutcheons which combined to enhance the impact and effect of the coffin furniture assemblage. Lead, tin, brass, and iron were used for the coffin furniture which could be gilt, tin-dipped (silvered), or painted. Many of the grips were ornate and heavy and were non-functional.

The most ubiquitous design on the oval grip-plates is the winged cherub motif set above a cartouche bordered with palm branches (Watts & Rahtz 1985, 172, fig 89, plate 62). Winged cherubs are also a common design on the associated grips (Reeves & Adams 1993, 87, fig 55; Cox 1996a, 102). Grips with a floral motif were also common. The winged cherub motif is recorded at all of the sites described below. Its popularity as a funerary furnishing motif spanned all levels of society. It is found in the large, dynastic vault at Hinton St George and the Sackville Vault at Withyham, Sussex (Litten 1991, 208, figs 101 & 46, plate 13) as well as in the smaller family vaults and brick graves at St Augustine the Less, Bristol and at St Oswald's Priory churchyard in Gloucester. There are many nuances of design which probably represent different centres of production and differing economic costs. It occurs throughout the 18th and early 19th centuries. There are many other grip-plate and grip decorations. The Christ Church, Spitalfields reports have established a type-series for coffin-furniture for the south east (Reeve and Adams 1993, 77, appendix D). The large collection of material recovered from Bristol has many parallels with Spitalfields in addition to items which do not occur at the London site (Boore 1986, 213). There is a requirement for more work, especially in the provinces, to record post-medieval burials and their furnishings, particularly for the late 17th and early 18th centuries. This would help to prevent duplication of repetitive material and perhaps establish regional types reflecting centres of production and manufacture.

Bristol churches and graveyards

The intensity of intramural burial vaults and brick graves in the church of St Augustine the Less is not an isolated occurrence within the city of Bristol. The extent of intramural vaults elsewhere cannot be proven without removal of the latest floor levels. An indication of their presence can be determined by the existence of monuments, ledger stones, and wall tablets within the church. Internal below-ground alterations, watching briefs, surveys, and archaeological impact assessments have confirmed the existence of burial vaults and brick graves throughout the city. Vaults have been recorded in five churches, including St Augustine the Less, and in eight churchyards. The following sites are prefixed by the Bristol Urban Archaeological Database (BUAD) reference number (J Brett, pers comm). Excavation of the church of St Mary-le-Port in 1962–3 (BUAD 358) revealed brick-built family vaults of the 18th and 19th century and associated coffin furniture (Watts & Rahtz 1985, 181 and 193, plates 60–2 and 66, figs 88–91; Litten 1985a microfiche MF8/A2–8/A5). The report includes a contemporary account of an exhumation and examination in 1814 of a body in a lead coffin from a vault of 17th century date (Watts & Rahtz 1985, 181). Burial vaults and brick graves are recorded in St Nicholas (BUAD 2831) (Dawson 1981, 18), St James (Dawson 1981, 19), and in Bristol Cathedral (W Rodwell, pers comm). Brick vaults and graves have also been recorded in several churchyards; St Michael the Archangel (BUAD 539), St Thomas (BUAD 1728), Brunswick Square (BUAD 389), Old Market Street (BUAD 3037), Holy Cross (Temple) (BUAD 3143), and the Moravian Chapel (BUAD 471). All of the above, excepting Temple Church, contained or still retain articulated human skeletons, coffins including lead shells, and coffin furniture. The burial ground of the Moravian Church (ST 58717 73420) which had been cleared in 1973 (Dawson 1982, 42) was discovered during redevelopment in 1993 to retain extensive burials. Several family rectangular vaults and brick graves complete with their original occupants were still in situ. A watching brief allowed for limited recording of the burial features and the retrieval of a sample of coffin furniture. The remains of over 200 individuals were reinterred at Canford Cemetery, Bristol (J Brett, pers comm). Brick graves are also known in the churchyard to the west of St Peter's church in Castle Park, Bristol.

Many of the above examples of vaults were only partly recorded due to the constraints of the terms of a watching brief or because of limited access and funding. Most of the features are of the 18th and 19th century. It is most probable that all of the churches and the burial grounds in the city of Bristol contain some brick-built vaults and graves. The density of their occurrence may be inferred by sepulchral features perhaps correlated with the status of the church and parish during the period 1650–1850. The concern is not only for their existence but also for their continuing susceptibility to the ongoing threat of destruction without any prior recording or defence. The collation of the disparate information both archaeological, documentary, and visual from an examination of Sites and Monuments Records and the developing Archaeological Databases, urban and rural, by county would allow for an assessment of the situation. This could create a register of sites, which could then be appraised according to status and listed in terms of priority and potential threat and the need for preservation. 'The three ecclesiastical 'Rs' (Reordering, Restoration and Redundancy) have opened new chapters for the archaeologist, and the present trend of archaeology in churches in use, together with the increasing involvement of diocesan archaeological advisers at DAC level in the matter of reordering and restoration schemes, is to be welcomed' (Litten 1985b, 9). Funerary archaeology has imposed new responsibilities for a finite body of evidence which offers a unique and potentially rich source of information and artefacts concerning life and death in post-medieval Britain.

Examples from Gloucester

The responsibilities of the funerary archaeologist are not confined or limited to the high status burials of the rising middle classes and landed gentry of the 17th, 18th, and 19th centuries. The modest churchyard of St Oswald's Priory in Gloucester (Heighway & Bryant forthcoming) contained the remains of two rectangular and one shouldered brick graves of the 18th century among the earth cut graves. One triple coffin was recorded and a considerable amount of coffin furniture. It included ornate iron grips and other iron fittings associated with single-shell wooden coffins and possible anti-resurrectionist safeguards (Richardson 1988, 81; Reeve & Adams 1993, 82 and appendix F). The iron coffin furniture, bearing traces of black paint, was similar to material associated with higher status vault burials found in Bristol and elsewhere in Gloucester (see the Creswicke vault, below). It is apparent that, as in many aspects of life, then as now, coffins and coffin furniture of similar design but different materials were available from the manufacturers to meet the requirements, aspira-

tions, and financial resources of all levels of society (Boore & Heighway forthcoming). Similar iron coffin furniture associated with single-shell wooden coffins and belonging to 'non-related infiltrators' was recorded in the 18th century Atkyns vault in St Kenelm's church at Sapperton, near Stroud, Gloucestershire (Heighway & Litten 1994, 125). Vaults and brick graves are recorded in several urban churches and churchyards in the city of Gloucester (C Heighway, pers comm).

St Nicholas' Church, Bathampton

A group of twenty-nine 19th century 'walled graves', all coffin-shaped except one, which was rectangular, were recorded in the churchyard of St Nicholas, Bathampton near Bath, Bath & North East Somerset (ST 777666) (Cox & Stock 1995, 131). The graves were all constructed with the local Bath stone ashlar, a material recorded elsewhere in Bath for burial features (ibid, 135). The use of Bath stone, a readily available local source material and relatively easily worked, may have been given added impetus by the local Allen family who owned the manor of Bathampton from the early 18th century and who had interests in Bath stone quarrying. In addition to the walled graves, 26 earth graves were also recorded. The circumstances of the recording of the burials in advance of the construction of a meeting hall, were less than ideal. However a remarkable amount of evidence for 19th century funerary practice in this area was obtained, in spite of limited time and working in conjunction with contractors and local undertakers who relocated coffins and coffin furniture into other graves which were not threatened by piling (ibid, 133 and 137). The shafts or walled graves were capped with roughly dressed Bath stone which lay beneath chest tombs constructed of Bath stone and Pennant Sandstone from the Bristol area, ledgers or headstones. The latter had been removed prior to archaeological recording. The walled graves contained square-section iron bars to support succeeding interments. Two of the graves varied from the single width coffin shape. Grave 11 was of double (Fig 6.3) and Grave 20 of three coffin widths while retaining the external coffin shape. Both vaults contained a single or double metal joist arranged longitudinally to sub-divide the internal area. The joist provided strengthening for the vault walls and would have supported the capping stones (ibid, 136, figs 4 and 138, plate 1).

There were 42 coffins recorded with c 29 representing triple-shell coffins. One lead shell was decorated with cross-hatching. The remains of a well-preserved outer elm case from a triple-shell coffin was decorated with triple panelled design of scrolls defined with brass upholstery pins, all later conserved at Bristol City Museum and Art Gallery (Fig 6.4). Twenty one depositum plates were recorded dating from 1813 to 1879. Both cast-iron and copper

Figure 6.3 St Nicholas churchyard, Bathampton, Bath & North East Somerset. A double width walled grave made of Bath stone ashlar, early 19th century (photo: Bournemouth University, courtesy of the Vicar and Churchwardens of Bathampton)

Figure 6.4 Exceptionally well-preserved and decorated coffin sides from the outer case of a triple-shell coffin from St Nicholas churchyard, Bathampton, Bath & North East Somerset (photo: Bournemouth University, courtesy of the Vicar and Churchwardens of Bathampton)

alloy grips decorated with scrolls, floral motifs, and winged cherubs, and iron grips bearing the legend, Joseph Hands of London, with pattern number and date of design registration 1839, were found. These grips are also known in Bristol and London. Remnants of fabric covering from the outer case of triple-shell coffins (see Fig 6.4), either baize or velvet, survived as did material from inner coffin furnishings. The presence of winding sheets and one shroud were observed which were subsequently removed by the undertakers prior to the reburial of the skeletons. Osteological analysis of some of the skeletons recorded the occurrence of osteoarthritis, oral periodontal disease, and the existence of 19th century dentures constructed with a mixture of natural 'Waterloo' and ceramic teeth sprung with gold springs (*ibid*, 141, plate 3). A combination of depositum plate details, information from both churchyard and church monuments, burial registers, and other documentary sources allowed for identification of most of the burials and some demographic and historical analysis of the sample. The walled-grave burials were of high economic and social status including several high-ranking retired military officers and their families (*ibid*, 142 and appendix).

Creswicke vault, St Mary's Church, Bitton

The appearance of a hole in the floor of the nave of St Mary's Church, Bitton (ST 68206933) in south Gloucestershire led to the discovery of the Creswicke family vault (Fig 6.5). A survey was carried out in 1989 as part of the Faculty granted to the parochial church council to repair the floor of the central aisle and seal the vault (Boore 1989, 248). St Mary's dates back to the Norman period. It contains a 13th century chapel on the north and a 14th century west tower and chancel. The Reverends H T Ellacombe and H N Ellacombe, father and son incumbents between 1817 to 1916, also carried out internal alterations. This included the installation of the hammerbeam nave roof, erected in *c* 1867 with timbers reused from a ship wrecked in the Bristol Channel (Gerrish 1970, 5). The church contains a hatchment on the south nave wall to Henry Creswicke who died in 1806 and several worn ledger stones to the Creswicke family dating from 1732 (Ellacombe 1881, 27). Sir Henry Creswicke, died 1668, was a burgess and mayor of Bristol and enjoyed a grand funeral with full heraldic ceremony in the city (McGrath 1955, 126). The family

Figure 6.5   The Creswicke vault at St Mary's Church, Bitton, South Gloucestershire, c late 18th century (photo: E J Boore, courtesy of the Vicar and Churchwardens of Bitton, South Gloucestershire)

acquired Hanham Court near Bitton in the 17th century. Francis Creswicke is recorded as being buried at St Mary's in 1732. It was probably Francis who had the family vault constructed to receive the remains of his wife Mary who died in 1720. The family continued to use the vault until the middle of the 19th century where interment would have been presided over by the Rev H T Ellacombe. Humphry Creswicke, died 1856, was buried in the churchyard at Bitton. At this time Hanham Court has been acquired by Thomas White and the surviving Creswicke family had left to live in Canada (Ellacombe 1881, 139).

The amount of time for the survey was severely limited. Environmental conditions, through lack of ventilation, penetrating damp, restricted light, and a humid atmosphere made recording difficult. The interior of the vault was illuminated by a single electric light on an extension lead and boosted with flashlamps. The vault entrance was located below the central aisle 13.25 m to the west of the chancel arch and 3.35 m south of the nave north wall and had been temporarily closed with a reused headstone made of Pennant Sandstone. The inscription was dedicated to Samuel Jones (died 1688). Ledger stones were recorded c 0.06 m to the west and c 0.5 m to the east of the opening. The ledgers were heavily worn. The first ledger to the east contains the name of Henry Creswicke (died 1806), Mary his wife (died 1799), and possibly their daughter Mary Hill (died 1834) though much more of the inscription remains to be deciphered. A second adjacent ledger commemorates Francis Creswicke (died 1732) and his wife Mary (died 1720), their son

Henry (died 1744) and his wife Helen (died 1757) (Ellacombe 1881, 27). On the south wall of the nave there is a wall tablet with the names Samuel Pearsall (died 1800), Susannah Creswicke (died 1779), and Sarah Creswicke (died 1803).

The vault opening measured 0.55 × 0.50 m and revealed a set of five steps leading down into the vault (Fig 6.6). These were capped with narrow slabs of Pennant Sandstone over blocks of Oolitic Limestone, and the steps measured 1.08 × 0.30 × 0.25 m and descended overall for 1.20 m. The walls of the entrance were constructed of dressed courses of white Lias Limestone. The flat roof of the entrance projected into the barrel-vaulted roof in a semi-circular arch. This feature was constructed of ashlar blocks of Oolitic Limestone. The bottom step stopped at a height of 0.55 m above the floor of the vault. This probably facilitated the handling of coffins which were either carried down the steps or were lowered down on rolling bars as used in the Sackville vault at Withyham in Sussex (Litten 1991, 208). The overall internal dimensions of the entrance were 2.50 × 1.08 × 1.20 m and the steps led into the north west corner of a rectangular burial vault which measured 4.15 × 2.50 m. The top of the wall from floor level to the beginning of the springing of the roof was 1.45 m and 1.84 m at the apex of the roof. The vault was aligned north–south with its barrel-vaulted roof pitched west–east. The local yellow-white and grey-blue Lias Limestone with some Oolitic Limestone was the main stone used in the vault construction. The walls and roof were built of roughly dressed blocks of Lias and bonded in pale grey-brown lime mortar, and the floor was

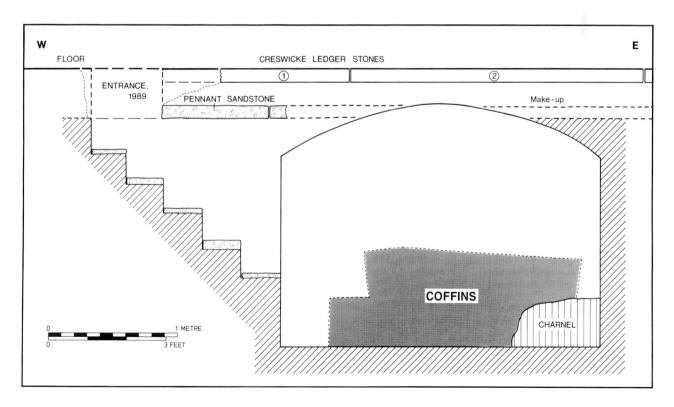

Figure 6.6   Section of the Creswicke vault at St Mary's Church, Bitton, South Gloucestershire (courtesy of City of Bristol Museums and Art Gallery)

constructed of Pennant Sandstone flagstones. The barrel-vaulted roof was constructed inside the north and south end walls, springing from the longer east and west walls. The side and end walls were well pointed while the smearing of mortar on the roof underside resulted from its construction over a wood template (Litten 1986, 6). The Lethieullier family vault at St Mary's Church in Little Ilford, Essex of 18th century date is of similar construction (Redknap 1985, 161).

Immediately against the north wall of the vault at the foot of the entrance steps were the remains of an articulated adult burial (Fig 6.7). The burial lay with its head to the west in the north-west corner of the vault and was surrounded and partly buried beneath a granular deposit of decayed wooden coffin remains. This deposit spread throughout the floor of the vault and varied in depth from 0.01 to 0.30m. It was not possible to sex the burial as no attempt was made to disturb the remains and there was no sign of a coffin plate. The height of the skeleton was c 1.75m (5'9"). It would appear to have been the last interment placed in the vault in a single-shell wooden coffin and is probably 19th century in date.

To the south of the entrance there was a lead shell lying on its side, decorated with a diaper pattern on the top or lid side of the coffin. The head end lay to the west while beneath the foot end there was a rectangular breast-plate. This coffin was an intact lead shell for an adult burial. Further south in the vault, c 0.50m, were four lead shells: all were adult

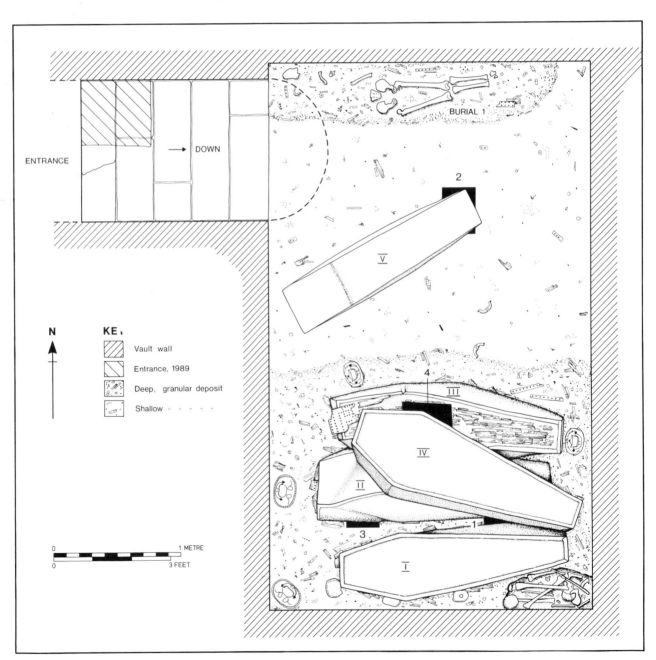

Figure 6.7   Plan of the Creswicke vault at St Mary's Church, Bitton, South Gloucestershire (courtesy of City of Bristol Museums and Art Gallery)

burials and lay with their heads to the west. One was in pristine condition and lay almost parallel, 0.06 m north of the south wall, and towards its foot end it overlay a breast-plate. Its lid was covered with a fine hard skin of a pale yellow mortar-like substance, perhaps an added precaution to seal in the occupant who may have died from an infectious disease (J Litten, pers comm). A second coffin lay 0.10 m north of and parallel to the first, its top side facing towards it so the weight of a further coffin had pushed the second one over on its side towards the first. A breast-plate was partly overlaid by the second coffin at its head end, while its foot end also overlay the first breast-plate.

Immediately to the north lay a third lead shell which partly overlay the base and north side of the second coffin. The third and second coffins were badly dented and buckled by the weight of the overlying fourth lead shell. The effect of this had caused, or at least contributed to, the bursting apart of the north-west corner of the third shell. This damaged lead shell was right side up, albeit buckled, and retained substantial remains of the outer wooden case which originally enclosed the inner lead shell. At the head end there were surviving upholstery pins which would have held the baize or velvet covering of the outer wooden case. The pins had originally been laid in regular patterns. A breast-plate lay above the outer case remains, although it was badly damaged by the overlying fourth coffin which lay straddled across the second and third shells. The fourth lead shell was also in pristine condition and clearly exhibited the sealing joint between the enclosing sides and lid of the coffin. It also had diaper decoration on its north west face at the head end.

All five lead shells were made of high quality lead. The surrounding granular deposit, upholstery pins, and fabric fragments were the remains of the outer cases from the triple-shell coffins. The lack of ventilation inside the vault and the humid atmosphere combined with gases associated with the decomposition and small animal incursion would all have hastened the decay of the outer wooden cases (Litten 1985b, 12). The re-opening of the vault and movement of coffins would also have contributed further to their decay.

In addition to the decayed remnants of the outer cases there were considerable remains of coffin furniture surrounding the lead shells. This consisted in the main of grips and grip-plates. Both lay around the floor in a haphazard manner and it was not possible to specifically associate individual coffins with coffin furniture. The decorative motifs on the grips were variations on winged cherub heads and were either cast brass or iron grips with wrap around copper-alloy decoration (Fig 6.8). They date to the 18th and early 19th centuries and have also been found in Bristol at St Mary-le-Port and St Augustine the Less (Watts & Rahtz 1985, plate 62, fig 89; Boore 1985, 32), Christ Church, Spitalfields, London (Reeve & Adams 1993, 83, appendix D), and

at St Nicholas, Bathampton, Bath & North East Somerset (Cox & Stock 1995, 138). The grip-plates were made of stamped tin-plate and were of two distinct decorative forms. An oval repoussé gilt plate decorated with winged cherub heads was surrounded by clouds and sun-rays, a ubiquitous design which has been recorded in many vaults throughout the country. An oval plate bordered with a floral design around a central sarcophagus motif was also recorded. These grip-plates lay around the north side of the third lead shell, discussed above. Coffin-furniture was extensively manufactured throughout the country, particularly in Birmingham and London as well as Bristol and Dublin (Church & Smith 1966, 622; Litten 1985b, 13).

The appearance of the lead shells suggested that they were not in their original positions. The subsequent rearrangement of coffins to make way for others occurred at the Poulett vault at Hinton St George, Somerset (Litten, Dawson & Boore 1988, 257). Other possibilities such as stacking of the coffins, also recorded at Hinton St George, and their subsequent collapse as the outer shells decayed, may explain the deposition of the lead shells in the Creswicke vault. The lack of external damage to the lead shells, with the exception of one, may argue against the casual treatment of the coffins within the vault as recorded at Christ Church, Spitalfields, London (Adams & Reeve 1987, 247). The depth of granular deposit in the southern half of the vault suggested that the triple-shell coffins were located here originally, allowing room for others to follow. The stack appeared to have slowly toppled northwards.

It was possible to record the four depositum plates indicated on plan which enabled identification of at least four of the burials if not their particular association with a lead shell. Three depositum plates were rectangular and made of brass while a fourth was trapezium shaped and of copper alloy. All possessed narrow decorative borders with floral motifs. Two were also decorated with a crown of life motif in the centre above the epitaph. The depositum plates commemorated Mary Creswicke (died 1799), Henry Creswicke (died 1806), Mary Mathilda Creswicke (died 1809), and Mary Hill (died 1834). Henry Creswicke and Mary were husband and wife, and Mary Hill was their daughter who had married John Hill (died 1833), possibly the occupant of the fifth lead shell. Mary Mathilda Creswicke was Henry and Mary's daughter-in-law who had married Humphry Creswicke, brother of Mary Hill. Humphry (died 1856) was buried in Bitton churchyard (Ellacombe 1881, 139).

The burial registers for St Mary's record the actual date of interment (BRO, P/B/R/1 [d] and P/B/R/4 [a]). The length of time between death and interment in the vault was exactly nine days for all the above except for Mary Mathilda who was buried eight days after she died. The latter died on 25 July 1809, one day later than her mother-in-law Mary,

Figure 6.8b

Figures 6.8a, b & c   Grips and grip-plates from the 18th and 19th century contexts at St Augustine the Less (photos: Bournemouth University)

Figure 6.8a

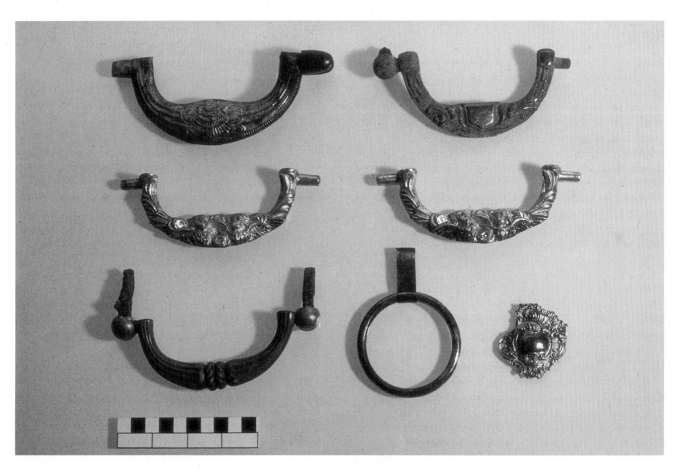

Figure 6.8c

who died on 26 July 1799. Both were buried on 2 August, exactly ten years apart. The funeral ceremony for Mary Hill (nee Creswicke) was performed by H T Ellacombe who was curate at the time (BRO P/B/R/4 [a]).

The funeral would have been an occasion of some ceremony with attendants for the triple-shell coffin covered in baize or velvet and gilt coffin furniture, presenting a spectacular sight. The instructions left by Edward Colston (1636–1721), the Bristol merchant, member of Parliament and well-known philanthropist, for his funeral and his detailed estimate, give a fascinating insight into the funerary customs of the day. The total cost came to £213 17s 2d in the early 18th century (Wilkins 1920, 80). Edward Colston was buried at All Saints Church in Corn Street, Bristol. The elaborate ceremony and procession was still continuing this century with funerals of eminent people like Joseph Fry, founder of Fry's chocolate firm, in 1913, in Bristol (Fisher & Ford 1985, 171–3).

The lack of a depositum plate on the extended burial near the entrance made identification impossible. The burial may have been that of a servant of the Creswicke family interred in the family vault as recorded in the Poulett vault at Hinton St George, Somerset (Litten et al 1988, 257). Alternatively the burial may have had no relationship with the Creswicke family and it may represent someone who had paid for the privilege of vault burial in a pre-existing vault. The reuse of vaults was not uncommon and is recorded in Bristol and north Gloucestershire (Boore 1985, 29; Heighway & Litten 1994, 125). In the south-east corner of the vault, between a lead shell and the south wall, there was a substantial charnel deposit. The charnel consisted mainly of the long bones from adult skeletons and at least six skulls. The charnel had been fairly carefully piled in the corner to a height of c 0.80 m and probably represent some earlier members of the Creswicke family interred in single shell coffins. The skeletons may be the remains of those Creswickes commemorated on the second ledger stone to the east of the vault entrance. In due course interment in single-shell coffins would have decayed in the conditions prevalent in the vault.

Poulett vault, Hinton St George

The Poulett family vault at Hinton St George in south Somerset is a tripartite structure and a prime example of Litten's Type 1 burial vault; 'the large dynastic vaults, either beneath a sidechapel or aisle, more usually associated with noble families' (Litten 1991, 211). The vault was first examined in 1981 after a visit by J W S Litten to advise the incumbent, churchwardens, and church architect on the condition of the vault and its contents (Litten 1981). A second survey carried out in 1987 allowed for an investigation of the eastern vault which had previously been sealed by a later wall when the

vault was extended westwards in 1814 (Litten et al 1988). The Poulett family have been associated with Hinton St George since 1429 and their former ancestral home survives in the south-west corner of the parish (Pevsner 1958, 198). The family vault extends below the north transept and north-east chapel of the parish church (ST 41831270). Most of the church dates to the 15th century. The Poulett Memorial Chapel was rebuilt in 1814 by Sir Jeffry Wyatville for John, 4th Earl Poulett and the transept remodelled as the Poulett Pew. At the same time the family monuments were re-erected, and the western extension to the vault was constructed (Fig 6.9). The monuments include the tomb chest with effigies built in about 1540 by Sir Hugh Poulett for his father, Sir Amyas (died 1537), the monument to Sir Amyas II (died 1588) removed with his body from St Martin-in-the-Fields in 1728, and those to Sir Anthony (died 1600) and his wife Katherine (died 1601), John Baron Poulett (died 1649), John 1st Earl Poulett (died 1743), and other later memorials.

The west vault is entered through Wyatville's Ham-stone portico enclosed by a contemporary paved and railed courtyard. Studded oak doors open into a staircase leading down to a large brick chamber (20 × 13 ft/6.09 × 3.96 m) with quadripartite vaulting occupying the entire area beneath the north aisle. There are seventeen coffins occupying shelf space designed for 24. All of the coffins are extremely well preserved. This is due to Sir Jeffry Wyatville's ventilation system as well as constant maintenance by the Poulett family (Litten 1986, 7). The use of shelves was generally confined to the vaults of noble families such as the 1810 extension to the Cavendish vault at Derby Cathedral (Litten 1985b, 10) and the Sackville vault, Withyham, Sussex (Litten 1991, 209). Several coffins, including Sophia (died 1811), first wife of John, 4th Earl Poulett, have been removed here from the 16th century vault to the east. All seventeen interments are in triple-shell coffins. The coffin furniture is of high quality for the 19th century and the coffin of Rosa, Dowager Countess Poulett, retains the coronet recorded at her funeral in 1915. The last coffin to be deposited contains George, eighth and last Earl Poulett, who died without issue in 1973.

To the east of Wyatville's vault is a 17th century brick-built chamber, probably a later entrance to the original 16th century vault. This may have been built either by Sir Hugh (died 1572) or Sir Anthony Poulett (died 1600). Both eastern chambers are built of brick and provided with elliptical barrel vaults, subsequently divided by a partial north–south wall. The 17th century room is occupied by three interments with two triple-shell coffins to the south, the uppermost resting on the remains of an oak frame. The upper coffin of Colonel William, second son of the 4th Earl, who died in 1805, is enhanced with ornate coffin furniture. A double line of upholstery pins frames the lid and sides. The edges are joined by regularly-spaced false hinges

Figure 6.9   The 1814 extension with shelving and entrance to the Poulett vault, Hinton St George in South Somerset, designed by Sir Jeffry Wyatville (photo: E J Boore, courtesy of the Vicar and Churchwardens of Hinton St George, Somerset and with acknowledgement to the Countess Poulett)

decorated with gadrooning. One surviving central grip-plate bears a coronet. A fragment of the rich red velvet which once covered the coffin survives below one of the breast-plates. Against the north wall is a lead shell with an inscription to Bernard Hutchins (died 1733), a servant and close friend of the family.

The eastern chamber, constructed of rendered brick (15 × 10 ft/4.57 × 3.05 m), contains at least 22 coffins which were poorly stacked in the re-arrangement of 1814. A small coffin by the north wall has collapsed under the weight of two larger ones and these in turn have toppled the stacks southwards. There was at least one, possibly two, anthropomorphic lead shells. One identified example was partially buried by the stack against the north wall. Contrary to normal practice its foot faces west and may be the coffin of Sir Amyas Poulett (died 1537). It is not unusual for coffins to be repositioned in private burial vaults. Three of the lead shells possessed decorative borders to the lids and would not have been contained in outer wooden cases (Litten 1991, 96, colour plate 9). One lead case, that of a child, near the south wall of the vault, bears the monogram VP above a winged cherub's head. On top of the stack is the richly decorated triple-shell coffin of John, 1st Earl Poulett (died 1743). The gilt coffin furniture consisted of grips and grip-plates decorated with

winged cherubs surmounted by an earl's coronet in appliqué with the side(s) enhanced with sunburst escutcheons (Fig 6.10).

Current position, concerns, and conclusions

The excavations at the church of St Augustine the Less, Bristol in 1983–4 recovered a vast quantity of coffin furniture, coffin fragments, and several complete lead shells. At the time there was little published comparative material. The survival of three trade catalogues of coffin furniture of the late 18th and early 19th century period in the Victoria and Albert Museum has provided a terminology and date range (Litten 1991, 107). A major exhibition at the Victoria and Albert Museum in 1992, 'The Art of Death – Objects from the English Death Ritual 1500–1800' also focused attention on the significance of artefactual remains within 'Christian ritual and behaviour in England during the 16th to 18th centuries' (Llewellyn 1991, 57). Other important publications have examined the English and European wider funerary tradition and architecture (Litten 1991; Curl 1993). The archaeological excavation and recording of the parochial vaults beneath Christ Church, Spital-fields has provided a major type-series for

Figure 6.10   The inner 16th century Poulett vault, remodelled in the 19th century, containing an anthropomorphic lead shell, lead shells with decorative borders, and the triple-shell coffin of John 1st Earl Poulett (died1743) (photo: E J Boore, courtesy of the Vicar and Churchwardens of Hinton St George, Somerset and with acknowledgement to the Countess Poulett)

undertaking techniques and funerary practice for coffins and coffin furniture for the period 1729–1859 (Reeve & Adams 1993, 77–91, appendix D, microfiche M2–M3; Cox 1996a, 98–105). The Spitalfields project also examined the anthropological aspects of the occupants of the vaults, correlating the named individuals with documentary sources and skeletal examination (Molleson & Cox 1993; Cox 1996a).

There is an increasing body of knowledge concerning the occupants of post-medieval burial vaults and brick grave burials in relation to vault construction, coffins, and coffin-furniture (Litten 1991, 107; Reeve & Adams 1993, 77; Cox 1996a, 98). Further work in the regions, although on a smaller scale, has also been reported in north Wales (Shoesmith 1981), Canterbury (Tatton-Brown 1980), Bristol (Watts & Rahtz 1985; Boore 1985), Norwich (Goodall 1993), Humberside (Mytum 1988), and in North Yorkshire (Harding 1987). Other work, particularly in the south of England, is in preparation while discussion continues around ethical and religious attitudes to the investigation and recording of burials in the post-medieval period (Cox 1996b). The threat to post-medieval burial deposits throughout Britain has not diminished and is increasing particularly in the urban centres where land is at a premium (Cox 1996b, 8).

The burial vault, brick grave, walled grave, and earth grave of the post-medieval period and their occupants cannot be seen in isolation to the associated sepulchral remains. The ledger stones, wall tablets, hatchments, memorials, headstones, and textiles, combined with documentary references, are a rich source of evidence. The burial vault may be an apartment associated with death but seen in its context it encapsulates the hopes and aspirations, religious and secular of those who built it, those who commemorate it, those whose responsibility it is to maintain it, and, most importantly, those who occupy it. Where preservation is not possible it is essential that archaeological, anthropological, and historical disciplines are enlisted to record, retrieve, and preserve the wealth of information contained and available in vault burial and thereby contribute to our knowledge of life and death in post-medieval Britain.

Acknowledgements

I am indebted to Julian Litten for his encouragement and advice during the excavations at the church of St Augustine the Less, Bristol in 1983 and 1984, for his continuing support, and for sharing his immense knowledge of burial vaults, funerary practice, and funerary archaeology. Also to Dr Margaret Cox for her help and support. I am most grateful to Julian Litten, Dr Roger Price, and Dr Warwick Rodwell for their comments on the text. Thanks and appreciation are owed to all those who worked on the sites mentioned and to Ann Linge for the plans and illustrations and to my former colleagues at Bristol City Museum and Art Gallery. I am also grateful to Jonathan Brett for information from the Bristol Urban Archaeological Database. I am pleased to acknowledge the assistance and forbearance of the incumbents, churchwardens, and relatives of the burial vaults visited, and of course the occupants.

My greatest debts and warmest appreciation are to Gill Heavens whose tolerance and perseverance was both remarkable in producing the text and for her continuing motivation and encouragement, and to the late Mrs Ivy May Boore. My grateful thanks are extended to Noel O'Donnell for providing access to information technology.

7 'To the praise of the dead, and anatomie': the analysis of post-medieval burials at St Nicholas, Sevenoaks, Kent Angela Boyle and Graham Keevill

With a contribution by Margaret Cox, Paul Kneller and Robert Haslam

Introduction

The Parochial Church Council of St Nicholas, Sevenoaks' (PCC) *Building for the Gospel* project created a suite of parish rooms as an undercroft below the existing floor levels. This involved excavation of the space below the floor to a depth of *c* 4m thereby destroying all archaeological deposits within the medieval parish church. The PCC was responsible, under archaeological supervision, for the removal and storage of all existing fittings, the modern floor, and associated rubble make-up. As a condition of the planning permission and Faculty granted for this development the entire church was excavated, with the exception of the present day vestry, west tower, and north and south porches. The vestry was excavated during subsequent work

in March and April of 1994. The ethical issues raised by this type of excavation will not be dealt with here as they are discussed in detail elsewhere (Boyle forthcoming).

The work at St Nicholas, Sevenoaks involved near-total excavation of the interior of the church along with watching briefs to various external works (Fig. 7.1). The excavation revealed the structural history in some detail as well as the pattern of burial on the site over the centuries. There do not appear to have been any total excavations within Kentish parish churches. Equally there has been relatively little archaeological work within church cemeteries. The project at St Nicholas, Sevenoaks, therefore attains added significance within a regional archaeological context. The work should also be viewed in a national research framework as

The Parish Church as it was before restoration in 1810.
(1797).

Figure 7.1   A drawing of St Nicholas, Sevenoaks in 1797 (from the south) by M Petrie FSA (Centre for Kentish Studies, Maidstone, P330/28/3; with acknowledgment to Rev. Miles Thompson)

the latest in a series of major excavations within parish churches in use, such as Barton-on-Humber (Rodwell & Rodwell 1982), Rivenhall (Rodwell & Rodwell 1986, 1995), Christ Church, Spitalfields (Reeve & Adams 1993), and Tong Church (Swann 1993).

St Nicholas, Sevenoaks first appears in documentary sources in the *Textus Roffensis* of 1122 and, not surprisingly, the main thrust of the excavation was aimed at recovering evidence of the earliest church structure (potentially pre-Conquest) and tracing its development through time. The study of the resulting human remains and associated artefacts and coffin fittings, particularly of the post-medieval period, was always seen as an issue of lower priority.

Late medieval documents relating to the Church are quite rare, but the parish records survive from the mid 16th century onwards and Sevenoaks was clearly affected by the social, political, and spiritual upheaval and change that took place during this period (see Killingray 1990, 5–9 for a useful summary). The archiepiscopal palace at Knowle passed into secular hands, and the administration and patronage of the parish underwent considerable change. A great number of documents relating to the 17th to 18th centuries survive, including memorials, wills, and other biographical materials. This chapter will not analyse such material in detail.

The existing superstructure of the church is largely 15th century (Perpendicular) in external appearance, although 14th century Decorated work is evident in the north aisle. Inside, the 13th century nave arcades are the earliest visible parts of the church (Newman 1976, 510–11), while the 14th century font is an important survival (Killingray 1990, 4). The physical situation of the church at the 'top of the town' is accentuated by the fine west tower. There may originally have been a tower on the north side of the church; Knocker (1926, 66) provides a critical reference to this. The building was probably neglected for much of the post-medieval period (see Yates 1986, 124–5), although galleries were inserted at the west end of the nave and in both aisles in 1798 (op cit, 122).

The successive restorations of St Nicholas Church in 1812–14 and 1877–8 (Yates 1986) involved the clearance of much of the interior arrangement of the church such as box pews and galleries. Old doors were blocked and new ones opened, the organ was moved, and the bellchamber was moved higher up in the tower. The 1877–8 work was the most destructive archaeologically, because the ground level was lowered over the entire interior of the church. A number of intramural burials were disinterred and two of the larger burial vaults were totally rearranged. Rodwell (1989, 114–6) has admirably summarized the deleterious effects of ground lowering on archaeological deposits within churches. The notes made in 1840 by W P Griffiths FSA, a local ecclesiologist who visited many Kent churches before restoration (Yates 1986), offer assistance in reconstructing pre-Victorian arrangements within the church but they cannot replace the lost floor levels of the medieval church. During the 20th century the north porch and a new vestry were added and roofs were replaced.

Building for the Gospel: redevelopment at St Nicholas Church

The 1980s and 1990s have seen a marked increase in developments within historic churches. These generally arise because the buildings are poorly suited to the perceived requirements of modern congregations and patterns of worship. A strong evangelical trend within the Church of England also recognises that a church cannot be regarded solely as a historic artefact: it must also be a place of fellowship and praise, a living symbol of God's purpose. As David Killingray wrote of Sevenoaks in 1990:

> A major problem is how to adapt that building to make it suitable for Christian worship and fellowship in the twenty-first century but in a way that is sympathetic to its traditional setting and sensitive to local interests. This is a challenge for the Christian family at St Nicholas (Killingray 1990, 13).

Archaeologists, historians, and others may not always be comfortable with church developments, but it is incumbent on them to recognise the legitimate needs and wishes of parish authorities and congregations.

The PCC of St Nicholas, Sevenoaks faced just such problems of space in the 1980s. They established a project, *Building for the Gospel*, intending to create a suite of parish rooms as an undercroft below the current church floor. They hoped thereby to give the church 'the capacity to be used seven days a week in the service of Christ in Sevenoaks' (Preface to Killingray 1990 by Rector Miles Thomson).

As the quotation above makes clear, the PCC were aware of their responsibilities to St Nicholas' past as well as its present and future. That past was clearly one of considerable significance, even if the early history of the church was imperfectly understood. It was obvious that some form of archaeological work would be needed in advance of the development so that its impact on the historic fabric and archaeological levels could be assessed. It was also clear that an archaeological input would be needed during the construction programme. The task of devising an appropriate archaeological response to the *Building for the Gospel* project exercised many minds in the early 1990s.

The work undertaken at Sevenoaks was considerable on any scale, and, perhaps more importantly, clearly not reversible. It is therefore worth reconsidering that work in the light of the so-called 'Maidstone Decision' or 'The judgement of the Court of Arches in the case of St Luke the Evangelist Maidstone (1994) [3 WLR 1165]' (Council for British Archaeology 1997c, 10) which indicated four considerations which a Chancellor should have in mind when determining proposals to alter a church. These considerations are worth quoting here:

1 The persons most concerned with worship in a church are those who worship there regularly, although other members of the Church who are not such regular worshippers may also be concerned.

2 Where a church is listed there is a strong presumption against change which would adversely affect its character as a building of special architectural or historical interest. In order to override that presumption there must be evidence of sufficient weight to show a necessity for such a change for some compelling reason, which could include the pastoral well-being of the church. There will be many instances where works are required for liturgical purposes, which are compatible with the historic character and appearance of the building and are reversible. They may be following a particular liturgical fashion, such as the introduction of a nave altar, and be acceptable in conservation terms. A distinction has however to be drawn between cases of that kind, and cases where the works will adversely affect the character of the building. The changes proposed may be in accordance with a particular liturgical fashion but cases which fall within the latter category will have to meet the test of necessity, which we have set out above, to have a prospect of being authorised.

3 Whether a church is listed or not a Chancellor should always have in mind not only the religious interests but also the aesthetic, architectural and communal interests relevant to the church in question.

4 Although the present and future needs of worshippers must be given proper weight, a change which is permanent and cannot be reversed is to be avoided wherever possible.

In the light of this judgement, it is debatable whether the kind of development undertaken at Sevenoaks would now be granted a faculty.

Excavation

Following an evaluation designed to determine the survival of medieval floor layers an excavation ran for twelve weeks from mid-September to mid-December 1993, with a professional staff of nine directed by Mike Webber. The research aims particularly focused on the historic development of the church and the possibility of an Anglo-Saxon origin. Aspects of specific interest included possible evidence for a pre-Conquest church, the relationship of structural phases identified below ground to the standing fabric and architecture, the arrangement of the church through time, both in terms of structural sequence and internal fixtures, fittings, and liturgy, and the burial archaeology.

The last was an obvious issue, if difficult to quantify in terms of resources and priorities. It was clear that burial had occurred throughout the later medieval and post-medieval periods (Fig 7.2), but it was also recognized that 15th century or earlier graves could be found in the aisles at least, and that such graves would probably have been external to the contemporary church. The potential for late Saxon burials was also recognized. All matters relating to burial archaeology were therefore of fundamental importance, including osteological analysis of the skeletal remains, evidence for burial practice, coffins and their furniture, and structures such as vaults and shafts. To all intents and purposes post-medieval, and, in particular, 18th and 19th century burials were not seen as archaeological. It was decided that they should be removed by a professional clearance company while the archaeological excavation progressed.

At the same time, however, it was recognized that the statistical validity of osteological studies depended on the availability of large numbers of relatively complete skeletons, preferably with a fairly tight date-range (cf Rodwell 1989, 171–2). It was by no means guaranteed that this condition could be met at St Nicholas. Furthermore, the sample was unlikely to be representative of the cemetery population as a whole: burial within the church was normally reserved for people of high status and wealth. This problem could be exacerbated by finding graves which had formerly been in the churchyard but which had been 'taken into' the church during later extensions. Suffice it to say here that all parties accepted that post-medieval and later graves and skeletons were of a lower priority than medieval ones. It was felt that the later material could be dealt with by making a reasonably detailed skeletal/grave record on site, leaving more time at a later stage to concentrate on medieval material. Survival of the later bones for study was important to this strategy, but this is a difficult issue for most Church authorities: the presumption (especially in Diocesan Faculties) is usually for reburial. In this instance the Chancellor directed that 'more recent burials should be disposed of discreetly'. The first author of this paper, an osteologist, was on site for most of the excavation so that low resolution recording of skeletons could occur during excavation, lifting, and processing. The methodology for the analysis of the skeletal material will be considered in some detail below.

It is worth emphasizing that the excavation brief was put together before the publication of the report on Christ Church, Spitalfields and at the

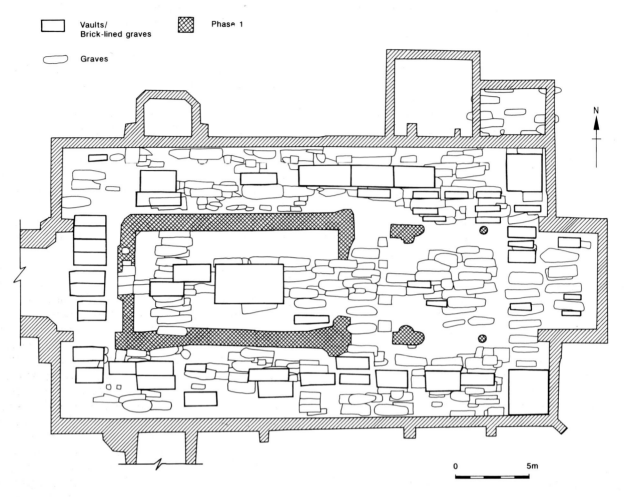

☐ Vaults/
  Brick-lined graves

▨ Phase 1

⬭ Graves

N

0   5m

Figure 7.2   Plan showing post-medieval graves and vaults (Oxford Archaeological Unit)

time it was by no means widely accepted that post-medieval burials were of particular archaeological interest. There was then, and still is now, marked uncertainty on the part of curatorial authorities as to the value of such material. A considerable financial investment is necessary to cover aspects of conservation, analysis, and storage of both skeletal remains and coffin fittings. At the time of writing the Sevenoaks archive has an uncertain future, no Kent museum has yet agreed to accept the material, and, even were a museum willing to do so it is unclear where the funding would come from for such an undertaking.

The original plan was to record all well-preserved wooden and lead coffins *in situ* and to have them removed complete and unopened for reburial by specialist contractors. It was originally intended that this should be carried out after the completion of the archaeological investigations. However, because of time constraints and the need to remove lead coffins in order to record and excavate earlier features, it was agreed that the Oxford Archaeological Unit (OAU) should work in tandem with the contractors employed to remove lead coffins from the building. The archaeological director was assured that this would cause no inconvenience to

the progress of the excavation, and that there would be no risk to health or morale.

It was clear that wooden coffins and the outer shells of lead coffins would not survive the move, but the PCC was reluctant to allow archaeological removal of coffin furniture. However, once it was discovered that the method to be employed in the removal of the coffins involved the opening and removal of the contents, it was agreed by the PCC, the County Archaeologist, and OAU that the furniture should be removed, and the removal of the contents should be archaeologically monitored. OAU staff felt that the method of removal was morally questionable and, on a more practical level, involved considerable destruction of potential archaeological information. The speed and methods employed during this process, and the depth at which several of the coffins lay, necessitated rapid recording and implementation of a sampling strategy. This was governed by the amount of time available and the willingness of staff to undertake the most unpleasant tasks necessary. This resulted in a somewhat subjective strategy, with textile samples alone being taken from individuals with surviving soft tissue, while several skeletonized burials were examined and recorded in greater detail.

Health and safety advice suggested that the risk of smallpox was low and that lead would only be a problem in confined spaces. Similar assurances were received from the contractors employed to remove the coffins. Protective clothing was used by those immediately involved in the work. Dr Susan Young (formerly) of the Communicable Diseases Surveillance Centre monitored site conditions after discussion with the County Archaeologist, Dr John Williams, who considered recording of the coffin contents to be worthwhile. All but two of the volunteers were kept off-site during this phase of work, and a viewing platform for the public at the west end of the church was closed. Lead coffins were only recorded photographically, as the process of removal produced dangerously sharp edges which were likely to cause injury to staff recording in confined spaces. When the lead coffins were actually opened the only people present on site were Dr Young, the first author, and the contractors, all of whom had had smallpox vaccinations. In addition protective suits, masks, and gloves were worn. It was only after the bodies had been checked for smallpox lesions and 'cleared' that the other staff were allowed to return to the site and resume work. Remains with surviving soft tissue were immediately reburied in new wooden coffins obtained from the local undertaker.

Stratigraphy and post-excavation methodology

It soon became clear during excavation that Victorian levelling for replacement of the floor had cut into natural deposits, except where they had been truncated previously by earlier features. The effect of post-medieval and Victorian vault burial within the nave and aisles was also quickly apparent. Such features covered much of the excavated interior space, and they had often removed all trace of earlier archaeology. Nevertheless a significant number of medieval burials were found (*contra* Rodwell 1989, 158). Earlier floors and other deposits were also preserved in a few isolated areas (physically and stratigraphically), and there was some evidence for pre-Victorian internal arrangements within the church.

Internal dating evidence for the stratigraphy was very variable indeed. On the one hand many later burials (largely 18th and 19th century) can be specifically dated by coffin plates giving the year of death. The stylistic development of coffin furniture is quite well known, and illegible plates may still be given a *terminus post quem*. Undertakers' pattern books of the period can be used in the typological study and dating of the furniture. Many of the latest contexts can, therefore, be dated with a very high degree of confidence. Unfortunately, and interesting though this study undoubtedly is, this is exactly the aspect of the excavation which had been identified from the outset as having a lower priority than the (possible) Saxon, medieval, and early post-medieval levels.

Dating of pre- 17th or 18th century contexts becomes much more difficult. Archaeological dating traditionally relies on finds evidence, especially pottery. The assemblage from St Nicholas, however, is very small considering the very extensive nature of the excavations. This is perhaps not so surprising in view of the fact that people would not have been likely to deposit refuse in such a context. Only 103 sherds (total weight 739g) were recovered, mostly from grave fills and cleaning layers over scarcely identifiable grave cuts (see below). The truncation of all levels during the Victorian lowering of the floors must have removed much pottery, but even so such a small assemblage is disappointing.

Other finds offer some assistance, including ceramic building materials (largely tile) and the non-coffin small finds. Once again quantities are small and the number of contexts restricted, and the finds (especially tile) tend to be from contexts in the middle and upper part of the sequence rather in the earlier medieval levels. To some degree, therefore, it was inevitable that the dating sequence would be at least partly externally derived, rather than relying on the internal evidence of the excavations themselves. Relevant external data include the architectural affinities of the church (both in the surviving superstructure and in parallels for the excavated evidence of plan development), the few specific documented dates, and comparative information on coffin furniture and other aspects of burial archaeology.

The stratigraphy largely consisted of vertical relationships between graves, or between graves and structural elements or other features. Floors or distinguishable horizons sealing graves or groups of graves were rare, and the perennial problem of identifying grave cuts in homogenous and regularly redistributed grave earths was encountered throughout the excavation (Rodwell 1989, 146–7; 169–70: Kjolbe-Biddle 1975, 89–92). This was less of a problem with the post-medieval and later vaults and brick-lined graves, where the very solidity of the mortuary structure produced clear definition (though even here the earth cuts for the structures were not always apparent). Typically, however, earlier graves could only be defined at all adequately when the skeleton itself was exposed.

Definition of the burial sequence and its phasing therefore had to be achieved by analysis of coffin typology and stratigraphy. Grave fills also appeared to differ through time and area between fairly clean sandy fills in earlier, extramural graves, and later or intramural ones containing mortar and building material fragments. Stratigraphic matrices were drafted on-site during the excavations, but these matrices were not the place for interpretative phasing. This work was undertaken at a second level of data capture, using typologies and fill types, again largely on-site. Fortunately it was possible to phase virtually all graves in this way, although an element of doubt was inevitable in some cases where very late graves or other features directly overlay a grave which appeared to be typologically early (ie medieval) but which had no other stratigraphic relationship other than with the natural subsoil. The phased groups then had to be placed in a chronological system of periods related to the structural sequence.

Among vault groups stratigraphic rules appeared to be inverted, as was the case at Christ Church, Spitalfields (Reeve & Adams 1993). The re-ordering of coffins within a vault, for instance, could easily lead to a coffin dated to, say, 1790, lying stratigraphically above one dated to 1800. Historical evidence suggests that sextons frequently commissioned the re-ordering of burials to create additional space for burials within crypts (Cox 1996a). As already mentioned the two larger burial vaults, located at the east end of the north and south aisles, were in fact totally re-arranged during the restoration work of 1877–8.

The majority of the 18th and 19th century burials were contained in elaborate and distinctive coffins, many with clear personal identifications in the form of coffin plates. These were identified and separated from the remaining burials. They were planned and it was found that there were very few cases where 18th century studded coffins cut others of the same type. Apart from those contained within vaults, the incidence of directly superimposed burials were few. Where these had occurred and the lower burial(s) remained largely undisturbed, or there was evidence for the presence of coffin wood separating the skeletal remains, a double or group grave was inferred.

Vaults and brick-lined graves proliferated throughout the country in the 18th and 19th centuries, and Sevenoaks was no exception. The Burial Boards Act prohibited intramural burial in the 1850s and the law was variously reinforced by pastoral measures. The vaults and brick lined graves of St Nicholas were permanently closed in 1878, by which time no fewer than 37 had been constructed.

Not all of the vaults were post-medieval. The vault located in front of the chancel may be identified with that of David Valtropkyn who was buried in 1474. It was subsequently cleared and re-used. During the 17th century large family vaults were built in both St Peter's chapel, belonging to the Lambard family, and the Chantry, built by Sir George Scott and later used by the Amherst family. These vaults continued in use until the 19th century.

A degree of data selection inevitably occurred during the excavations. The specific case of lead coffins has already been referred to. Some skeletal remains within vaults also had to be removed with a less than full *in situ* record due to pressures of time, the depth of vaults, and the restricted working space. It was not always possible to separate charnel from *in situ* skeletal remains in vaults for the same reasons. The watching briefs by definition involved a lower level of data recovery.

Some data selection was also involved during processing and analysis in post-excavation. Work has concentrated on the medieval and earlier post-medieval sequence, with less analysis of the later post-medieval and Victorian material as well as the later skeletal remains and finds.

The human remains

Methodology

The original specification required that the human remains (here defined as human skeletal material) be assessed and recorded on site by an osteologist while excavation proceeded. Only basic skeletal data was recorded at this stage, including preservation and completeness, age, sex, stature and potential for further detailed analysis. It was a further condition of the specification that the skeletal remains would receive long-term storage in an ossuary to be provided by the PCC and would therefore be available for detailed analysis in the future. The recording of metrical, non-metrical and dental data, and pathological condition was to be undertaken only following MAP 2-style assessment (English Heritage 1991) and the selection of individual skeletons or groups of skeletons. It was envisaged that where individuals of particular significance, either intrinsically or pathologically, required more detailed analysis, special provision would have to be made. A similar approach to recording of a large body of material was applied during the excavation of a Quaker cemetery at Kingston-upon-Thames (Bashford & Pollard, this volume). The major problem inherent in low resolution recording is in relation to the calculation of prevalence, for example, the incidence of pathology or non-metric traits (Waldron 1994). Charnel deposits were quantified by context and the minimum number of individuals estimated. In the initial stages of excavation the requirements for the basic recording of skeletal data were complied with. However, as the policy of the PCC on reburial and retention was revised during the excavation it was decided to increase the level of recording as far as possible to incorporate pathology, dental data, and selected metric measurements. The PCC decided that an ossuary for long-term storage of the skeletal remains would not be provided. The definition of long-term storage was to become a significant issue: the archaeologists believed it meant permanent storage while the PCC saw it as a short- to medium-term alternative to immediate reburial.

The post-medieval sample

This section deals with information recovered from all the burials from the period *c* 1550–1875.

Although it has been possible, to a degree, to refine the dating of many of the post-medieval burials to the extent where they can be placed in a hundred year period, the population here is discussed as a single uniform group which is summarized in Table 7.1. Biographic details for named individuals were recovered from coffin plates. A further 109 individuals were commemorated by memorials within the church but could not be related to an individual grave. Given that the majority of named individuals who were actually recovered were also commemorated by memorials it may be fair to assume that the majority of the 109 were definitely buried in the church. It is conceivable that a proportion of these would have been disturbed during restoration work in the 19th century.

A further 48 individuals who were buried in lead coffins were not osteologically examined because the retention of substantial amounts of body tissue necessitated their immediate reburial. These individuals were all identifiable and appear in the Appendix which details the names, age at death, and date of death as recovered from associated coffin plates. All of the skeletons which appear in Table 7.1 have been examined osteologically at the very least, using the low resolution method which is explained above. A further sixteen individuals from the vestry have not yet been examined and they do not appear in the table. There appears to be an under-representation of sub-adults and this may, in part, be related to preservation. However, as was demonstrated at Christ Church, Spitalfields (Molleson & Cox 1993), and is evident at St Bride's, Fleet Street (Scheuer, this volume) it is possible that the bias is an artefact of burial practice which skews the demographic representativeness of the sample. Neonates and infants in particular did not survive well and often only tooth buds were recovered. The bones of children were also poorly preserved, unlike those at Christ Church which survived better than those of older individuals (Molleson & Cox 1993). This applied to burials in wooden and lead coffins as much as to those in simple grave cuts. The high number of unsexed adults also requires qualification. At least 256 burials took place during the post-medieval period and a substantial number of these necessitated the construction of individual brick-lined graves and vaults. The construction of these features combined with the density of burial inevitably caused marked truncation of skeletons in virtually all periods. Therefore it was often the case that only the bones of the legs or feet survived. Further difficulties were caused by the extremely variable level of preservation of skeletal remains. It seems clear that burial in a wooden coffin actually accelerated the process of decay and disintegration whereas lead shells took a very long time to break down if deposited in the soil (Litten 1991, 86).

A proportion of skeletons survived only as crystalline debris (brushite) which had a white powdery appearance and this was also seen at Spitalfields (Molleson & Cox 1993, 10). In these cases the outline of the body was often clearly visible. A number of burials in lead coffins were so well preserved (hair, skin, internal organs etc) that they were not considered suitable for osteological examination. Hair survived in the form of eyebrows, facial, and body hair. Fragments of periosteum were also present on a number of dry bone specimens. Purple staining of bone, as at Spitalfields, was believed to be due to colonisation by species of the yeast group of fungi (op cit, 13). Examples of this were also quite common at St Nicholas and often seemed to occur in conjunction with the recrystallization of bone mineral (brushite) which caused the bone surface to break up. This seemed to affect teeth in particular.

Dental health and the evidence for dentistry

The dentition of approximately 58 post-medieval adult individuals has been recorded in detail. Caries rates, abscess rates, and the level of ante mortem tooth loss have been calculated for the purposes of this article and the results appear in Table 7.2.

Unfortunately it has not been possible at this stage to break the sample down into age groups. No less than 26 individuals had one or more dental cavities. The caries rate may actually have been much higher and is probably obscured by the level of ante mortem tooth loss. Forty-four individuals had lost one or more tooth in life. Four individuals had lost 30 or more of their teeth during life and dental extraction should be seen as a definite possibility. At Spitalfields it was argued that 'many of the teeth lost ante-mortem would have been extracted using either primitive forceps or the key or pelican. Both types of instrument were available' (Bell 1786, cited in Molleson & Cox 1993, 53). Only

Table 7.1: The post-medieval sample

	Males	Females	Adults of unknown sex	Sub-adults	Total
Wooden coffins/earth graves	38	30	59	10	137
Named individuals in lead coffins	11	22		3	36
Un-named individuals in lead coffins	6	9		4	19
Total	55	61	59	17	192

four individuals in the sample suffered from abscesses. One of these individuals, who had two abscesses, belonged to the named sample. His dentition is of considerable interest, exhibiting as it does the only clear evidence of dentistry, other than extractions. Three fillings were present. The occlusal surfaces of both maxillary second molars had been filled: one with a grey metallic material and the other with gold. A second gold filling was present in the labial surface of the left maxillary canine at the cement-enamel junction; these are discussed further in Appendix 7.2. Restorations of this type were also extremely rare at Christ Church, probably because they were very expensive. The single example from St Nicholas was the skull of Charles Whitworth, Earl, Viscount of Adbaston, Baron Adbaston in the county of Stafford, Lord of Newport Pratt in the county of Galway

in the peerage of Ireland, Knight Grand Cross of the Bath, Privy Counsellor, Lord Lieutenant of Ireland. He died in May 1825 aged 71 years (see Fig 7.3).

Two pairs of dentures (Fig 7.4) were recovered from a lead coffin within the central brick-built vault which was the burying place of the Nouaille family. The coffin contained the remains of Maria West who died in September 1785 aged 75 years. This individual was extremely well preserved and was not examined osteologically. It was therefore impossible to determine whether one or both pairs actually belonged to the individual with whom they were interred. The dentures were virtually identical to each other and also comparable to some of the examples from Christ Church, Spitalfields (Molleson & Cox 1993, 53–60). They were complete 'over-dentures', consisting of probable swaged gold-alloy bases, of low quality as some staining has occurred. The upper prosthesis consisted of a base of a size which suggests that it would have partially covered the hard palate. The teeth were entirely carved from porcelain (mesial and lateral incisors, canines, and first premolars). The second premolar and molar dentition were replaced by blocks of a brown material which was in part covered by a white concretion (possibly ivory). This material was

Table 7.2: Prevalence of dental pathology

Ante mortem tooth loss	Caries	Abscess
529/1394	113/803	5/1236
37.95%	14.08%	0.41%

Figure 7.3   Coffin of Charles Whitworth, Earl (photo: Oxford Archaeological Unit)

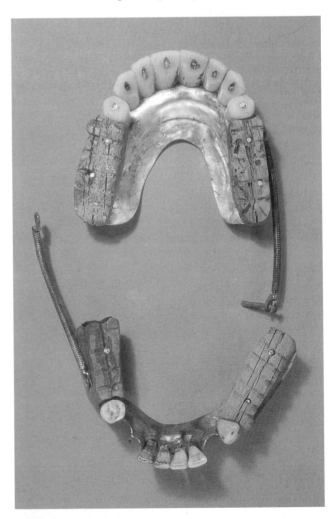

Figure 7.4   False teeth associated with the burial of Maria West (photo: Oxford Archaeological Unit)

decorated by a series of horizontal and vertical lines and crosses. In common with the porcelain teeth, the wooden blocks were fixed to the plate by gold pins (two for each block, whereas individual teeth had a pin each). A gold spring was attached to each side by means of a rotary pin which was fixed to the 'ivory' block. The porcelain teeth showed little sign of wear. The lower prosthesis had a smaller base which again appeared to have extended over the alveolus. The molar dentition was again represented by blocks of ivory. The anterior teeth in this instance were real. Mesial and lateral incisors and first premolars were present. It is not clear how these were fixed. The plate had been fashioned around the canines which were presumably present in the jaw when the denture was fitted. The second set varied only in the fact that the lower plate had mesial and lateral incisors, right first premolar, and left second premolar. The plate had been fashioned around both canines, and the lower left first premolar.

Stature

It has been possible to calculate the stature of 77 post-medieval individuals using the formulae of Trotter and Gleser (1952, reproduced in Brothwell 1981, 101). The stature of 34 adult males ranged from 1.62m to 1.83m with an average of 1.73m. The stature of 33 adult females ranged from 1.49m to 1.72m with an average of 1.61m. At Spitalfields the mean stature of the females varied, depending on the formula used, between 154.04 and 158.52cm and for males between 167.91 and 170.27cm (Molleson & Cox 1993, 24). Although the sample sizes were small, this suggests that the Sevenoaks sample were generally taller than those from London.

The named individuals

Biographical details of the named individuals whose coffins were identified appear in Appendix 7.1. Date of burial ranged from 1648 to 1854, and while the majority were adults aged between 19 and 102 years there were seven children, the youngest of which was Charlotte Anna Lambard aged 14 months. It is noteworthy that no less than 37 of the adults were aged upwards of 60 years when they died. Documentary evidence concerning a considerable number of the named individuals has been recovered and this has been largely due to the detailed research carried out by Richard Bailey for which the authors are most grateful. Only selected examples are referred to here.

Notable family groups were present and these included both the Amhersts and the Lambards. Famous members of the Amherst family included Jeffrey who was born in January 1717 and died in August 1797 aged 80 years. Lord Amherst was described thus on his coffin plate: 'Amherst Jeffrey, The Right Honourable, Lord Amherst, Night [sic] of the Order of the Bath, Baron of Holmesdale, Baron of Montreal, Field Marshal, Governor General of Canada, Commander in Chief of the British Forces in North America.' A portrait of Jeffrey Amherst was painted by Gainsborough and is part of the collection of the National Portrait Gallery in London. His son John, who died in February 1788 aged 39 years, was Admiral of the Blue Squadron of His Majesty's Fleet.

Famous Lambards include William who was the author of the first county history, A perambulation around Kent which was written in 1576, and although he was originally buried in Greenwich his remains were later exhumed for reburial in St Nicholas Church.

There are two Austens listed in the Appendix, Frances and Anne, who were husband and wife. 'Old Frances Austen' was the great uncle of the novelist Jane and we first hear of her visiting Kent in July 1788 when she made a visit to the Red House with her parents and sister (Smithers 1981, 27). Frances died aged 93 and there is a portrait of him in the Graves Art Gallery, Sheffield which is attributed to Ozias Humphreys although its date is unknown. Unfortunately the coffin in which Frances Austen had been buried was damaged and the surviving bones were much disturbed (see Fig 7.5). They were, however, identified as male and mild vertebral osteophytes were noted. His remains were deposited on top of the coffin of his wife whose remains were also in a very poor state of preservation. These remains were clearly those of a young female who was approximately 1.57m (5'1.5") tall. Two of her 24 teeth had gross carious lesions. Anne Austen was aged 29 years when she died in 1747.

Dame Margaret Boswell is described by Lansberry in his study of 17th century Sevenoaks widows as 'the only member of the gentry to appear in these wills' (1984, 285). She witnessed the will of one Parnell Hunt (K.A.O. PRS. W 8.108). A Lady Margaret Boswell is commemorated in a memorial inside the church which records that she was buried on the 31 August 1682 and was '20 years relict [widow] of Sir William Boswell, Ambassador at the Hague'. In her own will the heir to her land was her cousin, William Bosville, but she gave the largest legacies to six women and left the remainder of her personal estate to Elizabeth and Ann Worsley (Lansberry 1985, 292; PRO Prob. 11.370 f.94).

On-going analysis and future potential

At the time of writing it has not been possible to examine all of the individuals in detail, although it is hoped that further work may be undertaken in the future. However, it is far from clear how much time remains available as the PCC are now extremely anxious to rebury all of the skeletal remains regardless of the level of analysis that has been carried out. The potential, particularly for named individuals, has been clearly demonstrated in the case of Christ Church, Spitalfields (Molleson & Cox 1993; Cox 1996a).

The analysis of the textiles will be carried out at Bradford University under the guidance of Rob Janaway who analysed the assemblage from Christ Church (Janaway 1993, 92–119). Some detail of this analysis is discussed by Janaway (this volume). Detailed analysis on a selection of the coffin plates has been undertaken at Bradford University and a study of the survival and decomposition of human hair from a variety of sites, including St Nicholas, is in progress and is being carried out by Andrew Wilson, also of Bradford University.

The assemblage of coffin furniture from St Nicholas is undoubtedly one of the most important so far recovered, and if it does not challenge the Christ Church Spitalfields material in sheer quantity (Reeve & Adams 1993, 83–91, 144–7, and microfiche M2 and M3) it does so in quality and diversity: many designs and typological groups are present at St Nicholas but not at Spitalfields. Therefore as much work as possible has been done on this material within the overall project constraints of time and resources. A basic catalogue of the material has been produced and where possible

Figure 7.5   Coffin plate of Frances Austen (photo: Oxford Archaeological Unit)

examples have been cross-referenced to types recovered from Spitalfields. It is hoped that it will be possible to produce illustrations of the types not known elsewhere in order that a detailed country-wide corpus might be produced, albeit unpublished. This work is in part being made possible with the kind assistance of Jez Reeve who has provided the authors with a copy of the detailed archive drawings from Christ Church which were produced for inclusion on microfiche in the existing publication (Reeve & Adams 1993, microfiche M2 and M3).

Certain aspects of burial ritual are worthy of further analysis. A number of wooden coffins at St Nicholas were found to contain traces of flower petals and these appeared to survive both above and below the human remains. Examples were found in both 18th and 19th century graves. At present little discussion of this aspect of Christian burial ritual is to be found in the archaeological literature, though it is touched upon in this volume by Cox. Their study may indicate the season in which burial took place, and their obvious presence in predominantly later burials prompts the consideration that evidence for similar inclusions may be present in less visible form within earlier graves. Floral tributes in the form of wreaths were also recovered and in one example bunches of lavender and rosemary had been deposited within a coffin. It contained the burial of Peter Nouaille, a Huguenot, who died in August 1845 aged 79 years.

Conclusions

The full potential of the post-medieval material from St Nicholas is unlikely ever to be fully realised, for a number of reasons. The absence of a research agenda specific to post-medieval burial was crucial during the production of the archaeological brief. Some still argue that such material is clearly not archaeological and therefore does not merit archaeological attention. This was certainly the consensus view prior to the excavation at St Nicholas. However, even if it is retrospectively argued that the material is worthy of some level of analysis then we are faced with different problems. Should the developer be expected to pay for such analysis, and, indeed, if this is so should they then foot the bill for long-term storage of the archive in a museum? The production of a corpus of material, as described above in relation to coffin furniture, would go some way towards alleviating this problem. The issue of the human remains is much more problematic. We would not necessarily advocate the permanent storage of post-medieval burial groups, particularly in view of the related ethical and moral issues. It is generally the presumption of the church that such remains will be reburied, and generally as quickly as possible. It is the view of the authors that this is entirely understandable in the case of recent remains which may well have surviving descendants.

We are fortunate that the excavations at sites such as Spitalfields, St Bride's and St Barnabas (see Scheuer, this volume; and Black & Scheuer, unpublished), St Nicholas, and, most recently, Kingston-upon-Thames have stimulated much thought-provoking debate (eg Cox 1996b; Reeve & Cox forthcoming; Downes & Pollard forthcoming; Reeve, pers comm) and it is now imperative that archaeologists decide just how such material should be approached. Issues such as ethics, health and safety both psychological (see Thompson, this volume) and physical (see Kneller and Young, this volume), the recommended level of involvement, and the formulation of realistic research questions all need to be urgently addressed.

The archive

The archive from this project contains all the primary data (the Site Archive) and post-excavation analyses (the Research Archive: for definitions see English Heritage 1991), arranged according to guidelines issued by the Royal Commission on the Historical Monuments of England and OAU's standard Archive Department procedures. At the time of writing (May 1996) the archive was at the Oxford offices of OAU pending arrangements for transfer to a museum in Kent. It is to be hoped that once the debate over funding, level of analysis, and the reburial of skeletal remains is resolved that a full publication will follow.

Acknowledgements

The authors would like to thank Dr Susan Young for her help and advice, Annemarie Cromarty who worked on the dating of the burials, and Richard Bailey who has been studying the documentary sources. The project team was augmented by volunteer assistants, with a principal team of six and others participating. Backfill deposits of vaults and brick-lined graves were removed by contractors, for which OAU is most grateful. Research aims were set out in a document produced by David Miles, Director of OAU, and approved by Dr John Williams of Kent County Council. The dental study was possible courtesy of OAU and undertaken by the Investigative Support Unit, School of Conservation Sciences, Bournemouth University. We are confident that as a man of his time, Earl Whitworth would have supported the notion that his remains would enhance future scientific enquiry.

Appendix 7.1

Alphabetical list of named individuals identified

Name	Age at death	Year of death	Name	Age at death	Year of death
Alexander, Elizabeth		1838	Lambard, Thomas		
Amherst, Elizabeth		1752	MacDonald, Louisa	19	1833
Amherst, Elizabeth	32	1776	*Malloy, Mary Ann	95	1796
*Amherst, Elizabeth		1830	McMurdo, Jane B	42	1813
Amherst, Jeffrey	73	1750	Mellish, Elizabeth	75	1807
Amherst, Jeffrey	80	1797	*Nash, Susannah	83	1814
Amherst, John	39	1788	Nicoll, Elizabeth	81	1700
*Amherst, Margaret	17	1735	*Nouaille, Anne	74	1848
*Amherst, William	49	1781	Nouaille, Milo Philipe		
*Austen, Anne	29	1747	Nouaille, Peter	79	1845
*Austen, Frances	92	1791	*Petley, Catherine Ellen	2 years 6 months	1852
Bosville, James	72	1740			
Bosville, Jane	55	1728	Petley, Charles	50	1765
Boswell, Margaret		1682	*Petley, Charles Carter	50	1830
Bulkeley, Harriet	77	1848	*Petley, Elizabeth	91	1822
Burton, Henrietta	66	1831	*Petley, Ellen	57	1839
*Cranston, Anne	73	1780	Petley, Jane	49	1698
*Curteis, Thomas	69	1775	*Petley, John	34	1792
*Davis, Margaret	89	1777	*Petley, Judith	77	1834
Dodgin, Susanna Louisa	27	1825	Petley, Twisden	12	1773
Dummelow, Selina	39	1854	Plaistow, Mary	102	1844
*Everest, Ester	57	1778	*Randolph, Jane	81	1836
*Farnaby, Francis	19	1720	*Roussigny, Alice	75	1765
Farnaby, Mary		1765	*Saint John, Sarah	95	1755
Fermor, Henry	29	1780	Scott, George		1648
Fermor, John	54	1773	*Scott, Elizabeth		1672
*Fermor, John William	2	1790	Spencer, Harry Foche	72	1817
Fermor, John Shurley		1791	Spencer Crowther, James	8	1787
Gardiner, William	80	1793	Spencer Crowther, Thomas		1790
Hardy, Edward		1797	Streatfield, Henry	37	1817
Hilton, William Henry	40	1831	Streatfield, Jane Ann	85	1834
Hughes, Harriet	90	1837	*Streatfield, Martha		1763
Hughes, Louisa Bethia	55	1839	Streatfield, Sarah	44	1767
*Lambard, Aurea		1828	Streatfield, Thomas	84	1802
Lambard, Charles		1828	West, Maria	75	1851
*Lambard, Charlotte Anna	14 months	1839	*Weston, Mary	75	1785
*Lambard, Grace	55	1778	Whitmore, Jane		1793
Lambard, Jane	82	1780	*Whitworth, Charles	71	1825
*Lambard, Mary	80	1734	Willard, Charles		
*Lambard, Multon	78	1826	Francis Frederick	34	1841
*Lambard, Sophia		1787	Willard, Charles	81	1843
*Lambard, Thomas	64	1770	Wrainch, Hannah Maria Catlyn	43	1793
*Lambard, Thomas	52	1811			

* These individuals were examined osteologically
Gaps in the appendix indicate coffin plates whose inscriptions could not be fully deciphered.

Appendix 7.2 *Margaret Cox, Paul Kneller, and Robert Haslam*

Dental restorations

Introduction

Two of the three dental restorations observed in the maxilla of Earl Whitworth (discussed above) who died in May 1825 aged 71 years are shown in Figure 7.6. As stated above, such restorations are extremely rare in the archaeological literature for this period (see Whittaker in Molleson & Cox 1993, 49–63), reflecting the expensive nature of such treatment and the small number of either controlled exhumations or archaeological excavations where such evidence is likely to be recovered. The details of these restorations and the methods employed will be described in full elsewhere (Cox, Kneller, Haslam, and Boyle in preparation); what follows are preliminary results.

A comprehensive history of dentistry in England can be found in Bennion (1986) and the historical background that follows is derived from that work. As late as the 18th century, carious teeth were still attributed by many to the toothworm, at which time the work of dentists such as Garengeot (1688–1759 and Hunter (1728–93) began to cast doubt upon the creature's existence. Whatever the agent of decay, drills for removing carious material from teeth are described by Galen (AD 130–200) and again from the 16th century. By the late 18th century many different designs existed, some of which were more effective than others. Decayed tooth was also removed by files, chisels, spoons, or knives (Bennion 1986, 65–72). By the mid 19th century, some practitioners were combining the two using the drill first. While the design history of such instruments is known, the extent and chronology of their use is not. Contemporaneously, a wide range of filling materials were in use ranging from wax, resin, lead, gold, and tin. Dental compounds were introduced in the 19th century (op cit, 75–80).

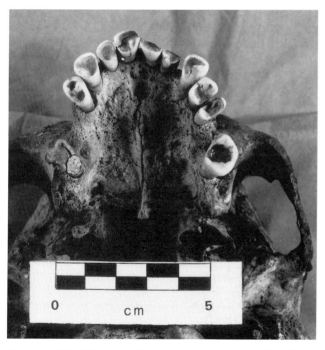

Figure 7.6 The maxillary dentition of Earl Whitworth, showing the tin filling in his upper left second molar and the gold filling in his upper right second molar. Note also the crack which probably occurred as a result of the excavation of the carious tooth prior to restoration (photo: Bournemouth University)

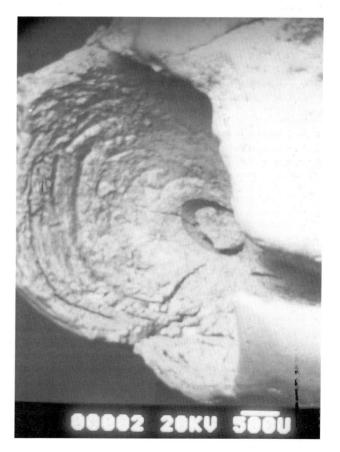

Figure 7.7 SEM micrograph of the upper right second molar, of Earl Whitworth, prior to insertion of the gold filling. (The scale bar is 500 microns.) Note the circular lesions created by the excavation of carious material using a blunt-edged instrument (Bournemouth University)

97

Figure 7.8a   *Figure 7.8b*

SEM micrographs illustrating the gold foil used for the filling. (The scale bars represent 500 microns) (a) shows the filling as compacted into the tooth, note also the crushing and deformation on the occlusal surface; (b) reveals a close-up of the folded foil (Bournemouth University)

Earl Whitworth's remains include three dental restorations of differing materials and sites providing an opportunity to examine a range of dental techniques and materials that must have been in use at some time between *c* 1775 and 1825.

Removal of carious tissue

The gold restoration from the upper right second molar conveniently fell out of the tooth during examination. This provided an opportunity to examine the tooth, using scanning electron microscopy (SEM), in order to assess the method of excavation. This appears to have been achieved using two different implements to excavate the carious tissue. There are roughly parallel U-shaped marks running around the tooth (Fig 7.7), denoting a blunt edged instrument, with other vertical marks running down into the cavity. The latter are V-shaped in profile, suggesting the use of a sharp and pointed tool. There is no evidence of the uniform marks one might expect to be associated with a drill.

It is interesting to note that this tooth appears to have split, possibly as a result of the excavation (Figs 7.6 and 7.7). The split extends from the centre of the excavated area in a labial direction stopping

short of the enamel. An alternative explanation is that the split could have occurred as a result of the dental practitioner using an alloy of mercury and silver for the filling. This medium was known to expand, resulting in teeth splitting (op cit, 77). If this was the case it is possible that the gold filling may have been a replacement.

Filling materials

The filling materials used in the occlusal surface of the upper right second molar and the anterior enamel/cementum junction of the lower left canine were examined using an energy dispersive X-ray detector fitted to the SEM. As expected, these comprise high carat gold foil (see Figs 7.8 and 7.9 which show the folds of the foil). This was usually rolled into cylinders before being pushed into the cavity (*ibid*), however, the micrographs give no indication that this was undertaken in either case. The filling in the molar appears to have been applied in one go, while two applications appear to have been used for the canine (examined after being sectioned and polished; Figs 7.9 and 7.10), the first being much less firmly compressed than the latter. This filling

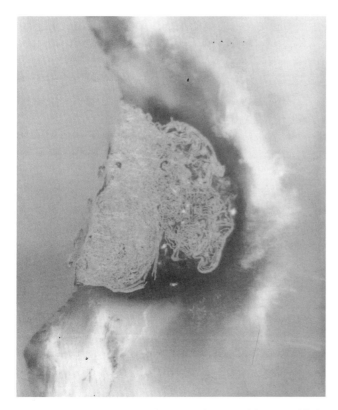

Figure 7.9 A section of Earl Whitworth's upper left canine showing the filling at the enamel cementum junction. Taken using a low powered microscope at ×10 magnification, it shows that the gold foil filling has been applied in two stages and that the first application was not well fitted (Bournemouth University)

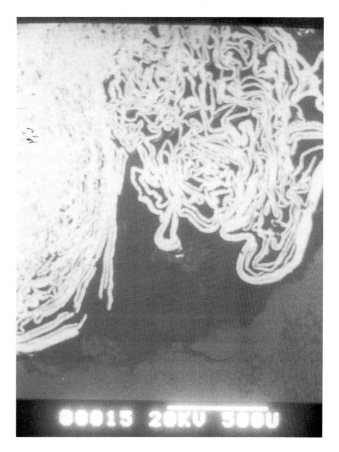

Figure 7.10   A SEM micrograph showing detail of the canine filling and the different levels of compaction of the gold foil. (Scale is indicated by the 500 microns scale bar) (Bournemouth University)

does not appear to fit very well although there is no evidence that carious decay continued after the restoration. Gold had been in use as a filling material since at least 1516, though only rarely, and was evident in two individuals at Christ Church, Spitalfields interred prior to 1809 (Whittaker in Molleson & Cox 1993).

The third filling, in the occlusal surface of the upper left second molar, was also analysed initially by an energy dispersive X-ray detector fitted to the SEM. Further analysis was undertaken using atomic absorption spectrometry. Both sets of results show that the filling material was tin with no deliberately added elements. Little is published about the use of tin as a filling material but it is known that in 1848 an alloy of pure tin was mixed with cadmium, apparently designed to control the

shrinkage believed to occur when using tin alone (Bennion 1986, 77). Clearly the Sevenoaks example predates this. However, no shrinkage had occurred to this rather shallow filling which was securely fitted into the tooth.

Conclusion

This small study on the dental restoration undertaken during the lifetime of Earl Whitworth demonstrates the immense importance and scientific and historical potential of the skeletal remains from St Nicholas, Sevenoaks. It is to be hoped that this potential will be realised and that the collection will not be reinterred prior to an appropriate programme of scientific and historical research.

8 Age at death and cause of death of the people buried in St Bride's Church, Fleet Street, London

Louise Scheuer

Introduction

The lead coffin burials from St Bride's Church, Fleet Street have been known to skeletal biologists for over 40 years. The present collection consists of over 200 skeletons of known sex and age at death. There has been much basic work on the skeletal reconstruction of the sample. Levels of sexual dimorphism were studied using the scapula (Bainbridge & Genoves 1956), the long bones (Steel 1963), and the innominate (Genoves 1956; Day & Pitcher-Wilmott 1975; MacLaughlin & Bruce 1986). Berry (1975) examined the incidence of non-metric skeletal variants in the skull and Miles (1958, 1963) studied the assessment of age from the dentition. Examination of the pathology of the vertebral column included a study of the incidence of Schmorl's nodes by Saluja *et al* (1986) and of spina bifida occulta by Saluja (1988). Current techniques for sex determination and estimation of age at death were tested by MacLaughlin (1987). The juvenile skeletons were used by Bowman *et al* (1992a) to compare biological and chronological age and Huda & Bowman (1994, 1995) used perikymata counts to identify ten comingled young juveniles. However, apart from Harvey (1968) and Forbes (1972), little work has been done on the historical and social background of the people buried at St Bride's. The present study used contemporary documentary data to examine age at death, interval between death and burial, occupation, and cause of death in an attempt to discover how representative the present skeletal collection is of the population of which the individuals formed a part. The problems encountered in interpretation of the documentary data are discussed.

Historical background

The site where St Bride's Church now stands has a traceable history from Roman times and a succession of churches has stood there, the first probably built during the 7th century (Morgan 1973). An historical exhibition in the crypt has recently been updated. Designed by Sir Christopher Wren, the seventh church was opened in 1675 and replaced the previous one destroyed in the Fire of London. Except for the steeple, it too was destroyed in an air-raid on the night of 29 December 1940. The present church is a rebuilt copy of Wren's church and was rededicated in 1957. A mandatory architectural survey before its construction involved an excavation of the crypts beneath the church. For almost two centuries the parish had used these crypts for burials, but they were sealed up in the early 1850s in an attempt to allay public fear of infection from the dead. For further details see Milne (1997).

The opening of the crypts revealed a large quantity of human remains including a medieval charnel house and nearly 300 burials from the 18th and 19th centuries. Many of the latter were typical triple case lead coffins with an inner and an outer wooden layer enclosing a middle lead shell (Litten 1991). A joint excavation team from the Museum of London, the Natural History Museum, and the University of Cambridge were responsible for preserving the skeletons for scientific study, but unfortunately proper archaeological records of the excavations have not been preserved. For unknown reasons certain coffins were put aside. The damaged coffin of Samuel Richardson has only recently been excavated (Scheuer & Bowman 1994), and there are still some undamaged coffins that remain unopened.

A survey of the burial registers from the period, and of the church records from the 1950s, reveals that the present collection consists of less than half of the individuals interred in the crypt. The fate of the remaining burials is not known in detail. Eight cases of adipocere formation and other examples of incomplete skeletonization were reburied (Redpath 1955). Many individuals were buried in wooden coffins and their remains were either irreparably damaged, or had coffin plates that were illegible or missing. The preserved skeletal remains were originally housed in metal munitions boxes but were later transferred to plastic boxes. In the 1960s an illustrated catalogue was prepared which included skeletal details, some pathologies, and occasional background historical information (Powers unpubl). Gradually however, the condition of the bones started to deteriorate partly due to comingling after prolonged use, and partly to damage caused by the heavy coffin plates lying in the same boxes. From 1990 to 1995 a programme of conservation and re-evaluation of the collection was carried out, funded by the Leverhulme Trust.

Skeletal material

The collection is now stored in its own bone room in the crypt. It consists of the remains of 227 persons who were interred in coffins which bore plates detailing the name, and therefore sex, age at death, and date of death of each individual. Each skeleton is contained in purpose-built cranial and post-cranial boxes and the associated coffin plates are preserved separately. A report and microfiche has been prepared detailing the known historical data and the skeletal remains of each individual (Scheuer & Black 1995). The dates of birth ranged from 1676 to 1840 and dates of death from 1740 to 1852 (Fig 8.1). Most individuals were born between 1750 and 1789 and the majority of the burials took place between 1810 and 1849. The adults greatly outnumbered the juveniles, who comprised only 6.6% of the total (Table 8.1), a result similar to that found in Christ Church, Spitalfields (Molleson & Cox 1993). The majority of the bones are well preserved but a few are poor and fragmentary.

Documentary sources

The coffin plate was always the primary source of documentation employed and an example is shown in Figure 8.2. Additional information was available from parish registers, many of which are preserved in Guildhall Library in the City of London. They contain hand-written records of baptisms, marriages, and burials conducted at the City churches (Fig 8.3). For some of the period there is also information concerning occupation, abode, and other details. During the late 18th century John Pridden, bookseller, was churchwarden at St Bride's, and as well as keeping a meticulous record in the church registers, he also gave details at the end of each year of interesting events concerning the church and the neighbourhood around St Bride's. In 1787 there is a graphic description of a fire in the house of Mr Warboys, silversmith, of 96 Fleet Street, whose occupant perished while the servant escaped the flames by climbing across the roofs of nearby houses. A particularly hard winter in 1788 necessitated 'two special warming machines, called buzaglas' being placed in the church. Pridden died at the age of 80 and was himself interred in the crypt in 1807.

The parish registers are available on microfilm on application to the Mormon Church in Salt Lake City and the main facts have been collated to contribute to the International Genealogical Index

Table 8.1: Numbers of adults and juveniles in the St Bride's documented collection, 1740–1852

	Number	Range of age at death
Juveniles <19yrs		
Males	12	1 day – 17 years
Females	3	3 yrs. 4 mths – 18 years
Total	15 (6.6% of total)	
Adults		
Males	109	20 years – 88 years
Females	103	19 years – 91 years
Total	212 (93.4% of total)	

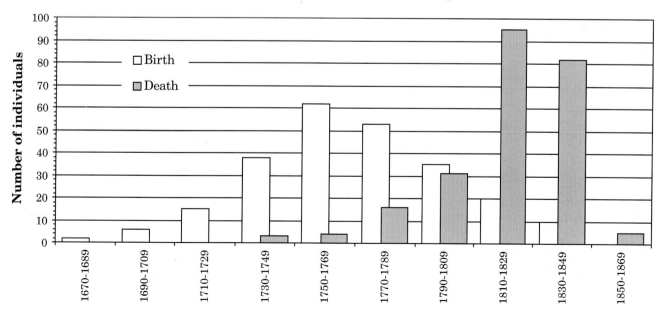

Dates of birth and death sample

Figure 8.1   Dates of birth and death of the St Bride's documented collection

(IGI) which is available on microfiche at Guildhall Library.

After 1837 it became a legal requirement in the United Kingdom to register births, marriages, and deaths, and copies of these entries may be viewed at

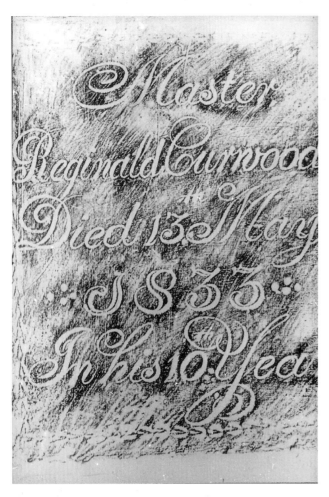

Figure 8.2   Rubbing from a lead coffin plate: 'Master Reginald Curwood, Died 13th May, 1833, In his 10th Year' (photo: L Scheuer)

the Office of National Statistics at Myddleton St, Islington, London EC1. Death certificates were obtained for the last 13% of the St Bride's burials and these give the date and place of death, sex, age at death and cause of death, the latter sometimes certified by a doctor.

For a few individuals a copy of the last will and testament was examined in the Probate Division of the Public Record Office in Chancery Lane and, for two unusual cases, reports in newspapers of the time were read at the British Newpaper Library in Colindale, north London. The most famous person whose remains lie in the collection is Samuel Richardson (Fig 8.4), the author and printer, about whom there is a great deal of primary documentary evidence. The bulk of his letters remain unpublished in the Victoria and Albert Museum and 82 letters from Dr George Cheyne, his physician until 1743, were examined in Edinburgh University Library (Laing Manuscript). Several portraits exist, including two by Joseph Highmore, which hang in the National Portrait Gallery and Stationers' Hall. His will is preserved in the Public Record Office.

Age at death

The parish registers for St Bride's Church for the whole period of the skeletal collection are incomplete, but a particularly good record exists for a restricted period from 1820 until 1849. The name, age at death, abode, date of burial, place of burial, and cause of death were given for 99% of all the individuals who were buried in the parish. It therefore provides mortality information for this populous inner London parish in the first half of the 19th century (Forbes 1972).

Figure 8.5 shows the percentage distribution of age at death for the whole of the period of the

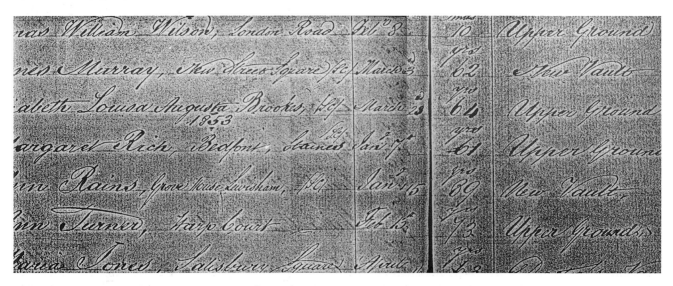

Figure 8.3   Facing pages of part of St Bride's burial register. It shows the entry for Margaret Rich as buried in the Upper Ground cemetery and whose coffin was actually interred in the crypt (photo: L Scheuer)

Figure 8.4 Portrait of Samuel Richardson, dated 1747, by Joseph Highmore which hangs in Stationers' Hall. The companion portrait of Elizabeth Leake, his second wife, was destroyed when the Hall was damaged in the same air-raid that demolished St Bride's (by kind permission of the Worshipful Company of Stationers and Newspaper Makers)

the skeletal collection, all those documented as having been interred in the crypt, and those individuals buried in the two outside cemeteries (Fig 8.6). The aim of examining the three different groups was to see how accurately the age at death profile of the present skeletal collection represented the population of which it formed a part. Firstly, was the collection representative of the total crypt population of which it formed less than half (42%) and secondly, how representative was it of the general population in St Bride's parish? The answer to this has important implications when making assumptions about whole populations from the excavation of partial crypt or cemetery burials where there are no documentary numerical data.

The major differences between the three profiles are in the numbers of child deaths below the age of five years and the peak of adult age at death. The 10% of child burials in the skeletal collection is less than half of that in the crypt group, and less than a third of that in the outside cemeteries. The peak of adult deaths of both the collection and crypt groups lie in the 60–69 years group, whereas in the cemetery population, so many children and young adults died early that there were fewer people surviving into old age. This is reflected in the almost flat part of the cemetery profile from 39 to 79 years. It is clear that the present skeletal collection is certainly not representative of the population of St Bride's parish as a whole although it has more in common with the crypt population, but even here there are far fewer child burials. The differences between the total crypt numbers and those of the cemetery are more striking, with the latter containing over 40% of persons under 20 years of age as against 28% in the crypt.

The reasons for the differences are not immediately obvious. The number of child burials is not consistent with the expected mortality rates for the time (Landers 1993). If the collection were used as a guide the number of children dying under five years of age would be underestimated by half to two-thirds. This discrepancy could be due to either a lower rate of child mortality in the crypt group, or that the crypt population buried their children elsewhere. Possible reasons for this are discussed by Cox (1996a) where the age at death profile for the Spitalfields' crypt burials is similar to the one at St Bride's.

The people who were interred in the crypt were almost certainly of a higher socio-economic status than those buried in the cemetery and this is reflected in the type of burial. Funeral expenses for a lead coffin burial in the crypt would have cost considerably more than a wooden coffin burial more commonly found in an outside cemetery (Litten 1991). The nutrition of the crypt population individuals would have been better and they would also have lived in less crowded surroundings than the poorer section of the community. These conditions would, in some measure, have mitigated against the higher mortality of the cemetery group.

collection and also for that between 1820 and 1849. As the general shape of the two age profiles was similar, the latter restricted time period was chosen for further analysis. Four thousand five hundred and twenty entries were transcribed and classified according to place of burial and cause of death. Four thousand two hundred and eight persons, 93% of the total burials for the period, were buried in the outside cemeteries. The Upper Ground cemetery was the churchyard immediately surrounding St Bride's and the Lower Ground Cemetery, recently excavated (Miles, pers comm), was in Farringdon Street. (The Upper Ground cemetery is commemorated in the name of the street parallel to the Thames on the south side of Blackfriars Bridge.) Three hundred and twelve persons (7% of the total) were interred in the crypt but the remains of only 131 of this group now remain in the collection (Table 8.2). An age at death profile was drawn for three groups of individuals: those comprising

In summary, the differences in age at death between the skeletal collection and the rest of the people interred in the crypt are due to factors that are primarily logistical and connected with unknown details of excavation. The much bigger differences between the crypt and cemetery popula-tion is more likely to be due to the gap in the socio-economic status of the two groups. However, the incompleteness of the crypt excavation could have caused as serious a bias in the results as that introduced by class difference between crypt and cemetery.

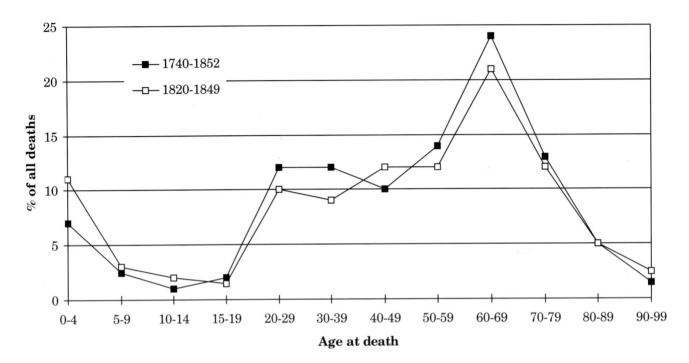

Figure 8.5 Age at death profiles for the skeletal collection for 1740–1852 and for 1820–49

Table 8.2: Numbers and percentages in different age groups for skeletal collection, total crypt population and St Bride's parish between 1820 and 1849

Age	Skeletal collection		Total crypt		Parish	
	N	%	N	%	N	%
0–4	14	10.7	63	20.2	1442	32.2
5–9	4	3.1	7	2.3	190	4.2
10–14	2	1.5	8	2.6	89	2.0
15–19	1	0.8	9	2.9	93	2.1
20–29	13	9.9	18	5.8	279	6.2
30–39	12	9.2	35	11.2	406	9.1
40–49	16	12.2	36	11.5	446	10.0
50–59	16	12.2	35	11.2	463	10.3
60–69	28	21.4	46	14.7	477	10.7
70–79	16	12.2	41	13.1	409	9.1
80–89	7	5.3	12	3.9	170	3.8
90+	2	1.5	2	0.6	13	0.3
	131	100.0	312	100.0	4477	100.0
Unknown					43	
Total	131		312		4520	

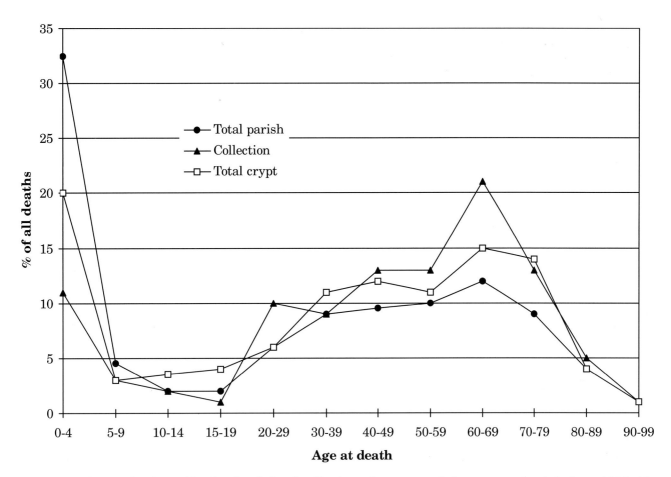

Figure 8.6   Age at death profiles for the skeletal collection, the crypt and the cemetery burials from 1820–49

Occupation

In theory, indications of the socio-economic status of the people buried in the crypt could be assessed by occupation. There were, however, problems with these data. Firstly, information was only available for 27% of the adult males, the women and children usually being described in relation to the husband or father (see Appendix). Secondly, interpretation of the actual occupation in this period is far from straightforward. For example, John L . . . is described at the time of his death as a coal merchant. As his obituary was published in the *Gentleman's Magazine* it is more likely that he was the owner of a considerable business rather than a manual worker. Also many people changed their occupation frequently. George R . . . is described as a confectioner on the baptismal certificate of his first child and as a venison dealer on that of his second. The occupations and trades of London in the 18th century are described by George (1965) and the problems and pitfalls of interpretation in the historical context are discussed by Cox (1995a).

National data on the distribution of occupation was not officially collected by the state until the census of 1841, which cuts out most of the St Bride's period. Before then, some incomplete data can be gleaned from church records, trade directories, and land tax returns but these are unlikely to throw light on the poorest section of the community. Lindert (1980) and Lindert & Williamson (1982, 1983) have surveyed some of this information but warn that there may be errors in their estimates.

Trying to relate occupation from the skeletal evidence is still more unreliable. There are difficulties both from the interpretation angle and also from the infrequency with which occupation manifests itself on the skeleton. Stirland (1991) reviewed the problems in attempting to diagnose occupation-related pathologies in the absence of documentary evidence. Clinical studies have emphasized that classification by work, rather than by actual task, has made correlation between lesions and occupation far from unequivocal. Although there is some information on occupation at St Bride's (see Appendix), the paucity of the data indicates that any conclusions drawn from it should be viewed with caution.

Interval between death and burial

For 221 (97%) of the individuals in the collection the time that elapsed between death and burial was calculated from the information on the coffin plate and in the burial registers. It varied from two to seventeen days (mean 7.2 ± 1.82 days). Because of a common fear at the time of being buried alive, some individuals requested in their wills that a minimum time should elapse between their death and funeral (Litten 1991). A fairly long interval would also have been necessary for the arrangements for the elaborate funerals of the time, rituals associated with mourning, and time taken for relatives to travel (Cecil 1991; Litten 1991; Llewellyn 1991).

Cause of death

Cause of death was available for 163 (69%) of individuals in the collection (Table 8.3). This information was available from the parish registers and, after 1837, from death certificates, although civil registration only covered the last 13% of the deaths. There are problems with both the interpretation and classification of these data. This is in part due to inaccuracies of notification of cause of death. The published London Bills of Mortality were compiled from information obtained by Searchers in each parish, lay people whose job it was to view the corpse and ascertain the cause of death, and age, of the deceased. Burial registers for the parish were also written up by lay people whose medical knowledge must have been, at best, sketchy. While some of the terms are unambiguous, many, for example 'spasms' and 'brain fever' are non-specific and difficult to interpret in relation to modern medical terminology. Positive correlation between this documentary evidence and examination of the skeletons is difficult as most of the diseases had caused the death of the individual before they manifested on the skeleton.

None of the previous attempts at a classification are entirely satisfactory. Forbes (1972), in a survey of the St Bride's burial registers, merely lists some of the more common causes of death and does not attempt any sort of classification. For example, 'decline', an almost certain synonym for pulmonary tuberculosis, is listed separately from consumption, chest diseases, and lung diseases. McKeown's (1976) classification of mortality from 1848 to 1854 is more useful although not strictly applicable to the St Bride's collection as it covers a time period after the beginning of civil registration in the second half of the 19th century. His two main categories were those diseases that were caused by, or independent of, micro-organisms. The first included airborne diseases, such as tuberculosis and influenza, and water- and food-borne diseases, such as cholera and typhoid. The second category included cardiovascular and other diseases, but the largest section was prematurity and other diseases of infancy. It is obvious from the burial records that many of the infant deaths were due to infectious diseases, such as measles and whooping cough, and so these overlap with the first category. Landers (1993), in an analysis of the high potential model of

metropolitan mortality between 1675 and 1824, classifies causes of death into consumption, fevers, diseases incidental to infancy, smallpox, and all others. This omits many of the adult causes of death that are recorded for St Bride's.

Because of these previous unsatisfactory classifications, cause of death in the St Bride's sample has been arbitrarily listed under headings in order of frequency (Tables 8.4 & 8.5). There are unavoidable inconsistencies in both lists and therefore some misclassifications. It is likely, for example, that at least some of the deaths in childbirth were from puerpural fever, although this term was not used as such until 1850 (Dudfield 1924). There is a separate category of unspecified 'fever' that could include these cases and also probably some of the infectious diseases which have not been mentioned by name.

Establishment of cause of death was also hampered by conflicts in the historical source material itself. Some of these were minor and unintentional such as a slight difference in date between the coffin plate and the burial register, possibly caused by an error in transcription, or by differences

Table 8.3: Numbers and percentages of stated cause of death 1820–49

	Total number	Number known	%
Juveniles	25	21	84
Adult males	109	77	71
Adult females	103	65	63
	237	163	

NB An extra 10 juveniles whose skeletons were comingled, but whose cause of death is known from burial registers have been added to the total of juveniles in Table 8.1.

Table 8.4: Number of total known causes of death in different categories

	Number	%
Respiratory diseases	52	32.0
Circulatory diseases	33	20.3
Old age	22	13.5
Fits	11	6.7
Gastro-intestinal disease	8	5.0
Childbirth/childbed	7	4.0
Cancer	6	3.7
Infectious disease	4	2.5
Miscellaneous	20	12.3
	163	100.0

between the cause of death as stated in the burial register and that stated on the death certificate. In the majority of cases these two documents were consistent, but examples of discrepancies are shown in Table 8.6. In the first case (a male of 26 years) the two terms agree. The second case (a female of 28 years) two different causes of death are given. This woman could well have had both tuberculosis and hepatitis, but the burial register probably reflects the report from the family to the church official of a more obvious cause of demise, whereas the death certificate would have been a medical opinion. The third case (a female of 43 years) is unusual in that the burial register states a more specific and recognizably modern medical term than does the death certificate.

Some of the conflicts in the source material were thought to be intentional 'mistakes' made for family or social reasons. One of these concerns a young man of 24 years who committed suicide in 1821 (Bowman, *et al* 1992b). The death, caused by a gunshot wound, was confirmed both from the skeletal evidence (Fig 8.7) and from a contemporary newspaper report of the inquest. The paraphrasing of the word suicide to 'suddenly found dead' in the church documents is curious and may reflect the ambiguous attitude of the ecclesiastical authorities towards suicide. (For further discussion of suicide during this period see Cox, this volume, and Mac-Donald and Murphy 1990.) Also the verdict of 'mental derangement' at the inquest would have facilitated the interment in consecrated ground rather than a burial in a segregated area that was more usual for admitted suicides. A similar case of burial of a suicide at Christ Church, Spitalfields in 1852 is discussed by Cox, *et al* (1990).

The last person to be interred in the crypt, whose skeletal remains and coffin plate are in the collection, was stated in the burial register to be buried in the Upper Ground cemetery (see Fig 8.3). This is probably another case of wilful misleading about the true facts. The interment possibly took place in January 1853 after the crypts should have been sealed, but she was probably placed there so that she could lie near her relatives even though this was then contrary to regulations.

In spite of these problems, a number of observations seem worthy of note. Nearly a third of the stated causes of death were from respiratory disease, of which the majority were from tuberculo-

Table 8.5: Causes of death in miscellaneous category

Fever	4
Inflammation	4
Accidents	3
Gout	2
Teething	2
Suicide	1
Stone	1
Erysipelas	1
*Complication of......	1
Suddenly by getting up in a hot night and refreshing himself at his chamber window	1

*illegible in register

Table 8.6: Cause of death from burial register and death certificates

Date of death	Sex	Age	Burial Reg.	Death Certificate
28/12/1838	M	26	Decline	Phthisis pulmonaris
12/01/1848	F	28	Decline	Jaundice from chronic hepatitis
27/04/1844	F	43	Influenza	Debility and nervous fever

Figure 8.7 Bullet exit wound in the left parietal bone (there is a metopic suture). Note typical bevelled edge and radiating fractures

108

sis. Less than 95% of the skeletons showed any signs of bone lesions even on the ribs. Manchester (1991) confirmed that the diagnostic criteria for tuberculosis in skeletal remains are inadequate as the disease is only diagnosable at an advanced stage of osseous development. Skeletal signs of tuberculosis have also been studied by Kelley & Micozzi (1984), Pfeiffer (1991), Manchester & Roberts (1987), and Roberts *et al* (1994).

The mean age for the considerable number of individuals for which the terms 'old age', 'aged', and 'decay' are given is probably similar to contemporary usage. The term 'cancer' was first used at St Bride's in 1806 and may mean specifically breast cancer. There is almost certainly a case of carcinoma of the prostate showing widespread lesions of the typical 'sunburst' type, especially in the vertebral column and innominate bone (Waldron 1997). This was presumably unrecognized and the cause of death is stated as 'of age' although the man was only 59 years of age when he died.

There is no recorded case of smallpox, and only one recorded case of typhus, as a cause of death in both the juvenile and adult groups. (The typhus death was a debtor in the Fleet prison.) This is difficult to reconcile with Landers' 1993 reports that smallpox and typhus were endemic in the population, at least up to 1824, and therefore a major contributor to mortality totals, especially in the juvenile age range.

The most satisfactory example of positive correlation between documentary and skeletal evidence was that of Samuel Richardson. Examination of his skeleton and descriptions from his doctor enabled a post mortem diagnosis of DISH (Diffuse Ideopathic Skeletal Hyperostosis) to be made, a disease only recognizable in life since the advent of radiology (Scheuer 1995). The descriptions of his movements by contemporaries led Brophy (1974) to believe that he suffered, for a number of years before his death, from Parkinson's disease. As this does not manifest on the skeleton it was not possible to confirm this suggestion. However, his height was confirmed by extrapolation from long bone lengths, and his neck pathology and dental condition were corroborated from his own descriptions in his letters (Scheuer & Bowman 1994).

Conclusions

This survey of the St Bride's skeletal collection has highlighted some of the problems associated with both using it as an example of a particular population, and of trying to correlate documentary and skeletal evidence. It is important to recognise that the skeletons that belong to a particular skeletal collection consist solely of the bones of that collection, and may well not be representative of either a smaller or larger group to which they appear to bear a relation. It is likely that the present skeletal

collection at St Bride's does not adequately represent even all the people interred in the crypt as it was biased at the time of excavation, and inadequate recording has made the factors responsible difficult to assess. Drawing conclusions about the health status of the general population of the parish from the limited set of data is likely to be flawed. It is obvious from the documentary evidence alone that there were greater numbers of children buried in the cemetery than in the crypt. An important factor influencing these numbers must have been the higher socio-economic status of the crypt population. However, there may be other reasons, as yet unknown, concerning the burial of the children that have contributed to this.

The present survey was hampered primarily by incomplete historical data on occupation, by difficulties of interpretation, and differences in the use and significance of terminology through time. Careful assessment of data is essential and any conclusions should be viewed with caution. Difficulties in interpretation of the data almost certainly added to the inaccuracies of classification of cause of death. One should also be aware that discrepancies in the historical record could be due to either unintentional errrors, or to wilful misleading for personal reasons. Positive correlation between documentary and skeletal evidence in individual cases is possible, but must be rare. This is because firstly relatively few diseases manifest on the skeleton and secondly, documentary evidence is usually limited to well-known individuals or to unusual cases. In the study of Samuel Richardson's skeleton, while it was not possible to confirm a suggestion of Parkinson's disease, much of the documentary evidence was confirmed and a possible cause for undiagnosed symptoms was suggested. The suicide case was unusual enough for there to have been a newspaper report and a will while the skeletal evidence was unequivocal.

In spite of these limitations the St Bride's skeletal collection represents a valuable source of documented material. Further work on occupation and cause of death by specialized medical historians could provide a clearer picture of the life histories of these people. Comparisons with other recent studies on populations of similar temporal affinities (Molleson & Cox 1993; Saunders, *et al* 1993) could make further observations more valuable. Finally, all methods of skeletal identification require rigorous standards of testing to ensure both their validity and reliability. Forensic osteologists always need a sample of known biological identity for the fair assessment of any new method of age at death estimation and sex determination.

Acknowledgements

Part of this work was given as a paper at the American Association of Physical Anthropologists meeting in Toronto in April 1993 and subsequently published as Chapter IV, pp 49–70, in *Grave Reflections – Portraying the Past through Cemetery Studies*, Shelley R Saunders & Ann Herring (eds) (1995), Toronto: Canadian Scholars' Press Inc. Thanks are due to Canon John Oates for continued access to the St Bride's skeletal remains, and to Margaret Cox for helpful discussion on the subject of 19th century suicide.

Appendix 8.1

St Bride's – male occupations
DOD – Date of Death
AAD – Age at Death
Included are the occupations of women as given on
death certificates (eg spinster, widow) or as wife/
widow of a named husband, and juveniles or women
where the occupation of the father or husband is
given.

No	Name	DOD	AAD	Occupation
3/44	Isambard Stephen Rains	1841	6 yrs	Son of Henry Rains, paper manufacturer
9/181	Mary Devey	1840	3 yrs 4 mths	Daughter of William Roger Devey, brass founder
14/10	Thomas Devey	1837	36 yrs	Clerk in the Council Office
15/12	Wm. Roger Devey	1842	34 yrs	Brass founder
20/177	Samuel Holden	1740	64 yrs	Governor of the Bank of England
21/73	George Fry White	1841	1 yr	Son of George White, upholsterer
45/84	Elizabeth Marriott Edkins	1851	51 yrs	Wife of Samuel Sabine Edkins, silversmith
47/96	Simeon Pope	1804	63 yrs	Lottery Office Keeper, Ludgate Hill
50/57	Wm. Charles Newcomb	1849	22 yrs	Land Surveyor
51/50	Henry Newcomb	1838	25 yrs	Gentleman
52/50	Louisa Ann Newcomb	1838	21 yrs	Spinster
58/172	John Blades	1829	77 yrs	Sheriff of London and Middlesex
61/43	Edwin Charlton	1848	24 yrs	Son of Edwin Charlton – Secretary
64/85	Edward Blakemore Searle	1830	41 yrs	Licensed victualler
69/69	Juliana Isherwood	1848	28 yrs	Widow of James Isherwood, upholsterer
71/21	Edward Rodwell	1823	68 yrs	Skinner
84/47	Henry Lee	1843	63 yrs	Gentleman
87/62	Alexander Macintosh	1841	23 yrs	Printer
90/23	William Lambert	1810	58 yrs	Gentleman
100/60	Robert Waithman	1835	46 yrs	Lord Major of London 1823–4
112/170	John Benjamin Varley	1836	65 yrs	Jeweller
117/191	Margaret Rich	1852	61 yrs	Wife of George Rich, venison dealer
118/34	William Rich	1811	56 yrs	? Pastry cook
120/40	Anne Sabine	1851	51 yrs	Spinster
127/28	John Lucas	1790	51 yrs	Coal merchant. Member Common Council of Ward of Farringdon Without
131/52	John Clare	1829	75 yrs	Vicar of St. Bride's 1802–29
136/17	William Skuse	1795	82 yrs	Shoemaker
138/56	Martin Cutler	1836	60 yrs	? Corn factor
139/70	Henry Frederick Cutler	1835	53 yrs	? Corn chandler/dealer
149/133	William Snoxell	1831	63 yrs	? Venetian blind maker
158/180	Henry Dunderdale	1840	70 yrs	Merchant

No	Name	DOD	AAD	Occupation
161/178	John Jolliffe	1771	75 yrs	Member of Parliament for Petersfield, Hampshire
166/149	Richard Tallamach	1816	72 yrs	? Solicitor
168/116	Letitia Phipps	1839	57 yrs	Single woman
169/116	Warner Phipps	1828	60 yrs	Secretary of Albion Fire and Life Assurance Co
182/159	Sarah Moxon Walker	1850	72 yrs	Widow of William Walker, Surgeon
188/184	Henry Eley	1794	63 yrs	Gold beater
191/156	Henry Dolamore	1838	42 yrs	Licensed victualler of the Cheshire Cheese, Wine Office Court, Fleet St
216/90	James Pemeller	1837	77 yrs	Packing case manufacturer
224/106	George John Tofft	1846	45 yrs	Jeweller
231/91	Sutton Simpson	1847	64 yrs	Isinglass merchant
233/64	Charles Joseph Eggleton	1837	53 yrs	Late Ward Beadle
235/83	Susannah Linton	1840	63 yrs	Widow
239/103	Zachary Edwards	1841	35 yrs	Gentleman
240/65	James Murray	1852	62 yrs	Baker
243/76	John Pridden	1807	80 yrs	Book seller. Church Warden at St Bride's
244/–	Samuel Richardson	1761	71 yrs	Novelist and printer. Master of Stationers' Company, 1754–5

9   Eschatology, burial practice and continuity: a retrospection from Christ Church, Spitalfields

Margaret Cox

Introduction

The excavation (1984–6) of the crypt beneath Christ Church, Spitalfields has possibly been written about more than any other funerary excavation of the later 20th century (for principal publications see Reeve and Adams 1993; Molleson and Cox 1993; Cox 1996a). However, since the completion of the Spitalfields Project (1988) a corpus of relevant literature has been published, much of which raises retrospective questions of this and other recently excavated post-medieval burial sites. As Kselman (1993, 3) observed 'Death and dying have become fashionable topics in recent years'.

The purpose of this chapter is not to rewrite the results of the Spitalfields Project but to extend previous discussion of the Spitalfields' evidence with contemporary accounts of formal and informal funerary practices. Further, it seeks to review some contemporary Anglican funerary rites in England in the context of a wider religious background, in particular those of contemporary Catholic France. As appropriate, these are examined briefly in order to consider the possibility that parallel pre-Reformation funerary rites might have survived subsequent doctrinal changes in England and that some pre-Christian or parallel sets of beliefs and practices might survive into the post-medieval period. However, the main aim of this chapter is to raise the awareness of funerary archaeologists to the possibilities that exist within post-medieval funerary archaeology, and that of earlier periods, and to suggest that research and sampling strategies need to reflect these more appropriately than they do at present.

Christ Church, Spitalfields

Christ Church, Spitalfields, designed by Nicholas Hawksmoor, was consecrated in 1729 and its vaults were utilized as a repository for approximately 1,000 interments between 1729 and 1857. This period saw the character of the burial group change from one that was largely of Huguenot descent and middle class, with livelihoods based upon the silk industry, to 'English' and upper working class. Christ Church was surrounded on the east and south sides by a graveyard in which approximately 67,000 individuals were buried. These were not excavated. As part of the refurbishment and restoration of this English Baroque church, it was decided to increase the space available for toilets and central heating plant by removing burials from the crypt. Consequently, between 1984–6, archaeological excavation took place recovering 987 burials, 387 of which had surviving associated coffin plates identifying them as named individuals. This was followed by a period of post-excavation analysis with the result that we were able to understand more about life, health, and death in 18th and 19th century Spitalfields as it affected a middle class Anglican sample, consider the associated funerary industry, and examine the reliability of a wide range of archaeological and osteological methodologies (see Reeve and Adams 1993; Molleson and Cox 1993; Cox 1996a for further details).

One of the important results of the Spitalfields project was that it provided a corpus of data about the era defined by Ariès (1981) as the transition from the period when the dying had been concerned with their fate in the afterlife, a concentration on the 'self' to a shift in the 19th century, when the focus moved to the 'other' and separation from loved ones. Ariès' inward focus has justifiably been criticized by numerous historians for neglecting the major ecclesiastical, political, and socio-economic changes within which this shift took place and it is this dynamic urbanizing and increasingly secular context which makes the subjects of death, burial, and eschatology in this period so interesting and, very often, so complex.

Funerals as composite rituals

For most people, and for many scholars, the value of the Spitalfields Project was not its immense contribution to science, but that in exploring this particular mortuary context it was possible to put people and humanity back into an increasingly sterile archaeology. This fact alone may account for its wide public appeal. To develop this theme further it is worth considering the following point (Richardson 1988, 17):

What was thought of as a decent funeral was a composite ritual. Other than the coffin and religious service, most of its components were provided within the community – without recourse to

112

undertaker or churchman. Apart from the burial service it was composed of secular rituals – which included physical attention to the corpse, watching, waking and viewing the corpse, some form of refreshment, and lay ceremonial surrounding the transport of the coffin to the grave.

The principle of shared lay-clerical participation in the care of the sick, the dying, and the dead was accepted by the Church and Christian Europe between the late 9th and the 11th centuries AD, particularly following the sacrament of St Denis (Paxton 1990, 197). This replaced a situation where the clergy appear to have been at the centre of rituals which reached into the lives of the laity (op cit, 126). Following the Reformation, and exacerbated by Renaissance philosophy and political revolution, this particular rite of passage (with baptism and marriage) witnessed 'diversity and dialogue within a continually contested conversation about religious and secular solemnities' (Cressy 1997, 379). Lay-clerical control of dying and burial continued throughout the post-medieval period when gradually (particularly over the last 100 years or so) a slow process of attrition has resulted from the commercialization and secularization of both death and disposal. (Discussion of this process is outside the scope of this chapter but see Cannadine 1981.)

Inhibitions and restricted vision

It is important to note that active control of, and participation in, death and burial by the lay community and (to a lesser extent) the clergy is not an experience familiar to many practising historians or archaeologists in England. La Rochefoucauld (Pleiade 1957, cited in McManners 1981a, 1) noted that 'One cannot look directly at the sun or at death'. McManners used this quotation in the context of scholars as external observers attempting to understand the secular and theological significance of death, and all that surrounds it, in the past. For many modern scholars, this situation is exacerbated further by the fact that as would-be observers we are generally so far removed from such ritual, both in practice and appreciation, that the surviving material culture of funerary rites becomes potentially indecipherable. Coupled with this, as a generation and culturally, we seem to be afflicted by an apparent inability to confront death in our own lives (Cox 1996b; Parker Pearson 1995, 17) or 'look directly at death' as either a biological or sociocultural phenomenon. If this complex position is accepted as reflecting the status quo, it is important that we should be aware of our shortcomings and limitations as they will inevitably impair and inhibit our ability to interpret the past.

It is salutary to consider that many of the aspects noted by Richardson (above) are generally invisible archaeologically, and in terms of the experience of the family, mourners, and community were of far greater spiritual and emotional significance than the material accoutrements of and within the coffin. The relationship between material culture from mortuary contexts and dynamic ritual and belief systems is difficult if not impossible to interpret with confidence (for example, the forces behind the shift from widespread cremation to inhumation in the Roman Empire during the 2nd century AD). Similarly, in a post-medieval context, eschatological issues may remain invisible unless particularly sought. When combined with the fact that those involved with the Spitalfields Project were products of an increasingly sceptical and secular society, and predominantly of a generation in which death is depersonalized, pre-packed, and commercialized, a society which has lost touch with both the folk and religious traditions of death, these factors inhibit our ability to bring the human experience of death and mourning back into archaeology.

There is also a tendency by archaeologists working in the later historic period to over-rely on contemporary religious doctrine and dogma as representing the belief systems determining the cultural behaviour represented by the archaeological record. It is frequently inferred, often by omission, that beliefs were commonly held through society. Clark (1982) examined the gap between orthodox and popular belief. He argued that official and folk theology exist in a state of conflict and symbiosis. Richardson observed that in post-Reformation England this can be seen in burial practices reflecting elements of Catholic doctrine officially expunged from the Anglican Church at the Reformation (1988, 7–8). This argument could be extended to suggest that some aspects of vernacular burial belief and practice may not reflect Christian doctrine but to be part of an older or parallel set of beliefs.

From death to burial

The rites of passage that accompany and effect a change in a person as they pass from one cosmic or social world to another (van Gennep 1960) are structured around preliminal, liminal, and postliminal states. Preparing the corpse for the grave in the post-medieval period (laying-out, 'streeking', or rendering last offices; Richardson 1988, 17) included washing the corpse, plugging orifices, closing the eyes and mouth, straightening the limbs, and dressing it in a winding sheet, shroud, or the individual's own clothes. In Christian texts, such practices can be traced back to Palestine, where the New Testament mentions the persistence of Jewish burial practice which includes washing and anointing the body and the use of herbs and linen cloth (Paxton 1990, 21).

What follows is a review of some aspects of continuity in death, mourning, burial, and eschatology both before and during the 18th and 19th centuries, aspects hinted at by the funerary archaeology of Christ Church, Spitalfields. This discussion is not all-encompassing as such areas as transporting coffins to burial grounds, funerary textiles, and the funeral itself are discussed elsewhere in this volume (see, for example, Litten and Janaway). Equally it goes into more depth for some aspects than others reflecting current professional pre-occupations and the author's particular research interests.

Lay and religious absolution

Many of the activities involved with pre- and post-burial belief and practice will leave no discernible archaeological trace. Some such customs evident in 18th century England were also extant in contemporary Catholic France. These included covering the pictures and bee-hives of the deceased with a black cloth, striking wine barrels in the cellar of the deceased three times, and stopping mill sails (if the deceased was a miller) in the position of the cross (McManners 1981a, 270). That such customs existed on both sides of the Channel at this period suggests that they were not local but part of a more widespread system of beliefs, one which defied or ran parallel to contemporary and local religious influence.

Washing the corpse

Washing the corpse was liturgically prescribed and incorporated into Christian ritual from at least the 6th century (op cit, 38), where it was conflated with forgiveness (Gelasian No 1627 op cit, 62). What is not generally recognized is that washing the dead may also have signified a lay-absolution (Richardson 1988, 19). During the post-medieval period laying-out and midwifery were usually undertaken by the same women in both England (ibid) and Catholic France (McManners 1981a & Kselman 1993). Kselman (1993, 51) notes that '... washing of the dead, in an age when bathing was uncommon, parallels the cleaning of the new-born and recalls the ritual of baptism, which also marks the individual for a new state of being'. It is also interesting to speculate whether washing the dead today, in our increasingly secular society, is carried out solely for reasons of hygiene. Research by Richardson in rural Suffolk in the early 1980s concluded that for those involved with this activity, washing the dead was '... resonant with meaning, the washing of the corpse involved [cleansing] not only the sweat of death, but the sins of the earthly life' (1988, 19).

Anointing the dead

Clearly, washing a corpse leaves no archaeological trace, unlike anointing the dead with oil, a custom which is believed to strengthen and separate the

individual from the community (Paxton 1990, 89). Anointing had spread to England from Ireland by the 8th century (op cit, 203) and evidence for its practice might be recoverable archaeologically where soft tissue and/or textiles survive. As the study of lipids in archaeology develops (Evershed 1991, 1992, 1995) this type of application becomes a possibility and the extent and chronology of anointing could be examined.

Funerary textiles

At Spitalfields, the generally well laid out skeletons attest to the practice of such offices as those described above (Janaway in Reeve and Adams 1993) and the survival of some textiles demonstrates the use of a wide range of funerary attire. These are discussed in depth in Janaway, this volume. Other accoutrements of the preparation process included ribbons or cloths which could be wrapped around the head going beneath the chin, hold arms to sides, or big toes together. At Spitalfields some of these were recovered. They were either brocaded or plain silk ribbons or torn-up strips of cloth (ibid).

In one case a pad which had been bound to the loins of an individual was recovered. This was presumed to have been used to absorb decomposition fluid expelled from the body and to have been forgotten by the person responsible for washing the corpse (ibid). An alternative explanation could be that the deceased may have been incontinent in life and that this pad was a residue of life's necessities. Alternatively, such a pad could have been used in life for protecting a pressure sore and retained (Susan Young, pers comm).

It was and is usual for orifices to be plugged rather than using pads to absorb the fluids upon release. Theoretically, where textiles survive, such plugs could also be recovered. However, if the significance of such textiles is not appreciated and considered as part of a textile sampling strategy they are unlikely to be recognized, recorded or recovered.

While the position of the body and surviving textiles and coins attest that bodies were prepared for the grave, what is not obviously apparent from the archaeology is the significance of these rituals. Laying-out was generally assumed to have taken place, as today, for reasons of hygiene and to facilitate viewing by mourners (Fig 9.1) but it seems likely that deep-rooted, cross-cultural, and generally more profound explanations are likely, ones possibly rooted in pre-Christian tradition.

The significance of linen

Research into the funerary textiles recovered from Christ Church placed the coffin furnishings and burial attire into a taphonomic, commercial,

Figure 9.1   Mourners paying their last respects: The Old Master, *by James Hayllar (1883) (copyright: City of Nottingham Museums, Castle Museum and Art Gallery)*

industrial, and legal context (Janaway in Reeve & Adams 1993, 93–119). At Christ Church, those textiles of known date that survive indicate that the 1666 (18 & 19 Car II c4) and 1680 Acts for Burial in Woollen (32 Car II c1), which banned the use of materials other than wool for burial attire and imposed a fine for non-compliance,[1] were complied with in respect of clothing specifically made for burials, despite the Acts being removed from the statute book in 1814 (54 Geo III c78). Ordinary clothes were sometimes worn (as recognised in the phraseology of the Acts) and in such cases, as would be expected, various fabrics, including linen, were used (op cit, 119) both before and after 1814. Some of these have survived as part of the archaeological record.

At Spitalfields, what was not considered, and is indeed difficult to deduce, is the possibility that the use of specific textiles might transcend the law and have either religious or folk significance. In the high medieval period and beyond, linen was the most popular material used for burial attire (whether winding sheet or shroud). While Litten argues that the use of linen was a matter of socio-economic status (1991, 72), and Gittings seems to suggest that it was a cloth of convenience (ie a sheet taken from the linen cupboard, 1984, 111), Richardson considers that it reflected both religious and subsequently popular belief that Christ was buried

in linen (as was popular during the early Roman Empire, Paxton 1990, 23). Consequently, folklorists believe that burial in linen was considered to be lucky (Richardson 1988, 21). Richardson argues that the Acts for Burial in Woollen, which incurred a fine of £5 if breached (Gittings 1984, 113), may have caused distress to the poor (Richardson 1988, 21). The socio-economic status of the majority of those interred at Christ Church (Molleson & Cox 1993: Cox 1996a) was such that this fine may not have been, generally, beyond their reach. Therefore it seems likely that if the surviving textiles were representative, and not an artefact of taphonomic processes, people would seem to have been more concerned with not paying a fine than being buried in linen.

The repeal of the Acts in 1814 was followed, at Spitalfields, by the use of different fabric types, but interestingly still excluded linen except as used for ordinary clothing (Janaway in Reeve and Adams 1993, 119). Janaway (pers comm) considers this to reflect that between the late 17th and early 19th centuries, a wider choice of textiles became available, reflecting both imperialism and industrialization. The evidence from Spitalfields seems to suggest that the use of linen had no apparent religious or popular significance either between 1729 and 1814, or thereafter. However, it should be remembered that Christ Church is a Protestant burial ground and that Catholics and/or non-conformists may have felt and acted differently. Stock (this volume) notes that following the first Woollen Act, and contrary to a Quaker instruction of 1678 to Friends, Abraham Hodgson buried his daughter in linen in the late 17th century, and was fined according to the particular circumstances. It seems that Quakers had no objection to obeying the Acts because they were directed by Parliament and not the Anglican Church.

Floral corpse dressing

One area of popular culture which could survive in the archaeological record is that of dressing the corpse with flowers and herbs. Corpse dressing dates from at least Shakespeare's time (mentioned in *Hamlet*) and it extended through the 17th century when 'the body was wrapped up with flowers and herbs in a winding sheet' (Francis Tate, cited in Cressy 1997, 428): at this time only the very rich were buried in coffins. Interestingly, c 1675 Joshua Stopford noted that 'casting flowers or herbs into graves was a popish practice derived from heathen customs' (cited op cit, 402), hinting at a pre-Christian origin.

Into the early 18th century mourners carried a sprig of rosemary which they cast into the grave after the coffin (Misson cited op cit, 454). Specific herbs were used to denote specific emotions and symbols, rosemary for fidelity in love and remembrance, and box for the life everlasting: generally evergreens were associated with the 'evergreen' memory (Richardson 1988, 21). Gittings (1984, 111), Litten (1991, 72), and Cressy (1997, 454) suggest that herbs were also used to mask the smells associated with putrefaction and autolysis. However, this seems extremely unlikely simply because they would have been ineffective, and known to be so, as attested by Pepys in his diary (referring to the death of his uncle Robert) of 6 July 1661 (Porter 1993).

McManners (1981a) and Kselman (1993) make no mention of this practice in 18th and 19th century France, although it appears that flowers might have been thrown into the grave in the 18th century. Whether the invisibility of floral corpse dressing in France is a reflection of it not being a Catholic rite, or simply that such a custom either never existed, or had died out, is unclear. By way of contrast, Richardson (1988, 22) notes that the custom was still referred to in rural Lincolnshire in the 1870s.

While no plant remains were attributed to this practice at Spitalfields, they were at St Nicholas, Sevenoaks (Boyle & Keevill, this volume) and at St Barnabas, London (Black & Scheuer, unpublished). The abundance of mattresses and pillows at Spitalfields, stuffed with a variety of materials including hay and straw (Janaway 1993, 103), combined with the wood-shavings and sawdust used as sanitizing media for absorbing body fluids, could have masked the presence of floral corpse dressing. This was not specifically sought as part of a plant macrofossil sampling strategy and analysis. The absence or non-retrieval of such evidence from dated coffins at Spitalfields is unfortunate as the opportunity and evidence to examine this practice through time might have existed. Nevertheless, it must be remembered that since this excavation (1984–6) archaeological priorities and strategies have changed, in part reflecting some of the issues raised at Spitalfields.

Although its extent is unknown, the practice of lining graves with flowers existed in England until the late 19th century. An example was the grave of the mother of the novelist Mrs Humphrey Ward whose funeral took place in the Lake District in 1888. The grave was lined with ivy, moss, and white flowers (cited in Jalland 1996, 223) and such a practice could be detected archaeologically if soil samples were taken specifically to detect plant remains in grave fills. It is worth considering whether the late 19th century trend of placing flowers on graves at funerals in both England and France (Litten 1991, 170), but rejected by Quakers who forbade the practice in 1873 (Stock, this volume), might perhaps represent an adaptation of earlier practice involving flowers and herbs. If so, it might be indicative of the increasing commercial exploitation and control of death (see Cannadine 1981) and the transition from overcrowded graveyards, reflecting the power and role of the Church in death and burial, to the aesthetically pleasing garden cemeteries of the period which reflected not only a physical distance from the Church but increasing non-conformity and secularism. It is worth considering the prudent advice of Taylor (1989) when deliberating on such matters:

we should examine changing forms in the discourse and material culture of death not simply as evidence of changing 'attitudes', but as cultural forms which sought to reframe death, to assert new structures of experience and the moral authority of those who stood behind such forms.

Feasting

Communal feasting at funerals is known from the pre-Christian Roman Empire, both on the day of a funeral and on special occasions thereafter when it was particularly seen as a means of re-establishing the integrity of the family (Paxton 1990, 23). In early Christian Europe it was considered to reinstate normal conditions of social and family life from which the bereaved had been removed during the period between death and burial (op cit, 6). It is also associated with taking a final communion, traditionally part of the last rites of the Church (formalized by the Council of Trent, op cit, 194). In post-Reformation England, having a final meal or drink in the presence of the deceased was retained, and presently constitutes taking refreshment after the funeral. Protestant or lay-theological retention of the function underlying some aspects of the final communion might have been achieved via the concept and practice of sin-eating, or having a drink to wash away the sins of the dead (Richardson 1988, 9). While it would be easy for us to dismiss non-doctrinal practice and belief as superstition, as Richardson points out (op cit, 21), we should not ignore the metaphysical dimension of such beliefs and practices, or disparage their importance in the popular culture of the time.

Grave goods

A French custom that could be construed as a ritual offering associated with death and thereafter, and which should be detectable archaeologically, is the practice that, at a funeral, a ceramic stoup containing holy water which was kept by the coffin prior to the funeral would be thrown into the grave on top of the coffin and interred with it (Kselman 1993, 275). This may be a long-standing Catholic tradition and one lost to England as a consequence of the Reformation. It should also be considered whether broken pottery recovered from a post-medieval (or earlier) grave would be classified as a 'ritual deposit', as it clearly was in post-medieval France, or as residual material. The archaeologist must be aware of the possible significance of such deposits if the evidence is to be interpreted meaningfully. Furthermore, they should be wary of unquestioningly applying different interpretations to such evidence from different periods because this is as likely to reflect their preconceptions as any real difference in the underlying significance of funerary deposits.

The naive archaeological adage that the presence of grave goods with a burial indicated a non-Christian burial no longer holds good. A range of both personal and apparently functional objects were recovered at Christ Church (Reeve and Adams 1993). These included jewellery, dental prostheses, a turned box-wood barrel containing a third party's extracted molars, and what appeared to be a medicine bottle. Little is known of the rationale dictating such practice, if indeed such an action is dictated by reason rather than emotion. An example of such an emotive response was the experience of the author, who vividly remembers the horror she felt when the undertaker responsible for her mother's funeral offered to remove her wedding ring prior to closing the coffin. It seemed, and still seems, both sacrilegious and inhuman to remove something so personal and precious and deny the deceased that comfort in death.

An indication of the desire to be buried with selected objects, in this case reminders of the family, is apparent in the diary of John Horsley whose wife died in 1852. Elvira Horsley personally cut locks of her husband's and children's hair which she placed in a red velvet bag to be hung around her neck after her death. She also asked her husband to encase his letters to her in a pine box which also accompanied her to the grave (Jalland 1996, 214).

As demonstrated above, it is worth considering that the presence of objects within a grave can reflect either the wishes of the deceased or of the bereaved. Potentially the range of such objects, of both an organic and/or inorganic nature, could facilitate long-term survival in appropriate burial environments. However, an awareness of their possible presence is a prerequisite to both appropriate sampling, recognition, and recovery.

Post-burial rites

Archaeologically 'invisible' rites following the interment of the deceased which continued into 19th century France included, on the day after the funeral, washing the bedding and clothing of the deceased, apparently reflecting a belief that if any stains remained another member of the family would be dead within the year (Kselman 1993, 55).

The straw from mattresses was usually burnt in both France and England. The artist Christopher Wood wrote of a similar burial practice he witnessed in St Ives, Cornwall in 1928. He observed, in a letter, that the mattress, clothes, and bedstead of the deceased were carried down to the beach and burnt while witnesses mused on the life of the dead person (Faulks 1996, 69). Few other records of this practice have been traced from either Protestant or non-conformist England. Perhaps some practices were so commonplace as to deny them a written record.

Such burial practices as those mentioned here are generally attributed to a fear of contagion and belief that the dead would not rest if they were not performed (Kselman 1993, 55), however, their value as a community bonding and/or mourning event should not be discounted or underestimated.

Conflated rites of passage

Baptism and death/burial

The Christian rituals associated with both baptism and death reflect their nature as rites of separation, transition, and incorporation. While in Christian England today (as in 18th and 19th century London) the rites associated with baptism and burial are quite distinct, it would appear that this has not always been the case. The early Christian mausoleum-baptistry served a dual function (Binski 1996, 32) and there are very marked similarities in the symbolism underlying both rituals reflecting that both are prerequisites for salvation.

It is interesting to consider the development of the baptism of infants as the norm. Paxton (1990, 35), suggests that, while known from the 3rd century, the baptism of infants became more common after the influence of Augustine in the late 5th to early 6th centuries. What is clear from Paxton's research (mainly liturgical), is that baptism generally took place at a time when death appeared to be imminent for the majority of early Christians and, that into the 9th century, it was an alternative to penance and communion prior to death (op cit, 130).

Archaeological indicators of the relationship between baptism and death/burial exist. Stocker (1997, 24) draws attention to the possible significance of large numbers of apparently ritual burials of font bowls at the end of their life, often beneath the replacement. He speculates that this long-lived practice reflected their value as material symbols of the cycle of birth, death, and resurrection. Of possible relevance to this was the pre-Reformation custom where children who died before the age of one month were buried in swaddling clothes, wearing the chrisom cloth of their baptism as a headband (Litten, 1991, 61), see Figure 9.2. A further link between baptism and burial practice may also be hinted at by the custom of placing pennies wrapped in linen upon the navel of the new-born child as part of post-natal ritual (Richardson 1988, 19). Richardson questions whether the coincidence extends beyond the fact that placing pennies upon the eyes of the deceased and the navel of the new-

Figure 9.2   Lydia Dwight on her deathbed, engraved John Dwight 1674 (copyright: Trustees of the Victoria & Albert Museum)

born may have been both carried out by the same person (*ibid*). At Spitalfields, in only one case, pennies, presumed to have been used to close the eyes, were also taken to the grave. It is also interesting to note the role played by coins in pre-Christian Roman burial rites where they were placed in the mouth of the deceased (to pay Charon) as a part of Roman *viaticum*. John Aubrey noted that a deviation of this practice was still evident in the oral tradition in Wales, the West Country and the North: 'I heard 'em tell that in the old time, they used to put a penny in the dead person's mouth to give to St Peter' (*sic*, cited in Cressy 1997, 402). Indeed, this was still a surviving tradition in London in the 1970s (Richardson, pers comm). The *viaticum* in Christian liturgy denotes the reception of the Eucharist as a sign of membership of the Christian community (Paxton 1990, 33).

Disposal of those on the margin of society

The non-baptised

The use of the chrisom in burial might also have been practised to demonstrate baptism, thus ensuring that the child, unlike the non-baptised, would be accorded a Christian burial. Protestant and Catholic dogma both assert that infants are corrupted by original sin prior to baptism, and consequently refusal to bury the non-baptised in consecrated ground was practised by both the Protestant and Catholic Church. An early 18th century French example saw the foetus of a pregnant suicide unceremoniously removed from its mother's womb and interred with other unbaptised children in a burial ground (as a punishment for suicide, the mother's remains were strung up on the gallows) (McManners 1981a, 409). A 19th century case extended to refusing to bury a non-baptised stillborn infant with its mother (who had died as a consequence of the birth) in consecrated ground (Kselman 1993, 190). Despite such examples from France, cases where stillbirths and neonates were accorded normal funerary rites are known from 17th century England and beyond (Harding 1989, and this volume).

The presence of a stillbirth, 'Master Chauvet', within Christ Church (1754) may attest to the practice by midwives of performing *in utero* baptisms, carried out with the sanction of the Church (Towler and Bramall 1986, 59). This was the only administration of the sacraments the Church permitted to be undertaken by women (Binski 1996, 56). It should, however, be considered that as this full-term baby appears not to have been given a Christian name, he may not have been baptised at all and yet was still accorded a Christian burial.

Master Chauvet was interred within his family's vault beneath Christ Church (his mother survived his birth). His presence in the crypt suggests that an oath sworn by midwives in the 17th century was at least in part redundant by the 18th: 'If a child be deadborn, you shall see it buried in such a secret place as neither hog, dog nor any other beast may come unto it . . .' (*sic*, Gittings 1984, 83). Perhaps at Christ Church the incumbent decided to interpret religious doctrine with humanity, unlike the situation in France, described above, where as Kselman asserts (op cit, 193), such unfeeling interpretation of dogma contributed to the rise of the anti-clerical movement in the 19th century. In England in the late 20th century, the Anglican church is known generally to view the burial of the non-baptised infant and child with compassion. However, from the author's personal experience, the fear that this might not be the case is still pervasive among concerned elderly grandparents of non-baptised grandchildren.

It is possible to determine if a baby survives birth, by about a day, using scanning electron microscopy to assess if there is a neonatal line in the developing deciduous dentition. This line reflects a change in the incremental growth of both dentine and enamel, which grows at a rate of approximately 4μm per day. It is caused by the physiological upset and changed metabolic activity associated with birth (Whittaker & MacDonald 1989, 61). If such analysis has been undertaken on Master Chauvet it remains unpublished. Such analysis is routinely applied in a forensic context but rarely to archaeological material. It has immense archaeological potential in understanding the significance of the burial of neonates in unusual contexts and determining if stillbirths are accorded specific burial rites. It could also be useful in examining the emotive and complex issue of potential infanticide victims, particularly from Roman contexts.

The burial of suicides

Suicide is essentially an individual gesture, the response to which is a cultural phenomenon (MacDonald 1986). The term was coined to provide a morally neutral designation for the act of voluntary death (Droge & Tabor 1992, 4) which through the medieval period and beyond had pejorative connotations. Societies' reponses to suicide have ranged in the past from being regarded as a noble act, to a sinful one, to the present, where in the west it is seen as indicative of a psychological or social disorder. Consequently, its treatment in society, both past and present, is an extremely interesting subject for which there is an enormous literature covering the last 400 years (culminating in MacDonald and Murphy 1990), but which, with the exception of work examining Christians and Jews in antiquity (Droge & Tabor 1992) has received little attention by the historians and archaeologists of earlier periods. The standard textbook on death and burial in the Roman world makes no mention of the subject (Toynbee 1971 and 1996; Philpott 1991),

yet it appears that suicides, like criminals, forfeited their right to formal burial (Hopkins 1983, 215), at least in 2nd century AD Italy.

It appears that formalizing the idea that voluntary death was a sin and a crime was a late Christian development which took its impetus from Augustine's polemics. These seem to have been based upon Plato's Pythagorean argument in the *Phaedo*, that to sever the bond between soul and body was to usurp a privilege that belonged to God (Droge & Tabor 1992, 5). This was translated into canon law as a result of three 6th-century Church councils. Between the 6th century and the Reformation, ecclesiastical proscription was incorporated into secular law by the emerging nation states and this was extended to include dishonouring the corpse.

The 16th century saw suicide as an '. . . offence against Nature, God and the King' (Gittings 1984, 72). The Middle Ages saw both intense theological condemnation and folkloric abhorrence of suicide (MacDonald and Murphy 1990, 2). This view was formalized by the coining of the word suicide in the 1630s (MacDonald 1986, 53), although it did not become common usage until the mid 18th century. Prior to that the use of terms such as *felo de se* (self murder) exemplifies the common perception of the action that was embedded into ecclesiastic and civil law and from which only idiots and those who were *non compos mentis* were spared punishment (*ibid*).

In England, prior to the 1823 Suicide Act (4 Geo IV c52), suicides who were considered by the Coroner's jury to be of sound mind were subject to non-Christian burial coupled with physical punishment of the corpse (Gittings 1984, 72). Suicides were generally interred near a cross-road, in a prone position, with a stake thrust through their body (MacDonald 1986, 53), a post mortem punishment also accorded to some executed criminals and alleged vampires. Known locations of such burials, some as early as the Anglo-Saxon era, are discussed by Halliday (1997). The denial of a Christian burial was coupled with the confiscation by the Crown of the individual's property (the latter element dating from the 13th century; Macdonald 1986, 54). The 19th century Act still forbade burial of *felo de se* suicides within consecrated ground, but also forbade cross-roads burial, and decreed that the bodies of suicides should be buried within 24 hours of the inquest and between the hours of nine and twelve at night (Forbes 1979, 121). Catholic France similarly confiscated goods and also humiliated the body of the deceased by dragging it along, in public view, on a hurdle (McManners 1981a, 410) as they did for condemned criminals.

The prone burial of suicides (ie face downwards) in the Middle Ages is interesting and it might be worth considering if there could be a continuity between this custom and that of prone burial in late Roman and Anglo-Saxon England. While the significance of prone (almost always adult) burials of both men and women in the archaeological record from

120

both periods continues to generate debate (Harman *et al* 1981; Philpott 1991), particularly their frequent siting (often in groups) around the edges of burial grounds (see Harding, this volume), the literature appears devoid of discussion of the possibility of a connection with the practice of prone inhumation of suicides from at least medieval times. Paxton (1990) makes no reference to the attitude of the early Church to suicide. Sixth-century canon laws forbade traditional Christian burial rites for suicides and this appears to have been reiterated *c* 1000 (Daniell 1997, 105). It is impossible to know if churchmen were responsible for disseminating the idea that suicide was the handiwork of Satan, or if they merely validated ancient popular conviction (MacDonald 1986, 55).

It is interesting to note that in 17th century England very few suicides (9%) were deemed to be *non compos mentis*, whereas by the 1720s 75% were, and by the end of the 18th century 97% (MacDonald 1986, 98). The period saw a gradual transition from the late 17th century, where the coroner's jury seemed reluctant to impose property confiscation and where, in cases of *felo de se*, property was regularly undervalued, particularly for male suicides with dependent families. It is also apparent that it was not uncommon for the *felo de se* verdict to be used as a means of punishing someone for another crime where the suicide was seen as a means of avoiding punishment (op cit, 93). Similar practice took place in contemporary France whereby criminals who committed suicide to avoid punishments received two types of post mortem punishment, that for the crime itself and that for suicide. The example of a thief who was hung by the neck for his original crime and by his feet for committing suicide exemplifies such practice (McManners 1981a, 409), as does the pregnant suicide victim described above.

The general transition evident in England from the late 17th century towards a more humane treatment of suicides, involved a highly discriminatory, class-biased use of the *non compos mentis* verdict by juries (op cit, 77). Even such commentators as the *Connoisseur* noted that suicide by a 'pistol genteelly mounted' (Fig 9.3a&b) might result in burial in Westminster Abbey while the 'pennyless poor dog' might be excluded from the churchyard (1755, cited in MacDonald 1986, 78). This trend is apparent in the archaeological record. A 24 year old bridegroom who had committed suicide was buried under the aisle of St Bride's Church, Fleet Street, London in 1821 (Bowman *et al* 1992b). This young man was reported as having suffered from 'mental derangement' by the Coroner (op cit, 94). A 57 year old male suicide interred within the vaults beneath Christ Church in 1852 was considered to have been the result of 'temporary insanity' (Cox *et al* 1990). In both cases, death was from pistol wounds to the head.

In the Spitalfields example (Figure 9.3), an abundance of surviving historical documentation allowed a reconstruction of the circumstances precipitating the event (discussed in full in Cox *et al* 1990). This was so detailed that it facilitated modern psychiatric and psychological enquiry into the victim's mental health. The individual concerned, William Leschallas, had made a previous attempt to take his own life. The Coroner clearly viewed this with some sympathy but had an individual made repeated suicide attempts two centuries previously, the jurors would have viewed this

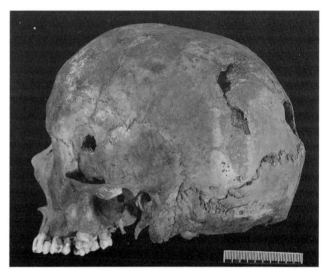

Figure 9.3a   The skull of William Leschallas showing the fatal consequences of a 'pistol genteelly mounted'. The lesion on the left frontal region (Fig 9.3b) is the result of his earlier suicide attempt (photo: The Natural History Museum, London)

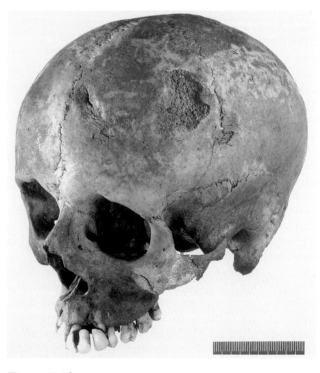

Figure 9.3b

as premeditation of a crime (MacDonald 1986, 91). A modern (1980s) specialist psychiatric opinion concluded that Leschallas may have been suffering from a severe psychotic depressive illness, *involutional melancholia*, a condition precipitated by a 'major life event', which he is known to have experienced[2] (Cox *et al* 1990). The symptoms he displayed are uncommon and considered by modern specialists to be unlikely to represent an invention by his family and friends (either to secure him a Christian burial or his estate for his heirs).

It seems that the bodies of suicides were particularly vulnerable to being stolen by the resurrectionists prior to the 1823 Suicide Act. Richardson (1988, 195) considered this to reflect the fact that they rarely received the usual post-mortem ministrations of friends and relatives and that their frequently hasty interment meant that their bodies were likely to be fresher and more valuable to the anatomy schools. Whatever the reason, it would appear that this was done with a degree of public sanction: '... I therefore propose ... that whether lunatic or not lunatic, the body be delivered for dissection' (*Gentleman's Magazine*, 1754, xxiv, 507). Demonstrating the mixed emotions that suicide invoked at this time, the same correspondent goes on to argue that the goods of the deceased should not be forfeit to the Crown (as was legally required) because of the hardship imposed upon his dependants.

Following the 1832 Anatomy Act (75 Will IV c75) which requisitioned for dissection the bodies of those who could not afford to pay for their funeral, the corpses of suicides could still be vulnerable to dissection and desecration, reflecting the fact that some still shared the view expressed in the 16th century that suicide was an '... offence against Nature, God and the King' (Gittings 1984, 72). Nevertheless, the period from the Reformation into the 19th century saw the gradual decriminalization and secularization of suicide, and the erosion of the '... last vestiges of supernatural significance ...' (MacDonald 1986, 93). Only such views as those held by John Wesley, who held that (like much human behaviour he sought to repress or punish) suicide was the work of Satan (op cit, 83), bucked the trend. How influential his rhetoric would have been in this respect is impossible to assess. Generally, a similar transition occurred in Catholic France, one which is attributed as a manifestation of enlightened humanism (McManners 1981a, 410).

It is worth noting that whatever views the Church and courts held, the folk view that suicide was wrong is evident in the continued popularity of ritual punishment of suicides well into the 19th century. Despite the fact that scientism, developing scientific enquiry and understanding, reshaped many common assumptions in the 19th century, this may also reflect the continuation of an important link between theology and cosmology for ordinary people (MacDonald 1986, 89). Perhaps the fact that, both before and after the 1823 Suicide Act,

non compos mentis suicides were usually buried on the northern edge of churchyards alongside the non-baptised and executed criminals suggests an element of continuing reticence to a total change of stance on the part of the Church. Similarly, in France some churches had similar special areas for the interment of Protestants and suicides (Kselman 1993, 196). Binski (1996, 56) likens the burial of individuals around the perimeter of the churchyard to limbo, a periphery of Hell, and assumes an earthly equivalent for those who were spiritually or socially marginalized (see Harding, this volume).

Eternal rest

It is unclear when a horror of damage to and disturbance of the corpse became embedded into social consciousness. The issue of bodily resurrection, while abnormal and transgressive to Christ's contemporaries, whether Jew, Gentile, or Greco-Roman (Binski 1996, 9), was a subject of debate amongst early Christians. St Paul argued in its favour. The Catholic doctrine of bodily resurrection, though developed by St Augustine, St Jerome, and Tertullian, was recognised as important by the 4th-century Christian writer Eusebius, when he talks of the Romans burning and scattering the charred remains of early Christian martyrs (at Lyon) to prevent their resurrection (op cit, 11).

Skeletons with the head removed and placed between the thighs or feet have been recovered in this country from late Romano-British contexts and Anglo-Saxon cemeteries (Harman *et al* 1981; Philpott 1991, 74–5). This tradition is also mentioned in Geoffrey of Burton's 12th century *Life and Miracles of St Modwenna* (O'Brien 1996, 163). However, the significance of such practices, both spiritual, religious, and social, is unclear as is the issue of whether such mutilation took place prior to, or after death. Headlessness has a similar history, and is often assumed to indicate an execution, ritual, or judicial killing (*ibid*). The importance of the anatomically correct position of the head in burial and resurrection is exemplified in the *Collectio Canonum Hibernesis* (Wasserschleben 1885, 206–7, cited in O'Brien 1996, 163).

It is tempting (but dangerous) to speculate that if such treatment of corpses was some sort of pagan or cultural form of post mortem punishment, it might have been absorbed into Christian culture and folk belief up to the period of the Reformation and beyond. It seems to have been eventually transferred from being the penalty for murder, or other serious breaches of the law, to that for poverty (with the 1832 Anatomy Act: see Richardson 1988).

French philosophers of the Enlightenment noted that many Christian observances associated with death and burial had parallels among other peoples, both Classical and contemporary. For example, they remarked upon the similarities between All Soul's Day processions and springtime festivals

122

for the dead of both the Romans and Chinese. Jesuit missionaries had also reported the remarkable similarities in funerary rites between Native Americans and the Classical world (eg burying weapons and animals with the dead). Their discussion dwelt upon both continuity, and deep-rooted human convictions that transcend cultural boundaries (McManners 1981a, 295–8).

It seems that the human corpse was believed to possess both sentience and spiritual power (Richardson 1988). Post mortem punishment may have been inflicted upon the corpses of criminals during the Roman period (Philpott 1991, 77–89) and is known from the Tudor period when an act of 1540 allowed surgeons to have the bodies of four criminals a year for dissection (Gittings 1984, 74). This was reinforced by the Murder Act of 1752 (25 Geo II c37) which stipulated that all murderers' bodies had to go to the Surgeon's Company for dissection before burial. Richardson (1988, 28) considers that activities such as quartering executed traitors and dissecting executed criminals, could be seen as representing a gross assault upon the integrity and identity of the body and, therefore, upon the repose of the soul (op cit, 76) constituting a deliberate judicial breach of society-wide norms and values (op cit, 28). This long tradition facilitating judicial dismemberment was believed to punish offenders by damning their eternal souls and denying them rest as a consequence of dismemberment, which was also believed to deny the possibility of resurrection on the Day of Judgement. In the 17th century, churchyards and sepulchres were considered to be the dormitories of Christians sleeping, expecting to be raised by the last trumpet (Cressy 1997, 385) and Samuel Cork (early 17th century) preached Jesus 'takes care of all the bones . . . that none shall be found wanting when he comes to raise their bodies again at the last day' (cited in Cressy 1997, 385). That this view continued is evidenced in contemporary literature associated with the debate preceding the socially divisive and inhuman consequences of the 1832 Anatomy Act:

> We covet a lengthened if not permanent residence in the grave . . . It seems, indeed, to be a prevalent notion that the body must be preserved in some way or other, that it must be suffered to rest in peace, quietly to await the general resurrection. (London Medical Gazette 1827–8(1)672, cited in Richardson 1988, 75)

Through the centuries Christianity has shown wide variation in its interpretation of eschatology. Souls are ultimately purified or undergo bodily punishment in purgatory. It might be that the apparent abhorrence of post-mortem bodily dissection reflected a perceived need for the body to remain intact during purgation so that complete bodily resurrection could be ensured (Llewellyn 1991, 57, following Richardson 1988). Purgatory was shunned by Protestants at the Reformation when they held that salvation, and possibly resurrection, was achieved by Christ and obtained by faith alone.

The general abhorrence of being disturbed after death, and particularly being subject to dissection, possibly reflects the fact that, despite Church and State having cast purgatory aside in England, Protestants continued to believe in the basic Christian tenet that resurrection would be associated with the 'Second Coming' of Christ. This involved revivifying the material particles of the dead body (Fig 9.4). This notion seems to have persisted through much of our period, only gradually being replaced by the theological argument that the resurrected body would be of a new order. Despite this, it seems that for some literal belief in physical resurrection has continued well into the 20th century. This is demonstrated by the concern expressed by two

Figure 9.4   Lydia Dwight resurrected, by John Dwight 1674 (copyright: Trustees of the Victoria & Albert Museum)

elderly Scottish women who were overheard worrying about whether their shrouds would meet at the back when they had to stand in front of the congregation at the Day of Judgement (McAdam, pers comm). Richardson (1988, 7–8) argues that discrepancies between official and lay theology seen in burial practice may represent post mortem customs designed to ensure the fate of the deceased's soul, despite the official position.

As discussed above, official Protestant attitudes to death, disposal, and the afterlife were significantly different from those of Catholics (Jupp 1990, 2). However, the position in post-medieval France seems to have changed from that of the earlier period. Dissection was practised from at least the 14th century where Ariès (1981, 361) notes that techniques aimed at reduction of the body to a skeleton displayed a curious indifference to the body as a whole. By the late 16th century, allusions seem to exist to the body being left intact (op cit, 363) and these continue into the 18th century (op cit, 364). The growth of medical science and the increasing interest in anatomy in France (a physician of Louis XVI boasted that he had dissected 1,200 cadavers; op cit, 368) seems not to have been accompanied by a legitimate source of cadavers prior to the mid 19th century. In 18th and early 19th century France, the activities of the body-snatchers in burial grounds caused immense public outcry at a crime which was perceived as offensive to humanity and which violated religion. The activities of body-snatchers were a serious problem in those cities with active medical faculties and led to the construction of 15 foot high walls with locked gates preventing unauthorized access (McManners 1981a, 304). The bodies of executed criminals appear not to have been requisitioned for dissection but were instead either left to rot or burnt alongside the records of their trial (Ariès 1981, 44). No research specifically dedicated to dissection/resurrection in France has been found.

It is interesting that the general attitude to body-snatching in France is at odds with that reflected in the acceptance of the normal practice of burial. For the majority, this entailed burial in pits, with several of one's contemporaries, for a period of between five and ten years after which one's bones were exhumed and placed in a charnel house, as in pre-Reformation England (McManners 1981a, 308). Clearly, the former was contrary to accepted practice and disrespectful while the latter was neither.

Also interesting is that in France abhorrence of dissection was accompanied by a general tolerance of the dislocation of mortal remains from one place of burial to another. Until 1805 (Kselman 1993, 183) ordinary graves and subsequently space in an ossuary (discussed above), were available to all free of charge. Either temporary or perpetual concessions were also available for purchase, but were very expensive. Thereafter costs of perpetual concessions were reduced and their use became widespread, a practice which facilitated the development of funerary monuments such as vaults, chest tombs, and ornate headstones and markers and led to the development of a proprietary attitude towards family tombs (op cit, 187). From the 19th century threats to repossess graves were objected to on the grounds that they conflicted with established social progress and equality following the Revolution. French burial practice of the late 18th and 19th century demonstrates how the poor sought individual autonomy and equal treatment with the wealthy in death as in life (op cit, 188) (apparent during and after the French Revolution) while in England, Parliament denied the very poor the right to eternal rest free from the menace of dissection (1832 Anatomy Act).

The closure of overcrowded urban burial grounds in 19th century France and the transfer of remains to other burial grounds away from residential areas (largely a response to epidemic disease) restructured relations between the geography of the living and the dead (op cit, 176) and was generally accepted as necessary by the populace. However, similar practice in rural areas caused some outrage which appears to reflect the fact that 'cemeteries were emblems of family and local identity that allowed people to observe and recall their continuity through time' (op cit, 178), rather than any intrinsic belief in the sanctity of the corpse as in England. Such a view had been seen earlier in the century (1805) when grave-diggers exhumed the dead (selling off the coffin boards and shrouds; op cit, 173), raising objections which were apparently based upon the risk to public health rather than a lack of respect for the dead. It would appear that in France the dislocation of burials and dissection of remains effected a mixed response reflecting a variety of factors.

In England the horror of the activities of the 'resurrection-men', or grave robbers supplying the medical schools with cadavers for dissection in the 18th and early 19th centuries, and the subsequent outrage at the consequences of the 1832 Anatomy Act was very real and significant (Richardson 1988). Fear of 'death on the parish' (in the workhouse) followed the Act (Richardson 1988, 279–81) and is perhaps still evident in the attitude of the elderly working class of today, many of whom avidly save to ensure that they can afford to pay for their funeral, and who increasingly subscribe to the financial services industry which is presently selling expensive pre-paid funeral plans (presently unregulated).

It is interesting to observe that the Quakers seemed less concerned with the significance of their mortal remains and their resurrection than Anglicans. Dobbs (1995, cited in Stock, this volume) notes '. . . the way in which the dead would be raised, the type of body with which they would be resurrected . . . they felt it unnecessary to discuss, leaving it, instead, to God'. The recent response of the Kingston-upon-Thames Friends to the proposed clearance of an 18th and 19th century Quaker burial ground suggests that this attitude is evidently still extant today:

We have no objection should a full archaeological investigation take place. Neither do we object to the use of any [skeletal] remains as a teaching resource. We would prefer the remains to be cremated and the ashes passed on to us for disposal at a Quaker cemetery, rather than be reinterred in separate containers [as had been proposed]. (Kingston Friends Trust, Monthly Meeting Minute 96.6)

Archaeological evidence of measures taken to avoid dissection was apparent at Christ Church (see Molleson and Cox 1993: Cox 1996a). This included the use of an iron Patent Coffin for an infant burial (coffins which once sealed could not be opened, see Richardson 1988, 81–2; Litten 1991, 110–11), a *mort-safe* (see Cox 1996a, 107), chains and iron straps around coffins, and iron bars within coffins. Evidence also survived of the successful efforts of resurrection-men, acting with the collusion of undertakers, in the form of sealed coffins which were empty of the intended corpse but full of building rubble.

It was not until 1944 that the Church of England (Upper and Lower Houses of the Convocation of Canterbury) formalized a more relaxed view of the doctrinal position in respect of 'completeness' and the resurrection of the body when they decreed that cremation did not preclude resurrection (Jupp 1990, 19). Some historians consider that today most Protestants believe in unconditional entry into heaven,

scorn purgatory, and dismiss the resurrection of the body (op cit, 22). Work undertaken by Richardson and Hurwitz (1995) on attitudes among whole body donors for dissection suggests that, even among a group predisposed to the notion of bodily dissection, there is a multiplicity of views about the role of the body, including those who consider it to be a vehicle of the soul. Their sample will inevitably also reflect a religious and socio-economic bias but the results suggest that attitudes to the body are enormously varied.

It is worth considering recent and current practice of the Church of England concerning such matters. That numerous church burial grounds, graveyards, and crypts have been subject to clearance over the last fifteen years would seem to suggest that the Church, as custodian of the burial place, has few qualms about disturbing burials if it is necessary for development (as at St Nicholas' Church, Bathampton; Cox & Stock 1995; Fig 9.5) or essential repairs. That this position might be changing is indicated by a recent judgement of the Arches Court of Canterbury (26 October 1995) concerning a proposed extension to the Church of St Michael and All Angels at Tettenhall Regis. As discussed in Reeve & Cox (in press), the Court and Chancellor found that disruption of burials should not take place without ascertaining the views of relatives (even distant ones) of those whose ancestors have or may have been buried there, and of parishioners (even non-churchgoers). A similar

Figure 9.5   St Nicholas Church and graveyard, Bathampton showing the modern extension to the Church (photo: M Cox)

judgement, discussed in Boyle and Keevill (this volume), would also seem to be indicative of a shift in the attitude of the Church. Further to this, while in the early 1980s the Church was prepared to grant a faculty which directed that the remains of those who abhorred dissection and believed in bodily resurrection should be cremated (Christ Church, Spitalfields), recent changes in that position (see Reeve, this volume) are also reflected in the detail of the Tettenhall Judgement.

Perhaps representing the same ambiguity and sensitivity to the rights of the dead and concerns of the living are recent reactions in the press to the activities of the artist Anthony Noel-Kelly whose art involves the use of illicitly procured cadavers, their dissection, and public display (*THES*, April 18 1997: *Times* April 10, 1997). Is it possible that these recent displays of feeling and sensitivity in respect of the repose and dignity of the dead, and the needs of the living, are signs of the slow reversal of the secularism and commercialism of the last 150 years, possibly reflecting a concern for human dignity and humanity rather than eschatology. Alternatively, they might reflect feelings which have been present throughout the last 150 years but which have not been reflected in official practice.

Final thoughts

It is easy to be constrained in our understanding of the archaeology of the recent past by an uncritical application of both theological or other doctrine and dogma and to ignore the power and practice of both lay theology and folk tradition. The potential value of applying ethnographic, archaeological (pre-Christian and pre-Reformation) and anthropological analogy, and ethno-archaeological principles, to post-medieval funerary archaeology is all too easily forgotten. The archaeological contribution to studies of death and disposal, of all periods, through material culture, is potentially invaluable, and must operate within clearly defined conceptual frameworks (Bell 1997). That said, such scholarship can only be extended, deepened and enriched by an awareness of what is apparent from historical sources and anthropological/ethnographic analogy. Such awareness should lead to the application of sampling strategies appropriate to the recovery of a greater range of artefacts and ecofacts than those presently operating, strategies which could significantly enhance our understanding of funerary rites and burial practice.

It is unfortunate that the author, along with many practising archaeologists in England would have struggled to understand either the spiritual or the lay significance of her own great-grandmothers' funerary rites – on contemporary terms. It would appear that for a variety of reasons La Rochefoucauld's comment 'One cannot look directly at . . . death' may apply to many scholars, both in respect of our present and the recent past. This being so, can we hope to apply either appropriate sampling strategies or meaningful interpretation to material culture associated with funerary archaeology from either earlier historic or prehistoric eras? If we are to have any hope of altering this unsatisfactory situation we must develop an awareness of the complexity and diversity of rites of passage accompanying death and disposal through the scholarship of those from other disciplines. Further, we must adopt a broad, multidisciplinary approach to our research if we are to do justice to the finite, precious, and, in these days of commercial development-driven archaeology, expensive archaeological resource.

Acknowledgements

The Christ Church Project was funded by the Wellcome Trust, English Heritage, the Greater London Council, and the Leverhulme Foundation. The motivation for this paper came from reflective hindsight which was stimulated by the work of John McManners and Thomas Kselman looking at death and funerary practice in Catholic France, alongside the burgeoning literature on death and burial. It would not have been possible without the compassionate work of Ruth Richardson. Ruth Richardson, Vanessa Harding, and Ellen McAdam are all thanked for their provocative and thoughtful comments which contributed to the final form of this paper. However, it should be noted that any shortcomings or erroneous conclusions are those of the author.

Notes

1   Following a 1660 prohibition on wool exports, these Acts were designed to increase the home demand for woollen manufacture.
2   His paper mills on the River Medway burnt down: a serious loss for a paper manufacturer and exporter.

Part II   The archaeological contribution: case studies

ii   A nonconformist view: the Quakers

By the middle of the 19th century, the term 'dissenter' (which had acquired a somewhat contemptuous flavour) was replaced by 'nonconformist', that is, a member of a religious body which had separated from the Established Church in England. Our main period of concern is one by which many nonconformist groups had became well established. These included Baptists, Presbyterians, Congregationalists, Methodists, and Quakers, to whom increasing tolerance was shown although they remained subject to the Test and Corporation Acts until 1828 and other prejudicial acts until the later 19th century.

While our understanding of funerary practice is biased towards the Anglican, it is worth considering that a religious census conducted in 1851 showed that approximately half of all churchgoers were nonconformists. Our lack of knowledge of nonconformist doctrine and practice possibly reflects (in traditional historiographical style) a 20th century decline whereby nonconformity attracts a proportionately smaller membership and consequently, less academic interest.

That this section concentrates on the burial practice of the Religious Society of Friends is purely coincidental reflecting recent opportunities to examine two Quaker burial grounds and the research that such opportunities has generated. The first site was in Bathford, near Bath, the second in Kingston-upon-Thames. Gwynne Stock's appraisal of Quaker burial doctrine and practice was inspired by the watching brief he undertook at Bathford in the early 1990s. Such was the contemporary lack of interest in nonconformist burials that the site, which was to be destroyed for development,

was not even accorded the dignity of an official watching brief. Fortunately, some curators are more enlightened to the value of post-medieval funerary archaeology than others, and archaeologists often learn retrospectively from the omissions of others. Consequently and subsequently, when the burial ground in Kingston-upon-Thames was to be cleared for housing, a full programme of archaeological works was implemented.

The chapters in this section all demonstrate that there was, in matters of burial practice, a degree of nonconformity amongst these nonconformists. While in some respects the burial practice of Quakers reveals a degree of dissension, proscribed by Quaker doctrine, from that of the Established Church, in others it apes the Anglican tradition, particularly in the context of demonstrating socio-economic status and values. Gwynne Stock's technical background is reflected in his extremely important reporting of much information on coffin fittings from Bathford. This aspect has previously been largely ignored by archaeologists in favour of a traditionally stylistic and metallurgical approach to such artefacts. Helen Start and Lucy Kirk's chapter on the health and mortality of the Quakers buried at Kingston-upon-Thames, not surprisingly, illustrates a group of people not dissimilar from those excavated from contemporary Anglican sites.

The contributions of Louise Bashford, Tony Pollard, Helen Start, and Lucy Kirk all develop notions first expressed in this volume by Angela Boyle and Graham Keevill; that some archaeologists are not entirely comfortable with the concept and practice of excavating and examining the more recently dead, and their long-term curation. It is reassuring to see an openness and honesty about issues which our culture is notoriously inept at expressing.

10 Quaker burial: doctrine and practice *Gwynne Stock*

Introduction

This paper addresses the subject of Quaker funerary and burial procedures by combining doctrinal, historical, and archaeological evidence, enabling comparisons to be made between how things were expected to be done (the doctrine or theory), and how things were done (the practice). The latter can most effectively be studied by an appropriate research-driven programme of archaeological work. Some information can also be retrieved from archaeological observation and recording during commercial clearance of burial grounds.

The anticipated position was that Quaker simplicity would contrast strongly with the socially structured Anglican practice, but the evidence presented below demonstrates that not all Quakers conformed.

Quaker background and beliefs

The Religious Society of Friends had its origins in the mid 17th century, in the unsettled religious and social climate of the Civil War. Their founder was George Fox (1624–91). The name Quaker is said to have originated from Justice Bennett of Derby, 'th[a]t first called Us Quakers because wee bid th[e]m tremble att the Word of God & this was in the year 1650' (*sic*) (Penney 1911, vol 2, 4).

Who are the Quakers?, a 1996 Friends House, London 'outreach' leaflet, includes the following:

There are about 240,000 Quakers world-wide. They differ in language, culture and national allegiance, in form of worship, and even in beliefs. What they have in common is their search for a real experience of God's love and power in the everyday world.

Meeting for worship is at the centre of Quaker life. It begins as Quakers sit in the meeting room, gathering together in a silence that grows deeper as it progresses. Here they open themselves to the love of God and to that of God in each other. The meeting house is simple. There are no ornaments or religious symbols. Neither is there an appointed minister or pastor. The responsibility for the meeting belongs to all. Anyone may speak when he or she feels inspired to do so; this is known as vocal ministry. These meetings for worship are open to all and visitors are particularly welcome . . .

Quaker business meetings, known as 'meetings for church affairs' are open to all members and often to attenders. They are meetings for worship and everyone present has a part to play in the decision-making process. The matter under discussion is not resolved by voting. The 'clerk', who conducts the meeting, listens to what is said and takes account of the general feeling. A minute is then made, read and approved during the meeting and so records the united decision.

'Simplicity' is a Quaker characteristic reflected in the advice that 'Gravestones should be such that there is no distinction between rich and poor' (*Book of Discipline* 1995, 15.20) and that 'There should not be any rigid pattern for the conduct of funerals' (op cit, 17.03). Early Quakers also avoided the use of titles, especially those with ecclesiastical connotations (Clarkson 1807, vol 1, 320). Place names would usually have been recorded, for example, as John Street for Saint John Street, Ives for St Ives, Bury for Bury St Edmunds, and even Auckland for Bishop Auckland, perhaps now confusing places half a world apart.

Proposals dated 1659 in the name of George Fox urged:

All friends who are not provided may speedily provide them selves Burying places Convenient, that thereby a testament may stand against the Superstisious Idolizing of those places Cal[l]ed holy grownd, formerly used to that purpose [*sic*] (MSS Portfolio 36/19, Friends House Library).

All ground is 'God's ground', and so consecrated 'holy ground' is unnecessary, making any convenient piece of land acceptable for burial. Figure 10.1 shows one such site at Kingsweston, north Bristol (NGR ST 5401 7796) which dates from 1690 (Trusts and Trust Properties 1870). That date is also recorded in an incised stone above the entrance (Fig 10.2). Housing development has surrounded the burial ground, which was formerly in a rural locality, but it is still available for interment.

Quaker organisation

It is beyond the scope of this paper to discuss the detailed committee structure of the Religious Society of Friends (*Book of Discipline* 1995, 8.04), but a simplified version is as follows.

- Most individuals belong to a local *Particular* or *Preparative Meeting* (op cit, 4.29), several of which prepare business for *Monthly Meeting*,

Figure 10.1   Quaker burial ground at Kingsweston, Bristol (photo: G Stock)

the primary meeting for church affairs (op cit, 4.01). 'Church' in this context denotes religious organisation and not a building; a Quaker place of worship being a Meeting House.

- *Monthly Meeting* boundaries are notional, in that they do not necessarily follow any county, parish, or other boundary, but simply and, usually conveniently, enclose a group of local meetings.

- *Six Weeks Meeting* dates from 1671 and, although a meeting of London Friends, is included here because it has a responsibility for property and financial affairs, and its minutes shed considerable light on burial practices. It engaged on occasion in national affairs (*Book of Discipline* 1995, 7.01; White 1971).

- *Meeting for Sufferings*, its name derived from the 17th century sufferings of Friends due to persecution, is the standing representative body entrusted with the general care of matters affecting Yearly Meeting (op cit, 7.02).

- *Yearly Meeting*, when in session, is the final constitutional authority.

- *General Meeting*, formerly part of the business structure called Quarterly Meeting, comprises several Monthly Meetings, its main purpose now being for conference, inspiration, and broad oversight of that area (op cit, 5.01).

A Clerk chairs the meetings for church affairs and is the principal contact for the Meeting (op cit, 3.12). Elders are responsible for the spiritual growth of the Meeting (op cit, 12.12) and Overseers for more temporal matters (op cit, 12.13), although there is overlap. All are positions of responsibility, not authority, and are usually held for three years, thereby ensuring an effective, but non-hierarchical structure. There is equality of the sexes throughout the Society.

Quaker record-making and keeping is of a very high order, and Quaker attitude to historical research is encapsulated in the report of Library Committee in *Yearly Meeting Proceedings* (Religious Society of Friends 1977, 840), and quoted in *Your Meeting's Records* (Religious Society of Friends 1986, 15):

And it is through historical study, as well in other ways, that Friends are enabled to learn about themselves: and self-knowledge (rather than inherited myth) is a good discipline in itself and an essential prelude to right action.

Figure 10.2   Quaker burial ground at Kingsweston, Bristol showing incised stone with date of establishment (photo: G Stock)

The doctrine of Quaker burial procedures

The doctrine or theory of Quaker burial procedures is as prescribed in The *Book of Discipline*, the generic name for all attempts of the Religious Society of Friends to codify the Yearly Meeting rules and regulations, whether in manuscript or printed form (see Appendix 10.1 for a full chronology and bibliography). The *Book of Discipline* represents the expectations of Friends, and enables comparison with contemporary practice, as evidenced by archaeological observations and by the use of other historical sources.

The current definitive statement of beliefs and procedures is the 1995 *Book of Discipline*. Revisions have been made approximately each generation since it was first issued, in manuscript form in 1738, under the name 'Christian and Brotherly Advices' (*Book of Discipline* 1738), and is usually called the *Book of Extracts*. The first printed edition followed in 1783. Before 1738, minutes of advice and counsel were sent out to Quarterly Meetings

(now called General Meetings) and Monthly Meetings annually by Yearly Meeting.

A query dating from 1682 asking 'What friends in the Ministry, in their respective Counties, departed this Life since the last Yearly Meeting?' was intended to produce factual information from meetings throughout the country. Such meetings were able to call upon the local knowledge of Friends (*Book of Discipline* 1968, 701). Queries like this, together with advice to Friends such as 'all former Records relating to Marriages, Births and Burials, be collected, and kept together by the Direction of their respective Quarterly Meetings' (*Book of Discipline*, 1738), were the basis of the *Book of Discipline*.

Six versions of the *Book of Discipline* (1738) have been examined to ascertain the reliability of the compilations. The manuscript sections applicable to this research were found to be substantially alike, implying diligence on the part of local individuals. References are from the Westminster version (Friends House Library Archive 11 b 7), taken here to be potentially the most reliable source, as it lies nearest the origin of the information.

Days and months

An awareness of Quaker terminology for days of the week, and for months, is necessary to understand fully the records and monumental inscriptions. Friends were advised in 1691 (*Book of Discipline*, 1738) to 'keep to their wonted Example and Testimony against the superstitious Observation of the Days' (*sic*), and in 1697 (op cit) 'that all Friends keep to the Simplicity of Truth in calling the Months, & Days by Scripture Names, & not by Heathen,' (*sic*). The days were to be called First (Sunday) to Seventh (Saturday), because the common names were of heathen origin. The months were similarly treated for the same reasons, although September, October, November, and December were acceptable because the names were derived from Latin numbers and were the seventh to tenth months of the Julian calendar. They ceased to be so from 1752 when under the Gregorian calendar they became the ninth to the twelfth months and so could no longer be regarded as statements of truth (Nickalls 1952, xiii–xiv).

Burial procedure

Legal status of land used for burial

The importance of formalizing legal ownership of property was minuted in the *Book of Discipline* (1738):

Advised that Friends in the several Quarterly and Monthly Meetings take Special care that the Titles of Friends Meeting Houses and Burial

Grounds be made Secure according to Law; This Meeting understanding there is a Deficiency in this Respect in some Places (1703).

(The date 1703 at the end of a quotation indicates that the extract is from business transacted in that year, rather than from a published source, such as a *Book of Discipline* for later years.) An entry in the margin dated 1737 reminded Friends 'Titles to be looked into and Secured & to keep Records thereof'. All property belonging to the Yearly Meeting is held in trust to be used for its charitable purposes, either generally or for specific uses as determined by its donor (*Book of Discipline* 1995, 15.01).

Gravestones

The term 'gravestone' is used in this paper as a generic name for 'tombstone' and 'monument', except when it is a part of a quotation. Under the heading 'Concerning Tombstones' in the *Book of Discipline* (1738) the following comment and advice was expounded:

This Meeting being informed, That Friends in some places have gone into the vain, & empty Custom of erecting Monuments over the dead Bodies of Friends, by Stones, Inscriptions, Tombstones &c, and being very desirous Friends should keep a commendable Plainness and Simplicity in this, as well as other Respects; It's therefore the Advice of this Meeting, That all such Monuments as are already in being over dead Bodies of Friends, should be removed as much as may be, with Discretion and Conveniency: And that none be any where made, or set up by, or over the dead Bodies of Friends, or others in Friends Burying-places for time to come (*sic*) (1717).

Forty-eight years later there was a plea for the advice to be heeded with the words 'The observance of the foregoing Minute earnestly recommended' (1765). The following year, Yearly Meeting recorded:

This Meeting being informed, that since the Advice lately issued in order to excite friends to be a proper Regard to our Testimony against Grave-Stones, divers have accordingly been removed; and being desirous that the Revival of this Concern may be effectual; We earnestly recommend the Removal of them may become general, & that an Answer may be transmitted to our next Yearly Meeting, how far the said Advice is comply'd with (1766).

Yearly Meeting minutes for 1767 do not record any response to the above.

Yearly Meeting (1847–56, vol 26), ostensibly for pragmatic reasons, relented in 1850 on the advice against gravestones that had dated from 1717 with the minute:

This Meeting, after serious and deliberate consideration of the subject, is renewedly of the judgement, that our religious Society has a sound Christian testimony to bear against the erection of monuments, as well as against all inscriptions of a eulogistic character over the graves of their deceased friends. Nevertheless, it is of the opinion, that it is no violation of such testimony to place over or beside a grave a plain stone, the inscription on which is confined to a simple record of the name, age, and date of the decease of the individual interred. The object in this instance is simply to define the position of the grave, with a view to the satisfaction of surviving relatives, and the preventing of its premature re-opening.

Friends are therefore left at liberty to adopt the use of such stones in any of our burial grounds; it being distinctly understood that, in all cases, they are to be provided and put down under the direction of the Monthly Meeting; so that, in each particular burial ground, such an entire uniformity may be preserved, in respect to the materials, size and form of the stones, as well as in the mode of placing them, as may effectually guard against any distinction being made in that place between the rich and the poor (1850).

The first paragraph was not included after 1911, and the second has changed little since 1850.

Mourning

Friends were advised in *Book of Discipline* (1738):

Not to imitate the World in Mourning Habits . . . According to the primitive Innocency [*Book of Discipline* (1822, 116) deletes 'innocency'] & Simplicity of Friends, it is the Advice of this Meeting. That no Friends imitate the World in any Distinction of Habit or otherwise, as Marks, or tokens of Mourning for the Dead (1717).

Further advice was noted in 1718, 1724, and 1745:

Advice against Men & Women imitating the World in making a Shew of Mourning for the Dead, in their Apparel (1718).

A Caution against imitating the vain Custom of wearing, or giving Mourning, & all extravagant Expenses, about the Interment of the Deceased (1724).

And whereas a Custom hath of late prevailed with some amongst us wearing Mourning at the Funerals of their Relations, contrary to the ancient Practice, & repeated Advice of Friends; 'Tis desired that Friends every where would discorage such a Custom: and such public [ministering] Friends, whose Company may be desired at

Funerals, are requested to signify to the persons concerned, the Uneasyness & Difficulty they are put under, by Reason of such Appearances, which by their Presence they may be supposed to countenance (1745).

The *Book of Discipline* (1783) repeats, with some paraphrasing, the above advice regarding mourning (1717 and 1724). The 1718 item does not appear, but is combined with that of 1824 to become 1824 PE (part of the Printed Epistle for that year). An addition forming part of the Printed Epistle for 1751 recounts:

Whilst others are putting on external marks of sorrow for the loss which this nation hath so lately sustained, let us demonstrate the sincerity of our sorrow, and express our gratitude and duty, in a manner becoming our holy proffession; for a conformity in externals, not agreeable to our principles, and contrary to the practice of our worthy ancients, will but expose us to the observation and pity of wise and discerning men (1751 PE).

The above may refer to the mourning associated with the death of Frederick Louis, Prince of Wales in 1751, but no confirmation has been found in the records.

Simplicity

Simplicity is perhaps taken to an extreme with the rewording of the advice in the *Book of Discipline* (1849, 352) against the use of mourning garments:

In connection with our Christian testimony to plainness of speech, behaviour, and apparel, our attention has been especially turned to the practice of wearing garments on the occasion of the decease of relatives and friends: and we feel concerned to offer an affectionate caution to our members against this obvious conformity to the vain and oppressive customs of the world.

The above wording remained until the *Book of Discipline* (1906), when it again became 'the practice of wearing *mourning* garments'.

According to Litten (1991, 170) floral tributes made their appearance in the late 1860s. Some Friends had apparently followed the fashion, and in 1911:

. . . are cautioned against the lavish use of flowers at funerals, and are encouraged to avoid display and needless expenditure as inconsistent with Christian simplicity. By yielding to worldly custom in these matters, many have involved themselves in pecuniary difficulty and brought a heavy burden upon their families.

The theme was further developed in 1925 under the heading 'Burials And Mourning':

Thinking in this way of death, we feel that therefrom arises a practice of reverent simplicity in respect to the outward facts attending death, which simplicity we earnestly commend to Friends everywhere. The funerals of Friends should be held in a spirit of quiet peace and trust. Natural sorrow there will be, especially for friends taken away in youth and in the strength of their days, but often our thoughts may be one of great thankfulness for lives which have borne witness to the upholding power of Christ.

Public cemeteries

The use of a public cemetery as an alternative to 'one of our own burial grounds' is first mentioned in the 1861 *Book of Discipline* (211). However, *Yearly Meeting* 1847–1856 (vol 26, 1852, 358) says that 'The subject of Burials in London and other large towns is continued under the care of Meeting for Sufferings to report thereon to our next Yearly Meeting'. The result of the deliberation was minuted in *Yearly Meeting* 1847–1856 (vol 26, 1853, 401):

This Meeting is informed that several cases have recently occurred of Bills being introduced into Parliament for the establishment of Public Cemeteries, accompanied by provisions of an Ecclesiastical character affecting the Christian testimonies of our religious [*sic*] Society. It is recommended that Friends in the respect of localities where such measures are contemplated, should give early attention to the subject as far as may be to protect their members in the faithful maintenance of a testimony in this respect, and where further attention is required that they communicate with their Correspondents in London as early as practicable.

Cremation

Cremation is first mentioned in the 1906 *Book of Discipline*, but only where printed on the Burial Note as an alternative to burial. Yearly Meeting did not discuss the matter until 1934, when a letter was received from the Clerk of Sussex, Surrey and Hants Quarterly Meeting asking Meeting for Sufferings for the guidance of Friends in respect to the 'right ordering' of meetings when held in connection with cremations (*Yearly Meeting* 1934, 184).

A committee was appointed to look into the question, and the recommendations, summarized below, were approved by Yearly Meeting in 1935 (op cit, 181) and a copy sent to every Monthly Meeting Clerk:

In the first place the wishes of the family or expressed by the deceased Friend should be ascertained . . . The alternative plans suggested below may guide relatives in forming their judgement:

The actual cremation could be carried on entirely independently of the Meetings for Worship . . . A Meeting for Worship if held at a Crematorium would proceed as at a graveside . . . The Meeting for Worship might be held as a memorial service. Such gatherings often prove very helpful and solemn occasions, especially when held in the Meeting House where the deceased Friend habitually attended . . . Ashes may be buried in a graveyard or cemetery, or placed in a casket in a columbarium, the inscription outside the niche recording the name and further particulars as relatives may desire. Ashes may be scattered, and if so, it is important that the Burial Note should state when and where the ashes are scattered, and if so desired some record or inscription might be put up at the Crematorium or the Meeting House.

Civil registration

The Registration Act 1836 (6 & 7 William IV c 86) created the system for a national register of all births, marriages, and deaths in England and Wales. The office of Registrar General was also established (Smale 1994, 12). The 1834 *Book of Discipline* (223–4) shows that just prior to that date, the procedure of the Religious Society of Friends was as follows:

In every monthly meeting one or more proper persons are to be appointed to give out birth notes, and burial notes; who are to fill them up agreeably to the prescribed forms, or to take care that the same be properly done; also to enter into the check margin of each note, the name of the person to whom such notes are delivered, and the other requisite particulars; the check margins are to be carefully preserved. No burial is to take place before the issuing of a burial note. . .

No mistake that happens to be made in a register, is to be erased, but to be corrected by drawing a line through the same, so as to leave it legible; and what should have been written, is to be inserted near it, and to be authenticated by the registrar's signing the initials of his name thereto. No contractions are to be used either in filling up any of the foregoing forms, or in the registers, except that in the latter, dates may be expressed in figures.

It is interesting that it was thought necessary to state that 'dates may be expressed in figures', when the Quaker expectation was that dates would only be expressed in figures and not in names of pagan origin. The words in question are not part of text of

the Parochial Registers Act (Rose's Act), 1812 (52 Geo III c 146), and therefore appear to be of Quaker origin, not simply transcribed from the Act. A great part of the 1836 Act was repealed by the Births and Deaths Registration Act 1874 (37 & 38 Vict c 88), the first to specify procedures, many of which still apply (Smale 1994, 12).

The Parochial Registers Act 1812 had required that registers of burials be made and kept by the rector, vicar, curate, or officiating minister of every parish. The removal of that requirement, from Friends' point of view, resulted in 'a mode free from objection in reference to our religious testimonies' (*Book of Discipline* 1861, 128).

The Registration of Burials Act, 1864 (27 & 28 Vict c 97) required that all burials in any burial-ground in England, not previously by law required to be registered, should be registered in books to be provided for each burial-ground, by the persons to whom the same belonged, and to be kept according to the laws then in force by which registers were previously required to be kept by rectors, vicars, or curates of parishes or ecclesiastical districts in England. Much of the 1864 Act remains in force (Draycott and Carr 1996, 2279).

Women at funerals

The 1802 revision and the 1822 supplement of the *Book of Discipline* repeat the advice on mourning habits, and add the following, which includes the first specific reference to Quaker attitudes to the involvement of women at funerals.

Having observed that, in imitation of a custom prevailing of late in the nation, diverse under our religious proffession [*sic*] have discouraged the female sex from attending the burial of their relations, by not inviting them thereto with the men; which is neither agreeable to the practice of our worthy predecessors, nor a decent token of respect, if health permits, it becomes both sexes for their deceased relations and friends, on these solemn occasions; we are therefore concerned to recommend that friends in general, and ministers, elders, and overseers in particular, would tenderly advise against any conformity amongst us, with the modern custom of the world in this respect; as well as in that of putting on black, or any other garments approaching to that colour, by way of distinction on such occasions; which we as people are well known to have always had a testimony against (1782).

The 1861 *Book of Discipline* (127) rephrases the above to read:

It is advised that women Friends should not be induced, by the desire to imitate prevailing customs or otherwise, to refrain from attending the burial of their relations, agreeably to the practice of our worthy predecessors, and as a becoming token of respect to the deceased.

The 1906 *Book of Discipline* (164) replaces the former double negative with a positive statement that 'Women Friends [are] Encouraged to be Present at Funerals'. Further involvement is advocated when 'Preparative Meetings are advised to appoint small committees of at least one man and one woman Friend, who should be informed when a death takes place and be prepared to consult with the relatives or friends of the deceased as to the holding of the funeral, and to acquaint Friends in the district' (*Book of Discipline* 1917, 116).

Quaker burial practice

The doctrine or theory of Quaker burial procedures described above is here compared and contrasted with the practice, verified by archaeological observations of burial grounds, both above and below ground, archaeological reports, Quaker archives and records, other than those already discussed, antiquarian comment and description, local authority records, and personal communication. Comparisons can thereby be made between how things were expected to be done and how things were done.

Funerals and coffins

The *Journal* of the Friends' Historical Society (Penney 1911, vol 15, 45) quotes George Fox, *An Encouragement to trust in the Lord* (1682, 12):

And all you that say, That we Bury like Dogs, because that we have not superfluous and needless things upon our Coffin, and white and black Cloth with Scutcheons, and do not go in Black, and hang Scarfs upon our Hats, and white Scarfs over our Shoulders, and give gold Rings, and have Sprigs of Rosemary in our hands, and Ring the Bells. How dare you say that we Bury our People like Dogs, because we cannot Bury them after the vain Pomps and Glory of the World?

A printed *Notice to Undertakers* (vol K [9a] Friends House Library), resulting from a Six Weeks Meeting Minute (vol 20, 279) dated 22nd 4th Month 1844, was presumably due to the apparent digressions in the intervening years.

Undertakers having the Superintendence of Funerals in the Burying-Grounds belonging to Friends, are requested to pay particular attention to the following Rule. 'All Interments in the Burial-Grounds of Friends are to be conducted strictly in accordance with the practice of the Society, and no Mourning-Coaches, Pall, Feathers, Black or Covered Coffin, or Coffin with Black

Furniture, Scarves, Hat-bands, Staves, Black Mourning-Cloaks or Mutes will be allowed.'

The words 'Floral Decorations' were added to a revised and re-issued version 12th month 22nd, 1873.

The records and recollections of James Jenkins (1753–1831), 'An obscure Englishman. A Quaker.' (Frost 1984), include fascinating contemporary glimpses of the actual practice of Quaker burial. This extract shows that custom had a strong influence on all:

My poor dear Sam died on the 23rd and on the 26th (1793) [month not given] I buried him at Newbury, with a piece of the shroud hanging outside of the coffin, agreeably to the custom of the place, and which (I understood) is there done, by way of proof that the penury of the relatives of the deceased is not so great, as to preclude their buying for the dead, the needful attire (op cit, 249–50).

Woodger (1994, 36) mentions 'a sample of sawdust from one of the coffins' from the Jubilee Line Extension Project 'which may represent the residue of some form of packing'. Clean deal sawdust has been used as an absorbent material in the base of coffins (Stock, this volume), and the use of sawdust in coffins is discussed by Molleson & Cox (1993, 11). Wood shavings were found in coffins at Bathford (Stock, this volume), and the effect of that substance on biological decay is discussed by Nawrocki (1995, 54).

The alternative use of sawdust described below may help to interpret archaeological evidence in the future, should any residue be identified outside the coffin.

2nd Mo 1799. Jn° Goad was a Linen-draper, in Bishopsgate Street, and supposed to be rich; by no means could it be said that he was decently interred in Long-Lane burial-ground, for, such an interment I never before saw, nor hope to see again; before the procession arrived there, I beheld a man pumping the water out of the grave, but it scarcely emptied, when it sprang up again, and to conceal it from the view of the company, a considerable quantity of sawdust was thrown upon it . . . soon after this, fell in, a great deal of earth from one side of the grave, and the corpse being then put down was literally interred in mud (Frost 1984, 309–10).

Burial in woollen

The Burial in Woollen Acts (1666, 1678, 1680, repealed 1814) required by law an affidavit to be sworn before a Justice or a clergyman within eight days of the funeral. Failure to do so incurred a penalty of £5 on the estate of every person not buried in woollen, of which £2 10s went to the poor and £2 10s to the informer. The fine could be reduced to £2 10s by collusion with an informer (Tate 1969, 67–9).

Six Weeks Meeting Minutes, Volume 1, recorded on 30th 5th Month [July] 1678:

> The Act for burying in Wollen being presented to the Consideration of the meeting – Doe agree: that the Complyance therewith as to burying in wollen, is a Civill matter, & fit to be done – and to procuring the makeing of Oath thereof, they meddle not therew[i]th but leave it to friends in the Truth, & this to be sent to each [London] Monthly Meeting.

Friends were thus content to comply with the law, because the Established Church was not involved, but, swearing the affidavit, especially if before a clergyman in the absence of a Justice, was contrary to the *Book of Discipline* (1737, 333):

> Concerning Oaths 1693 – Advised That our Christian Testimony be faithfully maintained against the Burden and Imposition of Oaths.

Penney (*Journal*, Friends Historical Society 1911, 106), quotes an un-Quakerly episode printed in 1881:

> Abraham Hodgson near Halifax, a quaker buryed a daughter in linnen, gave 50 shillings to the poor according to the act, went to Justice ffarrer, informed him of it, and claimed the other 50 shillings to himself as informer, prosecutes the business with much zeal.

Graves

Clarkson (1807, vol 2, 33–4) states that:

> The Quakers have no sepulchres or arched vaults under ground for the reception of their dead. There have been here and there vaults, and here and there graves with sides of brick; but coffins containing their bodies are usually committed to the dust.
>
> Quakers are sometimes buried near their relations, but more frequently otherwise. In places where their population is thin, and the burial ground large, a relation is buried next to a relation if it be desired. In other places, however, the graves are usually dug in rows, and the bodies deposited in them, not as their relations lie, but as they happen to be opened in succession, without any attention to family-connections . . . by this process a small piece of ground will be longer in filling, no room being lost . . .

The above is quoted by Montagu (1840, 23–4), who is in turn quoted by Jalland (1996, 220). Clarkson

may have taken his information from the minutes of Six Weeks Meeting, which a generation before had identified problems with graves and burial grounds (*Six Weeks Meeting Minutes* vol 14, 132, 16th 8th Month 1774):

> This Meeting being informed that an Attempt has lately been made to build a Vault in one of our Burial Grounds belonging to this City [London], and taking the same into Consideration, Do hereby direct the Grave-diggers of the respective Burial Grounds, that they shall not permit, or suffer any Vault, or Arch, to be built, Grave Stone set up, or Tomb erected, in any Burial Ground belonging to this Meeting.

In spite of the above, the author, when visiting the Kingston-upon-Thames Quaker burial ground on 27 September 1996, during archaeological exhumation for development, observed two abutting large brick vault-like structures with openings to the north (see Bashford & Pollard, this volume). Other examples of walled graves were found at Bathford (Stock, this volume). A memorial tablet from the Kingston vault-like structures bore the name 'Mrs S BARNARD'. The titles 'Mrs' or 'Mr', as contractions of Mistress or Master, were not normally used by Quakers (Clarkson 1807, vol 1, 311).

The report of an archaeological excavation carried out on the Friends' Burial Ground on the south of the High Street, Staines, Surrey (NGR: TQ 035 715) 1975–6, as part of the council's Central Redevelopment Scheme, recorded:

> In all there were 78 graves, many of which contained more than one burial. The first interment was John Winstone in 1849, the last Charles Ashby in 1944 . . . The burials were removed to a communal grave at Jordans [Quaker] Burial Ground in Buckinghamshire (Crouch & Shanks 1984, 5).
>
> Thirty-four graves were excavated, of which 31 were brick-lined and had been used for up to four burials, one upon the other, separated by a flagstone floor, with an average size of 2–2.5m long, 1m wide and 1.5–2.5m deep . . . Either wood or lead coffins were used with brass handles [grips] and fittings: the handles showed many variations of design (retained for possible future study). Some of the burials had been placed in shallow graves between brick vaults (op cit, 26).

In the first phase of the excavation at the southern end of the site in 1975, the levels proved in the main to be undisturbed, 'despite the presence of several deep brick-lined graves' (op cit, 5). The work in 1976 encountered 'heavy disturbance of most of the site by the digging of graves in the 19th century [which] meant that it was only in the small area outside the graveyard, to the extreme north of the site, that archaeological data could be retrieved' (op cit, 130). Figures 9 and 14 (op cit, 15 and 25) showed the axis of the graves to be north–south, and, where apparent from coffin-shaped graves, head south.

The O'Meara Street, Southwark, London SE1 (NGR: TQ 3239 8012) Jubilee Line Extension Project Report (Woodger 1994) noted that the site contained residual human skeletal remains and coffin fragments associated with a former Quaker burial ground that was largely cleared in 1860. A contemporary account included in Beck and Ball (1869) refers to:

... the compulsory sale of New Park meeting house and burial ground in 1860 [the O'Meara Street site] for the formation of New Southwark Street.

This was carefully dug over under the superintendence of a Friend who attended daily whilst the work was in progress, and about a thousand skeletons and nineteen entire lead coffins were dug up. All wood coffins had disappeared. The bones were packed in 111 shells of ordinary size, and carried by hearse to the Long Lane burial-ground, Bermondsey. Here two large deep pits were dug and the remains re-interred (op cit, 222).

The consequence of post-medieval burial activity is again commented upon (see Staines above) by Woodger (1994, 37):

the Roman sequence had been considerably disturbed by the excavation of graves, burial pits, and other destructive features in the 18th century.

The author assisted Professor Philip Rahtz and Lorna Watts in April 1996, during part of a rescue excavation of a burial ground in the curtilage of a former Quaker meeting house in Helmsley, North Yorkshire (NGR: SE 614 837). Other than a general level reduction of approximately 430mm, the ground was further disturbed only by foundation trenches. The axis of the ten graves revealed was approximately east–west with head east. Post-excavation analysis of the site is continuing.

The volumes of Six Weeks Meeting Minutes (Friends House Library) record the following:

Volume 17, 531, 19th 11th Month 1798: This Meeting taking into consideration the present irregular mode of burying Corps ... desires that the following friends to make enquiry thereinto, and report what improvement may be adopted to another meeting. [6 names]
Volume 17, 534, 31st 12th Month 1798: The Committee on Regulation of Burial Grounds is continued. [7 additional names]
Volume 17, 538–9, 11th 2nd Month 1799: The Committee on Burial Grounds and this Meeting recommends to the several Monthly Meetings within whose district the grounds are situated,

that they exercise suitable care from time to time that the ground be made use of to the greatest advantage it is capable of, ... the Grave diggers not to break it up in an irregular manner, but that they keep as much as the situation of the several grounds will admit to, one regular plan.

James Jenkins comments on graves thus:

On the 17th of the 12th Mo. [1795], died my father in-law Benj^m Lamb, of a mortification in his bowels, and was buried at Bunhill-fields in a grave made purposely deep, in order to hold others of the family, but, probably made so in vain, in a place where the dead are stowed away upon one another, with all the inattention of promiscuous inndecency. 10 mo. 14. 1820. I understand that this practice has been for some years discontinued (op cit, 154).
1802: I happened to be at Chipping Norton soon after [Thomas Wagstaffe's] decease about which time, his brother, Richd Wagstaffe of that place, also died, and it was told me with evident symptoms of disgust, that the two brothers had been buried in the same grave 'which (said the friends) is but half a grave to each.' I replied, that had he been buried in London, probably he would have had allotted to him but one third of a grave; ... that his coffin might have been laid upon that of a young woman, and that of an old woman placed upon his; the recital of my supposition, seemed not a little to shock the feelings. [I am assured that this practice is discontinued, both at Bunhill-fields, & Whitechapel, where they now bury in rows] (op cit, 397–8).

Gravestones

Yearly Meeting advice in 1717 to remove gravestones (Book of Discipline 1738) was as a result of nearly half a century of efforts elsewhere. Bristol Men's Meeting [Monthly Meeting], in a minute dated 20th 12th month [February] 1670 records:

Tis ordered that for the future no burying stones bee put at graves of any that may for the future bee buryed in our burying place [at that time, Redcliff Pit]. ... twas the request of this meeting that the gravestones should bee removed out of our graveyard [sic] (Mortimer 1971, 40).

George Borrow (1862, 515) visiting Quakers' Yard 'burying-place' near Treharris, Mid Glamorgan in 1854, observed:

The Quakers are no friends to tombstones, and the only visible evidence that this was a place of burial was a single flag stone, with half-obliterated inscription, which with some difficulty I deciphered, and was as follows:

138

To the Memory of Thomas Edmunds
Who died April the ninth 1802 aged 60 years.
And of Mary Edmunds
Who died January the fourth 1810 aged 70.

James Jenkins (Frost 1984, 548) recounts:

On 3mo 26th 1816 was buried at Newbury, in Berkshire aged 79. Dan[l] Fossick, of Crooked-lane, wire-merchant one of my old acquaintances . . . his wife was a native of that town, and in a bricked-grave of her family his remains were now put after those of her own, and two of their sons, having previously deposited. At the head of his grave, is placed a stone well-filled with inscriptions, but containing a strange admixture with respect to some of the dates being numerical, whilst others are expressed January, Feby &c. . . . the first were placed there before the Society-law forbade the erection of new, and directed the removal of old grave-stones, the second after its direction with respect to the names of the months &c. So that it seems like a two-fold breach of Society rule.

Braithwaite (1961, 417) quotes from a Minute [not cited]: 'the use of tombstones is of no service to the deceased'.

Women at funerals

An example of the direct involvement of Quaker women with the conduct of funerals was described by James Jenkins.

On first day [presumed to be the 1st of March (Friday), but could alternatively be an un-dated Sunday], 3rd Mo. 1816': [Mary Sterry's] remains were taken into morning meeting at Devonshire house [Bishopsgate, London], and from thence to Long-lane for interment, and where (I was informed) Mary Stacey said a few words in the line of exhortation. At the meeting, Eliz[h] Fry (wife of Joseph) knelt down and deliberately chanted a sweet prayer, after which we were addressed by Mary Stacey, Sarah Rudd, Sam[l] Southall, Wm Rickman, and Ann Capper . . . then Mary Sanderson in prayer, and lastly an address full of persuasion to good works, from Elizabeth Fry, aforesaid (Frost 1984, 555).

Resurrection

Dobbs (1995, 314) concludes:

For their beliefs concerning the resurrection of the dead, the day of judgement, and Christ's coming 'without us' to judge the quick and the dead, the Quakers turned to the Scriptures, from which they quoted freely. As to the actual way in which the dead would be raised, the type of body with which they would be resurrected, or the form of the day of judgement, they felt it unnecessary to discuss, leaving it, instead, to God.

Expected position

Based on the advice of the Religious Society of Friends, the following statements would be expected to be true:

- There are no extant gravestones dated before 1850.
- Gravestones are simple and of uniform design, in a particular burial ground.
- Gravestone inscriptions contain only name, date, and age.
- The month is depicted on gravestones as a number, not a name.
- Burial practice does not show any distinction between rich and poor.
- Grave axis does not need to adhere to what is often believed to be indicative of a 'Christian burial' – east–west, with head west.
- Graves are laid out in a regular plan.
- There are no vaults or other burial structures.
- There is no rigid pattern for the conduct of funerals.

Observed position

Although stone removal was advised nationally by Yearly Meeting from 1717, it was instigated by some meetings half a century earlier. However, throughout the time up to 1850 when there was a relaxation, it has been shown that there was considerable inertia. Legible inscriptions noted on extant gravestones (629), in Bristol and Frenchay Monthly Meeting, comprising Bedminster (ex Quakers Friars), Frenchay, Kingsweston, Lower Hazel, and Portishead demonstrate that 19.8% (125) pre-date 1850. Those pre-dating 1840 (83) accounted for 13.1%. The earliest was dated 1756. A much larger sample would be needed for confirmation, but meanwhile it is suggested here that caution should be exercised regarding Butler's statement (1978, xiii) 'In the years following [1850] a number of stones were erected in relation to those who had died previous to 1850': there are probably too many to have all been added retrospectively.

The above sample of 629 revealed 48 (7.6%) instances of named months; six were 19th century, 42 were 20th century. Judging by the condition of the stone in 1854 as described by Borrow (1862, 515) it had been there for more than four years; note too that the months were named, and the words 'To the Memory of', exceed the 'name, age and date of death' advice.

Some Quakers have been found to have spent well in excess of what would be required for the advocated simplicity of funeral and burial site. It is suggested here that because not all Friends had Quaker spouses or relations, there could be pressure from peers, business associates, friends (with a small f), and non-Quaker relations, to provide 'what was due according to the status of the deceased and the status of the bereaved' (Gittings 1984, 88–9).

There is a common view that a Christian burial is indicated by east–west alignment of a grave, with head west. Quakers belong to a Christian organisation (not necessarily as Christian individuals), but have no reason for or against using such an alignment for burial.

The statement by Fassnidge (1992, 24) that 'early Quakers cared little where their mortal remains were buried so long as it was not in a churchyard; the important thing was to have no truck with the Anglican church', and that by Milligan and Thomas (1983, 26), 'Friends have seldom felt a sentimental attachment to burial grounds', is endorsed by the Quakers (Religious Society of Friends 1992a) and the 1995 *Book of Discipline* (15.10):

> Disused burial grounds – especially those where there is no meeting house adjacent – have sometimes proved burdensome to monthly meeting. In such cases the possibility of sale should be considered, with due regard to the use to which the ground would be put.

Milligan and Thomas (1983, 3) suggest 'the reputation of Friends for full and efficient registration is not as justified as could be wished'. This is borne out archaeologically by evidence from coffin (name) plates, of individuals whose names do not appear in the records (observed, Stock, this volume). White (1971, 55) also confirms that:

> Attempts were made to keep very careful records of burials. Grave-makers [an often-used term, more versatile than 'grave-digger'] were supplied with registers which were to indicate names, dates and places of burials. Sometimes these books were not fully kept as desired, and sometimes they were lost, so that the exact spots where some eminent Friends were buried are not known. This puts them on a nice equality with those whose bones had been moved when the disused burial grounds were acquired by Authorities for other purposes, and those whose headstones were cheerfully displaced by 20th century Friends so as to convert graveyards into gardens or playgrounds.

Judging by the number of non-members, disownments, and abodes at death, out of the area, those interred in a Quaker burial ground are not necessarily members of the Religious Society of Friends. Non-members in the Bathford burial ground accounted for 28 (11.6%) of the 241 registered interments (Stock, this volume).

Public cemeteries, like Quaker burial grounds, appear to be largely laid out for efficient use of the available space, with the axes of the graves to suit the plan at a given location. A particular choice of grave axis could be made if space were available on that axis. An area for Quaker burials has been reserved in Mere Cemetery, Wiltshire (Fig 10.3).

Figure 10.4 illustrates that the chronological insertion of graves does not necessarily conform to an ordered spatial plan. The head to foot sequence is more common than the side by side configuration. From the health and safety point of view the former is preferable (consider two funerals on the same day) as side by side open graves would be logistically hazardous when lowering the coffin. Tree roots, rock, walled graves, and ground-water, together with pressure from families, all have a part to play in the layout. Grave-makers would probably be more aware of the problems than a committee intent on efficiency of space-filling.

A letter in *The Friend* (1996, vol 154, no 44, 24) asked about the custom of Quakers being buried standing up. This is an often-heard 'statement of fact' but the responses suggested that the subjective impression given by small flat gravestones was its origin. The custom is not supported by archaeological observations to date.

Cremation did not appear to cause any misgivings. For a detailed discussion of the history of cremation in England, see Jupp (1990).

The Quakers already had an effective structure for recording for their own use, and welcomed the advent of civil registration, because it removed the Church's monopoly and any need for involvement with the Church.

The form of the present-day Quaker funeral is explained in the leaflet *Quaker Funerals* (Religious Society of Friends 1992b) for the benefit of those who are unfamiliar with Quaker ways:

> The Meeting for Worship on the occasion of a funeral or memorial meeting held after the manner of the Society of Friends has no set form. It may be held either in a convenient meeting place or at the graveside, or both. Gathering together in silence, all present are invited to enter into the communion of prayer, bearing in mind those who are bereaved.
>
> The silence may be broken by vocal prayer, by the reading of a passage from the Bible or other helpful words, as well as spoken messages, some of which may testify to the qualities which the deceased by the grace of God displayed in life. Anyone who feels moved may speak.
>
> In this way loving remembrance and thankfulness may rightly find expression, together with thoughts of comfort and sympathy for those left behind. Whether in silence or otherwise, all who are present may help by their thought and

prayer, in the fellowship into which we are brought together by the Spirit of Christ.

The meeting ends with the shaking of hands.

The above, in practice today, does not exclude the use of music, or hymn singing, or some flowers, or a more structured 'programmed' approach; what it does exclude is the need for an ordained priest to control matters.

Conclusion

It can be seen that theoretical simplicity belies the complexities of practice, at least in some instances.

- Despite advice to the contrary, gravestones dated 1717 to 1850 do exist.
- Named, rather than numbered months are sometimes used on gravestones, again contrary to advice.
- The alignment of graves makes best use of the available space.
- Spatial and chronological arrangement of graves is often at variance.
- Lead coffins, walled graves, and other structures can be found in Quaker burial grounds.
- Those interred in a Quaker burial ground are not necessarily members of the Religious Society of Friends.

- Public cemeteries are non-Church and are therefore acceptable to Quakers.
- The re-burial of unidentified human remains, with a ceremony conducted by a priest, is not necessarily appropriate.
- In the event of potential disturbance of a Quaker (or any other) burial ground, ahead of exhumation there should be 'a well-considered archaeological assessment and evaluation combined with a preceding programme of historical research' (Cox & Stock 1995, 146).
- No archaeological evidence has so far been found to support the often-heard statement 'Quakers are buried standing up'.
- Yearly Meeting has a moderating effect on the other meetings, certainly regarding burial practice.
- The findings endorse the conclusion of Ubelaker (1995, 47) that:

  Historic mortuary [burial ground] sites offer new challenges and exciting new possibilities to supplement the existing written record.

A much larger sample is needed for confirmation of the above conclusions. The author is continuing his research, and endeavouring to communicate enthusiasm for such work in post-medieval burial practice, both archaeological and historical.

Figure 10.3   Mere Cemetery, Wiltshire, which has an area for Quaker burials (photo: G Stock)

* = Grave with contiguous horizontal and vertical graves dated plus and minus one year. |Date Date| = Grave group with same date.

```
        1917  *1842 *1842  1885  1855         1895
  1906  *1838 *1838  1875  1832  1867         1858
  1914  *1829 *1829  1871  *1829 1893  1907
  1864  1907  1867   1860  *1830 *1873 *1874 1907
  1938  1854  1842   1879  1842  1868  1845  1832
  1899        1867   1863  1856  1860  1858  1901
  1909  1854  1835   1859  1867  1862  1878  1933
        *1830 *1829  1859  1835  1876  1899
  1926  1829  1839   1820  1879  1865  1882  1920
        1833  1866   1835  1924  1883  1885  1912
        1837  *1831  1825  1814  1817  1851  1907
  1927  1833  *1831  1832  1929  1905  1856  1904
        1861  1855   1865  1832  1938  1918  1896  1847
        1882  1926   1868  1946        1924  1834
  1941  1858  1823   1840  1822        1905  1861  1859
  1860  *1839 *1940  1885  1922  1908  1876  1827  1816
  1945  1852  1927   *1919 *1920 1903  1893  1864  1859
  1920  1880  1920   1837  1866  1890  *1868 1860  1875
  1912        1913   1858  *1863 1885  *1869 1881  1907
        1920  1903   1854  *1862 1868  1829  1819  1840
        1924  1838   1831  1891  *1861 *1863 *1863 1824
        *1907 *1860  1845  1851  *1860 *1860 1845  1816
        *1906 *1860  1848  *1859 *1858 1856  1836  *1859
        1892  *1858  1900  *1859 *1860 1838  *1858 *1858
        *1863 *1857 *1856 *1856 *1856 *1855 *1855 *1855
        *1862 *1855 *1855 *1854 *1854 *1854 *1855 1860
        1892  *1855 *1854 *1853 *1853 *1853 *1852 *1851
        1915  1853  *1851 *1851 *1851 *1851 *1851 *1851
              *1850 *1850 *1849 *1848 *1849 *1848 *1847
        *1850 *1849 *1848 *1848 *1848 *1847 *1846 *1847
        *1898 *1848 *1846 *1846 *1846 *1846 *1846 *1845
        *1898 *1846 *1846 *1846 1838  *1845 *1844 *1845
        1885  1848  *1845 *1845 1856  *1844 *1844 *1843
        *1843 *1843 *1843 *1843 *1842 *1843 *1842 *1842
 *1841 *1842 *1842 *1842 *1841 *1841 *1841 *1840 *1840 *1840
 *1841 *1841 *1840 *1840 *1840 *1839 *1839 *1839 *1839 *1839
 *1838 *1838 *1838 *1838 1842  *1838 *1838 *1837 *1837 *1837
 *1837 *1837 *1837 *1837 *1837 *1836 *1836 *1836 *1836 *1836
 *1835 *1835 *1835 *1835 *1835 *1835 *1834 *1834 *1834 *1834
 *1834 *1834 *1833 *1833 *1833 *1833 *1833 *1833 *1832 *1832
 *1834 *1834 *1832 *1832 *1832 *1832 *1832 *1832 *1831 *1831
 *1834 *1834 *1831 *1831 *1831 *1830 *1830 *1830 *1830 *1829
 *1834 *1833 *1829 *1829 *1829 *1829 *1828 *1828 *1828 *1828
```

Figure 10.4 Quakers Friars, Bristol, interments: year of first interment in grave, derived from Plan SF / PL / 1 (Bristol Record Office)

Acknowledgements

Grateful thanks are due to Margaret Cox, who recognised the potential of my earlier research material, and encouraged and guided me to make something of it; the late Harold Fassnidge, who was the Custodian of Records for North Somerset and Wilts Monthly Meeting and who introduced me to the Religious Society of Friends; Roger Angerson and Kathleen Cottrell (Bristol and Frenchay Monthly Meeting) for the benefit of their knowledge of Quaker ways; Malcolm Thomas (Friends House Librarian) who together with Sylvia Carlyle, Rosamond Cummins, Peter Daniels, Tabatha Driver, Josef Keith and Edward H Milligan (former Friends House Librarian) guided me through the Quaker records. And many more. . .

Appendix 10.1

Chronology of *The Book of Discipline*

1668–90 *A Book of Several Things Relating to the Service of Truth to be taken notice of by Friends at Monthly and Quarterly Meetings.* [An earlier attempt in manuscript to organise minutes and advice.]

until 1738 Separate items distributed.

1738 Manuscript Compilation distributed to Quarterly and Monthly Meetings: *Christian and Brotherly Advices* ('Book of Extracts')

1783 First Printed Edition: *London Yearly Meeting, Extracts from the Minutes and Advices*

1792 *Supplement* [this, and subsequent revisions, printed]

1802 *Extracts from the Minutes and Advices of the Yearly Meeting of Friends*

1822 *Supplement*

1834 *Rules of Discipline of the Religious Society of Friends with Advices*

1849 *Supplement*, including Marriage and Registration Acts 1836

1861 Divided into chapters and later, 3 parts: *Christian Doctrine, Christian Practice* and *Church Government*

1883 *Book of Christian Discipline of the Religious Society of Friends* divided into three parts: *Christian Doctrine, Christian Practice* and *Church Government*

1906 *Christian Discipline of the Religious Society of Friends in Great Britain and Australia*: Vol. 1: *Doctrine and Practice*; Vol. 2: *Church Government*

1911 *Christian Discipline of the Religious Society of Friends* Part II *Christian Practice*

1917 *Christian Discipline of the Religious Society of Friends* with Part I *Christian Doctrine* [1883]; Part II *Christian Practice* [1911]; Part III *Church Government*

1921 1st Part (*Christian Doctrine*) became *Christian life, faith and thought* (the 1st Part of *Christian Discipline*)

1925 *Christian Practice* (Part II), being the 2nd part of *Christian Discipline of the Religious Society of Friends in Great Britain*

1931 *Church Government* (Part III of *Christian Discipline*)

1960 *Christian Life, Faith and Thought* and *Christian Practice* together became *Christian Faith and Practice*

1968 Revision of *Church Government*

1980 Reprint of *Church Government* with subsequent amendments

1990 Supplement to the 1980 printing of *Church Government*

1995 *Quaker Faith and Practice: The book of Christian discipline of the Yearly Meeting of the Religious Society of Friends (Quakers) in Britain*

11 The 18th and early 19th century Quaker burial ground at Bathford, Bath and North-East Somerset *Gwynne Stock*

Introduction

The construction of the Batheaston bypass by the Highways Agency required the complete removal of the Quaker burial ground in the parish of Bathford (ST 7851 6710), see Figure 11.1. This was carried out in fifteen days from 6 December 1993. The archaeological evaluation of the route of the road noted the presence of the burial ground, but opinion of the post-medieval site was such that no archaeological involvement was requested at the Public Inquiry in 1990. Consequently, no responsibility was placed upon the Highways Agency to go beyond the statutory requirements of exhumation (Garratt-Frost *et al* 1992; Smale 1994). The author was granted permission to carry out an un-funded, solo, watching brief. The human skeletal remains were exhumed and were re-interred at Haycombe Cemetery, Bath on 22 December 1993 with no ceremony and no Quaker present. Some information regarding Quaker funerary and burial practices, which would have otherwise been lost, was recorded.

The site

Location

Bathford was formerly in the historic county of Somerset; during the exhumation, in the District of Wansdyke in the County of Avon, and now in Bath and North East Somerset. The parish of Bathford is incidental to the Quaker burial ground within its bounds. The former site of the burial ground is now within the area of the roundabout at the eastern end of the Batheaston bypass.

Geology

The site lay on alluvial deposits containing some belemnites in the lower level, 30 metres to the east of the River Avon, some 100 metres downstream of the confluence with the By Brook. The area was subject to flooding, but there was no significant sign of silt in the walled grave cavities, contrary to that which might have been expected. The burial ground was reasonably level but it was not possible to make measurements, due to the accumulation of rubbish. In elevation the burial ground formed a wedge, relative to the natural slope of the ground towards the river. The local geology was described as 'Lower and Middle Jurassic undivided, in foundered areas' (IGS Sheet 265, Bath).

History

The lists of Trusts and Trust Properties (1870) in Friends House Library (Book of Deeds 64), and Wiltshire Record Office (1699/42B) record that, in a Deed dated 19 October 1734, a piece of land 'Was acquired by purchase in 1734 of John Cowling. It [in 1870] adjoins the south side of the Turnpike Road leading from Bath to Devizes, and is within a few yards of the GWR, which crosses the road near this spot'. It further states that 'It is not now in use; the last interment was in 1845'. The first recorded burial was in 1703 (Burial Digest for Bristol and Somerset Quarterly Meeting, Friends House Library). The site was sold to Avondale House in 1933 and compulsorily acquired by land exchange in 1993.

The measurements described in the 1734 Deed as '54 feet next to the London Road and 52 feet towards the river' agreed closely with the 1993 dimensions. Additionally, according to a questionnaire sent to local Quaker Meetings regarding the 1843 *Bill for the Improvement of Health in Towns* (MS vol 74, Friends House Library), the Bathford

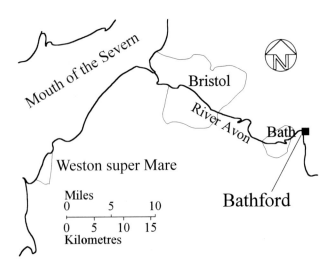

Figure 11.1   Location of Bathford, Bath & North-East Somerset

144

burial ground interments had an average depth of six feet; the actual range of depths was found to be from about one metre to a little over three metres (3 to 10 feet, an average of 6½ feet). The same questionnaire also indicated that the area was 2397 square feet, which should have been the available area within the walls. It was therefore considered unlikely that any burials would have taken place beyond the present wall. That proved to be so, when the surrounding land was excavated for road-building.

The archaeology

The watching brief facilitated recording the layout of the Quaker burial ground which had been in use from 1703 to 1845. It also demonstrated that the burial practices in some instances were far from the advocated simplicity of Friends (Stock, this volume). The walled graves were constructed with Bath stone ashlar, and ten of the inhumations were in lead coffins.

The approximate north–south axis of the graves is, however, in keeping with Quaker doctrine, whereas the east–west 'liturgical' alignment of the Established Church was considered unnecessary. The walled graves, three earth burials, and the lead coffins were aligned 180 degrees from the other burials. No reason for this arrangement has been discovered.

Gravestones

The only stones remaining were two pennant ledgers (1.8m×0.9m) in the north-east corner, associated with two walled graves (W10 and W11). It transpired that one rectangular stone had no inscription and a curved broken one was upside-down and the only characters remaining were insufficient for identification. Three other ledgers, with incised inscriptions, had already been removed to the adjoining hotel grounds, where they had been built-in to various structures, as had the stone from above the old burial ground entrance with the inscription 'FRIEND'S [sic] BURIAL GROUND/ 1734'. The style of lettering and condition might suggest that it was not of mid 18th century origin, but more likely to have been created as a result of the recommendation that (Bristol 24th of 4th mo. 1868, Trusts & Trust Properties, 1870):

Where Burial Grounds are disused or detached from Meeting Houses, care should be taken to have the ownership publicly notified, and the date when acquired. That where such are walled, a substantial stone tablet should be secured in the outer wall abutting on the public thoroughfare, with the words FRIENDS' BURIAL GROUND / (DATE).

The detail from a print dated c 1845 (Figure 11.2) showing the burial ground entrance without the stone, also supports that theory.

One headstone, inscribed 'Elizabeth Spencer 1748', had been re-used as a capping stone for a walled grave W2 (Fig 11.3). Quakers preferred to use numbers for the months, as the name origins were pagan (Stock, this volume). However, all of the surviving inscriptions used the named months. Possible explanations are that the doctrinal position was largely ignored or that a non-Quaker mason was not briefed, contrary to standard practice.

The graves (Fig 11.4)

A puzzling aspect of the burial ground was that there appeared to be few signs of grave-cuts. The sections created by the machine excavation often revealed stratified layers (rather than mixed earth), which appeared to be natural, but which were interspersed with graves. It was not possible to ascertain whether or not all interments were encoffined due to the degree of disintegration.

As Quaker doctrine advocated simplicity in burial (Stock, this volume), it was a surprise to find that some had apparently considered it desirable to have lead coffins and walled graves of Bath-stone ashlar associated with their final resting places. Such features were found in the Anglican churchyard of St Nicholas, Bathampton to the west just across the River Avon (Cox & Stock 1995). Similar contradiction of doctrine was also evident at the Quaker burial ground at Kingston-upon-Thames (Bashford and Pollard, this volume).

In this paper, the terminology for describing graves is as defined by the Interpretation Act 1889 (52 & 53 Vict c 63) and cited in The Local Authorities' Cemetery Order 1977 (SI 1977 No 204, p2): 'vault' means a chamber provided for the reception of human remains or cremated human remains, together with access thereto; 'walled grave' means a grave the sides of which are lined with walls.

Registers held by Local Authority cemeteries often have headings for grave types as 'earth' and 'walled', a clear distinction. The terminology is evolving (see Litten 1991, 207; Cox & Stock 1995, 133–7; O'Brien, not necessarily with post-medieval graves in mind, 1996, 163). More and more variants are coming to light, and alternative and additional descriptions have had to be used. All examples of structures at Bathford fall into the category of 'walled grave', the remainder being 'earth graves'.

The walled graves were constructed with Bath stone ashlar, of which the quality of dressing was very variable, although generally reasonable where visible. The mortaring techniques were often slapdash. The several different forms are described below:

Figure 11.2   Bathford burial ground, c 1845 (by kind permission of Godfrey Laurence)

Figure 11.3   Bathford: 1748 headstone used as a capping stone on a walled grave (photo: G Stock)

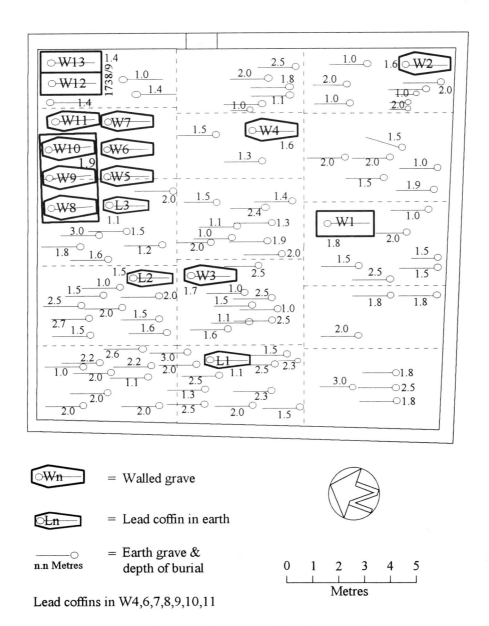

= Walled grave

= Lead coffin in earth

—————o
n.n Metres

= Earth grave &
depth of burial

0 1 2 3 4 5

Metres

Lead coffins in W4,6,7,8,9,10,11

Figure 11.4   Bathford burial ground: location of graves within the ground

- Walled grave W1, was a rectangular, buried (1.8m below the surface) walled grave for two coffins with separating iron bars.
- W2 was a coffin-shaped buried walled grave (1m below ground) with space for two coffins and holes for separating iron bars. The base was pennant sandstone. All others were built directly on earth.
- W3 was a buried (1.7m below ground) coffin-shaped 'unitary' walled grave. The term 'unitary' is suggested to describe a cist-like self-contained unit of space for one coffin. Figure 11.5 shows a plan of the more mechanically-sound notch method of construction of the foot end. This, and the head end, were the only examples. Compare the corners in Figure 11.6.
- W4/5/6/7 were each buried (0.3–0.5m) coffin-shaped walled graves with space for three coffins, with separating iron bars.

Foot end

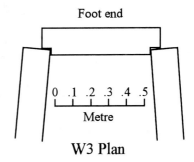

0 .1 .2 .3 .4 .5

Metre

W3 Plan

Figure 11.5   Bathford burial ground: walled grave construction

- W8/9/10 (Fig 11.6) a complex of three buried coffin-shaped structures with two-cavity, walled graves (unitary space for six coffins in all),

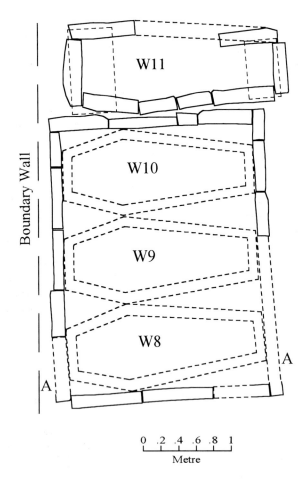

0 .2 .4 .6 .8 1
Metre

Section A - A

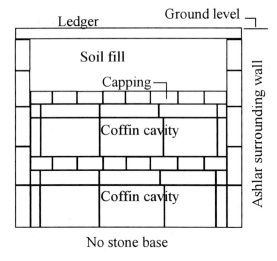

Figure 11.6 Bathford burial ground: walled graves 8–11

surrounded by an ashlar wall which extended to ground level.

- W11 (Fig 11.6) was a single cavity in the form of a shaft from ground level, with iron bars used to separate the coffins, similar to those found at Bathampton (Cox & Stock 1995, 136). It was also the only structure to be fully in conformity with Litten's (1991) description of 'shaft grave'.

- W12/13 consisted of buried, paired rectangular walled graves, with sufficient space for two coffins in each, but with no provision for bars.
- W12 had an incised date of '1738/9' which matched the Register entry for Ann Tylee 25 02 1738/9 (old and new style dates, 11th or 2nd month, February).

It is believed that the unitary form of post-medieval walled grave has not previously appeared in published literature, but it has also been seen in St Swithun's Anglican churchyard, Bathford while grave-digging (Arthur Cannings, pers comm).

Coffins

The surviving materials were wood and lead and the forms of construction were, in Litten's terminology (1991,100) triple case (inner wood coffin/lead shell/outer wood case), double case (wood inner coffin and lead outer case), and single case wood. All were single-break (coffin-shaped). The wood, where observed, was elm, and although no complete wooden coffin survived, from the available evidence it appeared that the method of construction matched the example illustrated in Reeve & Adams (1993, 79). No nails had survived, and the former presence showed only in the staining and distortion of the wood. No decorative beading or end-grain covering survived in a recognisable form. Kerfing, saw-cuts on the insides of the sides to facilitate bending at the widest part (shoulder), was noted.

The above form of construction also matched the description of coffin-making given to the author in 1994 by Arthur Cannings of Bathford, a retired carpenter with experience of coffin-making (and occasional grave-digging):

The head end of each side was held in a vertical vice and a kettle of boiling water poured over the kerfed area to *test* it round to fit the required shape (the rotted floor boards below bore witness to the process!). Planks were sawn with a straight saw using a pit. The usual thickness was three-quarters of an inch or slightly less when finished. The bottom was of interior dimensions, the top *overstood* and so covered overall. The sides and ends splayed slightly from bottom to top and a *pattern* was used to set the angle. The sides were outside the bottom and the ends, so head and foot end-grain showed. Bottoms of ends were nailed to the end-grain of the bottom.

Sides were nailed to the sides of the ends and of the bottom. Nails at about two inch intervals were cut type or oval, punched in and filled with putty, coloured to match the wood. Mouldings, fixed with panel pins, were usually applied around the upper parts of the sides and ends.

A more costly version had mouldings giving an impression of panelling. The finish was usually wax polish, occasionally (oak) French polished. Varnish was not used.

Joints and knots were sealed with pitch which was heated in the adjacent blacksmith's shop. The pitch had a tendency to ignite! Clean deal sawdust was obtained, to provide an inch or two of absorbent material in the base. An additional thickness of sawdust/shavings served as a pillow.

Alternatively, a separate pillow was bought in. Side linings, which initially lay outside, were fixed with three-eighth tacks along the upper edges, they were then folded over to cover the tacks and tucked inside. Separate end linings were applied in the same manner, and the side and end linings were united inside by folding.

The breast/name plate was obtained, and the lettering was painted on by John Francis (Tom) Cannings [brother], using a quick-drying paint. A total of eight grips were fitted, head, foot, and three each side. The top was finally secured with eight one and three-quarter inch Number 10 steel screws. A pattern was used to locate the screws in the centre of the upper part of the sides. The screws were hidden by 'mushroom' shaped covers.

All ten lead coffins appeared to have been constructed in a similar manner. Figure 11.7 shows the four component parts. A base with integral head and foot, of internal dimensions other than the extremities of the head and foot, extended some 15mm to form a lip to fold over the lid. Two sides were of external dimensions, plus a lip of some 15mm, to fold over the lid. The lid was of internal dimensions, and flat. The joints of the base and vertical portions of the ends were butted with the sides and continuously soldered internally, resulting in a right-angled external finish. The vertical portions were usually chamfered. The lid joints were most commonly wiped and radiused. The internal soldering indicates that the wooden coffin

was placed in a pre-fabricated lead shell. No patterning was seen on any surface. The form of construction matched none of the nine Spitalfields types (Reeve & Adams 1993, 84–5). What appeared to be a square hole (the edges were somewhat corroded) was noticed centrally under the coffin name-plate of one lead coffin. Such a hole would have negated any other attempt to create a sealed container.

Lead thickness was from 2–3mm and its condition was all stages from sound to oxidized to totally corroded. Analysis of samples of lead sheet and of solder by University of Bristol Interface Analysis Centre, using a Scanning Electron Microscope and Windowless Energy Dispersive X-ray Analysis, revealed the former to be of almost pure lead, and the solder predominantly tin, together with small amounts of lead and trace amounts of copper (Leon Black, pers comm). Of the ten lead coffins, eight were in walled graves and two were buried in the earth.

Coffin furnishings

Grips (handles) and grip-plates (backing plates with hinge fittings and fixings for attaching to the coffin) were recovered. Both ferrous and non-ferrous examples were present, and their distribution was such that if their use had a strict chronological basis, a strict spatial/chronological order of burial, as is suggested by Quaker doctrine, would seem unlikely (Stock, this volume). None bore any makers' name, but there were 24 design variations, some quite subtle, mostly based on the basic forms in Figure 11.8. These items were originally designed for the furniture trade in the 18th century (Julian Litten, pers comm). The high quality pressed tin grip-plate which had a ferrous grip was probably made by Thomas Pickering of Southwark *c* 1775 (Fig 11.9; Julian Litten, pers comm). The decorative assembly is shown in Figure 11.10 and dated 1775–1815 (Julian Litten, pers comm). The only item to approximate to the Spitalfields examples was that described as 'Type 01 grip' by Reeve and Adams (1993, 144, and microfiche 3).

The Spitalfields grips and grip plates (Reeve & Adams 1993, 144–5) were classified separately, with no indication of hinging or securing techniques, which themselves exhibited interesting variation at Bathford. The methods of preventing the grip swinging more than ninety degrees are illustrated in Figure 11.11, where the stop is on the hinge socket, and in Figure 11.12, where the stop is on the grip. The component parts are united using either an iron pin (Fig 11.13), or threaded stud and square nut (Fig 11.14), or by looped and splayed strip (Fig 11.15). The last two examples give an indication of the thickness of the coffin wood. Other methods involved burring and/or brazing. It can be seen that the grips were intended only for steadying (and decorative) purposes, certainly not for lifting!

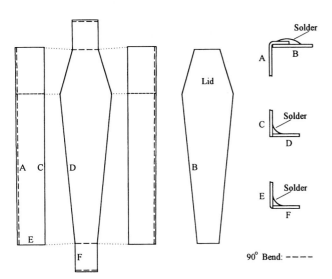

Figure 11.7   Bathford burial ground: lead coffin (shell) construction

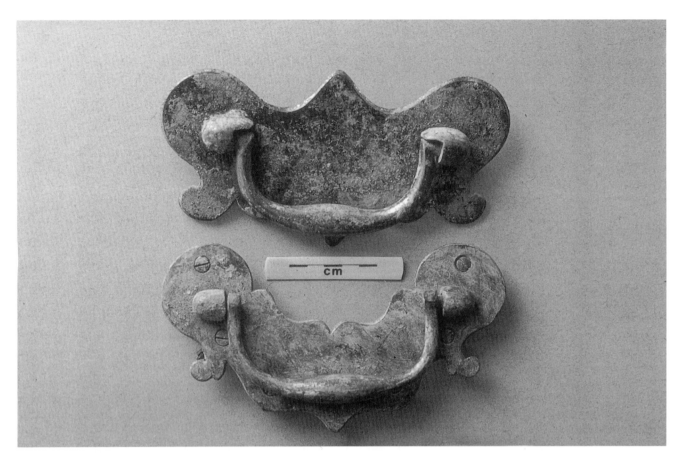

Figure 11.8   Bathford burial ground: pair of grips made for the furniture trade, 18th century (photo: G Stock)

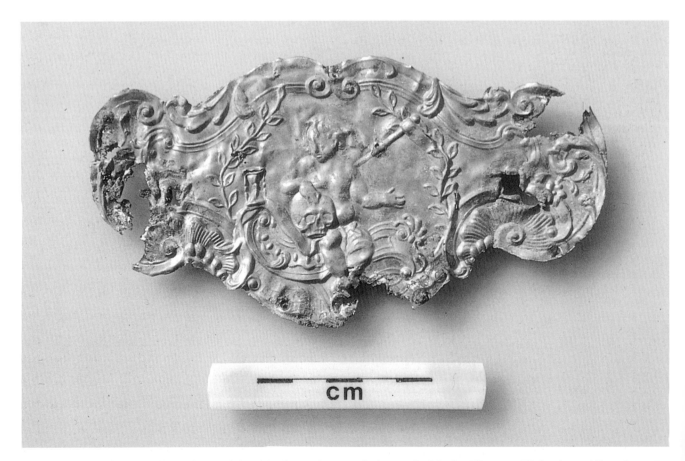

Figure 11.9   Bathford burial ground: grip plate of pressed tin, probably by Thomas Pickering of Southwark, c 1775 (photo: G Stock)

Figure 11.10   Bathford burial ground: decorative grip assembly, 1775–1815 (photo: G Stock)

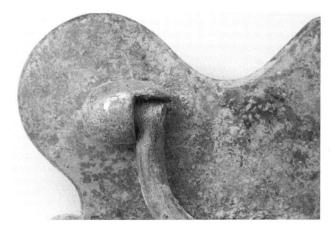

Figure 11.11   Bathford burial ground: detail of a stop on a grip socket (photo: G Stock)

Figure 11.12   Bathford burial ground: detail of a stop on a grip (photo: G Stock)

Eight coffin name plates were found; all were non-ferrous, the most usual shape being the shield, but examples of two small rectangular plates with clipped corners were also found. No other attachments were seen.

The presence of a textile cladding of the outer case was noted in some instances, by scraps sandwiched between copper-alloy grip-plates, coffin plates, and coffin wood: its survival was perhaps due to the properties of copper, as 'copper ions act as biocidal agents, thereby limiting the main agents

of biological decay' (Janaway 1987, 136). It was noticed that the best survival of wood and textile occurred where those materials were penetrated by the copper, in addition to the two-dimensional contact.

Fragments of textile linings also survived, but there were no signs of any other decoration. Pitch was present in the remains of two coffins, as were wood shavings. It was not possible to tell if the shavings had been loose, or within a mattress cover. No 'grave goods' were recovered.

Figure 11.13   Bathford burial ground: detail of iron pin fixing (photo: G Stock)

Figure 11.15   Bathford burial ground: detail of splayed fixing and survival of wood (photo: G Stock)

Figure 11.14   Bathford burial ground: detail of threaded stud and square nut fixing (photo: G Stock)

The inhumations

Of the 241 individuals recorded in the burial records (to 1836), the approximate three-dimensional locations of 102 were plotted. The preservation ranged from very good to totally disintegrated. There being no qualified osteologist present, no osteological analysis took place. All skeletons, where observed, were supine with hands at sides and with legs straight. This was the position of 90% of the Spitalfields remains (Molleson & Cox 1993, 197).

Little evidence of burial attire remained; examples of woven textile, felt, and flock were noted, but not further identified. The skeleton in one lead coffin had what appeared to be the remains of a cloth over the face, which has been termed by Litten (1991, 40) a *sudarium*, but there was insufficient survival of textile to identify shroud, winding-sheet, or any other actual form of dress.

A sample of 185 records of dates of death and burial derived from the Burial Digests revealed that 47% of burials were within three days of death,

and a further 40% within six days (Fig 11.16). Reference to the burial records demonstrated that Sunday was the most common day for burial (Fig 11.17). That trend was repeated in the records of the Spitalfields named sample (Cox 1996a), Bathampton (Stock, unpublished), and in the parish of Tormarton ten miles to the north (Stock, unpublished).

Conclusion

The archaeological recording of the commercial clearance of this burial ground, albeit a solo watching brief, enabled the acquisition of new knowledge regarding 18th and early 19th century Quaker funerary and burial practices. The archaeological evidence showed that, at Bathford at least, some of the practices, certainly with regard to walled graves, lead coffins, and large memorial stones, were at variance with the advocated simplicity of Quaker ways (Stock, this volume). Such evidence should provide a valuable basis for further research to ascertain whether or not Bathford was typical. Further, and perhaps of greater significance, it clearly demonstrates both the potential of post-medieval burial sites and the deserving case they present for a thorough and considered archaeological response by curators in the future.

Acknowledgements

The Highways Agency allowed me to be present at the burial ground clearance, and I thank Neil Hawkins and Kenneth Petch for their support, and also David Carmichael, (Sir Alexander Gibb & Partners), to whom I was responsible, and who made me very welome. Grateful thanks are also due to Alan Bratt, Environmental Health Officer, the former Wansdyke District Council; John Crutcher, Superintendent of Cemeteries, Bath; Edward Rowe, Department of the Environment; and Vince

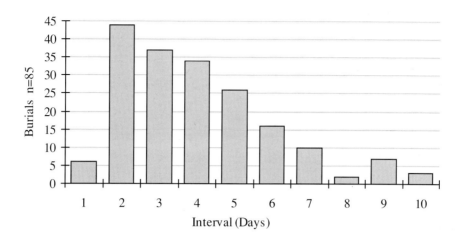

Figure 11.16   Bathford burial ground: interval plotted between death and burial

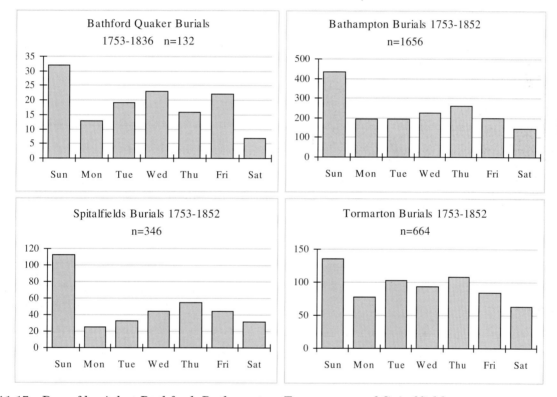

Figure 11.17   Day of burial at Bathford, Bathampton, Tormarton, and Spitalfields

Russett, Archaeological Officer, the former County of Avon, for their invaluable help and advice. The cooperation, interest, and enthusiasm of Bernard Milner (Turfsoil Ltd), is especially appreciated. Valuable post-exhumation help was generously given by Julian Litten, funerary historian, regarding coffin furniture; Geoffrey Allen and Leon Black, University of Bristol, Interface Analysis Centre, for the analysis of the coffin lead. Arthur Cannings, Bathford shared his experience of coffin-making, and Godfrey Laurence, Bathford allowed me to photograph and publish his *c* 1845 Bathford print. Margaret Cox and Harold Fassnidge; the staff of Friends House Library, Malcolm Thomas (Librarian), Sylvia Carlyle, Rosamond Cummins, Peter Daniels, Tabatha Driver, Josef Keith, and Edward H Milligan (former Librarian) also had a very significant part to play here.

12 'In the burying place' – the excavation of a Quaker burial ground *Louise Bashford and Tony Pollard*

Introduction

The excavation of a Quaker burial ground in London Road, Kingston-upon-Thames, over a period of ten weeks in Autumn 1996, was motivated by the need to remove all human remains from the ground beneath a vacant lot which had been selected for residential development (Fig 12.1). The site's earlier role as a Quaker burial ground was historically recorded, and had been confirmed during an evaluation carried out by MoLAS (Miller 1993), which had identified a number of graves in the northern part of the site.

This paper is not intended as a definitive statement on the excavation, with post-excavation analysis presently on-going. However, it does hope to achieve more than a conventional interim report. This is not to say that a summary consideration of the excavation results is not presented here, but what this paper also does is give room to issues which do not always find their way into excavation reports. Included in this discussion is a consideration of attitudes toward the recently dead, and ethical issues related to commercial archaeology and the dead. On a more project-specific level this paper also discusses some of the problems related to this excavation and some drawbacks of the strategy adopted. It is hoped that these observations will be of use to those undertaking burial ground excavations in the future.

The somewhat unconventional approach of this contribution is perhaps in keeping with the nature of the site itself; a nonconformist burial ground. The excavation provided a rare opportunity to investigate an early Quaker community through analysis of their burial practices and physical remains. Archaeological excavation of this type of post-medieval burial ground is unprecedented, and obviously required an approach geared towards the specific requirements of this unusual site. In order to

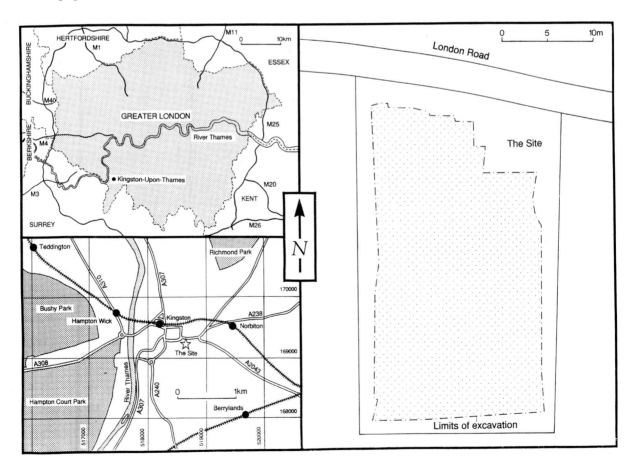

Figure 12.1   Location plan of the Quaker burial ground at London Road, Kingston upon Thames (illustration: Rob Goller)

maximize the value of the data recovered the brief and specification provided by the Greater London Archaeology Advisory Service (English Heritage) and Margaret Cox (1996c) identified various avenues of research to be addressed during the course of the excavation and subsequent post-excavation analysis of the burial ground, in relation to what we knew of standard contemporary burial practices. The main research topics relating to the excavation method and burial ground analysis were pre-burial ground land-use, topographic development of the burial ground, burial rites, and undertaking practices. The background to the project and the issues relating to it are discussed below, since many of these have a wider bearing on the practice of post-medieval burial ground excavation in Britain.

Approaches to excavation

A lack of excavated precedents for this type of burial ground and financial restraints led to the adoption of a partially experimental excavation strategy, based upon the division of the site into two areas, which were designated high and low resolution. This division was intended to speed up the excavation process, a critical factor dictated by financial and time constraints, while also maximizing the value of the data recovered. It was intended that skeletal material from each area would receive differential treatment on site and a different level of recording and osteological analysis. The area selected for high resolution treatment consisted of a sample believed, on the basis of preliminary documentary research, to provide a cross-section of the interred population through the chronological development of the burial ground, and included all burials within north–south strips constituting 30% of the total area available. Any skeletons surviving in an exceptional state of preservation, showing signs of unusual pathology, or with legible coffin plates from the remainder of the site, were also to be treated as high resolution. This strategy unwittingly introduced a bias into the results, for a number of reasons. Firstly, it was quickly realised that the site extended beyond the excavation boundaries and the skeletal sample was therefore incomplete. Secondly, the high resolution area contained not only the greatest density of burials, resulting in a high resolution sample that was larger than the 30% intended, but also contained a high number of skeletons which were either incomplete due to truncation, or were badly preserved. Alterations were also made to the definition of high resolution on site, largely as a result of time constraints. In addition, differential preservation meant that the definition of high resolution was again changed at the analysis stage, with better-preserved skeletons favoured over poorly preserved examples, thus resulting in an analysed sample which differed greatly from the excavated high resolution sample.

A single-context recording system was employed on the site, but was found to be time-consuming and often uninformative during the course of this rescue excavation; grave cuts varied only in their dimensions, and fills were of uniform character. With hindsight, separate context sheets for grave cut, fill, coffin, and skeleton, in addition to recording sheets for osteology and palaeopathology, may not have been necessary for this type of site: recording the grave contents on a single burial sheet, with additional sheets for recording osteology/palaeopathology and noteworthy coffins would have been equally useful.

History of the burial ground

The Quakers are excellent record-keepers and the availability of documentary sources relating to the site made a valuable contribution to the project, representing a human dimension of special interest to archaeologists more accustomed to dealing with largely anonymous burial groups. Documentary research carried out by Gwen Jones brought the Quaker community to life in a manner which could never have been achieved by archaeology alone.

The most informative records were the minutes of the Men's Monthly Meetings, and the registers of births, marriages, and burials.[1] From these documents the broad history of the burial ground could be reconstructed. In 1663 the Quakers leased and subsequently bought a garden and orchard for use as a burial ground. At that time, gardens and orchards were favoured for burial of nonconformists, who did not wish to be interred in parish churchyards (Steele 1973, 674–7). The first person interred was Ann Stevens in 1664, and the area available for burials was increased in 1683, 1687, 1691, and 1739. In 1691, the minutes record a clause for enlarging the burial ground; 'and the burying place to be taken off straight from before the gate to the next row of trees straight up to the brick wall next to the field . . . and that a fence be made between the burying place and the garden let to John Green . . .' (Men's Minutes, held in the Library of Society of Friends [LSOF], Minutes of 5 November, 1691). The final interment was made in 1814, when another plot of land was adopted as a burial ground, and the London Road burial ground fell out of use.

The historical documents are both exciting and tantalizing. A vast body of data has been generated from the Quaker records, but very little of it is correlated in the archaeological record, since, quite naturally, a certain amount of pre-knowledge of local topography is assumed. Unfortunately, with many of the contemporary landmarks either destroyed or buried outside the site boundary, the detail of much of the records is lost to us. They tell us of the inception, expansion, and decline of the burial ground, its boundaries, problems with trespassers, and the presence of walls, fences, paths, trees, a vine and arbour, a house and barn, and a well, none of which were found on the site.[2] A well discovered at the northern end of the site was back-filled in the 16th century and therefore pre-dates the burial ground. Former boundaries may be inferred where burial density suddenly alters, or a number of graves are set in line, for example immediately south of burials 1199 to 1322 (Fig 12.2). To the west of burial 1199 there is an apparent boundary extending to the north and south-west, and part of the western edge of the site may be seen where burials are lacking to the west of the vault.

The surviving Quaker records document 497 burials at the London Road site, and a total of 364 burials were located during the excavation. On site it was clear that not all of the burials were recorded in the Quaker records since initials and dates recovered from wooden and lead coffins did not correspond with the registers (Fig 12.3). It was also apparent that the burial ground extends beyond the excavated site perimeter, and its exact boundaries are therefore unclear, although the northern extent is known from indirect evidence in the Men's Minutes, which state that the vault 'lyeth about 28 yards in measure from the North Wall that now abuts against the road or highway leading from Kingston Town to London, wherein is now a door, leading into said Burying Ground from the road or highway there' (LSOF, Minutes Volume 3 (1745–78): 2, memorandum entered on 9 January 1745). This would place the northern boundary approximately 2m outside the excavated area, beneath the existing pavement of London Road. Growth of the burial ground was limited to the south and east by contemporary buildings, but it is uncertain how far it extends to the west, or how many burials remain outside the excavated area.

Quaker burial practices

The first features exposed during the excavation were two brick-built structures located toward the centre of the site. One of these was related to a much later building but the other was instantly recognisable as a burial vault, its collapsed roof only partially covering the lead coffins within (Fig 12.4). Across the site in general, some of the issues relevant to our research aims became immediately apparent, since burials intensively occupied the available land and there was a wide variation in the preferred orientation (see Fig 12.2). Burial density was a major feature on the site; graves were both closely spaced and heavily intercut, although frequency varied within the excavated area.

The early phases of the burial ground saw reuse of previous grave cuts as in the cases of burials 1020 and 1052, 1048 and 1053, and 1122 and 1135. The secondary burials within these cuts lie immediately above the initial interment, but do not appear to have been contemporary. It is therefore assumed that grave markers were used in these early peri-

ods, in the manner described by Stock, this volume. The occurrence of truncated burials surprised modern Quakers visiting the site, and indeed, it is believed that the idea was abhorrent to the contemporary Quakers, since 'no Friends [were to] level any grave in the burying ground without order of the meeting' (LSOF, Minutes of August 1693) and (one of the elders was to) 'oversee the opening of any ground in the burying ground' (LSOF, Minutes of October 1693). Where possible, and where space was limited, preference appears to have been for reuse of cuts rather than risking truncation of previous interments. The historical sources give instances of the 'levelling' of graves in the early phases of the burial ground, probably resulting in periodic clearance of grave markers, which were finally banned in Quakerism in the yearly meeting of 1717, when the *Rules of Discipline* state that '... Friends ... have gone into the vain custom of erecting monuments over the dead bodies of friends by stones, inscriptions etc ... all such monuments should be removed, and that none be any where made or set up at, near, or over, the dead bodies of friends or others, in friends burying places for time to come' (Steele 1973, 677, quoting *Rules of Discipline* (3rd edition, 1834), 70). Although these clearances, along with repeated changes in both grave-diggers and site boundaries, would have made it increasingly difficult to recall and pinpoint the exact location of previous burials, the primary cause of inter-cutting burials was probably spatial pressure, experienced despite periodic expansion of the burial ground.

The extent of truncation varied enormously. Often only the extremities of the skeleton were affected, but in some cases it was difficult to determine whether we were dealing with articulated or disarticulated remains, the deciding factor being the presence of coffin furniture or signs of a grave cut. Although Stock has stated that reburial of unidentified remains should have been unnecessary in Quakerism (Stock, this volume), disturbed remains at Kingston had been treated respectfully by grave-diggers; charnel was placed in pits excavated in the base of the grave cut (Fig 12.5), with the recent burial placed above. These pits were often difficult to identify, having been cut into the natural subsoil with no visible edges. The majority were found by tapping the base of the grave cut in order to locate hollow sounds, which were then investigated, resulting in the discovery of pits such as that shown in Figure 12.5. Consideration of the stratigraphy then enabled much of the charnel to be reunited with the remainder of the skeleton. Only in the case of disturbed infant remains had the charnel not been given a secondary burial, but was lost in the grave fill. Careful recording of charnel recovered from each grave has resulted in the discovery of several infant burials which were so heavily truncated as to render their grave cuts invisible during excavation and others were discovered by sieving the dried bulk samples taken from apparently

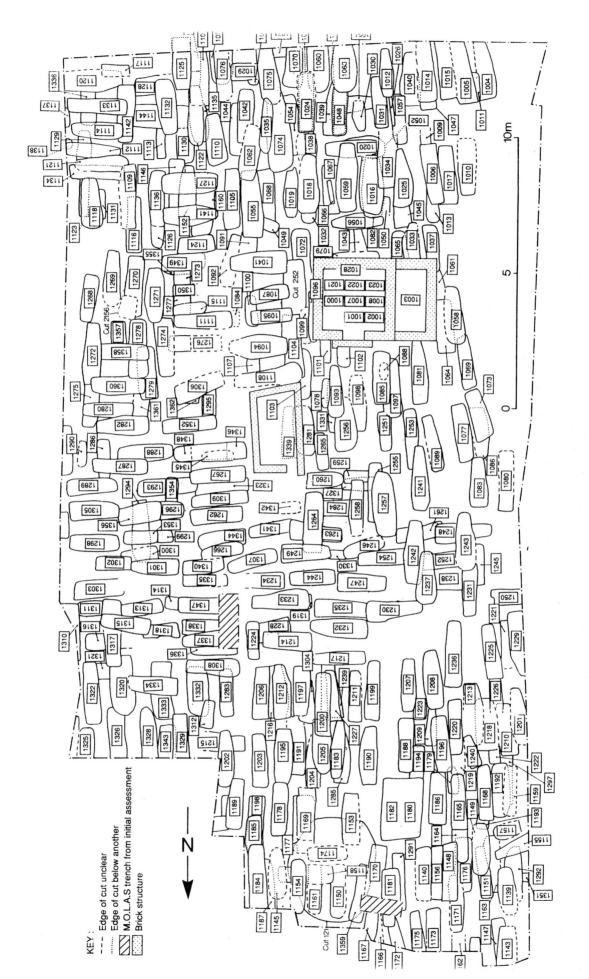

Figure 12.2   Plan of all excavated burials at London Road. The circular feature at the northern end of the site is a medieval well (illustration: Rob Goller)

158

Figure 12.3 Excavated grave showing biographical details indicated by studs attached to the coffin lid (photo: Archaeology South-East)

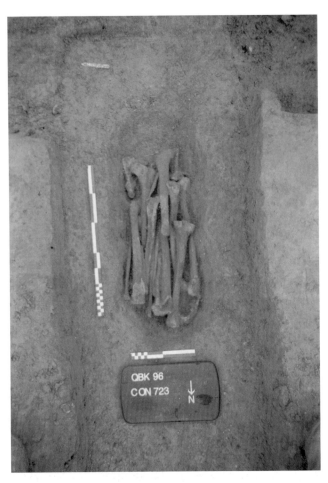

Figure 12.5 Charnel pit found beneath another burial, this contained partial remains of five individuals (photo: Archaeology South-East)

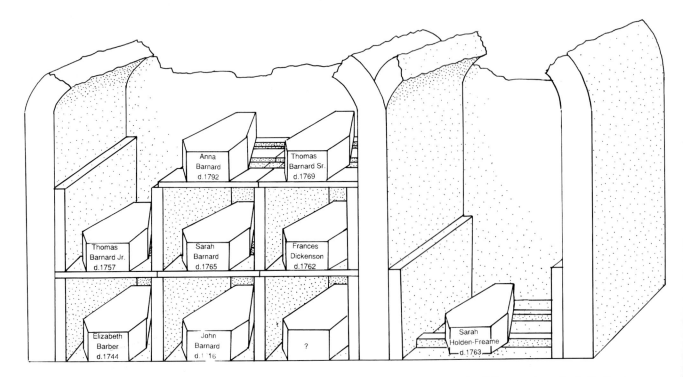

Figure 12.4 Reconstruction of the Barnard vault, looking south, not to scale (illustration: Rob Goller)

empty cuts. The size of charnel pits also varied according to the quantity of remains requiring secondary burial, from a single shovelful to pits large enough to hold their own extended burial.

Burial orientation (Fig 12.6) was the main indicator that this burial ground was nonconformist in character. North–south burials comprised 55% of the total, with others oriented south–north or west–east. Only 10% of skeletons were oriented east–west in the traditional Christian manner. Orientation within the burial ground appears to have resulted from a series of influences. The topography of the burial ground was one factor, with alignment affected by the presence of walls, paths, and trees which were gradually removed as the burial ground was enlarged.[3] In addition to this, burials were initially spaced in such a way as to avoid earlier interments. This can be seen in the southern portion of the site, where a series of west–east burials have been inserted between rows of north–south and south–north ones (Fig 12.6). The strength of Quaker beliefs must have changed over time, and there may have been times when the group needed to promote a greater sense of unity by distancing themselves from established traditions, visible in the burial ground through burial alignment. Changes in the grave-digger may have affected orientation, since grave-diggers were not always members of the Quaker community and may have occasionally enforced their own views on the group. In the late 18th century the burial registers record a number of non-Quaker interments in this burial ground, representing adults married into the community who may have been given different rites.

Orientation has been a useful indicator of possible phasing, with widespread changes in burial alignment in different areas such as the north-eastern corner and central east–west strip (Fig 12.2), suggesting development of the burial ground, either due to the factors mentioned previously or to documented enlargement of the burial area. Four broad alterations have been identified, based on biographical data extracted from coffin lids, analysis of the matrix, and patterns appearing in the burial ground. For convenience, these phases have been associated with the burial ground expansions mentioned in the Minutes, but the results of this analysis are adversely affected by the limited number of dated burials, the rapid expansion of the burial ground, and the limited size of the excavated sample. Without knowing the full extent of the burial ground boundary, it is unclear how the remainder of the burial ground will affect the phasing. Further problems with site phasing result from the early Quaker practice of burying within private gardens and orchards, mentioned in early Quaker records across the country (Steele 1973, 674–7). In the Minutes of 1678, one grave-digger was ordered to cease making private arrangements for burials, which were from then on only to be allowed with the permission of the community elders. It is not clear whether this was a check on overcrowding, or to

prevent burial taking place within the orchard, which lay outside the bounds of the burial ground at that time.

Bodily attitude did not vary greatly across the site, the majority of individuals being laid in a supine position with arms by the side, indicating that the limbs had been tied. Occasionally arms were found in different positions, usually with one lying extended below the pelvis, and the other either extended on top of the pelvis or folded across the body. Instances of feet and hands being crossed were identified, and sometimes one of the legs was bent with knee facing outwards. These positions are consistent with the corpse being placed in the coffin after the period of rigor mortis had elapsed, and imply minimal post mortem arrangement of the body. In one case, the body was apparently laid on its side in a semi-flexed position, and infants were interred in extended or crouched positions.

Preservation conditions varied from grave to grave, but in general organic materials did not survive well, to the relief of the excavators. Occasional tufts of hair or patches of skin-like periosteum were found on the burials, with soft tissue surviving on the individuals interred in lead coffins. No soft tissue samples were retained for hygiene and financial reasons. Lead coffins were dealt with by exhumation contractors, and trained osteologists examined the interments (see Start & Kirk, this volume).

Scant evidence for burial dress was recovered, usually limited to examples of shroud pins occurring around the skull. Partial remains of burial attire were preserved in three of the lead coffins, including the remnants of a leather cap associated with two skeletons, leather ties in the sternum area of another, and cuff-links with one individual. These fragments would be more consistent with day-wear than specific funerary attire (see Janaway, this volume). Litten has associated day-clothes with cases of infectious disease, although Janaway has found that there may be a variety of reasons for burial in non-funerary attire, which is only to be expected given the variety of human character (see Litten, and Janaway, this volume). The lead coffins contained only traces of winding sheets, and occasional imprints of mattresses, pillows, and coffin linings were noted but not retained. No evidence was found that personal items other than clothing were interred with the body. A pipe damper found in one coffin may have been the property of the grave-digger, and lost by him during grave preparation.

At the time of writing, the coffins are undergoing analysis (Richmond, forthcoming). Interim results of this work suggest that these Quakers were buried in a variety of caskets, reflecting the common types of burial container prevalent in the 17th and 18th centuries. Although the *Rules of Discipline* imply that the Quakers frowned on ostentatious displays within the burial ground (Steele 1973, 677) this attitude did not apply below ground at Kingston, and coffin types were

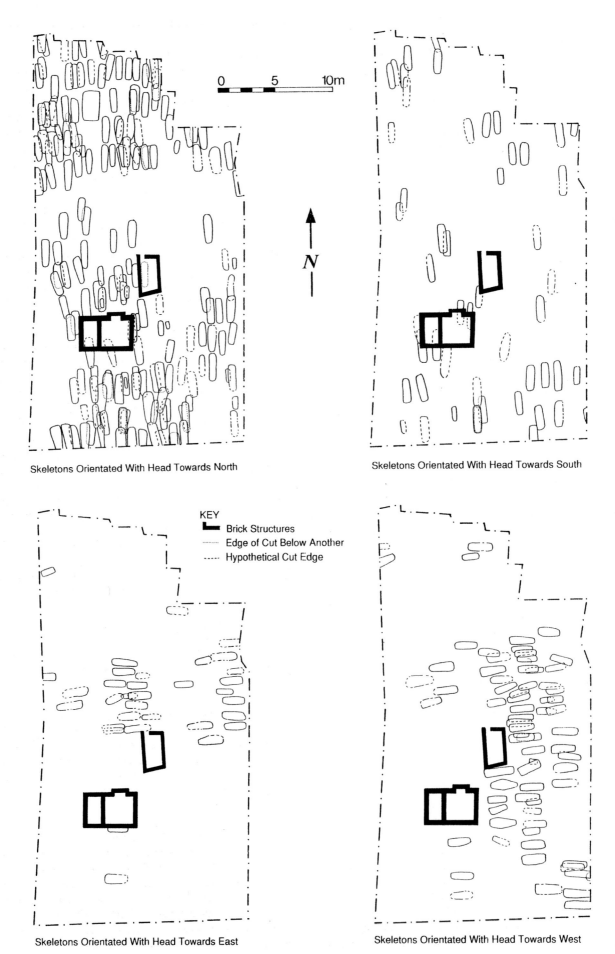

0   5   10m

N

Skeletons Orientated With Head Towards North

Skeletons Orientated With Head Towards South

KEY
▟ Brick Structures
.... Edge of Cut Below Another
- - - - Hypothetical Cut Edge

Skeletons Orientated With Head Towards East

Skeletons Orientated With Head Towards West

Figure 12.6   Burials arranged according to orientation which may indicate phasing (illustration: Rob Goller) noticeably different, reflecting the social status of the individual within. This accords with those Quaker burials examined by Stock (this volume). At Kingston, most burials were encased in wooden containers, ranging from a plain rectangular box to those retaining evidence of decorative upholstery studs and fragments of cloth, with finely-decorated grips and escutcheons. Examples of wooden coffins with viewing windows were discovered, as well as those with breastplates or informative studding. Sixteen lead coffins were found, some with evidence of triple-shell construction and decoration. Occasional inscriptions contained biographical data ranging from initials, date and/or age at death (see Fig 12.3), to full name, age, and date of death with additional family information. The finery on some of these coffins must have been intended to create an impression upon mourners; the funeral march may have been less glorious than those for individuals of comparative status from other religious denominations, for reasons of formality, but informal mourners would still stand at the graveside. In the Minutes of 1710, 'It is desired that 2 deals be bought for the service of friends to stand on when the corpse are laid in the graves' (LSOF, Minutes of 6 February, 1710).

The Barnard Vault

The most ostentatious burials were undoubtedly those within the brick burial vault containing ten members of the Barnard family. This was built by Thomas Barnard in 1744 and was of typical mid 18th century brick construction with vertical walls and a barrel-vaulted roof (see Fig 12.4). Typical structures of this time would have had an entrance in the eastern side (Litten 1985b), but in keeping with nonconformist practice across the site, this example had a stepped entrance in the centre of the northern side. An annexe was constructed prior to 1762, when the body of Sarah Holden-Freame was interred. This did not have an entrance but was completely enclosed, and appears to follow the fashion for brick graves seen elsewhere (Boore 1986; this volume; Cox & Stock 1995). The family members were each interred in lead coffins encased in individual cells consisting of brick dividing walls overlain by stone slabs, onto which was inscribed the name of the occupant. An infant, named simply Baby Barber Barnard, who died in 1742, was interred within a small coffin-shaped brick-lined vault built into the dividing wall between two adults, one of whom was its mother, Elizabeth Barber. Although Elizabeth's coffin contained two inscriptions, the date of her death is inconsistent. A brass plate attached to the wooden outer coffin read, 'Eliz Barber/ Died 19th Octr 1743 Aged 23', while a lead plate underneath this read 'Within this case /lies the body of /Elizabeth Barber/ Daughter of /Thos. Barnard Gent /Died Octr ye 20th 1744 /Aged 23 years'. Elizabeth is not recorded in the burial registers, so her date of death cannot be confirmed, and it is assumed that the outer coffin is a simple mistake, since she would otherwise have had to be moved from elsewhere for interment in the vault, constructed as it was in April 1744. However, Elizabeth's grandfather, John, who was a prominent Quaker and who died in Bramsott, Hampshire in 1715 (Challen 1958) must have been removed from his original resting-place. His coffin lay in the centre of the lowest tier of the vault, and is inscribed 'John Barnard/ Died March 21st 1716/ In the 75th year of his age'. Since the vault was not built until 1744, the decision to move him into the vault from wherever he was interred originally may imply the desire to strengthen ancestral ties in Kingston. Although the motives underlying this act may never be fully understood, it does appear to reflect the the need to demonstrate ancestral links and familial bonding. Similar cases were found at Christ Church, Spitalfields (Molleson & Cox 1993).

The vault attests the prominence of the family within this community. Thomas himself was a linen draper, with estates in London, Sussex, Surrey, and Essex. His father John had been a prominent Quaker and his brother, also John, had a distinguished political career. He was MP for London, Sheriff, Lord Mayor in 1737, held the title of 'Father of the City', his statue was erected on the Royal Exchange in 1747, and he was buried in the chancel of Mortlake church in 1764. The Kingston vault was built with the permission of the Quaker community, who 'having viewed the ground . . . where he proposes to make a large grave or vault for the burying of his family and apprehending that it will not incommode any graves already made agree that Thomas Barnard may proceed therein when he thinks proper' (LSOF, Minutes of 11 October, 1743). This early example of a planning condition was clearly infringed as the vault did in fact cut through a number of previous burials but this appears to have been overlooked: Thomas paid £10 to the Quaker meeting for granting him planning permission (LSOF, Minutes of 23 November 1745/6).

Case studies

Other than the discovery of the burial vault, there were several interesting and curious burials in this burial ground which serve to cast light on the character of both this community and its contemporary society.

During the excavation a number of cuts were encountered which were certainly grave cuts, due to their size, shape, and the presence of coffin furniture, but which contained no skeletal remains. It is possible that the skeleton had decayed to such an extent that only traces of the coffin remained. However, Anna Barnard's lead coffin may infer a different explanation. Anna died in 1792, and was the last Barnard to be buried in the vault. In addition to modern breaks caused by lifting the coffin,

162

the sealing of the coffin displayed old breaks indicating that it had been peeled back at the head end, which lay closest to the vault entrance. The coffin contained no skeletal remains, although the discovery of blonde hair, possibly a wig, in the base of the coffin suggests that it did originally contain her body. The vault was abandoned following Anna's burial and it is plausible that body-snatchers had removed her body (see Richardson, 1988, for further details on the activities of the 'Resurrectionists').

Another curiosity was the discovery of two skeletons deposited within the same grave cut (Fig 12.7). Both were laid out as interments but were deposited with a quantity of ash, suggesting that they had been partially burnt. The upper one consisted of a mature adult male skeleton complete and unburnt up to the cervical vertebrae, with a small oval area of burnt and fragmentary bone, ash, and charcoal deposited in place of the head. The lower skeleton was a mature adult of indeterminate sex whose skeleton was complete to the upper thoracic region, above which the torso was completely missing. A layer of ash was deposited with this skeleton but no apparent attempt had been made to reconstruct the upper body. The burnt material included burnt human bone as well as the bones of small mammals, 'twiggy' charcoal, and fragments of a

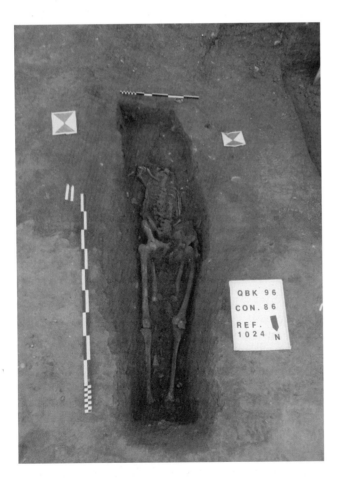

Figure 12.7   Grave containing two individuals thought to have been partially burnt (photo: Archaeology South-East)

clay pipe. Although no signs of burning were found on either skeleton, the ash was apparently intended to represent the remainder of the body. It is thought that the condition of these two skeletons may be the result of an accident, perhaps a building fire, with a sample of the charred remains being recovered and placed in the coffin. According to the retired Home Office pathologist, Professor Bernard Knight, this type of burning is possible: partial but complete burning of an individual can occur which has little effect on either the rest of the body or on the surrounding area (B Knight, pers comm).

Four walnuts were found in association with one lead coffin. Three were found inside the coffin, placed along the central axis of the body in the mouth, and between the knees and feet. The fourth had fallen out of the partially decayed base of the coffin. These walnuts are significant because they may indicate post mortem interment of items for specific symbolic reasons and may be compared with the discovery of common box and holly interred in a coffin from St Barnabus (Black & Sheuer, unpublished). Although the intention of the symbolism is unknown, the meaning may be sought in folk medicine. Walnuts are associated with mental illness and madness, due to the similarity in appearance between a shelled walnut and the human brain. Superstitions surrounding walnuts include the avoidance of both sitting beneath a walnut tree and of eating the fruit because these both lead to madness (Allen 1995). It is therefore interesting to postulate whether these finds indicate the interment of an individual suffering from some form of mental illness or epilepsy.

Reuse of grave cuts has already been mentioned, but purposeful interment of two coffins within the same grave may also have occurred contemporaneously. One lead coffin without a lid was deposited in a deep grave with a second, highly decorative lead coffin placed above it. The depth of this grave indicates that the two lead coffins were purposefully interred together, and is one of several examples of double graves within the burial ground. In each case, it is assumed that the burials were contemporary, but relatedness cannot be proved. The ash burials have already been mentioned. In addition, two adults were placed side-by-side in a large rectangular grave cut. Three cases of double interments involving infants placed on top of adult female coffins were found, and one case of a neonate apparently interred with an infant.

Very little evidence was found to suggest that special areas had been set aside for particular reasons in this burial ground. A concentration of four infants was located immediately to the east of the vault, which may relate to a particular family. Although it is tempting to suggest that a high incidence of child mortality in a locality may be the result of an epidemic, the circumstances of burial did not support this. The fact that the burials appeared to partially truncate one another and displayed a variance in orientation is more indicative of interment over a longer period of time than would be expected in the case of an epidemic.

A concentration of six lead coffins was located to the south of the vault, and a single one was found two metres to the east. Their alignment and close proximity implies either that they were deposited at more or less the same time, or that there was some other reason for this concentration. They are deposited later than most burials in this area and although they are not inscribed, they have produced osteological evidence suggesting that at least one of them is related to the Barnard family members interred in the vault. A skeletal trait of this family is the occurrence of an extra vertebral element (see Start & Kirk, this volume), also occurring in two lead coffins interred to the south of the Barnard vault. That a family plot had been established in the area of the vault is given credence by the discovery of Jane Gambles, the sister of Thomas Barnard, buried immediately to the west of the vault annexe.

Commercial archaeology and the dead

With the exception of a small number of research excavations carried out by university archaeology departments and projects initiated by bodies such as English Heritage, field archaeology is today a largely commercial affair, with the government's introduction of PPG 16 in November 1990 (HMSO) providing guidelines which, in theory at least, should make developers responsible for ensuring that archaeological deposits are either preserved *in situ* or by record (excavation). The importance of developer-funded projects has been mirrored by the growth of commercial field units, both as independent commercial concerns and those embedded in university archaeology departments. Archaeological units operate within a free market where competitive tendering can lead to situations where projects are usually awarded to units who submit the lowest quotation. There is increasing concern that this environment may have a detrimental effect on the quality of the archaeological work carried out, and it is here that the importance of clear research aims and excavation strategies become most apparent. At Kingston, high standards were established and maintained from the outset through the active participation of a number of interested parties in the preparation of the specification through to the monitoring of the field project and post-excavation, notably by the Greater London Archaeology Advisory Service of English Heritage, Margaret Cox, and Trevor Anderson.

Prior to excavation, the London Road site was merely a vacant lot or gap site, similar to many which await redevelopment in urban areas such as Kingston-upon-Thames. This particular site had been ear-marked for the construction of residential flats, for which planning permission had been granted, on the condition that due consideration was given to the presence of human remains. The

developer was initially advised to remove only those remains which lay within the foot-print of the proposed building, however, rather than have human burials beneath a residential building the developers preferred to have the site cleared. Thus, the dead had to make way for the living. Although a commercial exhumation contractor was initially approached to clear the site it was recognized that the buried individuals should be removed under archaeologically controlled conditions. Archaeology South-East were subsequently commissioned by the landowner to excavate the site, assisted by the exhumation contractors.

The excavation of any burial ground requires a particular set of skills, not necessarily utilized on other types of site, most obviously in the fields of palaeopathology and osteology. Excavation of a post-medieval burial ground is a more daunting prospect than usual, since health and safety issues are of paramount importance, with the potential for soft tissue preservation and resulting possible hazards being of special concern (see Young, Kneller, and Thompson, all this volume). The welfare of the staff is another concern when emotional stress arises from the nature of the material they must deal with.

The disturbance and removal of human remains, even by archaeologists, is an emotive issue. Prior to any burial ground clearance Home Office regulations (The Disused Burial Grounds [Amendment] Act 1981 [section 1 (2)]) stipulate that an advert must appear in local and national newspapers for six consecutive weeks prior to commencement of work in order to allow any living relatives to express an interest in the remains of their ancestors, with the wishes of the interested party being taken into account when it comes to reburial. However it is rare for anyone to come forward and no-one did at Kingston. The living Quaker community (Religious Society of Friends) of Kingston-upon-Thames were approached and showed great interest in, and concern with, the project. They readily granted permission for the removal of the remains, on the proviso that they were cremated and presented to the Religious Society of Friends for reburial. Permission was also given for the retention of palaeopathologically interesting remains by a suitable archaeological institution and these are now held by the School of Conservation Sciences Bournemouth University.

Although the time and labour required to excavate individual burials had been carefully calculated prior to commencement of the project this allowance was found to be inadequate when it came to the practicalities of excavation. The excavation strategy included the rapid removal of some of the human remains. However, the human response to this type of work could not be adequately foreseen, and progress was hindered by the cautious and respectful approach of the excavators. Despite attempts to hurry the work along the excavation took several weeks longer than anticipated and programming and financial considerations caused the Project Manager some discomfort. Archaeologists in general will obviously become more accustomed to working with post-medieval burials as curators become more aware of the potential of these sites, but as yet the archaeological investigation of such sites is still a relatively new sub-discipline and any such excavation is likely to involve a fair proportion of people working on this type of site for the first time. The effect of post-medieval burial ground excavation on excavators therefore needs to be addressed.

The human response

The effect of working with the dead on the emotions of the archaeologist has long been an interest of one of the authors (Pollard 1991, 1992) and the opportunity to explore the relationship between the living and the dead at Kingston could not be ignored. The osteologists were invited to write about their experiences of the project to be included in a forthcoming book on the subject (Downes & Pollard forthcoming). These experiences are also touched upon in Start & Kirk (this volume). The psychological effects of the excavation mentioned in this paper are based on the experiences of the excavation team itself.

Although the excavators were deliberately kept away from the area where those human remains found within lead coffins were processed, the effects of the excavation soon began to tell, as excavators reported nightmares and a general lowering of spirits. The causes of this have not been examined in detail for this project (but see Reeve & Adams 1993; Morris 1994; Cox 1994; Huggins 1994; Cox 1996b; Boyle forthcoming), and no long-term effects have been noted. Some thought should be given to whether psychological effects result from the nature of the work, and a distinction should be drawn between the actual process of excavation, and what could be described as the morbid nature of the work undertaken. Burial grounds and cemeteries are essentially repetitive sites to dig, consisting as they do of numerous graves of very similar character. Excavation can seem a never-ending task and the Project Manager (Tony Pollard) distinctly remembers, during one site visit, the daunting feeling that all the dead in the world were appearing before him as grave after grave was revealed by excavation. It may be the case that repetitive work can lead to nightmares and bouts of depression, since many an archaeologist during an excavation will claim to dream of cobble-stones, flint flakes, or any other archaeological feature if their excavation requires their attention for any length of time. However, cobble-stones and 'endless trowelling' dreams do not generally involve activities other than those taking place on site during the day; dreams experienced at Kingston were active, surreal, and disturbing for not being explanatory. They involved images and sensations which resulted in feelings of horror, persecution, and the sense of feeling trapped, and imply subconscious thought processes which explored the morality of the work. More than anything else, the dreams are difficult to articulate, as any nightmares are.

In spite of the experiences recounted above the project was found to be a rewarding experience by the majority of those taking part, although it is obviously not a branch of archaeology which appeals to everyone. The research potential of the site was by and large fulfilled, although the ability of the documentary sources to cast light on the archaeological remains and the practical application of the sampling strategy (see Start & Kirk, this volume) did not quite live up to expectations.

Conclusions

The site at London Road has provided a valuable lesson in the techniques appropriate to post-medieval burial ground excavation. Certain aspects of the excavation posed practical difficulties, which only exacerbated the stress to the excavators caused by excavation of the recently dead. Attempts at a consistent sampling strategy were hampered by differential preservation and the extent of truncation, and organic remains had to be disposed of for reasons of hygiene and finance. However, the information recovered by this excavation is enhanced by the wealth of historical data examined. This has in itself led to problems, and we have had to overcome the temptation to make inferences about the archaeology from historical information, rather than use the historical data to supplement the archaeological data.

The picture evoked by excavation of this Quaker community reflects the historical image of a self-conscious community in close contact with those of other religious denominations, evidenced by the occurrence of rich merchants among the interments and the occasions of Quakers marrying outside the community in the 18th century. The burial ground itself seems perhaps more reminiscent of medieval precedents than other post-medieval excavations (Spitalfields, Reeve & Adams 1993; St Brides, Scheuer, this volume; St Barnabas, Black & Scheuer, unpublished) in its preference for wooden coffins. However, this reflects both that the Kingston site is earlier than other quoted post-medieval cemeteries, and that the Kingston excavation is more representative of the relative economic and social status of members of the community. The more extensive use of lead coffins in later post-medieval cemeteries reflects both economic status, since the wealthier part of a population is usually interred intramurally, and the legal imposition of lead coffins for intramural burials after 1815, the year after the Kingston burial ground was replaced (see Molleson & Cox 1993 for details). Our expectations of post-medieval burial ground samples are understandably coloured by the spectacular results of the well-documented Christ Church, Spitalfields excavations (Reeve & Adams 1993; Molleson & Cox 1993). That site and others discussed in papers in this volume (Scheuer, Boore, and Boyle & Keevill) create the impression of a post-medieval preference for interment within 'structural' graves, for example vaults, crypts, or brick graves (St Augustine-the-Less, Boore 1986; Bathampton, Cox & Stock 1995). However, intermural burials also imply a degree of prosperity which was not reflected in all parishes, and the 'common' populace would have been buried in earth graves in the 18th and 19th centuries. It is important to remember that the majority of those sites mentioned above reflect the elite burial area of a parish, either intra- or extra-murally. For example, the excavated Christ Church sample is only c 1.5% of the total burials in the parish (Molleson & Cox 1993).

One problem encountered was the lack of precedent for this type of burial ground. While the value of crypts for post-medieval funerary studies is becoming more widely acknowledged, especially since Christ Church, Spitalfields, graveyards have not been widely recognised for the variety of data they contain. Many are still in use and/or are cleared without archaeological involvement, therefore less is known of burial grounds and 'common' funerals than of contemporary crypts and burial vaults.

The Kingston excavation also highlighted a number of problems associated with this type of site. Firstly, practical problems arose from the beginning. The need to excavate the site in segments due to a lack of space to store spoil meant that an overview of the site was not possible until the last few days, and pacing the work was therefore difficult. Slow progress on individual skeletons was initially attributed to 'getting used to the site', but it was eventually realised that this was a reflection of respect on the part of the excavators. In reality, no differentiation was made on-site between high and low resolution excavation, each skeleton being accorded equal care.

In addition, the primary purpose of excavation was to remove all trace of human remains, essentially for economic reasons. This site was derelict and an ideal location for re-development, lying as it does in an urban area, but the issue of whether the burial ground should have been disturbed had been taken out of the hands of the curators, who recognised that given the depth of overburden, excavation could have been avoided. A Zionist chapel had after all occupied most of the site from the late 19th century with very little damage to the skeletal remains. The over-riding issue was one of how the present and future occupants would feel when they realised that they were living on top of a disused burial ground, and whether this would have a detrimental effect upon the value of the property. Whatever the ethical issues involved in the clearance of this burial ground, it cannot be doubted that had

the clearance been left to commercial exhumation contractors then the opportunity to obtain a valuable insight into this population would have been lost, and it is to the developer's credit that they recognised this fact and provided funds for the project. Excavation can therefore be thought of as more than preserving the site on paper, its record in effect serving as the final memorial to those buried on this site.

Although the modern Quakers gave their support to the project, the Minutes of the early meetings detail the concern felt by Friends that non-members were using their burial ground as an access route, and that buildings being erected at the boundary of the site were too close to the burial ground. Was this due to 'respect for the dead' or simple territorialism? The 17th and 18th century Quakers at Kingston disliked the idea of truncation, and requested that both permission be sought for burials to take place, and that elder Friends be present during burial, indicating that the attitudes towards burial have altered within the community over time. How would the original Quakers have reacted to this excavation?

The archaeologists' reaction was a general sense of unease. Discussion on the ethics of this type of operation in Britain have focused on lead coffins (eg Cox 1994 & 1996b; Huggins 1994; Morris 1994; Boyle forthcoming), because where soft tissue survives the remains they contain are recognisably human, and reactions to their removal evoke similar emotions to the trauma experienced during exhumation of modern remains in criminal cases (see Cox 1995b). We have found that these reactions do not just apply to the excavation of lead coffins. In prehistoric or early historic burials the presence of grave goods serves to draw attention away from human remains, which in the majority of cases are themselves treated as artefacts (see Downes & Pollard forthcoming). The absence of grave goods at Kingston removed this cushion and the archaeologists were forced to confront directly their attitudes toward the dead. The feeling that they were involved in a direct confrontation with the recently deceased rather than an objective archaeological excavation was exacerbated in the case of graves with biographical information (see Fig 12.3), where the name and age of the individual was known. This stressed the fact that the remains of the dead were human beings with lives, experiences, and feelings not dissimilar from our own.

Mixed emotions focused on whether excavation was appropriate and on issues of hygiene. Although the lead coffins were uncovered by us, it was a relief that they were 'dealt with' by the exhumation contractors and osteologists. On site, the excavators treated all skeletons with equal care. Responses polarized, ranging from those who apparently experienced no compunction, expressed through flippancy, to those who experienced repeatedly disturbed dreams, progressive depression, and/or stress-induced illness. Personal relationships became very strained over the ten weeks of excavation and during the post-excavation process, although the extent to which this may be the natural result of a lengthy excavation is impossible to assess. On site, symptoms were likened to the cases in North America where people have experienced problems attributed to living on the site of former native burial grounds. Have we experienced our own version of miasma?

Acknowledgements

The authors would like to thank Rushmon Ltd for funding the project, and especially Guy Thatch for his cooperation and assistance during the project. The project was monitored by Jez Reeve and Ken Whittaker of the Greater London Archaeology Advisory Service, both of whom provided encouragement and valuable advice throughout the project. Margaret Cox provided advice and assistance and the opportunity to take part in the Grave Concerns Conference. The documentary research was carried out by Gwen Jones, osteological work was carried out by Lucy Kirk and Helen Start, with external advice provided by Trevor Anderson, and the coffin furniture is being analysed by Mel Richmond. Their reports on this work will appear in the final excavation report. Greg Priestley-Bell and Louise Bashford supervised the fieldwork, Tony Pollard was Project Manager, and Luke Barber ensured the smooth running of post-excavation work. The illustrations were drawn by Rob Goller.

Notes

1　Men's Minutes held in the Library of the Society of Friends, London (LSOF). Registers held at the Public Record Office, Kew. PRO RG6 1240, PRO RG6 831, PRO RG 841, PRO RG 837 and 427, PRO RG6 541.
2　Men's Minutes held in the Library of the Society of Friends, London. Dates include Minutes of 29 January, 1673, 26 October 1676, 28 July, 1681, 2 September 1685, 5 January 1687, 3 February 1687, 7 April 1687, etc.
3　LSOF, Minutes of 26 October 1676, 2 September 1685, 5 January 1687, 3 February 1687, 5 November 1691, 7 October 1739.

13 'The bodies of Friends' – the osteological analysis of a Quaker burial ground *Helen Start and Lucy Kirk*

Introduction

This paper is concerned with the analysis of the human skeletal remains recovered during the excavation of the Quaker burial ground, London Road, Kingston-upon-Thames (Bashford and Pollard, this volume). The overall project specification was designed by English Heritage (1996) and Margaret Cox (1996c); the latter also formulated the specification for the osteological analysis. The osteological research aims can be summarized as follows:

- To establish the biologically-determined demographic structure of the Quaker sample.
- To assess through biological methods the interrelatedness of the Quaker group.
- To investigate and interpret pathological manifestations and patterns within the sample.
- To compare the biological assessment of the Quaker sample with the historical picture of the group provided by documentary sources.
- To provide a detailed record of this skeletal group prior to the cremation of the majority of the remains in accordance with the wishes of the present-day Quaker community of Kingston-upon-Thames.

High and low resolution analysis

The strategy employed in the excavation and subsequent post-excavation analysis of this site was experimental. It followed a policy which divided the site into two areas, high and low resolution. The skeletal material from each area was to receive different on-site treatment and a different level of osteological analysis and recording. The high resolution skeletal sample was to consist of approximately 30% of the whole, which was to encompass a chronological sample, plus any skeletons of special interest, with legible coffin plates, unusual pathology, or in an exceptionally good state of preservation, regardless of their position within the cemetery.

Low resolution skeletal recording included a skeletal and dental inventory, age and sex assessments, gross pathological observations, and basic metrical recording for use in the determination of stature and sex. The high resolution sample was subject to the same recording criteria with the addition of detailed descriptions of pathological manifestations

and differential diagnosis, additional metrical recording, and a study of non-metric traits.

Demography

The aim of the low resolution analysis was to provide enough information to reconstruct the demography of the excavated sample. As discussed by Bashford and Pollard (this volume) the excavation revealed that the burial ground continued under standing buildings to the west. Historical documents record a minimum of 497 individuals buried at the site so the excavated sample of 360 individuals clearly represents only a percentage of those buried. Demographic interpretations are therefore based on a majority sample, not the entire buried sample. The basic parameters of a demographic investigation are age and sex, and these were established during the course of low resolution analyses.

Sex estimation

Standard osteological techniques were used in the multi-factorial assessment of biological sex (Steele & Bramblett 1988; Chamberlain 1994; Buikstra & Ubelaker 1994). Individuals were assigned to the M?, F?, or ? categories where incompleteness, poor preservation, or ambiguous results prohibited definitive assignment to either sex.

Age estimation

Age at death was also established using standard osteological techniques (Miles 1962; Lovejoy *et al* 1985; Buikstra & Ubelaker 1994). Assignment to an age category was made on the basis of a combination of all possible methods.

The problems with assigning specific age-at-death assessments to adults are widely known (Saunders 1992; Molleson & Cox 1993), and in order to avoid introducing bias into the sample broad age categories were employed. Sub-adult age-at-death estimations can be made with a greater degree of accuracy, and narrower categories can be safely employed. The age categories employed are summarized in Table 13.1.

There were 65 individuals in the sub-adult categories FE–3, and 295 individuals in the adult categories 4–6. Some individuals have been assigned across a range of age categories as the result of incompleteness, poor preservation, or an age-at-death assessment falling between two categories.

Re-distributed totals

In order to compare the osteological and historical data and examine demographic patterns, such as mortality and life expectancy, the results were proportionally redistributed to single age categories (Chamberlain 1994). Briefly, the number of individuals in each adult age category was added together, and a fraction was then calculated by dividing the totals for each adult age group by the total number of adults. The numbers of individuals spread across age categories were then multiplied by the resulting fractions, and the results added to the totals for each age category. To facilitate the examination of demographic trends, the F? individuals were treated as F, and the M? as M. The redistributed results appear in Table 13.2.

Comparisons of historical and osteological data

Individuals

The Kingston-upon-Thames project provided a welcome opportunity to compare the osteological data with detailed historical records. Due to its relatively small size, this group does not offer the exceptional opportunities for testing osteological techniques provided by the Christ Church Spitalfields project (Molleson & Cox 1993). However, there are several valuable insights to be drawn from this study. It was possible to identify sixteen skeletons of known age from coffin plates and studs but due to the state

of preservation it has only been possible to make osteological assessments of age in thirteen of these individuals. Known ages and osteological assessments are compared in Table 13.3.

Examination of the results shown in Table 13.3 reveals several trends worth commenting upon. The first observation is that molar attrition was an unreliable indicator of chronological age. This finding highlights the need for research into attrition in post-medieval dentition as the current methods are not appropriate (Miles 1962; Brothwell 1981). Secondly, two patterns become apparent when comparing auricular surface age assessments with chronological age. Younger adults tend to be over-aged and older adults tend to be under-aged by Lovejoy et al's (1985) method. The trend from Kingston was also observed at Spitalfields (Molleson & Cox 1993). Both samples support work on a large collection of known-age adults, which found that this method has a uniform tendency to over-age younger individuals and under-age older individuals (Murray & Murray 1991).

The small number of individuals of known chronological age at death prohibits any statistically significant examination of the results presented in Table 13.3. However, it is interesting that the adults tend to fall into three groups of young, prime, and older ages. The mean age of the adults below the age of 30 is 23.25 and they form 30.8% of this sample; the second cluster of adults falls between the ages of 30 and 45, the mean age of this group is 37 and they form 38.5% of this sample. Finally there is a second cluster of adults of considerably older ages who have a mean age at death of 83 and form 30.8% of the sample. Almost 70% of these people died before they were 45. This is interesting because most of them were found in lead coffins and were members of the Barnard family, known to be wealthy and presumably with a high standard of living, yet this did not protect them from the probability of dying relatively young. Also of interest are

Table 13.1: Age categories

Age category	Description	Years
FE	Fetus	Before birth
NE	Neonate	Birth–11 months
1	Infant 1	1–5
2	Infant 2	6–11
3	Juvenile	12–17
4	Young Adult*	
5	Prime Adult*	
6	Mature Adult*	

*assignments were based on the biological appearance of the skeleton (ie a biologically 'old'-looking skeleton can belong to an individual not chronologically 'old' in years)

Table 13.2: Redistributed age and sex totals

Age	?	M	F
FE–NE	4.6	0.0	0.0
Infant 1	22.0	0.0	0.0
Infant 2	22.8	0.0	0.0
Juvenile	15.9	0.0	0.0
Young Adult	5.4	23.4	28.8
Prime Adult	10.8	32.5	62.8
Mature Adult	13.9	51.6	65.5
Totals	95.4	107.5	157.1

The totals are fractional or include 'part people' as an artefact of the redistribution of the unknown-age adults into the known-age categories described above.

Table 13.3: Individuals of known age with biological assessments

| Skeleton reference number | Osteological results | | | | | |
	Osteological sex	Molar attrition	Auricular surface	Pubic symphysis	Clavicle epiphyseal union	Known age
1003	F	18–24	25–29	–	>30	23
1021	F	20–32	30–34	–	–30+	23
1190	?	18–32	30–34	–	<30	23
1217		18–32	30–34	–	–30+	24
1000	M	30–38	30–34	22–35	>30	30
1271		18–24	30–34	–	–	35
1232		36–44	–	–	–	37
1218		–	–	–	–	39
1008	F	18–32	40–44	–	>30	44
1022	M	–	40–44	26–45	>30	75
1132		52–58	45–49	–	–	81
1183	F	–	–	–	>30	82
1002	M	–	60+	–	>30	94

the ages of the older adults who did live past 45. It was clearly quite possible to live into your 70s, 80s, or even 90s during this period; this trend is borne out by reference to the Bills of Mortality for London which also include those living to 100 and beyond. It was not possible to compare individuals of known sex with the osteological findings because in the majority of cases this information was not available.

The thirteen individuals in Table 13.3 who could be tied directly to known historical individuals were the exception. In the majority of cases it was not possible for individuals in the ground to be linked with specific individuals in the historical records.

Sample level

On a broader level it was possible to compare the results of the osteological reconstruction of the demographic structure of the burial ground sample with the historical record. After 1721 it became standard to record age at death in the burial register, whereas previously this information was recorded only haphazardly. A total of 146 individuals of known age at death and sex have been identified from the burial register (Jones, pers comm). Of this total, 103 came directly from the burial register, and the remaining 43 were calculated through a comparison of the birth and burial registers.

In order to compare the demographic patterns produced by the osteologically-aged sample and historically-aged at death it was necessary to define the broad age categories already described (young, prime, and mature adult) with chronological age ranges. Chronological age categories used by some osteologists were employed and these are defined as: young adult (18–29 years); prime adult (30–44 years), and mature adult (45+) (Chamberlain 1994 and pers comm). These age categories broadly reflect the three clusters of ages evident in Table 13.3 and were therefore considered appropriate.

Discussion

The most dramatic difference occurs in the youngest age categories (birth to age five) with the low level of individuals in the osteological sample. The under-representation of young children is not uncommon in archaeological samples. The explanations most commonly given for this phenomenon are differential preservation and incompleteness of the excavated sample (Henderson 1987; Boddington 1987). With reference to Kingston, several individuals under five survived only as tooth crowns retrieved through dry sieving grave fills, and therefore preservation of infants was clearly poor. It is therefore not possible to attach any significance to the small number of foetal to age five remains in the sample.

From the age of six to seventeen, the crude percentages are very similar for the historical and osteological samples. This suggests that these sections of the sample are proportionally represented by the skeletal remains, and that there are no unusual population dynamics within these age categories.

For the young and prime adult categories the percentages are greater for the osteological sample than for the historical, but in the mature adult category the percentages are almost identical. There are several possible explanations for this. Many factors of a physical, chemical, and biological nature combine to affect the preservation of bone, and it is possible that the age of an individual may affect decay (Henderson 1987). For example, at Christ Church, Spitalfields the tendency was for younger individuals (including infants and juveniles) to be better preserved (Molleson & Cox 1993). However, during the course of the excavation at Kingston there was no noticeable difference in preservation between adult age categories (Bashford & Kirk forthcoming). The incompleteness of the sample could also be responsible for producing this bias.

Alternatively, a non-archaeological explanation could be one or more epidemics of an acute disease (ie resolved so quickly, either by death or recovery, that it does not affect the bones), that would not be detected osteologically, for example smallpox (*variola major*). The burial ground at Kingston was in use between 1664 and 1814, and the demographic patterns discussed here are based on a percentage sub-sample from this total sample, not a cross-section of the living population at any one point in time. Brief demographic fluctuations, like an epidemic, are unlikely to be detected because they are balanced, or masked, by the long use of the burial ground by a 'normal' population. Any demographic fluctuations are more likely to be detected in the osteological sample if it proves possible to phase the site through time and link demographic statistics to these phases.

Another explanation could be that a bias is introduced by the lack of ages in the burial register before 1721. The majority of the historically known sample (146 individuals) are from the period following this date. Historical records suggest that the majority of burials occurred during the early period of Quaker use of the site (Jones, pers comm). For example by 1687, only 23 years after the first burial, 214 interments had been made. By 1739, only 18 years after age at death became routinely recorded, 399 burials had been made: thus 80% of the total recorded burials occurred in the first 75 years of use of the cemetery.

The Quaker group was most successful and active, in terms of membership numbers, attendance at meetings, and adherence to Quaker practice, in its earlier phases. In the 18th century this situation changed and there was a general decline in the Quaker movement compounded by increased population mobility (Jones, pers comm). In addition, the burial ground expanded beyond the site boundary and the skeletal sample is therefore incomplete (Bashford & Pollard this volume).

Finally, the comparison of the osteologically-determined demographic picture with the historical would not be complete without an appraisal of osteological ageing techniques. As previously noted, past workers have commented on the tendency for osteological techniques to under-age older adults.

Table 13.4: Stature estimates

Stature	?	M	F
Average (cm)	166.2	168.7	160.3
Range (cm)	152–186	154.5–190	139.5–174.5
Average (inches)	5'5"	5'6"	5'4"
Range (inches)	5'–6'1"	5'1"–6'2"	4'6"–5'6"

The over-representation of young and prime adults in the osteologically-determined demographic picture may simply be due to the assessment of individuals as biologically younger than their chronological age. In other words, some of the individuals put in the young and prime adult categories by the osteologists may have been in fact older than their assessed ages, and should have been in the mature adult category.

Stature Estimates

Stature was calculated using standard stature estimate formulae after Trotter and Gleser (1958). The results shown in Table 13.4 reveal a degree of sexual dimorphism as would be expected in a sample of this size.

For the purposes of this study, osteological data from the sample at Christ Church, Spitalfields (Molleson & Cox 1993) has provided a useful comparison. The stature estimates obtained from the Kingston sample are very comparable with those produced for the Spitalfields collection. As would be expected, these two post-medieval samples from a similar geographical area were of a very similar average stature. It could be surmised that this is due to a similar sample affiliation, health, and environmental conditions.

Familial relationships

Relatedness is examined osteologically through the investigation of non-metric traits. Non-metric traits (Buikstra & Ubelaker 1994) are also known as epigenetic traits (Berry & Searle 1963) or discontinuous traits. They are described as minor morphological variations in the human skeleton (Berry & Berry 1967). They commonly take one of the four forms set out below (after Buikstra & Ubelaker 1994):

- Ossicles, or small bones, that occur within cranial sutures.
- Proliferative ossifications such as bony spurs or bridges.
- Ossification failure, for example the retention of the metopic suture.
- Variation in foramen number and location.

Several studies have shown that the manifestation of non-metric traits are subject to some degree of familial inheritance (Sjøvold 1977 and 1984; Saunders & Popovich 1978). The primary aim of this investigation was concerned with the possibility of establishing inter-group relatedness through the statistical examination of biological distance in the high resolution sample. The frequencies of occurrence of non-metric traits are used by osteologists to measure the biological distance between two groups of people. At Kingston the two groups of people compared were the adult males and adult females from the high resolution sample.

The choice of which non-metric traits were chosen for study was influenced by the potential each trait offered in addressing the stated research aims, and financial limitations. Cranial non-metric traits were considered to offer the best potential to answer the research aims posed by the specification. They are more highly canalised than noncranial morphological variations, and were better represented than dental traits in the Kingston skeletal sample. Seventeen cranial non-metric traits were selected for study. The heritability of each trait was of prime importance, as was ease and reliability of scoring. Sjøvold's 1984 study of a European post-medieval sample with known familial relationships was used as a basis for selecting the most heritable cranial non-metric traits.

Methodology

Once all the data had been collected, and totals calculated for the expression or non-expression of each trait, the t-test was used to determine any correlations with age. Traits which did show a significant correlation to age were excluded from the calculations of biological distance because their inclusion may have masked the true measure of divergence.

Calculation of the mean measure of divergence (MMD) was done following Sjøvold (1977) and Tyrrell (1997). The significance of the results was then tested through the calculation of the standard deviation of the MMD. If the MMD is significant, or the males and females are significantly different in their genetic make-up and therefore assumed to be not closely related, the MMD will be more than or equal to twice its standard deviation (Sjøvold 1977). The results of the measures of divergence for each trait, the MMD, and the standard deviation of the MMD appear in Table 13.5.

Interpretation

Statistical analysis of the results implies that the females and males of the group are not significantly different from, and therefore are closely related to each other (MMD=0.012, $2 \times$ standard deviation =0.138). This osteological result matches the historical picture of a close-knit community where marriage within the Religious Society of Friends was encouraged (Jones, pers comm). However, there are several limitations to the interpretation which can be drawn from analysis of the relatedness of this skeletal sample. These are discussed in Kirk & Start (forthcoming).

Health and disease

The significance of an investigation of the pathology of a group of archaeological human remains has been eloquently stated by Wells (1964, 64):

Table 13.5: Non-metric traits in males and females

Non-metric trait	Female		Male	
	number observed	number expressing trait	number observed	number expressing trait
Metopic suture	39	5	28	1
Supra-orbital foramen	13	3	10	2
Coronal ossicle	32	0	26	4
Bregmatic bone	26	0	19	0
Parietal foramen	33	21	24	17
Epiteric bone	15	0	16	1
Lamboid ossicle	29	1	21	4
Os inca	35	0	22	0
Palatine torus	22	1	16	0
Maxillary tori	24	2	16	0
Mandibular tori	38	0	27	1

The pattern of disease or injury that affects any group of people is never a matter of chance. It is invariably the expression of stresses and strains to which they were exposed, a response to everything in their environment and behaviour.

Palaeopathological investigation offers information about health and disease at the sample level. This data can then be examined in relation to, and provide further evidence of, other cultural and environmental factors, for example occupational stress (Bridges 1991 and 1994), diet and nutrition (Cohen & Armelagos 1984; Goodman & Rose 1991), or socio-economic status (Goodman & Dobney, 1991).

It was during the investigation of pathology that one of the problems with the dual high and low resolution approach to recording and analysis became apparent. As specified in the original project brief, on-site low resolution analysis included recording gross pathology and dental disease for all individuals. This provided crude totals of individuals affected by six broad classifications of pathology, namely joint disease, trauma, congenital and developmental conditions, metabolic disease, infective disease, and dental disease (Table 13.6).

However, in the study of pathology at a sample level, it is crucial to calculate prevalence rates and undertake detailed recording and diagnosis of pathological conditions. Unfortunately, time and financial constraints did not allow for post-excavation analysis at this level to be applied to the whole sample. Therefore, it was only possible to investigate prevalence of disease in the high resolution sample.

Pathology will be discussed first at the sample level and then at the individual level through the presentation of particularly interesting cases.

Diet and nutritional health

Two main categories of pathological conditions offer the potential to reconstruct the dietary and nutritional health of the Kingston Quakers. These are dental disease and metabolic disorders, although both can reflect varied aetiology.

Dental disease

Dental recording was undertaken at the low resolution stage of analysis, and dental disease has therefore been investigated for the whole sample. Post mortem loss and intercutting of graves in the burial ground have resulted in the exclusion of some individuals from this area of the study due to non-survival of dental evidence. In total 3858 teeth and 4149 sockets were examined.

The most common form of dental disease in the sample from Kingston-upon-Thames was ante mortem tooth loss (AMTL). Of the individuals it was possible to assess, 89% (161 of 182) had lost one

or more teeth before death. The reduced sample size of 182 is due to post mortem loss (PMTL) of the maxilla and mandible. AMTL was common to all age categories, and the very high percentage in the sample as a whole greatly reduced the potential value of the investigation of the condition by age category.

AMTL was also calculated on the number affected/number observed basis in order to investigate which teeth were most commonly affected. This statistic is calculated on the basis of sockets present in the sample, and the results appear in Table 13.7. Interpretation of the results allows several observations. In general, more mandibular than maxillary teeth were lost ante mortem, although this could be due to the better survival of mandibular sockets. A pattern common to mandibular and maxillary teeth is a greater loss of molar than anterior teeth ante mortem (Lukacs 1989).

There are several possible causes for the loss of teeth ante mortem and these include severe periodontal disease, systemic conditions such as syphilis and leprosy, nutritional deficiencies such as scurvy, or trauma to the teeth or jaws. A more common reason for AMTL is tooth decay (caries) and this is discussed in detail below.

In order to present the most reflective and accurate picture of dental health for this sample, loose teeth have been included in the totals for the investigation of caries. Of the individuals it was possible to assess for caries, 64% (96 of 151) had carious lesions in one or more teeth. The reduced sample size of 151 is due again to PMTL, and also to the very high prevalence of AMTL. At the number affected/number observed sample level 1561 maxillary and 2297 mandibular teeth, including loose teeth, were available for study. Age-specific patterns were again not investigated due to the high

Table 13.6: Crude pathological totals

Pathological classification	Number of individuals
Dental	158
Joint	46
Enthesopathies	17
Trauma	13
Congenital	12
Infective	10
Metabolic	8

Table 13.7: Dental disease

	Caries	AMTL	Abscess	Congenital
No. affected	210.0	1436.0	3.00	27.0
No. observed	3858.0	4149.0	4149.00	4149.0
Percentage	5.4	34.6	0.07	0.7

prevalence of carious lesions throughout the sample as a whole. Further, constraints on the available time for this study prohibited the investigation of carious lesions by their position on the tooth. Of all maxillary teeth observed, 7.1% showed carious lesions as opposed to 4.1% of all mandibular teeth. These statistics are unlikely to reflect differing sample sizes (1637 maxillary and 2512 mandibular). The pattern of less involvement of the anterior teeth observed for AMTL is less marked for the observation of carious lesions with, unusually, the maxillary canine most affected. However, apart from this one deviation, the pattern of more involvement towards the posterior teeth is again broadly true. The lower observed prevalence rates for caries are probably due to the very high percentages of AMTL. As mentioned above, caries is a cause of AMTL. Obviously if a carious tooth is lost ante mortem, it cannot appear in the skeletal record for this sample as a carious tooth.

Even though 63% of individuals had at least one carious tooth, only 5.4% of total teeth had carious lesions. When compared to some other post-medieval samples this is a relatively low prevalence rate. For example, at Christ Church, Spitalfields (Whittaker, in Molleson & Cox 1993), 17.9% of teeth showed carious lesions. There are several possible reasons for this discrepancy between the rates at Kingston and those at Spitalfields. The sample sizes are different, with only 100 individuals selected for analysis at Spitalfields. Also, Whittaker excluded individuals with less than twelve teeth from his study. A further possibility is related to diet. Quaker beliefs included a simple lifestyle, and rejected trappings of wealth. The evidence from their teeth may suggest that these values were influential on their diet, making them less likely to have tooth decay, giving them less sugars and highly processed carbohydrates like white flour.

Untreated caries involving total destruction of the tooth crown often leads to infection and abscessing. However at Kingston only three teeth, or 0.2% of the whole sample, showed signs of abscesses despite the widespread occurrence of caries. This may suggest that many of the teeth lost ante mortem were extracted before infection could attack the pulp, providing indirect evidence for dentistry.

No direct evidence for dentistry, such as fillings or dentures, was recovered from this sample. This lack of evidence for dental restoration and prostheses is surprising given the evidence for dentistry recovered from Spitalfields (Molleson & Cox 1993), St Brides (Scheuer, this volume), and St Nicholas, Sevenoaks (Boyle & Keevill, this volume). Perhaps the Quakers did not consider dentures to be necessary, or maybe considered them excessive or vain.

Metabolic disorders

These were limited to only two cases of rickets, both affecting sub-adults, one case of *cribra orbitalia*

affecting a female adult, and three cases of Diffuse Ideopathic Skeletal Hyperostosis (DISH) affecting adult males.

Diffuse Ideopathic Skeletal Hyperostosis is a disease of unknown aetiology. Its manifestation is age- and sex-related with mature adult males most commonly affected in archaeological samples (Rogers *et al* 1985). Suggested factors responsible for the manifestation of the disease include a diet rich in proteins and fats, and late onset of diabetes (Waldron 1985).

Two children, aged 7–8 and 11–12, sub-adults from the Kingston sample, display evidence of rickets. Rickets is a systemic childhood disease. One cause of rickets is a deficiency of vitamin D, essential for the successful mineralization processes of the organic matrix of bone. It is possible for a dietary deficiency of food containing vitamin D to produce rickets, however, many workers believe the absence of adequate exposure to sunlight is the most common factor in its aetiology (Stuart-Macadam 1989). Additionally, a dietary deficiency of calcium can be involved in the aetiology of rickets, with a connection commonly seen between artificial feeding of infants and the appearance of rickets (Molleson & Cox 1993).

It is possible that poor preservation is responsible for the relatively low prevalence of rickets among children from Kingston where many individuals in the younger age categories were present in the sample only as tooth crowns. At Spitalfields there was a high prevalence rate among infants and a very small one among children and adults, but at Spitalfields infant remains were well-preserved. This trend is also apparent at Kingston, where none of the better-preserved adult skeletons revealed signs of healed childhood rickets, or indeed the adult version of the disease, osteomalacia. A possible interpretation of this data is a diet adequate in calcium and the procurers of vitamin D, combined with a lifestyle which entailed adequate exposure to sunlight for most of the Quaker sample.

Iron deficiency anaemia

Only one possible case of iron deficiency anaemia was recovered from the skeletal sample from Kingston, in an adult female. Pitting of the bone, characteristic of *cribra orbitalia*, was present in both the left and right orbits of this individual. Again, the aetiology of this skeletal lesion is not fully understood, but it is considered to be representative of episodes of childhood iron deficiency anaemia (Stuart-Macadam 1989). It is possible that more manifestations of this disease were present in the Kingston sample but they were not observed due to post mortem damage to the fragile orbits of crania. Iron deficiency anaemia could therefore be more common in the living sample than the one observed case (of 362) would suggest.

174

Frequencies of disease

Overall, the prevalence rates in six broad categories of disease are relatively low (see Table 13.8). Only four individuals from the sample show bone changes thought to be the result of an infective disease process. Sample level prevalence of trauma is relatively low but the problems caused by poor preservation, post mortem damage, and inter-cutting may have affected these results. Both congenital and developmental conditions were evident at Kingston. Included in the sample were examples of spinal congenital abnormalities, extra thoracic or cervical vertebrae totalling 25 rather than the usual 24, sacralization of the fifth lumbar vertebrae, and a scoliotic, or S-shaped, spine.

The highest prevalence was joint disease in the spine. In order to assess any patterns in the manifestation of spinal joint disease, prevalence rates were calculated by age, sex, and area of the spine affected. The most obvious pattern was the higher prevalence of spinal joint disease in the older age categories. This reflects the widely known correlation between age and spinal joint disease (Ortner & Putscher 1984; Bridges 1991 and 1994).

The sample shows relatively low levels of joint disease in all age categories, as shown in Table 13.9. This could be interpreted as indicating a lifestyle, common to most of the sample, that did not involve overtly physical repetitive occupations: this is in keeping with the historical evidence which suggests that mercantile occupations were common among the Quakers at Kingston (Jones, pers comm).

In summary, there is an absence of diseases taken to indicate poor diet or living conditions often prevalent in urban populations. The overall picture of disease at Kingston therefore indicates a remarkably healthy post-medieval sample.

Case studies

In addition to the above, several individual cases of specific pathological conditions shed light on the Quaker community at Kingston and enrich the palaeopathological study of the history of disease.

Table 13.8: Disease rates (%)

	Trauma		Joint		Enthesopathies		Infective		Metabolic		Congenital	
Skull	–		–		–		–		0.9 (1/117)		1.7 (2/117)	
Vertebrae	2.6 (2/76)		47.4 (36/76)		–		–		3.9 (3/76)		6.6 (5/76)	
	L	R	L	R	L	R	L	R	L	R	L	R
Pelvis	1 (1/101)	1 (1/96)	4 (4/101)	3.1 (3/96)	1 (1/101)	1 (1/96)	2 (2/101)	2.1 (2/96)	1 (1/101)	1 (1/96)	–	1 (1/96)
Clavicle	–	–	5.2 (4/78)	5 (4/80)	–	–	1.3 (1/78)	1.3 (1/80)	1.3 (1/78)	1.3 (1/80)	1.3 (1/78)	1.3 (1/80)
Scapula			6.1 (5/82)	7.4 (6/81)	–	–	1.2 (1/82)	–	1.2 (1/82)	1.2 (1/81)	1.2 (1/82)	1.2 (1/81)
Ribs	5 (2/40)	5.6 (2/36)	2.5 (1/40)	2.8 (1/36)	–	–	2.5 (1/40)	2.8 (1/36)	5 (2/40)	5.6 (2/36)	2.5 (1/40)	–
Humerus	–	–	7.9 (9/114)	9 (10/111)	0.9 (1/114)	1.8 (2/111)	0.9 (1/114)	2.7 (3/111)	0.9 (1/114)	0.9 (1/111)	1.8 (2/114)	1.8 (2/111)
Radius	–	–	4.1 (4/98)	5 (5/99)	–	–	2 (2/98)	–	1 (1/96)	1 (1/99)	1 (1/98)	1 (1/99)
Ulna	–	–	3.9 (4/103)	4.9 (5/101)	1.9 (2/103)	1 (1/101)	1 (1/103)	2 (2/101)	1 (1/103)	1 (1/101)	1 (1/103)	1 (1/101)
Carpus	–	3.3 (1/30)	6.3 (1/16)	3.3 (1/30)	–	–	–	–	–	3.3 (1/30)	–	–
Femur	–	0.9 (1/110)	6.5 (7/108)	5.5 (6/110)	12 (13/108)	10 (11/110)	0.9 (1/108)	1.8 (2/110)	2.8 (3/108)	2.7 (3/110)	–	–
Tibia	1 (1/97)	1.1 (1/95)	4.1 (4/97)	4.2 (4/95)	5.2 (5/97)	4.2 (4/95)	1 (1/97)	1.1 (1/95)	3.1 (3/97)	3.2 (3/95)	–	–
Fibula	–	1.2 (1/85)	1.1 (1/87)	1.2 (1/85)	1.1 (1/87)	1.2 (1/85)	–	–	3.4 (3/87)	3.5 (3/85)	–	–
Tarsus	–	9 (1/11)	–	–	37.5 (3/8)	18.2 (2/11)	12.5 (1/8)	9 (1/11)	–	–	–	–

Table 13.9:   Joint disease in the Kingston sample

Joint		No. observed	Percentage
		Prevalence rates	
		No. affected	
Shoulder	left	5/57	8.7
	right	6/50	12.0
Elbow	left	3/72	4.2
	right	3/72	4.2
Wrist	left	0/44	0.0
	right	1/17	5.9
Hand	left	1/26	3.8
	right	1/26	3.8
Hip	left	3/84	3.6
	right	5/77	6.5
Knee	left	5/68	7.4
	right	5/66	7.6
Ankle	left	0/47	0.0
	right	1/48	2.1
Foot	left	0/7	0.0
	right	0/9	0.0

Figure 13.1   Skeleton 1098, from the London Road site, demonstrating the skeletal changes associated with syphilis (photo: Archaeology South-East)

Skeleton 1098

Individual 1098 was an adult male and presents one of the most advanced levels of skeletal change caused by venereal syphilis yet recovered from the British archaeological record (M Cox & T Anderson, pers comm). The appearance of *caries sicca* is characteristic of venereal syphilis and allows a definitive diagnosis. Other related changes appear throughout the skeleton including periosteal and lamellar new bone evidencing repeated infection on all the surviving long bones (Fig 13.1).

The recovery of an individual with advanced venereal syphilis has implications for our understanding of the Quaker group within which he lived and died. He appears to have been accorded the same burial rites as everyone else in the burial ground. In the post-medieval period the sexually transmitted nature of venereal syphilis was understood, and during the 18th and 19th centuries it was treated with mercurial ointments. The community who buried at London Road clearly accepted this individual who would have been understood to have a sexually-transmitted disease, and who may well have needed considerable levels of care. The final stages of syphilis can produce dementia, and the level of bony alteration in this individual suggests his condition was long-standing and that this dementia could have affected him.

Skeleton 1020

Individual 1020 was an adult male with deformities of both upper arms and his cranium. Both humerii were abnormally short, though circumference and diameter measurements are within the normal range for this sample. The bones of the lower arm and the rest of the skeleton that were present were morphologically normal. The cranium of this individual is abnormally broad resulting in a markedly brachycephalic shape.

The cause of these abnormalities is not yet certain. Several possibilities have been investigated and these include congenital dwarfing conditions like achondroplasia and a condition known as *humerus varus* deformity, but further research and radiographic investigation will be required before a differential diagnosis can be made. This, and other interesting pathological examples along with named individuals, have been retained for further study, with the blessing of the present-day Quaker community.

Skeleton 1125

Individual 1125 suffered unusual traumatic injury and subsequent complications to both elbows, the like of which has rarely been recovered from the archaeological record. The distal end of the right humerus, and the entire right ulna and radius are of abnormal morphology. Preliminary observations of the abnormal bone surface suggest a fracture to the medial epicondyle that sheared the medial-most part of the bone from its normal alignment. Articulation of the joint in the dry bone allows the observation that this injury and the subsequent bone remodelling resulted in severely limited movement with the elbow flexed at 90 degrees. The shortening of the radius and ulna suggest that the trauma involved neurological structures and resulted in the premature fusion of the epiphyses of the two bones. It can be surmised from this that the injury occurred during childhood. The left elbow displays changes of a very similar nature.

The pattern of injury and subsequent healing observed at the elbows of this individual is suggestive of a fall forward broken by out-stretched arms, with the dynamic force suffered at the elbows causing the observed bone fractures and proposed neurological damage. This individual is of particular interest to modern medicine since it provides evidence of the complications that can arise from an untreated complex childhood traumatic injury (T Anderson, pers comm).

Quality of life

Analyses of disease among the high resolution sample allows some comments to be made regarding the environment and culture of this community. As is clear from the case studies just discussed, individuals with severe conditions formed part of this society and were accorded equal value at least in terms of burial. Neither dietary deficiency nor excess are prevalent, and osteological signals of poor living conditions are rare. The Quakers present an osteological picture of a generally healthy sample which mirrors the historical picture of a thriving, generally middle-class community.

Although the historical record provided information about occupations, it was not possible to directly correlate this information with individual burials. At the sample level no significant pathological patterns could be tied to the historical record. The conclusion has been reached that questions concerning occupation in this community are best addressed by the historian and not the osteologist.

Conclusions

This site offered the opportunity to compare osteological data with the historical record with varying degrees of success. The experimental approach to the excavation of a post-medieval burial site, with two different levels of recording and analysis, allowed the excavation of 362 skeletons in ten weeks. Problems were encountered with the dual recording and analysis system including the introduction of biases in the composition of the sample, and limited assessment of the prevalence of disease, but it would not have possible to excavate every skeleton to the high resolution level in the limited time available. This dual system was an experimental compromise that produced far more information than would otherwise have been possible.

Final comments

The excavation and, more particularly, the osteological analysis of this burial ground presented unusual working conditions and constraints. The first difficulty encountered was the application of the dual high and low resolution recording system both on site and during the subsequent post-excavation analysis of the skeletal material.

At the end of the excavation, the 30% area of the ground selected for high resolution had produced approximately 56% of the total skeletal material. This clearly exceeded the 30% originally intended to receive a high resolution level of analysis. However, during the low resolution analysis it became clear that some of the material recorded at high resolution level on site was not well enough preserved to merit high resolution analysis. Similarly, a percentage of the low resolution material from site was in a good state of preservation and suitable for high resolution work. Consequently decisions were made to change the site designation of low and high resolution skeletons during the analysis stage, in order that the project objectives could be met within the financial constraints of the project.

The specified factors of pathology, legible coffin plates, and preservation formed the basis of these decisions, as did the desire to retain an even spread across the site from north to south reflecting anticipated chronological use of the site. It was not possible to base decisions solely on comparisons between the state of preservation of the material over the whole site. This would have resulted in a bias towards the southern due to the poorer preservation at the northern end. When analysing the material from the northern end of the site, the standards applied when deciding whether high resolution work was possible were adjusted accordingly. The high resolution skeletal material was reduced to approximately 37% of the total.

The selective nature of this re-assignment of material was necessary in order to achieve the project aims and succeeded in doing so. However, the authors are aware that the resulting skeletal sample subjected to a high resolution level of analysis was heavily biased. This bias may have affected the demographic profile of the group and the prevalence rates of pathological conditions, since all individuals displaying unusual pathology were selected. Having said that, it should be remembered that all cemetery samples are biased in respect of completeness, differential survival etc.

Another issue to be considered at this site was the nature of the buried remains, historical in date, and the presence of lead coffins. For all members of the excavating team this experience was a first. The specification required that most of the osteological analysis should be carried out during the excavation and facilities had been provided for the purpose by The Necropolis Company at their nearby premises. The analyses were therefore carried out in the surroundings of a busy undertakers. Archaeologists, particularly osteoarchaeologists, are accustomed to working with the physical remains of death and this usually means skeletal remains of some antiquity. This site presented the opportunity to work with more recent remains of known individuals and the presence of soft tissue. (It should be noted that the only soft tissue surviving consisted of brain tissue and ligamentous attachments and due to the time and financial constraints of the project these were not sampled for analysis.) Added to this was the unusual nature of the working environment.

Work was primarily undertaken in a garage used for storage, a disused coffin-manufacturing workshop, and a disused embalming room (Fig 13.2). In this environment and being constantly surrounded by the undertakers' daily routine, recent death suddenly became both a consideration and an issue. This provoked an emotional response which could not be ignored but which is difficult to express or quantify. This response was not, however, unwelcome because in turn it caused a re-examination of osteological motivations of the modern approach to archaeological death (Kirk & Start forthcoming).

One tentative conclusion reached was that if burial grounds are to be cleared then the archaeological excavation of those areas should be respectful, maintaining the individuality of the interred remains. The sense of unease experienced in these surroundings was never completely overcome but the familiar nature of osteological analysis enabled the work to be carried out, indeed the desire to immerse oneself in work has never been felt more strongly.

Acknowledgements

We gratefully acknowledge the advice and support offered throughout the project by Dr Margaret Cox, Jez Reeve, Ken Whittaker, Trevor Anderson, and Dr Tony Pollard. Gwen Jones undertook the historical analysis and The Necropolis Company assisted with lead coffins and provided accommodation. This project was funded by Rushmon Ltd.

Figure 13.2 Working conditions in the undertakers' premises: an unusual working environment (photo: Archaeology South-East)

Part III   Hazards for the archaeologist

Hazards for the archaeologist

Health and safety policies and risk assessment are now generally a part of everyday archaeological practice reflecting a plethora of legislation, regulation, and codes of practice. While many aspects of archaeology (for example deeply stratified urban sites) present their own particular range of hazards, funerary archaeology is perhaps one of the most complex. Following the excavation at Christ Church, Spitalfields it appears to have developed its own mythology.

Paul Kneller's contribution to these proceedings is an overview of some of the complex legislation and regulations which currently dictate health and safety policy for archaeologists. As is appropriate, he concentrates on those particular hazards that might be relevant in a church or funerary context. Possibly the most particular of all is the complex issue of smallpox and funerary archaeology contributed by Susan Young whose epidemiological and communicable diseases background ensure that she probably understands the complexity of this issue better than any other person. Susan concludes that while the risk of anyone contracting smallpox is extremely remote, the potential threat to the population at large, from this globally eradicated disease, is such that it has to be taken seriously.

Current legislation and legal precedents are not only concerned with the physical health of the workforce and the population at large but also their psychological well-being. As indicated in Part II of this volume and in the Christ Church publications, there is anecdotal evidence that suggests that some archaeologists might experience post-traumatic stress disorder (PTSD) as a result of engaging with the more recently deceased. It is to be hoped that the impact of such work will not be as long-lasting as that experienced by the author Gabriel García Márquez when he witnessed the exhumation of tombs beneath a convent. These he described 45 years later in *Of love and demons* (1995, 3–4) where he concludes: 'Almost half a century later I can still feel the confusion produced in me'. While psychology examines and categorizes this newly labelled but ancient disorder, archaeologists can usefully come to terms with their own humanity and accept that it is not only acceptable but desirable to express negative emotions, discomfort, and distress when they occur.

For a few archaeologists, acceptance of the legitimacy of concepts such as PTSD is culturally abhorrent in much the same way as is their acceptance of health and safety protocols which protect physical well-being. Unfortunately, though now a minority view, 'macho-archaeology' still exists and it is regrettable that it can occasionally be seen among those in senior positions, whose power ensures that such an ethos can be insidiously imposed upon and transferred to those more junior and less experienced.

James Thompson's valuable chapter sets out to demystify emotional distress and PTSD experienced in the arena of exposure to the dead from a psychologist's perspective. Some readers might be surprised at the complexity of human responses to the dead body. There is a tendency to assume that the discomfort experienced by archaeologists working in a forensic or post-medieval funerary context simply reflects a horror of sights of putrefaction and autolysis. This contribution corrects that misconception and stresses that without a controlled scientific study, it is impossible to establish either the presence or extent of the risk of archaeologists experiencing PTSD.

14 Health and safety in church and funerary archaeology *Paul Kneller*

Introduction

Church and funerary archaeology present the archaeological unit's safety officer with a number of problems (the term 'unit' is used throughout but includes all groups of archaeologists who undertake fieldwork). While being specific to church and funerary archaeologists these problems can be relevant to those involved on construction sites, in scientific laboratories, and in the general office environment. This paper examines the safety problems that present themselves to the various occupational roles within church and funerary archaeology, current legislation including recent changes, and how these may affect archaeologists. The aspect of funerary archaeology that renders it different from many other types of archaeology is that it usually involves either removal of, or exposure to, human remains. Obviously this introduces a range of biological and psychological risks that are not normally relevant to archaeologists.

The first task is to examine the extent of the problem, that is to determine whether archaeology is a high risk occupation and if funerary work is a still greater risk. The normal way for the safety professional to compare occupational risks is to use the published statistics from the Health and Safety Executive (1996a). However, this is not possible for archaeology as it is too small a profession to be one of the Standard Occupational Classifications used in these statistics. The same situation applies to the Department of Health statistics compiled by the Public Health Laboratory Service (Dr R Smith, pers comm) and the Scottish Centre for Infection and Environmental Health (Dr S Adams, pers comm). The Council for British Archaeology stated that in July 1991 only 1682 people were employed in archaeology (CBA 1997a), consequently understanding the extent of the problem is much greater but even if we cannot find exact statistics we can draw conclusions from the other occupational groups that perform similar tasks. As can be seen from Table 14.1, serious accidents in the UK workforce as a whole present a cause for concern.

There are of course a large number of tasks performed by the church or funerary archaeologist and some are performed by enthusiastic amateurs. Many are also performed by other archaeologists, so this paper may also be of use to a wider readership. If these groups of field workers are to be protected then a number of safety rules should be understood and adhered to.

The workforce must be protected for a number of reasons. A lack of safety management could lead to physical or emotional damage to the workforce, prosecution for the unit or site manager, or simply loss of working time and over-running of the project with associated financial implications.

The first step in the safety management process is to inform the appropriate authority that archaeological work (evaluation or excavation) is proposed in a church or cemetery context. Assuming that the appropriate authority from either religious or secular authorities has been obtained (for a full discussion of the law and burial archaeology see Garratt-Frost *et al* 1992), then the next step is to inform the local Environmental Health Department (EHD). Interestingly, it may come as a surprise to some Environmental Health Officers (EHO) that what is proposed is within their jurisdiction. Except for archaeology on some building sites (which is Health and Safety Executive controlled), the EHD is the regulatory authority, especially where there may be disturbance of buried or interred remains.

The EHO will require the production of a safety policy and an outline of the work, together with a risk assessment for each stage of the work. Risk assessments are required under several sets of regulations, for example:

- Management of Work Regulations 1992 (HMSO 1992a)
- Control of Substances Hazardous to Health 1994 (HMSO 1994a)
- Manual Handling Operation Regulations 1992 (HMSO 1992b)
- Construction, Design & Management Regulations 1994 (HMSO 1994b)
- Personal Protective Equipment Regulations 1992 (HMSO 1992c)
- Control of Lead at Work Regulations 1980 (HMSO 1980)

Table 14.1: Injuries reported to HSE enforcement authorities in 1993–4 (HSE 1996a)

	Injuries	Fatalities
Employed	151,900	245
Self employed	3,900	51
Member of the public	11,700	107
Total	167,500	403

Most modern UK safety legislation is now framed to require assessment. That is, instead of requiring action if, and only if, an exact or specific condition occurs these new regulations require a 'suitable and sufficient' assessment to be made and acted upon to provide a safe working environment. In this way prosecution of employers, unit managers, or even individual archaeologists is straightforward if an accident occurs because a safe working environment had not been provided or maintained. One defence against this could be that the unit had done as much as was reasonably practicable, and to prove this the risk assessment could be used. 'Reasonably practicable' is a phrase often used when discussing safety matters and is taken to have a particular meaning. Where an employer has a statutory duty which is amended by the phrase 'as far as reasonably practicable', then the employer is only in breach of that duty if the occurrence was reasonably foreseeable. A calculation weighing the risk against expenditure is allowed, if the risk is very small compared to the expenditure, and then a defence of 'reasonable practicability' could be used. However, it is a requirement that employers should keep up to date with the legislation, HSE publications, and other technical publications which affect their workforce.

The risk assessment process

Risk assessments are performed by everyone every day and not even considered. A good example of this is the complicated calculation involved in the act of crossing the road. In order to achieve this safely,

consideration must be given to the width of the road, road surface and weather conditions, the distance to, speed of, and number of oncoming cars, and the pedestrian's own speed. This calculation is performed millions of times a day, mostly correctly. So suitable and sufficient risk assessments in safety are not necessarily problematical: guidance can be found in the HSE document *5 steps to risk assessment* (1994).

As can be seen in Figure 14.1, the process can be a simple iterative one of information gathering and evaluation. In the area of safety the words 'risk' and 'hazard' have precise meanings. The hazard is the potential damage that may be done during the operation, including any waste produced or if the process goes wrong. The risk of an operation is the likelihood that a hazard may occur. There may of course be more than one hazard (and therefore more than one risk) associated with each activity. If the case of a person crossing the road is reconsidered then the major hazard involved is that of being knocked down and this risk increases the more often the road is crossed. If the person never crossed the road then there would be no risk. The workplace risk assessment should be performed by a competent person and would need to be recorded if more than four persons are employed at that workplace.

Hazards in church and funerary archaeology

Church and funerary archaeology present most of the normal hazards associated with archaeology

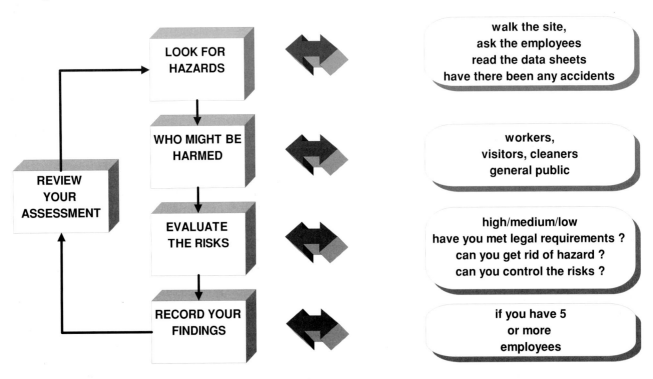

Figure 14.1   The risk assessment process (after HSE 1994)

Figure 14.2   Archaeologist in safety equipment: filtered air flow face mask with waist mounted pump and filter units for dust and organic vapours, disposable breatheable coveralls, gloves, and boots (photo: P Kneller)

and some additional ones. This may make some types of the work a medium- to high-risk activity.

Archaeologists of all types are concerned with a number of common activities and most would consider themselves proficient at some, including trenching (see below), manual handling, and the erection and use of tower scaffolds.

The church or funerary archaeologist may face a large number of additional hazards during the course of the project. One of the major risks is that of the microbiological hazard. A 'suitable and sufficient risk assessment' must be made under the Control of Substances Hazardous to Health Regulations 1994. Suitable guidance can be found in the Approved Code of Practice L5 (HSE 1997) and other information regarding the required facilities from the Advisory Committee on Dangerous Pathogens (HSE 1995). In the biological agents section of the Approved Codes of Practice (ACOP) there is a requirement to assess if biological exposure may result not from the work itself but is incidental to it. It gives the examples of agriculture, sewage purification, and health care but church or funerary

archaeology could also come in this category. Under section 12 of the ACOP, the assessment should include consideration of the biological agents present, their hazard group, the diseases they cause, and how these are transmitted. Thought should also be given to the likelihood of disinfection resistance and spore or cyst formation. The minimization of the number of people exposed should also be evaluated, as should be the likelihood of exposure and consequent disease and the identification of any immuno-compromising conditions that would elevate the risk (including pregnancy). Also required is the examination of the control measures used to reduce exposure, including ventilation and protective equipment and clothing together with the associated monitoring systems. The need for medical surveillance is also assessed.

The major microbiological hazards faced by archaeologists are:

- Weil's disease
- Lyme disease
- ornithosis
- histoplasmosis
- tetanus
- fungal spores and moulds
- food-borne diseases
- anthrax
- smallpox

The biological hazards presented to the archaeologist can be placed in two categories. The first are those that exist in large numbers of places, such as old buildings, river sides, farms and so on, with the church and its associated crypt just another of these. These could include Weil's disease, Lyme disease, ornithosis, histoplasmosis, reactions to spores and moulds, tetanus, and food-borne diseases. The second category is that of the risks associated with buried remains and this group includes smallpox and anthrax.

In the primary group the first three are all zoonoses, that is they are associated with animals or birds and information is given about their occupational risk by HSE 1993.

Risks associated with general working environments

Weil's disease

Weil's disease is the most serious form of the family of diseases known as leptospirosis. The bacterium that causes it infects animals including rats, cattle, cats, and dogs and any of these can transmit it to humans. Weil's disease is caused by *Leptospira icterohaemorrhagiae*, is usually associated with rats, and amounts to about one third of all reported leptospira infections. Although leptospirosis is a notifiable disease and reportable by law if an occupational link is suspected, it is very hard to diagnose,

Table 14.2: Table of infections in the United Kingdom by year. Numbers in brackets indicate deaths. (Sources: Public Health Laboratory Service and Scottish Centre for Infection and Environmental Health)

	1992	1993	1994	1995
Anthrax (England & Wales)	0	0	0	1
(Scotland)	0	0	0	0
Leptospirosis (England & Wales)	52 (2)	47 (1)	20 (1)	20 (0)
(Scotland)	5 (0)	4 (0)	3 (0)	2 (0)
Lyme disease (England & Wales)	18	44	25	n/a
(Scotland)	4	9	9	5
Tetanus (England & Wales)	7	8	5	6
(Scotland)	n/a	n/a	n/a	n/a
Ornithosis (England & Wales)	338	369	494	435
(Scotland)	n/a	n/a	n/a	n/a

especially in the early stages. This often means that confirmation by the public health laboratories and therefore inclusion in the statistics (see Table 14.2) occurs in only about 5% of the estimated cases (Loss Prevention Council 1994, 30–32).

After an incubation period of up to fourteen days, the usual symptoms include a flu-like early stage, often followed by jaundice and occasional death in untreated cases. The bacteria are spread in the urine of affected animals and can survive in damp conditions or in water for four to five weeks. They enter humans via open wounds or via water through the mucus membranes.

Traditionally the most at-risk occupational group was the sewer worker but risk assessment leading to altered working practices has reduced the numbers of affected workers significantly. The risk of contracting Weil's disease exists when working anywhere that is likely to have a population of rats, and a large number of urban and rural church sites will come into this category.

Lyme disease

This is caused by the inoculation of the bacterium *Borrelia burgdorferi* after being bitten by a deer (or occasionally sheep) tick. The bacterium reproduces at the bite site to produce a red rash, then migrates to the lymph nodes and into the bloodstream and may produce cardiac or neurological complications some weeks or months later. The tick tends to attach itself to the highest part of its surroundings and then be brushed off by a passing animal or human. The tick will normally migrate upwards and towards damp soft skin, then bite. Workers should examine behind the knees, between fingers and toes, under arms, in navels, in or behind ears, and where elastic or waistbands stop further movement (Lyme Disease Network 1996). If ticks are found they should be removed carefully with tweezers, grabbing the tick as close to the skin as possible and twisting in an anticlockwise direction.

Vaseline or alcohol or a lighted match should not be used as these will encourage the transmission of the bacterium. Inform your doctor if flu-like symptoms occur after a tick bite. The areas most affected by Lyme disease are the New Forest and the west coast of Scotland.

Ornithosis

This is a bacterial infection caused by the organism *Chlamydia psittaci*. It is acquired via contact with infected birds or their droppings and is often called Psittacosis. The disease is widespread in the wild and domestic bird population, including pigeons. The average number of cases per year is about 400, some of these will be from domestic situations but for most the source will be unknown. The incubation period is anywhere between four to fourteen days resulting in fever, headache, joint and muscle pain, and occasionally pneumonia and hepatitis (HSE 1993). Death is rare but can occur in the immuno-challenged sector of the population, including pregnant women. The organism can survive for many months in dry and dusty droppings and inhalation of these is the normal transmission route. Respiratory protection is required where disturbance of bird droppings is inevitable. Care should be taken when removing overalls, etc, and a good standard of personal hygiene should be enforced. If the conditions are correct for the transmission of ornithosis then it is possible that fungal spores associated with mammals or birds will also be present, as discussed below.

Histoplasmosis

This is a fungus infection of the lung caused by inhalation of the spores of the fungus *Histoplasmosa capsulatum* that can be found in bird and, more often, in bat droppings. In most cases either no or mild flu-like symptoms are produced but occasionally severe lung infections can occur and can persist for between one to six months. Reporting of this disease is assumed to be poor and consequently it is a rare disease. Again, the immuno-suppressed population are at greater risk and allowance should be made in the risk assessment. As with all occupational illnesses provision of information on the type of work and location is vital for correct diagnosis. Avoidance of transmission is possible by the correct use of suitable personal protective equipment.

Other fungal spores and moulds

The conditions for moulds and the accompanying spore formation are often found in church buildings as these have the correct humidity and temperature for mould growth, now exacerbated by the use of central heating systems in buildings that were not designed to house them. It is normally the spores of the moulds that cause a reaction in humans. The extent of the reaction depends on the human sensitivity. One group, the atopic, is more likely to become sensitized to spores whereas the other, the non-topic, is less likely to be become sensitized but may react more seriously. The spores can be responsible for asthma, rhinitis, and alveolitis. Spores vary greatly in size and it is their size that determines the affected site within the respiratory system. Spores larger than 10 microns in size will normally be trapped by the nasal hairs, those between 10 and 4 microns can lodge in the bronchi and smaller ones in the alveoli.

On exposure to some spores allergenic reactions are common. Sensitivity is produced by exposure to enough allergen to produce antibodies and from then on any exposure will result in this altered excessive reaction. The atopic group, between 10–20% of the population, are sensitized at an early age, often to a number of materials. The time taken for the symptoms to occur and their duration is short for this group of individuals. For the non-topic group, the time of occurrence of symptoms is longer and they may often last for 24 hours. In both cases the symptoms are wheezing, sneezing, and congestion of the tissues.

The most common fungi that will be found in buildings that present a health hazard are shown in Table 14.3. Protection from these respiratory sensitizers can be obtained by wearing respiratory protective equipment of the correct grade, at probable classification of P3.

Tetanus

Tetanus, also called lockjaw, is an anaerobically propagated bacillus and its toxins produce its characteristic effect. The spores of the bacilli are found in soil, and the body can be innoculated with them through open wounds. The tetanus victim is not infectious and effective protection is provided by immunization. The routine immunization scheme was started in 1961 so all field workers should have some protection that should be boosted by re-immunization at no more than ten-year intervals. Part of every employment interview should ask for proof of tetanus protection. The risk to the working archaeologist may be small but the outcome could be very serious (see Table 14.2).

Food-borne diseases

The most likely disease to afflict the archaeologist is one of the food-borne or hygiene-related ones (CBA 1997b). These include dysentery, paratyphoid, and gardiasis and those caused by *E. coli.* and *cryptospodidium parvum*. The reported cases (all occupations) number on average 70,000 per year but there is an estimated under-reporting of about ten times.

These illnesses come from many sources, from the home, restaurants, sandwich bars, and some from the workplace. The peripatetic nature of archaeological work can lead to problems. The provision of 'suitable and sufficient' sanitary and catering facilities, kept in good order, is vital to reduce the risk of these diseases. Most of the food-borne diseases are debilitating for only a short time but can often be easily spread among the other workers by poor hygiene. The result of these diseases could be reduced resistance to other infection and serious

Table 14.3: The site affected by various spores found in buildings (Institute of Environmental Health Officers 1985, 13, Table 1)

Type of mould	Rhinitis	Asthma	Disease Alveolitis	Infection
Penicillium spp	yes	yes	yes	yes
Serpula lacrymans (dry rot)	yes	yes		
Aspergillus spp (especially *A. Fumigatus* and *A. Niger*)	yes	yes	yes	yes
Mucor spp	yes	yes		yes
Cladosporium spp	yes	yes		

loss of working days to the project. Some cases are notifiable to the local health authority.

The risk of infection from human burial and interments

A number of papers have been written of the risks presented to the archaeologist during the investigation of buried or interred human remains (Waldron 1985; Baxter *et al* 1988). The pathogenic risk presented by bodies buried in plague pits is small, because the use of coffins was unlikely and without this protection the normal soil microbial action will inactivate these agents. Where wooden coffins were used there can be an increased risk due to the very occasional good preservation of bodies and materials (see Young, this volume). The highest risk category is that of the sealed lead coffin. The condition of the contents of these coffins vary greatly. The body may be completely skeletonized, completely dessicated, completely preserved, or in any condition between these extremes (see Molleson & Cox 1993). If any soft tissue remains the hazard presented should be treated as potentially severe (Healing *et al* 1995) and suitable protective systems should be used. It is not only the human remains themselves that may present a risk but also the coffin linings and pads, and the result of the body's decomposition, a viscous black liquid. The greatest potential risk presented by this activity is that of contracting anthrax or smallpox.

Anthrax

Anthrax is a disease that affects many animals. In the context of church and funerary archaeology the normal potential source would be from burials and interments and the materials used in the coffins. Anthrax is caused by a spore-forming bacillus *Bacillus anthracis* and three types of disease can result from infection. The most common form of anthrax affects the skin and is transmitted by spores entering broken skin or mucus membranes. The signs and symptoms of this disease are a painless boil on the skin that turns black after three or four days. The other forms enter via the respiratory and ingested routes often beginning with a high fever occurring between one and six days of inhaling the spores, followed by severe stomach pain, diarrhoea, and vomiting (HSE 1997). All forms could lead to death if untreated or treatment is delayed. However anthrax is a rare disease in the United Kingdom (see Table 14.2). The risk for the archaeologist associated with working with the remains of a recorded anthrax death are thought to be small. A higher risk is gained from the well-preserved horse hair or woollen materials used in the coffin pads, pillows, and packing.

The possibility of infection from this sort of material is hard to quantify but it is reported that the bacillus has been isolated from the roof insulation of Kings Cross station that was constructed 110 years earlier. In a well-documented case anthrax spores have been found to be infectious after fifty years in soil (Turnbull *et al* 1996).

A suitable and sufficient risk assessment must be performed when exposure to coffin contents is possible. The minimum precautions are to wear the correct level of protective equipment (see below) and to provide information to the workforce.

Smallpox

The risk and hazards associated with this disease are dealt with elsewhere in this volume by Dr Susan Young. It is enough to say that even if the risk is small there is a requirement to assess the risk involved, the risk reduction process, and the process involved if smallpox is suspected. These should be clearly understood by all that are potentially exposed.

Non-biological physical hazards

Other hazards that may be found in funerary archaeology include manual handling, repetitive strain injury, and post traumatic stress. An assessment of the manual handling requirements of the project is vital to decide on an appropriate handling strategy. There might be the possibility of having to move lead coffins weighing up to one third of a ton. These may be on the ground, presenting a lifting problem, or stored at heights, sometimes above shoulder height. The coffins may have to be manoeuvred through narrow, poorly lit passages with uneven floors and often upstairs. Each one of these situations presents a handling problem, especially if the coffin is in poor condition. A risk assessment is required under the *Manual Handling Regulations 1992* (HSE 1992) and is likely to require the use of hoists, trolleys, and movers.

Repetitive strain injury (RSI)

RSI is caused by the repeated restricted movement of one part of the body, often the wrist, as in archaeologists trowelling during excavation. This particular RSI is associated with pain in the tendons in the hand, wrist, and forearms. The number of cases of disability in the UK workforce due to this tenosynovitis rose from 423 in 1989–90 to 800 in 1993–4 and, of these, the number having a 14% or greater disability has risen from 8% to 35% in the same time period.

Post-traumatic stress disorder

It is a contentious issue as to whether the emotional disturbance experienced by some archaeologists can be classified as being post-traumatic stress disorder (PTSD). There are a number of classifications which are often based on the fact that the person had been exposed to a catastrophic stressor that was outside the usual human experience, such as war, earthquakes, factory explosions, or aeroplane crashes (Friedman 1997). The exposure of an archaeologist to a well-preserved or decomposing body may come within these ranges of experience. Another consideration as to whether any emotional damage may occur is the personal circumstances of the archaeologist. If the worker had recently lost a child, the effect of working with a child's coffin may be considerably more disturbing. The clinical experience of PTSD is that the most difficult cases are those where prior early, severe, or unresolved traumatic experiences were exacerbated by more recent trauma (Baldwin, pers comm). Care must therefore be taken in the allocation of work if a worker's prior experience is known. Monitoring by a specialist and daily or weekly group debriefings may help to recognise or reduce symptoms. This subject is discussed in detail by Thompson (this volume).

Construction Design and Management (Welfare) Regulations 1996

The major change in the legal position to affect the archaeologist in recent years is that of the *Construction Design and Management (Welfare) Regulations 1996* (HSE 1996b). These are designed to provide adequate welfare facilities on construction sites which last more than 30 days and employ more than four persons, but in some cases archaeological excavations will be classified as construction sites, ie excavations on existing building sites. Other sites may also come under these regulations as a construction site is defined as: 'any site where the principal work activity is any of these; construction, alteration, conversion, fitting, . . . decommissioning, demolition or dismantling of a structure' or 'the preparation for any intended structure, including site clearance or the removal of any part of the structure' (HSE 1996b, 2) (Fig 14.3).

The regulations then go on to define what a 'structure' is: the list includes earth-retaining structures and those designed to preserve or alter any natural feature, and 'any structure similar to those on the list'. Could this be interpreted as meaning hill-forts and barrows? Perhaps only a test case will decide this. But what of those green field sites? There has been a general agreement from the HSE that it would be very difficult to have two sets of standards, so even if not strictly covered the same conditions would be expected on all sites. It is suggested that a rule of equivalence not regulation should be followed by unit managers.

There are 35 sections and ten schedules in the Regulations, each specifying particular areas of activity. Some of the more relevant ones for the archaeologist will include those on excavations and welfare facilities. Under the section on excavation there has been a change in the shoring rules: there is now no minimum depth before shoring must be used. In the past if the trench went below 1.2 metres then shoring was required, now a suitable and sufficient risk assessment must be made for each and every trench. This is so that all practical steps should be taken so that no excavation (so far as reasonably practicable) should collapse and that no person shall be trapped or buried by any fall of material.

The consideration given to the welfare facilities of site workers is extended. It is the duty of the employer and the person in charge of the site to ensure that the following provisions are made. There should be suitable and sufficient sanitary conveniences, either separate male and female or individual units together with associated washing facilities. These should include hot and cold or warm water (which shall be a piped supply so far as reasonably practicable), soap, and a means of drying. There may be a requirement for showers depending on the type of work carried out, though if lead coffins were being moved this would already be a requirement. There must be on site a rest room with suitable arrangements for smokers and non-smokers, this should also have an adequate supply of drinking water and cups and, most British of all, a means of boiling water.

Disposal of materials from the excavation site

Part of the health and safety strategy of the excavation site must be the destination of all the materials to be removed from the site. Some of these materials will be carefully protected and sent for post-excavation treatment, others may be seen as material to be disposed of, ie large amounts of rubble or rotten wood. Anything which is not required or reused is waste, and its movement and/or final destination will be controlled, some specifically, such as clinical waste, and some under general waste regulations. Specific cases from church or funerary excavations may include the disposal of coffin liquor, disposable paper suits, and respiratory protection equipment (canisters and dust masks). These may all be classified as clinical waste. Clinical waste will have to be collected and incinerated by approved contractors, and this significant expenditure will have to be included in the project costs. Any lead from coffins (the property of the landowner) can be stored carefully and then recycled. Some recycling contractors may require the lead to be disinfected before storage. Builders' rubble and the rotting wood from coffins, etc, can be disposed of by agreement with the local waste regulation

188

Figure 14.3 A normal archaeological excavation: how many potential safety problems can you see? (photo: Museum of London Archaeology Service)

authority, and payment for this will also have to be included in the project costs. The last category is liquid wastes. These may include the normal sanitary wastes from toilets and showers and the wastes from the equipment cleaning and decontamination systems. Approval and, depending on the area, a licence is required for disposal into sewers. For areas where no mains sewerage exists great care must be taken when disposing of decontaminating fluids as a relatively small amount can disrupt the efficient working of septic tanks.

Conclusion

What effect does the above have on church and funerary archaeology? The major requirements are to assess, react, and, most importantly, to protect. The risks involved in this type of archaeology may be low but some of the hazards are very serious. The protective systems and the welfare facilities needed will enforce the same professional standards of care shown to artefacts to be shown to the workers. This may have serious financial implications to the smaller archaeological units and it may be that in the future the required safety equipment will result in specialized units for particular activities, including funerary archaeology. As can be seen from Figure 14.2 the appearance of the archaeologist will change in the near future. The cost of this equipment, its maintenance, and disposal, per person/usage will have to be included in estimates for work. Failure to do so and then the subsequent purchase enforced by the safety authorities is likely to lead to a drastic over-running of budget, as would a successful claim for damages from an injured employee or visitor. The Loss Prevention Council who produce reports to aid insurance risk assessment have stated that 'in the event of a claim for damages an employer would have a poor defence if there was a clear occupational link and no evidence of risk assessment having been performed' (1994, 31).

Every year there are about 120,000 civil actions for damages made by TUC-affiliated unions, compared to about 1800 criminal cases brought by the enforcing authorities. It is clearly vital that the collecting of information, its assessment, and enforcement of subsequent local safety rules, are as much a part of the experience of the archaeologist as the interpretation of archaeology.

Note

By today's standards, Figure 14.3 shows at least eight potential safety problems: worker on a plank between a step-ladder and stone steps; long extension leads training near edges (what voltages are used?); unsecured pole ladder; poor working practice on overhanging steel structures; single planks used as walkways; no evidence of barriers to prevent workers carrying out tasks above others; general clutter around the storage area, and how stable is the shed?; worker standing on a chair to produce drawings. The Museum of London Archaeology Service are thanked for their permission to use this illustration.

15 Archaeology and smallpox *Susan E J Young*

Few facts are available about the archaeology of smallpox, but theories about virus survival abound and feelings run high. For thousands of years smallpox (*variola*) afflicted humankind and killed or scarred a high proportion of its victims. It has now been eradicated from the world, so why are we still concerned about it? Archaeologists expect to handle the remains of people who have died through the millennia and the state of preservation in which these remains will be found can only be guessed at before they are exposed, however educated that guess may be.

Devastating epidemics of smallpox (*variola major*) occurred in all parts of the world. Princes and peasants were equally affected: this disease was no respecter of rank or privilege. Mortality rates of 40–60% were reported for severe forms of smallpox rising to over 90% in particularly susceptible individuals. A milder form of the disease (*variola minor*) also caused major outbreaks but these had a very much lower mortality rate of 1% or so. Recovery from smallpox conferred life-long immunity, and the last known case of naturally acquired *variola major* occurred in Bangladesh in 1975. *Variola minor* persisted in the Horn of Africa until 1977 when the last case was diagnosed in Somalia. In 1979 the World Health Organisation certified the global eradication of smallpox and this was ratified by the World Health Assembly in 1980.

A very brief description of this terrifying disease might be helpful. The patient became highly infectious particularly after the appearance of a characteristic deep-seated rash. This rash, which was typically distributed centrifugally (Fig 15.1), evolved through a pustular stage to crusts. In the majority of cases the rash was most dense on those areas of skin which were commonly uncovered, such as the face and limbs, and less dense on the trunk. In some cases the rash was sparse at all times, yet in others the pustular eruption was almost confluent. In very severe cases the rash might have been haemorrhagic, or death might even have occurred before the true rash appeared. These early deaths apart, a fatal outcome might occur at the height of the rash, or in the convalescent phase from secondary bacterial infection of the lesions. Scarring was often gross and blindness was a common complication. No treatment existed to cure smallpox, only supportive care was available. Reduction of spread of infection depended on stringent isolation of cases and quarantine measures until vaccination became an effective method of control.

Like any epidemic disease, incidence varied from time to time and from place to place. Transmission occurred through face to face contact with the respiratory secretions, or direct contact with the skin lesions of patients and also from materials contaminated by these exudates.

An individual was infectious until all the scabs had separated. Scabs carried the infectious virus for long periods, and there are many anecdotes of outbreaks of smallpox associated with contaminated bedding and clothing. Populations of American Indians were exterminated in epidemics of severe smallpox transmitted by infected blankets from traders and soldiers.

It is impossible to be sure of diagnoses made in past centuries, but the meticulous historian of smallpox Dr Donald Hopkins (1983) suggests that it was an important disease in the 2nd millennium BC, and the view that the Pharaoh Rameses V died of smallpox in 1160 BC is common. Others prefer to find evidence for it only after the 1st century AD.

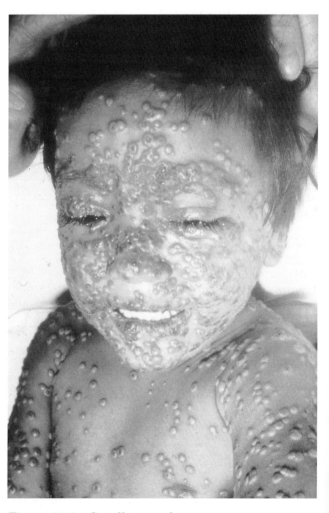

Figure 15.1 Smallpox rash

Galen knew the disease in the 2nd century AD, as was suggested by Al-Razi, the great physician from Baghdad, who gave what is generally accepted as a clear description of smallpox in the 10th century AD. Certainly the geographical distribution and momentum of smallpox outbreaks increased as the centuries passed. It was not until the end of the 18th century, when Edward Jenner, a doctor in Gloucestershire, introduced vaccination in 1796, that control of this disease at last became a real possibility. Vaccination finally enabled the conquest of smallpox and this is so far the only infectious disease to be eradicated from the globe.

Smallpox was widespread in Europe in the 16th century and was probably its most devastating epidemic disease. How much smallpox was there in this country? It has been estimated that in the 17th century Britain suffered severely from the disease and that 5% of all deaths in London were due to this disease. Considering that some people had mild infections and a significant proportion of those affected recovered, albeit with gross scarring, the total number of cases would have been enormous. Estimates of the number of smallpox deaths are stark: Baxby (1981) suggests that between one in eight and one in fourteen of adult deaths and one in three child deaths were likely to have been from this disease in the 18th century.

Looking at some of the available data we may get a feeling for the effects of smallpox. These data have been tabulated in different ways over the years and construction of a unified presentation is impractical. Some figures were collated on a geographical basis, some concern deaths, others relate to the number of notified cases. There are interruptions in recording which coincide with major wars. Nevertheless perhaps the following tabulations will serve to make illustrative points, taking the figures at face value and recognising that even for a disease associated with a characteristic rash ascertainment may well underestimate the number of deaths caused by smallpox.

Using data from Bills of Mortality in London from 1730–1839 (Table 15.1), smallpox deaths ranged from about 300 to almost 4000 per annum during this period. In each decade the proportion of total deaths in London which were attributed to smallpox varied and were as high as 18.4% in 1796 and as low as 1.5% in 1834. Decade peaks occurred in 1736, 1746, 1752, 1763, 1772, 1781, 1796, 1800, 1812, 1825, and 1838. Inapparent major epidemics associated with more than 3000 deaths occurred in 1757 and 1768.

Later mortality data extracted from the Registrar General's Returns for London from 1840–1909 (Table 15.2) show that up to 1885 the number of smallpox deaths fluctuated widely, ranging from 46 to almost 8000 a year. Annual totals exceeded 1500 deaths caused by smallpox in 1838, when 3817 deaths were recorded, in 1844, 1863, 1877–8 and 1881. In 1871–2 a major outbreak of *variola major* caused 9698 deaths.

After 1885 numbers fell dramatically with less than 100 deaths in most years, but two big outbreaks occurred, one in 1893 (206 deaths) and the other in 1901–2 (1,542 deaths). From 1907–13 records show zeros or less than ten smallpox deaths annually, showing that this disease persisted into the 20th century, and still caused significant numbers of deaths.

After 1920 the data are presented as notified cases and deaths for England and Wales (Table 15.3). Notified cases ranged between 14,764 in 1927 and 179 in 1934. Over 2000 cases were notified a year for ten consecutive years from 1923 to 1932. The number of deaths between 1920 and 1940 ranged from 0–53 per annum. Clearly a milder form of smallpox was present in the country: *variola minor*, also known as alastrim, was endemic.

The data for 1950–79 are presented as cases and deaths in Great Britain (Table 15.4). Small outbreaks still occurred and these were associated with

Table 15.1: London Bills of Mortality: 1730–1839. Range of smallpox deaths as a proportion of total deaths

Decade	Highest	Lowest
1730–39	10.9%	4.7%
1740–49	11.5%	5.2%
1750–59	17.2%	4.0%
1760–69	13.7%	7.2%
1770–79	15.3%	4.8%
1780–89	16.9%	3.5%
1790–99	18.4%	3.1%
1800–09	10.4%	3.7%
1910–19	7.0%	2.1%
1820–29	5.4%	2.8%
1830–39	4.3%	1.5% (data for three years missing)

Table 15.2: Range of annual smallpox deaths in London: 1840–1909. Registrar General's Returns

Decade	Highest annual	Lowest annual	Decade total
1840–49	1804	257	8631
1850–59	1158	156	6751
1860–69	1996	217	8272
1870–79	7012	46	16,041
1880–89	2371	1	5266
1890–99	206	1	432
1900–09	1300	0	1596

cases imported from overseas brought by travellers, servicemen and immigrants.

From 1950–4 there were 220 cases with 26 deaths, then followed three years with no smallpox. In the six years from 1957–62 there were 82 cases with 29 deaths. Then an outbreak of *variola minor* occurred in 1966 with 71 cases and no deaths. Two cases were recorded in 1967 and one in 1968 with no deaths. In 1973 there were five cases and two deaths and finally in 1978 the world's last two cases occurred in Birmingham with one death. Both of the last two incidents resulted from laboratory infection of the primary cases.

Can the smallpox virus have survived with human remains and their associated materials? It is a large tough virus which has been shown to survive in dried crusts for at least thirteen years under laboratory conditions (Wolff and Croon 1968) and this survival has been attributed to favourable dry conditions of storage. Other workers have demonstrated decreasing amounts of virus in crusts taken from patients and retested for virus viability over a period of 417 days (Downie and Dumbell 1947). Based on his own work Dr Nakano, of the WHO Collaborating Center for Smallpox and Other Poxvirus Infections, in the Centers for Disease Control, Atlanta, believes that a realistic survival time for infectious smallpox virus particles at temperate ambient temperatures is less than two years, although virus survival could possibly be very much longer if victims had been buried in areas where permafrost exists. We have recently seen on television (Channel 4, *Horizon*, 'Ice Mummies', February 1997) how remarkably bodies have been preserved in ice.

Table 15.3: Smallpox notified cases and deaths: 1920–39, England and Wales

Dates	Notified Cases	Deaths
1920–24	7755	82
1925–29	53,639	166
1930–34	20,343	48
1935–39	33	3

Table 15.4: Smallpox notified cases and deaths: 1950–79, Great Britain

Dates	Notified Cases	Deaths
1950–54	220	26
1955–59	11	3
1960–64	71	26
1965–69	74	0
1970–74	5	2
1975–79	2	1

In April 1983 a large number of well-preserved 16th century mummies were discovered in a 'suspended passageway' in the church of Saint Domenico Maggiore, in Naples (Fornaciari 1985, 215). Not only were the individuals well preserved but they were personally identifiable and information was available on their lives and causes of death. Interestingly, Professors Fornaciari and Marchetti of Pisa, who worked on these mummies, reported in 1986 that they had been able to demonstrate the presence of smallpox virus particles by electron microscopy and protein A-gold immunostaining in skin lesions taken from a mummified child with 'a diffuse vesiculo-pustular rash with the appearance and regional distribution of severe smallpox' (Fornaciari and Marchetti 1986, 625). Information was not given concerning the viability of this virus. In Professor Fornaciari's preliminary report in 1985, he described this unembalmed child's skin lesions as 'dry and their contents showed a crystalline aspect. The lesions affected the whole skin thickness and reached the periostium on the skull and ribs' (Fornaciari 1985, 223).

Stearn & Stearn (1945, 36) commenting on an outbreak of smallpox in Quebec in 1854, suggested that this had been caused by disturbance of the earth, for laying sewerage and water pipes, in a cemetery where hundreds of Canadian Indians had been interred during an intense outbreak of smallpox when one in four inhabitants died, in 1702–3. It is impossible to say whether the 1854 outbreak 'in the immediate vicinity' of the cemetery 'which was more severe and fatal there than in other parts of the city and suburbs' (*ibid*) was in fact related to the exhumations as smallpox was clearly present in the community at the time.

It is now medically accepted that risk of infection from exhumed human remains relates to 'modern infections' rather than the great plagues of the past. In what conditions might there be reasonable cause for concern? Human remains have been laid to rest in an enormous variety of conditions: bogs, sodden soil, sand, caves, catacombs, brick-lined voids, crypts, and even fields. Although decaying to dry bones occurs in the vast majority of cases over a short time other states may be found. Liquefaction and resultant brittle dried black material on bones or even the presence of a viscid black fluid in the coffin is not uncommon. Soft tissue preservation is unpredictable. Skin may be well-preserved ranging through dry mummification (Fig 15.2) with or without evidence of insect activity and tanning, to remains with the superficial appearance of a freshly interred body. Temperature, ventilation, moisture, pH, and coffin structure could all be expected to influence preservation of tissues to some degree though the role of each is as yet undefined. Some degree of preservation is commoner in lead-shelled coffins stored in relatively dry cool conditions but this generalization is by no means absolute. The effects of lead or zinc outer shells, disinfecting and absorbent materials including vegetable matter,

Figure 15.2   Mummified body from a crypt burial (photo: The Natural History Museum, London)

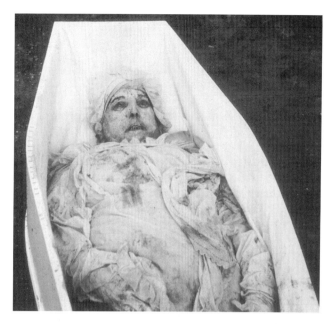

Figure 15.3   Well-preserved female, died 1839, exhumed 1996. Wooden coffin, brick-lined grave in a cemetery (photo: Susan Young)

Figure 15.4   Well-preserved female, died 1844, exhumed 1996. Lead coffin, brick-lined grave in a cemetery (photo: Susan Young)

and of embalming procedures are virtually unexplored. However, it is clear that well-preserved skin and soft tissues are found in a wide variety of conditions and it is only in such circumstances that the smallpox virus could conceivably have survived.

The author has personally seen full skin preservation to such a degree that the body was flexible and a pale colour when exposed after being interred for 150–200 years in crypts. This type of preservation has also been seen very occasionally in earth burials, in the south of England (Figs 15.3, 15.4, 15.5, 15.6, and 15.7). These bodies, whose coffin clothes were also beautifully preserved and often hardly discoloured, were interred both in simple wood coffins and, more often, in elaborate lead-enclosed coffins in brick-lined graves (without brick-lined floors) in a cemetery. The age at death ranged from a baby to 78 years old and the bodies showed no external evidence of any embalming procedure. Within hours of exposure, the skin darkened and unpleasant penetrating odours developed.

Fenner *et al* (1988) point out that although the smallpox virus does not cause persistent infection in humans (the only host), the *variola* virus in scabs is very resistant to inactivation especially at moderate temperatures and out of sunlight. Razzell (1976) suggested that interred corpses might be a possible source of infectious virus, but Fenner *et al* (1988) felt that the only evidence for this was anecdotal and came from situations in which the possibility of infection by direct contact with cases of smallpox could not be excluded. They concluded that the likelihood of the virus still surviving in scabs or associated with corpses or coffins in a form that might give rise to new cases of smallpox is now extremely remote. This reflects the length of time that has elapsed since there were numerous smallpox deaths in temperate climates, and that the topic does not lend itself to scientific investigation.

194

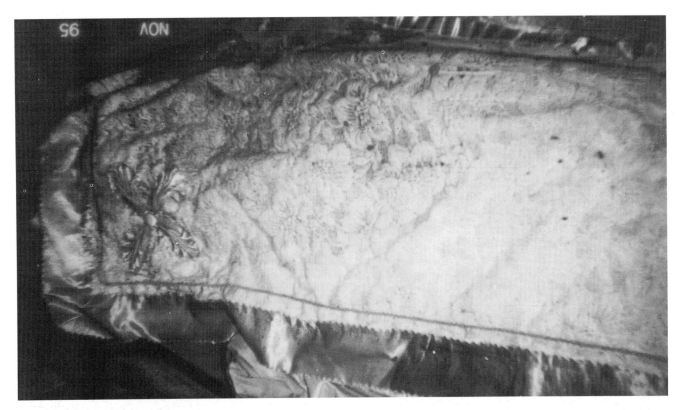

Figure 15.5   Cloth covering male in lead coffin, died 1847, exhumed 1995. Brick-lined grave in a cemetery (see also Figures 15.6 and 15.7) (photo: Susan Young)

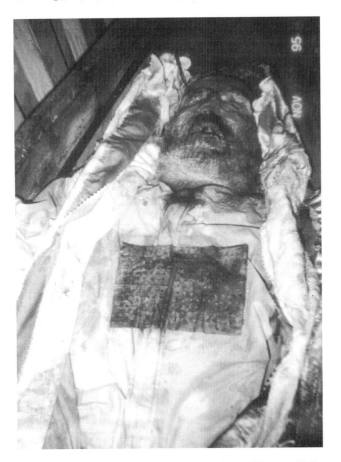

Figure 15.6   Well-preserved male from Figure 15.5, died 1847, exhumed 1995, brick-lined grave in a cemetery. Rectangular perforated material was next to skin (?poultice) (photo: Susan Young)

Nevertheless, because it is impossible to foretell the condition and state of soft tissue preservation within coffins before they are opened, it is prudent to consider whether smallpox might present an infectious hazard and to seek medical help if a visible rash, appropriately distributed on well-preserved skin is revealed (Figs 15.8, 15.9, 15.10, and 15.11).

Earthen burials, where moist conditions inevitably occur, are generally considered likely to shorten virus survival but the rate of decay in virus titres in dry airy conditions such as crypts is questioned by Meers (1985) and Zuckerman (1984). The latter has expressed the need for caution when handling well-preserved corpses, in the absence of reliable virus survival data.

Smallpox virus was present in high titres in the lesions of patients with the disease. Therefore, even in temperate climates we need to consider whether there are reasonable grounds for recommending personal protective measures and equipment for use when working with exhumed human remains. From a practical point of view, plans are needed to ensure the safety of workers, whether they are archaeologists or others. Burials under the open sky, that is those that have been subjected to the vagaries of weather since interment, are very rarely associated with significant survival of skin or soft tissues. When making risk assessments and drawing up codes of practice for the health and safety of workers it seems unreasonable to impose severe restrictions in such circumstances, but the proviso stands: should there be significant skin preserva-

Figure 15.7   Hand of male in Figures 15.5 and 15.6 (photo: Susan Young)

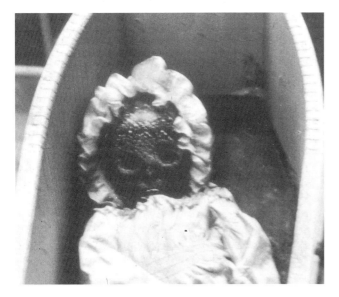

Figure 15.8   Well-preserved child eight days after exhumation by vandals in 1986, crypt burial (photo: Susan Young)

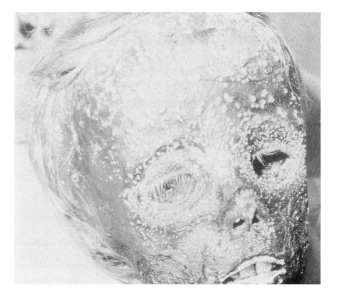

Figure 15.9   Child, close-up of suspicious rash on face (see also Figures 15.8 and 15.10) (photo: Susan Young)

tion, especially with apparent skin lesions, it would be wise to seek medical advice quickly. Unlike archaeologists and perhaps forensic pathologists, most medical practitioners rarely see bodies centuries after death, but in the United Kingdom the local Consultant for Communicable Disease Control

or appointed deputy is the person responsible for making decisions on action in such a situation.

Burials in mausoleums and brick-lined graves present a hazard situation intermediate between regular earth burials and those beneath churches. Occasionally well-preserved remains will be found

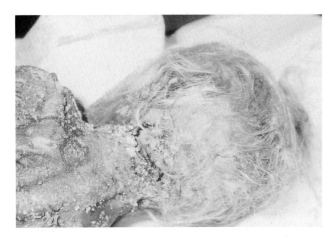

Figure 15.10 Child, close-up of head and shoulders (see also Figures 15.8 and 15.9) (photo: Susan Young)

Figure 15.11 Child, trunk showing few lesions (see also Figures 15.8, 15.9 and 15.10) (photo: Susan Young)

but action and planning are basically as for simple earth burials.

A very different situation pertains in crypts under churches. Here ventilation is restricted, coffins tend to be in disarray and decaying, damage may have been left by vandals, charcoal and rubble backfill may hide the burials, and, as only the wealthy were interred in crypts and private vaults, the standard of coffin manufacture is usually high. Triple-shells are commonly encountered. A significant proportion of coffins, perhaps 0.5 to 1%, can be expected to contain variably well-preserved remains. Because the effect of any agent liberated from coffins in such conditions will be relatively much more concentrated than out in the open air it seems prudent to be more stringent in planning protection for workers. Any bodies with significant skin preservation should be subjected to an urgent medical inspection for evidence of suspicious rash. When coffins are opened, accidentally or intentionally, the author considers that any workers present should already have a visible scar from a past primary smallpox vaccination (Baxter *et al* 1995). Alternatively high-quality respiratory protective equipment is needed although this will hamper what may well be very strenuous physical work. Nowadays, it is absolutely unacceptable to offer primary vaccination to adults. For the individual the risk of potentially serious complications of vaccination itself greatly outweighs the remote risk of viable smallpox virus being released.

The author is well aware that although time passes without trouble and our perceptions of the risk change, others feel differently, and that these suggestions in themselves raise a number of problems for the future. The previously vaccinated workforce is ageing! But unless the question of infectious risk can be confidently settled we must be pragmatic. We all have to respond positively to the requirement for risk assessments and to observe current Control of Substances Hazardous to Health (COSHH) regulations, (the control of substances hazardous to health includes microbiological risks) and to reasonable demands for the protection of workers and the general public. To release the smallpox virus again into the community, however remote that possibility, would be a global disaster and, to quote Dr Waldron, 'no archaeologist still less his medical advisors – would wish to enter history with that on his conscience' (1985, 794).

Contacts with archaeologists since the excavation of the crypt at Spitalfields in 1985 have given the author a fresh dimension to a working life concerned mainly with infectious diseases and she is grateful for that opportunity and has much to be thankful for. She had never suspected how remarkably preserved some human remains could be long after death. But well-preserved bodies have been exhumed throughout the ages; they used to be thought the remains of saints. The venerable Bede recorded that when St Cuthbert, one-time Bishop of Northumbria, was exhumed in 687, eleven years after his death, the monks expected to find his flesh reduced to dust and his remains withered, but they found the body whole and incorrupt. Furthermore, all the vestments in which he was clothed appeared spotless, but wonderfully fresh and fair. We may still uncover human remains in a remarkable state of preservation to this day so it behoves us to be cautious.

16　Bodies, minds, and human remains

James Thompson

The process whereby a person becomes a body has always been mysterious. We are used to the everyday experience of interacting with people who express their thoughts, react to our inquiries, behave as we behave, and form the basis of our strongest attachments. When a person dies there is a strong sense of something having slipped away, that something being the force which has given them life. Different cultures and different individuals have evolved different explanations to account for what happens when an individual dies. The religious notion of a continuing soul seeks to suggest that in some disembodied way the essential features of the dead person are preserved. The rationalist tradition says that the concept of a person depends upon the correct functioning of the body and when a person dies then there is no person left, and that the sets of behaviours which went into creating our notion of a person have ceased to be.

Whatever the nature of people's beliefs about death it is certainly the case that most people when confronted with a dead body go through a series of emotions. We have so much experience of associating people with their bodies that even the simplest depictions of a body, particularly of the face, are capable of arousing expectations, creating reactions, and making us wish to interact in some way. Evidence derived from the behaviour of recently born children suggests that we have an innate preference for looking at face-like objects and that we are very quick to ascribe emotional states to particular facial displays. It is probable that the particular facial configuration of children is quick to elicit parental responses from us. Certainly toys, dolls, and cartoon figures tend to accentuate those sorts of characteristics so that relatively rounded features with large eyes proportional to the face and body and large heads proportional to the body tend to be a common feature of cartoon characters. The power of body shapes to arouse sexual feelings is well known and obvious and most people are able to form preliminary impressions about another person even when they have seen them very briefly. The height of a person may contribute to feelings of dominance or submission, their general attractiveness can have an influence on how we respond to them and some body shapes are generally seen as more sexually attractive than others.

While live bodies and particularly faces possess immense power to generate emotions and expectations, dead bodies maintain a good element of this

power and add to it some new dimensions. Dead bodies may elicit sympathy, pity, disgust, and contempt. The process whereby a body decomposes may seem dreadful and disgusting to many observers and yet at the same time may have its fascination as well as its legitimate scientific interest.

Any person who comes into contact with human remains will go through some form of personal and philosophical adjustment to the issue of how minds and bodies relate. When people carry out the task of body handling either as emergency workers, mortuary attendants, or archaeologists certain sorts of psychological impacts or adjustments are likely to happen. First of all the sight of a human body will engender a range of strong emotions as already discussed. The observer may be able to state at an intellectual level that they are handling 'just flesh and bones' but there are many stimuli which are likely to engender sympathetic responses and speculations about the person concerned. Dead bodies may sometimes resemble people whom the observer knows or have artefacts or clothing which the observer recognizes or can strongly associate with. Associations of this sort make it much harder for the observer to maintain emotional detachment and make it much more likely that the experience will have personal relevance and personal impact.

It is said that most people most of the time maintain an illusion of immortality. They assume that they will be healthy and well and that they will not suffer accidents or serious illnesses. There is a tendency for people to believe that they will live longer than the average person. This optimistic personal bias which is probably very helpful in everyday life is severely questioned by having to deal with bodies, particularly when there are many bodies to be dealt with all at once, and it is clear that the dead were ordinary people and no different in terms of their life chances from the person who is handling the body.

The archaeological approach to human bodies differs from emergency body recovery work in several ways. These may potentially determine the extent of psychological impact. First, the impact of emergencies is likely to be far more vivid. Rescue teams working at the site of car or plane crashes will come upon the wounded as well as the very recently dead. They may well hear people begging for help. They may struggle to free people trapped in debris, and may have to talk to and encourage the injured for many hours, often in rescue efforts which are unsuccessful. All this increases the psychological burden of the work. Second, the 'unfairness' of sudden death has a profound impact, particularly when there are any similarities between the victims and the rescuers. Police who worked at the Bradford fire disaster were affected because they could not use their familiar psychological defence that they were dealing with criminals who had brought about their own misfortune, but had to confront the fact that ordinary law-abiding people had lost their lives needlessly. Third, deaths from 'natural causes' may be seen as more acceptable, and not something that could have been avoided as in the case of an accident. Fourth, the sheer passage of time might might insulate archaeologists from those similarities ('a person just like me') which disturb emergency rescue workers.

Although these reflections can only be speculative in the absence of long-term studies on archaeologists, it would appear that the predicted impact of body recovery work will be less on archaeologists than upon rescue workers. However, one factor which might put archaeologists more at risk is the guilty feeling that their work has disturbed the dead. Although much of value can be learnt from funerary and forensic archaeology and the subsequent study of human remains, it is unlikely to be seen as heroic as saving lives. It is unclear how important this factor might be. Certainly many rescue workers also feel that their interventions often do not achieve very much. There is some evidence that the impact on such workers is much more severe when they have not been able to save any lives, which is often the case. That is not to say that many archaeologists will not experience long-lasting painful memories of some aspects of their work. One would expect such effects and for some people they may be long-lasting, with a negative impact on their general psychological well-being (see Bashford & Pollard, this volume). However, it would be very wrong to assume, simply from a description of the work, that most people involved in exhumations and the discovery of human remains will be permanently traumatized by such experiences. Eventually these matters will have to be resolved by proper research studies carried out on archaeologists working in a funerary and/or forensic context.

In considering the effects of events upon people it is probably useful to study three categories: threat, loss, and horror. Threat relates to the perceived probability of receiving an injury or being killed. It is the most obvious impact in near-miss phenomena in which people survive an accident but have had to undergo a period of personal threat. Loss refers to loss of possessions, loss of cherished ideals, loss of bodily limbs and functions, and, of course, loss of life. Such losses are likely to generate depressive and bereavement reactions. Horror relates to the experience of seeing dreadful things happen, generally involving injury and death to human beings, although the observer him or herself is not under threat and has not suffered personal loss. Naturally all these dimensions are psychological in terms of their content but horror could be argued to be the most psychological of the lot, since there is no physiological startle response as in the case of threat, as horror is purely about the mental associations with observed events. Put plainly, if horror could be elicited by the sight of flesh then virtually the entire population would be traumatized by walking past a butcher's shop. Horror results when the flesh that is seen and touched obviously relates to an identifiable person. Even in the case of the butcher's shop care is taken to remove parts of the animal's body which make the animal recognizable, such as the head. Special language is used to distinguish the meat of dead animals from the living animal itself. These precautions and artifices make it possible for a large majority of the population to eat animal meat with relatively few qualms. Few such adaptations are readily available for the sight of dead bodies, though there are plentiful euphemisms about death itself.

For many years it has been known that particular events, including life threat, the experience of loss, and of horror, could engender strong reactions in human beings. There are many accounts in early literature of the psychological incapacity of people who had witnessed combat and who, though physically unharmed, were incapable of functioning because of the horror of what they had experienced. Post-traumatic stress disorder is no more than a new jargon phrase for an old condition. There are good accounts in Homer's *Iliad*, and Shakespeare described it well in *Henry IV, Part I Act II* where it would appear that Hotspur suffered from the condition. There are further accounts in Pepys' diary (although on my reading he had a relatively mild reaction to the Great Fire of London, was able to continue functioning very well, and his descriptions are worthy of mention only because he writes so well, and was recording his personal reactions in a private diary). The condition has been variously described as 'soldier's heart', 'nostalgia', 'railway spine', 'shell shock', 'battle neurosis', 'combat fatigue' etc (Trimble, 1981). It has always been recognized that troubling memories were an important component of the disorder, and that sufferers responded with anxiety, arousal, and avoidance. Given that the condition has an extensive history, it is perhaps surprising that there has been less agreement on the definition of the condition. The current diagnostic lists attempt to gather together the most common psychological reactions to sudden massive stress, though the way in which this is done owes as much to committee processes as to the collection of good epidemiological data.

The lists provided by the American Psychiatric Association (1994) at least have the merit of trying to be precise about what is involved in the disorder even though this is at the risk of reducing a human suffering to a number of items on a checklist required for the purposes of American health insurance claims. The essential features of the disorder as described in the diagnostic manual involve either direct personal experience of threat of death or serious injury, witnessing the death or injury of others, or learning about such things from a family member or close associates. In this sense people involved in body recovery and archaeological tasks involving bodies could be said to be exposed to the late effects of a death to another person. Post-traumatic stress disorder is unusual in that instead of just describing the symptoms it is linked as a matter of definition to its presumed cause, a dreadful event which the sufferer has witnessed or experienced. In addition to witnessing or experiencing the dreadful event the person's response should involve either intense fear or helplessness or horror.

The diagnostic manual then goes on to list three categories of symptoms. The first is about the re-experiencing of the event either by intrusive recollections, distressing dreams, the feeling that the event is re-occurring, and psychological distress and physical bodily reactions when exposed to something that reminds the person of the traumatic event.

The second major category relates to the persistent avoidance of stimuli associated with the trauma. So, for example, this would include efforts to avoid thoughts, feelings, or conversations associated with the event, also avoiding activities, places, or people related to it, an inability to recall important aspects of the event, a markedly diminished interest or participation in usual activities, feelings of detachment or estrangement from others, a restricted range of affections such as an inability to have loving feelings, and a sense of a foreshortened future.

The final category relates to symptoms of arousal such as difficulty falling or staying asleep, irritability or outbursts of anger, difficulty concentrating, being extremely vigilant, and easily startled.

Finally, for one to be able to make a diagnosis of post-traumatic stress disorder the symptoms should have lasted for more than a month and have caused clinically significant distress or impairment in one's normal life. As with most diagnoses a list may help to give an indication of the sorts of behaviours which should be investigated, but ultimately the diagnosis is based upon the statements and behaviour of the sufferer as elicited at interview. There is no gold standard that proves the diagnosis, but by gathering interview observations, questionnaire responses, and the accounts of family and friends, a composite picture can be created to substantiate the diagnosis.

Much more data can be obtained on post-traumatic stress disorder from a number of sources. A good and very large source book, though somewhat dated by publication delays, is Wilson and Raphael (1993) which contains 84 chapters by most of the authors active in this field. It contains useful diversity in one unwieldy volume.

For perpetual updates in the field one should look at the *Journal of Traumatic Stress*. Green (1994) has produced a very good review, though she has excluded reports on treatment. She notes that very many people experience potentially traumatic events, but only about 25% of them go on to develop PTSD. This rate may be lower for accidents, at about 12%, and higher for rape, at about 80%. About half those who develop the disorder may still have it decades later. Most studies find a dose-response relationship between the severity of the stressor and the degree of consequent psychological distress. The vulnerability factors are low education and social class, pre-existing psychiatric problems, and female gender. Most patients with PTSD will also have major depression, other anxiety disorders, and possibly substance abuse and sexual dysfunction, which suggests that PTSD is too narrow a focus for studying post trauma reactions.

Of course, the diagnostic manual is largely describing behaviour and making an assumption that it is connected with the precipitating event, but otherwise does not offer any hypotheses as to what is going on in the person. In the case of someone who is handling bodies, we know from the accounts of people in psychological treatment that the primary difficulty relates to seeing a person transformed into a body, and the whole paradox of the relationship between personality and flesh being made evident in this particularly gruesome way. It is well known from anatomy lessons that the psychological impact of the dissection of a cadaver can be reduced somewhat by covering or removing the head and hands of the body. Indeed the standard measure of intrusive recall, a questionnaire developed by Horowitz and his associates (Horowitz *et al* 1979), used the recollections of medical students one week after their first dissection of a corpse as one of the base rate measures for intrusive recall. Although the numbers themselves have no absolute meaning, it is usual for patients who present at a stress clinic to have levels of reported intrusive recollection which are four times as high as that experienced by the students a week after their first dissection.

Several studies have now been carried out about the impact of body recovery work (Thompson *et al* 1991; Thompson 1993) and from these it is possible to identify some general findings. First of all the traumatic effects are likely to be brought about by the first fifteen minutes of body recovery work, that is to say once a person has come across body parts they stand a risk of being traumatized and there do not appear to be additional effects of continued exposure unless other special factors intervene. This suggests that in terms of public health it makes more sense to have a dedicated team who conduct the whole duty from start to finish, rather than distributing it among a large number of people because that would simply increase the numbers who might be likely to be traumatized. These issues take on particular importance now that employers must include the possibility of 'psychiatric damage' within their duty of care to their employees (Walker *v* Northumberland County Council, November 1994). Although the case referred to a social worker whose breakdown was attributed to overwork, it potentially increases the scope of employee litigation, and cases are currently being brought by emergency service workers in which they claim that their psychological reactions to emergency body recovery duties were not properly handled by their employing authorities.

Preparation for the work begins with the screening of the people who are taking part. There is no reliable measure of human resilience, but as a general rule those who on personality questionnaires report themselves as being of a worrying disposition anyway, are more likely to be affected. There is also evidence that people who have had previous psychological problems are more at risk. In general women are somewhat more likely to be affected than men, and education and marriage or close personal relationships are both protective factors in the sense that having a knowledge of what is happening and a sense of mastery through education is helpful, and marriage in the sense of having a supportive partner is a positive protective factor. As a general rule such groups are paid volunteers, and it is probably wise to do potentially disturbing work only with those who are willing to undertake it.

Preparation for the task involves a number of factors. The key thing is to explain why the job needs to be done, how it's going to be done, how it will be completed and what the end result will be. The work of Alexander (1991 and 1993) looking at the recovery of bodies after the Piper Alpha explosion showed that a well conducted and well managed body recovery operation could actually somewhat improve the psychological state of police workers by virtue of good management, direction, and support of the people involved. In addition to explaining the purpose of the task, familiarization and training with all necessary equipment and techniques is also a helpful approach. Another helpful technique is to allow the group to discuss and formulate its own preferred way of working. For example, police teams often have to search fields by making a long cordon and then looking for either murder weapons or possibly the murder victim's body. Naturally individual officers fear that they will be the one who will first come upon the victim and wonder how they will cope with that particular shock. It may be better to have self-directed teams who search whole areas together, thus being on hand to give each other support, and being able to pace the work to suit their needs. Within the work setting itself it is important for the leaders of the group to be involved in doing the tasks and to show that they are willing to participate. At the end of the working day good practice suggests that there should be a formal and then an informal debriefing. The formal debriefing is about the technicalities of the task, the data collected, problems with equipment, and so on. The informal debriefing, which is generally held together with a communal meal and drinks, is about the emotional reactions of the group. This will include personal disclosures as to which parts of the task were found the most difficult, and a general discussion of the psychological demands of the duty, together with support and encouragement from the group as a whole. Sometimes an outside helper or facilitator is useful at some of those meetings, though once groups are functioning together well they may resent such outside assistance. If team members do not report for duty, particular care should be taken to call them up and find out how they are and if necessary to visit them, and also to keep them informed about the progress of the group.

At the completion of the task it is helpful to have some sort of formal farewell ceremony which recognizes the contribution of every single team member, which explains the outcome of the work and the contribution it has made, and which gives an indication of any further follow-up programmes.

It is difficult to be precise about the number of people who are likely to be adversely affected by body recovery work. Using composite figures from fire fighters, police officers, and ambulance workers the rate of post-traumatic stress disorder might be estimated at around 5–7%. This may be an underestimate in that many professional groups find a stress diagnosis to be stigmatizing, and tend instead to release their staff members with more physical diagnoses such as back pain. However the likely rate is probably in the order of 5–15%. It should be remembered therefore that the main human response to adversity is one of resilience and coping.

Studies of ways of coping conducted on disaster survivors suggest that there is no single technique which is reliably associated with low distress but two of them stand out as being particularly helpful (Charlton & Thompson 1996). The first of these is called 'positive reappraisal' which is essentially a coping technique which relies on concentrating upon the benefits of the experience, the personal learning which the person has taken from it, and seeing the events in as positive a light as possible. The other helpful approach is called 'distancing', in which the person tries not to make too much of the event and tries to place it in perspective. By far the least successful way of coping is labelled 'escape avoidance' which is not to think about the events at all and to avoid all reminders of them. These techniques can only be indicative, but it does appear that, quite separately from any effects of personality, the above mentioned ways of coping seem to reduce people's distress.

Since the condition is difficult to treat, remedies abound. As usual, controlled trials are few. Solomon *et al* (1992) found that out of 255 English language reports up to the end of 1991 only eleven were randomized clinical trials that used the most detailed diagnostic criteria. The drug studies showed modest gains, while behavioural techniques involving direct therapeutic exposure were more powerful, but more apt to cause complications in patients suffering from other psychiatric disorders. Cognitive therapy, psychodynamic therapy, and hypnosis showed some promise, but required far more research and longer term follow-ups. However, most studies had limitations and there was insufficient concordance in therapy outcome measures for it to be possible to give absolutely firm statements about the power of the different therapeutic procedures.

In the case where someone, after body recovery work, is showing the symptoms which appear to constitute a stress disorder then the first step is an assessment of their condition. This is normally done in an interview of 90 minutes together with some questionnaire analysis. If a person's distress is such that they require psychological treatment then it is likely that the most helpful approach will involve a technique which requires them to re-experience some of the events in a particular controlled way. (Thompson *et al* 1995a and 1995b). Typically they would give an account of the most difficult aspects of their experience and recount them in detail under guidance while tape recordings are made. They would then play those tape recordings several times between sessions which serves to reduce their emotional impact. On subsequent sessions they would again discuss other troubling aspects of the experience and make further tape recordings and particular attention would be paid by the therapist to what those events meant for the sufferer, that is to say the interpretation placed upon them by the patient. Treatment typically takes about eight sessions and results in a 60% reduction in reported symptoms. Within each patient group people differ in their rates of recovery and some predictions can be made about this on the basis of other known facts about the patients. The initial risk factors are also reasonable predictors of treatment outcome, and people do best when they have not had a previous history of psychological problems, when they are well supported in their lives, and probably also when they are seen within months rather than years of the precipitating event.

In summary, we now have a much better understanding of the psychological impact of body recovery work. Although disabling disorders probably only affect a minority, such work distresses the majority of people for some time. The impact of these duties can be reduced by good management before, during, and after the event. The main area where benefit can be obtained is the way that groups are managed during the event itself. The disorder, which is essentially a stress response, is relatively easy to detect, particularly by those close to the individual. The individuals themselves may sometimes not realize or deny what is happening to them. Treatments are available which have high rates of effectiveness and are reasonably quick, though they are still quite demanding of therapists' time.

As a final point it must be understood that the diagnostic labels are partly misleading in this regard. Any normal and sensible human being will be made thoughtful when faced with human remains. It is quite natural to be saddened by these sights and for the experience of body recovery to have some impact on a person's perception of life. Publilius Syrus (*c* 43BC, Antioch) said 'We are all equal in the presence of death'. Archaeologists will understand that better than most people.

Part IV   Concerns, priorities, and the way forward

Concerns, priorities, and the way forward

Of all the areas covered in this volume this is the one that is perhaps least satisfactory, simply because there are so many concerns and research priorities that it is not possible to do justice to more than a few. Nevertheless, those aspects which are addressed provide the reader with an idea of the complexity of some of the issues facing archaeological curators and consultants, the extent of historical coverage of death and burial in post-medieval England, and the enormous potential of scientific, particularly submacroscopic, analysis of human bone.

Vanessa Harding gallantly takes us through a massive historical literature and considers areas which require more research. She focuses on the puzzling lack of research looking at death and disposal from a gender perspective. This is a surprising situation given the gender delineation which governed (and still does) the treatment and disposal of the dead in post-medieval England (and elsewhere) and which must have to some extent predetermined and formalized experience.

Jez Reeve tackles the practical aspects of the extent of the extant archaeological resource in London, suggesting pragmatic and economically robust approaches to archaeological examination of burial grounds and crypts which may be destined for reuse necessitating clearance of burials. Above all Jez reminds us of the true significance of the resource, that it represents people's lives and experiences, their sense of belonging, and their contribution to society.

Even more bravely, Lynne Bell and Julia Lee-Thorp examine submacroscopic and bio-molecular advances in the study of human remains. A vast and burgeoning subject area, the authors understandably deal with their own particular research areas in depth but, usefully, discuss them in a non-specialist way and direct the reader to relevant literature in other areas. Of considerable importance for future research, Lynne and Julia make a good case for a reappraisal of curatorial policy towards the availability of small samples of appropriate material to *bona fide* researchers for destructive, but massively informative, microscopic and bio-molecular techniques. The existing and seemingly widespread curatorial policy of facilitating macroscopic research, which is no more illuminating than microscopic analysis, simply because it does not require destructive sampling, is eloquently put under the microscope.

The issue of whether archaeologists should excavate more recent burials was much debated at the *Grave Concerns* conference largely in response to provocative comments made by Ruth Richardson. Unfortunately, these have not been articulated in a paper for these proceedings and consequently the issue of ethics and funerary archaeology remains largely unexplored. Bill White, however, has responded to key aspects of these proceedings from the floor. In particular he examines changing attitudes to disturbing the dead through the post-medieval period and argues for a continuation of scientific examination of human remains from archaeological contexts.

17 Research priorities: an historian's perspective

Vanessa Harding

Introduction

The history of death is a diverse field of study. There is no single narrative to which we all contribute our quota of primary research, accumulating data and detail until we have 'the full picture'. It is not just that archaeologists, art historians, historians, and others are working on different source materials, which themselves influence the approach and the kinds of questions posed. We cannot set a simple agenda for research because we are pursuing quite diverse ends: most of us, in some sense, want to answer questions about past societies, but for some the study of death is a means and for others it is more of an end in itself – that is, the interest lies primarily in the information about practices and attitudes relating to death, not in the way in which these may be interpreted and incorporated into a larger picture. And for some, of course, the study of past societies and the processes of change is itself a means to an end, the knowledge that empowers us to change modern society.

The development of the history of death

Over the past twenty years, the historical study of death has come a long way. Philippe Ariès's sweeping and idiosyncratic account of attitudes towards death in western society from antiquity to modern times, *L'homme devant la mort*, was published in 1977. While it did not either initiate the historical study of death (he had already published in this area), nor set an agenda for further research, it has been an influential work, especially after its appearance in English as *The hour of our death*, in 1981. The two-fold theme of the book must be familiar to most: a model of change over time, and the belief that modern attitudes to death and dying need to be appraised, evaluated, and perhaps revised. The main shortcoming is usually felt to be the difficulty of understanding and distinguishing Ariès's proposed five stages in the history of attitudes to death, which is partly (for us) a question of translation. 'La mort apprivoisée' and 'la mort inversée', describing the first and fifth stages, are both difficult to translate: rendering them as 'the tame death' and 'the invisible death' does not do justice to the complexity of the ideas or the contrast between them (Ariès 1981; Whaley 1981, 5–7; McManners 1981b, 118–21). Many historians, however, are uncomfortable with the five-stage model

itself, particularly given Ariès's lack of specificity as to time and place, and his use of impressionistic generalization rather than quantification. His assumption of a very broad eschatological continuum in western thought is much more problematic for countries experiencing a successful Protestant reformation in the early modern period. For these reasons, it has not had such a fundamental influence on English approaches to its subject as, say, Lawrence Stone's arguments about the invention of childhood and affective family relations in the early modern period have to that area of enquiry. Historians have not explicitly set out to challenge and disprove Ariès's model with empirical data and argument, as they undoubtedly have with the history of the family.

Nevertheless the overall view – that modern attitudes to death are very different to those of past societies, that we can trace their evolution over a long period of time, and that in some ways modern attitudes are less 'healthy' than those of past societies – has been quite influential. We have implicitly accepted a distinction between 'traditional' and 'modern' attitudes to death, and tried to establish when the change occurred, whether through arguments about individualism, secularization, or the discourse of public health. We have also, sometimes unconsciously, accepted the idea that a society's attitudes to death can and should be the subject of moral judgment: that some societies handle the question of death better than others, and that our own society is one that has some problems with it. It is possible that this aspect of Ariès's work has had more influence outside the realm of history, in that of sociology, in the sense of presenting a world view of the past which influences prescriptions for the present and future, and its message chimed with contemporary concerns in that discipline about death in our own society (Houlbrooke 1989, 5–6). Certainly, while there may be some debate about the value of Ariès's book as an historical account, it has helped to locate the history of death firmly in the sphere of action, and to establish the idea of a modern failure to deal with death in popular consciousness.

Despite challenge from an early date, such as David Cannadine's essay on 'Grief and mourning in modern Britain' which appeared in 1981, and argued strongly that the Victorian celebration of death was not necessarily as universally accepted at the time or as therapeutic as has been assumed, the view persists. At least part of the purpose of the

Victoria and Albert Museum's *Art of Death* exhibition in 1992 was to contrast the cultural and material responses to death of the 16th to 18th centuries with those of our own times (Litten 1991, 1–4; Llewellyn 1991, 136; Llewellyn 1997). The implication certainly seemed to be that past societies were culturally rich and articulate in the face of death where ours is poor, and that we need to do something about it.

Ariès's book was published in English in 1981, the same year as Joachim Whaley's collection, *Mirrors of Mortality*, in which Cannadine's essay appears. Though less famous in the outside world, this collection must be known to every serious scholar in the subject, both for its introduction and for the studies it includes. These range widely in topic and period, but also in approach, from the usefully empirical to the more reflective or theoretical. In Whaley's view 'the historical study of attitudes to death is thus a relatively new field', and the aim of the collection was 'an attempt to stimulate a more general discussion of the significance of death in human history' (Whaley 1981, 13), and it certainly gave a useful starting point. Together, Whaley's introduction and McManners' contribution on 'Death and the French historians' provide an invaluable introduction to the French historiography of this subject.

In the 1980s and 1990s, the historical study of death became a much more popular field, though even in 1988 Ruth Richardson could say that 'death studies as a discipline are in their infancy in Britain' (Richardson 1988, xiv). The way in which it has developed has some parallels with women's history, in which early, generalizing, politically engaged studies were followed by a reaction towards empirical research and specificity, withdrawing to some extent from the political aspects of the subject. The new research took in a much wider range of enquiries and sources than the first approaches had suggested, greatly enriching the conception of the subject. The results of these enquiries could subsequently be incorporated in a new, informed, general perspective which is now an accepted part of the mainstream. No-one can now write social history without being aware of the agendas and findings of women's history (cf Hufton 1995) At the same time, there is a still a debate over whether there is a discipline at all: is women's history a subject or an approach?

Similarly, with the history of death, early generalization has been supplemented by more precise enquiry, in a number of fields. We are recognizing the need to set empirical research and the conclusions drawn from it in a very specific social, geographical, and chronological context. The biomedical, demographic, and art-historical agendas have been drawn into the subject. Even so, we are not yet able to write a general account of death (or mortality) in the early modern and modern periods. Although the subject has been more explicitly acknowledged in the writing of social and cultural history of early modern and modern England, the insights we may have gained from the study of death – into the world view and motivations of our ancestors – have yet to be incorporated into the mainstream of historical writing.

Recent and current research on death in the post-medieval period

The actual focus of research and writing on death varies with the period being examined: not only with the source material, but with the existing historical discourses and concerns. Death studies in the post-medieval period can draw on a much richer range of written records (official, judicial, commercial, personal), than is available for preceding periods. Documentary history thus plays a larger, indeed a dominant, part in the whole. The question of language and textual analysis becomes very important, as literary sources proliferate. From the perspective of archaeological investigation, there can be a tendency to view historical research as simply the collection of data from documentary sources, to inform the project planning and complement the data retrieved archaeologically. While documentary research of this kind should certainly play a part in any archaeological investigation in the period of written records, historians of death more often address wider issues, and their research is directed towards answering questions set by other historical concerns and shaped by the evidence available to them.

At the same time the artefactual evidence also proliferates: the furnishings of death, commemorative sculpture and representation, mourning items, grave goods. The art-historical or material culture approach is in fact one of the oldest, in that 17th-century antiquaries were recording tombs and monuments of their present and recent past, creating a rich written and visual record on which we now draw. It has become more conscious of cultural history in a broad sense, rather than relying on traditional analysis by patron, artist, and so on (cf Llewellyn 1991, 7–8), but it may still need to be defended both from becoming antiquarianism and from being dismissed as antiquarianism.[1]

However, though the documentary and material sources for the study of death may multiply as the time nears the present, there are increasing difficulties with the excavation of burial sites and the scientific investigation of bodily remains. It is not a shortage of material – survival is almost too good, both in terms of quantity and physical preservation – but a question of how we deal with it. Examination of human remains and burial contexts may be (or have been) a staple of prehistoric and early archaeology, but it is not so easy to be objective about the bodies and burials of the more recently deceased. Archaeology is still driven by rescue priorities, and powerfully influenced by the sense of destruction, but it is also affected by long-standing taboos concerning the body (see Thompson, this volume), and by anxieties about the respect that is or ought to be paid to the dead and their wishes (Cox 1996b). It may not be considered improper to enquire into attitudes to death; it is considered at least dubious to disturb the corpse itself.

Our perception of what is 'post-medieval' is a construction rather than an objective reality. Post-medieval archaeology has always had the problem of being defined in relation to other periods in which the importance of the discipline and its contribution was much better established, and has not always demonstrated its own justifications for the focus and parameters of research. Historians and art historians have been able to defend their periodization by drawing on large defining concepts, such as Reformation and Renaissance, even if those are now less secure than they once were.

If the distinction between medieval and post-medieval is open to question, there may be a better case for later divisions. French and other continental studies use the idea of a social and cultural, as well as political, 'ancien régime', stressing a discontinuity at the revolutionary and Napoleonic eras. There is a strong tendency in recent English historical writing to take 'the long 18th century' as a coherent unit of study and location of change. This view looks for some kind of break with the past in the 1660s or 1680s, and another in the 1820s or 1830s. There is perhaps a slight irony that these dates are more obviously ones of political change (the Restoration of 1660 or the 1688 Revolution, and the 1832 Reform Act) but are used to define a period of social and cultural change. In broad cultural terms, the idea of the long 18th century draws something from continental ideas of Enlightenment, and from the social and material changes of the pre-industrial period (see for example Borsay 1989). There are several other justifications, however, for looking for some break in the later 17th century of importance to the history of death. One of these is the epidemiological: epidemic plague disappeared from England in around 1670, to be replaced as a major cause of death by tuberculosis and smallpox (Dobson 1996). Another is the religious, with the toleration of a range of Protestant churches after 1688, and also the return of Jewish settlements and communities.

The idea of the long 18th century, and indeed much of the historiography of the early modern and modern periods, consciously or unconsciously focuses on the modernization of society and social attitudes. This is certainly central to the history of death. Whether we characterize modernity as the advance of capitalism, consumerism, individualism, secularization, or the impact of scientific rationalism, it is obviously an issue in all our enquiries into death in this period. The idea of modernity is hardly a 'hidden agenda', and is probably inescapably present in all our approaches; provided we remain conscious of it, and the influence it may have on the questions and conclusions of our research, it need not subvert the enquiry.

Historians of the early modern and modern periods who study death have tended to follow one of two paths, the biomedical and demographic, looking at the mechanics of mortality, the causes and incidence of death; or the socio-cultural (attitudes to death, ritual behaviour, treatment of the body). Although I will consider these separately below, they cannot of course be neatly separated. It has long been taken for granted that the incidence of mortality affects the way death is viewed, whether one is considering high pre-modern infant mortality or the exceptional slaughter of epidemics or wars (Whaley 1981, 11; Cannadine 1981, 196–202). Nor can the biomedical and the socio-cultural aspects of death be simply dichotomized as fact and response: the incidence of mortality is influenced by social factors, including attitudes to death. This is obviously true in the case of suicide (Durkheim 1897; MacDonald & Murphy 1990). It is also true of involuntary deaths, sometimes in a truly dialectical way: for example, in the 16th century, metropolitan elites learned to leave London in advance of the plague epidemics; they learned this by reading the Bills of Mortality, which we take as primary source material for the incidence of epidemic death. By quitting London, they altered the geography and incidence of mortality in later epidemics (Slack 1985, 151–64). Similarly, medical interventions are provoked by and subsequently modify death statistics.

Death and demography

The history of mortality as a biomedical or demographic phenomenon has itself quite a long tradition, but in this country the last twenty years have seen significant developments, with the work of the Cambridge Group for the History of Population and Social Structure and with the Wellcome Trust's involvement in funding research into the history of medicine. Together these have contributed enormously to the level and quality of information now in the public domain about mortality in past societies, especially in the post-medieval period. Though some of these researches initially focused on quantifying or measuring the phenomenon of death, their implications are much wider than the provision of statistical material, and some of the best social and cultural history has resulted from them.

In the case of the Cambridge Group, long-term funding made possible the collection and analysis of huge quantities of data, and established methodologies, practices, and conclusions that benefit ongoing research. Wrigley and Schofield's *Population history of England, 1541–1871* was published in 1981, and established a model of population change in the early modern and modern periods that now dominates our perspective. The picture of growth, stagnation, decline, recovery, and renewed rapid growth between the mid 16th and the later 18th centuries is now largely integrated into the social and economic history of the period. Even though their view played down the importance of changes in mortality in determining population change (giving primacy to nuptiality and fertility), mortality statistics constitute a significant part of the data. A more recent critique of their findings (Razzell 1994) re-emphasizes the role of mortality in demographic change, especially in the 18th-century, and suggests a rather different chronology of growth, but notwithstanding these disagreements, in consequence of all this work we have a frame of reference within which to set our own researches into aspects of death. We are now well informed about overall death rates and life expectancies, the ages at which people died, and the reasons for local variations. We know much more about how and when death occurs; we have a precise enough sense of normal mortality rates that we can identify crisis years and measure the severity of the crisis. We know that death varied with the season of the year, being highest in late winter and early spring and lowest in midsummer, and also that this pattern was modified in distinctive ways by different epidemic diseases (Wrigley & Schofield 1981, 293; Landers 1993, 203–41).

Though much was established, further directions for research were indicated, such as the detailed local investigation or the exploration of different causes of death. Several studies have highlighted infant mortality, one of the most striking differences between vital regimes in the 20th and earlier centuries, and one that has coloured our view of our ancestors' relationship to death and to one another. In *The world we have lost* (Laslett 1965, 1983), one of the founding works of historical demography as social history and of the Cambridge Group's approach, Peter Laslett examined the perception and the phenomenon of child mortality in the pre-modern period, concluding that although high, it was not as high as had sometimes been suggested. Later research, such as Roger Finlay's 1981 study of early modern London, showed that there could be extreme variation according to local conditions of wealth and salubrity (Finlay 1981). Even such an important component of past mortality levels has thus been shown to be more complex and variable than once assumed.

Another very fruitful area of study has been plague, also something we think of as a characteristic feature of early modern mortality. Many of our visual and verbal images of death in the 16th and 17th centuries are derived either from the London Bills of Mortality, or from literary accounts of epidemics, such as Dekker's plague pamphlets and Defoe's *Journal of the Plague Year* (Healy 1993; Defoe 1986). The plague pit, with all its implications of a brutalized attitude to death and the dead, has a secure place in the popular imagination. The modern study of plague has been in part a statistical and epidemiological investigation (Creighton 1894, Shrewsbury 1970; Sutherland 1972), and estimating levels of mortality in different epidemics and localities remains an important part of the subject. But the recent studies have also explored the social geography of plague mortality in much greater detail (Slack 1985; Champion 1995), and have considered the social impact of epidemics, including the impact on burial practices (Slack 1986; Harding 1993).

The Cambridge Group's researches have at times interlocked with the areas covered by the Wellcome Trust's support for research into historical epidemiology, the analysis of the distribution of death in society and over time. This is part of a wider concern with the history of health and medicine, now a very sophisticated discipline contributing to social and cultural history. The Wellcome Trust has funded units, posts, and projects at a number of different universities and centres, resulting in a range of important studies. John Landers' substantial work, *Death and the metropolis, 1670–1830* (Landers 1993) is based in part on a Cambridge Group PhD on death among the Quaker community in London, but also on further researches funded by the Wellcome Trust, using quantitative analysis of the Bills of Mortality. Among his findings are a marked divergence between London and the rest of the country in terms of mortality experience in the 18th century, the result, most probably, of deteriorating living standards and conditions in the capital. He shows, however, that in the later 18th century survival rates improved, especially among the young; medical activity could have contributed to this, and to the decline of smallpox and typhus as killers (Landers 1993, 351–7). Another Wellcome-funded project is now studying the geography of disease and mortality in the capital in the 19th and early 20th centuries, using the even more plentiful figures of the Officers of Health.[2] Our understanding of what death was in the past is being reshaped by studies of this kind.

Mortality in London has certainly received attention, but probably not unduly: it must constitute a significant element in any attempt to write an account of the experience of mortality in English history. As the home of approximately one tenth of the population in 1700, the capital's death rates had a significant impact on national statistics. It was the first great urban centre, and if it is agreed that the urbanization of the provinces in the 18th and 19th centuries changed the incidence of death in England, then London's experience will be instructive. Such things as the rise of the undertaking profession (see Litten 1991, and this volume) and the cemetery movement (see Rugg, this volume) either developed first in London or were influenced by London's needs and problems. The role of London is also fundamental to the question of modernization, however this may be characterized (Wrigley 1967). Nevertheless, there could undoubtedly be more studies of mortality in the provinces, firmly located in their local context.

The cultural history of death

If quantification plays an important part in the bio-medical and demographic approaches to death, it is also present in socio-cultural studies. A recent study of suicide in early modern England begins with the words 'this is a work of social and cultural history'; but it includes tables and statistical analyses, if on a lesser scale than some of the works cited above, and sets itself in the demographic context established by Wrigley and Schofield (MacDonald & Murphy 1990, vi, 252). Statistics do not explicitly feature in all approaches, however, and some discussions of emotions and attitudes are essentially qualitative not quantitative: as Houlbrooke points out, 'grief is something which historians cannot readily measure' (1989, 14). Although there is no single social and cultural history of death in the post-medieval period, the subject illuminates several areas of contemporary historical debate, such as the Reformation, the social role of ritual and ceremony, the development of the family and affective relations, and discourses of the body; the last two especially are important for arguments about the modernization of society and attitudes. There have been a number of important focused studies, in many cases using source material not previously explored in this way.

One of the most runaway successes in recent English early modern history has been the attack on one of the defining thresholds between medievalism and modernity, the Reformation. A number of studies, culminating in Eamonn Duffy's powerful and influential *The stripping of the altars* (Duffy 1992), affirmed the reluctant response of the English people to reform of doctrine and practice; with important implications, of course, for the study of death. We have characterized medieval religion as focused on purgatory and on appeasing and protective practices such as prayers for the dead and large-scale post mortem benefactions. Protestant doctrine condemned the idea of intercession for the dead and brought to an end the elaborate structure of chantries, obits, and commemorative practices. The departed soul could neither benefit from nor confer benefits on the living; the dead ceased to exist as a meaningful human category. However, prescription was not practice, and the argument of the revisionists is that many people went on believing, and, as far as possible, acting on the teaching and practices of the pre-Reformation church. While the suppression of the chantries can be documented, the suppression of the chantry mentality was more problematic. There is much evidence from around the country of the slow disappearance of physical features and practices associated with a Catholic view of salvation. Even in London much traditional practice survived in the post-Reformation funeral (Harding 1989; Harding forthcoming). The implications of Reformation revisionism have not yet been fully incorporated into our thinking about death in the 16th century, but we may be able to move towards a less crude contrasting of medieval and reformed religious practice, without neglecting the real changes that did take place. Since this paper was presented, a major new study of ritual, religion, and the life-cycle in early modern England has appeared (Cressy 1997), exploring many of these important themes.

With a better understanding of the 16th and 17th centuries, we should be aiming to move forward into the later 17th, 18th, and 19th centuries and look more closely at the different approaches to death of the independent and nonconformist churches. At least until recently, religion was a less important topic of enquiry for historians of this period; the history of nonconformity was left to its committed chroniclers, and that of Anglicanism largely neglected, compared with the attention paid to both of these in the period before 1660 (though there are now some detailed studies: Jacob 1993, Walsh *et al* 1993). The views of the Quakers on burial location were remarkable at the time, and the papers in this volume make an important contribution to our understanding of their practice, but there are other areas also worth study. General and Particular Baptists had quite distinct views on the availability of salvation; is this true of other churches? Did Methodists and Anglicans differ in their views of the resurrection of the body and the integrity of the corpse? We apply these kinds of questions to early Protestant churches or movements, and find significance for the study of death in the answers; we ought to do the same for the period after 1700. If indeed we find that the differences between 18th and 19th century churches are not focused on salvation, then religion itself has come to mean something very different. We must also consider more fully the implications of atheism and unbelief for the study of death and burial, as McManners has done for France (McManners 1981a).

Consideration of the changing role of religion leads almost naturally into the wider investigation of the place of death in discourses of continuity, change, and the transition to modernity, though only a few of the many important research contributions in this area can be cited here. A well-received and widely-read study is Clare Gittings' *Death, burial and the individual in early modern England* (Gittings 1984). Drawing on wills and probate accounts, which she demonstrated are a rich source of information on the costs and character of funerals, she reasserted the importance of documentary history, alongside art and artefactual history, for the material culture of death and burial. In some ways it is a more convincing picture of continuity than of change, and the initial contention that funeral ritual in the early modern period displayed 'a changing conception of the self and a heightened sense of individuality' (op cit, 14) is not sustained throughout the book. This suggests that if we are seeking significant change in attitudes, we should focus on the period after the mid-17th century.

The thesis of qualitative change over time is fundamental to MacDonald and Murphy's study of suicide in early modern England, *Sleepless souls* (MacDonald & Murphy 1990), which studies the period 1500–1800. They argue that attitudes to suicide 'first hardened [in the Tudor and early Stuart period] and then grew more tolerant and sympathetic', with a noted decline in severity after 1660 (op cit, 5). They explain this with reference to two other interlocked discourses, the rise of the modern state and the history of the body. Those who took their own lives committed a crime against the state, and they were symbolically punished for this through their bodies and their posterity; only slowly, and piecemeal, was the rigour of punishment disarmed, and the reasons for this seem to have been complex. The book is obviously about death, but in terms of my original distinctions it falls into the category of the study of death as a means to a larger historiographical end. The same could be said of John McManners' *Death and the Enlightenment* (McManners 1981a), which studies changing attitudes to death in 18th century France. Although it is set in a different national and cultural context, and MacDonald and Murphy limited their examination and conclusions to England, the two works have a certain amount in common. McManners engages with the idea of Enlightenment and the intellectual culture of 18th century French society, and the impact of theological-intellectual controversies such as Jansenism. He looks at attitudes to death as part of a broadly defined and evolving culture; and if Enlightenment can be seen as a synonym for modernity, or at least modernization, that's what the book is about.

Historical discourses of the body have much to offer historians of death, in terms of direct insights and ways of deconstructing apparently unquestionable concepts. Research into death and burial could equally well be summarized as an enquiry into 'the much wider field of coherent, socially recognized practices, expressed through the use of the body, and having and being perceived to have a public resonance' (this phrase was used of an investigation into the body in the French Revolution: Outram 1989, 22). We also owe them 'the insight that the history of bodies and the history of political structures cannot be separated' (Outram 1989, 21), and many of the accounts of death in the 18th and 19th centuries focus on power. Historians of earlier periods have been more concerned with community and identity than with power, but the reverse may be true of the modern historians.

The ownership of the body is part of the history of suicide; so too is the state's appropriation of the monopoly of violence. These issues are equally relevant to the issue of capital punishment. Crime and judicial punishment have been important topics in 18th century studies for some time, and this has recently produced two major works on execution in England, Harry Potter's *Hanging in judgment* (Potter 1993), and Vic Gattrell's *The hanging tree*

(Gattrell 1994), while Richard Evans has just completed a history of capital punishment in modern Germany from 1600 (Evans 1996). The power of the state and popular attitudes to the meaning of death and the body are also explored in Ruth Richardson's *Death, dissection and the destitute* (Richardson 1988). The 1832 Anatomy Act reclassified the bodies of paupers as dissection material, formerly a punishment reserved for executed felons, in the interests of medical science (and largely for the benefit of the middle classes). The book therefore examines power relations and questions of property and commodity in relation to the human body, and argues that the Act created a new reason to fear death.

Setting research priorities?

The recent historiography of death itself suggests some areas for further research, such as the role of religion, perhaps neglected as we consider social practices. It could also be useful if early-modernists and modernists borrowed more from one another's agendas, so that the former discussed power more than they do, and the latter community and identity. One topic which could bridge the gap and offer a promising way into questions of power and the role of the state in the early modern period is the Burial in Woollen Act of 1678, encapsulating mercantilist economic legislation and the claims of the state to intervene in private behaviour of citizens. This is also obviously one of several areas in which archaeologists and historians could collaborate, to their mutual benefit.

A more substantial suggestion to consider, for both historians and archaeologists, is that we should pay more attention to the role of gender in our approaches and conceptions. We are not yet tackling the study of death with the sensitivity to gender issues that is being applied in other areas of social and cultural history. Just as we now look at writings of 20 or 30 years ago on social and cultural history and note, with some incredulity, when they fail to pay much attention to gender, we may in the future come to look at more recent studies of death and ask why they do not discuss it either.

Obviously there are some areas where gender is already a part of the structure of enquiry. Any analysis of a burial population will begin by making a distinction between males and females. Biological anthropology certainly aims to distinguish males from females on grounds of physical difference (though even here it would be interesting to consider whether the use of metrical criteria for distinction might not owe something to gender stereotyping). Analyses of life expectancy, causes of death, and vital regimes have always had to take account of the different characteristics of these for men and women, though in practice historical life expectancy is often expressed without differentiation. Similarly, in documentary research, we have long recognised that in England at least male and female willmakers are not equivalent social categories. Far fewer women than men made wills in the early modern period, and most of the women willmakers were widows. Men and women had different property rights, might recognise different relationships and responsibilities, and inevitably made different sorts of wills.

But we have not yet applied our knowledge of the different experiences that men and women had of death to a serious consideration of whether they had different attitudes to it. Until the rise of the medical professions and commercial funeral provision, women probably encountered death in its physical reality more often than men; they nursed the sick and had to deal with deaths occurring within their own households, and the professional searchers and layers-out of the dead were normally women. Women were surely present at most deathbeds. They may well have had a sharper perception of the danger of death in their middle years than men did: men were then at their healthiest, but women were encountering death in relation to their own infant children, and were also at risk in childbirth. Although death in childbirth was not a statistically strong possibility (Schofield 1986), it was probably consciously feared because its incidence was prominent and striking. Historians have discussed whether parents loved and mourned their children, and the myth of parental indifference has largely been dispersed (Houlbrooke 1984, 134–45), but we have not fully addressed the question of different male and female attitudes. Much of the autobiographical writing, at least before the 18th century, is by men, and it is clear that men grieved for wives and children; but the different remarriage possibilities for men and women, not to mention the prevailing view of the subordination and dependence of women in the marriage relationship, must have affected the view of the death of a spouse, both in prospect and retrospect (Laurence 1989). Women remarried less quickly and less frequently than men; a wife's social and economic position was more likely to deteriorate with the death of her husband than vice versa (Laslett 1983, 113, 115). Women may have lived longer but they were more likely to die alone.

It is possible that men and women had different views of salvation and the afterlife too; it was perhaps an extreme view to doubt whether men's and women's souls were equal (Fraser 1984, 3), but many medieval and later writers were cautious or ambivalent about the nature and importance of women's spirituality. We accept that men and women might have had different kinds of religious experience, mystical, charismatic, and so on; although it is very possible that these differences reflected the constructions of gender in contemporary society, this applies to the more general argument as well. Women were enthusiastic Catholics, but they were also enthusiastic Protestants, and arguably the emphasis on election for salvation

rather than the accumulation of merit (with its dependence on works and benefaction) offered them a clearer sense of personal identity in their approach to death and the afterlife. The proliferation of nonconformist sects in the mid 17th century certainly gave a few women a prominent role (Crawford 1993). The early modern construction of witchcraft provides a very striking intersection of ideas about gender, religion, death, and the role of the body in sin and salvation (Laurence 1994, 193–224). Ideas of the masculine and the feminine informed past practices relating to death, and an awareness of them can clearly benefit both historical and archaeological enquiry.

Conclusion

Historians of death, as well as historians of the body (Outram 1989, 21), may well see their role as informing and empowering action in the modern world. This paper began by noting the view that the study of death in history has a moral purpose, in that it should lead us critically to question and improve the way in which we deal with it today. Many more of the historians than are specifically identified here make some reference to the modern-world relevance of their own work. That has to be a personal position, but as long as it is held as critically and consciously as any intellectual position, it does not compromise the historian's approach. We should however resist the temptation to characterize the modern age as particularly inept or inarticulate in the face of death, simply because our responses and practices differ greatly from those of the past. However, if indeed it is true that 'death has become a taboo subject in our time' (Houlbrooke 1989, ii), historians can perhaps contribute to dissolving those constraints, through their examination of death in the past.

Historians may also have something to contribute to another important contemporary debate. Certainly the historical issue of the ownership of the body, discussed above, connects with the concerns of archaeologists and others over the way in which the bodies of the dead of more recent centuries should be treated (Morris 1994; Cox 1994; Parker-Pearson 1995; Cox 1996b). If we can examine and understand attitudes to the body, including the dead body, in the past, we may help to set a rational framework for discussing how we should deal with the present bodily remains of past populations. It will remain an emotive issue, but this approach may provide a useful perspective.

Without wishing to give 'an historian's view' on the subject, I do think it worth noting that one part of the problem facing us today concerns a phenomenon that is new in historical terms: the probability of long-term preservation. At different moments in the past, some humans have sought to preserve their bodies indefinitely, but only a few have succeeded in doing so. There seems to be increased

212

attention to the preservation and integrity of the corpse in the modern period, diverging markedly from the expectation of decomposition and restoration to the natural elements which characterises earlier periods. There had always been embalming, for the few, and the protection of a perpetual resting-place for rather more, but for most people death was followed by dissolution: the sentiment 'I leave my body to the earth from whence it came' expressed a reality. At a time, however, when probably more people were losing faith in the idea of a literal resurrection, the lead-lined coffins and burial vaults of the 18th and 19th centuries ensured the long-term survival of their physical remains.

However, even if it is clear that these individuals wanted their bodies to remain intact, this historical fact does not oblige us to submit to the tyranny of perpetual preservation, when the question of graveyard and vault clearance arises. In many cases, decisions are made for us, but when there is any choice, we should be able to make it rationally. It is important to respect the record of the past, but historians are bound to recognise that the choices people made then, however genuinely felt, were conditioned by the society and culture they lived in. To act as if the sensibilities of the dead must be paramount in this matter is to give them a power of veto that exceeds anything they could command in life. It may also be a way of displacing attention from an unexpressed fear of the body, in which the greater preservation of post-medieval bodies may play a part. There is in any case a pleasing irony in all this, undermining the efforts of those who have imposed on posterity their own desire for physical survival. It now appears that DNA, the real stuff of

immortality in the late 20th century, is destroyed by the fluids of decay which are trapped in a lead coffin, and is more likely to survive in bodies buried in the earth.[3]

Acknowledgements

My research on death has benefited from insights and information from many historians and archaeologists, including Richard Evans, John Henderson, Ralph Houlbrooke, and Peter Jones. In writing this paper I particularly valued the contribution of Dorothy Porter, with whom I have had many spirited discussions on science, medicine, and modernity.

Notes

1   Julian Litten, a self-styled antiquarian, makes, in practice, the best defence of antiquarianism in his excellently researched and structured paper in this volume. It is not a fascination with the phenomenon that I would criticize in other antiquarians, only an absence of method and judgment.
2   'Mortality in the Metropolis, 1860–1920' (team leader W E Luckin), based at the Centre for Metropolitan History, Institute of Historical Research, University of London. See Centre for Metropolitan History Annual Report 1995–6.
3   Black & Scheuer, unpublished. Work at St Barnabas, West Kensington suggests that DNA does not survive in bone in lead coffins. Interment in a lead coffin was made mandatory for intramural burials, for hygiene reasons, after 1815 (Cox 1996a), but the origin of the practice, and the popular perception of it, is surely as a preserver of the body contained within, not the health of the environment outside.

18 A view from the metropolis: post-medieval burials in London *Jez Reeve*

Introduction

In England the pressure to develop land to provide for increased housing and social needs, trade, and industrial functions is nowhere more intense than in London. Land which is no longer used for its original purpose comes into view when sites are sought for these developments. Disused burial grounds, graveyards and cemeteries, and even crypts and vaults underneath churches are increasingly viewed as possible sites for redevelopment. There is some protective legislative framework (Garratt-Frost *et al* 1992; Reeve 1997), but there are no government or church directives which identify how the ethical and religious considerations should be addressed, unlike in Scotland (Historic Scotland 1997). Archaeologists often act as frontline advisors and service providers when the development of burial grounds is proposed. What they can offer is advice on what hidden knowledge might lie in disused burial grounds and how to release it, if the imperative to disturb these ancient burial grounds is pursued. This is not to endorse the wholesale clearance of burial grounds; on the contrary, as they represent the physical and spiritual remains of past societies they should be treated with respect. This respect should be exhibited by determining ways of avoiding clearance before moving on to careful consideration of strategies which might honour the dead through acknowledging the value of their remains to understanding the past. What level of archaeological intervention is appropriate to each case is examined elsewhere (Reeve & Cox forthcoming).

Perspective

I live in London. I did not always live there, but work has brought me there for the second time in my life. Now that I am becoming more established I am getting to know some of the other people who have made London their home. I am getting to know some of the Londoners who say they have always been here and how the neighbourhood in which I live has changed with the changing of governments and housing styles, and with money changing hands. I live next to one of the first extramural cemeteries (Fig 18.1) to be laid out in the 'Age of Sanitary Improvement', as some of the Victorians referred to it. It is there that people like me, with their own intricate history of arrival and sur-

vival, are buried. It used to be a place to go for polite walks, to meander past the vast array of names set down on grand and lesser stone monuments, but it has become rather overgrown and the houses and blocks of flats have come right up to the perimeter walls, making it less open and perhaps less relevant than it used to be. How many stories are contained within that wall? If it were all to be cleared away tomorrow what would be lost? This is the question this contribution will address.

This discussion will outline how some of these stories can be put in context and identify how the post-medieval burial ground might answer other questions about London, about human experience and the nature of decay. The quantity and extent of burial in London will be examined, as will its significance for archaeology and the implications for land management now and for the future. Examples of some crypts and graveyards which have already been assessed for archaeological potential or physically examined will be discussed, as will areas of further research. The issue of cremation, in the 18th and 19th centuries and in the present, will be touched upon and an attempt made to set out a statement of what this means for the archaeology of buried remains in London.

Quantity and extent of burials in London

Vanessa Harding's excellent paper 'And one more may be laid there: the location of burials in Early Modern London' (1989) investigated the period 1550–1666, immediately preceding the period of this volume. It examined the power of personal choice in selecting a burial location, the availability of burial space, the price and perceived status of various locations, and concluded that the 'living Londoners did not shun the company of the dead' (op cit, 123). Harding also observed that the concepts of parish and community were strong determinants when it came to choosing a burial location (a factor also evident from 1729–1852 at Christchurch, Spitalfields [Molleson & Cox 1993]). These observations came from a detailed study of 300 wills covering a 100-year period, in which recurrent episodes of plague caused substantial fluctuations in the regular provision of burial space. There was always the need to maintain and provide for new burial space and this was reflected in the extensions to older burial grounds and

Figure 18.1   Tower Hamlets Cemetery, London (photo: Jez Reeve)

the laying out of new ones in this and subsequent periods.

A long campaign by sanitary reformers against the abuses associated with burials in the over-crowded churchyards and burial-grounds of London, especially those of body-snatching and the dangers to health, culminated in the Burial Act of 1852 (15 & 16 Vict c 85). Prime movers in this campaign included George Frederick Carden. He had recognised the need for a Grand National Cemetery and presented the idea to Parliament on Thursday 13 May 1830.

The petition is that of Mr George Frederick Carden, Barrister, of the Inner Temple; and he calls the attention of the House to what he very properly terms the indecent and unhealthy practice of interring human bodies in churches and churchyards in the heart of this populous City, in which not less than 40,000 burials take place in the course of the year. He states that in many churchyards the number of interments is so great, that time is not afforded for the decomposition of bodies; and that, in consequence, many shocking spectacles present themselves to the public eye in those places, and that a putrid and most unhealthy exhalation is sent from them to the surrounding neighbourhood; and he prays that the House will take this important subject into consideration, and appoint a committee to enquire into the present system of interment in the Metropolis; and also to consider a plan which he proposes as a remedy for this great nuisance. (General Cemetery Company 1830, 15)

He continued to lobby Parliament and in 1832 an Act was passed to licence a new non-denominational burial ground for London. Seventy-seven acres of land off the Harrow Road were taken for use as the Kensal Green Cemetery and were consecrated on 24 January 1833. It was the first extensive burial ground in England and its size contrasted markedly with the 80 or so churchyards and burial grounds with identifiable foundation dates from the 1600s in the combined gazetteers of Mrs Isabella Holmes (Mrs Basil Holmes; Holmes 1896) and Hugh Mellor (Mellor 1985).

Mrs Holmes reported on the valiant efforts of George Alfred Walker, a surgeon of Drury Lane who wrote *Gatherings from Graveyards, particularly those of London* . . . (Walker 1839), noting details of causes of death and illness directly attributable to contact with human remains in a state of putrefaction. He described the state of St Ann's, Soho thus:

. . . it is walled in on the side next to Prince's St; close to this wall is the bone house, rotten coffin wood and fragments of bone are scattered about. Some graves are only partly filled up, and left in that state, intended, probably, for paupers. The ground is very full, and is considerably raised above its original level; it is overlooked by houses thickly inhabited. . . . (Walker 1839, 207)

Some of Walker's descriptions were thought at the time to be exaggerations, but they were fully corroborated in the evidence before the Parliamentary Committee which sat in 1842. Several Acts were born out of this Committee, the 1848 City of London Sewers Act (11 & 12 Vict c 163) which required new coffins in vaults to be made of lead or lead-lined, the 1851 Act which gave the Commissioners of Sewers powers to remove bodies from burial grounds and re-inter them outside the City boundaries (14 & 15 Vict c 91), the Metropolitan Interments Act of 1850 which effectively barred any further burial within the 63 City churchyards (13 & 14 Vict c 52), and the culminating Burial Act of 1852.

The 1852 Burial Act required each vestry to set up a burial board to provide adequate burial grounds for its area and residents, stating that, if new burial space were needed, this would have to be outside London's built-up area and no nearer than 100 yards to any dwelling (Fig 18.2). In practical terms this meant that new cemeteries in the metropolis had to be large to sustain the increasing population; a fact which is most easily illustrated by the flurry of cemetery foundations from 1832 to 1900. During this period 2,333 acres of land were laid out as cemeteries, many of 20 acres or more

with the largest being the joint cemeteries of St Pancras and Islington of 182 acres. A further 471 acres were laid out as cemeteries between then and 1947 (Mellor 1985). The Bishop of Manchester had earlier been reported as observing on the increase of dedications of burial grounds: 'Here is another hundred acres of land withdrawn from the food-producing area of this country for ever' (Jamieson, 1816, 61).

In 1896 Isabella Holmes was engaged by the London County Council's Parks Committee to assess the extent of burial space in London, both that which was still in use, either for burial or as public gardens or playgrounds, and that which had disappeared from view. She used Roque's map of 1742–5 to identify the location of the older burial-grounds, along with the returns drawn up by Edwin Chadwick in his report to the House of Lords in 1843 (Chadwick 1843), and the location of grounds closed by Order of Council in 1853, 1854, and still open in 1855. Her extensive visits and inquiries resulted in a gazetteer of 364 burial-grounds (Holmes 1896).

Mrs Holmes makes a number of assertions regarding the density and frequency of burials in some churchyards. It is not clear whether this information has been gleaned with reference to burial registers or from hearsay. In the case of St Ann's, Soho the figure computes at 46 burials per square yard, which hardly seems possible, even taking the

Figure 18.2   Tower Hamlets Cemetery, London (photo: Jez Reeve)

vault space under the church into account. These levels of burials were also mentioned by Edwin Chadwick in 1843 when he reported to Parliament that 100,000 corpses occupied just four acres in Bunhill Fields. These high figures contrast with recent projections for desirable burial densities made by the London Planning Advisory Committee in *Planning for Burial Space in London*, a consultation draft circulated in February 1997 (1997b); both are set out in Table 18.1.

At the time of Holmes' survey at least another 113 burial grounds had been overtaken by development in the form of public buildings, new streets, and railways and by private developments (Fig 18.3). Some of these have since been redeveloped and the burial-grounds which had been built over have been archaeologically excavated, eg The Mint, excavated 1985 and Spital Square; excavated 1984. Some have been cleared commercially, notably the crypts of St Marylebone; St Anne's, Limehouse; St George's, Camberwell; St Botolph's, Aldgate; and St John's, Wapping.

The number of burials in the metropolis varies wildly in estimation, but a conservative estimate of those buried in cemeteries laid out between 1600 and 1900 at 2,500 per acre would gross around six million. Examining the quantity of post-medieval burials in London enables us to get a feel for the size and variety of the whole and helps to come to a strategic view, which is archaeologically intelligent, given that burial space is still a problem.

In his article *Cemetery Overload* Ben Griffiths, reporting for the journal *Planning* (21 Feb 1997), was perhaps unaware that his chosen title was a truism for London. He summarized the findings of

the London Planning Advisory Committee's *Burial space needs in London*, based on work undertaken by the University of York which had been funded by ESRC (Dunk & Rugg 1994). The conclusions of this report were:

- that 20,000 burial spaces were still required every year despite the fact the 70% of people now opt for cremation
- that inner London would run out of burial space in the next nine years
- that even in 2016 for an estimated 53,300 deaths 12,000 burial spaces would still be required

These statistics were based on an analysis of population levels and mortality projections, taking into account the particular requirements of Jews, Catholics, and Muslims living in the metropolis. Four suggestions were made in the report to remedy this situation and are now being investigated. All might impact on what could be called the archaeological resource. These were:

- increasing the depth of new graves to accommodate more coffins
- limit exclusive burial rights to 50 years
- promote the choice of cremation
- elective reuse of graves over 100 years old (requiring legislative change)

This survey and the desire of parochial church councils to clear vaults under churches and parts of their adjoining churchyards to accommodate new building developments will most certainly mean that wholesale and limited clearances of post-medieval burial-grounds will continue and increase. The Necropolis Company (founded in 1852, originally as part of cemetery ownership) now proclaims itself as 'Exhumation Engineer Specialists' and has already been commissioned to clear or part-clear 48 burial grounds and crypts in London. What is the archaeologically intelligent response to this situation?

Table 18.1: Density of burial in some London cemeteries

Acres	Name	Period	# per year	# per acre
38.0	Brompton Cemetery	1840–89	3,163	4,079
0.5	St Ann's Soho	160 years	689	220,480
0.5	Whitfields Tabernacle Tottenham	97 years	309	60,000
33.0	City and Tower Hamlets Cemetery	1841–89	5,146	7,485
0.75	New Bunhill Fields, Deverell St	1826–38	555	7,500
17.0	Deptford Cemetery	1858–1889	1,613	2,941
	Profile of London Cemetery Provision	1997 projection		800–2,000

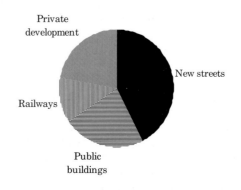

Figure 18.3 Burial grounds overtaken by development in 1896 (after Mrs Basil Holmes)

Examples of London investigations

In order to examine what has already been done in this field I have to return to my life as a Londoner. I was involved once before in the lives of past Londoners when I was employed by a parochial church council to supervise the crypt clearance of a church in the East End of London. This project, which first came to my attention in 1983, had stumbled at a number of hurdles so I had gone to Italy to seek my fortune there. While involved in an excavation of a medieval house in a medieval town in Northern Italy I was called back to organise the excavations of Christ Church, Spitalfields. The easy comparisons between the immigrant-filled streets of Spitalfields in 1984 and the immigrant-filled vaults of Christ Church struck a chord of continuity just as the formal excavation of a Ferrarese house had done in Italy.

Christ Church, Spitalfields

At Christ Church, Spitalfields, a full-scale excavation of the crypt was bravely envisaged in the course of restoration work. The results of this endeavour are now internationally famous. The project which was scheduled to take just six months took nearer three times that to complete. The unforeseen difficulties of extracting 250 tonnes of rubble, 16 tonnes of lead, the remains of approximately 1,000 human beings, and the thousands of small finds by hand from the constrained spaces and tunnels used as vaults was compounded by the regular monitoring of blood lead levels and the now famous smallpox scare (see Young, this volume). Thankfully, a similar project planned today would not have to revisit the unknowns which confounded the original Christ Church timetable.

Thirteen years later the excavations at Christ Church are still acting as the benchmark for studies of post-medieval burials (Molleson & Cox 1993; Reeve & Adams 1993). From some points of view this is entirely appropriate, as Margaret Cox has demonstrated in her articulate description of *Life and Death in Spitalfields* (1996). However this opportunity to review the benefits and highlight where further research avenues might prove fruitful is timely.

Burial space was (and to some extent still is) a commodity marketed locally with increased rates of two-times or more levied at non-parishioners or residents buried in the parish burial ground and also as a tax on those parishioners choosing to be buried outside the parish. The results of this and the premium on space have been demonstrated above; *c* 68,000 burials were made at Christ Church between 1729 and 1859, with only 38% of those interred in the crypt coming from the parish of Spitalfields itself (Molleson & Cox 1993). Other aspects of the trade in burials were touched on in *Across the Styx* (Reeve & Adams 1993), such as body-snatching

and the funeral itself. These have been examined elsewhere in Ruth Richardson's *Death, Dissection and the Destitute* (1988) and Julian Litten's *The English Way of Death: the common funeral since 1450* (1991). With hindsight, at Christ Church the archaeological evidence for the activities of sextons and churchwardens is a subject that could have been examined in more depth. The different manner in which space was organised in the eastern parochial vault as opposed to the Peck vault (Fig 18.4) merits some discussion. Are we looking at different people's work signatures or attitudes to people in life expressed in death? The archaeological evidence for one of the Peck coffins is that it rotted where it lay, having been dropped down the steps of the family vault. The responses elsewhere in the crypt to the need to maximize space and subsequently seal the vaults entirely resulted in various space management techniques.

The most notable research area which now appears to be lacking, but was outside of most archaeologists' consciousness in the early 1980s, is the analysis of the processes of decay. The method and rates of recording and excavation were such that detailed inferences cannot be soundly made retrospectively. However the retention of the material collected from the excavations, held in the Museum of London and at the Natural History Museum may yet act as the subject of further study in this area. In the same way the reference collection of funeral furniture and grave-goods, although described in the published accounts (Reeve & Adams 1993; Boore 1995), could act as the basis for more detailed archaeological and historical research into the nature and mechanics of the undertaking industry. The 4,000 small finds collected at Christ Church have already defined 273 different design motifs (1729–1852) observed on coffin furniture and decoration: surely these should act as a reference collection for any future studies.

Other crypts and graveyards have come up for clearance in the last thirteen years. Some have been dealt with exclusively by commercial clearance companies, one or two have been tackled jointly by archaeological contractors and clearance undertakers, and others have had detailed assessment of their archaeological potential undertaken to inform on appropriate mitigation strategies.

St Botolph's, Bishopsgate

At St Botolph's, Bishopsgate both small-scale intrusive investigations, which examined the extent of deposits and their level of preservation, and very detailed historical research were combined into the formulation of an archaeological research design for the proposed crypt clearance (Gilchrist & Reeve 1991). Through analysing the extant manuscripts (burial, birth, and marriage registers, burial fee account books, Searchers Reports, Vestry minutes, churchwarden's account books, Vestry Clerk's

Figure 18.4   (Top) Eastern parochial vault, Christ Church, Spitalfields: orderly space management; (Bottom) Peck vault, Christ Church, Spitalfields: evidence of less respectful disposal (photos: Christ Church, Spitalfields Archaeological Project)

Census books, and Registers of Inhabitants) it was possible to put forward a proposal for a multi-disciplinary investigation which would involve archaeologists, medically-trained staff, and undertakers (Fig 18.5). This resulted in the proposal for selective targeting of the most likely informative material through archaeological supervision and recording of the crypt contents with appropriately-skilled personnel designated to specific on-site tasks. The working regime, outlined in the project design, further took into account some of the negative effects on health of this sort of work by combining on- and off-site days with necessary computer and other data analysis in an integrated programme of recording and continual assessment.

The documentary research revealed exceptionally useful information, with burial registers from as early as 1600 (although civil registration of burials only became mandatory in the 1830s), details of causes of death for the parish (Fig 18.6) which had been collected in Searchers' reports for 1792–1800, and details of relative costs for burials recorded in the burial fee account books. This wealth of information provided the context for justifying the selective approach to the archaeological recording and analysis of the physical contents of the crypt. Without the knowledge that the biographical information on individual coffins was still surviving it would have been hard to justify much in the way of archaeological involvement in the crypt clearance. It was thus possible to develop this study from a

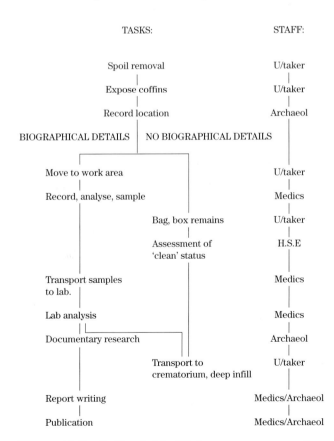

Figure 18.5 St Botolph's, Bishopsgate: proposed crypt clearance, outline methodology

solely historical analysis of documentary evidence into an integrated multi-disciplinary investigation because the quality of the historical sources was combined with a high level of material preservation, particularly the survival of dated biographical information in the form of coffin plates. This proposal has not yet been carried out for a number of reasons, although some of the ideas outlined in the research design have been implemented at other sites.

St Luke's, Old Street

The crypt and some of the graveyard at St Luke's, Old Street will be cleared if a new development proposal goes ahead to convert the remains of the upstanding walls and tower to a series of rehearsal and educational spaces for the London Symphony Orchestra. As part of a feasibility study an initial desk-based assessment was undertaken (MoLAS 1996) which identified the extant documentary record and outlined the general research potential of the human remains. In order to refine these general statements it was necessary to examine the vaults by breaking through one of the blocking walls and assess the likely survival and integrity of the remains themselves. A subsequent paper was drawn up by the archaeological consultant (Cox 1996d) which made recommendations for an archaeological mitigation strategy based on the poor levels of preservation, the incompleteness and disturbed nature of the actual remains. What the desk-based assessment did not achieve was a statement of how the remains in the crypt could achieve the potential identified from the documentary records. The consultant's report (*ibid*) considered such factors as relative completeness, condition, rarity, and group value of the crypt and graveyard remains in order to move from the general statements of potential made in the desk-based assessment to a practical assessment of the site's potential. It was clear from the examination of the crypt that due to the evidence of frequent movements and more recent vandalism in the crypt, combined with the high level of damp and the poor state of repair of the derelict building that the completeness of the crypt as a mortuary deposit was very much in question. The levels of preservation were observably poor and the site could not be considered rare in the context of London. As far as group value was concerned, although the development proposal included partial clearance of the graveyard, which, in principle, could enhance the potential value of both groups of material, the poor condition and incompleteness of both diminish this aspect.

The proposals for archaeological mitigation have thus become more modest than the desk-based assessment might have suggested with an archaeological watching-brief level of recording for most of the crypt clearance. This would examine the issues of preservation and taphonomy, quantify the buri-

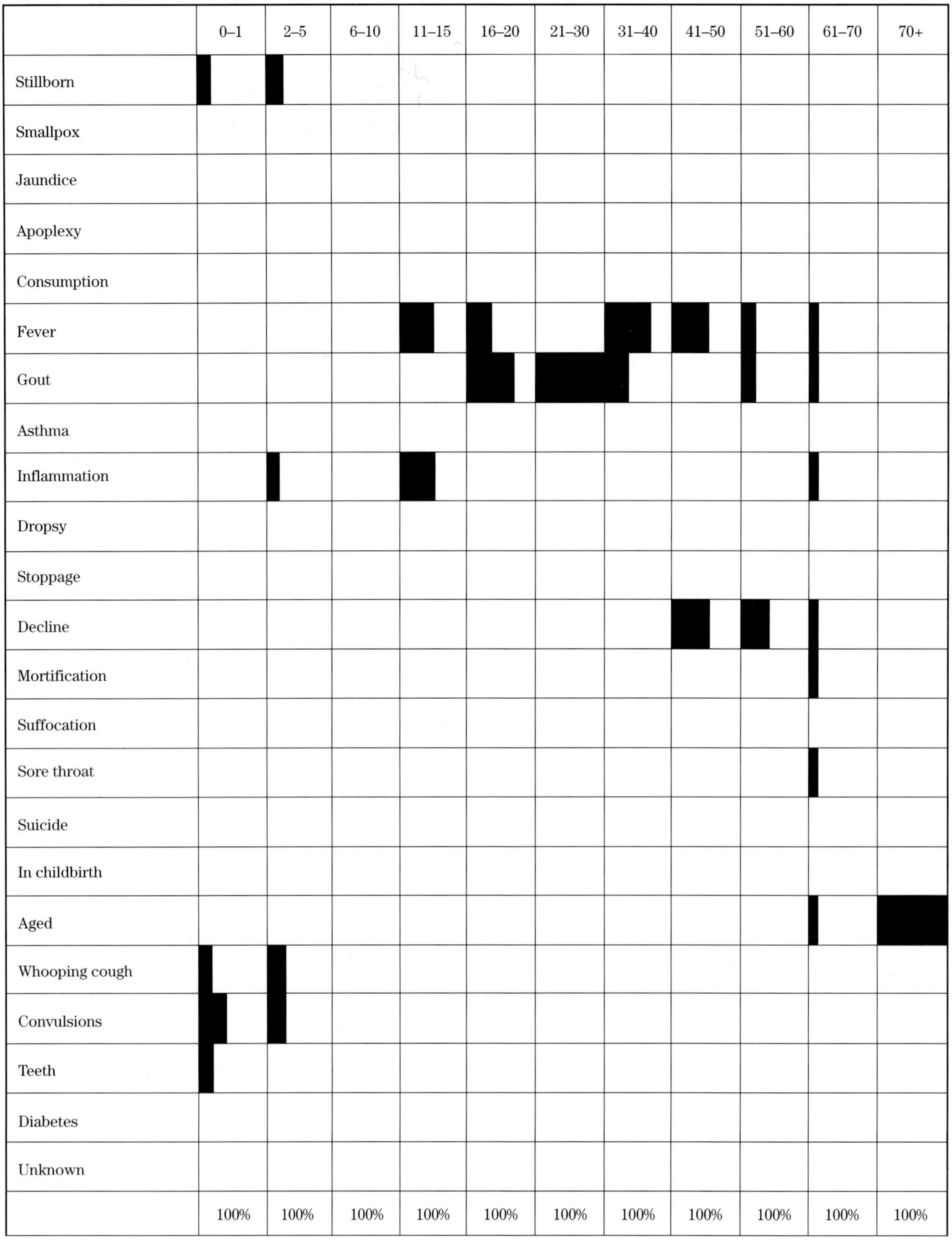

	0–1	2–5	6–10	11–15	16–20	21–30	31–40	41–50	51–60	61–70	70+
Stillborn	■	■									
Smallpox											
Jaundice											
Apoplexy											
Consumption											
Fever				■	■		■	■	■	■	
Gout					■	■				■	
Asthma											
Inflammation		■		■						■	
Dropsy											
Stoppage											
Decline								■	■	■	
Mortification										■	
Suffocation											
Sore throat										■	
Suicide											
In childbirth											
Aged										■	■
Whooping cough	■	■									
Convulsions	■	■									
Teeth	■										
Diabetes											
Unknown											
	100%	100%	100%	100%	100%	100%	100%	100%	100%	100%	100%

Figure 18.6   St Botolph's, Bishopsgate: researchers' report of crypt population, cause of death 1792–1800, % of female deaths by age group

als in the crypt, and record legible details which might contribute to analysis of crypt usage. In the churchyard the uppermost levels of that part of the graveyard to be cleared (above and below the turf-line) would be recorded and land-use patterns in relation to dated events (as recorded from grave-yard memorials) would be defined.

These examples of investigations and assessments of the material culture of crypt contexts and their skeletal samples demonstrate that, from a situation before 1984 when there was no such thing as a research design for post-medieval crypt or grave-yard clearances, it has been possible, because of one total archaeological crypt clearance and others partial, to provide a more considered evaluation of the archaeological potential of certain categories of material, in particular of human remains, and their relative value. There are no stock justifications for excavating post-medieval burial grounds; they all have to be researched and consultation needs to take place widely before assessing the appropriateness of archaeological involvement.

Research priorities

As examined above the relationship between the historical documentation and the condition of the material is the critical factor in the decision to progress to any form of archaeological recording and analysis in the study of post-medieval burial contexts. Just because it may be possible to record/measure/photograph something does not mean that it should be done. It may only be reasonable to attempt to address one or two key issues on a burial site because of the levels of documentary evidence and survival of archaeological material. The size of sample which might need to be investigated will be dependent upon the nature of the research question(s) that can be addressed (Reeve & Cox forthcoming), although the issue of detailed treatment of human remains has been dealt with (McKinley & Roberts 1993). In London, in particular, even the subject of death has been relatively well researched by the Centre for Metropolitan History in their 'Mortality in the Metropolis 1860–1920' project. The Centre was set up in 1987 to concentrate on studies which characterized London, in the late 19th and early 20th centuries, and set it within a wider context in comparison with other metropolises. Without due reference to appropriate expertise in the form of historians, economists, town planners, scientists, art historians, and others when considering what the relevant research questions for each site are, the value of the archaeology could be squandered. Although the medical profession has not really taken the opportunity as yet to become a regular part of this process there are clearly a number of areas where archaeological studies can combine with those of medical research. The study of the histories of medicine, disease, and dentistry may be obvious areas but, if archaeologists are going to be able to contribute to such highly specialized areas as the study of DNA, they would be advised to work closely with appropriate research laboratories.

A recent paper (Reeve & Cox forthcoming) identifies three major research headings: funerary archaeology, osteoarchaeology, and the complex issue of burial environments, preservation, and taphonomy. These headings could usefully be extended to include those of archaeological methodology and the evidence for known historic events. Other useful statements of research issues can be found in the CBA publication *Church Archaeology: Research Directions for the Future* (Blair & Pyrah 1996), especially in the articles by O'Brien and Roberts, and Rodwell. The human experience of living in a certain climate, subject to the vagaries of politics and laws, access to wealth, and the downside of societal prejudice are all valid topics of research which might be addressed through the targeted archaeological analysis of post-medieval burials. It is almost impossible to sub-divide the headings into neat disparate groups of research issues as so many will overlap. However it is useful to list some of the areas of research which examination of the post-medieval burial ground might contribute to (see Table 18.2).

Cremation: past and present

The issue of cremation and eventual disposal of human remains, whether contemporaneous with time of death or in subsequent disposal of excavated remains, has been addressed both in the 19th century and more recently in a local government advisor's report (LPAC 1997a). Attitudes towards this form of disposal can colour the approach taken by archaeologists to the need to archive excavated remains.

The development and acceptance of cremation as a method of disposal is worth considering briefly. In 1873, Professor Brunetti of Padua exhibited a model of his cremation furnace at the great exhibition of Vienna. It followed his own tests in open furnace cremation in 1869 and 1870. What followed in England was the establishment in 1874 of 'The Cremation Society of England' whose president Sir Henry Thompson had visited the great exhibition in Vienna and become an untiring advocate of cremation. It was not until 1885 that the first legal English cremation took place in Woking. From as early as 1866 papers and monographs were advocating cremation as a hygienic solution to what was seen as a burial crisis, with titles such as *On the origins of cremation or the burning of the dead* (Jamieson 1816), *Pagan cremation or Christian Burial* (Pollock 1846), *Cremation considered in reference to the Resurrection* (Grindon 1874), *Spade versus Torch or, the Perils of Cremation, with a glance into the Wherefore of Man* (Munday 1875), *The Disposal of the Dead, a plea for cremation* (Ber-

Table 18.2: Research issues in post-medieval burial archaeology

Major headings:

Funerary archaeology

Osteoarchaeology

Burial environments and preservation, taphonomy and diagenesis

Archaeological methodology

Evidence for known historical events (eg epidemics, climatological fluctuations)

Sub-headings:

Funerary studies (charnel pits, mass graves structure, artefact developments, taxonomies)

Palaeodemography and demography (rural/urban, incomers/indigenous, religious/lay, institutional/free, wealthy/poor

Biological anthropology

Pathology

Epidemiology

Osteological methodology (pathology, age and sex, stature)

Biomolecular analyses (eg DNA, lipids, Y chromosome etc)

Social and gender archaeology

Forensic science

Clinical medicine

Archaeological theory and practice

Curation procedures and environments (both in situ and in museums)

The English funeral

Ownership and choice of vaults and private chapels

Industrialization (transition) through artefact/diet/fashion/technology

Socio-economic development (local customs)

Historical events (eg Big Stink, Anatomy Act)

Environmental change (eg Little Ice Age)

Epidemics/multiple deaths

Migration (ethnicity/rural-urban interface)

Land use (practice v liturgy, graveyard morphology, location of interments to memorials

Re-ordering (reflecting law, robbing, tidying, maintenance)

Burials as entities (intrinsic interest)

Genealogical studies

(Adapted from Reeve & Cox forthcoming)

mingham, 1881), *Cholera treatment and Cure: With remarks on the danger of premature interment and suggestions for cheap and healthy cremation* (Cornish 1884), *Cremation versus burial: an appeal to reason against prejudice* (Holder 1891), and *Earth burial and cremation: The history of earth-burial with its attendant evils etc.* (Cobb 1892).

The strong objections that the practice of cremation was pagan and would interfere with a person's resurrection were almost eclipsed by the objection that cremation might destroy the evidence of administered poisons, the list being given by Sir Henry Thompson as morphia, aconite, atropine, strychnine, prussic acid, arsenic, antimony, and mercury (Thompson 1889). These objections were to be overcome both through public debate and the compelling need for a sanitary method of disposing of the dead, but not formally until the 1902 Cremation Act (2 Edw 7 c 8), amended in 1952 (15 & 16 Geo 6+Eliz 2 c 31). The current statistic that 70% of people in London opt for cremation demonstrates that the ground has now shifted (LPAC 1997a). (A more detailed discussion of this change in process can be found in Jupp, 1990.) The ban on Catholics being cremated was only lifted in 1963, while, according to the LPAC research, Jews find cremation and reuse of graves unacceptable and the majority of Muslims and Buddhists (90%) are buried, as opposed to the majority of Hindus (90%) and Sikhs (84%) who opt for cremation.

These statistics have been highlighted to make it clear that in arguing against cremation of the human remains from part or wholesale churchyard clearances just on the grounds that it would have been against religious or personally-held beliefs presupposes that these are known. The debates on the subject did not start (in this country) until very recently and since then, despite the obstacles which were described in the papers of the late 19th and early 20th centuries, its use by choice has been increasing rapidly. It seems that Leopold Hartley Grindon, who described himself as a 'Truth Seeker' in 1874, has had his rhetorical question answered:

> Few, probably, of the people now living in England, will ever be called upon to decide which is best, but it may be well for everyone to ask himself the question in some serious moment. 'Is it better to be reduced rapidly to ashes, or to be nailed down in a wooden box, and left for worms to worry?' (Grindon 1874, 22)

The case for selected samples of human bones being archived as reference and teaching collections has to be made in the face of diminishing storage space and the sometimes stated wishes of the parent church to return the remains of their parishioners to the location of the church, albeit for convenience, in the reduced form of cremated remains. The only large and detailed excavation of human remains from this period is that of Christ Church, Spitalfields (*c* 1,000 skeletons). It is the unique nature of the knowledge base which the bones from Christ Church represent that make it a justifiable case for long-term curation rather than cremation. The original Faculty identified cremation as the eventual means of disposal prior to reinterment in the grounds of the church for the excavated human remains. Since then it has become apparent that the bones themselves are still capable of generating further research and acting as a reference for future studies. This, coupled with the changes in attitude to the preservation of remains, has justified a request to the Diocese to consider issuing a new Faculty which will secure the collection for the future within the accessible confines of a sensitive institution.

London and burial clearances

In London, English Heritage is plotting the location of all disused burial grounds and known cemeteries and graveyards onto the Greater London Sites and Monuments Record at the Greater London Archaeology Advisory Service. Using the historical documentation of foundation and closure dates, where they exist, this information can be referred to in advice to potential developers on inquiries regarding the impact of planning proposals. In order to establish the relative importance of each site, using the criteria of completeness, condition, rarity, and group value a desk-based assessment will automatically be sought before advice on what level, if any, of destruction is considered appropriate to each proposal.

Whether it is through the planning system (with reference to the Disused Burial Act 1884 and the Burial Act 1857) or through the Church of England Faculty procedures the treatment of human remains should always receive the same respect and careful considerations.

It is certainly not appropriate to consider the archaeological examination and recording of all human remains in London. However, it is appropriate, in the first instance, to interrogate each proposed part or wholesale clearance of burials to assess whether there are research issues which can justifiably be addressed by targeted examination and analysis with specialists from other key disciplines. If every proposed clearance is assessed in this way, using the types of research criteria outlined here and in Reeve & Cox (forthcoming) it will be possible to identify, through repeated consideration, whether the type of exercise which was heroically conceived by the Friends of Christ Church, Spitalfields in 1981 for the crypt of Christ Church ever needs to be repeated.

We owe it to all the Londoners whose lives and works have contributed to making London what it now is and whose mortal remains have been properly disposed of in the custom and religion of the day to justify any disturbance and unasked-for examination.

Conclusion

There is more to this debate than being a Londoner, or even a teller of Londoners' tales. If the clearance of burial sites continues at its present rate, what will be lost will be respect for those who have gone before, and acknowledgement of their contribution in shaping the world in which we all live. However, the archaeological inferences which can be made from mortal remains can inform on the minutiae of each individual's contribution and reflect more than the seasons and the politics, the privations and the choices which were lived. They can inform on the collective experience of being human in a small corner of the universe.

Appendix 18.1

Index to London cemeteries and burial-grounds (after Holmes 1896; Mellor 1985)

This index has combined the basic information from Isabella Holmes' book *The London burial grounds: notes on their history from the earliest times to the present day* (1896) and *London Cemeteries: an illustrated guide and gazetteer* (Mellow 1985). This list is more comprehensive for the inner boroughs than the outer ones. All those mentioned on this index are plotted on the Greater London Sites and Monuments Record, held by the Greater London Archaeology Advisory service, English Heritage, at 23 Savile Row, London W1X 1AB.

This list is arranged alphabetically, by dedication, significant first letter, road, district, or other significant key word, in that order. Entries with asterisks are listed by both names given, ie Baptist (Unitarian) is listed under 'B' and 'U'.

Cemetery	Foundation	Owner	Acreage	Source
Abney Park Cemetery	1840	Hackney	32	Hugh Mellor 1985
Acton Cemetery	1895	Ealing	16.5	Hugh Mellor 1985
Aldgate burial-ground, Cartwright St	1615		0.13	Holmes 1896
All Hallows churchyard, London Wall				Holmes 1896
All Hallows, Tower Hill, Barking				Holmes 1896
All Hallows, Lombard St				Holmes 1896
All Hallows, Mark Lane, Staining				Holmes 1896
All Hallows the Great, Upper Thames St				Holmes 1896
All Hallows the Less, Upper Thames St				Holmes 1896
All Saints churchyard, Deptford Lower Road	1840		1	Holmes 1896
All Saints churchyard, Fulham			2	Holmes 1896
All Saints churchyard, High St Wandsworth			0.25	Holmes 1896
All Saints churchyard, Poplar			4	Holmes 1896
All Souls Cemetery, Kensal Green, Kensington	1833		69	Holmes 1896
All Souls Roman Catholic burial-ground, Cadogan Terrace, Chelsea	1811		1.5	Holmes 1896
Alperton (Wembley) Cemetery	1917	Brent	10	Hugh Mellor 1985
Augustine Friars (cloisters)				Holmes 1896
Bancroft Almshouses burial-ground of the Mile End Road	c 1872		0.5	Holmes 1896
Baptist burial-ground, Bandy Leg Walk (subsequently Guildford St), Southwark	c 1729		1000 sq yds	Holmes 1896
Baptist burial-ground, Broad St, Wapping	c 1756		200 sq yds	Holmes 1896
*Baptist (Unitarian) chapel burial-ground, Church St, Greenwich			0.25	Holmes 1896
*Baptist chapel-ground, East St, Walworth			400 sq yds	Holmes 1896
Baptist burial ground, North St, Wandsworth				Holmes 1896
Baptist chapel ground, Bow			0.33	Holmes 1896
Baptist chapel ground, Mare St			500 sq yds	Holmes 1896

Cemetery	Foundation	Owner	Acreage	Source
Barkingside Cemetery	1923/1954	Redbridge	8/13.5	Hugh Mellor 1985
Barnes Common Cemetery	1854	Richmond	2	Hugh Mellor 1985
Battersea New Cemetery	1891	Wandsworth	70	Hugh Mellor 1985
Bath St, the poor ground	1662		0.25	Holmes 1896
*Beaumont burial ground, Shandy St (also East London Cemetery)			2.25	Holmes 1896
Beckenham Cemetery	1877	Bromley	5	Hugh Mellor 1985
Benedictine Nunnery cemetery, Fulham Palace Road, Hammersmith	c 1829		(168 sq yards)	Holmes 1896
Bexleyheath Cemetery	1876	Bexley	5.25	Hugh Mellor 1985
Bridewell burial-ground			900 sq yds	Holmes 1896
Brockley Cemetery	1858	Lewisham	21	Hugh Mellor 1985
Brockley Hill Cemetery	1905	Bromley	6.25	Hugh Mellor 1985
Brompton Cemetery	1840	DoE	39	Hugh Mellor 1985
*Brunswick Wesleyan chapel ground, Threecolt Lane			450 sq yds	Holmes 1896
Bunhill Fields	c 1665	City	5	Hugh Mellor 1985
Butler's burial-ground, Horselydown	1822		1440 sq yds	Holmes 1896
Camberwell Cemetery	1865	Southwark	29.5	Hugh Mellor 1985
Camberwell New Cemetery	1927	Southwark	61	Hugh Mellor 1985
*The Cemetery of the Convent (Nazareth House), Hammersmith Road			(108 sq yards)	Holmes 1896
Chapel of Ease, Holloway Road, additional ground			4	Holmes 1896
Chapel Graveyard, Collier's Rents, Long Lane	1729		620 sq yds	Holmes 1896
*Chapel Royal churchyard (St Mary's), Savoy			0.25	Holmes 1896
Charlton Cemetery	1855	Greenwich	14.5	Hugh Mellor 1985
Old Charterhouse graveyard	1828		0.33	Holmes 1896
New Charterhouse burial-ground			0.25	Holmes 1896
Charterhouse Square, Holborn	1349		13	Holmes 1896
Chelsea Hospital Graveyard, Queen's Road, Chelsea			1.33	Holmes 1896
Chingford Mount Cemetery	1884	Waltham Forest	41.5	Hugh Mellor 1985
Chiswick Old Cemetery	1888	Hounslow	9	Hugh Mellor 1985
Chiswick New Cemetery	1933	Hounslow	6.5	Hugh Mellor 1985
Christ Church, Newgate St				Holmes 1896
Christ Church, Newgate St, additional ground				Holmes 1896
Christ Church churchyard, Blackfriars Bridge Road	1737		1.5	Holmes 1896
Christ Church churchyard, Spitalfields	1729		1.75	Holmes 1896
Christ Church churchyard, Union Road, Rotherhithe			700 sq yds	Holmes 1896
Christ Church churchyard, Victoria St, Westminster			7,000 sq yds	Holmes 1896
Christ's Hospital burial-ground				Holmes 1896

Cemetery	Foundation	Owner	Acreage	Source
Church St, Rotherhithe, additional ground			1.25	Holmes 1896
City of London Cemetery	1856	City	130 (+46 reserve)	Hugh Mellor 1985
Congregational burial-ground, Old Gravel Lane			140 sq yds	Holmes 1896
Congregational chapel ground, Greenwich Road	1800		0.25	Holmes 1896
Congregational chapel ground, Lower Norwood			0.33	Holmes 1896
Congregational chapel ground, Maze Hill, Greenwich			500 sq yds	Holmes 1896
Congregational chapel ground, New Road, Cannon St Road			0.33	Holmes 1896
Cripplegate poor ground	1636			Holmes 1896
*Cross Bones (also St Saviour's), Redcross St, Southwark, additional ground	c 1620		1000 sq yds	Holmes 1896
Croydon Cemetery, Mitcham Road	1876	Croydon	43	Hugh Mellor 1985
Crystal Palace District Cemetery	1880	Beckenham Crematorium Company	30	Hugh Mellor 1985
Danish burial-ground, Wellclose Square				Holmes 1896
*Deadman's Place burial-ground (also Park St)			0.5	Holmes 1896
Denmark Row chapel ground, Coldharbour Lane				Holmes 1896
Deptford Cemetery	1858		17	Holmes 1896
Drury Lane, additional ground			0.25	Holmes 1896
Dulwich burial-ground	c 1700		1.5 roods	Holmes 1896
Ealing & Old Brentford Cemetery	1861	Ealing	24	Hugh Mellor 1985
*Earlham Hall (Maberley chapel ground), Balls Pond Road			270 sq yds	Holmes 1896
East Hill burial-ground, Wandsworth	1680		0.5	Holmes 1896
East London Cemetery	1872	The East London Cemetery Company	35	Hugh Mellor 1985
*East London Cemetery, Shandy St (also Beaumont burial ground)			2.25	Holmes 1896
East Sheen Cemetery	1903	Richmond	16	Hugh Mellor 1985
*East St Baptist chapel ground, Walworth			400 sq yds	Holmes 1896
Eastcote Lane Cemetery	1900	Harrow	3.5	Hugh Mellor 1985
Ebenezer burial-ground, Long Lane, Bermondsey	1796		220 sq yds	Holmes 1896
Ebenezer burial-ground, St George's St			220 sq yds	Holmes 1896
Edmonton Cemetery	1884	Enfield	30	Hugh Mellor 1985
Edmonton & Southgate Cemetery	1880	Enfield	11	Hugh Mellor 1985
Eltham Cemetery & Crematorium	1935	Greenwich	27.5	Hugh Mellor 1985
Enon chapel yard, High St, Woolwich			112 sq yds	Holmes 1896

Cemetery	Foundation	Owner	Acreage	Source
Esher St Congregational chapel ground			480 sq yds	Holmes 1896
Friends burial-ground, Baker's Row	1687		1	Holmes 1896
Friends burial-ground, Bunhill Row	1661		0.5	Holmes 1896
Friends burial-ground, Long Lane, Bermondsey	1697		0.25	Holmes 1896
Friends burial-ground, High St, Deptford			360 sq yds	Holmes 1896
Friends burial-ground, Hammersmith			(300yds)	Holmes 1896
Friends burial-ground, Peckham Rye	1821		470 sq yds	Holmes 1896
Friends burial-ground, Brook St, Ratcliff	1666		800 sq yds	Holmes 1896
Friends burial-ground, Park St, Stoke Newington	1827		0.75	Holmes 1896
Friends burial-ground, High St, Wandsworth			400 sq yds	Holmes 1896
Fulham Cemetery	1865	Hammersmith	13	Hugh Mellor 1985
German Lutheran Church, Little Alie St				Holmes 1896
Gibraltar Walk burial-ground, Bethnal Green Road	1796		0.75	Holmes 1896
*Globe Road Chapel burial-ground (also Mile End cemetery)			670 sq yds	Holmes 1896
Golden Lane burial-ground, Bunhill, the City	1833		1.25	Holmes 1896
Golders Green Crematorium	1902	The London Cremation Company	12	Hugh Mellor 1985
Greenwich Cemetery	1856	Greenwich	22.5	Hugh Mellor 1985
Greenwich Cemetery, Royal Hospital	1857	Greenwich	6	Hugh Mellor 1985
Greenwich Hospital burial-ground			4	Holmes 1896
Greenwich Hospital Cemetery, Westcombe, Greenwich	1857		6	Holmes 1896
Greyfriars, burial-ground of the				Holmes 1896
Grove Park Cemetery	1935	Lewisham	33	Hugh Mellor 1985
Gunnersbury Cemetery	1936	Kensington	22	Hugh Mellor 1985
Guy's Hospital burial-ground, Nelson St	1696		0.5	Holmes 1896
Hackney Road, old burial-ground			0.5	Holmes 1896
Hammersmith Cemetery	1869	Hammersmith	17	Hugh Mellor 1985
Hammersmith New Cemetery	1926	Hammersmith	26	Hugh Mellor 1985
Hampstead Cemetery	1876		19.5	Holmes 1896
Harrow Cemetery	1887	Harrow	7	Hugh Mellor 1985
Hendon Cemetery	1899	Barnet	40	Hugh Mellor 1985
Highgate Cemetery	1839	Pinemarsh Ltd for the Friends of Highgate Cemetery	37	Hugh Mellor 1985
Holly Lane burial-ground, Hampstead	1812		1.25	Holmes 1896
Holy Trinity churchyard, Brompton			3.5	Holmes 1896
Holy Trinity churchyard, nr Commercial Docks Pier	1838		1	Holmes 1896
Holy Trinity churchyard, Minories	c 1348		302 sq yds	Holmes 1896
Holy Trinity churchyard, Tredegar Square			0.75	Holmes 1896

Cemetery	Foundation	Owner	Acreage	Source
*Holywell Mount burial-ground, behind St James church, Curtain Road	c 1666		0.33	Holmes 1896
Independent burial-ground, Wandsworth				Holmes 1896
*Independent chapel-ground, Mare St (also called St Thomas' Square burial ground	1888		0.66	Holmes 1896
Isleworth Cemetery	1879	Hounslow	2.5	Hugh Mellor 1985
Islington chapel ground, Church St, Bunhill Fields	1788		1	Holmes 1896
Jarratt Lane Cemetery, Wandsworth	1808		1.75	Holmes 1896
Jewish burial-ground, Balls Pond Road			1.25	Holmes 1896
Jewish burial-ground, 70 Bancroft Road			1650 sq yds	Holmes 1896
Jewish burial-ground, Grove St	1788		2.25	Holmes 1896
Jewish burial-ground, Hoxton St	1700		0.25	Holmes 1896
Jewish burial-ground, Mile End Road			0.75	Holmes 1896
Jewish burial-ground, Brady St, Bethnal Green	1796		4	Holmes 1896
Jewish burial-ground, Fulham Road, Chelsea	1813		0.5	Holmes 1896
Jewish Cemetery, Alderney Road E1	1697	The United Synagogue	1.25	Hugh Mellor 1985
Jewish Cemetery, Brady St E1	1761	The United Synagogue	c 4	Hugh Mellor 1985
Jewish Cemetery, East Ham E6	1919	The United Synagogue	25	Hugh Mellor 1985
Jewish Cemetery, Fulham Road SW3	1815	The Western Synagogue	c 1	Hugh Mellor 1985
Jewish Cemetery, Hoop Lane NW11	1895	The Western Synagogue	16.5	Hugh Mellor 1985
Jewish Cemetery, Kingsbury Road N1	1840	The Western Synagogue	c 0.5	Hugh Mellor 1985
Jewish Cemetery, Lauriston Road E9	1788	The United Synagogue	2.25	Hugh Mellor 1985
Jewish Cemetery, Montague Road N18	1884	Federation Burial Society & the Western Synagogue	c 20	Hugh Mellor 1985
Jewish Cemetery, Plashet Park E6	1896	The United Synagogue	14	Hugh Mellor 1985
Jewish Cemetery, Rowan Road SW16	1915	West End Chesed V'Emeth Burial Society	5.5	Hugh Mellor 1985
Jewish Cemetery, West Ham E15	1857	The United Synagogue	10.5	Hugh Mellor 1985
Jewish Cemetery, Willesden	1873	The United Synagogue	23	Hugh Mellor 1985
Jewish Old Sephardi Cemetery, Mile End Road E1	1657	Spanish and Portuguese Jew's Congregation	1.5	Hugh Mellor 1985

Cemetery	Foundation	Owner	Acreage	Source
Jewish New Sephardi Cemetery, Mile End Road E1	1733	Spanish and Portuguese Jew's Congregation	c 1	Hugh Mellor 1985
*Keldy's burial-ground (also called North East London cemetery/Peel Grove)	1796		4	Holmes 1896
Kensal Green Cemetery	1832	The General Cemetery Company	77	Hugh Mellor 1985
Kensington Hanwell Cemetery	1855	Kensington	19	Hugh Mellor 1985
Kingston Cemetery	1855	Kingston	27.5	Hugh Mellor 1985
Knightsbridge Green, Westminster				Holmes 1896
Kings Road old burial-ground, Chelsea	1736		0.75	Holmes 1896
Lambeth Cemetery	1854	Lambeth	41	Hugh Mellor 1985
Lee Cemetery, Hither Green	1873		10	Holmes 1896
Lee Cemetery	1873	Lewisham	65	Hugh Mellor 1985
Lee old churchyard				Holmes 1896
Lewisham Cemetery	1858		15.5	Holmes 1896
Lillie Road Pest Field			4	Holmes 1896
*Lock burial-ground, Tabard St (also St George's recreation ground)			0.25	Holmes 1896
London Hospital burial-ground			1.5	Holmes 1896
*Maberley chapel ground (now called Earlham Hall), Balls Pond Road			270 sq yds	Holmes 1896
Manor Park Cemetery	1874	Manor Park Cemetery Company	58	Hugh Mellor 1985
Merton & Sutton Joint Cemetery	1947	Merton & Sutton Joint Cemetery Board	57.5 (only 23 in use)	Hugh Mellor 1985
Millbank Penitentiary burial-ground			432 sq yds	Holmes 1896
*Mile End cemetery (also Globe Road Chapel burial-ground)			670 sq yds	Holmes 1896
Mile End New Town burial-ground, Hanbury St			250 sq yds	Holmes 1896
Mitcham Cemetery	1883	Merton	7	Hugh Mellor 1985
Mitcham Cemetery	1929	Merton	18	Hugh Mellor 1985
Moravian burial-ground, Milman's Row, Chelsea				Holmes 1896
Morden College cemetery, Blackheath	1695		0.25	Holmes 1896
Old Mortlake Cemetery	1854	Richmond	6	Hugh Mellor 1985
Mortlake Roman Catholic Cemetery	1852	Southwark Roman Catholic Diocesan Corporation	13	Hugh Mellor 1985
*Nazareth House (The Cemetery of the Convent), Hammersmith Road			(108 sq yards)	Holmes 1896
New Bunhill Fields, Deverell St, New Kent Road (also Hoole and Martin's)	c 1820		0.75	Holmes 1896

Cemetery	Foundation	Owner	Acreage	Source
New Southgate Cemetery (The Great Northern Cemetery)	1861	New Southgate Cemetery and Crematorium Ltd	60	Hugh Mellor 1985
New West End Baptist Chapel ground, King St, Hammersmith			0.25	Holmes 1896
Newgate burial-ground				Holmes 1896
North Sheen Cemetery	1926	Hammersmith	26	Hugh Mellor 1985
*North East London cemetery (also called Peel Grove burial-ground/Keldy's)	1796		4	Holmes 1896
Nunhead Cemetery	1840	Southwark	52	Hugh Mellor 1985
Paddington Cemetery	1855	Westminster	24	Hugh Mellor 1985
Paddington Cemetery (Mill Hill)	1936	Westminster	26	Hugh Mellor 1985
Paddington old burial-ground,			3	Holmes 1896
Paradise Row burial ground, High St, Lambeth, additional ground	1705		1.5	Holmes 1896
*Park St burial-ground (also Deadman's Place)			0.5	Holmes 1896
*Peel Grove burial-ground (also called North East London cemetery/Keldy's)	1796		4	Holmes 1896
Pinner Cemetery	1933	Harrow	22.5	Hugh Mellor 1985
*Poplar Chapel churchyard (St Matthias')			1.25	Holmes 1896
Portugal St, additional ground			0.5	Holmes 1896
Plaistow Cemetery	1892	Bromley	4	Hugh Mellor 1985
Plumstead cemetery, Wickham Lane, Plumstead	1890		32.25	Holmes 1896
Providence chapel burial-ground, Shoreditch Tabernacle				Holmes 1896
Putney burial-ground, Upper Richmond Road	1763		1	Holmes 1896
Putney Lower Common Cemetery	1855	Wandsworth	3	Hugh Mellor 1985
Putney Vale Cemetery	1891	Wandsworth	45	Hugh Mellor 1985
Queens Road Cemetery Croydon	1861	Croydon	26	Hugh Mellor 1985
Retreat Place, Hackney	1812			Holmes 1896
RC burial-ground, Commercial Road			0.5	Holmes 1896
RC Ground, New Road, Woolwich			0.25	Holmes 1896
RC ground, Parker's Row	1833		300 sq yds	Holmes 1896
RC ground, Wade's Place			1300 sq yds	Holmes 1896
Regent's St Baptist chapel ground, Kennington Road				Holmes 1896
Richmond Cemetery	1853	Richmond	c 15	Hugh Mellor 1985
Royal Hospital Chelsea burial-ground	1692	The Royal Hospital	1	Hugh Mellor 1985
Russell Court, Catherine St, additional ground			430 sq yds	Holmes 1896
St Alban's, Wood St				Holmes 1896
St Alphege Churchyard, Greenwich	c 1716		2,740 sq yds	Holmes 1896
St Alphege, Greenwich, additional ground	1833		2.5	Holmes 1896

Cemetery	Foundation Owner	Acreage	Source
St Alphege's, London Wall			Holmes 1896
St Andrews, Holborn			Holmes 1896
St Andrew's burial-ground, Grays Inn Road		1.25	Holmes 1896
St Andrew Undershaft, Leadenhall St			Holmes 1896
St Andrew by the Wardrobe, Queen Victoria St			Holmes 1896
St Ann, Blackfriars			Holmes 1896
St Ann's churchyard, Soho	1892	0.5	Holmes 1896
St Ann and St Agnes, Gresham St			Holmes 1896
St Anne's churchyard, Limehouse	1730	3	Holmes 1896
St Antholin, Watling St			Holmes 1896
St Barnabas churchyard, Homerton		0.75	Holmes 1896
St Bartholemew's hospital ground		0.33	Holmes 1896
St Bartholomew the Great			Holmes 1896
St Bartholomew the Less			Holmes 1896
St Batholomews churchyard, near Cambridge Road, Bethnal Green		1	Holmes 1896
St Bartholomew's churchyard, Sydenham		0.75	Holmes 1896
St Benet Fink, Threadneedle St			Holmes 1896
St Benet Sherehog, Pancras Lane			Holmes 1896
St Botolph's churchyard, Aldersgate St			Holmes 1896
St Botolph's churchyard, Aldgate		0.25	Holmes 1896
St Botolph's churchyard, Bishopsgate		0.5	Holmes 1896
St Botolph's, Billingsgate, Botolph Lane			Holmes 1896
St Bride's churchyard, Fleet St			Holmes 1896
St Bride's, Fleet St, additional ground	1610	750 sq yds	Holmes 1896
St Catherine Cree, Leadenhall St			Holmes 1896
St Christopher le Stocks			Holmes 1896
St Clement, Eastcheap			Holmes 1896
St Clement Danes churchyard		0.25	Holmes 1896
St Dionys, Backchurch, Lime St			Holmes 1896
St Dunstan's churchyard, Stepney Mile End Old Town	c 1666	6	Holmes 1896
St Dunstan's in the East, Lower Thames St			Holmes 1896
St Dunstan's in the West, Fetter Lane, additional ground		4750 sq feet	Holmes 1896
St Edmund the King and Martyr, Lombard St			Holmes 1896
St Elizabeth, Franciscan Convent, burial ground, Portobello Road, Kensington	1862	0.25	Holmes 1896
St Ethelburga, Bishopsgate			Holmes 1896
St Gabriel, Fenchurch St			Holmes 1896
St George, Botolph Lane			Holmes 1896
St George's burial-ground, Bayswater Road		5	Holmes 1896
St George's burial-ground, Bloomsbury	1714	1.25	Holmes 1896

Cemetery	Foundation Owner	Acreage	Source
St George's burial-ground, Mount St, Hanover Square	1730	1.25	Holmes 1896
St George's churchyard, Battersea Park Road		0.75	Holmes 1896
St George's churchyard, Borough	1882	1	Holmes 1896
St George's churchyard, Camberwell	1824		Holmes 1896
St George's churchyard (in the East)	1730	3	Holmes 1896
*St George's (also St Marylebone), Paddington St (south side), Marylebone	1733	2.25	Holmes 1896
*St George's recreation ground, Tabard St (also the Lock burial ground)		0.25	Holmes 1896
St George's Wesleyan chapel ground, Cable ST			Holmes 1896
St Giles, Cripplegate			Holmes 1896
St Giles churchyard	1628	1	Holmes 1896
St Giles churchyard, Camberwell	c 1717	3.25	Holmes 1896
St Giles in the Fields burial-ground	1803	6	Holmes 1896
St Helen, Bishopsgate			Holmes 1896
St James, Garlickhithe			Holmes 1896
St James's burial-ground, Hampstead Road	1887	3	Holmes 1896
St James's burial-ground, Pentonville Road		1	Holmes 1896
St James's cemetery, Highgate	1839	38	Holmes 1896
St James's churchyard, Bermondsey, Jamaica Road		1.75	Holmes 1896
St James's churchyard, Clerkenwell	1673	0.75	Holmes 1896
St James's churchyard, Duke St			Holmes 1896
St James's churchyard, Piccadilly		0.50	Holmes 1896
St James's churchyard, Ratcliff		1	Holmes 1896
*St James church, Holywell Mount burial-ground, Curtain Road	c 1666	0.33	Holmes 1896
St James's the Less, Old Ford Road		1	Holmes 1896
St James's middle ground, Bowling Green Lane, Rosoman St, Holborn, additional ground	1775	0.25	Holmes 1896
St James's workhouse-ground, Poland St		0.25	Holmes 1896
St John's, Horseferry Road, Westminster, additional ground	1627	1.5	Holmes 1896
St John, Watling St			Holmes 1896
St John's churchyard, Clerkenwell		320 sq yds	Holmes 1896
St John's, Clerkenwell, Holborn, additional ground	1775	0.25	Holmes 1896
St John's churchyard, Hampstead		1.5	Holmes 1896
St John's churchyard, Hoxton		1.25	Holmes 1896
St John's churchyard, Waltham Green, Fulham		0.5	Holmes 1896
St John's churchyard, Wapping	1617	600 sq yds	Holmes 1896
St John's, Wapping, additional ground		0.5	Holmes 1896
St John's churchyard, Waterloo Bridge Road		1	Holmes 1896
St John's at Hackney churchyard		6	Holmes 1896

Cemetery	Foundation	Owner	Acreage	Source
St John the Baptist churchyard, Lee, Eltham			3	Holmes 1896
St John's Episcopal chapel ground, Walworth	1843		6400 sq yds	Holmes 1896
St John the Evangelist churchyard, Smith Square			0.25	Holmes 1896
*St John's and St Olave's, Horselydown, additional ground	1888		0.5	Holmes 1896
St John Zachary, Gresham St				Holmes 1896
St John's RC burial-ground			0.5	Holmes 1896
St John of Jerusalem, South Hackney	1831		0.75	Holmes 1896
St John's Wood chapel ground, Marylebone			6	Holmes 1896
St Katharine Coleman churchyard, Fenchurch St				Holmes 1896
St Lawrence Jewry, Guildhall				Holmes 1896
St Lawrence Pountney, Cannon St				Holmes 1896
St Leonard, Fish St Hill				Holmes 1896
St Leonard's, Foster Lane, additional ground			0.5	Holmes 1896
St Leonard's churchyard, Shoreditch			1.5	Holmes 1896
St Leonard's churchyard, Streatham	1731		1.25	Holmes 1896
St Luke's churchyard, Charlton			0.5	Holmes 1896
St Luke's churchyard (old church, Embankment) Chelsea			0.25	Holmes 1896
St Luke's churchyard (new church in Robert St), Chelsea	1812		2.25	Holmes 1896
St Luke's churchyard, Norwood			1	Holmes 1896
St Luke's churchyard, Old St			1.75	Holmes 1896
St Magnus the Martyr, London Bridge				Holmes 1896
St Margaret, Lothbury				Holmes 1896
St Margaret's churchyard			2.25	Holmes 1896
St Margaret's churchyard, Lee			1.5	Holmes 1896
St Margaret Pattens, Rood Lane				Holmes 1896
St Mark's churchyard, Kennington			1.75	Holmes 1896
St Martin, Ludgate				Holmes 1896
St Martin's churchyard			0.33	Holmes 1896
St Martin Orgar, Cannon St				Holmes 1896
St Martin Outwich, Camomile St	1538			Holmes 1896
St Martin Pomeroy (St Olave, Jewry), Ironmonger Lane				Holmes 1896
St Martin Vintry, Queen St				Holmes 1896
St Martins-in-the-fields burial ground	1805		1.75	Holmes 1896
St Mary, Abchurch Lane				Holmes 1896
St Mary, Aldermary				Holmes 1896
St Mary's Cemetery, Battersea	1860	Wandsworth	8.5	Hugh Mellor 1985
St Mary's churchyard, Battersea			0.75	Holmes 1896
St Mary's churchyard, Bow			2716 sq yds	Holmes 1896
St Mary's churchyard, Bromley by Bow			1.25	Holmes 1896

Cemetery	Foundation	Owner	Acreage	Source
St Mary's churchyard, Haggerston			1.33	Holmes 1896
St Mary's churchyard, Hammersmith Road, Fulham			0.5	Holmes 1896
St Mary's churchyard, Islington	c 1793		1.33	Holmes 1896
St Mary's churchyard Lambeth	c 1623		0.5	Holmes 1896
St Mary's churchyard, Lewisham			2	Holmes 1896
St Mary's churchyard, Newington	pre 1757		1.25	Holmes 1896
St Mary's churchyard, Paddington			1	Holmes 1896
St Mary's churchyard, Putney			0.5	Holmes 1896
St Mary's churchyard, Rotherhithe			0.75	Holmes 1896
*St Mary's churchyard (Chapel Royal), Savoy			0.25	Holmes 1896
St Mary's churchyard, Stoke Newington			0.75	Holmes 1896
St Mary's churchyard, Whitechapel			0.75	Holmes 1896
St Mary's churchyard, Woolwich			3	Holmes 1896
St Mary Abbots churchyard, Kensington			1.25	Holmes 1896
St Mary's Aldermanbury churchyard				Holmes 1896
St Mary at Hill, Eastcheap				Holmes 1896
St Mary Somerset, Thames St				Holmes 1896
St Mary Staining, Oat Lane				Holmes 1896
St Mary Woolnoth, Lombard St				Holmes 1896
St Mary's Roman Catholic church ground, Finsbury Square				Holmes 1896
St Mary's Roman Catholic Cemetery, Kensal Green	1858	St Mary's Catholic Cemetery Company	29	Hugh Mellor 1985
St Marylebone burial-ground, Paddington St (north side), St Marylebone	1772		0.75	Holmes 1896
St Marylebone Episcopal chapel ground, St Marylebone			0.33	Holmes 1896
*St Marylebone (also St George's), Paddington St (south side), Marylebone	1733		2.25	Holmes 1896
St Marylebone Cemetery	1854	Westminster	33	Hugh Mellor 1985
St Mary-le-Strand churchyard			200 sq yds	Holmes 1896
St Mary Magdalene's churchyard, Bermondsey	c 1738		1.5	Holmes 1896
St Matthew, Friday St				Holmes 1896
St Matthew's churchyard, Bethnal Green	1746		2	Holmes 1896
St Matthew's churchyard, Brixton	1824		2	Holmes 1896
*St Matthias' churchyard, (Poplar Chapel)			1.25	Holmes 1896
St Michael, Cornhill				Holmes 1896
St Michael, Queenhithe				Holmes 1896
St Michael Bassishaw, Basinghall St				Holmes 1896
St Michael Paternoster Royal, College Hill				Holmes 1896
St Mildred, Bread St				Holmes 1896
St Mildred, Poultry	1420			Holmes 1896
St Nicholas churchyard, Deptford			0.75	Holmes 1896
St Nicholas churchyard, Lower Tooting			2	Holmes 1896

Cemetery	Foundation	Owner	Acreage	Source
St Nicholas churchyard, Plumstead			4	Holmes 1896
St Nicholas Acons, Lombard St				Holmes 1896
St Nicholas Cole Abbey, Queen Victoria St				Holmes 1896
St Olave's, Hart St				Holmes 1896
St Olave's churchyard, Tooley St			634 sq yds	Holmes 1896
St Olave's churchyards, Silver St				Holmes 1896
*St Olave's and St John's, Horselydown, additional ground	1888		0.5	Holmes 1896
St Pancras, Pancras Lane				Holmes 1896
St Pancras burial-ground, St Pancras Road	17??			Holmes 1896
St Pancras & Islington Cemetery	1854	Camden & Islington	182	Hugh Mellor 1985
St Patrick's Roman Catholic Cemetery	1868	St Mary's Catholic Cemetery Company	43	Hugh Mellor 1985
St Paul's Cathedral churchyard, City			1.5	Holmes 1896
St Paul's churchyard, Clapham			1.5	Holmes 1896
St Paul's churchyard, Covent Garden	1631		0.75	Holmes 1896
St Paul's churchyard, Deptford			2.5	Holmes 1896
St Paul's churchyard, Hammersmith	1631		1	Holmes 1896
St Paul's churchyard, Shadwell	1671		0.75	Holmes 1896
St Peter, Cornhill				Holmes 1896
St Peter's, Paul's Wharf				Holmes 1896
St Peter ad Vincula churchyard in the Tower			525 sq yds	Holmes 1896
St Peter Cheap, Wood St				Holmes 1896
St Peter's churchyard, Black Lion Lane, Hammersmith			(1,800yds)	Holmes 1896
St Peter's churchyard, Hackney road			0.25	Holmes 1896
St Peter's churchyard, Walworth			1.25	Holmes 1896
St Saviour's churchyard, Southwark			0.25	Holmes 1896
*St Saviour's (also Cross Bones), Redcross St, Southwark, additional ground	c 1620		1000 sq yds	Holmes 1896
St Saviour's (also St Saviour's Almshouse burial-ground), Park St, Southwark, additional ground	c 1732		0.25	Holmes 1896
St Sepulchre's churchyard, Holborn				Holmes 1896
St Stephen, Coleman St				Holmes 1896
St Stephen, Walbrook				Holmes 1896
St Swithin, Cannon St				Holmes 1896
St Thomas' churchyard			787 sq yds	Holmes 1896
St Thomas's churchyard, Charlton	1854		1	Holmes 1896
St Thomas' churchyard burial-ground, St Thomas's St			1770 sq yds	Holmes 1896
St Thomas the Apostle, Queen St				Holmes 1896
St Thomas' Roman Catholic Cemetery, Fulham	1849	Westminster Roman Catholic Archdiocesan Trustee	c 0.5	Hugh Mellor 1985

Cemetery	Foundation	Owner	Acreage	Source
*St Thomas' Square burial ground, Mare St (also called Independent chapel ground)	1888		0.66	Holmes 1896
St Vedast, Foster Lane				Holmes 1896
Salem chapel yard, Powis St, Woolwich			300 sq yds	Holmes 1896
Sheen's burial-ground, Church Lane, Whitechapel	c 1763		0.5	Holmes 1896
*South Metropolitan or Norwood Cemetery	1837	Lambeth	39	Hugh Mellor 1985
Spa fields burial-ground, Xmas St, Clerkenwell			1.75	Holmes 1896
Stepney Meeting House burial-ground, Whitehorse St			0.5	Holmes 1896
Stepney pest field (Stepney Mount)	c 1665			Holmes 1896
Streatham Cemetery	1892	Lambeth	36	Hugh Mellor 1985
Streatham Park Cemetery	1909	The Great Southern Group	70	Hugh Mellor 1985
Stockwell Green Congregational chapel ground			0.25	Holmes 1896
Sutherland Congregational chapel-ground, Walworth	c 1889		300 sq yds	Holmes 1896
Sutton Cemetery	1889	Sutton	19.5	Hugh Mellor 1985
Swedish burial-ground, Princes Square			0.5	Holmes 1896
Teddington Cemetery	1879	Richmond	9	Hugh Mellor 1985
Temple churchyard				Holmes 1896
Lower Tooting chapel ground	1688		260 sq yds	Holmes 1896
Tottenham Cemetery	1856	Haringey	56	Hugh Mellor 1985
Trinity Congregational chapel-ground, East India Dock Road			0.33	Holmes 1896
Tower Hamlets Cemetery	1841	GLC	33	Hugh Mellor 1985
Twickenham Cemetery	1868	Richmond	20	Hugh Mellor 1985
Union Chapel Graveyard, Sun St, Woolwich			0.33	Holmes 1896
Union Chapel ground, Streatham Hill			500 sq yds	Holmes 1896
*Unitarian (Baptist) chapel burial-ground, Church St, Greenwich			0.25	Holmes 1896
Unitarian Church new gravel pit chapel ground, Chatham Place,			0.75	Holmes 1896
Victoria Park Cemetery			11	Holmes 1896
Vincent Square, Westminster			8	Holmes 1896
Walthamstow Cemetery	1872	Waltham Forest	11	Hugh Mellor 1985
Wandsworth Cemetery	1878	Wandsworth	34	Hugh Mellor 1985
Well St burial-ground			0.75	Holmes 1896
Wellington St, Greenwich, additional ground	1884		0.75	Holmes 1896
West Hackney churchyard, Stoke Newington Road	1824		1.5	Holmes 1896
West Ham Cemetery	1857	Newham	20	Hugh Mellor 1985

Cemetery	Foundation	Owner	Acreage	Source
Westminster Abbey churchyard				Holmes 1896
Westminster Cemetery	1854	Westminster	23	Hugh Mellor 1985
Wesleyan Chapel burial-ground, Waterloo St, Hammersmith			(5,000yds)	Holmes 1896
Wesleyan chapel graveyard (Southwark), Long Lane, Bermondsey	1808		900 sq yds	Holmes 1896
Wesleyan chapel ground, City Road			0.5	Holmes 1896
Wesleyan chapel ground, Liverpool St, Kings Cross			225 sq yds	Holmes 1896
Wesleyan chapel ground, Stafford St, Peckham			336 sq yds	Holmes 1896
Wesleyan chapel yard, William St, Woolwich			0.25	Holmes 1896
*Brunswick Wesleyan chapel ground, Threecolt Lane			450 sq yds	Holmes 1896
Whitechapel Road (called the workhouse burial ground), additional ground	1796		0.5	Holmes 1896
Willesden Cemetery	1891	Brent	26	Hugh Mellor 1985
Whitfield Tabernacle burial-ground, Tottenham Court Road	1895		0.5	Holmes 1896
Wimbledon Cemetery	1896	Merton	28	Hugh Mellor 1985
Woodgrange Park Cemetery	1890	Tottenham Park Cemetery Company	28	Hugh Mellor 1985
Woolwich Cemetery	1856	Greenwich	32.5	Hugh Mellor 1985
Wycliffe burial-ground, Philpott St, Stepney	1831		0.75	Holmes 1896
York St chapel-ground, Walworth			700 sq yds	Holmes 1896

19 Advances and constraints in the study of human skeletal remains: a joint perspective

Lynne S Bell and Julia A Lee-Thorp

Introduction

In this chapter we describe advances made in the study of human skeletal remains at the submacroscopic level, particularly in the understanding of skeletal preservation and the survival of biogenic signals. We go on to describe recent improvements in sampling protocols and to discuss the current investigative constraints placed upon researchers. It is not intended to be an exhaustive account of analytical methods applicable to skeletal remains, rather it represents the areas of most interest to the authors. It is aimed at the nonspecialist in order to provide a flavour or overview of the potential and opportunities which arise from these approaches. Where possible useful review articles and papers have been indicated for readers to pursue their interests further, as have review articles of topics not sufficiently covered by this chapter. We contend that future work is very much dependent on the realization that much can be gained from such invasive analyses and that access to historically well-defined and well-excavated material is largely the only way, on the one hand, to thoroughly test and develop current methodologies, and, on the other, to extend our knowledge of past communities beyond the scope of macroscopic osteological reconstructions. It is therefore suggested that a national policy be established for the collective examination of human skeletal remains, where provisions and guidelines are given to facilitate the inclusion of invasive analyses.

Notional states of preservation

It is useful to introduce the discussion by defining what is meant by preservation. Preservation is usually defined by the level of investigation. Gross studies judge preservation at the macroscopic level. Hence, survival of soft tissues in either a partially hydrated or mummified form will be considered well preserved, while bodies which exhibit only remnants of such soft tissues will be considered relatively less well preserved. This relativism stands true for the macroscopic assessment of skeletal material where bone which is intact and maintains good macromorphology will be considered well preserved, while bone which has suffered post mortem surface damage or breakage will be considered poorly preserved. In the context of archaeological excavation it is known that within one site a range of gross preservation states may exist together and this was well illustrated at the Christ Church, Spitalfields excavation (Molleson & Cox 1993; Cox 1996a). However, the natural agencies which control this diversity of gross preservation are still poorly understood and gross preservation may not be freely translated to infer microstructural, isotopic, and DNA survival.

In order to discuss submacroscopic preservation states it is necessary to define the associated terminology. Over the past decade there has been a general consensus that much of what is observed in terms of post mortem change is caused by the interaction of the skeletonized body with the soil and the soil's microflora, eg bacteria and fungi (Kyle 1986; Pate & Hutton 1988; Grupe *et al* 1993). Diagenesis is a geochemical term used originally to refer to the physical, physicochemical, and biochemical events which occur during the formation of a sedimentary deposit and this term has been adopted and utilized by archaeologists and geochemists to describe post mortem alteration to skeletal tissues. Such diagenetic events are here understood to include:

> . . . compaction, dessication, deformation, corrosion, bleaching, oxidation reduction, crystal inversion, recrystallization, intercrystalline bonding, cementation, decementation, mineral growth and mineral replacement, particle accretion, flocculation, sediment mixing, boring, decomposition and synthesis of organic compounds . . . incorportation of biota . . . and excludes the effects of high temperature and pressure. (Lapedes 1978, 153)

Presumably this term was applied to archaeological material because faunal remains can constitute a greater or lesser percentage of a sedimentary deposit. However, the term has introduced an implicit assumption that decay processes which affect the integrity of the skeletal tissues are solely post-burial phenomena. This assumption can be seen in experimental protocols where diagenetic processes have been modelled on bone which has been initially defleshed, ie the experiment begins at the point of skeletonization (Wedl 1864; Marchiafava *et al* 1974; Hackett 1981; Ascenci & Silverstrini 1984; Yoshino *et al* 1991). Other workers simply state that soil bacteria, fungi, and humics are the agents by which bone has been changed (Piepenbrink 1986; Piepenbrink & Schutowski 1987). This approach makes sense only if one considers bone and teeth to be no more than depositional artefacts subject soley to the effects of soil cofactors, while being totally unaffected by the endogenous microflora of soft tissue decay. Recently, the notional primacy of soil-related co-factors has been questioned and an argument made for the redefinition of diagenesis, where preburial history is included: specifically immediate death history and soft tissue decay (see below).

Microstructural preservation

Much of what follows concerns bone, but the discussion is also relevant to the dental tissues, particularly dentine and cementum. Bone is a dynamic tissue in that it is constantly remodelling throughout life. Dentine and cementum are essentially accretionary tissues and do not turn over in the way that bone does, although under certain circumstances cementum does have a limited capacity to remodel. The only hard tissue which does not remodel after formation and maturation is enamel. Bone, in life, is a highly vascularized tissue and contains large numbers of encased single cells, known as osteocytes, which form an interconnecting cellular network throughout the bone. The bone itself is a two-phase system with both an organic and a mineral phase. During normal bone turnover, packets of bone will increase their local mineral density over time, by increasing the proportions of mineral relative to the decreasing organic phase. This process is known as bone maturation. After death the body usually skeletonizes, via decomposition processes, leaving an empty array of vascular and cellular spaces intracortically and this level of microstructural integrity or micromorphology would be described as well preserved (Fig 19.1).

In the previous century and well into the present, diagenetic change to skeletal microstructure was observed only as a curiosity. The original description and first important histological study was undertaken by Wedl as early as 1864, and described post mortem microstructural change (latterly known as diagenesis) in dentine and bone. The microstructural alteration in this case consisted of small boring canals which invaded the circumferential aspect of affected specimens without apparent regard to the microstructure they were penetrating. Wedl considered that the invading micro-organism was probably a fungus. The antiquity of this type of post mortem alteration was quickly established as being considerable, it being observed in fossil bone and teeth over 90 million years in age (Roux 1887; Schaffer 1895, 1889, 1890). Many histological studies followed which essentially described two additional basic morphological types of microstructural alteration thought to be caused by either the combined or separate actions of soil bacteria and fungi

on bone and dentine (Falin 1961; Marchiafava et al 1974; Piepenbrink 1986; Garland 1989; Yoshino et al 1991) and as 'pseudocaries' in enamel (Poole & Tratman 1978). The environmental contexts in which these diagenetically altered specimens were derived were all subsurface and included limestone caves, a range of terrestrial contexts, and marine deposition. One important point to note, however, is that microstructurally intact bone and teeth from spatially related skeletons could equally cohabit such environments. Hence, the depositional environment does not seem to be *the* defining factor in the occurrence and morphological type of microstructural diagenetic change. Additionally, given the variation of preservation from material of varying ages, many workers felt that time was an unimportant factor in the process of these changes since no apparent rate constant existed. This idea was supported by experimental data based on defleshed specimens which showed bacterial and fungal changes to microstructure occurring at any time between 15 days to 15 years, or not at all (Syssovena 1958; Marchiafava et al 1974; Hackett 1981; Yoshino et al 1991).

While this remarkable variation in microstructural preservation states was established as existing in bone and teeth, such changes were viewed as the microstructural embodiment of contamination for other analytical techniques, eg trace element, isotopic, and DNA analyses (Bell 1990; Bell et al

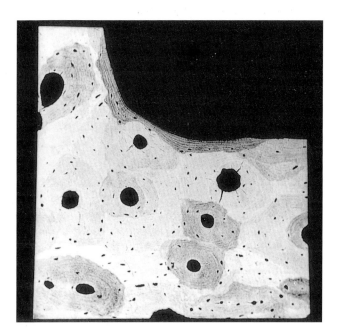

Figure 19.1 Transverse section of normal cortical type bone prepared from a cadaver. Younger osteonal systems can be seen as relatively less dense (darker), while older osteonal systems appear increased in density (whiter). A new packet of bone can be seen forming at the top of the micrograph appearing least dense (darkest). SEM/BSE image. Field width 950 microns (image provided by Hard Tissue Unit, University College London)

240

1991; Hagelberg *et al* 1991a; Grupe *et al* 1993). This is likely to be a true perception, since if bone microstructure has been altered by the chemical challenge of invading microflora, then both the mineral and organic phase of bone will have been changed. Hagelberg *et al* (1991a) observed that a relationship appeared to exist between microstructural integrity and DNA recovery, and suggested that microstructural preservation might be used as a bridge to predictively gauge DNA preservation. This observation was applied by Richards *et al* (1995) on a range of archaeological skeletal material and confirmed that microstructural preservation can be a good indicator of DNA survival.

Recent work by Bell and co-workers, however, has suggested that the variability in outcomes of change to skeletal material might be better explained if the diagenetic pathway is redefined and expanded to include immediate death history decay phenomena as well as the currently held post-depositional/skeletonization phenomena. A sensitive scanning electron microscopical method known as backscattered electron imaging (SEM/BSE) was used to provide information on skeletal microstucture and relative density. Hence, any diagenetic changes seen were at the level of microstructural alteration and changes in localized mineral density. Bell (1990) confirmed the observations made by previous authors, finding a common bacterial alteration in archaeological specimens from terrestrial contexts. These changes were documented in bone and teeth (Figs 19.2 & 19.3) and extended to identify a unique marine change in the crew of the *Mary Rose* wreck (Fig 19.4) (Bell *et al* 1991). This latter change was similar to the change documented by Arnaud *et al* (1978), but was seen to affect only those individuals who had been exposed

on the sea bed for a considerable period of time (Bell 1996). Specimens which had been buried within a few months were unaffected by such post mortem change and maintained good micromorphology.

While the *Mary Rose* changes are best considered to be post-skeletonization phenomena caused by

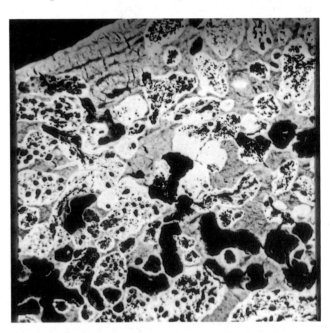

Figure 19.2   Transverse section of lateral midshaft archaeological tibia. A small region of the sub-periosteal lamellae has been preserved intact, as has a single osteocyte lacuna. Areas which appear very bright and very dark represent the typical bacterial post mortem / diagenetic change of increased and relatively decreased density to that of bone (seen as mid-grey). SEM / BSE image. Field width 145 microns

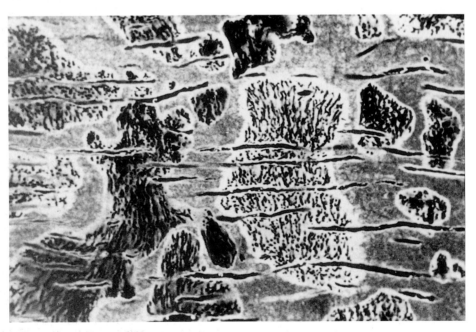

Figure 19.3   Bacterial diagenetic foci of increased and decreased density present in archaeological radicular dentine. Note the dentine tubules crossing laterally through these diagenetic foci. SEM / BSE image. Field width 170 microns

Figure 19.4   Typical Mary Rose and intertidal marine post mortem/diagenetic change. Tunnels can be seen penetrating the neck of the tooth and undermining the enamel for a short distance. These invasive tubules have many orientations within the dentine and cementum. The enamel always remained unaffected. SEM/BSE image. Field width 430 microns

endolithic microboring, the distribution of bacterial changes in buried specimens from terrestrial contexts cannot be similarly ascribed. The terrestrial changes were located around vascular pathways but the inner lamellae of Haversian canals within osteonal systems remained unaffected, yet the connecting canaliculae, which once contained the osteocyte filapodia, were enlarged with the cell spaces themselves (osteocyte lacunae) appearing to act as initial foci for these dramatic microstructural and density changes. This suggested that the geochemical model for diagenetic change to bone might not be mediated by soil bacteria, but might instead be a result of endogenous gut bacterial overgrowth directly into the portal vein onwards into the entire vasculature of the dead individual.

Bone (as previously stated) is a dynamic tissue and, being highly vascularized, would soon act as a receiving site for such a bacterial migration. It has

been demonstrated elsewhere that gut bacteria can rapidly transmigrate from the gut, via the vasculature, to all the major organs of the body within 24 hours post mortem (Dolan *et al* 1971; Kellerman *et al* 1976; Mainous *et al* 1991). With this in mind Bell *et al* (1996) examined a set of forensic specimens with known post mortem intervals (3 months to 83 years) and known environmental contexts in order to ascertain the speed of post mortem change and its relationship to the depositing environment, if any. This study brought forward the time of known onset of post mortem or diagenetic change for whole body decay in three morphological types of post mortem microstructural change and also established a new morphological type. The earliest change was documented three months post mortem seen in a tibial fragment recovered from a carnivore scat and may therefore represent gut demineralization via ingestion (Andrews 1990). The typical bacterial change was observed fifteen months post mortem and the marine change, previously observed in the *Mary Rose* material, was found to exist identically in a specimen retrieved from an intertidal zone after two years of post mortem immersion.

The results from this study indicate that the speed of microstructural change can be fast, being hypothesized to occur three days post mortem in temperate environments, and that the depositing environment can be retrospectively determined by the action of the invading microflora on the affected hard tissues. This is useful not only for the better understanding of site formation processes, but also to document the early death history of the body itself. If the role of the post mortem vasculature is central to the promotion of certain distributions of bacterial change, then any disruption at death to these pathways may indicate death type. This opens the way for the proper use of something which was considered little more than irksome contamination, providing valuable, and, until recently, unobtainable information on the immediate death history, potential death type, and the depositing environment.

Histopathology

Palaeopathological studies of skeletal tissues are usually based upon macroscopic and radiological appraisal. Macroscopic analysis of pathological conditions which affect the skeleton are founded upon studies of gross pathology undertaken at the turn of this century (Greig 1931) and have been comprehensively and successfully applied to archaeological populations (eg Ortner & Putschar 1984). However, relatively little use has been made of histology, the microstructural appearance of tissues, which constitutes a powerful diagnostic tool in modern medicine. This represents a serious shortfall at the level of successful diagnosis for archaeological series or for the presentation of important

242

individual case studies, since vital information is simply being left out of the interpretative equation. For example, studies by Bell & Jones (1991) and Aaron *et al* (1992) on Pagetic bone have demonstrated that microstructural interpretation can add a useful tier of diagnostic information, even when that skeletal material has undergone extensive diagenetic microstructural alteration, or when gross preservation is extremely poor (Fig 19.5).

Preservation and significance of stable light isotope signatures

Almost twenty years ago a seminal study by van der Merwe and Vogel showed that stable carbon isotope ratios ($^{13}C/^{12}C$) in archaeological bone collagen could chart precisely the expansion of maize agriculture in prehistoric woodland North America (van der Merwe & Vogel 1978). Since this ground-breaking study isotopic tools have become widely used for reconstructing past human diets. The toolkit has expanded to include nitrogen isotopes ($^{15}N/^{14}N$), and, rather more recently, carbon isotopes from the mineral phase of calcified tissues. These techniques use patterned shifts in the natural abundance ratios of $^{13}C/^{12}C$ and $^{15}N/^{14}N$, known as fractionation, and trace the pathways of these essential elements of life as they are cycled through biochemical pathways in foodwebs and into animal or human tissues.

The rationale for isotopes as tracers of human diets runs along these lines. Carbon and nitrogen isotope ratios in the bones, teeth, and other tissues of consumers, be they animal or human, reflect the isotopic composition of their foods. Carbon isotopes distinguish between several different plant sources at the base of the foodweb, on the basis of the degree of discrimination (or fractionation) against the heavier ^{13}C isotope occurring in various photosynthetic pathways. Thus terrestrial plants using the Calvin-Benson pathway (or C_3 because the first product is a molecule with 3 carbon atoms) have low or depleted $^{13}C/^{12}C$ ratios compared to marine phytoplankton, and differ even more markedly from tropical grasses (following the C_4 pathway) (Smith and Epstein 1971). Almost all plants in temperate regions of the world, including northern and central Europe and the winter rainfall Mediterranean region, follow the C_3 pathway, but within this general confine isotope values vary according to environmental variables such as temperature, moisture, ambient temperatures, and special conditions within closed forests (see van Klinken *et al* forthcoming). Nitrogen isotopes reflect mainly trophic level (the place of organisms in the foodweb), since there exists a consistent enrichment effect with each trophic level (Schoeninger & De Niro 1984), although this pattern is disrupted in arid regions (Ambrose 1991; Sealy *et al* 1987).

These kinds of differences are reflected in all the tissues of consumers since diet-tissue isotopic shifts are consistent and fairly well-known, although they vary for different tissues. Skeletal tissues, especially bone, have been most widely used for these purposes because of their survival in archaeological contexts. Many studies have used carbon and nitrogen values in the main organic phase of bone – Type 1 collagen – to determine, for instance, the amounts and kind of marine foods included in the diets of various groups or the amounts of cereal foods in the diets of agriculturalists. Some of these possibilities, drawn from a number of studies, are summarized in Figure 19.6, together with appropriate references.

The advantage of this kind of chemical 'tracer' approach in past human foodwebs is that quantitative information is obtained about what was actually eaten, rather than what was discarded, as is the case with habitation debris. Further important advantages inherent in isotopic approaches are that they reflect individual and group choices and can be used to compare dietary differences along with gender, age, and status divisions in past communities. For instance, Katzenberg *et al* (1993) showed that nitrogen isotopes are elevated in nursing infants, and a curve of isotope values against age (of infant and juvenile skeletons) may reveal information about age of weaning and other early dietary practices in prehistoric groups. These methods may also be used to test assumptions and models of human

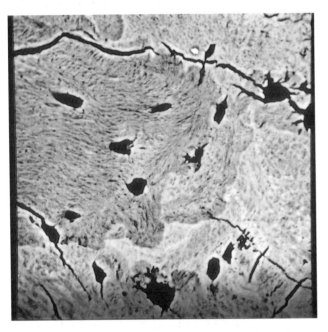

Figure 19.5 Archaeological Pagetic specimen in tranverse section exhibiting good pathological micromorphology. A hypermineralized reversal line can be clearly seen with the characteristic scalloped outline of osteoclastic resorption lacunae. The outline of these lacunae are irregular as is the arrangement and orientation of collagen, particularly in the less mature packet of bone seen centre field. The osteocyte lacunae are enlarged and irregular in their morphology. SEM/BSE image. Field width 185 microns

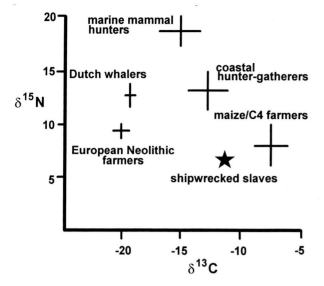

Figure 19.6 Typical stable carbon (13C/12C) and nitrogen (15N/14N) isotope ratios for bone collagen from prehistoric groups with a variety of subsistence patterns, adapted from Sealy et al *(1995). The data are drawn from a number of sources: Schoeninger et al (1983), Sealy & van der Merwe (1986), and Cox & Sealy (forthcoming). Isotopic data for each subsistence group is plotted as a mean and standard deviation, with the exception of the group of shipwrecked slaves. Although both were excavated in the South Western Cape Province, isotopic values for the slaves' bones are clearly different from the coastal hunter-gatherer skeletons. Isotope ratios are conventionally expressed in the d notation in parts per thousand (per mil), relative to the PDB international standard in the case of carbon, and atmospheric nitrogen standard in the case of nitrogen, as:*

$$\delta^{13}C\ (\permil) = (R_{sample} - R_{ref})/R_{ref} \times 1000,\ where\ R =$$

$$^{13}C/^{12}C\ and\ \delta^{15}N\ (\permil) = (R_{sample} - R_{ref})/R_{ref} \times 1000,$$

where $R = {}^{15}N/{}^{14}N$

behaviour, as Sealy and van der Merwe (1986) showed in their study based in the western Cape of South Africa, where isotopic comparison of coastal and inland skeletons indicated a residence pattern which which did not support a seasonal mobility model postulated on the basis of presence and absence of food debris and other indirect indicators (Parkington 1972). Recent studies have used the differences between formation and turnover time of various skeletal elements to document dietary and geographic shifts during an individual's life; this approach is particularly applicable for emigrants or immigrants (Sealy *et al* 1995; Cox & Sealy, forthcoming).

The two over-arching concerns in the application of isotopic tools to archaeological problems are, firstly, a sound understanding of the isotopic effects occurring along metabolic pathways, and, secondly, ways of determining whether the original, in vivo, biological isotopic signatures remain intact. In the first case we quite obviously need to understand the

tool in order to apply it properly, and the advances over the last 20 or so years document our gradual progress towards this end. We have now reached a point where we can begin to address rather more subtle questions about past human diets, such as gender differences, and in geographic areas where clear-cut isotopic differences between various foods are often lacking, such as in Europe. The second point highlights again one of the principal concerns of this paper, the issues of preservation and diagenesis.

Carbon isotopic composition of the diet is reflected in both the organic and mineral phases of bone, but, until fairly recently, most archaeological studies have concentrated on collagen as sample material. Historically this is partly because it is a fairly straightforward procedure to extract purified bone collagen from archaeological skeletons, as long as it has not been degraded by the post mortem action of bacteria (see above), or dissolved away by exposure to water and heat. Conversely, it was believed for a long time that the bone mineral, a biological apatite in which the isotopic dietary signal is held in carbonate ions substituted within the crystal structure, undergoes fairly rapid reorganization and exchange which renders it useless for isotopic dietary reconstructions (this history is reviewed in detail in Lee-Thorp 1989). Collagen can survive under optimal conditions for fairly long periods of time. Small amounts, barely enough for analysis, have been found in Neanderthals more than 40,000 years old (Bocherens *et al* 1991; Fizet *et al* 1995). Ambrose recently assessed the prospects for collagen survival and isotopic dietary reconstructions in Middle Palaeolithic material (ages up to ~70,000 years) from cool Central European locations as good, and those in warm Middle Eastern contexts as poor (Ambrose forthcoming). A great deal of work has gone into refining collagen purification methods and testing them, as these are concerns shared by isotopic researchers and radiocarbon chemists.

However, almost exclusive use of collagen as sample material threw up some puzzling aspects related to our (then) incomplete understanding of the isotopic relationship between body tissues and diets of various kinds. Subsequent work has shown that some earlier assumptions were too simplistic. The results of empirical field observations (Krueger & Sullivan 1984; Lee-Thorp *et al* 1989) and, more latterly, laboratory controlled dietary experiments (Ambrose & Norr 1993; Tiezsen & Fagre 1993), has clarified the isotopic relationships between macronutrient components of the diet and the two phases of bone. It appears that collagen isotope values preferentially reflect protein components, whereas apatite values reflect the entire, integrated diet. For example, Sealy and van der Merwe (1986) found that some individuals buried at coastal locations appeared to have – somewhat implausibly – a diet composed of 100% marine food. In this case, collagen isotope values were simply reflecting the dominant high protein component of the diet, and the contribution of other energy foods became apparent when the mineral phase was analysed (Lee-Thorp *et al* 1989). Studies are now beginning to use isotope values of both phases, in tandem, to better understand the complexities of past human diets.

Similarly, preservation of original isotopic signatures in the mineral phase is now better understood, and the picture is certainly not as bleak as it seemed earlier. Assumptions that apatite isotopic signatures were likely to be completely obscured by diagenesis were based largely on evidence which showed that mineral, especially in bone, can undergo fairly rapid increases in crystallinity after death; this process is usually attributed to recrystallization but it can also follow post mortem crystal maturation. Some early work using isotopic comparisons of collagen and apatite from the same individuals seemed to support the diagenesis model (Schoeninger & DeNiro 1982), *contra* earlier work by Sullivan and Krueger (1981), who had shown that predictable isotopic values were obtained when samples were subjected to decontamination procedures designed to eliminate added carbonates. A closer examination of these two apparently conflicting studies revealed several shortcomings and likely experimental artefacts in the method employed by Schoeninger and DeNiro (1982) which account pretty well for the differences (see Lee-Thorp 1989, forthcoming). Numbers of studies have demonstrated that for animals with known diets, expected carbon isotopic values are maintained in the mineral phase for very long periods indeed (Lee-Thorp & van der Merwe 1987; Lee-Thorp forthcoming), and preservation is especially good for enamel. Therefore it follows that in spite of changes in crystallinity, on the whole, original isotopic composition is often maintained in bone apatite and almost always in enamel. The impact of the bacterially-driven post mortem microstructural change on isotope values is unknown and is currently being investigated.

In mono-isotopic environments such as Europe (where plants are all C_3), the dual approach can be used as a trophic indicator, since the isotopic difference between collagen and apatite, usually called Delta (Δ) is diminished in high protein diets. Δ is normally about 7–8% for herbivorous diets, and about 4% for carnivorous diets. Together with nitrogen isotope ratios as trophic indicators, this kind of approach could be helpful in determining relative amounts of animal- or vegetable/cereal-based foods in the diet, and hence clarifying aspects of past subsistence, eg the importance of animal husbandry versus horticulture. Indeed, Ambrose, in reviewing the prospects for obtaining information about Neanderthal and Upper Palaeolithic human diets from isotopic analyses of bone and tooth enamel, has stressed that a dual approach using collagen and apatite analyses is essential in mono-isotopic environments (Ambrose forthcoming). Such applications would certainly extend the relevance of isotopic dietary tools in European archaeological contexts, which previously have been limited to questions about the presence or amounts of marine food in prehistoric diets (eg Mays 1997).

Future research must continue to develop our understanding of the preservational status of isotopic signatures in the organic and mineral phases of the skeletal tissues in a variety of contexts. One way to achieve this might be to carefully chart the course of crystallographic, mineral, and isotopic changes occurring after death and burial, using new Fourier Transform infra-red techniques commonly used in calcified tissue research, to probe the reorganization of ions within the crystal structure. Some progress has been made, but this kind of interdisciplinary work is in its infancy and has a long way to go. It seems, however, that a healthy 'pushme-pullyou' dynamic has been set up between isotopic dietary reconstructions and studies of post mortem changes occurring at the crystal or protein levels in calcified tissues, and that this will lead to advances in both areas.

DNA

DNA survives! This discovery has been perhaps one of the most exciting developments in archaeology since Libby was awarded the Nobel Prize in 1960 for development of the C-14 dating method.

The retrieval of DNA from bone was first established as possible when Hagelberg and co-workers, using the polymerase chain reaction (PCR) method, successfully amplified mitochondrial (mt) DNA from human material dated to about 300–500 years BP (Hagelberg *et al* 1989). Prior to this study it was considered impossible to obtain DNA from bone (Iscan 1988) and DNA had only been successfully retrieved from the skin of the extinct Quagga (Higuchi *et al* 1984), the skin and liver of an Egyptian mummy (Paabo 1985), 7000 year old brain tissue (Paabo *et al* 1988), and the skin of the extinct marsupial wolf (Thomas *et al* 1989). In 1991 Hagelberg and co-workers reported successful amplification of bone mtDNA from a 15 year old Caucasian murder victim (buried in a carpet for 8 years), which was subsequently co-matched to the mtDNA of the victim's immediate family in order to confirm identity (Hagelberg *et al* 1991b). The presentation of this new type of evidence was not only crucial to the eventual conviction of the murderer, but also firmly established the applicability of the PCR method to extract and amplify DNA from skeletal material, be it forensic or archaeological.

Since then further studies have successfully isolated mtDNA from skeletal material including the identification of Romanov family members from a mass grave site (Gill *et al* 1994), the establishment of the potential geographical and racial origins of the Pacific islanders (Hagelberg & Clegg 1993), and the retrieval of DNA from the American Civil War and Vietnam War soldiers (Fisher *et al* 1993;

Holland *et al* 1993). An extensive study of archaeological skeletal material from a 2000 year old Japanese double cemetery site revealed both different and shared maternal lineages within and between the two cemeteries (Shinoda & Kunisada 1994). Mitochondrial DNA was also successfully recovered from the 5000 year old mummified corpse of the Tyrolean Ice Man (Handt *et al* 1994), a staggering example of preservation under one of the most destructive natural agencies known to the planet. Other recent successes include the identification of ancient DNA belonging to the bacillus *Mycobacterium tuberculosis* (TB) in archaeological bones which exhibited gross osteological evidence of TB (Baren *et al* 1996; Taylor *et al* 1996). The findings of these two studies paves the way for the identification of soft tissue-related infections currently undetectable in the macroscopic analysis of skeletal material. Finally, work by Loreille *et al* (1997) managed to differentiate sheep from goat in Neolithic skeletal material on the basis of the biological specificity of the recovered mtDNA. Again, this study pushes out the boundaries of osteological research beyond the scope of macroscopic analysis, where it has been difficult and often impossible to differentiate between the skeletal remains of sheep and goat.

The longevity of DNA into the archaeological and fossil record has been the source of considerable controversy. Once it was established that DNA could survive in archaeological soft tissue and bone, other workers began reporting the successful recovery of DNA from vastly older specimens. Goldenberg *et al* (1991) recovered chloroplast DNA from a 17 million year old magnolia leaf, while Cano *et al* (1993) isolated and amplified DNA from an amber entombed weevil dating back to 120–135 million years! Even more staggering was the identification and subsequent regeneration of 25–40 million year old amber-entombed bacterial spores (Cano & Borucki 1995). However, recent work by Austin *et al* (1997) has cast doubt on the longevity of DNA and particularly the repeatability of the amber-entombed DNA results (*ibid*). In extensive studies of insects trapped in Oligocene Dominican amber and Quaternary East African copal they failed to find any credible evidence of DNA survival and suggested that the work of Cano and co-workers was an experimental artefact caused by contamination. Certainly, contamination is an extremely difficult and complex aspect of research into ancient DNA, largely because of the extreme sensitivity of the PCR method itself combined with the unpredictable preservation of ancient DNA and the presence of extraneous DNA from human handling, bacterial DNA, airborne DNA, memory, and carryover effects from the experimental apparatus and reagents (for a full discussion of this aspect see Francalacci, 1995). In Sykes's article 'Lights turn red on amber' (1997) the author wonders whether Austin and co-workers might be considered 'spoilsports', since due to their recent work with amber, the collective dream of literally recreating our past, embodied in the film *Jurassic Park*, appears to have stalled. However, for archaeological material, being considerably younger, the lights still remain promisingly green.

The survival of noncollagenous proteins, lipids and trace elements

This section is intended to identify briefly other investigative areas of research which are outside of the scope of this chapter and suggests further reading as a stepping-off point for the interested reader.

The most abundant protein in bone is collagen, but other smaller noncollagenous proteins (NCPs) reside in or are associated with the organic phase of bone, and some of these survive into the archaeological and fossil record (for further reading see Eglinton & Logan 1991; Childs & Pollard 1992; Tuross 1993). In the living skeleton lipids are found predominantly within the marrow cavity and in the vascular pathways of bone (Haversian canals). A smaller fraction can be recovered from demineralized bone and these too are known to survive into the archaeological record (see Eglinton & Logan 1991; Evershed *et al* 1995), and have been analysed isotopically to provide alternative information about diet. Trace element studies of the skeletal tissues represent another aspect of dietary investigation and a considerable literature exists representing many years of archaeologically based research. Good introductory papers are Sillen (1989), Sillen *et al* (1989), and Sandford (1992).

Research constraints

All the methods outlined above require invasive sectioning or sampling of skeletal material. The amounts are fairly small, having improved significantly over the past decade. Using modern equipment isotopic samples require approximately 2–4mgs for mineral and even less for collagen analyses, while DNA samples require single or multiple samples of 0.5gms. Sections for microscopy usually require a partial or complete, albeit thin, section which may bisect a bone or tooth. Some sampling methods require extremely tiny amounts and can be removed so that they are undetectable to the naked eye. Apart from microscopic sectioning, where the section can be stored or archived, all other samples are consumed in order to undertake these analyses. Such sampling is negatively referred to as 'destructive sampling' and is often resisted by curators and osteoarchaeologists.

Resistance to invasive sampling centres, fairly obviously, around the fact that the gross morphological appearance of the bone or tooth will be damaged and that biological information will be lost. This view is prevalent and presents two underlying themes. One is the entrenched supremacy of macroscopic analysis over all other methods, and the second is the often uncritical conservation of human skeletal material. These two themes are perfectly reflected in an article by DeGusta and White (1996), where the need to conserve skeletal material is balanced against the need to sample invasively. Much of what is suggested is heavily orientated towards conservation of the skeletal material, even suggesting unprovenanced material as the best starting point for invasive sampling since it has no intrinsic value to the gross osteologist. Further, an assumption is made that all skeletal collections are finite resources and therefore inherently rare. Much of this article is heavily inflenced by the current legal restraints placed upon excavation in the New World and the concomitant return of skeletal collections to historically disenfranchised peoples, otherwise known as the 'reburial issue' (Ubelaker & Grant 1989). In the context of archaeology in the United Kingdom and many European countries this article is, for the most part, inappropriate.

At the risk of sounding flippant, in Britain we are frankly knee-deep in human skeletal material. Based on statistics held by English Heritage, since the mid 70s in England alone skeletal excavations have produced over 54,000 skeletons and 11,000 cremations (S Mays, pers comm). Figures are not available for Scotland and Wales, but will significantly increase the previous statistic. These figures do not include the great number of crypt clearances which have been and are currently being undertaken by nonarchaeological agencies (see Cox 1996b). Clearly in Britain, aside from our unique skeletal collections such as the skeletal material recovered from the *Mary Rose* wreck (Rule 1983), human skeletal material is plentiful and will continue to be so, so long as the need for urban space increases (see Reeve, this volume). The concerns and recommendations of DeGusta and White (1996), while applicable to our rare collections, are hard to support unless the needs of the gross morphologist continue to outweigh the needs of the new

methodologies. If finite archaeological resources and research monies from national funding agencies are to be expended on human skeletal remains, then surely there should be explicit support for all avenues of research and that the best-preserved well-documented material be made available to all parties. Otherwise one is forced to ask the question, albeit cynically, why are we bothering to excavate skeletons at all? Clearly, curators are in a very difficult position trying to satisfy the needs of the many and might be better aided in their task by the establishment of a national protocol for the examination of archaeological human skeletal remains. A commendable first step towards the coherent development and management of human skeletal material has recently been published as a policy document by Historic Scotland (1997), where the value of approaches using invasive techniques is recognised and provision made for these procedures as a stated objective.

Future priorities

The submacroscopic methods outlined in this paper provide biological and taphonomic information which considerably extend the scope of macroscopic osteological reconstruction. The sampling requirements for these methods are modest, and some of them may be archived for reappraisal. We have tried to provide an idea of the scope and promise of these relatively new methods and stressed the need for ongoing development on well-documented and well-preserved material. Given the abundance of archaeological human skeletal material in the United Kingdom it should be possible to meet the needs of researchers and curators alike. The best way to do this might be to agree national guidelines as a matter of policy for the collective examination of archaeological human skeletal remains.

20 The excavation and study of human skeletal remains: a view from the floor *Bill White*

O lovely appearance of Death
What sight upon earth is so fair?
Not all the gay pageants that breathe
Can with a dead body compare.

On Seeing a Corpse by Charles Wesley (1707–88)

Bizarre though it may appear to most of us today, Wesley's close encounter with the freshly dead was, for him, a cause for rejoicing. The expectation was that the soul that until recently had animated that corpse had gone now to its reward in Heaven. Thus, such an occasion was a happy one although, one suspects, tinged a little with envy. Charles Wesley's response was a highly emotional one but not for him the risk of experiencing 'post-traumatic stress disorder' (of which more later, and Thompson, this volume).

Few among Wesley's contemporaries would have shared his extreme view but what they had in common with him was an easy familiarity with death. The point has been made frequently that the general population in Britain today lacks the routine acquaintance with the dead familiar to their forebears. Individual bereavements are inevitable but, as the result of advances in clinical medicine, the acquisition of a safe water supply, immunization, the growth in the pharmaceutical industry, and the scaling-down of warfare in Europe at the end of this century, the modern population as a whole does not confront death on a daily basis. Mercifully, death has ceased to be an ever-present fact of life and few people today have the regular experience of viewing dead friends and relatives. This otherwise welcome retreat from the need to face death in daily life brings in its wake new taboos (see Harding [2], this volume). Death is a subject generally shunned and the ethical and actual constraints on dealing directly with the dead on any basis are greater now than ever before.

The presumption in common law as well as in the apprehension of the public is that the buried dead ought not to be disturbed. At first sight this may seem at odds with the aims of archaeology, which include the excavation of the dead themselves along with the cultural materials that they generated. The irony is, of course, that it is chiefly the practice of the deliberate burial of the dead that has allowed their survival for long enough to be excavated and studied. Early societies, like some contemporary ones, that had no scrupulously observed burial rite but disposed of their dead by dereliction or exposure to scavengers have left only randomly-preserved remains, and our knowledge of their culture is all the poorer thereby. Any form of deliberate interment affords a degree of protection against predation, erosion, or other deleterious taphonomic processes and the potential for study is consequently at least partly intact.

In archaeology, too, the presumption may often be against excavation. It is argued that techniques to be developed in the future may be capable of extracting greater amounts of information from the same site than present methods of excavation and analysis afford (a view that English Heritage frequently takes and one supported by PPG16, DoE 1990). A dichotomy is involved here, however. How will these superior procedures be devised and developed if the opportunity for excavation is denied? There are limits to what can be achieved by computer modelling or in vitro experimentation and all techniques need to be tried and tested in the field. This is hardly to say that in the prevailing financial climate there is much scope for 'blue-sky' research in archaeology. In the area with which we are dealing, burial archaeology, such opportunities as do arise follow in the wake of property development or vault or cemetery clearance desired by the Church or secular owners for their own purposes. Here the internal market may raise its head in the invitation of tenders for the accomplishment of the said clearance. What was recognised at the *Grave Concerns* conference is that archaeologists do not often represent the driving force in the disturbance of graves of recent centuries.

Since it is the Christian church that is often responsible for initiating the clearance of vaults and certain cemeteries it is worth exploring the attitude of the Church over the centuries toward the disturbance of the burials in its care. In summary it would seem to be inconsistent, even contradictory, from the time of its founder. During the selection of the Disciples Jesus Christ remarked: 'Let the dead bury their dead', implying that dereliction was an acceptable practice (St Matthew; 8:22). Burials were invoked only for the more spectacular miracles: the literal resurrection of the dead bodies of Lazarus and Christ Himself. Thirty years ago Francis Celoria performed a survey of opinion toward disturbing and studying the Christian interred (Celoria 1966). He found that the attitude of the Church itself was very relaxed (interference in his own research on the burial of Lady Anne Mowbray came from a different quarter – the House of Lords – which is another story!). During the Middle Ages the Roman Catholic Church seems to have had no compunction about disturbing earlier burials when making new ones (Stapleton 1976). Land could be made available again by relegating a collection of skulls and those long bones deemed representative of the deceased to the charnel house, while the smaller bones were neglected and escaped reburial (op cit, 73). The scatter of disturbed bone can also be discerned in manuscript illuminations depicting grave-digging, such as in *Books of Hours* (Binski 1996). After the Norman Conquest the parish might clear away Christian Saxon inhumations in order to create space for new interments (Daniell 1997, 145–6). Similarly, in cemetery excavations there is frequent evidence of the complex inter-cutting of graves, no apparent attempt being made to avoid previous interments (*ibid*). By contrast considerable care could be exercised in the clearance of burials. A recent excavation in the City of London involved the site of St Katherine Coleman, one of the churches destroyed in the Great Fire. Although the area excavated included part of the original cemetery, revealing gravecuts both from the original burials and the exhumations, very few human bones were encountered. It appears that after the church was finally demolished around 1730 AD the original inhumations were carefully lifted for reburial elsewhere, only a few bones of the extremities of some skeletons going unnoticed (D Bluer, MoLAS, pers comm). By contrast, when London Bridge was opened in 1831 its medieval forerunner was demolished and the bones of those interred in its chapels were cast unceremoniously into the Thames (Hearsey 1961, 77).

The curious custom of bodily division and 'offal burial' was known among the peerage. Organs removed from the body after death, whether or not in pursuance of embalming, would be buried in locations separate from the body itself. While it was understandable that several different religious establishments might wish to share in the reflected glory of retaining the visceral organs of the distinguished deceased the Church did not always approve (Daniell 1997, 89, 92). What, however, were the implications of division of the body with regard to the hoped-for resurrection? However well-preserved Horatio Nelson's body was as the result of the legendary temporary steeping in brandy or of the deliberate embalming for the rare privilege of a commoner's State Funeral (Litten, this volume) he still lacked an eye and an arm. Similarly, an 80-year old amputee general interred at St Barnabas was unable to boast the full complement (Black & Scheuer unpublished). Conversely, amputated limbs might be accorded separate burial during the life of the donor (Celoria 1966). Richardson (1988) and others have stressed that those whose skeletons we study expected to lie in the ground forever. Some degree of decay was expected but how does this accord with demands for the literal resurrection of the body on Judgement Day? What was the

minimum percentage of the original bodily inventory required by the Christian Church in order to comply with the purposes of full physical resurrection? Reeve (this volume) has reiterated that although cremation as a means of disposal of the dead has a venerable history (and/or prehistory) it was resisted in this country by the established Church until late in the 19th century. Moreover, it did not become an acceptable rite within some parts of the Roman Catholic church until the 1960s (Jupp 1990). How are parishioners to keep pace with the theological vagaries of the church that happens to have the franchise over place of burial at the time during which they live and die?

It is an interesting coincidence that the period of burial covered by these proceedings is precisely that during which the tombs of English monarchs were prised open for inspection, although Henry VI had to wait until the present century (St John Hope 1911). During our period scientific examination was not the justification. Rarely was an attempt made to disguise the motive of idle or morbid curiosity. With the opening of the tomb of Edward I in Westminster Abbey in 1774 the spectators managed to strike lucky in that the body of the king was found in a state of almost complete preservation almost 500 years after his interment (Ayloffe 1774). Having satisfied their curiosity the researchers piously poured molten pitch into the king's coffin so that no future investigators might repeat their experience (Daniell 1997, 172). The only information that the privileged group bequeathed to those that followed after (at best to examine the monarch's now skeletonized form), is that the instruction by *Malleus scottorum* to boil up his bones, in order that in death he could lead further campaigns against the Scots, had been over-ridden and that instead the monks of Burgh-on-the-Sands had preserved his body perfectly. Often in the exhumation of the lower ranks there was no such pretence to a respectful and dignified examination. In the *Gentleman's Magazine* of April 1789 one T White, Esq mentions his presence at the opening of an anonymous 14th century tomb, wherein:

> . . . we were presented with a view of the body, laying in a liquor or pickle, somewhat resembling mushroom catchup but of a paler complexion and somewhat thicker consistence . . . I tasted it and found it to be aromatic, tho' not very pungent, partaking of the taste of catchup and of the pickle of Spanish olives. The body was totally perfect, no part appearing decayed but the throat and part of one arm. The flesh everywhere, except on the face and throat, appeared exceedingly white and firm, the face was of a dark colour, approaching black, the throat which was much lacerated was of the same colour [sic] (White 1789, 337–8).

The 'pickle' in question was not just body liquor but a marinade, resulting from the embalming fluids originally employed. It is relevant that an

18th century recipe for 'mushroom catchup' reveals not only mushrooms but vinegar (which would have provided an acidic medium which some putrefactive organisms would not have survived) and a variety of aromatic spices (each with its own bacteriostatic properties and used for that reason in embalming practice), though whether the addition of 'Spanish olives' would have made a contribution to the excellent preservation of the corpse observed is a matter for conjecture. This account literally may appear to be in poor taste but actually it becomes worse. After describing the close examination of the clothing of the deceased White mentions that 'Whether the legs were crossed or not must forever remain a doubt . . . for one of the gentlemen pushing a walking stick rather briskly from the knees to the ancles [sic], the left foot separated from the leg . . .' (*ibid*). Readers were not necessarily of such arrogance or strong stomach. An anonymous vicar wrote to deprecate White's 'unmanly, indecent and impious' behaviour and promised him that should White predecease him he would pursue him into the grave so as to poke at him with his own walking stick! ('Xenos', 1789, 617–8).

As we have seen, attitudes towards the disturbance, examination, and handling of the dead span a broad spectrum of morality and behaviour. Present-day encounters with the dead, especially where soft-tissue preservation is concerned, may give rise to crises of conscience, notable in presentations and discussions throughout the *Grave Concerns* conference as a whole, over laying hands upon the recent or ancient dead (Fig 20.1). Here one ventures to suggest that the development of an appropriate professional attitude toward the material presented might be useful. Most of us have encountered soft-tissue preservation upon our first acquaintance with Egyptian mummies, whether naturally or artificially preserved. Need we all be as sanguine and strong-stomached as those jaded investigators two hundred years ago? How far need we re-think our own attitude toward a familiarity with the remains of the ancient dead or with those who have died within living memory? Here it is necessary to consider those professions that may have to deal with the contemporary dying and the dead.

The issue raised is not restricted to those who deal with post-medieval remains. Many professional people experience an analogous moral and emotional dilemma in going about their working lives. All those involved in healthcare who are in direct contact with the sick may feel the need to suspend their emotional involvement to a greater or lesser extent to do their job effectively. Those performing autopsies similarly have to remain detached. Their professional body and the standard texts that apply make it clear that they should

Figure 20.1 Body with soft tissue preservation, Islington Green, London EC1 (photo: Museum of London Archaeology Service)

regard themselves as dealing with human patients who happen not to be able to make a vocal response to their investigators and who need to be treated with the maximum consideration and dignity possible under the circumstances. Here we might consider that these patients likewise have not given their permission for this perhaps unseemly handling but that the State itself has presumed to override their wishes (Fig 20.2). Forensic pathologists and archaeologists have to deal with the recently dead often under the most distressing of circumstances (Cox 1995b). Their efforts cannot eradicate the personal tragedies involved but a detached attitude helps them to provide results that serve the bereaved and society as a whole. At a greater remove from the corpse, are historians to be considered immune from an emotional response to a written account of a personal tragedy or of a wider catastrophe? The compassionate tone of Richardson's *Death, Dissection and the Destitute* (1988) would suggest that some at least are not. What all these professional researchers have in common is that they are concerned with humanity. In facing the dead all react with the maximum care, respect,

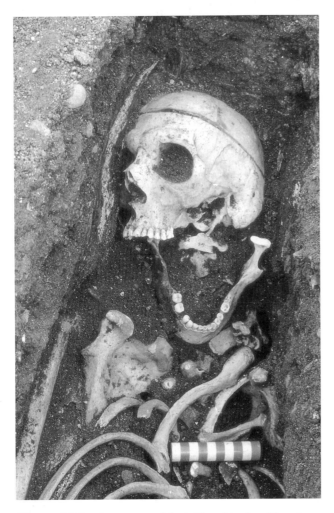

Figure 20.2   Autopsy subject, Farringdon Street, London EC4 (photo: Museum of London Archaeology Service)

and dignity possible under the circumstances; so must we all.

Richardson (op cit) is disturbed by what she describes as the 'commodification' of the dead. The difficulty lies in the absence of a proper legal standing. Certainly the notion of 'ownership' over the dead is an ethical problem, endlessly debated (Jones and Harris 1997). In the common law of England the dead cannot be 'owned' although the law comes into play when human remains are to be disturbed or removed. In Australia and the United States of America there have been recent changes in the law of ownership of excavated human remains as a sop to accusations of continuing colonial oppression. The North American Graves Protection Act of 1990 makes the assumption that any human bones unearthed are of ancestors of the local native American nation that now occupy the region in which the remains are found. The tribal administrators thus have the right of ownership and disposal of the excavated remains and this frequently results in reburial rather than scientific study. Inevitably this can lead to abuse such as the inappropriate reburial in tribal cemeteries of European skeletons disinterred in the area (White 1997). Human remains excavated in Winchester and thought to be Jewish were reburied in a Jewish cemetery before further investigation shed doubt upon their Jewish identity (Cox 1996b). Something similarly inappropriate may be involved when disinterred English skeletons are finally cremated, presumably in contravention of the wishes of the deceased, as Richardson has pointed out (1988; see also Cox 1996b).

The arguments for the excavation and study of human skeletal remains have been put perhaps most cogently and with greatest sensitivity by Paul Bahn (Bahn 1984 and 1986; Renfrew & Bahn 1996, 403–40). As well as adding to the general sum of human knowledge by the reconstruction of past lives there is also a utilitarian aspect of archaeological investigations of human burials. Specific problems can be addressed providing insight into population characteristics (sex ratio, mean age at death, physique), diet, health, genetic relationships and micro-evolution. There is a spin-off in the useful contribution such studies may make to other fields such as medicine and forensic science. The latter acknowledges the importance of studies on human skeletal remains in its desire to identify the deceased, simultaneously perhaps satisfying one family by ending uncertainty and permitting the grieving process to commence while giving another family fresh hope that a missing member may yet emerge alive. In palaeopathology the dead may genuinely teach the living. The study of disease in skeletons or bodies with preserved soft tissue can refine the knowledge of infection and other pathological processes. A greater understanding of how disease organisms have developed or mutated in the past may help in the devising of strategies to deal with new infections as they emerge. It would

Figure 20.3   Crypt excavation, Farringdon Street, London EC4 (photo: Museum of London Archaeology Service)

be advantageous not to be taken by surprise by the emergence of Lassa fever or the HIV or Ebola viruses. Young (this volume) provides us with a fascinating account of the virulence of smallpox in the recent past with its extinction in our lifetime. However, even here the contemporary outbreak of its close relative, Monkey Pox, infecting human populations in Africa renders it premature to consider destroying the final samples of smallpox virus held in laboratories in Russia and the United States of America (Stuttaford 1997).

Finally, the multi-disciplinary investigation at Christ Church, Spitalfields represents the pinnacle of what can be achieved through the archaeology of a post-medieval site (Reeve & Adams 1993; Molleson & Cox 1993). Such sites continue to be excavated and to extend the database of comparative material (eg Boyle and Keevil, this volume; Black & Scheuer unpublished; Conheeney & Miles forthcoming) (Fig 20.3). While some abuses and cases of disrespect for the dead may occur when burial

grounds are cleared (though not at the hands of archaeologists) the theft of human bones 'for occult purposes' (alleged at the *Grave Concerns* conference) has the ring of urban legend. Curiously, theft of body parts may be for the sake of art, as alleged in the on-going prosecution of the sculptor Anthony Noel-Kelly, under the 1984 Anatomy Act (*Independent* 1997). At least one outer-London site where a post-medieval burial ground was commercially cleared had only an archaeological watching brief, which did not allow the collection of the human remains present. From this some 1,500 coffin plates were recovered, tantalizingly revealing the potential for demography and methodological development that had been lost. Field archaeologists are neither the lackeys of the developers nor the new grave-robbers. When archaeologists are called onto a site it is always in the wake of a decision to disturb and remove burials. Their attentions then ensure that safe and respectful hands are available to complete the task.

Postscript

It is clear from the nature and extent of the contributions to this volume that the study of death and burial in post-medieval England is diverse in both scope and the number and range of disciplines involved. As areas of research some aspects have received good coverage in certain respects but others are either in their infancy or entirely neglected. Nevertheless, it is clear that the enormous potential of such research is at last beginning to be realized.

As stated in the papers of Julian Litten, Robert Janaway, and Vanessa Harding there is thus far a strong regional bias in work undertaken with emphasis on the south-east and London. There is also a dereliction of research into most aspects of nonconformity, with only the Quakers receiving much academic attention. As Vanessa Harding noted, studies of gender and death are almost entirely neglected. The challenge to scholars of all disciplines is enormous, matching the potential of available historical and archaeological material and data.

Many papers raise the spectrum of the ethics of disturbing the more recent dead, the effects of such work on archaeologists and historians, and the misguided notion of the right of the deceased to rest in peace forever. This issue is of fundamental importance to the progression of post-medieval funerary archaeology and it is imperative that English archaeology follows the lead of Historic Scotland (1997) and produces a policy concerned with the excavation and analysis of human remains. This subject deserves consideration in its own right rather than run the risk of being blighted and predetermined by changes in legislation as have affected the right of archaeologists to explore mortuary contexts in other countries. These have invariably arisen out of political and moral issues and grievances which have, in part, been diverted by channelling their potency into archaeology, often allowing the more fundamental issues to continue relatively unabated. It is imperative that this situation is pre-empted by positive action by those defining archaeological policy in consultation with field archaeologists and archaeological scientists. If those responsible for defining such policy in England fail to respond to this urgent need they must accept the fact that English archaeologists will produce their own policies which will be adopted by majority agreement of those that care and those that undertake such work.

Loss and change?

As this text was written, the editor was reflecting upon the events of a week which has seen the death of Diana, Princess of Wales. This national loss has seen Britain grieve and mourn in a more public and open manner than has been experienced this century. Many contributors to this volume have noted British taboos concerning death, our inability to see it other than in terms of scientific failure, and our lack of widely adopted modes of expressing public and private grief.

The loss to the nation of the Princess has reminded us of the immense and far-reaching value of public displays of humanity, grief and compassion. It would be an ironic coincidence if her death gives back to the British public an ability to mourn our dead and deal with death in a healthier manner than that which has recently prevailed. For the editor, it seems appropriate to further reflect that the only occasion during which her life overlapped with that of the Princess was when a scheme was proposed to excavate the crypt of a North London church in order to create a centre for homeless youngsters in the Kings Cross area. As it happens, the dead still rest in peace beneath that church and the centre was realised elsewhere.

Margaret Cox
September 1997

Bibliography

(Place of publication is London unless otherwise indicated)

Primary Sources

Act for Burial in Woollen 1666 (18 &19 Car II c4)
Act for Burial in Woollen 1680 (32 Car II c1)
Murder Act of 1752 (25 Geo II c37)
Act for Burial in Woollen 1814 (54 Geo III c78)
Suicide Act 1823 (4 Geo IV c52)
Anatomy Act 1832 (75 Will IV c75)
City of London Sewers Act 1848 (11 & 12 Vict c 163)
Metropolitan Interments Act 1850 (13 & 14 Vict c 52)
Sewers Act 1851 (14 & 15 Vict c 91)
Burial Act of 1852 (15 & 16 Vict c 85)
Disused Burial Act 1884 (47 + 48 Vict c 7) Burial Act 1857 / (20 + 21 Vict c 81)
Cremation Act 1902 (2 Edw 7 c 8)
Cremation Act 1952 (15 & 16 Geo 6 + Eliz 2 c 31)
Annual Reports of the Westgate Hill Cemetery Company, dates various, Local History Library, Newcastle Central Library.
Archives of London and Middlesex (Friends House Library): Westminster Monthly Meeting 11 b 7
Articles of Agreement of the Rusholme Road Cemetery Company, 1820, MS, Manchester
Archive Office
Bristol Record Office P/St Aug/R/6
Bristol Record Office P/St Aug/R/2(c)
Bristol Record Office P/B/R/1 [d]
Bristol Record Office P/B/R/4 [a]
British Museum, Trade card of William Boyce, c 1680, BM Negative Number 229190
British Museum, Trade card of Robert Green, 1752, BM Number 37021–2
British Museum, Trade card of Eleazor Malory, Joiner, c 1720
Guildhall Library, London, ledgers of Richard Carpenter, 1746–7
GL MS 66, f 13v
GL MS 818/1, f 27v
GL MS 9051/8, f 339
GL MS 9171/31, f 28
GL MS 7815
GL MS 9531/13, pt 2, f. 378
GL MS 4438, not foliated: entries for 2 & 9 September 1625, 7 November 1625
GL MS 9171/15, f 237
GL MS 9531/13, ff 90v–91
K.A.O. PRS. W 8.108
Litten Collection, Banting ledgers
MSS Portfolio 36/19 (1659) Friends House Library
newspaper clipping, undated (but probably 1845) and without a source, pasted into the *Scrapbook of John Green Crosse*, 1829–46, Norfolk Record Office, Norwich.
Norwich Church of England Burial Ground Company, 1845 handbill pasted into the *Scrapbook of John Green Crosse*, 1829–46, Norfolk Record Office, Norwich
Printed Epistles London: Friends House Library
PRO, PROB 11/62, f 364v
PRO Prob. 11.370 f.94)
Statutes at Large Vol 22 (1810–1812)
South Bristol Crematorium: Burial Registers for Avon View Cemetery
J Turner catalogue, Guildhall Library, London
Victoria & Albert Museum, c 1700 Trade card of William Grinly, V&A Negative Number JX1242
Victoria & Albert Museum, c 1710 Trade card of Christopher Gibson, V&A Negative Number JX897
Victoria & Albert Museum, 1783 pattern book by 'JB', issued by Tuesby & Cooper, Acc No E997 to E1011– 1903 (M 63e)
Victoria & Albert Museum, c 1810 Trade card of Jarvis' Patent Coffin, V&A Negative Numbers JX898 and JX1156
Victoria & Albert Museum, c 1821–4 catalogue by 'AT', Acc No E994 to E1021–1978
Victoria & Albert Museum, 1826 catalogue by 'EL', Acc No E3132–1910
Yearly Meeting Proceedings London: Friends House Library

Secondary Sources

Aaron, J, Rogers, J, & Kanis, J, 1992 Skeletal palaeopathology: palaeohistology of Pagets disease in a 16th century skeleton, *Amer J Physical Anthropology*, **89**, 325–31
Adams, M, & Reeve, J, 1987 Excavations at Christ Church, Spitalfields 1984–6, Antiquity, **61**, 232, 225–47
Alexander, D A, 1991 Reactions of police officers to body handling after a major disaster. A before and after comparison, *Brit J Psychiatry*, **159**, 547–55
Alexander, D A, 1993 Stress among body handlers. A long term follow up, *Brit J Psychiatry*, **163**, 806–8
Allen, A, 1995 *A Dictionary of Sussex Folk Medicine*, Newbury: Countryside Books
Ambrose, S H, 1991 Effects of diet, climate and physiology on nitrogen isotope abundances in terrestrial foodwebs, *J Arch Sci*, **18**, 293–317
Ambrose, S H forthcoming Prospects for stable isotopic analysis of Later Pleistocene hominid diets in West Asia and Europe, in T Akazawa, K Aoki, & O Bar-Yosef (eds), *Neanderthals and modern humans in West Asia*, New York
Ambrose, S H, & Norr, L, 1993 Carbon isotope evidence for routing of dietary protein to bone collagen, and whole diet to bone apatite carbonate: purified diet growth experiments, in J B Lambert, & G Grupe (eds), *Prehistoric Human Bone: Archaeology at the Molecular Level*, Berlin, 1–37
Andrews, P, 1990 *Owls, Caves and Fossils*
Archer, I W, 1991 *The pursuit of stability: social relations in Elizabethan London*, Cambridge: Cambridge University Press
Ariès, P, 1981 [1977] *The Hour of Our Death*, trans Helen Weaver, Penguin
Arnaud, G, Arnaud, S, Ascenzi, A, Bonnucci, E, & Graziani, G, 1978 On the problem of the preservation of human bone in seawater, *J Hum Evol*, **7**, 409–20

Arnold, A P, 1962 A list of Jews and their households in London, extracted from the census lists of 1695, *Jewish Hist Soc England Trans*, **24**, 134–50

Ascenzi, A, & Silverstrini, G, 1984 Bone-boring marine microorganisms: an experimental investigation, *J Hum Evol*, **13**, 531–6

Austin, J J, Ross, A J, Smith, A B, Fortey, R A, & Thomas, R H, 1997 Problems of reproducibility: does geologically ancient DNA survive in amber-preserved insects, *Proc Roy Soc*, **264**, 467–74

Ayloffe, J, 1774 An account of the body of Edward I as it appeared when his tomb was opened in 1774, *Archaeologia*, **3**, 401

Bahn, P G, 1984 Do not disturb? Archaeology and the rights of the dead, *J Applied Phil*, **1**, 213–25

Bahn, P G, 1986 The last rights? More on archaeology and the dead, *Oxford J Archaeol*, **5**, 255–71

Bailey, B, 1991 *The Resurrection Men – A History of the Trade in Corpses*

Bainbridge, D & Genoves, S T, 1956 A study of sex differences in the scapula, *J Roy Anthropol Inst*, **86**, 109–34

Bannerman, W B (ed), 1912 *The registers of St Mildred, Bread Street, and of St Margaret Moses, Friday Street, London*

Bannerman, W B (ed), 1913 *The registers of All Hallows Bread Street, and of St John the Evangelist, Friday Street, London*

Bannerman, W B (ed), 1914 *The registers of St Mary le Bowe, Cheapside, All Hallows Honey lane, and of St Pancras, Soper Lane, London*

Bannerman, W B (ed), 1916 *The registers of St Olave Hart Street, London, 1563-1700*

Barclay, R, 1965 *The Population of Orkney 1755–1961*, Kirkwall: W R Mackintosh

Barker, P, 1986 *Understanding Archaeological Excavation*, Batsford

Baron, H, Hummel, S, & Herrmann, B, 1996 Mycobacterium tuberculosis Complex DNA in ancient human bones, *J Arch Sci*, **23**, 667–71

Bashford, L, & Kirk, L, forthcoming *Excavation of a Quaker Burial Ground at London Road, Kingston-upon-Thames*

Baxby, D, 1981 *Jenner's Smallpox Vaccine*, Heinemann

Baxter, P J, Brazier, A M, Young, S E J, 1995 Is smallpox a hazard in church crypts? *Brit J Indust Medicine*, **45**, 359–60

Beck, W, & Ball, T F, 1869 *London Friends' Meetings with accounts of various Meeting-Houses and Burial-Grounds*, F Bowyer Kitto

Beier, A L, 1990 Social problems in Elizabethan London, in J Barry (ed), *The Tudor and Stuart town, a reader in English urban history, 1530–1688*, 121–38

Bell, B, 1786 *A system of surgery*, volume 4, Edinburgh & Co

Bell, E L, 1997 Documentary and comparative scholarly research: context in cemetery archaeology, in D A Poirier & N F Bellantoni (eds) *In Remembrance: Archaeology and Death*, Bergin & Garvey, Westport, Conn, 219–29

Bell, L S, 1990 Palaeopathology and diagenesis: an SEM evaluation of structural changes using back-scattered electron imaging, *J Arch Sci*, **17**, 85–102

Bell, L S, 1996 *Post Mortem Microstructural Change to the Skeleton*, unpublished PhD thesis, University of London

Bell, L S, Boyde, A, & Jones, S J, 1991 Diagenetic alteration to teeth *in situ* illustrated by back-scattered electron imaging, *Scanning*, **13**, 173–83

Bell, L S, & Jones, S J, 1991 Macroscopic and microscopic evaluation of archaeological pathological bone: backscattered electron imaging of putative Pagetic bone, *Int J Osteoarch*, **1**, 179–84

Bell, L S, Skinner, M F, & Jones, S J, 1996 The speed of post mortem change to the human skeleton and its taphonomic significance, *Forensic Science Int*, **82**, 129–40

Bennion, E, 1986 *Antique Dental Instruments*, Sotheby's

Bentham-Edwards, M, (ed), 1898 *The autobiography of Arthur Young*, Smith, Elder & Co

Bermingham, E J, 1881 *The Disposal of the Dead, a Plea for Cremation*

Berry, A C, 1975 Factors affecting the incidence of non-metrical skeletal variants, *J Anatomy*, **120**, 519-35

Berry, A C, & Berry, R J, 1967 Epigenetic Variation in the Human Cranium, *J Anatomy*, **101**, (2), 361–79

Berry, R J & Searl, A G 1963 Epigenetic Polymorphism of the Rodent Skeleton, *Proc Zoological Soc London*, **140**, 557–615

Bettey, J, 1996 St Augustine's Abbey, Bristol *Bristol Hist Assoc*, **88**, 1–2

Binski, P, 1996 *Medieval Death; ritual and representation*, British Museum Press

Bishop, J, 1864 *Strolls in the Brighton Extra-mural Cemetery*, Brighton

Black, S M, & Scheuer, J L, 1995 The St Bride's Documented Skeletal Collection, unpublished

Blair, J, & Pyrah, C, (eds), 1996 *Church Archaeology: Research Directions for the future*, CBA Res Rep **104**, York

Bocherens, H, Fizet, M, Mariotti, A, Lange-Badre, B, Vandermeersch, B, Borel, J P, & Bellon, G, 1991 Isotopic biogeochemistry of fossil vertebrate collagen: implications for the study of the fossil foodweb including Neanderthal man, *J Hum Evol*, **20**, 481–92

Boddington, A, 1987 From Bones to Population: The Problem of Numbers, in A Boddington *et al* (eds) 1987, 180–97

Boddington, A, Garland, A N, & Janaway, R C (eds), 1987 *Death, Decay and Reconstruction: Approaches to Archaeology and Forensic Science*, Manchester: Manchester University Press

Bond, C J, & Wilson, J M, 1977 Human Burials at the Central Garage, *Vale Evesham Hist Soc Res Pap*, **4**, 38–42

Book of Discipline – see Appendix 10.1 for full bibliographical details

Boore, E J, 1985 Excavations at St Augustine the Less, Bristol, 1983–4, *Bristol Avon Archaeol*, 4, 21–33

Boore, E J, 1986 The Church of St Augustine the Less, Bristol: an interim statement *Trans Bristol Gloucestershire Archaeol Soc*, **104**, 211–14

Boore, E J, 1989 St Augustine the Less and Bitton, Avon, in M Ponsford *et al*, Archaeology in Bristol 1986–9, *Trans Bristol Gloucestershire Archaeol Soc*, **107**, 246–9

Boore, E J, & Heighway, C M, (forthcoming) Post Medieval Coffins, in C M Heighway and R Bryant

Borrow, G, 1862 *Wild Wales*, Collins

Borsay, P 1989 *The English urban Renaissance: culture and society in the provincial town, 1660–1770*, Oxford: Oxford University Press

Boulton, J, 1987 *Neighbourhood and Society. A London suburb in the seventeenth century*, Cambridge

Bowman, J E, MacLaughlin, S M, & Scheuer, J L, 1992a The relationship between biological and chronological age in the juvenile remains from St Bride's Church, Fleet Street, *Annals Human Biol*, **19**, 216

Bowman, J E, MacLaughlin, S M, & Scheuer, J L, 1992b Burial of an early 19th century suicide in the crypt of St Bride's Church, Fleet Street, *Int J Osteoarchaeol*, **2**, 91–4

Boyle, A, forthcoming A grave disturbance: archaeological perceptions of the recently dead, in J Downes, & T Pollard (eds),

Braithwaite, W C, 1961 *The Second Period of Quakerism*, Cambridge: Cambridge University Press

Braudel, F, 1967 *Capitalism and material life 1400–1800*, Weidenfeld & Nicolson

Bridges, P S, 1991 Degenerative Joint Disease in Hunter-Gatherers and Agriculturists from the South-eastern United States, *Amer J Physical Anthropology*, **85**, 379–91

Bridges, P S, 1994 Vertebral Arthritis and Physical Activities in the Prehistoric South Eastern United States, *Amer J Physical Anthropology*, **93**, 83–93

Brièle, L, 1881 *Collection des documents pour servir a l'histoire des hopitaux de Paris*, vol I, Paris

Brigg, W (ed), 1890 *The register book of the parish of St Nicholas Acons, London, 1539–1812*, Leeds

Brophy, E B, 1974 *The Triumph of Craft*, Knoxville, University of Tennessee

Brothwell, D R, 1981 *Digging up bones*, third edition, British Museum

Brown, J K, & Jones, B 1997 *Yorkshire Snippets*, Bradford: Private publication

Buikstra, J E & Ubelaker, D H, 1994 *Standards for Data Collection From the Human Skeleton*, Arkansas Archaeological Survey Research Series 44, Fayetteville, Arkansas

Butler, L A S, 1978 St Martin's Church, Allerton Mauleverer, *Yorkshire Archaeol J*, **50**, 177–88

Campbell, C, 1987 *The Romantic Ethic and the Spirit of Modern Consumerism*, Oxford: Basil Blackwell

Campbell, R 1747 *The London Tradesman*

Cannadine, D, 1981 War and Death, Grief and Mourning in Modern Britain, in J Whaley 1981, 187–242

Cano, R J, & Borucki, M K, 1995 Revival and identification of bacterial spores in 25–40-million-year-old Dominican amber, *Science*, **268**, 1060–4

Cano, R J, Poinar, H N, Pienazek, N J, Acra, A, & Poinar, G O, 1993 Amplification and sequencing of DNA from a 120–135-million-year-old weevil, *Nature*, **363**, 536–8

Cecil, R, 1991 *The Mask of Death*, Lewes: The Book Guild Ltd

Celoria, F S, 1966 Burials and archaeology: a survey of attitudes to research, *Folklore*, **77**, 161–83

Centre for Metropolitan History *Annual Report* 1995–6

Chadwick, E, 1843 *A Supplementary Report on the Results of a Special Inquiry into the Practice of Interment in Towns*, House of Lords

Challen, W H, 1958 Thomas Barnard, Lords of the Manor of Southease, *Sussex Notes and Queries*, **XV**, (1), 31

Chamberlain, A, 1994 *Human Remains*, British Museum Press

Champion, J A I (ed), 1993 *Epidemic Disease in London*, University of London

Champion, J A I, 1995 *London's dreaded visitation. The social geography of the great Plague in 1665*, Historical Geography Research Series **31**

Charlton, F, & Thompson, J, 1996 Ways of coping with psychological distress after trauma, *Brit J Clinical Psychology*, **35**, 517–30

Chester, J L (ed) 1878 *The reiester booke of Saynte De'is Backchurch parish for maryages, christenynges, and buryalles begynnynge in the year of or lord God 1538*

Chester, J L (ed), 1882 *The parish registers of St Michael, Cornhill, London, containing the marriages, baptisms and burials from 1546 to 1754*

Chester, J L, & Armytage, G J (eds), 1883 *The parish registers of St.Antholin, Budge Row, London, containing the marriages, baptisms, and burials from 1538 to 1754; and of St. John Baptist on Wallbrook, London, containing the baptisms and burials from 1682 to 1754*

Childs, A M, & Pollard, A M, 1992 A review of the applications of immunochemistry to archaeological bone, *J Arch Sci*, **19**, 39–47

Church, R A, & Smith, B M D, 1966 Competition and Monopoly in the Coffin Furniture Industry 1870–1915, *Econ Hist Rev*, **XIX**, 621–41

Clark, D, 1982 *Between Pulpit and Pew: Folf Religion in a North Yorkshire fishing village*, Cambridge: Cambridge University Press

Clarkson, T, 1807 *A Portraiture of Quakerism*, 2 vols, Longman, Rees, & Jones

Cobb, A G, 1892 *Earth Burial and Cremation: The history of earth-burial with its attendant evils etc.*

Cohen, M, & Armelagos, G J, 1984 *Palaeopathology at the Origins of Agriculture*, Orlando, Florida

Collinson, J, 1791 *The History and Antiquities of the County of Somerset*, 3 vols, Bath, **11**, 165–8

Collinson, P, 1967 *The Elizabethan Puritan movement*

Collison, G, 1840 *Cemetery Interment*

Conheeney, J, & Miles, A W, forthcoming *A Post-medieval Population from London: Excavations at 75-82 Farringdon Street*, Museum of London

Cook, C, & Stevenson, J, 1980, *British Historical Facts*

Cooper, B B, 1843 *The Life of Sir Astley Cooper*

Corfield, P J, 1982 *The impact of English towns, 1700–1800*, Oxford University Press

Cornish, K H, 1884 *Cholera treatment and Cure: With remarks on the danger of premature interment and suggestions for cheap and healthy cremation*

Council for British Archaeology, 1997a *CBA fact sheet 5: A job in Archaeology*, York (http://britac3acuk/cba/cba/factsht5html)

Council for British Archaeology, 1997b *CBA fact sheet 8: Everything you always wanted to know about archaeological digs but were afraid to ask*, York (http://britac3acuk/cba/cba/factsht8html)

Council for British Archaeology, 1997c *DAC Archaeologists' information pack*, York

Cox, G, & Sealy, J, C, forthcoming Investigating identity and life histories: isotopic analysis and historical documentation of slave skeletons found on the Cape Town Foreshore, South Africa, *Int J Hist Arch*

Cox, M, 1994 On excavating the recent dead, *Brit Arch News*, **18** (November), 8

Cox, M, 1995a A dangerous assumption: anyone can be an historian! The lesson from Christ Church, Spitalfields, in S R Saunders, & A Herring (eds), *Grave Reflections–Portraying the Past through Cemetery Studies*, Toronto: Canadian Scholars Press, 19–29

Cox, M, 1995b Crime scene archaeology is one of the most frightening areas of archaeology in which to operate, *Field Archaeol*, **23**, 14–16

Cox, M, 1996a *Life and Death in Spitalfields 1700–1850* York: Council for British Archaeology

Cox, M, 1996b Crypt archaeology after Spitalfields: dealing with our recent dead, *Antiquity*, **71**, 8–10

Cox, M, 1996c Quaker Burial ground, Kingston-upon-Thames, Archaeological Specification, unpublished, Bournemouth University

Cox, M, 1996d St Lukes, Old Street, London: Archaeological Recommendations, unpublished, Bournemouth University

Cox, M, Molleson, T, & Waldron, T, 1990 Preconception and perception: The lessons of a 19th century suicide, *J Arch Sci*, **17**, 573–81

Cox, M, & Stock, G, 1995 Nineteenth Century Bath-Stone Walled Graves at St Nicholas's Church, Bathampton, *Somerset Archaeol Natur Hist Soc*, **138**, 131–50

Crawford, P, 1993 *Women and religion in England, 1500–1720*

Creighton, C, 1894 *A History of Epidemics in Britain*, 2 vols, Cambridge: Cambridge University Press

Cressy, D, 1997 *Birth, Marriage and Death: ritual, religion and the life-cycle in Tudor and Stuart England*, Oxford: Oxford University Press

Crouch, K R, & Shanks, S A, 1984 *Excavations in Staines 1975-76 The Friends Burial Ground Site*, Joint Publ **2**, London Middlesex Arch Soc & Surrey Archaeol Soc

Curl, J, 1972 *The Victorian celebration of death*, Newton Abbot: David & Charles

Curl, J S, 1993 *A Celebration of Death – An introduction to some of the buildings, monuments, and settings of funerary architecture in the Western European Tradition*

Dale, T C (ed), 1938 *The inhabitants of London in 1638*, 2 vols

Daniell, C, 1997 *Death and Burial in Medieval England*, Routledge

Dawson, D P, 1981 Archaeology and the Medieval Churches of Bristol, *Bristol Avon Archaeol Res Group Rev*, **2**, 9–23

Day, M H & Pitcher-Wilmott, R W, 1975 Sexual differentiation in the innominate bone studied by multivariate analysis, *Annals Human Biol*, **2**, 143–51

Defoe, D, 1645 *The Complete English Tradesman*

Defoe, D, 1722 (1986) *A journal of the Plague Year*, Harmondsworth: Penguin Classics

DeGusta, D, & White, T D, 1996 On the use of skeletal collections for DNA analysis, *Ancient Biomolecules*, **1**, 89–92

Department of the Environment, 1990 *Planning Policy Guidance No 16: Archaeology and Planning*

Dezallier-D'Agenville, A J, 1731 *Travels et Tours*, Victoria and Albert Museum (National Art Library) msss, Press Mark 86 N

Diamond, A S, 1962 The community of the resettlement, 1656-84, *Jewish Historical Soc Eng*, Miscellany **6**, 73–141

Dickens, C, 1839 (1983) *Nicholas Nickelby*, Harmondsworth: Penguin

Dickinson, J C, 1976 The Origins of St Augustine's, Bristol, in P McGrath & J Cannon (eds) *Essays in Bristol and Gloucestershire History* Bristol, 109–26

Diggins, J, 1978 *The bard of savagery: Thorstein Veblen and modern social theory*, Brighton: Harvester Press

Downie, A W, & Dumbell, K R, 1947 Survival of *variola* virus in dried exudate and crusts from smallpox patients, *Lancet*, **i**, 550–3

Dobbs, J P B, 1995 *Authority and the Early Quakers* unpublished D Phil thesis, University of Oxford

Dobson, M J, 1996 *Contours of death and disease in early modern England*, Cambridge: Cambridge University Press

Dolan, C T, Brown, A L, & Ritts, R E, 1971 Microbiological examination of post mortem tissues, *Archives Path*, **92**, 206–11

Downes, J, & Pollard, T, forthcoming a *The loved body's corruption: archaeological contributions to the study of human mortality*, Glasgow: Cruithne Press

Downes, J, & Pollard, T, forthcoming b Preface, in J Downes, & T Pollard above

Draycott, A T, & Carr, A P (eds), 1996 *Stone's Justices Manual*, **2**, Butterworth

Droge, A J, & Tabor, J D, 1992 *A Noble Death*, San Francisco: Harper

Dudfield, R, 1924 A survey of mortality due to childbearing in London from the 17th century, *Proc Roy Soc Medicine*, **17**, 59–72

Duffy, E, 1992 *The stripping of the altars: traditional religion in England, c 1400–1580*, Cambridge

Dunk, J, & Rugg, J, 1994 *The Management of Old Cemetery Land: Now and Future. A Report of the University of York Cemetery Research Group*, York: Shaw & Sons

Durkheim, E, 1897 (1951) *Le suicide*, trans J A Spaulding & G Simpson, Glencoe

Earle, P, 1994 *A city full of people: men and women of London, 1650–1750 The Ecclesiastical Art Review*, 1878, 1

Eglinton, G, & Logan, G A, 1991 Molecular preservation, *Phil Trans Roy Soc London B*, **333**, 315–28

Ellacombe, H T, 1881 *The History of the Parish of Bitton in the county of Gloucester*, 2 vols

English Heritage, 1991 *Management of Archaeological Projects*, 2nd edition

English Heritage, 1996 *Brief for an archaeological excavation: Former Friends burial ground, 84, London Road, Kingston Upon Thames*, unpublished

Evans, R J, 1996 *Rituals of retribution: capital punishment in Germany, 1600–1987*, Oxford: Oxford University Press

Evershed, R P, Heron, C, Charters, S, & Goad, L J, 1992 The survival of food residues: new methods of analysis, interpretation and application, *Proc Brit Acad*, **77**, 187–208

Evershed, R P, Heron, C, & Goad, L J, 1991 Epicuticular wax components preserved in potsherds as chemical indicators of leafy vegetables in ancient diets, *Antiquity*, **65**, 540–44

Evershed, R P, Turner-Walker, G, Hedges, R E M, Tuross, N, & Leyden, A, 1995 Preliminary results for the analysis of lipids in ancient bone, *J Arch Sci*, **22**, 277–90

Falin, L I, 1961 Histological and histochemical studies of human teeth of the Bronze and Stone Ages, *Archives Oral Biol*, **5**, 5–13

Fassnidge, H, 1992 *The Quakers of Melksham 1669–1950*, Bradford on Avon: Bradford on Avon Friends

Faulks, S, 1996 *The Fatal Englishman: Three Short Lives*, Vintage

Fenner, F, Henderson, D A, Arita, I, Jazek, Z, & Ladnyi, I D, 1988 *Smallpox and its Eradication*, World Health Organisation

Fenwick, J, 1825 *Substance of the Speech given at the General Meeting of the Various Denominations of Protestant Dissenters, of Newcastle upon Tyne, to take into Consideration the Propriety of Obtaining a New Place of Sepulture*, Local History Library, Newcastle Central Library

Fido, M, 1988, *Bodysnatchers: A History of the Resurrectionists 1742-1850*, Weidenfeld & Nicolson

Finch, J, 1991 'According to the Qualitie and Degree of the Person Deceased': funeral monuments and construction of social identities 1400–1750 *Scot Archaeol Rev*, **8**, 105–14

Finer, S E, 1952 *The Life and Times of Edwin Chadwick*, Methuen

Finlay, R A P, 1981 *Population and metropolis, the demography of London 1580–1650*, Cambridge: Cambridge University Press

First Annual Report of the Leeds General Cemetery Company, 1836, Brotherton Library, University of Leeds

Fisher, D L, Holland, M M, Mitchell, L, Sledzik, P S, Wilcox, A W, Wadhams, M, & Weedn, V W, 1993 Extraction, evaluation and amplification of DNA from decalcified and undecalcified United States Civil War bone, *J Forensic Sci*, **38**, 60–68

Fisher, J, & D, & Ford, M, & F, 1985 *Bristol on Old Postcards: Reflections of a bygone age*, **2**, 6–7

Fizet, M A, Mariotti, A, Bocherens, H, Lange-Badre, B, Vandermeersch, B, Borel, J P, & Bellon, G, 1995 Effect of diet, physiology and climate on carbon and nirogen isotopes of collagen in a Late Pleistocene anthropic palaeoecosystem: Marillac, Charente, France, *J Arch Sci*, **22**, 67–79

Flinn, M W (ed), 1965 *Report on the Sanitary Condition of the Labouring Population of Great Britain*, Edinburgh

Forbes, T R, 1972 Mortality books from 1820 to 1849 from the parish of St Bride, Fleet Street, London, *J Hist Medic Allied Sci*, **27**, 15–29

Forbes, T R, 1979 By what disease or casualty: the changing face of death in London, in C Webster *Health, Medicine and Mortality in the 16th Century*, Cambridge: Cambridge University Press, 117-39

Fornaciari, G, 1985 The mummies of the Abbey of Saint Domenico Maggiore in Naples, *Archivo per l'Anthropologia e la Etnologia*, **115**, 215–26

Fornaciari, G, & Marchetti, A, 1986, Intact smallpox virus particles in an Italian mummy of the sixteenth century, *Lancet*, **ii**, 625

Foucault, M, 1979 *Discipline and punish*, Harmondsworth: Penguin

Foucault, M, 1981–6 *The history of sexuality*, 3 vols, Penguin

Francalacci, P, 1995 DNA recovery from ancient tissues: problems and perspectives, *J Hum Evol*, **10**, 81–91

Frankenstein, S, & Rowlands, M, 1978 The internal structure and regional context of Early Iron Age society, *Bull Instit Archaeol*, **15**, 73–112

Fraser, A, 1984 *The weaker vessel. Woman's lot in seventeenth-century England*

French, A, 1985 *John Joseph Merlin*, GLC

Friedman, M J, *1997 Post-Traumatic Stress Disorder; An overview*, Dartmouth, MA (http://wwwdartmouthedu/dms/ptsd/overviewhtml)

Frost, J W (ed), 1984 *The Records and Recollections of James Jenkins*, New York: Edwin Mellen

Garciá Márquez, G, 1995 *Of love and demons*, New York

Garland, A N, 1989 Microscopical analysis of fossil bone, *Applied Geochem*, **4**, 215–29

Garland, A N, & Janaway, R C, 1989 The Taphonomy of Inhumation Burials, in C A Roberts, F Lee & J Bintliff (eds), 1989, 15–37

Garratt-Frost, S J, Harrison, G, & Logie, J G, 1992 *The Law and Burial Archaeology*, Institute of Field Archaeologists Technical Paper **11**, Birmingham

Gattrell, V, 1994 *The hanging tree: execution and the English people, 1770–1868*, Oxford: Oxford University Press

General Cemetery Company, 1830 *Prospectus of the General Cemetery Company for providing Places of Interment Secure from violation, inoffensive to public health and decency and ornamental to the Metropolis*

Genoves, S T 1956 *A study of sex differences in the human innominate bone (os coxae)*, PhD dissertation, Corpus Christi College, University of Cambridge

Gentleman's Magazine, 1826, **96**

Gentles, I 1996 Political funerals during the English Revolution, in S Porter (ed), *London and the Civil War*, 205–24

George, M D, 1965 *London Life in the 18th Century*, Penguin

Gerrish, J, 1970 *Church of St Mary, Bitton: A Short History*, Bristol

Gilchrist, R, & Morris, R, 1996 *Continuity, reaction and revival: church archaeology in England c1600–1800*, in Blair & Pyrah, 1996, 112–26

Gilchrist, R, & Reeve, J, 1991 *St Botolph's without Bishopsgate Project Design & Project Design for proposed Crypt Clearance*, unpublished

Gill, P, Ivanov, P L, Sullivan, K, Kimpton, C, Piercy, R, Benson, N, Tully, G, & Evett, I, 1994 Identification of the remains of the Romanov family, *Nature Genetics*, **6**, 130–35

Girouard, M, 1987 *A Country House Companion*

Gittings, C, 1984 *Death, Burial and the Individual in Early Modern England*, Routledge

Glass, D V, 1976 Socio-economic status and occupations in the city of London at the end of the seventeenth century, in P Clark (ed), *The early modern town, a reader*, 216–32, Routledge Kegan Paul

Goldenberg, E M, 1990 Amplification and analysis of Miocene plant fossil DNA, *Phil Trans Roy Soc B*, **333**, 419–27

Goodall, I H, 1993 Iron coffin fittings, in S Margeson, Norwich Households: The Medieval and Post Medieval Finds from Norwich Survey Excavations 1971–1978, *E Anglian Archaeol Rep*, **58**, 82, figs 45–6

Goodman, A H & Dobney, K, 1991 Epidemiological Studies of Dental Enamel Hypoplasias in Mexico and Bradford: Their Relevance to Archaeological Skeletal Studies, in H Bush & M Zvelebil, *Health in Past Societies*, BAR Int Ser **567**, 81–100

Goodman, A H, & Rose, J C, 1991 Dental Enamel Hypoplasias as Indicators of Nutritional Stress, in M A Kelley & C S Larson, *Advances in Dental Anthropology*, New York: Wiley-Liss, 279–93

Gordon, A, 1984 *Death is for the Living*, Edinburgh: Paul Harris

Grady, K, 1987 *The Georgian Public Buildings of Leeds and the West Riding*, Leeds

Gray, R, (ed) 1996 *Edgar Allan Poe*, Everyman's Poetry, **11**

Green, B L, 1994 Psychosocial research in traumatic stress: An update, *J Traumatic Stress*, **7**, 341–63

Green, V, 1797 *An Account of the Discovery of the Body of King John in the Cathedral Church of Worcester in July 1797*, Worcester

Grieg, D M, 1931 *Clinical Observations on Surgical Pathology of Bone*, Edinburgh and London

Griffiths, B, 1997 Cemetery overload, *Planning*, 21 February 1997

Grindon, L H, 1874 *Cremation considered in reference to the Resurrection*

Grundy, T, 1846 *Report of the subcommittee appointed to visit and examine into the formation and present management of various public cemeteries, and to provide plans and estimates for the Northampton General Cemetery Company*, unpaginated MS, Local Studies Room, Northampton Central Library

Grupe, G, Werringloer, U D, & Parsche, F, 1993 Initial stages of bone decomposition, in J B Lambert, & G Grupe (eds), *Prehistoric Human Bone: Archaeology at the Molecular Level*, Berlin, 257–74

Gwynn, R D, 1985 *Huguenot heritage: the history and contribution of the Huguenots in Britain*, Routledge Kegan Paul

Hackett, C J, 1981 Microscopical focal destruction (tunnels) in excavated human bones, *Medicine Sci Law*, **21**, 243–65

Hadfield, G, 1882 *The personal narrative of George Hadfield*, MS, Manchester Archive Office

Hagelberg, E, Bell, L S, Allen, T, Boyde, A, Jones, S J, & Clegg, J B, 1991a Analysis of ancient bone DNA: techniques and applications, *Phil Trans Roy Soc London B*, **333**, 399–407

Hagelberg, E, & Clegg, J B, 1993 Genetic polymorphisms in prehistoric Pacific islanders determined by analysis of ancient bone DNA, *Proc Roy Soc B*, **252**, 163–70

Hagelberg, E, Gray, I C, & Jeffreys, A J, 1991b Identification of the skeletal remains of a murder victim by DNA analysis, *Nature*, **352**, 427–9

Hagelberg, E, Sykes, B, & Hedges, R E M, 1989 Ancient bone DNA amplified, *Nature*, **342**, 485

Hall, D J, 1988 How we got our Book of Discipline: the story to 1863, *Friends' Quart*, **25**, (1), 32–9

Halliday, R, 1997 Criminal Graves and Rural Cross-roads, *Brit Arch*, **25**, 6

Handt, O, Richards, M, Trommsdorff, M, Kilger, C, Simanainen, J, Georgiev, O, Bauer, K, Stone, A, Hedges, R, Schaffner, W, Utermann, G, Sykes, B, & Paabo, S, 1994 Molecular genetic analyses of the Tyrolean Ice Man, *Science*, **264**, 1775–8

Harding, C J, 1987 Post-medieval Coffin Furniture, in J G Hurst and P A Rahtz (eds) *Wharram: A Study of Settlement in the Yorkshire Wolds, III: Wharram Percy: The Church of St Martin* by R D Bell, M W Beresford *et al*, *Soc Medieval Archaeol Monogr Ser*, **11**, 150–3, figs 166–7 and fiche

Harding, V, 1989 'And one more may be laid there': The location of burials in early modern London, *London J*, **14**, (2), 112–29

Harding, V, 1990 The population of London, 1550–1700: a review of the published evidence, *London J*, **15**, (2), 111–28

Harding, V 1992 Burial choice and burial location in medieval London, in S R Bassett (ed), *Death in towns: urban responses to the dying and the dead, 100–1600*, Leicester: Leicester Uni Press, 119–35

Harding, V 1993, Burial of the plague dead in early modern London, in J A I Champion (ed), *Epidemic Disease in London*, 53–64

Harding, V, forthcoming 'Living with the dead: funeral ceremonies and civic memory in early modern London', in G Chaix, (ed) *La Ville a la Renaissance. Espaces – Representations – Pouvoirs*

Hargrove, A E, 1847 *The Baneful Custom of Interment in Towns and the Present State of the York Graveyards*, York

Harmann, M, Molleson, T I, & Price, J L, 1981 Burials, Bodies and Beheadings in Romano-British and Anglo-Saxon Cemeteries, *Bull Brit Mus (Natural Hist) (Geol)*, **35**, 145–88

Harvey, W, 1968 Some dental and social conditions of 1696–1852 connected with St Bride's Church, Fleet Street, London, *Medic Hist*, **12**, 62–75

Hasluck, P, 1905 *Coffin-Making and Undertaking*, Cassell & Co

Heal, A, 1925 *London Tradesmen's Cards of the Eighteenth Century*, Batsford

Healing, T D, Hoffman, P N, & Young, S E J, 1995 The infection hazards of human cadavers, *CDR Review* **5**, R61–8

Health and Safety Executive, 1992 *Manual handling operations Regs 1992: guidance on the Regulations L23*, Sudbury

Health and Safety Executive, 1993 *The occupational zoonoses*, Sudbury

Health and Safety Executive, 1994 *5 steps to risk asssessment*, Sudbury

Health and Safety Executive, 1995 *Categorisation of biological agents according to hazard and categories of containment*, Sudbury

Health and Safety Executive, 1996a *Health and Safety Statistics 1994/95*, Sudbury

Health and Safety Executive, 1996b *A guide to the construction (health, safety and welfare) Regs 1996 INDG220*, Sudbury

Health and Safety Executive, 1997 *General COSHH ACOP/Biological agents ACOP L5*, Sudbury

Healy, M, 1993 'Discourses of the plague in early modern London', in J A I Champion (ed) 1993, 19–34

Hearsey, J E N, 1961 *Bridge, Church, and Palace in Old London*

Heighway, C M, & Bryant, R, forthcoming *The Anglo-Saxon Minster and Medieval Priory at St Oswald at Gloucester, CBA Res Rep*, York

Heighway, C M, & Litten, J W S, 1994 Investigations at St Kenelm's Church, Sapperton, *Trans Bristol Gloucestershire Archaeol Soc*, **CXII**, 111–26

Henderson, J, 1987 Factors Determining the State of Preservation of Human Remains, in A Boddington, A N Garland, & R C Janaway 1987, 43–54

Hicks, A, & Ward, A, 1991 St Nicholas Church, Sevenoaks, *Archaeology Canterbury*, **109**, 277–83

Higuchi, R, Bowman, B, Freidberger, M, Ryder, M, Wilson, O A, & A C, 1984 DNA sequences from the Quagga, an extinct member of the horse family, *Nature*, **312**, 282–4

Historic Scotland, 1997 *The treatment of human remains in archaeology*, Edinburgh

HMSO, 1980 Control of Lead at Work Regulations, **1248**

HMSO, 1990 Planning Policy Guidance **16** *Archaeology and planning*

HMSO, 1992a Management of Health and Safety at Work Regulations, **2051**

HMSO, 1992b Manual Handling Operations Regulations, **2793**

HMSO, 1992c Personal Protective Equipment Regulations, **2966**

HMSO, 1994a Control of Substances Hazardous to Health Regulations, **3246**

HMSO, 1994b Construction, Design and Management Regulations, **3140**

Holder, W, 1891 *Cremation versus burial: an appeal to reason against prejudice*

Holland, M M, Fisher, D L, Mitchell, L G, Rodriquez, W C, Canik, J J, Merril, C R, & Weedn, V W, 1993 Mitochondrial DNA sequence analysis of human skeletal remains: identification of remains from the Vietnam War, *J Forensic Sci*, **38**, 542–53

Holmes, Mrs B, 1896 *The London Burial Grounds: notes on their history from the earliest times to the present day*, The Gresham Press

Hood, T, 1827 *Mary's Ghost: a pathetic ballad*

Hopkins, D R, 1983 *Princes and Peasants, Smallpox in History*, University of Chicago Press

Hopkins, K, 1983 *Death and Renewal*, Cambridge: Cambridge University Press

Horowitz, M, Wilner, N, & Alvarez, W, 1979 Impact of events scale: A measure of subjective stress, *Psychosomatic Medicine*, **3**, 209–18

Houlbrooke, R A, 1984 *The English family, 1450–1700*, Longman

Houlbrooke, R A (ed), 1989 *Death, ritual and bereavement*, Routledge

Houston, R A, 1992 *The population history of Britain and Ireland, 1550–1750*, Cambridge: Cambridge University Press

Hubbard, G, 1985 *Quaker by Convincement*, Quaker Home Service

Huda, T F J & Bowman, J E, 1994 Variation in cross-striation number between striae in an archaeological population, *Int J Osteoarchaeol*, **4**, 49–52

Huda, T F J & Bowman, J E, 1995 Age determination from dental microstructure in juveniles, *Amer J Physical Anthropol*, **97**, 135–50

Hufton, O, 1995 *The prospect before her. A history of women in western Europe, vol 1, 1500–1800*, Harper Collins

Huggins, P, 1994, Opening Lead Coffins, *Brit Arch News*, **17** (October), 8

Hughes Clarke, A W (ed), 1938 *The register of St Clement Eastcheap, and St Martin Orgar, (ii)*

Hughes Clarke, A W (ed) 1943 *The registers of . . . St Michael Bassishaw, London, (ii) 1626–1735*

Hunt, B C, 1936 *The Development of the Business Corporation in England*, Cambridge, Mass

Hygienic Physician, A, 1890 *Earth to Earth Burial and Cremation*

Independent, 19 August 1997, 2, col 1

Institute of Environmental Health Officers, 1985 *Environmental Health Professional Practice*, vol **8** Moulds and fungal spores

Iscan, M Y, 1988 Rise of forensic anthropology, *Yearbook Physical Anthropology*, **31**, 203–30

Jacob, W M, 1993 *Lay people and religion in the early eighteenth century*, Cambridge: Cambridge University Press

Jalland, P, 1996 *Death in the Victorian Family*, Oxford: Oxford University Press

Jamieson, J D D, 1816 *On the origins of cremation or the burning of the dead from transactions of Royal Society*

Janaway, R C, 1987 The preservation of organic materials in association with metal artefacts deposited in inhumation graves, in A Boddington, A N Garland, & R C Janaway (eds) 1987, 127–48

Janaway, R C, 1993 The Textiles, in J Reeve, & M Adams (eds), 1993, 160–7

Janaway, R C, 1996a Textiles, in M Bell, P J Fowler, & S W Hillson (eds) *The Experimental Earthwork Project 1960–1992, CBA Res Rep* **100**, York

Janaway, R C, 1996b The decay of buried human remains and their associated materials, in J Hunter, C Roberts, & A Martin (eds), *Studies in Crime: An Introduction to Forensic Archaeology*, Batsford, 58–85

Janaway, R C, Bell, M, Blanchette, M, Docherty, C, Ryder, M, Hardman, S, Henderson, J, Hovmand, I, Edwards, G, & Thomas, R, forthcoming *Preservation and decay processes affecting 32 year old buried materials: the Wareham Experimental Earthwork*

Johnson, M C P, 1984 *The Churchyard Carvers' Art*, Bristol

Jones, D G, & Harris, R J, 1997 Contending for the dead, *Nature*, **386**, 15–16

Jones, E, 1980 London in the early 17th century: an ecological approach, *London J*, **6**, 123–33

Jupp, P, 1990 *From Dust to Ashes: The Replacement of Burial by Cremation in England 1840–1967*

Katzenberg, K A, Saunders, S R, & Fitzgerald, W R, 1993 Age differences in stable carbon and nitrogen isotope ratios in a population of prehistoric maize horticulturalists, *Amer J Physical Anthropol*, **90**, 267–81

Kellerman, G D, Waterman, N G, & Scharfenberger, L F, 1976 Demonstration in vitro of post mortem bacterial migration, *Amer J Clinical Pathology*, **66**, 911–15

Kelley, M A & Micozzi, M S, 1984 Rib lesions in chronic pulmonary tuberculosis, *Amer J Physical Anthropol*, **65**, 381–6

Killingray, D, 1990 *St Nicholas Church Sevenoaks, Kent – a Brief History*, Sevenoaks: St Nicholas Parish Church

Kirk, L, & Start, H, forthcoming The human osteology, in L Bashford, & L Kirk, forthcoming

Kjolbe-Biddle, B, 1975 A cathedral cemetery: problems in excavation and interpretation, *World Archaeology*, **7.1**, 87–107

Knocker, H W, 1926 Sevenoaks: the manor, church, and market, *Archaeology Canterbury*, **38**, 51–68

Krueger, H W, & Sullivan, C H, 1984 Models for carbon isotope fractionation between diet and bone, in J F Turnland, & P E Johnson (eds), *Stable Isotopes in Nutrition*, ACS Syposium Series, **258**, Washington DC, 205–22

Kselman, T A, 1993 *Death and the Afterlife in Modern France*, Princeton: Princeton University Press

Kyle, J H, 1986 Effect of post-burial contamination on the concentration of major and minor elements in human bones and teeth – the implication for palaeodietary research, *J Arch Sci*, **13**, 403–16

Laing, *Manuscript III*, 356, Special Collections Department, Edinburgh University Library

Lambarde, William, 1576 *A perambulation of Kent, containing the description, hystoire and customes of that shyre*, London, Henry Middleton for Robert Newbire 1st Edition (2nd edition 1596, Edward Bollifant, London)

Lamb, T, 1811 *On Burial Societies, & the Character of an Undertaker*, 2 vols

Landers, J, 1993 *Death and the Metropolis – Studies in the Demographic History of London 1670–1830*, Cambridge: Cambridge University Press

Lansberry, H C F, 1985 Free bench see-saw: Sevenoaks widows in the late seventeenth century, *Archaeology Canterbury*, **100**, 281–93

Lapedes, D N, 1978 *McGraw Hill Encyclopedia of the Geological Sciences*, New York

Laqueuer, T, 1983 Bodies, Death and Pauper Funerals, in *Representations*, **1**, 1, 109–31

Laqueuer, T W, 1993 Cemeteries, religion and the culture of capitalism, in J Garnett, & C Matthews (eds), *Revival and religion since 1700*, 183–200

Laslett, P, 1965 *The world we have lost*, Methuen

Laslett, P, 1983 *The world we have lost, further explored*, 3rd edition, Routledge

Laurence, A, 1989 Godly grief: individual responses to death in seventeenth-century Britain, in R A Houlbrooke 1989, 62–76

Laurence, A, 1994 *Women in England, 1500–1760. A social history*, Weidenfeld & Nicolson

Lawrence, S, 1988 'Entrepreneurs and private enterprise: the development of medical lecturing in London, 1775–1820', *Bull Hist Medicine*, **62** ·

Lee, W, 1852 *Report to the General Board of Health on an Inquiry Respecting the Condition of the Burial Grounds in the District of the Borough of Reading*

Lee-Thorp, J A, 1989 Stable carbon isotopes in deep time; the diets of fossil fauna and hominids, unpublished PhD thesis, University of Cape Town

Lee-Thorp, J A, forthcoming Preservation of biogenic carbon isotope signals in Plio-Pleistocene bone and tooth mineral, in S H Ambrose, & K A Katzenberg (eds), *Close to the Bone: Biogeochemistry and Paleodietary Analysis*, New York

Lee-Thorp, J A, & van der Merwe, N J, 1987 Carbon isotope analysis of fossil bone apatite, *S Afr J Sci*, **83**, 712–15

Lee-Thorp, J A, Sealy, J C, & van der Merwe, N J, 1989 Stable carbon isotope ratio differences between bone collagen and bone apatite and their relationship to diet, *J Arch Sci*, **16**, 585–99

Leibenstein, H, 1982 Bandwagon, Snob and Veblen effects in the theory of Consumers' Demand, in E Mansfield (ed) *Microeconomics: selected readings*, New York: Norton, 12–30

Leveson Gower, G W G (ed) 1877 *A register of all the christninges burialles and weddinges within the parish of St Peeters upon Cornhill begining at the raigne of our most soveraignes ladie Queen Elizabeth*, **1**

Lewis, R A, 1952 *Edwin Chadwick and the Public Health Movement*, Longman

Lindert, P H, 1980 English occupations, 1670–1811, *J Econ Hist*, **40**, 685–712

Lindert, P H & Williamson, J G, 1982 Revising England's social tables, 1688–1867, *Explor Econ Hist*, **19**, 385–408

Lindert, P H & Williamson, J G, 1983 English workers' living standards during the Industrial Revolution, *Econ Hist Rev*, **36**, 1–25

Linebaugh, P, 1977 The Tyburn riot against the surgeons, in D Hay et al, *Albion's Fatal Tree*, 65–117

Litten, J W S, 1981 *Report on the Poulett Burial Vaults in the Church of St George, Hinton St George, Somerset*, unpublished

Litten, J W S, 1985a Copper alloy coffin fittings, in L Watts and P Rahtz, *Mary-le-Port, Bristol Excavations 1962–63*, 169–74, microfiche 8/A2–8A5 *Bristol Mus Art Gallery Monogr*, **7**

Litten, J W S, 1985b Post Medieval Burial Vaults: Their Construction and Contents, *Bull CBA Churches Comm*, **23**, 9–17

Litten, J W S 1986 *The Dead Beneath our Feet: Burial in Churches, 1550–1850*, unpublished

Litten, J W S, 1991 *The English Way of Death: The Common Funeral since 1450*, Robert Hale

Litten, J W S, Dawson D P, & Boore, E J, 1988 The Poulett Vault, Hinton St George, *Somerset Archaeol Natur Hist Soc*, **132**, 256–9

Little, B, 1988 Vale of Tears, Arnos Vale Cemetery, Bristol, in N Pickford (ed) *Bristol Illustrated*, May, 52–3

Littledale, W A (ed), 1903 Marriages and burials, **ii** in *The registers of St Vedast, Foster Lane, and of St. Michael le Quern, London*

Littledale, W A (ed), 1912 Burials, St Bene't, 1619 to 1837; St Peter, 1607 to 1834, in **iv** *The registers of St Bene't and St Peter, Paul's Wharf, London*

Llewellyn, N, 1991 *The Art of Death – Visual Culture in the English Death Ritual c 1500–1800*, Reaktion Books

Llewellyn, N, 16 April 1997 interview on BBC Radio 3, *Nightwaves*

Lobel, M D, & Carus-Wilson, E M, 1975 *Historic Towns: Bristol*

London Planning Advisory Corporation, 1997a *Burial Space Needs in London*

London Planning Advisory Corporation, 1997b *Planning for Burial Space in London*

Loreille, O, Vigne, J, Hardy, C, Callou, C, & Treinen-Claustre, F, 1997 First distinction of sheep and goat archaeological bones by the means of their fossil mtDNA, *J Arch Sci*, **24**, 33–7

Loss Prevention Council, 1994 *Report SHE 12 Infectious Diseases at Work*

Lovejoy, C O, Meindl, R S, Meindl, R S, & Barton, T J, 1985 Multifactorial Determination of Skeletal Age at Death: A Method and Blind Test of its Accuracy, *Amer J Physical Anthropol*, **68**, 1–14

Lukacs, J R, 1989 Dental Pathology: Methods for Reconstructing Dietary Patterns, in M Y Iscan & K Kennedy (eds), *Reconstruction of Life From the Skeleton*, New York, 261–86

Lyme Disease Network of NJ Inc *Lyme disease – an overview*, (http://wwwlehighedu/lists/lymenet-1/overviewhtml) [Accessed 25 July 1996]

MacDonald, M, 1986 The secularization of suicide in England 1600-1800, *Past Present*, **111**, 50–100

MacDonald, M, & Murphy, T R, 1990 *Sleepless souls: suicide in modern England*, Oxford: Clarendon Press

McGrath, P, 1955 Merchants and Merchandise in Seventeenth Century Bristol, *Bristol Rec Soc*, **XIX**, 92–100

McKendrick, N, Brewer, J, & Plumb, J, 1982 *The birth of a consumer society: the commercialisation of Eighteenth Century England*, Europa

McKeown, T, 1976 *The Modern Rise of Population*, Edward Arnold

McKinley, J I, & Roberts, C M, 1993 *Excavation and post-excavation treatment of cremated and inhumed human remains*, IFA Technical Paper 13, Birmingham

MacLaughlin, S M & Bruce, M F, 1986 Population variation in sexual dimorphism in the human innominate, in M Pickford, & B Chiarelli (eds) *Sexual Dimorphism in fossil and living primates*, Firenze, 121–31

MacLaughlin, S M, 1987 *An evaluation of of current techniques for age and sex determination from adult human skeletal remains*, unpublished PhD dissertation, University of Aberdeen

McManners, J, 1981a *Death and the Enlightenment: Changing attitudes to death among Christians and unbelievers in eighteenth-century France*, Oxford: Oxford University Press

McManners, J, 1981b Death and the French historians, in J Whaley, 1981, 106–30

McMurray, W (ed), 1925 *The records of two city parishes, . . . SS Anne and Agnes, Aldersgate, and St John Zachary*

Mainous, M R, Tso, P, Berg, R D, & Deitch, E A, 1991 Studies of the route, magnitude and time course of bacterial translocation in a model of systemic inflammation, *Archives Surgery*, **126**, 33–37

Maitland, W, 1756 *The history and survey of London from its foundation to the present time*

Makins, C, 1833 letter to Edward Eddison, 2 September, MS, Leeds General Cemetery Company: miscellaneous correspondence, Brotherton Library, University of Leeds

Maltby, J, 1993 (1997) 'By this book': parishioners, the Prayer Book, and the established church, in P Marshall (ed), *The impact of the English Reformation, 1500-1640*, 257–78

Manchester, K, 1991 Tuberculosis and leprosy: evidence for interaction of disease, in D T Ortner, & A C Aufterheide (eds) *Human Paleopathology – Current Synthesis and Future Options*, 23–35, Washington D C and London: Smithsonian Institution Press

Manchester, K & Roberts, C A, 1987 *Palaeopathological evidence of leprosy and tuberculosis in Britain*, Bradford: University of Bradford

Manning, B, 1952 *The Protestant Dissenting Deputies*, Cambridge: Cambridge University Press

Manning, E, 1905 *Guide to the Birmingham General Cemetery*, Birmingham

Mant, A K, 1989 Knowledge acquired from post-war exhumations, in A Boddington, A N Garland, & R C Janaway (eds), 1989, 65–80

Marchiafara, V, Bonucci, L, & Ascenzi, A, 1974 Fungal osteoclasia: a model of dead bone resorption, *Calcified Tissue Res*, **14**, 195–210

Matthew's Annual Bristol Directory and Almanack, 1843, Bristol

Matthews, J, 1818 *Matthew's Annual Bristol Directory*, Bristol

May, T, 1996 *The Victorian Undertaker*, Princes Risborough

Mays, S A 1997 Carbon stable isotope ratios in medieval and later human skeletons from Northern England, *J Arch Sci*, **24**, 561–7

Meers, P D, 1985 Smallpox still entombed? *Lancet*; **i**, 1103

Mellor, H, 1985 *London Cemeteries: An illustrated Guide and Gazetteer*

Miles, A E W, 1958 The assessment of age from the dentition, *Proc Roy Soc Medicine*, **51**, 1057–60

Miles, A E W, 1962, Assessment of the Ages of a Population of Anglo Saxons from their Dentitions, *Proc Royal Soc Medicine*, **55**, 881–5

Miles, A E W, 1963 The dentition in the assessment of individual age in skeletal material, in D R Brothwell (ed) *Dental Anthropology*, Pergamon Press

Millar, A, 1759 *A Collection of the Yearly Bills of Mortality from 1657 to 1758 inclusive*

Miller, D, 1985 *Artefacts as categories: a study of ceramic variability in Central India*, Cambridge: Cambridge University Press

Miller, P, 1993 84, London Road, Kingston: An Archaeological Evaluation, unpublished, Museum of London Archaeology Service

Milligan, E H, & Thomas, M J, 1983 (1990) *My Ancestors were Quakers*, Society of Genealogists

Milne G, 1997 *St Brides Church London: archaeological research 1952–60 and 1992–5*, English Heritage

Milner, G, 1846 *On Cemetery Burial: or Sepulture Ancient and Modern*, Hull

Minute Book of the City Burial Grounds Institute and Père Lachaise of Sighthill, 24 March 1840, MS, Glasgow Archive Office

Minute Book of the Trustees of the St James Cemetery, 10 August 1825, MS, Liverpool Archive Office

Misson, N, 1719 *Memoirs and Observations of His Travels over England*, trans J Ozell

MoLAS, 1996 *Desk-based assessment of St Lukes, Old St*, unpublished

MoLAS, forthcoming a Excavations at the Mint

MoLAS, forthcoming b Excavations at Spital Square

Molleson, T, & Cox, M, 1993 *The Spitalfields Project Volume 2 – The Anthropology, The Middling Sort*, CBA Res Rep, **86**, York

Montagu, B, 1840 *The Funerals of the Quakers*, William Pickering

Morgan, D, 1973 *The Phoenix of Fleet Street*, Charles Knight & Co Ltd

Morley, J, 1971, *Death, Heaven and the Victorians*, University of Pittsburgh Press

Morris, C, 1994 Examine the dead gently, *Brit Arch News*, **17** (October), 9

Morris, R K, 1987 Parish Churches, in J Schofield and R H Leech (eds), *Urban Archaeology in Britain*, CBA Res Rep, **61**, 177–91 York

Mortimer, R (ed), 1971 *Minute Book of the Men's Meeting of the Society of Friends in Bristol 1667–1686*, Bristol Record Society, vol 26

Munday, J, 1875 *Spade versus Torch or, the Perils of Cremation, with a Glance into the Wherefore of Man*

Murray, K A & Murray, T, 1991 A Test of the Auricular Surface Ageing Technique, *J Forensic Sci*, **36**, 1162–9

Mytum, H C, 1988 A Newly Discovered Burial Vault in North Dalton Church, North Humberside, *Post-Medieval Archaeol*, **22**, 183–7

Mytum, H C, 1989 Public Health and Private Sentiment: the development of cemetery architecture and funerary monuments from the eighteenth century onwards, *World Archaeol*, **21**, 2, 283–97

Mytum, H C, 1990 A Study of Pembrokeshire Graveyards: cultural variability in material and language, *Bull CBA Churches Comm*, **27**, 6–11

Nawrocki, S P, 1995 Taphonomic processes in historic cemeteries, in A L Grauer (ed) *Bodies of Evidence – Reconstructing History through Skeletal Analysis*, New York: Wiley Liss, 49–68

Newman, J, 1976 *The Buildings of England: West Kent and the Weald*, 2nd edition

Nichols, J G (ed), 1848 *The diary of Henry Machyn, citizen and merchant-taylor of London, from AD 1550 to AD 1563*

Nicholls, J F, & Taylor, J, 1881 *Bristol Past and Present*, **2**, 237–43 Bristol

Nickalls, J L, 1952 *The Journal of George Fox*, Cambridge: Cambridge University Press

Notice to Undertakers, vol K (9a), London: Friends House Library

Nottingham Church Cemetery: Report of Directors, 1855 Local History Library, Nottingham Central Library

O'Brien, E, 1996 Past rites, future concerns, in J Blair, & C Pyrah (eds) 1996, York, 160–5

O'Brien, E, & Roberts, C, 1996 Archaeological Studies of Church Cemeteries: Past, Present and Future, in J Blair & C Pyrah (eds) 1996,159–66

Ortner, D J & Putschar, W G J, 1984 *Identification of Pathological Conditions in Human Skeletal Remains*, Washington: Smithsonian Institution Press

Paabo, S, 1985 Molecular cloning of ancient Eygptian mummy DNA, *Nature*, **314**, 644–5

Paabo, S, Gifford, J A, & Wilson, A C, 1988 Mitochondrial DNA sequences from a 7000 year old brain, *Nucleic Acids Res*, **16**, 9775–87

Panton, F, & Elder, J (eds), 1992 Interim report on work carried out in 1992 by the Canterbury Archaeological Trust, *Archaeology Canterbury*, **110**, 357–81

Parker Pearson, M, 1995 Ethics and the Dead in British Archaeology, *Field Archaeol*, **23**, 17–18

Parkington, J E, 1972 Seasonal mobility in the Later Stone Age, *Afr Stud*, **31**, 223–43

Pate, E D, & Hutton, J T, 1988 The use of soil chemistry data to address post mortem diagenesis in bone mineral, *J Arch Sci*, **15**, 729–39

Patel, N S, 1973 Pathology of Suicide, *Medicine Sci Law*, **2**, 103–9

Paxton, F S, 1990 *Christianising Death: the Creation of a Ritual Process in Early Medieval Europe*, New York: Cornell University Press

Penney, N (ed), 1911 *The Journal of George Fox*, Cambridge: Cambridge University Press

Pettegree, A, 1986 *Foreign Protestant communities in sixteenth-century London*, Oxford

264

Pevsner, N, 1958 *Buildings of England*, Harmondsworth: Penguin

Pfeiffer, S, 1991 Is paleopathology a relevant predictor of contemporary health patterns?, in D T Ortner and A C Aufterheide (eds) *Human Paleopathology – Current Synthesis and Future Options*, Washington D C and London: Smithsonian Institution Press, 12–17

Philpott, R, 1991 *Burial practice in Roman Britain: a survey of grave treatment and furnishing AD 43-410*, BAR Brit Ser 219, Oxford

Piepenbrink, H, 1986 Two examples of biogenous dead bone decomposition and their consequences for taphonomic interpretation, *J Arch Sci*, **13**, 417–30

Piepenbrink, H, & Schutowski, H, 1987 Decomposition of skeletal remains in desert dry soils, *J Hum Evol*, **2**, 481–91

Pollard, T, 1991 *Archaeological and popular perceptions of the dead*, unpublished, Scottish Archaeological Forum conference on Death, University of Glasgow 1990

Pollard, T, 1992 *The sarcophagus is leaking: death and the archaeologist*, unpublished, Theoretical Archaeology Group conference, University of Durham 1991

Pollard, T, 1996 *Method statement for archaeological excavation of Quaker burial ground, 84, London Road, Kingston-upon-Thames*, unpublished

Pollard, T, forthcoming The drowned and the saved: perspectives on the seas as grave, in J Downes, & T Pollard (eds), forthcoming

Pollock, A J, 1846 *Pagan Cremation or Christian Burial*

Poole, D F G, & Tratman, E K, 1978 Post mortem changes on human teeth from late upper Palaeolithic/Mesolithic occupants of an English limestone cave, *Archives Oral Biol*, **23**, 1115–20

Port, M (ed), 1986 *The Commissions for building Fifty New Churches*

Porter, R (ed), 1991 *George Cheyne: The English Malady (1733)*, Routledge

Porter, S, 1993 From Death to Burial in Seventeenth-Century England, *Local Historian*, **23**, (4), 199–204

Potter, H, 1993 *Hanging in judgment – Religion and the death penalty in England from the Bloody Code to Abolition*, SCM Press

Powers, R, Illustrations of the St Bride's Skeletal Collection London, unpublished, St Bride's Church

Prospectus of the Portsea Island Cemetery Company, 1830 Sanderson Collection, Local History Library, Portsmouth Central Library

Puckle, B, 1926 *Funeral Customs*, Werner Laurie

Quarterly Review, 1835 The Church and the Voluntary System, **LIII**, 174-215

Quarterly Review, 1844, **CXLVI**, 449

Raphael, B, 1986 *When Disaster Strikes: How Individuals and Communities Cope with Catastrophe*, New York: Basic Books

Razzell, P, 1976 Smallpox extinction – a note of caution, *New Scientist*, **71**, 35

Razzell, P, 1994 *Essays in English Population History*

Redknap, M, 1985 Little Ilford, St Mary the Virgin 1984, *London Archaeol*, **5**, 31–7

Redpath, W, 1955 A visit to Fleet Street, 21 April 1955, *West Lond Medical J*, **60**, 130–40

Reeve, J, 1997 Grave Expectations, in *Building Conservation Directory Special Report (The Conservation and Repair of Ecclesiastical Buildings)*, 4–6

Reeve, J, & Adams, M, 1993 *The Spitalfields Project Volume 1 The Archaeology, Across the Styx, CBA Res Rep*, **85** York

Reeve, J & Cox, M, forthcoming Research and our recent ancestors: Post-Medieval Burial Grounds: views and advice, in J Downes, & T Pollard (eds)

Religious Society of Friends, 1977 *Yearly Meeting Proceedings*

Religious Society of Friends, 1986 *Your Meeting's Records – Notes on creation, custody and use*

Religious Society of Friends, 1992a *Disused Burial Grounds*, leaflet

Religious Society of Friends, 1992b *Quaker Funerals*, leaflet

Religious Society of Friends, 1996 *Who are the Quakers?*, leaflet

Renfrew, C, & Bahn, P G, 1996 *Archaeology: Theories, Methods and Practice*

Report on a General Scheme of Extra-mural Sepulture for County Towns, 1851 [1348]

Reports on Burial Grounds, (1843) MS 74, Friends House Library

Richards, M B, Sykes, B C, & Hedges, R E M, 1995 Authenticating DNA extracted from ancient skeletal remains, *J Arch Sci*, **22**, 291–9

Richardson, R, 1988 *Death, Dissection and the Destitute*, Routledge Kegan Paul

Richardson, R, 1994 Sympathy, sensibility or hypocrisy: the etiquette of mourning. Paper presented at 'Sympathy, sensibility and judgement: notions of community 1750–1870' conference, Cambridge University, 5–6 August 1994

Richardson, R, & Hurwitz, B, 1995 Donor's attitudes towards body donation for dissection, *Lancet*, **346**, 277–9

Richmond, M, forthcoming The coffin furniture, in L Bashford, & L Kirk

Roberts, C, 1996 The biological evidence, or what the people say, in J Blair, & C Pyrah (eds), 1996, 166–181

Roberts, C, Lucy, D, & Manchester, K, 1994 Inflammatory lesions of ribs: an analysis of the Terry Collection, *Amer J Physical Anthropol*, **95**, 169–82

Roberts, C A, Lee, F, & Bintliff, J, (eds) 1989 *Burial Archaeology: Current Research, Methods and Developments, BAR Brit Ser*, **211**

Rodwell, W J, 1981 *The Archaeology of the English Church*, Batsford

Rodwell, W J, 1989 *Church Archaeology*, Batsford/English Heritage

Rodwell, W J, 1996, Church archaeology in retrospect and prospect, in J Blair, & C Pyrah (eds), 1996, 197–202

Rodwell, W J, 1997 Landmarks in church archaeology, in *Church Archaeol*, **1**, 5–16

Rodwell, W J, & Rodwell, K A, 1982 St Peter's Church, Barton-upon-Humber: excavation and structural study 1978-81, *Antiq J*, **62**.ii, 283–315

Rodwell, W J, & Rodwell, K A, 1986 *Rivenhall: investigation of a villa, church and village 1950-1977 Volume 1, Chelmsford Archaeological Trust Report 4, CBA Res Rep*, **55**, York

Rodwell, W J, & Rodwell, K A, 1993 *Rivenhall: investigation of a villa, church and village 1950–1977 Volume 2* – Specialist studies and index to volumes 1 and 2 *Chelmsford Archaeological Trust Report* **4.2**, *CBA Res Rep*, **80**, York

Rogers, J, Watt, I, & Dieppe, P, 1985 Palaeopathology of Spinal Osteophytosis, Vertebral Ankylosis and Vertebral Hyperostosis, *Annals Rheumatic Diseases*, **44**, 113–20

Roskams, S (ed), 1996 *Interpreting Stratigraphy 8: Papers presented at the eighth stratigraphy conference at York*, York: University of York

Roux, W, 1887, Uber eine Knochenlebende Gruppe von Faderpilzen (*Mycelites ossifragus*), *Z wiss Zool*, **45**, 227–54

Rowell, G, 1970 Nineteenth century attitudes and practices, in G Cope (ed) *Dying, death and disposal*, SPCK, 49–56

Rugg, J, 1992 *The emergence of early cemetery companies in Britain, 1820–53*, unpublished PhD thesis, University of Stirling

Rule, M H, 1983 *The Mary Rose: the Excavation and Raising of Henry VIII's Flagship*

Sabin, A, 1956 *The Registers of the Church of St Augustine the Less, Bristol, 1579–1700, Bristol Gloucestershire Arch Soc Records Section*, **3** Bristol

St John Hope, W H, 1911 The discovery of the remains of King Henry VI in St George's Chapel, Windsor Castle, *Archaeologia*, **62**, 533–42

Saluja, G, Fitzpatrick, K, Bruce, M, & Cross, J, 1986 Schmorl's nodes (intravertebral herniations of intervertebral disc tissue) in two historic British populations, *J Anatomy*, **145**, 87–96

Saluja, P G, 1988 The incidence of spina bifida occulta in a historic and a modern London population, *J Anatomy*, **158**, 91–3

Sandford, M K, 1992 A reconsideration of trace element analysis in prehistoric bone, in S R Saunders, & M A Katzenberg (eds), *Skeletal Biology of Past Peoples: Research Methods*, New York: Wiley Liss, 79–103

Saunders, S, 1992, Subadult Skeletons and Growth Related Studies, in S Saunders, & M A Katzenberg (eds), *Skeletal Biology of Past Peoples: Research Methods*, New York: Wiley Liss, 1–20

Saunders, S R, & Herring, A (eds) 1995 *Grave reflections: portraying the past through cemetery studies*, Toronto: Canadian Scholars Press

Saunders, S R, Hoppa, R, & Southern, R, 1993 Diaphyseal growth in a 19th century sample of subadults from St Thomas' Church, Belleville, Ontario, *Int J Osteoarchaeol*, **3**, 265–81

Saunders, S, & Popovich, F, 1978 A Family Study of Two Skeletal Variants: Atlas Bridging and Clinoid Bridging, *Amer J Physical Anthropol*, **49**, 193–203

Schaffer, J, 1889 Uber den feineren Bau fossiler knochen, *S B Akad Wiss Wien Math-nat III*, **98**, 319–82

Schaffer, J, 1890 Uber Roux'sche Kanale in menchlichen Zahnen, *S B Akad Wiss Wien Math-nat III*, **99**, 146–52

Schaffer, J, 1895 Bermerkungen zur Geschichte der Bohrkanale in Knochen und Zahnen, *Anat Anz*, **10**, 459–64

Scheuer, J L, 1995 Postmortem diagnosis of DISH (diffuse idiopathic skeletal hyperostosis) in a well-known 18th century person, *Clinical Anatomy*, **8**, 371

Scheuer, J L & Black, S M, 1995 *The St Bride's Documented Skeletal Collection*. Unpublished research report, St Bride's Church

Scheuer, J L & Bowman, J E, 1994 The health of the novelist and printer Samuel Richardson (1689–1761): A correlation of documentary and skeletal evidence, *J Roy Soc Medicine*, **87**, 352–5

Schoeninger, M J, & DeNiro, M J, 1982 Carbon isotope ratios of apatite from fossil bone cannot be used to reconstruct diets of animals, *Nature*, **297**, 577–8

Schoeninger, M J, & DeNiro, M J, 1984 Nitrogen and carbon isotopic composition of bone collagen from marine and terrestrial animals, *Geochimica et Cosmochimica Acta*, **48**, 625–39

Schoeninger, M J, DeNiro, M J, & Tauber, H, 1983 ^{15}N/^{14}N ratios of bone collagen reflect marine and terrestrial components of prehistoric human diet, *Science*, **220**, 1381–3

Schofield, R, 1986 Did the mothers really die? Three centuries of maternal mortality in 'The world we have lost', in L Bonfield, R M Smith, and K Wrightson (eds), *The world we have gained. Histories of population and social structure*, Oxford: Basil Blackwell, 231–60

Sealy, J C, Armstrong, R, & Schrire, C, 1995 Beyond lifetime averages: tracing life histories through isotopic analysis of different calcified tissues from archaeological human skeletons, *Antiquity*, **69**, 290–300

Sealy, J C, & van der Merwe, N J, 1986 Isotope assessment and the seasonal mobility hypothesis in the south-western Cape, South Africa, *Curr Anthrop*, **27**, 135–50

Sealy, J C, van der Merwe, N J, Lee-Thorp, J A, & Lanham, J L, 1987 Nitrogen isotopic ecology in southern Africa: implications for environmental and dietary tracing, *Geochimica et Cosmochimica Acta*, **51**, 2707–17

Shinoda, K, & Kunisada, T, 1994 Analysis of ancient Japanese society through mitochondrial DNA sequencing, *Int J Osteoarch*, **4**, 291–7

Shoesmith, R, 1981 Llangar Church, *Archaeol Cambrensis*, **CXXIX**, 64–132

Shrewsbury, J F D, 1970 *A history of bubonic plague in the British Isles*, Cambridge: Cambridge University Press

Sillen, A, 1989 Diagenesis of the inorganic phase of cortical bone, in T D Price (ed), *The Chemistry of Prehistoric Bone*, Cambridge: Cambridge University Press, 211–29

Sillen, A, Sealy, J C, & van der Merwe N J, 1989 Chemistry and palaeodietary research: no more easy answers, *Amer Antiquity*, **54**, 504–12

Six Weeks Meeting Minutes, 1843 Responses to a questionnaire regarding 'A bill for Improvement of Health in Towns, by removing the Interment of the Dead from their Precincts' 6 March 1843, Friends House Library

Sjøvold, T, 1977 Non Metrical Divergence Between Skeletal Populations, *Ossa*, **4** supplement 1, 1–117

Sjøvold, T, 1984 A Report on the Heritability of some Cranial Measurements and Non-Metric Traits, in G N Van Vark, & W W Howells (eds), *Multivariate Statistics in Physical Anthropology*, Reidel, Groningen, 223–48

Slack, P, 1985 *The impact of plague in Tudor and Stuart England*, Routledge Kegan Paul

Slack, P, 1986 Metropolitan government in crisis: the response to plague, in A L Beier, & R Finlay (eds) *London 1500–1700, the making of the metropolis*, Longman, 60–81

Smale, D A (ed), 1994 *Davies' Law of Burial, Cremation and Exhumation*, 6th ed (revised), Crayford: Shaw

Smith, B N, & Epstein, S, 1971 Two categories of 13C/12C ratios for higher plants, *Plant Physiol*, **47**, 380–4

Smith, J, 1850 *Report to the General Board of Health on a Preliminary Inquiry into the Sewerage, Drainage and Supply of Water, and the Sanitary Condition of the Town and Borough of Kingston-upon-Hull*

Smithers, D W, 1981 *Jane Austen in Kent*, Westerham: Hurtwood Publications

Solomon, S D, Gerrity, E T, & Muff, A M, 1992 Efficacy of treatments for post traumatic stress disorder, *J American Medical Assoc*, **268**, 633–8

Southall, K H, 1974 *Our Quaker Heritage*, Quaker Home Service

266

Spry, J H, 1832 A brief account of the excavation of the tomb of Henry IV in the cathedral of Canterbury, *Archaeologia*, **26**, 440–5

Stanley, A P, 1879 On the examination of the tombs of Richard II and Henry III in Westminster Abbey, *Archaeologia*, **45**, 309–26

Stapleton, H, 1976 Postscript, in P Addyman, & R Morris (eds), *The Archaeological Study of Churches*, CBA Res Rep **13**, 72–4

Start, H V, & Kirk, L, forthcoming Death at the Undertakers, in J Downes, & T Pollard (eds)

Steane, J, 1996 *The Mortality Patterns of the Skeletal Population of Saint Augustine the Less, Bristol* (BSc dissertation) Bournemouth University: unpublished

Steel, F L D, 1963 The sexing of long bones, with reference to the St Bride's series of identified skeletons, *J Roy Anthropol Instit*, **92**, 212–22

Steele, D G, & Bramblett, C A, 1988 *The Anatomy and Biology of the Human Skeleton*, Texas: A & M Press

Steele, D J, 1973 *Sources for non-conformist genealogy and family history*, vol. 2, Chichester: Philimore, 601–90

Stirland, A, 1991 Diagnosis of occupationally related pathology: Can it be done?, in D T Ortner and A C Aufterheide (eds) *Human Paleopathology – Current Synthesis and Future Options*, Washington D C and London: Smithsonian Institution Press, 40-47

Stock, G, 1996 *An Evaluation of Quaker Burial Practices*, research diploma dissertation, Bournemouth University, unpublished

Stocker, D, 1997 *Fons et origo*: the symbolic death, burial and resurrection of English font stones, *Church Archaeol*, **1**, 17–25

Stone, L, 1977 *The family, sex and marriage in England 1500–1800*, Weidenfeld & Nicolson

Strype, J, 1720 *A survey of the cities of London and Westminster . . . written at first in the year 1598 by John Stow, citizen and native of London, since reprinted and augmented . . . now lastly corrected, improved and very much enlarged*

Stuart-Macadam, P, 1989, Nutritional Deficiency Diseases: A Study of Scurvy, Rickets and Iron Deficiency Anaemia, in M Iscan, & K Kennedy (eds), *Reconstruction of Life From the Skeleton*, New York: Alan Liss, 201–22

Stuttaford, T, 27 May 1997 Monkey pox in Zaire raises vaccine worries, *The Times*, 12

Sullivan, C H, & Krueger, H W, 1981 Carbon isotope analysis of separate chemical phases in modern and fossil bone, *Nature*, **292**, 333–5

Sutherland, I, 1972 When was the great Plague? Mortality in London, 1563–1665, in D V Glass, & R Revelle, *Population and Social Change*, 287–320

Swann, A, 1993 Tong Church: A level three investigation, in P Ryder, *Medieval churches of West Yorkshire*, West Yorkshire Archaeology Service

Sykes, B, 1997 Lights turn red on amber, *Nature*, **386**, 764–5

Syssovena, P R, 1958 Post mortem changes to human teeth with time, *Sudebnd-Medisthinskaya Ekspertiza I Kriminalistika na Sletsshiviya*, **2**, 213–18 (Russian)

Tarlow, S, forthcoming Wormie clay and blessed sleep, in S Tarlow and S West (eds) *The familiar past?*, Routledge

Tate, W E, 1969 *The Parish Chest*, Chichester: Philimore

Tate Gallery, 1984 *The Pre-Raphaelites*

Tatton-Brown, T, 1980 The Roper Chantry in St Dunstan's Church, Canterbury, *Antiq J*, **LX**, Part II, 227–46

Taylor, G M, Crossey, M, Saldanha, J, & Waldron, T, 1996 DNA from *Mycobacterium tuberculosis* identified in medieval human remains using polymerase chain reaction, *J Arch Sci*, **23**, 789–98

Taylor, L, 1989 The Uses of Death in Europe, *Anthropol Quarterly*, **62**, 149–54

Thibaut-Payen, J, 1977 *Les morts, l'église, et l'état dans le ressort du Parlement de Paris au XVIIe et XVIIIe siècles*, Paris

Thomas, K, 1978 *Religion and the Decline of Magic: studies in popular belief in sixteenth and seventeenth century England*, Peregrine

Thomas, R H, Schaffner, W, Wilson, A C, & Paabo, S, 1989 DNA phylogeny of the extinct marsupial wolf, *Nature*, **340**, 465–7

Thomson, J A F, 1993 *The early Tudor church and society, 1485–1529*

Thompson, H, 1889 *Modern cremation, its history and practice. With information relating to the recently improved arrangements made by the Cremation Society of England*

Thompson, J, 1993 Psychological impact of body recovery duties, *J Royal Soc Medicine*, **86**, 628–9

Thompson, J, Charlton, P F C, Kerry, R, Lee, D, & Turner, S W, 1995a An open trial of exposure therapy based on deconditioning for post-traumatic stress disorder, *Brit J Clinical Psychology*, **34**, 407–16

Thompson, J, Chung, M C, Jackson, G, & Rosser, R, 1995b A comparative trial of psychotherapy in the treatment of post-trauma stress reactions, *Clinical Psychology and Psychotherapy*, **3**, 168–76

Thompson, J, & Solomon, M, 1991 Body recovery teams at disasters: Trauma or challenge?, *Anxiety Res*, **4**, 235–44

Thompson, J, & Suzuki, I, 1991 Stress in ambulance workers, *Disaster Management*, **4**, 193–7

Tiezsen, L L, & Fagre, T, 1993 Effect of diet quality and composition on the isotopic composition of respiratory CO_2, bone collagen, bioapatite and soft tissues, in J B Lambert, & G Grupe (eds), *Prehistoric Human Bone: Archaeology at the Molecular Level*, Berlin, 121–55

Todd, B J, 1985 The remarrying widow: a stereotype reconsidered, in M Prior (ed), *Women in English society, 1500–1800*, Cambridge, 54–92

Tolmie, M, 1977 *The triumph of the saints: the separate churches of London, 1616–1649*, Cambridge

Towler, J, & Bramall, J, 1986 *Midwives in History and Society*, Croom Helm

Toynbee, J M C 1971 (1996) *Death and Burial in the Roman World*, Thames & Hudson (Harvard University Press)

Trimble, M R, 1981 *Post-traumatic neurosis*, Chichester: Wiley

Trotter, M, & Gleiser, G C, 1958 A Re-evaluation of Estimation of Stature Based on Measurements of Stature Taken During Life and of Long Bones after Death, *Amer J Physical Anthropol*, **16**, 79–123

Trusts and Trust Properties, 1870, vested in Bristol and Somerset Quarterly Meeting and its Subordinate Meetings, Book of Deeds 64, Friends House Library, London

Turnbull, P, Bowen, J, & Mann, J, 1996 Stubborn contamination with anthrax spores, *Environmental Health*, June, 171–3

Tuross, N, 1993 The other molecules in ancient bone: noncollagenous proteins and DNA, in J B Lambert, & G Grupe (eds), *Prehistoric Human Bone: Archaeology at the Molecular Level*, Berlin, 275–92

Ubelaker, D H, 1995 Historic Cemetery Analysis: Practical Considerations, in A L Grauer (ed) *Bodies of Evidence – Reconstructing History through Skeletal Analysis*, New York, 37–48

Ubelaker, D H, & Grant, L G, 1989 Human skeletal remains: preservation or reburial, *Yearbook Physical Anthropol*, **32**, 249–87

van Gennep, A, 1960 *The rites of passage*, Translated by M. Vicedom, S. Kimball, University of Chicago Press

van der Merwe, N J, & Vogel, J C, 1978 ^{13}C content of human collagen as a measure of prehistoric diet in Woodland North America, *Nature*, **276**, 815–16

van Klinken, G J, Richards, M P, & Hedges, R E M, forthcoming Stable isotopic variations in past European human populations: environmental, ecophysiological and cultural effects, in S H Ambrose, & K A Katzenberg (eds), *Close to the bone: Biogeochemistry and Paleodietary Analysis*, New York

Veblen, T, 1957 (1925) *The Theory of the Leisure Class: an economic study of institutions*, Allen & Unwin

Verey, D, 1970 Gloucestershire 2 The Vale and the Forest of Dean in *Buildings of England*, 109–111

1788 The examination of Edward IV in his coffin at Windsor, *Vetusta Monumenta*, **3**

Waldron, H A 1985 Occupational Health and the Archaeologist, *Brit J Ind Medicine*, **42**, 793–4

Waldron, T A, 1985 DISH at Merton Priory: evidence for a 'new' occupational disease, *Brit Medical J*, **291**, 1762–3

Waldron, T, 1994 *Counting The Dead The Epidemiology of Skeletal Populations*, Chichester: Wiley

Waldron, T, 1997 A 19th century case of carcinoma of the prostate, with a note on the early history of the disease, *Int J Osteoarchaeol* 7:241–7

Walker, G, 1839 *Gatherings from graveyards, particularly those of London, with a concise History of the Modes of Interment among different Nations, from the earliest periods, and a detail of dangerous and fatal results produced by the Unwise and revolting custom of inhuming the Dead in the midst of the Living*

Walker, N, & Craddock, T, 1849 *History of Wisbech*, Wisbech

Walsh, J, Taylor, S, & Haydon, C (eds), 1993 *The Church of England, c 1689–1833, from Toleration to Tractarianism*, Cambridge: Cambridge University Press

Walters, H B, 1939 *London churches at the Reformation, with an account of their contents*

Wasserschleben, F W H (ed), 1885 *Die Irische Kanonensammlung*, Leipzig

Watt, I, 1957 *The rise of the novel: studies in Defoe, Richardson and Fielding*, Berkeley: University of California Press

Watts, L, & Rahtz, P, 1985 *Mary-le-Port, Bristol: Excavations 1962–1963, Bristol Mus Art Gallery Monograph*, **7** Bristol

Weatherill, L, 1988 *Consumer behaviour and material culture in Britain, 1660–1760*, Routledge

Weber, M, 1930 *The Protestant Ethic and the Spirit of Capitalism* (trans Talcott Parsons), Unwin

Wedl, C, 1864 Uber einen im Zahnbein und Knochen keimenden Pilz. Akademie der Wissenchaften in Wien. Sitzungsberichte Naturwissenchaftliche Klasse ABI, Mineralogie, *Biologie Erdkunde*, **50**, 171–93

Weever, J, 1631, *Ancient Funerall Monuments, & c*, Thomas Harper

Wells, C, 1964 *Bones, Bodies and Disease*, Bristol: Thames & Hudson

Wemyss Reid, T, 1883 *A Memoir of J D Heaton*

Whaley, J, 1981 *Mirrors of Mortality: essays in the social history of death*, Europa Publications

W H B, 1918 Barnardiston Vaults in Kedington Church, *Proc Suffolk Instit Archaeol Natur Hist*, **16**, Part 1, 44–7

Whellan, W, 1849 *History, Gazetteer and Directory of Northamptonshire*, Northampton

White, B, 1997 Letter, *New Sci*, 15th February 1997, 49

White, T, 1789 Curious leaden coffin found at Danbury in Essex, *Gentleman's Magazine*, **59**, 337–8

White, W M, 1971 *Six Weeks Meeting 1671–1971*

Whittaker, D K, & MacDonald, D G, 1989 *A Colour Atlas of Forensic Dentistry*, Wolfe Medical

Whittaker, D, 1993 Oral Health, in T Molleson, & M Cox 1993, 49–65

Wilkins, H J, 1920 *Edward Colston (1636–1721) A Chronological Account of his Life and Work* Bristol

Wilkinson, D, 1992a *Oxford Archaeological Unit Field Manual*, Oxford

Wilkinson, D, 1992b *St Nicholas Church, Sevenoaks: archaeological field evaluation*, Oxford Archaeological Unit

Willsher, B, 1985 *Understanding Scottish Graveyards*, Chambers

Willsher, B, 1992 Adam and Eve scenes on Kirkyard monuments in the Scottish Lowlands, *Proc Soc Antiq Scotl*, **122**, 413–51

Wilson, J P, & Raphael, B, (eds) 1993 *International Handbook of Traumatic Stress Syndromes*, New York and London: Plenum

Winstone, R, 1962 *Bristol in the 1880's*, 74–5, Bristol

Wohl, A, S 1983 *Endangered Lives*, Dent

Wolff, H L, & Croon, J J A B, 1968 Survival of smallpox virus (*Variola minor*) in natural circumstances, *Bull VMO*, **38**, 492–3

Woodger, A, 1994 *Jubilee Line Extension Project*, MOLAS

Woods, R, & Woodward, J (eds), 1984 *Urban Disease and Mortality in Nineteenth-Century England*, Batsford

Workwomans Guide, The 1832 (1975), New York

Wrigley, E A, 1967 A simple model of the importance of London in changing English economy and society, 1650-1750, *Past and Present*, **37**, 44–70

Wrigley, E A, & Schofield, R, 1981 *The population history of England, 1541–1871, a reconstruction*, Cambridge: Cambridge University Press

'Xenos', 1789 Lead coffin at Danbury, *Gentleman's Magazine*, **59**, 517–8

Yates, N, 1984 The major Kentish towns in the religious Census of 1851, *Archaeology Canterbury*, **100**, 399–423

Yates, N, 1986 The condition of Kentish churches before Victorian restoration, *Archaeology Canterbury*, **102**, 119–25

Yoshino, M, Kimijima, T, Miyasaka, S, Sato, H, & Seta, S, 1991 Microscopical study on estimation of time since death in human skeletal remains, *Forensic Sci Int*, **49**, 143–58

Zuckerman, A J, 1984 Palaeontology of smallpox, *Lancet*, **ii**, 1454

Index

Susan Vaughan

Illustrations are indicated by page numbers in *italics* or by *illus* where figures are scattered throughout the text. The following abbreviations have been used in this index: B & N E S – Bath and North East Somerset; C – century; d – died; *illus* – illustrated; m – married; n – note.